Apple Training Series

Mac OS X System Administration Reference, Volume 1

Schoun Regan, Ed.

Apple
Certified

Apple Training Series: Mac OS X System Administration Reference, Volume 1
Schoun Regan, Ed.
Copyright © 2006 Apple Computer, Inc. and Peachpit Press

Published by Peachpit Press. For information on Peachpit Press books, contact:

Peachpit Press
1249 Eighth Street
Berkeley, CA 94710
(510) 524-2178
Fax: (510) 524-2221
http://www.peachpit.com
To report errors, please send a note to errata@peachpit.com
Peachpit Press is a division of Pearson Education

Contributing Writers: Gordon Davisson, Arek Dreyer, Scott Neal, Priscilla Oppenheimer (Open Door Networks), Deborah Peer, David Pugh, Schoun Regan, Paul Suh, Jan Stewart, John Welch
Editors: Cheryl England and Whitney Walker
Managing Editor: Nancy Peterson
Series Editor: Serena Herr
Production Editor: Pat Christenson
Technical Reviewers: Deborah Peer, David Ekstrand, John Signa
Copy Editors: Hon Walker and Emily K. Wolman
Compositors: Danielle Foster and Jerry Ballew
Indexer: Jack Lewis
Cover Art Direction: Charlene Charles-Will
Cover Illustration: Alicia Buelow
Cover Production: George Mattingly/GMD

ISBN 0-321-36984-X
9 8 7 6 5 4 3 2 1
Printed and bound in the United States of America

To my daughter Amie and my son Dakota;
Every day, you two make me so very proud.

Acknowledgments I only edited what others wrote, and they deserve enormous thanks: John Signa, Deborah Peer, Paul Suh, David Ekstrand, Arek Dreyer, Scott Neal, John Welch, Gordon Davisson, Jan Stewart, and Priscilla Oppenheimer.

Special thanks to David Pugh for his invaluable assistance. This book would not have been completed without him.

Words sometimes need to be massaged. Whitney Walker attacks them, and this book is better because of it.

Thanks also to Rebecca Gulick and Tiffany Taylor for their patience.

Thanks to Susan for holding down the fort in my mental and physical absences. You are one of a kind, and I am so lucky.

As always, thanks to my friends Joel Rennich and Michael Bartosh. Driving down Pacific Coast Highway from San Francisco to Santa Barbara in a Jag on the way to a conference is an excellent way to kill an afternoon.

And finally a huge thanks Serena Herr. Can I get some sleep now?

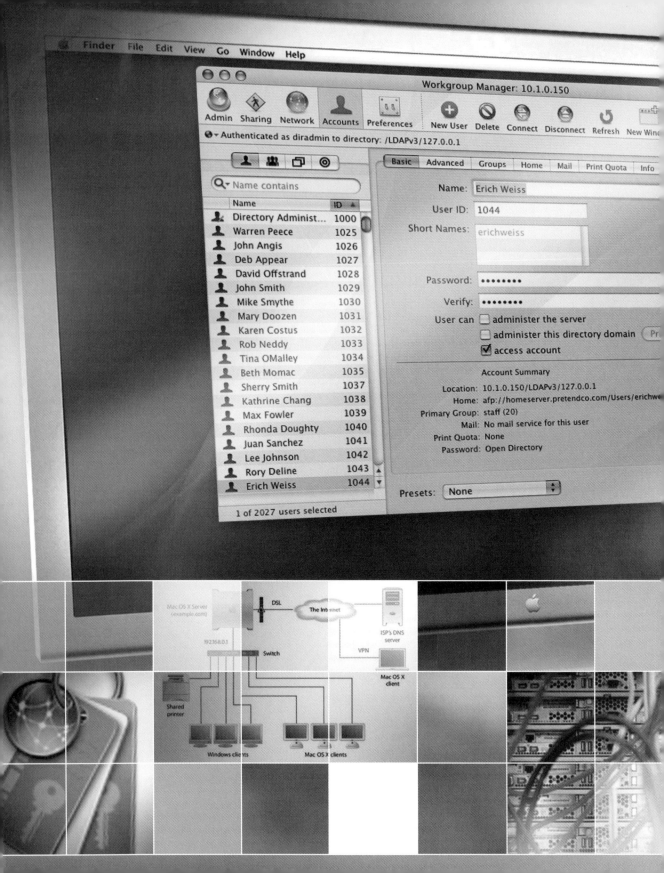

Contents at a Glance

Contents

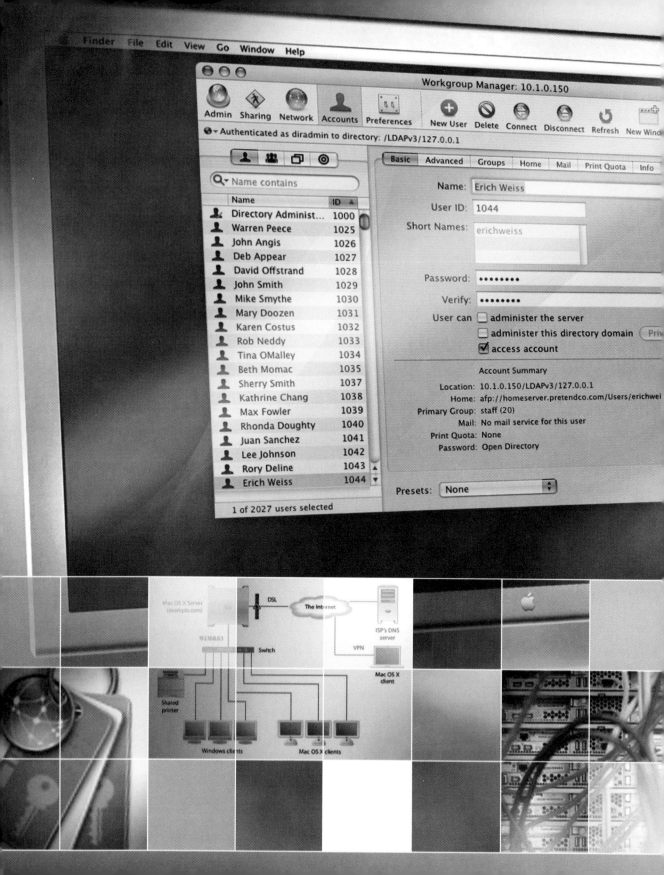

Getting Started

Congratulations on choosing the only Apple-certified reference guide to Mac OS X system administration. Designed as a companion to Apple's own Directory Services Integration, Administration for Client and Server, and Security Best Practices training courses, this comprehensive, self-paced guide will give administrators, support technicians, and ardent Mac users an in-depth look at the technical architecture of Mac OS X and Mac OS X Server. It also includes a section on networking and file services.

So whether you need to get your organization's Active Directory setup to work with Mac OS X, troubleshoot an existing network, or secure your Mac OS X computers to comply with government standards, here's the book to show you how.

The Methodology

Apple Training Series books emphasize hands-on training. The lessons contained within this book are designed to prepare system administrators for the tasks demanded of them by managing, merging, and editing directories, securing the network and systems, and troubleshooting networks and file services. To become truly proficient, you need to learn the theory behind each of these topics.

Lesson Structure

This reference guide is broken down into three parts, each bringing you into a world of configuration files, mechanisms, best practices, and integration:

▶ **Part 1, Directory Services Administration,** instructs you on configuring Mac OS X computers to use directory services and configuring Mac OS X Server to provide directory services in a mixed-platform environment. This section begins with a basic explanation of directory services and moves into more advanced topics, such as Active Directory integration, Workgroup Manager, Password Server management, Lightweight Directory Access Protocol (LDAP), single sign-on, Kerberos, and Open Directory replication.

▶ **Part 2, Security Administration,** deals with the implementation of security on your computers and your network to comply with standards. This section teaches you to configure your computers—both portable and desktop—and your network to conform to security standards. You'll benchmark security changes using common criteria tests and tools agreed upon by several nations throughout the world, explaining how Mac OS X can be further secured against attacks and snooping. Though this topic could fill several volumes, these lessons cover compliance and best practices, serving as an excellent starting point for those interested in securing their systems.

▶ **Part 3, Networking and File Services,** discusses routing tables, DNS fundamentals, and various file-sharing protocols and file systems. The lessons will help you streamline and head off issues before they escalate into something more serious. This section is critical for anyone preparing Mac OS X for use as a file server and covers a host of networking topics, from unmanaged networking to troubleshooting network issues, as well as understanding and managing file services—both local and remote connections.

► **Part 4, Appenixes,** Finally, two appendixes are included in this book: One serves as a reference guide to vi, the UNIX text-editing tool, and the other gives a short command-line refresher.

NOTE ► The exercises in this book are nondestructive if followed correctly. However, a few exercises are disruptive, in that they may turn certain network services off or on suddenly. Some exercises, if performed incorrectly, could result in data loss to some basic services, and even erase a disk or volume of a computer connected to the network on which the Mac OS X and/or Mac OS X Server resides. As such, it is recommended that you run through the exercises on Mac OS X computers that are not critical to your productivity or connected to a production network. Instructions are given for restoring your services back to their initial state, but reasonable caution is recommended. Apple Computer, Inc. and Peachpit Press are not responsible for any data loss or any damage to any equipment that occurs as a direct or indirect result of following procedures in this book.

Prerequisites

Because Mac OS X and Mac OS X Server contain several open-source initiatives, it is impossible to include all the possibilities and permutations here. First-time users of Mac OS X and Mac OS X Server may find the concepts in this book a bit unfamiliar, but that should not dissuade them from learning an integral part of Mac OS X. Seasoned administrators of Mac OS X, Windows, and UNIX will find this book extremely helpful in integrating their various systems to work in tandem.

Before undertaking the lessons in this book, you should have experience in the following areas:

► Apple Certified Technical Coordinator (ACTC) certification or equivalent knowledge

► Network and Internet topical knowledge

► Understanding of the purpose, function, and use of basic IP networking, including IP addresses, subnet masks, ports, and protocols

► Familiarity with the command line and Secure Shell Protocol (SSH)

Hardware Requirements

It is not necessary to have computers set up for this reference guide, although basic configuration requirements are listed below for readers who want to locate files, attempt commands, and adjust settings based on the lessons in this book. In order to follow along, you are expected to network your computers and provide basic services without prior instruction.

To complete the lessons in this book, you will need two Macintosh computers—one with Mac OS X version 10.4 installed and one with Mac OS X Server v10.4—and network cables and a switch to keep them connected via a small private local network. Although it is not required, a Microsoft Windows 2003 Advanced Server with the latest Service Packs installed will be helpful for completing certain exercises.

Before you set up Mac OS X and Mac OS X Server, you'll want to keep in mind that you should have temporary Internet access to download and install all necessary software updates using the Software Update mechanism in Mac OS X.

You will also need the following items, freely downloadable from Apple or on the Mac OS X/Mac OS X Server CD or DVD:

▶   Server Admin Tools package

▶   Developer Tools package

▶   Latest Mac OS X Server Combo Update package

Set up your client computer

In this exercise, you will ensure that your Mac OS X computer is properly configured.

1   Do a custom erase and install of Mac OS X, and add the X11 package if this is a computer that can have all of the data on it erased. *Do not erase a disk with data you want to keep!*

2   If this is a portable computer, ensure that the power cable is connected.

3   In the Welcome window, select your country of choice and click Continue.

4   In the Do You Already Own a Mac? window, select "Do not transfer my information" and click Continue.

5 In the Select Your Keyboard window, select your choice and click Continue.

6 In the Enter Your Apple ID window, leave the Apple ID and Password fields blank and click Continue.

7 In the Registration Information window, press Command-Q and skip the registration process.

8 In the "You have not finished setting up Mac OS X" dialog, click Skip.

You do not need to register with Apple for this book.

9 In the Create Your Account window, enter the following information:

Name: *Apple Admin*

Short Name: *apple*

Password: *apple*

Using the same word for the user name and password does not follow best practices. Because you will be using many different accounts and passwords throughout the book, the exercises use simple, easy-to-recall passwords.

10 Click Continue.

11 In the Select Time Zone window, click your time zone on the map, and then click Continue.

12 In the Set the Date and Time window, reset the time and date if either one is incorrect, and then click Save.

13 Click Continue.

14 In the Don't Forget to Register window, click Done.

The Setup Assistant will quit and the Finder will open.

At this point, your computer should be configured only with an administrator's name and password and basic settings such as date, time, and keyboard settings. Do not configure any network settings.

Configure preference settings and update software

Because you will be using multiple user accounts, you need to disable automatic login.

1   Open the Accounts pane of System Preferences.

2   Click the Lock button and authenticate as Apple Admin.

3   Click Login Options.

4   Deselect the "Automatically log in as" checkbox.

    Disabling automatic login is a basic security measure. If your computer logs in automatically, any person who starts the computer can access your files.

5   Select "Name and password" for "Display Login Window as."

6   Select the "Enable fast user switching" checkbox.

7   Click OK in the Warning sheet.

    During certain exercises, you will need to quickly switch between different user accounts. With Fast User Switching enabled, you will be able to log in a new user without having to log out the current user.

8   Click the Show All button to return to all System Preferences.

9   Open the Date & Time pane of System Preferences.

10 Deselect the checkbox for "Set date & time automatically" if it's selected.

11 Click the Show All button to return to all System Preferences.

12 Open the Network pane of System Preferences.

13 From the Show pop-up menu, choose Network Port Configurations.

14 Turn off all Port Configurations except Built-in Ethernet.

    This will ensure that you are not inadvertently connecting to a network other than the private network you are creating.

15 Click Apply Now.

16 Click the Show All button to return to all System Preferences.

17 Open the Sharing pane of System Preferences.

18 In the Computer Name field, enter *DS Client* and press the Tab key.

19 Quit System Preferences.

20 Temporarily connect to the Internet and run Software Update repeatedly to obtain all current software updates.

21 Download and install Server Admin Tools, if you do not already have them, from the Apple support site (www.apple.com/support).

22 Insert the Mac OS X v10.4 DVD and install the Developer Tools.

23 Install Remote Desktop Admin software if you have purchased it from Apple. (It is not necessary for this book but may help manage your remote server.)

24 Run Software Update repeatedly to update any final tools.

25 Disconnect from the Internet and connect to your local private switch to ensure that you are on a private network.

Configure Workgroup Manager

You can use Workgroup Manager in its default configuration to modify user and group records. However, in this course you will also use it to directly view and modify directory data. In order to do so, you need to enable the Inspector.

1 Open /Applications/Server/Workgroup Manager.

Typically, Workgroup Manager is used to administer a Mac OS X Server computer. However, you can skip connecting to a server and just manage the accounts in the local NetInfo database.

2   Choose Server > View Directories.

This command dismisses the Connect dialog and opens a Workgroup Manager window for the local directory.

3   In the "This is not a server directory node" warning sheet, select the "Do not show this warning again" checkbox and click OK.

The purpose of this warning is to remind you that you are editing directory data on a non–Mac OS X Server computer.

4   Choose Workgroup Manager > Preferences.

5   Select the "Show 'All Records' tab and Inspector" checkbox.

This option allows you to use Workgroup Manager to directly view and manipulate directory service data.

6   Click OK.

Notice that an Inspector button (a target) has been added next to the Users, Groups, and Computers buttons on the left. The Inspector is used to modify data directly.

7   Click OK in the warning sheet.

8   Quit Workgroup Manager.

Workgroup Manager is now configured to allow you to view native directory data.

Perform the initial server configuration
Later on in the directory services section, you will configure Mac OS X Server to provide directory services.

1   Do a custom erase and install of Mac OS X Server, and add the X11 package if this is a computer that can have all of the data on it erased. *Do not erase a disk with data you want to keep!*

2   If this is a portable computer, ensure that the power cable is connected.

3   In the Welcome window, select your country of choice and click Continue.

4   In the Select Your Keyboard Keyboard window, make your choice and click Continue.

5   In the Serial Number window, enter the serial number that came with your server software.

6   In the Administrator Account pane, create an administrator account with these settings:

Name: *First Administrator*

Short Name: *fadmin*

Password: *fadmin*

Using the same word for the user name and password does not follow best practices. Because you will be using many different accounts and passwords throughout the book, the exercises use simple, easy-to-recall passwords.

7   Click Continue.

8   In the Network Names pane, enter the following:

Computer Name: *C-serverbook*

Local Hostname: *C-serverbook*

9   Click Continue.

In the Network Interfaces list, make sure TCP/IP is selected for the Built-in Ethernet port and that all other checkboxes are deselected, and then click Continue.

10 In the TCP/IP Connection pane for Built-in Ethernet, configure your connection as follows:

Configure IPv4: *Manually*

IP Address: *10.1.10.1*

Subnet Mask: *255.255.0.0*

Router Address: *10.1.10.1*

DNS: *10.1.10.1*

Search Domains: *pretendco.com*

11 Click Continue.

12 In the Directory Usage pane, choose Standalone Server from the "Set directory usage to" pop-up menu and click Continue.

13 In the Services pane, leave all services off except Apple Remote Desktop and click Continue.

14 In the Time Zone pane, select your time zone and click Continue.

15 In the Network Time pane, make sure to deselect the "Use a network time server" checkbox if it's selected.

16 Click Continue.

17 Review your settings, make corrections if necessary, and then click Apply.

Server Assistant configures the server according to your instructions and then reboots the server.

18 After the server reboots, log in as First Administrator (password: *fadmin*).

19 Obtain the latest Mac OS X Server Combo update and install that update.

20 Install Developer Tools from the Mac OS X Server CD or DVD.

21 Open the Server Admin application located in /Applications/Server and authenticate as First Administrator.

22 Select your server from the list on the left, click the Settings button, and then choose Date & Time.

23 Double-check your time zone, changing it if necessary, and click Save.

24 Quit Server Admin.

Apple Certification Program

This book is an excellent preparation for the following exams:

▶ Directory Services Integration and Administration v10.4 Exam (9L0-611), worth four points

▶ Security Best Practices v10.4 Exam (9L0-612), worth three points

It also addresses networking and file-service objectives for both Mac OS X and Mac OS X Server. Successful completion of these two exams earns an Apple Certified System Administrator (ACSA) certification, which requires seven points. Before you take the tests, you should review this book and spend time setting up, configuring, and working with directory services and security methodology on both Mac OS X and Mac OS X Server.

You should also download and review the Skills Assessment Guide, which lists the exam objectives, the total number of items, the number of items per section, the required score to pass, and how to register. To download the Skills Assessment Guide, visit http://train.apple.com/certification.

Earning Apple technical certification shows employers that you have a high level of technical proficiency with Apple products. You'll also join a growing community of skilled professionals—Apple Mac OS X certification programs are among the fastest-growing certifications in the industry, with 300 percent growth in 2004.

Achieving any of the Mac OS X certifications also qualifies you to join the new Mac OS X Certification Alliance, a free benefit program that recognizes and supports the thousands of Mac OS X experts worldwide. For more information, visit http://train.apple.com/certification/macosx.

For those who prefer to learn in an instructor-led setting, Apple also offers training courses at Apple Authorized Training Centers across worldwide. These courses, which use the Apple Training Series books as their curriculum, are taught by Apple-certified trainers and balance concepts and lectures with hands-on labs and exercises. Apple Authorized Training Centers have been carefully selected and have met Apple's highest standards in all areas, including facilities, instructors, course delivery, and infrastructure. The goal of the program is to offer Apple customers, from beginners to the most seasoned professionals, the highest-quality training experience. To find an Apple Authorized Training Center near you, go to www.apple.com/training.

Part 1   Directory Services Administration

1

Time   This lesson takes approximately 1 hour to complete.

Goals   Understand the need for directory services to store system data such as user records

Identify what system data is appropriate to store using directory services

Learn the relationship between a requestor, such as an application, and directory services data

Learn how directory services enable data to be shared between multiple requestors

Understand how directory services allow requestors to retrieve data from multiple sources

Understanding Directory Services

In this first section of the book, Part 1: "Directory Services Administration," you will learn the benefits and features of directory services in Mac OS X version 10.4. This first lesson introduces you to the concept of directory services, how they are used to provide common data to multiple services, and the format of the most frequently used directory services data types.

If you have spent time setting up Mac OS X computers and servers, you have probably heard of directory services. However, since directory services work behind the scenes, most people aren't even be aware of their presence unless they are misconfigured. Then everyone knows, because their computers do not work properly.

Before Directory Services: Separate Files

Applications often ask for your identity and for a means of authenticating that identity with a user name and password. You propose an identity by entering a user name, which is then compared to a list of user names. Once the application finds a matching identity, authentication (proof of identity) is required. By entering a password, you are proposing a piece of information that can be used to authenticate against. Once your account has been authenticated, you are authorized—using your proposed identity—to gain access to resources needed while using the application.

Identification and authentication information (or methods) must be stored in a way that makes them easy for applications to access. For years, UNIX systems stored administrative information in a collection of files located in the /etc directory. This scheme required each computer to have its own local set of files for applications to find administrative information. If you're experienced with UNIX, you probably know about the files in the /etc directory—group, hosts, master.passwd, and so on.

For example, a UNIX application that needed to identify a user account and verify the password consulted the /etc/master.passwd file. For group information, it consulted the /etc/group file. This means of storing identification and authentication information was not very centralized, could not be easily distributed, and worked only with certain types of operating systems.

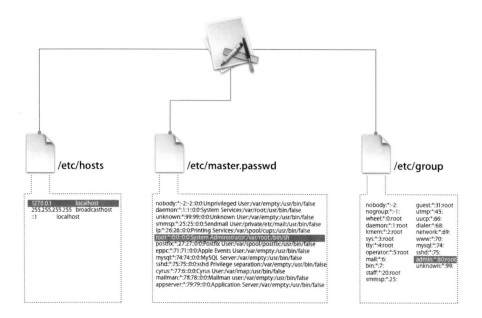

Another disadvantage of this method is that information was stored in a variety of places (in other words, files). If you wanted to add a user, you had to first add the user to the master.passwd file, then possibly edit the group file to add that user to various groups. Permitting users to change their passwords often involved a cumbersome method of using the command line. Meanwhile, the password itself was stored in the master.passwd file, along with the user information. Not only was this method difficult to manage, but it was also insecure by today's standards.

The first step to collecting and storing all the information in one centralized location was having all the necessary files inside the /etc directory, but individual files were not necessarily the best answer.

After Directory Services: Solidified Data Structure

Today, a directory service provides a central location for commonly requested identification and authentication information. It is the protocol(s), process(es), and data store(s) that provide a method for requesting and receiving data. Having the central data store, rather than scattered files, was integral to the bigger picture.

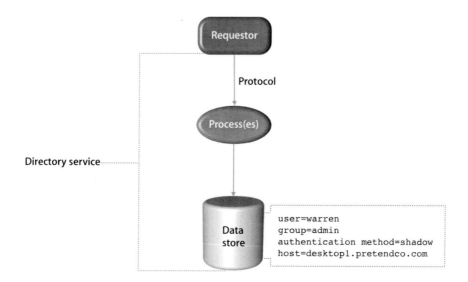

Centralized Data Store

Instead of requiring users to enter a user name and password each time they use a different application, requests can be made to a central directory service. By consolidating or centralizing this information, directory services simplify the interactions between applications (requestors) and the administrative data they create and use. Requestors no longer need to know how and where administrative data is stored: Directory services can retrieve the data for them. If a requestor needs the location of a user's home folder, it simply has directory services retrieve the information and then return it to the requestor, insulating the requestor from the details of how the information is stored.

This centralizing of information is particularly beneficial to administrators, because they don't have to maintain separate user account information on each individual's computer. Additionally, information does not have to be maintained in several different formats to support different client applications.

However, a distribution method must be in place to permit one computer to access directory information on another computer.

Distribution

Directory services provide a way to distribute identification and authentication information. They are either local (they are used only on your local computer) or remote (they reside on another computer and your computer must be configured to request information from them remotely).

Requestors can be configured to use common protocols to request that information through remote processes and, therefore, access remote data stores. Remote directory services enable you to distribute the information and make it available to more than one computer over a common protocol.

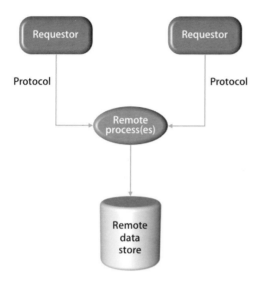

This method works well if all computers are running an identical operating system, but one more piece to the puzzle is needed to make directory services complete: a middleman.

Heterogeneous Integration

Directory services enable you to access identification and authentication information from a variety of data stores. The problem, however, is that having user information stored in many different places can pose an administrative challenge. A given user might have a record on many different computers, making tasks such as updating passwords or modifying user information more difficult and prone to error. In addition, users might need to remember several user names and passwords—often a different set for each service. As a result, administrators are forced to learn and understand many different tools for working with all the systems.

This problem is solved by using a standard set of processes that handle all directory-service calls. This "middleman" gives requestors a means of gathering information from a variety of directory services, using the processes and data stores of those services, without the requestor needing to know where the information came from or what format it was in. Furthermore, the information can be distributed so that it is visible on a network to the computers that need it and the administrators who manage it. In Mac OS X and Mac OS X Server, this "middleman" is called *Open Directory*.

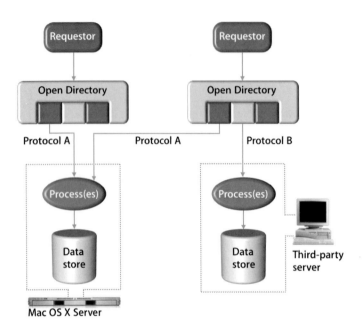

Defining Directory-Services Terminology

Now that you have seen the very basics of directory services and to avoid any confusion with similar terms used in different contexts, the following definitions apply to the terms used in the directory services lessons of this book:

▶ Directory service: Process(es), protocol(s), and data store(s) that provide a method for requesting data and receiving that data in a scalable, centralized, and distributable manner. An example of a complete directory service would be Lightweight Directory Access Protocol (LDAP), where the process is slapd, the protocol is LDAP, and the data store is a Berkeley DB database.

▶ Protocol: A common set of rules to request and receive data. For example, LDAP is a protocol for communicating between requestors and an LDAP directory.

▶ Process: Executables that handle client requests and retrieve data. Two examples are slapd (for accessing LDAP directories) and netinfod (for accessing NetInfo databases).

▶ Data store: A specialized read-optimized database, such as a set of flat files.

- ▶ Directory: A data store that follows a particular way of organizing data for a directory service. A Berkeley DB database that is structured to be accessed via LDAP is an LDAP directory.

- ▶ Directory domain: A logical grouping of data.

- ▶ Open Directory: Apple's overall name for the implementation of directory services in Mac OS X and Mac OS X Server.

- ▶ DirectoryService: The actual process that handles directory service calls in Mac OS X and Mac OS X Server, and passes those requests to other directory services based on a plug-in architecture.

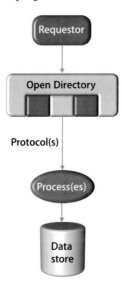

By defining certain aspects of the directory structure, it's easy to see how these pieces work together to provide the requestor with information from the data store.

Managing Directory Information

Directory services allow easy access and management of information by organizing data in *records*. Each record describes different kinds of entities in the database such as users, groups, or mounts. The information stored into each record is in plaintext format and is organized in attributes and related values.

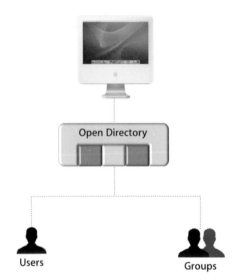

Mac OS X uses sets of predefined standard records called *record types,* which serve as a blueprint for standard entry into the directory data store (often referred to as the directory database). Some standard entries in the database are:

▶ User records, with attributes such as RecordName, RealName, UniqueID, GeneratedUID, and AuthenticationAuthority

▶ Group records, with attributes such as RecordName, RealName, PrimaryGroupID, GeneratedUID, and GroupMembers

▶ Mount records, with attributes such as RecordName, VFSLinkDir, VFSType, and VFSOpts

Each record type contains sets of predefined attributes and related values that define specific information for a specific entry, such as users. These attributes describe a characteristic type of information related to a record and are used to hold values (the actual data that an attribute contains).

As you will see throughout this section, there can be many different types of records and attributes can often have more than one value.

User Records

Every user account on the computer must contain enough information to uniquely identify and authenticate the user. Providing additional attributes, such as both the long name and short name, user ID, password type, primary group ID, shell type, and home folder location, will make for a richer user experience than just a plain login.

```
AuthenticationAuthority: ;ShadowHash;
AuthenticationHint:
NFSHomeDirectory: /Users/elle
Password: ********
Picture: /Library/User Pictures/Animals/Jaguar.tif
PrimaryGroupID: 501
RealName: Elle Bee
RecordName: elle
UniqueID: 501
GeneratedUID: C56D2D5C-7EB4-11D8-84F1-0030654CB2AC
UserShell: /bin/bash
```

When creating user accounts using Mac OS X and Mac OS X Server GUI tools such as the Accounts preferences pane and Workgroup Manager, certain attributes are necessary (and automatically generated unless otherwise noted). For a basic level of user experience, the following attributes should have values:

Attribute	Definition	Example Value
RecordName	The user's primary short name, used to identify the record in the database	susan
RealName	The user's long name	Susan Admin
UniqueID	The user ID used by standard UNIX file permissions	501
GeneratedUID	128-bit user ID; should be unique across multiple systems; used by access control list (ACL) permissions and group membership	C56D2D5C-7EB4-11D8-84F1-0030654CB2AC
Password	Crypt password	xwi/q8lhgFrYU
NFSHomeDirectory	Local file-system path to the user's home folder	/Users/susan
UserShell	The location of the default shell for command line	/bin/bash

MORE INFO ▶ The previous table lists key user-record attributes. Additional attributes will be discussed in Lesson 3, "Accessing Mac OS X Server Directory Services."

NOTE ▶ Standard UNIX file permissions are for user, group, and other. The permissions options are read, write, and execute. Bear in mind that users added with the GUI tools do not require a password, although the attribute will still be created. Also, the Accounts preferences pane automatically creates a home folder for every user on Mac OS X, whereas using Workgroup Manager to create local Mac OS X accounts does not.

Understanding Local Authentication

Because the operating system must always be able to authenticate a user even when the computer is not connected to a network, user passwords are stored locally on the computer in a scrambled form using either crypt or shadow hash.

Crypt

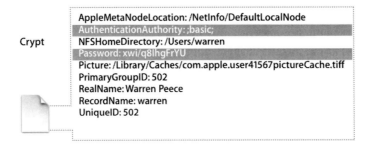

```
AppleMetaNodeLocation: /NetInfo/DefaultLocalNode
AuthenticationAuthority: ;basic;
NFSHomeDirectory: /Users/warren
Password: xwi/q8lhgFrYU
Picture: /Library/Caches/com.apple.user41567pictureCache.tiff
PrimaryGroupID: 502
RealName: Warren Peece
RecordName: warren
UniqueID: 502
```

Shadow password

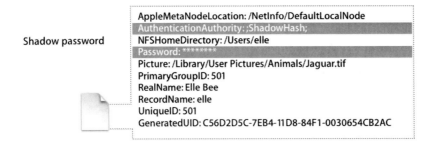

```
AppleMetaNodeLocation: /NetInfo/DefaultLocalNode
AuthenticationAuthority: ;ShadowHash;
NFSHomeDirectory: /Users/elle
Password: ********
Picture: /Library/User Pictures/Animals/Jaguar.tif
PrimaryGroupID: 501
RealName: Elle Bee
RecordName: elle
UniqueID: 501
GeneratedUID: C56D2D5C-7EB4-11D8-84F1-0030654CB2AC
```

Crypt Passwords

A crypt password is stored as a hash directly in the user account. Because user records are accessible by anyone using the computer (in the case of shared directory, potentially anyone on the network), crypt passwords are not very secure. Once another user has the hash, they can easily run cracking applications to reverse the hash into the users password using readily available tools, such as John the Ripper.

New accounts created in Mac OS X v10.3 or later no longer use crypt passwords. However, because older versions of Mac OS X expect to find passwords in crypt format, Mac OS X will still accept authentication using crypt passwords. The requestor (for example, the Login Window application) is responsible for authenticating user accounts that have crypt passwords by doing a crypt compare. However, the Login Window will change the password type from Crypt to Shadow the first time the user logs in with the old crypt password. It also creates a GeneratedUID for that user account if none exists.

When looking at a user record with a tool such as dscl, crypt passwords are denoted by the "basic" value in the AuthenticationAuthority attribute. The scrambled form of the password is found in the Password attribute. If there is no value for the AuthenticationAuthority attribute, then basic, or crypt, is assumed.

Shadow Passwords

A *shadow password* is stored as several hashes in a file. Because the password isn't stored directly in the user account, other users cannot access it, and it is more secure than a crypt password. The shadow password file for each user is named according to the user's GeneratedUID or RecordName and is stored in /var/db/shadow/hash. These files are accessible only by root. Earlier versions of Mac OS X stored an NTLM hash of the password, but Mac OS X v10.4 does not, a significant security gain.

> **NOTE** ► Shadow passwords are used only for local or mobile accounts.

The AuthenticationAuthority for a shadow password is ;ShadowHash; and you will see eight asterisks in the Password attribute, indicating that there is no password stored in this record. The DirectoryService process is the authoritative authentication agent for

Mac OS X (except in the case of crypt passwords or Kerberos authentication, which will be discussed in Lesson 2, "Accessing Local Directory Services"). This means that DirectoryService is responsible for authenticating user accounts that use shadow passwords.

While crypt passwords can be only 8 bytes in length, shadow passwords do not have that limitation. Furthermore, hashes for NT/LAN Manager are also stored in the shadow password file, providing additional compatibility. LAN Manager uses the first 14 characters of the shadow password; NT authentication uses the first 128 characters. These limitations are applicable only in the case of a Server Message Block (SMB) authentication. The SHA1 method, which you will learn more about later in this section, hashes the entire password.

Group Records

Advanced configurations and customizations might require additional information. Configuring workgroup management or setting up group folders requires access to different entities in the database. Group record types will provide all the attributes needed to support groups functionality in Mac OS X client computers.

```
GeneratedUID: C56D2D5C-7EB4-11D8-84F1-0030654CB2AC
GroupMembership: root elle
Password: *
PrimaryGroupID: 80
RealName: Administrators
RecordName: admin
GroupMembers: B12D5D56-7EB2-99D8-54C1-34929CB20A96
              4DAA0134-7699-11D8-84F1-87ABBC1378988
NestedGroups: F7D7D614-5C33-4183-B8A3-7F476F781DC8
              F8328B5C-1234-6BCE-A7B2-7F3423BDCA11
```

Like user records, group records contain attributes and values. The following table lists group attributes.

Attribute	Definition	Example Value
RecordName	Name associated with the group	admin
RealName	The group's full name	Administrators
PrimaryGroupID	Unique identifier for the group used by standard BSD file permissions	80
GenerateUID	128-bit group ID; should be unique across multiple systems; used by ACL permissions and group membership	C56D2D5C-7EB4-11D8-84F1-0030654CB2AC
GroupMembership	A list of short names of user records that are considered part of the group	root susan
GroupMembers	A list of generated UIDs of user records that are considered part of the group	B12D5D56-7EB2-99D8-54C1-34929CB20A964DAA0134-7699-11D8-84F1-87ABBC1378988
NestedGroups	A list of generated UIDs of group records that are considered part of the group	F7D7D614-5C33-4183-B8A3-7F476F781DC8F8328B5C-1234-6BCE-A7B2-7F3423BDCA11

A default installation of Mac OS X includes the creation of several system groups. One of the more important groups is Administrator. All members of this group have administrative capabilities on the computer.

memberd and Nested Groups

Mac OS X v10.4 also uses a new schema which permits the nesting of groups (Legacy UNIX groups, however, will retain their older style). The process now used to resolve group memberships is memberd, but it is not sufficient to manually edit groups so you should use dseditgroup for that task.

Creating User Accounts and Exploring Directory Services

User and group records are two of the more important types of system data stored using directory services. As you manage directory services, it is important to be able to identify the key components of both record types.

In this exercise, you will create two standard user accounts and then use the command-line utility dscl to explore the types of information in the user and group records in the local directory services database on Mac OS X.

1   On your client computer, log in as Apple Admin.

2   Open the Accounts pane of System Preferences and create a new user account for Warren Peece using the following values:

Name: *Warren Peece*

Short name: *warren*

Password: *2bornot2b*

Password hint: *Hamlet*

Do not give the account administrative authority.

3   Create a second user account for Isadora Jarr with the following values:

Name: *Isadora Jarr*

Short name: *isadora*

Password: *ml8ml8*

Password hint: *White Rabbit*

Give Isadora's account administrative authority.

4   Quit System Preferences.

Exploring Directory Services With dscl

The dscl utility is very useful for finding out what information is returned when DirectoryService requests are made. Since it is a command-line utility, it can be used remotely with ssh.

1   Open Terminal.

2   Display the manual page for dscl by typing *man dscl.*

3   Read the Description paragraph and then quit the man page (press Control-Z).

As described in the man page, you use the dscl command-line utility to access and set information in a directory domain. The format of the command is

dscl [*options*] datasource [*command*]

Without specifying a command, dscl operates in interactive mode. This is useful for browsing available directory data.

4   Run dscl in interactive mode by typing *dscl localhost.*

5   At the prompt (/>), type *list.*

A list of data paths is displayed. For example:

Bonjour

NetInfo

SLP

SMB

Search

Contact

6   At the prompt, type *cd Search.*

The prompt changes to indicate that you are now in a path that can be used to search directory services for information.

7   List the categories of records that can be searched by typing *ls.*

The ls command is the same as the list command. The records in a folder are organized in a hierarchy.

8   Change to the Users folder by typing *cd Users.*

9 List the records in the Users folder by typing *ls*.

You will see a record for each user account in the local database on this computer. Information that is normally stored in /etc/master.passwd (or /etc/group) on other UNIX systems is stored in these records.

10 Display Warren's user record by typing *read warren*.

Read the information for Warren's user record and identify the following fields:

▶ RealName (long name)

▶ RecordName (short name)

▶ UniqueID (UID)

▶ GeneratedUID

▶ NFSHomeDirectory (home directory path)

The Password attribute is listed, as well as the authentication method (Authentication-Authority), but the Password value is displayed as eight asterisks (********).

11 Display the user record for Isadora and compare it to Warren's.

Notice that the two records contain the same attributes, even though Isadora has an admin account. An account's authority is not determined by the account itself; it depends on whether it belongs to the admin group.

12 Navigate to the listing of group records by typing *cd ../Groups*.

Notice that navigating around in dscl is similar to using the command line to navigate the file system.

13 List the records in the Groups folder by typing *ls*.

You will see a record for each group in the local data store. This information would normally be stored in /etc/groups on other UNIX systems.

14 Display the contents of the admin group record. (The syntax of dscl on how to navigate and read records should be somewhat familiar now.)

In the GroupMembership field, you will see the short names of all the users who are members of the admin group (and are therefore administrators of the machine).

15 Quit dscl by typing q and pressing the Return key.

Using dscl to Modify Directory Data

In this scenario, it's best if your security policy states that user records should not include the password hint. This, of course, would be up to the administrator to specify. You can use dscl to modify the user records and remove the password hint.

1   Using root access (sudo), run the dscl command in interactive mode (sudo dscl localhost).

You don't need root access to view directory data, but you need root access to modify it. You can also modify data using dscl by authenticating in the command itself.

2   Navigate to the listing of user records.

3   Display Warren's user record.

Note the name of the attribute that contains the password hint.

4   Use the delete command to delete the attribute containing the hint.

The format of the delete command is

delete *path* [*key* [*val...*]]

where *path* is the path to the record that you want to modify, *key* is the attribute to modified, and *val* is the value to be deleted. If you do not specify a value, the attribute is deleted.

5   To delete the password hint from warren's user record, type *delete warren AuthenticationHint.*

6   Display Warren's user record again.

The AuthenticationHint attribute is now gone.

7   Delete the password hint from Isadora's user account.

8   Quit dscl.

9   Quit Terminal.

10 Log out.

Try logging in several times as Warren and Isadora with incorrect passwords and verify that a password hint is not displayed.

What You've Learned

▶   Directory services allow multiple processes to access common system data, such as user information.

▶   A centralized data store allows for easier maintenance by a system administrator.

▶   With data stored on a network server, multiple computers can access the same data.

▶   With proper configuration, the same user account can be used to log in on multiple computers on the network; the user is no longer tied to a single computer.

▶   User records, the most frequently used record type, stores information to uniquely identify a user. Group records define one or more users that should share certain system permissions.

References

Administration Guides

"Mac OS X Server Getting Started": http://images.apple.com/server/pdfs/Getting_Started_v10.4.pdf

"Upgrading and Migrating to Mac OS X Server v10.4 Tiger": http://images.apple.com/server/pdfs/Migration_v10.4.pdf

"Open Directory Administration": http://images.apple.com/server/pdfs/Open_Directory_v10.4.pdf

"User Management": http://images.apple.com/server/pdfs/User_Management_Admin_v10.4.pdf

"Mac OS X Server Command-Line Administration": http://images.apple.com/server/pdfs/Command_Line_v10.4.pdf

Books

Carter, Gerald. *LDAP System Administration* (O'Reilly, 2003).

URLs

Managing Users and groups on FreeBSD: http://www.perlcode.org/tutorials/sysadmin/managing_users.pod

Lesson Review

1. What is a directory service?

2. What is the primary benefit of a directory service?

3. What are the key user record attributes?

4. What is the difference between how crypt and shadow hash passwords are stored?

5. What is the default password type for Mac OS X v10.4?

6. What is the purpose of the GroupMembers attribute in a groups record?

7. What is the format of the Password value in an Open Directory user record?

8. What is the purpose of the PrimaryGroupID value in a group record?

Answers

1. A directory service is the process(es), protocol(s), and data store(s) that provide a method for requesting data and receiving that data in a scalable, centralized, and distributable manner.

2. A directory service provides a centralized location for commonly requested system information.

3. RecordName, RealName, UniqueID, GeneratedUID, Password, NFSHomeDirectory, and UserShell

4. A crypt password is stored as a hash in the user account. A shadow password is stored as several hashes in a file elsewhere.

5. hash

6. GroupMembers is a list of the generated UIDs for users and other groups that are members of the group.

7. If a password is stored in the user record, it is stored in crypt format.

8. It serves as a unique identifier for the group.

2

Time

This lesson takes approximately 2 hours to complete.

Goals

Understand the type of data stored in each of the BSD flat files and identify those used by the Open Directory plug-in

Use Directory Access to configure Open Directory on a Mac OS X computer to retrieve user records from BSD flat files

Modify data in the local NetInfo database with both Workgroup Manager and dscl

Understand how the DirectoryService process on Mac OS X uses plug-ins to access system information

Use the lookupd command-line tool to determine which agents, in what order, are used for a particular category of items

List the local data stores that Open Directory uses on Mac OS X

Use lookupd to search for different types of user information

Accessing Local Directory Services

This lesson introduces you to how Mac OS X accesses directory data stored on the computer, how to configure Mac OS X for local data access, and how to manipulate local directory data.

While directory services as a solution is well understood, the implementation of different vendors' directory services can vary. As mentioned in the previous lesson, the Apple implementation of directory services is called Open Directory. This lesson will provide the fundamentals on how Open Directory is implemented in Mac OS X. Although Open Directory is a very complex and broad subject, understanding this lesson is essential for progressing ever deeper into the heart of directory services on Mac OS X.

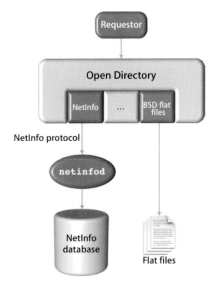

Understanding Local Data Stores

Open Directory in Mac OS X and Mac OS X Server provides system-level support for directory services as well as an extensible plug-in architecture that allows access to different data stores or other directory services. Like any directory service, it provides a standardized way for applications to request and receive information. Open Directory provides access to two local data stores—NetInfo and BSD flat files.

NetInfo

The NetInfo database is a repository for administrative information and is the default local data store in Mac OS X. It stores information that was traditionally found in configuration files in UNIX and some Apple-specific information, including the records for local users and groups, mount records, and possibly managed client settings. Some services that run on Mac OS X also use the local NetInfo database to store configuration information. For example, the Internet sharing feature (enabled in System Preferences) stores the Dynamic Host Configuration Protocol (DHCP) subnet information in the local NetInfo database. The NetInfo database is accessed through the netinfod process.

> **NOTE ▸** Regardless of how you have configured directory services to search for data, the local NetInfo database is always searched first.

This figure shows how traditional UNIX directory data was stored in several files (on the right) and how Mac OS X stores the data in the local NetInfo database (on the left).

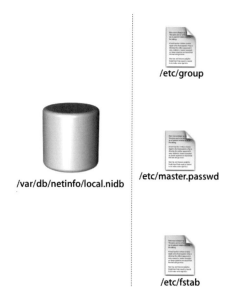

/etc/group

/var/db/netinfo/local.nidb

/etc/master.passwd

/etc/fstab

BSD Flat Files

In Mac OS X version 10.2 and later, directory services can also retrieve administrative data from Berkeley System Distribution's version of UNIX (BSD) configuration files, or flat files. This capability enables organizations that already have flat files to use copies of those existing files on Mac OS X computers. BSD flat files can be used alone or in conjunction with other directory services.

Mac OS X v10.2 also allowed you to use any BSD flat files and to customize the mappings of the attributes. Mac OS X v10.3 and later uses a fixed set of flat files. As such, no custom mapping of contents to Mac OS X record types or attributes is allowed.

Because NetInfo and flat files are the only two local data stores, inserting flat files into the directory services data path can be used to show how directory services can access more than one source of administration information. BSD flat files should not be used as a replacement for local directory services; however, in some cases they are used to augment the local NetInfo database by allowing users to log in who are missing from the local NetInfo database.

The following table lists the BSD configuration flat files.

Configuration File	Content
/etc/master.passwd	Users and crypt passwords
/etc/group	Groups
/etc/fstab	NFS mounts
/etc/hosts	Computer names and addresses
/etc/networks	Network names and addresses
/etc/services	TCP/IP service ports and protocols
/etc/protocols	IP protocol names and numbers
/etc/rpcs	ONC RPC servers
/etc/printcap	Printers
/etc/bootparams	Boot parameter settings

Configuration File	Content
/etc/bootp	bootp settings
/etc/aliases	Email aliases and distribution lists
/etc/netgroup	Network groups

You can edit the content of the flat files using any standard text editor.

Locating Standard UNIX Files Containing User and Group Data

To show that the BSD flat files still exist in Mac OS X and Mac OS X Server, follow these steps:

1 Log in to your computer with the local administrator account.

2 Open the Terminal application, type *sudo –s* to enter a root shell, and type the local administrator password when prompted.

3 Type *more /etc/master.passwd* and press the Return key to view the contents of the file.

4 If necessary, press the Space bar to move through the file.

Every user record in /etc/master.passwd on Mac OS X contains ten attributes, each separated by a colon (:). For example, the following line of code has ten attributes, although other variants of this file may have more or fewer attributes depending on the version of UNIX being used and/or the administrator's prerogative.

mysql:*:74:74::0:0:MySQL Server:/var/empty:/usr/bin/false

▶ The first attribute is the short user name (mysql).

▶ The second attribute is the account password. An asterisk (*) indicates no password is set for this user.

▶ The third and fourth attributes are the user and primary group IDs, respectively.

▶ The fifth attribute should be the account's general classification. (UNIX accounts lack this attribute.)

▶ The next two attributes are for the password change time (0) and account expiration time (0).

▶ The following attribute is the user's long name (MySQL Server).

▶ The next attribute is a pointer to the location of the home folder, if one exists (/var/empty).

▶ The final attribute is the default shell, if permitted (/usr/bin/false).

5 After viewing the /etc/master.passwd file, type *more /etc/group* to view the contents of the group file.

Modifying the NetInfo Database

The NetInfo database is organized hierarchically, much like a file system. Each folder has properties (referenced by property keys) and values (which depend on the property). The netinfod process provides access to the database, and the database is stored at /var/db/netinfo.

The following figure illustrates how netinfod reads from the local NetInfo database and writes to, in this case, netinfo.log. When managing the NetInfo database, you can use dscl or NetInfo Manager, although Workgroup Manager is better suited to the task.

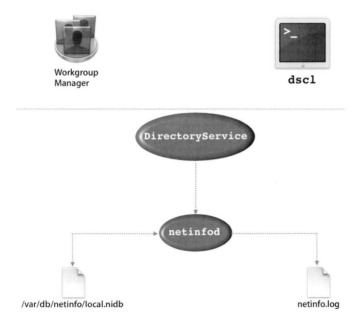

NOTE ▶ While NetInfo calls them properties, Workgroup Manager calls them attributes. This book will use the universal term *attributes,* since the term *properties* is more specific to NetInfo.

Using Command-Line Utilities

For command-line access to the NetInfo database, you can use the dscl utility. It includes commands to read, create, and manage NetInfo data. If used without any commands, dscl runs in an interactive mode, reading commands from standard input. Because dscl uses the DirectoryService process, it is able to access directory data from any of the directory services that Mac OS X supports.

The nicl utility is a legacy tool that works directly with the NetInfo database. Because nicl does not go through DirectoryService, it can be used to edit the NetInfo database directly. Unlike dscl, nicl can access only NetInfo data. You can use either dscl or nicl to edit directory data from the command line, but while dscl an edit both databases, nicl can be used in single user mode, (nicl –raw /var/db/netinfo/local.nidb). As a precautionary measure, you should backup your NetInfo database before editing by using the line nidump -r / . > ~/Documents/local.dump to dump a copy of the NetInfo database to your Documents folder.

Although you can use dscl to edit group information, Mac OS X includes dseditgroup for manipulating a group record. The format of the command is

dseditgroup [options] [parameters] *groupname*

where *groupname* is the group record being manipulated.

MORE INFO ▶ Refer to the man page for dseditgroup for a listing of valid options. Because of the new schema surrounding groups, it would be rather tedious to attempt to edit groups the way it was done in previous versions of Mac OS X. The dseditgroup command was created specifically for the purpose of managing groups, and should be used accordingly.

Using GUIs

If you prefer using a graphical user interface (GUI), you can use either Workgroup Manager or NetInfo Manager to view and change records, properties (attributes), and values in the NetInfo database. However, you should be aware of the differences between the two tools.

Workgroup Manager

Workgroup Manager ships with Mac OS X Server to enable you to administer user, group, and computer accounts; manage share points; and perform client-management functions for Mac OS X users. Workgroup Manager is also available online as part of the Server Admin Tools package (www.apple.com/downloads/macosx/apple/serveradmintools104.html).

This tool features an Inspector mode that provides an administrator full access to all of the information stored in either the Lightweight Directory Access Protocol (LDAP) or NetInfo databases. With the Inspector, you can directly manipulate the attributes and values that Workgroup Manager would have changed automatically for you. You are also able to select whether to view the raw LDAP attribute names as the LDAP server sees them, and/or the Open Directory names, after Directory Access has mapped them.

NetInfo Manager

NetInfo Manager ships as part of Mac OS X (/Applications/Utilities) and, like Workgroup Manager, it is used to view and modify directory data. However, it is limited to data in the NetInfo database. Also, it bypasses the DirectoryService process and accesses the NetInfo database directly.

> **TIP** Apple recommends that you use Workgroup Manager to access directory data whenever possible. It works with both LDAP and NetInfo directory domains, and provides an Open Directory view of the data and parameters.

Configuring the DirectoryService Process

You use the Directory Access application (located in /Applications/Utilities) to configure DirectoryService, thus allowing the possibility of searching more than the local NetInfo database (recall that Mac OS X always searches the local NetInfo database first, and this behavior cannot be changed using the Directory Access application). When more than two data stores are searched, you can also decide in what order they are searched.

Directory Access is also used to select which plug-ins to enable. For each plug-in, you can configure that service by selecting the service and clicking the Configure button. Activating
a particular plug-in simply allows DirectoryService to place requests using that plug-in; it does not guarantee that the referenced directory service or data store is enabled or configured properly.

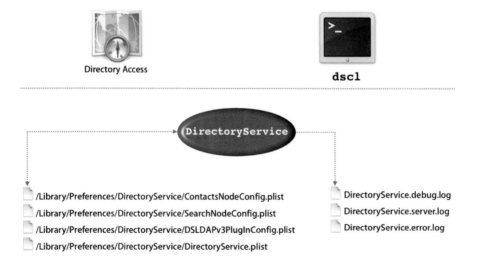

The BSD plug-in for DirectoryService (which doubles as the NIS plug-in) does not require any configuration when used strictly for enabling the searching of BSD files. Once it is enabled and the change applied, it will be eligible to be added to the search policies for both authentication and contacts.

Defining Search Policies

Use Directory Access to define the following search policies:

▶ Mac OS X uses the authentication search policy to locate and retrieve user authentication information and other administrative data from directory services or data stores.

▶ Mac OS X uses the contacts search policy to locate and retrieve name, address, and other contact information from directory services or data stores. Address Book uses this contact information, and other applications can be programmed to use it as well.

Each search policy consists of a list of *directory nodes* (also known as *directory domains*). The order of directory nodes in the list defines the search policy. Starting at the top of the list, Mac OS X searches each listed directory node in turn until it either finds the information it needs or reaches the end of the list without finding the information.

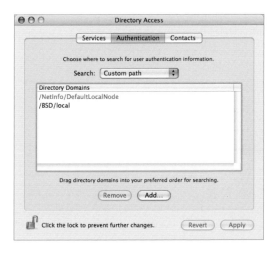

```
dscl localhost -read Search
```

You can set the authentication search policy and contacts search policy as follows:

▶ "Automatic" starts with the local directory domain and can include an LDAP directory supplied automatically by DHCP and NetInfo domains to which the computer is bound. An automatic search policy is the default setting for Mac OS X v10.2 and later, and offers the most flexibility for mobile computers.

▶   "Local directory" includes only the local directory domain.

▶   "Custom path" starts with the local directory domain and includes your choice of one or several LDAP directories, an Active Directory domain, NetInfo domains, BSD configuration files, and an NIS domain.

To verify that DirectoryService is using the configuration you specified in Directory Access, go to the command line and type *dscl localhost -read Search*. This will list the search policies that are configured (LSPSearchPath, CSPSearchPath, SearchPath, and NSPSearchPath) and the search policy that is being used (SearchPolicy).

Configuring Mac OS X to Use BSD Flat Files

You will configure the BSD Configuration Files Open Directory plug-in, and then create the required files to allow a user to log in using this type of directory request.

> **NOTE** ▶ If you do not know how to use sudo or how to edit files with a command-line application such as vi, pico, or emacs, you should skip this exercise. See Appendix A for more about vi.

1   In Terminal, make a copy of the existing /etc/master.passwd file, saving it as master.passwd.bkup.

Before you use a user list taken from another UNIX computer, you will need to edit the file to avoid conflicts. Enter the following command:

sudo cp /etc/master.passwd /etc/master.passwd.bkup

2   Create a root shell by typing *sudo -s.*

3   Use vi to open the file by typing *vi /etc/master.passwd.*

4   View the contents of the file as you scroll to the end of the file.

Every user record in /etc/master.passwd contains ten attributes, each separated by a colon (:).

5   Using Terminal, highlight the last line of text in the file.

It should look something like this:

securityagent:*:92:92::0:0:SecurityAgent:/var/empty:/usr/bin/false

6 Using vi, enter interactive mode, create a new line below the current line, and paste in the identical line.

You now have two identical lines of text at the end of the /etc/master.passwd file. You will be editing the last line to make some changes.

7 You will be changing a few attributes in this new line to a new user named Annie, so edit the file so it matches the following:

annie:*:600:600::0:0:Annie Whey:/Users/annie:/bin/bash

▶ The first attribute is the short user name (annie).

▶ The second attribute is the account password. You will use a command-line tool to change this later.

▶ The third and fourth attributes are the user ID (UID) and primary group ID (GID), respectively. Because the Apple Admin account already uses 501, you needed to change the values for Annie's account to a different value.

▶ The next attribute after the GID should be the account's general classification. The UNIX accounts lacked this attribute, so you needed to add one. (Don't worry about Annie's account not having any class; none of the other user accounts has any either.)

▶ The next two attributes are for the password change time (0) and account expiration time (0).

▶ The following attribute is the user's long name (Annie Whey).

▶ The next attribute is a pointer to the location of Annie's home folder (/Users/annie).

▶ The final attribute is the default shell (bash).

8 Save the changes and close the file.

9 Set a crypt password for Annie's user account in the BSD flat file by typing *sudo passwd -i file annie.*

The -i parameter specifies where the crypt password should be stored. In this case, -i file specifies that the password is to be set for the specified account (annie) in the BSD flat files (/etc/master.passwd is the default file).

10 When prompted for the new password, type *annie* and verify.

11 View Annie's entry in the /etc/master.passwd file again.

Notice how the password field has changed.

Enabling the BSD Open Directory Plug-in

Directory Access enables the BSD Open Directory plug-in to use the newly created passwd file.

1 Open Directory Access.

2 Select the "BSD Flat Files and NIS" checkbox in the Services pane.

3 In the Authentication pane, choose "Custom path" from the Search pop-up menu.

4 Click Add.

5 Select /BSD/local from the list of available directories.

6 Click Add.

7 Click Apply.

8 Quit Directory Access.

Testing BSD Configuration Files Setup

The BSD flat file is the only location where the Annie Whey account currently exists.

1 In Terminal, switch users to Annie Whey by typing *su annie*.

2 Enter Annie Whey's password, *annie*.

You might receive an error because Annie's home folder does not exist. However, notice the prompt changes to annie$.

3 Display the user ID for the current user by typing *id*.

This displays Annie's user ID, along with her group information.

4 Type *exit* and quit the Terminal application.

5   Log out as Apple Admin and log in as Annie Whey.

Once the desktop appears, you have successfully accessed user account information located in flat files you previously created.

Notice that Mac OS X automatically created a new home folder for Annie in /Users.

6   Log out as Annie and log back in as Apple Admin.

DirectoryService Troubleshooting

Max OS X includes command-line tools that are useful in confirming that DirectoryService is responding to requests and that those requests contain correct information. As you saw earlier, you can use dscl to find out how DirectoryService responds to requests. This tool will retrieve information from any of the DirectoryService plug-ins.

When troubleshooting, it may be necessary for you to view or edit the contents of your data stores. Again, you can use Workgroup Manager or dscl to view and modify the local NetInfo database, and you can use any text editor to view and modify the BSD flat files (located in the /etc directory), which are all owned by root.

You will follow a basic workflow to solve directory-service issues. For example, suppose you are unable to log in using an account that you set up in either the local NetInfo database or in the BSD flat files. Take these general steps to resolve the issue:

1.   Plan.

Before making any configuration changes, decide on the approach you will use to resolve the problem.

2.   Configure.

Open Directory Access and verify that the path for authentication includes the data store that contains the user account record. Oftentimes changes made to the plug-in require that the directory be removed from the authentication path and added back in, thus allowing DirectoryService to reread the authentication list.

3.   Test.

Use dscl to see how the DirectoryService process responds to requests. If you are trying to log in from a BSD utility (such as ssh), then use lookupd -q or lookupd -configuration to see how requests are handled.

4. Modify.

   If the requests return incorrect information or no information, then take a look at
   the data stores using Workgroup Manager and dscl for the local NetInfo database, or
   a text editor for the BSD flat files.

Using the DirectoryService Debug Log

Another good resource for looking at DirectoryService activity is the DirectoryService debug
log. To enable the log, go to Terminal and type *sudo killall -USR1 DirectoryService*.

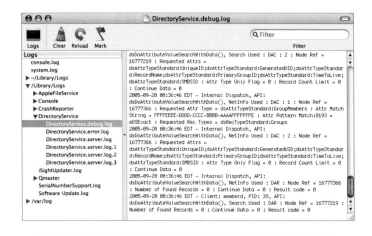

```
sudo killall -USR1 DirectoryService
```

Once the log is enabled, you can use Console to view the results. With Console, you
can filter local logs by command, error codes, or anything that is contained in the log.
You can also clear the screen or add flags to track new entries. If you need to locate
information in the debug logs of remote computers (using ssh, for example), you can
use the command-line utilities tail and grep to filter information found in /Library/Logs/
DirectoryService/DirectoryService.debug.log.

The debug log will continue to log information until disabled. To disable the log, use the
same command you used to enable it.

You can also use the following command to turn on API logging:

sudo killall -USR2 DirectoryService

The result is that any calls to the API will be logged in the /var/log/system.log. The USR2 logging will automatically turn itself off after 5 minutes.

> **MORE INFO ▶** The man pages for DirectoryService provide a list of error codes that you may see in the log files.

You can also log DirectoryService activity at startup by creating two files:

▶ /Library/Preferences/DirectoryService/.DSLogDebugAtStart

▶ /Library/Preferences/DirectoryService/.DSLogAPIAtStart

When DirectoryService detects these files at startup, log entries will be added to them. This is useful in evaluating what the computer is doing when it boots.

Enabling the DirectoryService Debug Log

By default, the DirectoryService debug log is not enabled. Use Terminal to enable the debug log on the DirectoryService process:

1 Log in as Apple Admin.

2 Open Terminal.

3 Send a USR1 signal to the DirectoryService process by entering *sudo killall -USR1 DirectoryService.*

Viewing and Marking Logs With Console

You can use Console to view and mark the debug log to track events that take place in the Finder:

1 Log out and log back in as Apple Admin so that the log contains information about the login.

2 Open Console (/Applications/Utilities).

3   Click the Logs button to display the list of logs.

4   Select DirectoryService.debug.log, located in the DirectoryService entry in /Library/Logs.

   Note the entries for the different processes that use DirectoryService.

5   Click Mark.

   This sets a time marker in the log display, enabling you to differentiate new log entries from the previous entries.

6   In the Finder, navigate to ~/Public/Drop Box.

7   Press Command-I to get info for the Drop Box folder.

8   Expand Ownership & Permissions.

9   Expand Details.

10   Close the Drop Box Info window.

11   In Console, view the DirectoryService.debug.log.

12   In the Filter field, type *dsGetRecordList.*

13   Locate an entry that contains Client:Finder.

   The Client portion of the entries indicates what process is making the requests. This enables you to see what processes are making directory service requests.

14   To disable the debug log for the DirectoryService process, send it the USR1 signal again.

15   In Terminal, send another USR1 signal to the DirectoryService process by typing *sudo killall -USR1 DirectoryService.*

16   Clear Console.

17   Perform some lookups in dscl and verify that debug messages are not being logged anymore.

Working With DirectoryService Plug-ins

The DirectoryService process is launched on demand during boot by the launchd process, which also restarts DirectoryService when it fails. DirectoryService provides a plug-in architecture and a public API so software developers can add functionality for any directory service.

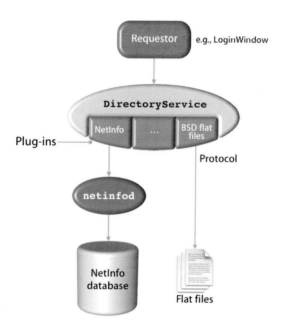

Local data stores are accessed through the BSD flat file and NIS and NetInfo plug-ins. (The NetInfo plug-in that is visible in Directory Access is used to bind a local NetInfo database to a parent NetInfo database and does not affect DirectoryService checking the local NetInfo database first.) Other plug-ins on Mac OS X provide support for remote directory services, as well as service discovery capabilities that search for resources such as file servers. The plug-ins for DirectoryService are configured using Directory Access and some can be configured via the command line, such as the Active Directory plug-in.

This plug-in architecture allows applications to query DirectoryService without needing to know the specifics of the underlying directory services. This means that you can change where Mac OS X and Mac OS X Server retrieve information regarding users and groups without affecting the rest of the operating system. DirectoryService acts as an intermediary that enables software developers to design software without concern for directory-service data store changes. It also allows system administrators to take advantage of the flexible architecture to create solutions that best fit their network.

Understanding lookupd

An additional process called lookupd interacts with DirectoryService and provides some similar services for system-level requests. The lookupd process uses agents that are extensions to the lookupd code to retrieve information about users, groups, and domain name system (DNS) configuration. Each agent is designed to locate a particular type of information. Command-line utilities such as ls and any network applications requiring DNS resolution use lookupd to retrieve DNS information.

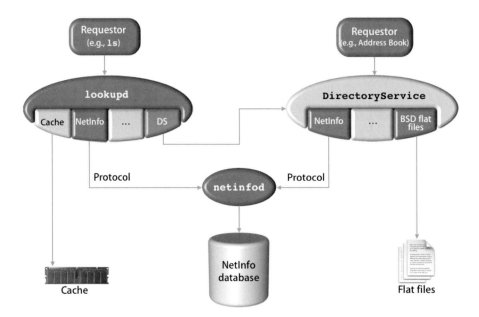

The following agents retrieve information for directory services:

▶   CacheAgent: The cache agent stores retrieved values; this improves performance by minimizing trips to other data sources.

- ▶ DNSAgent: The DNS agent queries a DNS server for host resolution, using the currently configured DNS server information.

- ▶ FFAgent: The flat file agent queries traditional UNIX flat files in the file system.

- ▶ NIAgent: The NetInfo agent queries the local NetInfo database and its parents.

- ▶ DSAgent: The directory-service agent queries DirectoryService.

You can configure which agents are used and the order in which they are searched, although the cache agent is typically searched first. Also, you can use lookupd to check what information is being retrieved from the DirectoryService process. These are both good troubleshooting steps when attempting to locate a problem with directory services not looking in the proper place.

Another point to consider is that the lookupd process can be configured to work with DirectoryService using DSAgent. Any process that uses lookupd would also search the DSAgent and, therefore, DirectoryService.

Because lookupd has a DNS agent, it is the DNS resolver for Mac OS X. It is, therefore, an acceptable tool for performing DNS lookups.

Comparing DirectoryService and lookupd

DirectoryService and lookupd are similar in that both have an architecture that allows for flexible configuration of various data stores. There are, however, significant differences between the two:

- ▶ The UNIX-based system calls of Mac OS X rely on lookupd to provide access to data stores, whereas native applications use the set programming functions implemented with DirectoryService.

- ▶ DirectoryService provides read and write support, whereas lookupd is read only.

- ▶ DirectoryService supports many authentication methods; lookupd only returns results for predefined attribute schemes.

- ▶ DirectoryService does not provide DNS resolution, a critical service to Mac OS X. This function is provided by lookupd.

These differences are summarized in the following table:

DirectoryService	lookupd
Used by native applications	Used by standard system calls
Read and write support	Read-only support
Full support for many authentication methods	Does not provide authentication support
No DNS support	Used to resolve DNS

Identifying lookupd Agents

Because different types of information might be stored in different places, you can configure a separate set of agents and a separate lookup order for each category of agents. When lookupd searches for user information, it looks in the cache first (using the CacheAgent), then the NetInfo database (using the NIAgent), and then DirectoryService (using the DSAgent). When lookupd searches for host information, it looks in the cache first, then the /etc/hosts file (using the FFAgent), then the DNS server (using the DNSAgent), then the NetInfo database, and, finally, the DirectoryService process.

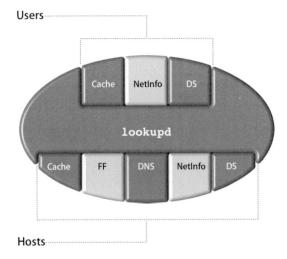

The lookupd process has a predefined default configuration. No configuration files are necessary. There are two methods for changing the configuration of lookupd:

▶   Create entries in the local NetInfo database.

▶   Create flat files with properly formatted configuration information.

While global settings affect the process as a whole, you can add further configuration information for each agent or category of agents. For example, the global timeout value for lookupd might be set to 30 seconds, but you could set the timeout value for the DNSAgent to be 15 seconds. The more specific settings will override the global values.

To determine the configuration of lookupd, type *lookupd –configuration* at the command line.

To change the values in the NetInfo database for lookupd and its agents, you can use Workgroup Manager (running locally) or through manual configuration files. Refer to the man page for lookupd for more information.

1   Open Workgroup Manager.

2   Choose Server > View Directories.

3   Click the Lock button and authenticate so that you can edit the local NetInfo database.

4   Click the Inspector button next to the Users, Groups, and Computers button.

5   Choose Locations from the Record Types pop-up menu.

6   Choose Server > New Record to create a new locations record.

7   Set the name of the new record to lookupd.

8   Within the lookupd record, create an attribute for each of the categories you want to edit. For example, to change how lookupd searches for users, click the New Attribute button, type *users* in the Attribute Name field, and click OK.

9   Within each attribute for the category you want to edit, define the property and the value. For example, to change the lookup order for users, create a new property called LookupOrder. For the values, enter the agent names in the order you want them used. To change the time agents, wait for a response, create a new property called Timeout, and give the value in seconds.

Working With lookupd and PAM

Although lookupd is able to do the work of identification, it cannot actually authenticate the user account. To solve this, Mac OS X provides a pluggable authentication module (PAM) that accesses the security framework. PAM is a set of libraries that handle authentication tasks for applications—in this case, BSD utilities and UNIX system calls. The primary purpose of PAM is to provide a layer of abstraction between the open-source system calls and the security framework that works directly with DirectoryService. The configuration for PAM-enabled services are stored in /etc/pam.d. The following figure illustrates how Mac OS X leverages a PAM to act on behalf of the requestor when talking to the security framework.

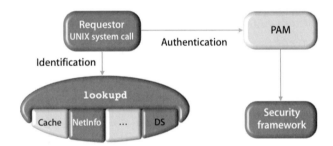

Examples of an ssh Login

There are two basic ways to do ssh login, depending on whether the user is in the NetInfo database or in BSD flat files. Both of these examples illustrate how the lookup process handles queries to the user data, depending on where that data is stored.

ssh Login of a User in the NetInfo Database

The lookupd process is used when a user logs in via the command line, referencing getpwent, getpwnam, and other various system calls, depending on the specific command, which can be ftp, ssh, su, or sudo. The login process may or may not use DirectoryService, depending on where the user record is stored and in what order the agents are used.

In this first example, the user record is located in the local NetInfo database. From a remote computer, the user (Warren) uses ssh to access a Mac OS X computer, which then uses lookupd to retrieve the user record. To perform the search, lookupd agents query data stores. First the cache is checked. If the user record is not found in the cache, the NetInfo agent queries the local NetInfo database. The record is found and returned to ssh, and the user is authenticated using PAM. DirectoryService is not used for this request.

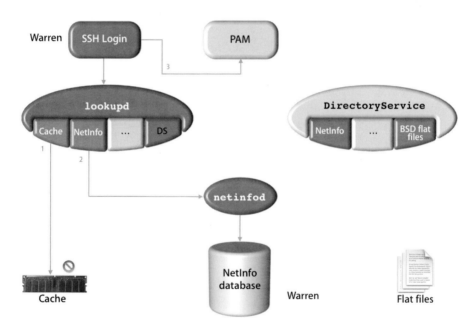

ssh Login of a User in BSD Flat Files

From a remote computer, the user (Tina) uses ssh to access a Mac OS X computer, which then uses lookupd to retrieve the user record. To perform the search, lookupd agents query data stores. First the cache is checked. If the user record is not found in the cache, the NetInfo agent queries the local NetInfo database. When the record is not found in the local NetInfo database, the DSAgent queries the DirectoryService process. Provided DirectoryService is configured to search the BSD flat files (along with the preceding default search in the NetInfo database) for authentication, the record is found and returned to ssh, and the account is authenticated with PAM.

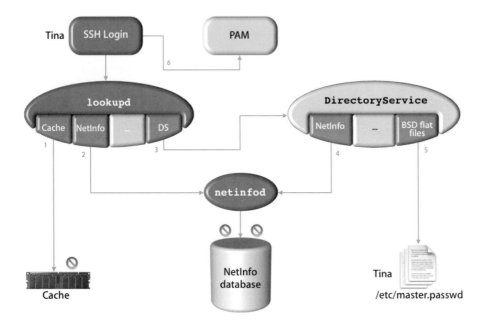

An alternative to this somewhat lengthy process would be to reconfigure lookupd to search the flat files using the FFAgent. This would require you to create a lookup order for lookupd in either a configuration file or in the NetInfo database.

Viewing the Current Configuration of lookupd

When you use the lookupd command to retrieve directory-service information, it is helpful to understand how lookupd is configured so that you know where the information is coming from.

1   Log in as Apple Admin.

2   Open Terminal.

3   Display the current configuration for lookupd by typing *lookupd -configuration*.

Notice that the configuration information is broken into sections, each ending with "_config_name:" and the type of configuration to which the preceding settings apply. The Global Configuration settings apply to all lookupd requests, unless a specific request type has a setting specified, in which case the global value is overridden.

DNS represents the DNS agent, FF the flat file agent, NI the NetInfo agent, and DS the DirectoryService agent.

4   Query the Directory Domain with lookupd by using the -q option with the lookupd command, which can query the currently running instance of lookupd. To do so, type

lookupd -q category -a key value

where *category* is the category of request being made (user, group, service, etc.), *key* is the record attribute being used to search, and *value* is the value being looked for in the key.

5   In Terminal, test the resolution of user names by typing *lookupd -q user -a name apple*.

This returns the user records that have a short name of apple. Since there is only one user account with the short name apple, only one user record will be displayed.

6   Locate the authentication_authority, generateduid, and passwd attributes.

They will look similar to the following:

authentication_authority: ;ShadowHash;

generateduid: A2B6A2A-1F56-11B9-8A22-0003935455BC

passwd: ********

The authentication_authority attribute specifies the type of password used (basic or shadow). If the user account was created by a prior version of Mac OS X, the authentication_authority would be set to Basic and the passwd attribute would contain an encrypted version of the password. When authentication_authority is set to ShadowHash, the generateduid attribute contains a unique ID for the user. A file in /var/db/shadow/hash with a name that matches the generateduid value contains the user's encrypted password. (The passwd value is set to ******** to indicate that it is not used.) If the authentication_authority attribute is blank, then a crypt password is used.

7   Switch to the root user by typing *sudo –s*.

8   Navigate to /var/db/shadow/hash.

9   List the contents of the hash folder.

For each user account set to use shadow hash passwords, there is a file named with the user account's generated user ID (GUID).

10 Display the contents of the file with the name that matches the GUID for the Apple Admin that you looked up in step 2.

The file contains a shadow hash of the user's password.

Running an Interactive Session With lookupd

By using the -d option with the lookupd command, you can begin an interactive session of lookupd. Using this option creates a second lookupd process on the machine, separate from the one that is normally running. This enables you to test lookupd settings interactively, without affecting the entire machine.

1   At the command prompt, type *lookupd -d*.

You will be presented with three lines of output similar to the following:

lookupd version 324.5 (root 2005.05.13 00:28:44 UTC)

Enter command name, "help", or "quit" to exit

>

Notice that the command prompt has changed. The > prompt indicates that you are now in a session with lookupd, and not at the command-line shell.

2   At the prompt, type ? to get a listing of all commands.

You will see a listing of all the commands you can enter in the lookupd prompt. All the queries that lookupd performs are represented here.

3   To test resolution of host names, at the prompt (>) type *userWithName* and press the Tab key.

The interactive lookupd session supports command completion. Press the Tab key or Space bar instead of the colon. This will fill in the colon and enable you to type in the argument.

4   Look up a user by typing *userWithName: apple.*

The result is a list of attributes for Apple's user account. Note the lookupd agent used. In this instance, it is the NIAgent.

5   Type *q* to quit the lookupd interactive session and quit the Terminal application.

What You've Learned

- Every user account on the computer must contain enough information to uniquely identify the user account, authenticate a user using the account, and identify what authority the user has.

- Open Directory is the Apple implementation of directory services in Mac OS X and Mac OS X Server.

- Every Mac OS X computer has a local directory called the local NetInfo database; it can also retrieve administrative data from BSD configuration files.

- Mac OS X v10.4 can use crypt passwords to authenticate a user account, but all new user accounts use shadow hash passwords, which are more secure on a local system.

- The DirectoryService process handles directory-service calls.

- The lookupd process provides support for requests from BSD command-line tools and performs the DNS resolution for the operating system.

- To resolve directory-service issues, you should first plan, and then configure, test, and modify.

- DSAgent is the lookupd agent that retrieves information from the DirectoryService process.

- Use the Directory Access tool to configure directory services on Mac OS X and define custom search paths for authentication and contact information.

References

Administration Guides

"Mac OS X Server Open Directory Administration": http://images.apple.com/server/pdfs/Open_Directory_v10.4.pdf

"Mac OS X Server User Management": http://images.apple.com/server/pdfs/User_Management_Admin_v10.4.pdf

"Mac OS X Server Command-Line Administration": http://images.apple.com/server/pdfs/Command_Line_v10.4.pdf

Apple Knowledge Base Documents

The following Knowledge Base documents (located at www.apple.com/support) provide further information on lookupd and local directories.

Document 30770, "Mac OS X: What is lookupd?"

Document 106499, "Mac OS X 10.1: Binding Local NetInfo Database to an NIS Domain"

Document 60038, "Mac OS X Server 1.x: What Is NetInfo?"

Document 107210, "Mac OS X, Mac OS X Server: How to Replace the NetInfo Database"

Books

Carter, Gerald. *LDAP System Administration* (O'Reilly, 2003).

URLs

Apple Developer Documentation on Open Directory: http://developer.apple.com/darwin/projects/opendirectory

Open Directory concepts and structure: http://developer.apple.com/documentation/networking/Conceptual/Open_Directory

Lesson Review

1. What tool is used to configure DirectoryService search policies for authentication?
2. What are the two local data stores for directory services on Mac OS X?
3. What tools can you use to modify data in the local NetInfo database?

4. What is the key difference between using Workgroup Manager and dscl versus NetInfo Manager and nicl to modify NetInfo data?

5. In a configuration displayed after you enter the lookupd command, when lookupd is used to retrieve service configuration data, what agents are used, and in what order are they used?

6. Using the same configuration settings, when lookupd retrieves user configuration data, what agents are used, and in what order?

7. When retrieving information through DirectoryService, which database is always searched first by default?

8. What is the role of lookupd?

9. What lookupd agents access NetInfo and BSD flat files?

10. What determines which lookupd agents are used when a configuration has not been specifically created for a particular type of lookup?

Answers

1. Directory Access

2. NetInfo and BSD flat files

3. Workgroup Manager, NetInfo Manager, dscl, and nicl

4. Workgroup Manager and dscl use DirectoryService to read and write data. NetInfo Manager and nicl access the NetInfo database directly.

5. The agents used, in order, are CacheAgent, FFAgent, NetInfo, and directory-service.

6. Since user requests don't have a specific configuration setting, the global settings are used: cache, NetInfo, and DirectoryService.

7. The local NetInfo database

8. lookupd is a DNS resolver on Mac OS X with more generalized abilities for search-ing and retrieving data. It is a process that can be used to look up various pieces of information—one of the most common in Mac OS X is DNS information.

9. The NI and FF agents are used to access NetInfo and BSD flat file data, respectively.

10. The Global Configuration settings define which agents are used for lookups that don't have a configuration specified.

3

Time	This lesson takes approximately 2 hours to complete.
Goals	Understand how data is structured and how entries are distinguished in an LDAP database
	Use command-line and GUI tools to search for a specific entries in a given LDAP database
	Use Directory Access to add a Mac OS X server providing directory services for user authentication
	Troubleshoot problems with Open Directory records retrieved from an LDAP database
	Interpret entries in a network user account to determine why a user is unable to log in correctly

Accessing Mac OS X Server Directory Services

Data is valuable only if it can be stored and accessed. With multiple vendors of directory services solutions competing for your business, you may worry that their disparate systems will not be able to interoperate and that it will be difficult for clients to support multiple vendors. Lightweight Directory Access Protocol (LDAP) addresses these concerns by providing a protocol that all vendors can support while still being able to differentiate themselves on the basis of additional features, over and above what a simple data access protocol dictates.

This lesson introduces you to the LDAP specification and explains Mac OS X support for this nearly universal protocol. In Lesson 2, "Accessing Local Directory Services," you saw how Open Directory provides a means of retrieving information from a local data store to identify and authenticate user accounts on the local computer. Now you'll learn how to request and retrieve identification information stored in an LDAP directory on the network, in particular, the LDAP directory on Mac OS X Server.

By accessing the directory in Mac OS X Server on your network, you can take advantage of features such as automounting share points, preferences management, and mobile user accounts.

Understanding LDAP

LDAP is an industry-standard method of accessing data from within a directory. If your organization already has a network directory service in place, it is likely that the directory is based on LDAP or is accessible via LDAP. LDAP is many things, and can be described in different ways. It is:

▶   An information model. It defines how data is accessed.

▶   A namespace. It defines how to distinguish one piece of data from another, similar to a URL.

▶   A protocol. It defines how a client can read, write, and search for data.

▶   A distribution model. LDAPv3 defines how to distribute the logical information model physically. This means that data can be partitioned and stored on multiple hosts, while still being one logical directory.

> **MORE INFO** ▶ The distribution model aspect of LDAP is not covered in this book. Please refer to the References section at the end of this lesson for more information.

▶   A way to standardize access to directory data, regardless of how or where that data is stored. This standardization, while simple in in concept, is quite complex in implementation, requiring standardized naming (the namespace) and standardized searching.

▶   Extensible. It can be customized to fit any organization's directory services needs.

LDAP Information Model

The basic unit of LDAP is an *entry,* or an instance of related attributes. It consists of one or more attributes and the values for those attributes in the following format:

attribute=value

LDAP uses the schema to define attributes, among other things. An object class specifies which attributes are required when populating the LDAP directory and which attributes will be allowed when populating the LDAP directory. This attribute definition provides data integrity.

Object classes are defined in the schema. Because LDAP is so customizable, the schema can be tailored to meet the needs of many different deployments.

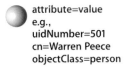

```
attribute=value
e.g.,
uidNumber=501
cn=Warren Peece
objectClass=person
```

The LDAP Tree

An LDAP directory is arranged in a hierarchy called a *tree*. In a tree, each entry can have entries beneath it. One useful aspect of LDAP is that the structure of an LDAP hierarchy is not strictly defined, so it is open to different implementations depending on the site. This can lead to confusion when attempting to understand someone else's deployment, because the hierarchy has been customized.

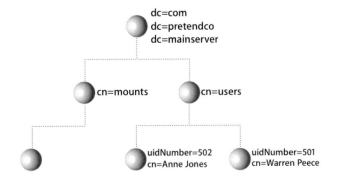

The attributes are usually an abbreviation or mnemonic for a typical characteristic. For instance, *dc* stands for *domain component* and *cn* stands for *common name*. These abbreviations can be used in several locations within the tree and may not be specific to each entry within each entry.

LDAP Namespace

Because the structure of an LDAP directory can be different at each site, you have to tell any LDAP client where to find an entry. To request a particular entry, the client uses the logical path to the entry or the *distinguished name (dn)*. This is similar to an absolute path in the Mac OS X file system. Here is an example of the dn for Warren Peece:

dn:uidNumber=501,cn=users,dc=mainserver,dc=pretendco,dc=com

The structure of the LDAP hierarchy is defined by the distinguished names.

In addition, one or more attributes in an entry can be used as the name of the entry itself. This is the entry's *relative distinguished name (rdn)*, which is similar to a relative path in the Mac OS X file system. For example

rdn:uidNumber=501

refers to all the attribute/value pairs in that entry.

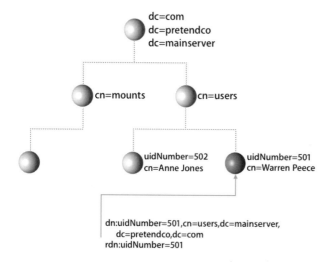

LDAP Search Parameters

When a requestor (such as a login window) asks for data, some parameters must be defined.

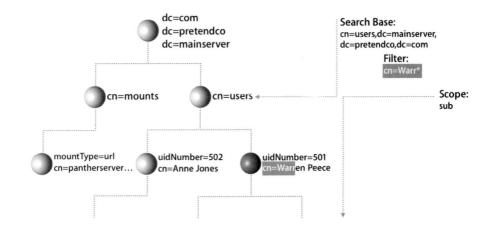

Search Base

The *search base* is the point in the tree where the requestor starts the search. For instance, the client might want to start searching at the entry cn=users. If this is the case, then the search base would be defined as

cn=users,dc=mainserver,dc=pretendco,dc=com

Scope

The *scope* defines how deep to go in the search. For instance, the search could be limited to the same level the search started, limited to the same level and one level below, or open to all levels below the one where the search started. This becomes important when searching a large LDAP database or using applications that frequently query the database. Walking down the entire tree consumes processor cycles and RAM, which can be avoided by refining the scope of the search.

Filter

Finally, a *filter* specifies the item that is being searched for. In Mac OS X, the filter is automatically constructed by the LDAPv3 plug-in. Filters, like scopes, can decrease the load on the directory by not searching entries that do not fit certain criteria. For example, a request might be made to find any cn entries under cn=users. However, since the information under cn=users may or may not be only user information, you can narrow the search to save time, which you're about to learn how to do.

LDAP Search Transactions

When searching the LDAP directory with a tool such as ldapsearch, you would limit the request by specifying the search base and filter. The following figure demonstrates how to search for the mount entries in the LDAP directory on mainserver.pretendco.com.

```
$ ldapsearch -LLL -x -H ldap://mainserver.pretendco.com
  -b dc=mainserver,dc=pretendco,dc=com "(objectClass=apple-group)"
  cn objectClass



dn: cn=admin,cn=groups,dc=mainserver,dc=pretendco,dc=com
cn: admin
objectClass: posixGroup
objectClass: apple-group
objectClass: extensibleObject

dn: cn=mktg,cn=groups,dc=mainserver,dc=pretendco,dc=com
objectClass: posixGroup
objectClass: apple-group
objectClass: extensibleObject
objectClass: top
cn: mktg
cn: marketing
```

Breaking down the line of code in the figure above, you can see it does the following:

▶   The -LLL option specifies that you want the output to be in standard LDAP Interchange Format (LDIF).

▶   The -x option tells ldapsearch to make a simple (non-SASL) bind to the directory.

▶   The -H option is used to specify the server (by URL) hosting the LDAP directory.

▶   The -b option is used to specify the search base. In this figure, the filter specifies that you are looking for any entries where the objectClass attribute is equal to apple-group.

At the end of the search command, you can specify which attributes you want displayed from the resulting entries. In this case, the attributes are the common name and the objectClass. By default, the search is performed at the level indicated by the search base and in all subtrees.

The results of the search are a listing of all the group entries (the dn, cn, and objectClass attributes listed) at the dc=mainserver,dc=pretendco,dc=com level and below. The information is displayed in standard LDIF.

You can also use the ldapsearch command to display information about the root or base dn of an LDAP tree. For example,

> ldapsearch -h "10.1.0.1" -x -a never -s base supportedSASLMechanisms namingContexts
> supportedLDAPVersion

will display the names of the SASL mechanisms, the naming contexts, and the versions of the LDAP protocol that are supported by the server named 10.1.0.1.

> **MORE INFO** ▶ To find out more about ldapsearch options such as -a, -s, or -h, please refer to the man page for ldapsearch.

Using the LDAPv3 Plug-in

Due to LDAP's broad adoption by most directory-service vendors, the Mac OS X DirectoryService LDAP plug-in allows Mac OS X to integrate with most directory-service environments. Mac OS X supports connecting to an LDAP server using version 2 or 3 of the LDAP protocol; however, the LDAPv3 plug-in supports only full read/write access to an LDAPv3 directory. The figure below illustrates that the directoryservice process uses the LDAPv3 plug-in to access an LDAP data store via the LDAP protocol.

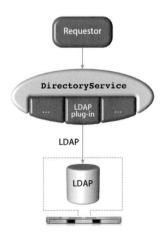

Directory Access is the primary tool for configuring the LDAPv3 plug-in. Within Directory Access, there are two ways to configure the LDAPv3 plug-in to access an LDAP server running on Mac OS X Server.

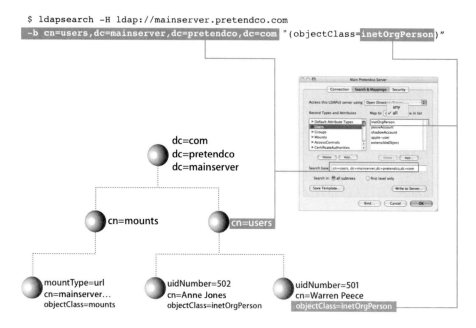

The first method is to use a DHCP-supplied LDAP server. To use this option, the LDAP configuration must be included with the information that your DHCP server provides. If an LDAP server's address and search base are provided by the DHCP server and pushed down over the appropriate option, Mac OS X will automatically bind to the server, and applications will have access to the directory's data through Open Directory without any additional configuration.

However, the server is not automatically added to the authentication or contacts search path by default. To be able to log in using user accounts on an LDAP server provided by DHCP, you must enable the checkbox for the "Add DHCP-supplied LDAP server to automatic search policies" option or manually add the server in the Authentication and Contacts panes, both of which can be accessed by editing the LDAPv3 plug-in using the Directory Access application.

MORE INFO ▶ The LDAP information on a DHCP server is pushed down to a DHCP client via Option 95. DHCP options are covered in the DHCP documentation "Request For Comments (RFC) 2131."

TIP ▶ To check what a Mac OS X computer using DHCP receives from the DHCP server, use the command ipconfig getpacket enX, where X can be 0 (for built-in Ethernet) or 1 (commonly for AirPort cards).

You can also create a configuration for the LDAPv3 plug-in and manually set the connection, search and mapping, and security parameters. If you're connecting to an LDAP server running on a Mac OS X server, you only need to provide the server address in the Connection pane and click one button to have Mac OS X automatically bind to the LDAP server.

If a more customized schema is used, you can choose to map record types and attributes to LDAP object classes and attributes. In the Search & Mappings pane, the "any" and "all" choices in the "Map to…items in list" pop-up menu (under the Edit menu of the LDAPv3 plug-in when selecting a configured LDAP server to which you are going to bind) define which object classes or attributes are necessary when returning a result. The default is "all," which means a search will return only those entries that contain all of the values listed on the right. If you choose "any," the search will return entries that have any of the values.

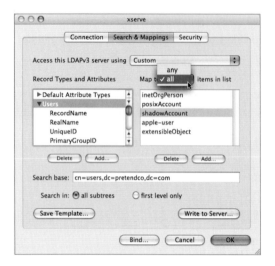

Whereas LDAP supports limiting the scope of a search to the base object (base) and one level down (one) or to all subtrees (sub), Directory Access does not offer all of these options. Directory Access will limit the scope of the search to all subtrees (sub) or to first level only (one), as shown in the figure below.

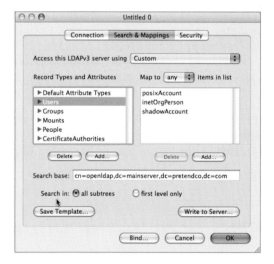

In the list of LDAP configurations, you can use Secure Sockets Layer (SSL) for the connection between your computer and the LDAP server by selecting the SSL option next to the LDAP configuration in the LDAPv3 plug-in. Other security options for an LDAP configuration can be selected by choosing the LDAP configuration you want to modify, and clicking the Edit button. Click the Security tab (as shown in the figure below) to see additional security options. The options that are available depend on the configuration and capabilities of the LDAP server.

If you select the "Use authentication when connecting" option, the LDAPv3 connection authenticates with the directory when it connects by providing a dn and password. The security options are explained further in Lesson 7, "Hosting OpenLDAP."

Troubleshooting the LDAP Connection

The components of a successful remote connection to an LDAP database include:

▶   An active connection to the server where the LDAP database is located

▶   A successful binding to the LDAP database

▶   An appropriate LDAP plug-in configuration

If you are experiencing problems with your LDAP connection, you should isolate it to one of these three areas.

First establish that you have an active connection to the server. Check your network connection, and make sure that you have configured the LDAP plug-in with the correct server address information. If you're using DHCP to receive this information from the server, use ipconfig to verify the configuration.

If you're not using DHCP to receive this information, use Directory Access to configure the LDAPv3 plug-in with the server address and search base. Verify that "Access this LDAPv3 server using Open Directory Server" is selected, and don't remap any of the record types and attributes.

If your connection to the server is working but you're still having problems, you should verify that the information you need is actually in the database. You can use:

▶ ldapsearch to make a request directly from the LDAP directory

▶ dscl to check if the attributes and associated values are correct

▶ Third-party tools, such as LDapper (http://www3.baylor.edu:80/~Carl_Bell/stuff. html) or LDAPManager (http://sourceforge.net/projects/ldapmanager)

▶ Directory Access to make sure Mac OS X will bind to the correct directory service.

Use these tools to search the directory for entries with objectClass=mount. This search will list the volumes that should be automounted. If the search returns the results you expect, then you have verified that the directory contains the correct information and that your client is receiving it correctly.

If the directory does not return correct information for mounts, verify that the file servers are functioning properly and that your user account has authorization to use the server (as well as enough user licenses).

If the requests are returning incorrect information or no information, tell your directory administrator to modify the directory using Workgroup Manager.

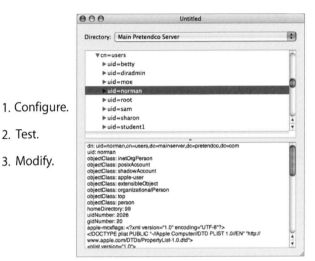

1. Configure.

2. Test.

3. Modify.

Mapping Open Directory Records to LDAP Entries

Open Directory contains predefined record types that are automatically mapped to LDAP entries on Mac OS X Server. When Open Directory receives requests for information, such as users or mounts, using the LDAPv3 plug-in builds the search at that time for that information based on the mappings. This is because Open Directory record types are also mapped to LDAP search bases and object classes. When the LDAP plug-in requests a particular piece of information, it knows where in the LDAP directory to find it based on the search base and one or more object classes. The plug-in also parses the results based on those same mappings. This presents a unified request for data from requestors to Open Directory, and thus the LDAP mappings are transparent to the requestor (or application) that originated the request.

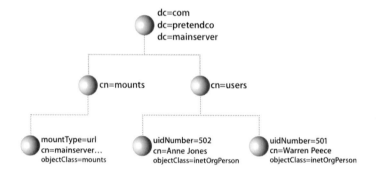

OD record	LDAP search base and object class
Users	-b cn=users,dc=mainserver,dc=pretendco,dc=com
	objectClass=inetOrgPerson
Mounts	-b cn=mounts,dc=mainserver,dc=pretendco,dc=com
	objectClass=mount

Mapping Open Directory Records to LDAP Attributes

Although the search base tells Open Directory how to query an LDAP server for a given type of entry, Open Directory must be told how to use the information found in the entry. For this reason, Open Directory attributes are mapped to LDAP attributes. The mapping tells Open Directory which LDAP attributes hold the specific data Open Directory is looking for.

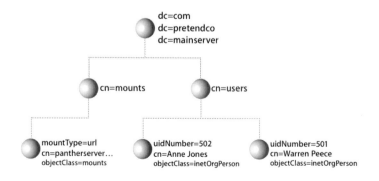

OD attributes for users	LDAP attributes -b cn=users,dc=mainserver,dc=pretendco,dc=com objectClass=inetOrgPerson	Sample values
RealName	cn	Warren Peece
UniqueID	uidNumber	501

Workgroup Manager defines all attributes as either Standard or Native attributes. Standard attributes are Open Directory attributes, and Native attributes are OpenLDAP attributes. You can choose to see either or both sets of attributes by clicking the Options button within the Inspector tab of Workgroup Manager. Each set of attributes can also be preceded by their respective prefixes; however, viewing the prefixes is not absolutely necessary to obtain a better understanding of the automatic mapping of attributes.

Default Initial Attribute Names in Mac OS X Server

Open Directory Attribute	Open LDAP Attribute	Example Value(s)
RecordName	uid	joel, jrennich, Joel Rennich (OpenLDAP will not use the third option here, (Joel Rennich) but will utilize the other two)
RealName	cn	Joel Rennich
UniqueID	uidnumber	1025
PrimaryGroupID	loginshell	20
AuthenticationAuthority	authAuthority	;ApplePasswordServer;0x435562f15e6b13 790000000200000002,1024 35 141955407 348052274487605267977838275353903615368713866674954475330117628625448617831608156595891393044850975624754694810041696640277531916627103042964159218202004509165343802623245099094910469711742864493866309759710768060442733807152390336249598135064942057151017885221346785848010386857229955540869959704843 root@homeserver.pretendco.com:10.0.1.150

Open Directory Attribute	Open LDAP Attribute	Example Value(s)
Password	userPassword	********
GeneratedUID	apple-generateduid	74C69B76-9CFD-4FF6-BE7D-90D8CD1AEEE5
HomeDirectory	apple-user-homeurl	\<home_dir>\<url>afp://homeserver.pretendco.com/Users\</url>\<path>joel\</path>\</home_dir>
NFSHomeDirectory	homeDirectory	/Network/Servers/homeserver.pretendco.com/Users/joel
UserShell	loginshell	/bin/bash
FirstName	givenName	Joel
LastName	sn	Rennich
MCXFlags	apple-mcxflags	\<?xml version="1.0" encoding="UTF-8"?> \<!DOCTYPE plist PUBLIC "-//Apple Computer//DTD PLIST 1.0//EN" "http://www.apple.com/DTDs/PropertyList-1.0.dtd"> \<plist version="1.0"> \<dict> \<key>simultaneous_login_enabled\</key> \<true/> \</dict> \</plist>

Understanding Similar LDAP Attributes

Although some LDAP attributes seem similar to Open Directory attributes, their uses are very different. The following definitions refer to a default configuration of the LDAPv3 plug-in on Mac OS X and a default configuration of the LDAP directory on Mac OS X Server:

▶ uid: This attribute in an LDAP directory refers to the short name of a user account. In Open Directory, this is one of the attributes mapped to RecordName. This attribute should not be confused with the user's ID used in the Mac OS X file system.

▶ uidNumber: This attribute is mapped to the UniqueID attribute in Open Directory, and the value is the same as the user's ID used in the file system. Much of the process of associating files to user accounts and determining authorization is done using the user's ID.

▶ apple-generateduid: This attribute is unique to Mac OS X. It maps to the Open Directory attribute GeneratedUID, and its value is a 128-bit value.

For user accounts, there are two available attributes for home folders in LDAP:

▶ homeDirectory: This LDAP attribute maps to the Open Directory attribute NFSHomeDirectory. The value of this attribute is the local file-system path to the user's home folder (for example, /Users/johnsigna).

▶ apple-user-homeurl: This attribute maps to the HomeDirectory attribute in Open Directory. The value of this attribute is a tagged entry that specifies the URL and share point for the location of a home folder, regardless of whether it is an Apple Filing Protocol (AFP) or SMB-based home folder.

It is critical that these attribute differences be understood. It's just human nature to see what we want to see, and mistakenly assume that UID stands for a user's ID value rather than the short name for a user account.

Networked User Attributes

LDAP and Open Directory make it possible to use network user accounts to store and administer account information in a remote data store, thus removing the need to handle many local accounts.

Network user accounts offer the following benefits:

▶   Network home folders enable administrators to provide users with a consistent, controlled interface while providing access to their documents from any computer.

▶   Administrators can manage clients by controlling permissions on mobile computers and reserve certain resources for specific groups or individuals.

▶   Administrators can secure computer usage in "open" environments, such as administrative offices, classrooms, kiosks, or computer labs.

In addition to the standard attributes for user accounts, network user accounts make use of the following attributes:

▶   HomeDirectory: The location of an AFP-based home folder in UTF-8 XML text. The value for this attribute must be accurate for network users to log in.

▶   MCXSettings: The managed preferences for the user, stored in a multivalued UTF-8 XML plist.

▶   MCXFlags: Determines whether the MCXSettings attribute is loaded, stored in a single valued UTF-8 XML plist.

Managed Client Attributes

The configurations for managed client and mobile account options are stored in the LDAP directory using the apple-mcxsettings and apple-mcxflags attributes. Each user, group, or computer account that has managed preferences enforced would have a base-64 value assigned to those attributes in the entry. The information is stored as encoded XML code that will be interpreted by the client computer when it binds to the LDAP server. The results are placed on the client based on the type of settings. Depending on the number of preferences managed, the mcxsettings value can be quite large. While this is not a problem, it does permit the administrator to paste the value into any text editor and manually edit any values he or she wants, then paste the string back into the value field.

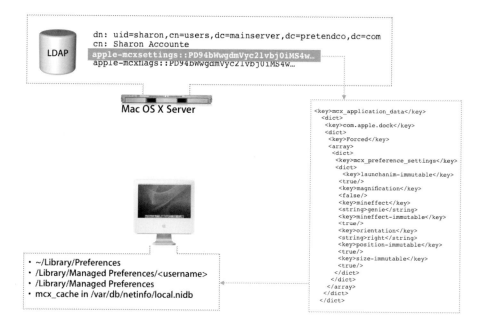

The managed preferences, when passed down to Mac OS X, can reside in several places:

▶ Managed preferences for the current user are placed in ~/Library/Preferences and include mobile account settings for the user.

▶ Managed login preferences are placed in /Library/Managed Preferences/username, where username is the name of the logged in user.

▶ Managed startup (boot) preferences are placed in /Library/Managed Preferences.

Managed group preferences are applied when the login window appears, and managed computer and mount settings are applied when the computer boots.

The data is also stored in mcx_cache in the local NetInfo database (/var/db/netinfo/local.nidb) for offline use. This information can be removed from the database using NetInfo Manager or Workgroup Manager running locally.

Working With Mount Records

Mac OS X computers using network user accounts need to access networked volumes at startup (prior to logging in). Open Directory specifies a *mount record*, which contains information about these network volumes so a startup process can automatically mount them, regardless of which user logs in.

Mac OS X computers prepared for use with network user accounts typically don't store this information in their local NetInfo database, as that information can become outdated and each Mac OS X computer's NetInfo database would need to be updated manually. At startup, the automount daemon queries Open Directory for mount records. In response, directoryservice plug-ins that have been preconfigured with remote server information search the databases on those servers for mount records. The automount daemon uses the information from any mount records that are returned to mount the appropriate volumes. This type of automount is supported for AFP and network file system (NFS), but not for SMB.

The following table lists a mount record's attributes.

Attribute	Purpose	Example Value
RecordName	The server's name and the full path to the folder that is to be mounted	mainserver.pretendco.com:/shared_folder
VFSType	The type of mount, set different for each protocol	For AFP, the value is url. For NFS, the value is nfs.
VFSLinkDir	The local folder where clients will mount the share point. Dynamically mounted share points always have a value of /Network/Servers/.	/Network/Servers/
VFS Opts (for AFP)	Mount options	Two values: net and afp://;AUTH=NO%20USER%20AUTHENT@mainserver.pretendco.com:/shared_folder
VFSOpts (for NFS)	Mount options	net

For some types of servers, you may not be able to rely on the mount record being stored on the server. You can add mount records to the client's local NetInfo database using dscl, NetInfo Manager, or Workgroup Manager.

If the computer won't boot to multiuser mode after you modify the mounts record, delete the record in single-user mode, restart the computer, and enter the data again.

If you can browse a computer but you cannot connect, try the following:

▶ Look for network problems. Check physical connections and try to ping the server. Try other services from the same server. If more than one protocol is affected, you should troubleshoot your network connection.

▶ If you get a login dialog but can't mount the volume, the connection is good and authentication is the most likely problem. Verify the user name and password. A good way to do this is using id and su from the command line.

▶ If you have a problem mounting from the Finder, try mounting from the command line. You may get more information from error messages.

▶ Verify the permissions of the folder you're mounting on.

▶ Verify that the URL you are using is correct.

Try connecting from a different computer. If the service appears on that computer, find out what is different. Look at Network preferences and Directory Access settings, for example.

Troubleshooting Home Directories

The majority of problems encountered come from users not being able to connect. This happens primarily at login, so a good idea is to check the directory-service binding first. Use dscl to verify that the Mac OS X computer is binding to the server and is able to access the data. If it is not binding, use an LDAP browsing utility such as LDapper or LDAPManager to verify that you have the correct server address and search base.

1. Make sure the client is bound to the correct directory.

    Your organization may be using two different LDAP servers: one for user account information and one for contact information (this is often the case). If the computer is binding to the server providing contact information, users will not have access to their user accounts. Use an LDAP browsing tool again to verify that the server to which the computer is binding is providing user accounts.

2. Try a different user account.

    If the problem is isolated to just one account, compare the values of the two accounts to isolate the cause of the problem.

3. Verify the file server is accessible.

    If a user is able to log in but unable to access the correct home folder, the file server might not be accessible, the mount record for the share point is absent or invalid, or the home directory attributes are incorrect.

    You can also run lookupd -q mount -a allMounts to help discover directory data issues with the mounts.

    NOTE ▶ If you place *.* in /etc/syslog.conf and add another file to receive that particular log, you'll end up getting lots of automount logging and afp / smb errors when loginwindow can't mount the home directory.

What You've Learned

▶ Lightweight Directory Access Protocol (LDAP) is an industry-standard way to access data from within a directory. It runs on Mac OS X Server.

▶ You can use the command-line tool ldapsearch to search for a specific entry in a given LDAP database, or use a GUI tool, such as LDapper, to search for a specific entry in a given LDAP database.

▶ Requestors need identification and authentication information that can be stored on Mac OS X Server.

▶ The LDAP directory on Mac OS X Server is accessed from a client using the LDAPv3 plug-in.

▶ Directory Access can be used to configure a Mac OS X client computer to bind to an LDAP server using address and search base values provided by DHCP or a Mac OS X server providing LDAP service.

▶ The dscl command-line tool verifies that a Mac OS X client computer is bound to a Mac OS X server providing directory services.

▶ Directory Access can add a Mac OS X server providing directory services to the list of servers used for user authentication so that a user can log in to the client computer using a user account stored on the server.

▶ The ipconfig command verifies that a client computer is receiving LDAP configuration information from a DHCP server.

▶ Directory Access can add a Mac OS X LDAP server to the list of directory servers for user authentication.

References
Administration Guides
"Mac OS X Server Open Directory Administration": http://images.apple.com/server/pdfs/Open_Directory_v10.4.pdf

"Mac OS X Server User Management": http://images.apple.com/server/pdfs/User_Management_Admin_v10.4.pdf

"Mac OS X Server Command-Line Administration": http://images.apple.com/server/pdfs/Command_Line_v10.4.pdf

Apple Knowledge Base Documents
The following Knowledge Base document (located at www.apple.com/support) provides further information about accessing LDAP data stores.

Document 107695, "Mac OS X Server v10.3 or later: Avoid spaces and long names in network home directory name, path"

Books
Carter, Gerald. *LDAP System Administration* (O'Reilly, 2003).

URLs

The application LDapper author's website: Carl Bell: http://carl-bell-2.baylor.edu/~Carl_Bell/stuff.html

The main OpenLDAP website: www.openldap.org

Lesson Review

1. What is the basic unit of an LDAP directory, and how are these units arranged?

2. What process allows Mac OS X to use the LDAP directory on Mac OS X Server?

3. Which command would you use to view the DHCP packet that the client accepted from the DHCP server?

4. What does the LDAP plug-in do? What tool in Mac OS X can you use to configure the LDAP plug-in?

5. If a client computer is having problems accessing an LDAP server provided by DHCP, what would be an appropriate early troubleshooting step to take?

6. What attribute in an LDAP user record maps to the Open Directory RecordName attribute?

7. What attribute in an Open Directory user record maps to the uidNumber attribute in an LDAP user record?

8. What are some of the advantages of a network user account?

9. Which attribute stores the managed preferences for network user accounts?

Answers

1. The basic unit of the LDAP directory is an entry, and entries are arranged in a hierarchy called a tree.

2. DirectoryService through the LDAPv3 plug-in

3. getpacket

4. The LDAP plug-in allows Mac OS X to integrate with LDAP directories. Use Directory Access to configure the LDAP plug-in.

5. Use ipconfig and verify that the LDAP url parameter provided by Option 95 contains the correct value for the server.

6. uid

7. UniqueID

8. Administrators can use network home directories to provide users with a consistent, controlled interface while providing access to their documents from any computer. You can control permissions on mobile computers and reserve certain resources for specific groups or individuals.

9. MCXSettings and MCXFlags

4

Time   This lesson takes approximately 2 hours to complete.

Goals   Integrate Mac OS X with a variety of third-party directory services

Use Directory Access to map required Open Directory attributes to unused attributes on an LDAP server

Use variables to supplement required attributes missing from an LDAP server

Provide mount records for a client computer retrieving records from an LDAP server

Enable a Mac OS X computer to automatically mount a file-server volume

Use NFS or file-sharing protocols to provide home folders

Integrating Mac OS X With Third-Party Directory Services

If your network uses a directory service other than the one provided with Mac OS X Server, don't worry—your Mac OS X computers can still integrate with that system. This lesson introduces several third-party directory services and explains how to integrate Mac OS X clients with them.

Since each directory service is different, Open Directory includes plug-ins to interact with them. To integrate Mac OS X with these services, you just need to configure the appropriate plug-in and address the attribute differences between Open Directory and the third-party directory service.

Binding a Mac OS X computer to an Open Directory server is a straightforward task requiring very little configuration. Connecting a Mac OS X computer to other directory servers requires a bit more work, but by following a simple, methodical approach, you can bind a Mac OS X computer to almost any LDAP server. You can also use third-party directory services to provide network home folders and client management policies.

Choosing a Third-Party Network Directory Service

Some organizations may prefer to use a directory service developed by manufacturers other than Apple, or they may already have a well-established infrastructure in place. When choosing an alternative to Apple's directory service, keep in mind that Open Directory is plug-in based. Apple has supplied plug-ins for various directory service protocols, such as Lightweight Directory Access Protocol (LDAP), Network Information Service (NIS), Active Directory, and NetInfo. In addition, manufacturers other than Apple can develop their own plug-ins to add features not available with the Apple plug-ins, such as ADmitMac, sold by Thursby Software.

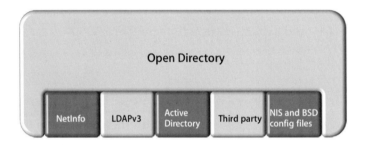

It is important to choose the plug-in that best fits the needs of your organization. In some cases, a plug-in may provide only a limited set of features that hinder the overall usability of Mac OS X. This lesson will look into the specifics of the NIS and LDAP plug-ins that Apple supplies.

> **NOTE ►** The Active Directory plug-in will be covered in Lesson 5, "Integrating Mac OS X With Active Directory."

Network Information Service

Administrators have long sought to have a centrally managed network directory service on their networks. In 1985 Sun Microsystems developed one of the earliest implementations to help support administrators deploying network file system (NFS) servers. Originally called Yellow Pages, the service eventually became known as Network Information Service, or NIS. However, the utilities were never updated to reflect the name change, so most NIS utilities start with the prefix yp.

With Mac OS X v10.2.5 and later, Apple has provided an NIS plug-in for Open Directory. As with other Open Directory plug-ins, it is configured with Directory Access. Although the NIS plug-in is disabled by default, it is simple to enable and configure. If you want to use the NIS plug-in to authenticate users, be sure to add the /BSD/domain name to the Authentication pane of Directory Access after configuring the plug-in. The figure below shows where to enable the BSD/NIS plug-in and the options available within the plug-in.

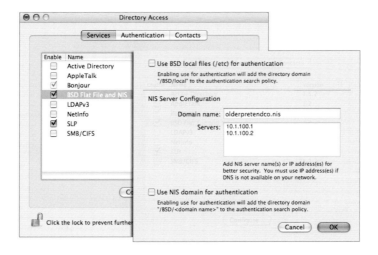

NOTE ▶ The NIS plug-in primarily supports legacy deployments and currently does not support NIS+ or the use of shadow files.

LDAP Integration Methodology and Workflow

You have learned how Mac OS X stores a set of attributes for every Mac OS X user, such as user name, password, home folder, and user ID. Mac OS X needs the specific data found in these attributes, regardless of the directory-service connection. Integrating Mac OS X with a directory service to provide these attributes is a multistep process.

Open Directory's directory service shares a common communication protocol with directory services from other vendors. Each vendor has the freedom to choose the directory data store of their choice and to build native tools to manage that directory data store. Through LDAP, a standards-based directory-service protocol, different vendors can operate together peacefully.

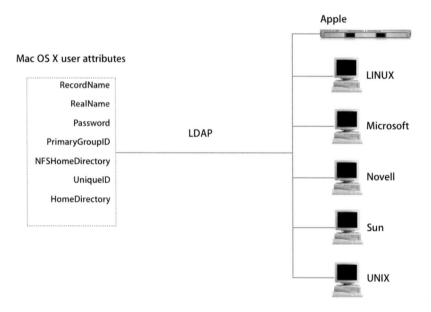

The rest of this lesson will focus on using Open Directory's LDAP directory-service protocol plug-in and the dynamics of getting the best Mac OS X experience possible from a non-Apple directory service.

By following a five-part LDAP workflow, you will greatly increase your chances of successfully integrating Mac OS X with a third-party directory service. This process helps to break down the mechanics of connecting and should expose common issues administrators face while reducing the guesswork in troubleshooting a directory.

1. Connect.
2. Understand.
3. Supplement.
4. Configure.
5. Test.

Step 1: Establish a Valid Connection

To integrate Mac OS X into any directory service, you should first establish a valid connection. There are several utilities available to assist administrators in connecting to a directory service over LDAP, such as LDAP Browser, LDapper, LDAPManager, and command-line utilities. They are all excellent methods of getting immediate feedback from your directory service.

When connecting to a directory service, administrators will have to determine the following:

▶ Does this directory service allow anonymous browsing or is user authentication required?

▶ Does this directory service require a secure connection with SSL?

▶ Is the LDAP server using a custom port?

If user authentication is required for a particular directory service, the user name will be a user's full distinguished name (dn). For example:

cn=John Smith,cn=Users,dc=mainserver,dc=pretendco,dc=com

Once connected, your browser will display output similar to that in the following figure:

If you cannot make a connection to the directory server, then there is no need to proceed further. You must prove a valid connection and be able to view all necessary attributes and their associated values, so check typing, DNS issues, and firewall settings as the first culprits in thwarting your initial attempts at a valid connection.

Step 2: Understand Your Directory

Once a connection has been established, take a look at the data that exists in the directory service. Start by determining where user records exist in the directory service. They may be distributed throughout the entire directory or be completely contained in one part of the directory. This, of course, is at the discretion of the LDAP administrator; therefore, when planning to deploy Mac OS X with third-party directory services, you should meet with the LDAP administrator and understand exactly how the LDAP structure is laid out for that particular directory service.

When configuring Mac OS X, Directory Access will prompt you to specify a search base. This search base is the dn of where the user records can be found in a particular directory service. For example:

cn=users,dc=mainserver,dc=pretendco,dc=com

Inspect the individual user records and see what attributes have been associated with the record. Also inspect the data associated with each attribute.

Remember, for Mac OS X to integrate with this directory service, the attributes listed in the figure must be mapped to user attributes in the directory service. The names of the attributes in the directory service do not have to match. The important thing is that the value for a user's primary group ID is 20 and the attribute gidNumber in the directory has the value 20 associated with it. In Directory Access, the attribute PrimaryGroupID is mapped (in one method or another) to gidNumber.

Upon further review of the user records in the directory, you will discover that certain required attributes for Mac OS X either do not exist or have incompatible data populated. Take note of these deficiencies and incompatibilities as you determine the correct schema for the directory service.

Step 3: Supplement Missing Data

Supplementing directory data is by far the most challenging part of integrating Mac OS X with a third-party directory. Knowing where the deficiencies are with your existing user records will be the key to your success. The missing data must be supplemented in one or more of these three methods:

- ▶ Repurposing existing fields
- ▶ Employing local mappings with static and variable attributes
- ▶ Modifying the schema of the directory

Regardless of the method administrators choose, they must plan their strategy and adequately test it prior to rolling out the solution. The major pros and cons of the three methods, which are detailed in the following sections, are summarized in this table.

	Flexibility	Directory admin required to help?	Impact to network install?	Impact to other platforms?
Repurpose	Limited number of attributes	Yes, to discover attributes and populate data for every user	Image should include all configuration settings	Might step on resources needed by other applications and platforms
Local mappings	Some, with variable mappings	No	Variables should be imaged while static mappings may need to be configured post image	None
Modify schema	Unlimited	Yes, to create new attributes and populate data for every user	Image should include all configuration settings	None

Repurpose Existing Unused Attributes

This method involves taking unused attributes that are already part of the current directory schema and putting Mac OS X–specific data in those attributes.

Repurposing requires cooperation with the LDAP administrator. The primary reason to repurpose is because it does not require any modification to the schema of the directory service. Different directory services and their administrators have different appetites for making schema modifications. In addition, it usually requires less setup time, which is valuable for smaller organizations.

This method is often the most attractive at the beginning and quickly becomes the least viable solution. In the long run, attribute reuse is more difficult to maintain: Not only must system administrators track what attributes were commandeered, but there is the risk of overwriting critical data required by other clients if those attributes are suddenly needed by the LDAP administrator.

In addition, attributes have certain requirements, and one attribute may be unable to store the data that you want to populate. For example, the attribute employeeID may be allowed to store only integers. Any attempt to store a text string such as /Users/myhome would result in an error, as it does not comply with the attribute limitations. Your LDAP browser will not display unused attributes. Each user record consists solely of attributes that contain specific data for that user. To discover all the available unused attributes, administrators usually consult the directory's schema with vendor-supplied tools for that directory service.

In the example in the following figure, two attributes that were not being used, secondaryFax and ipPhone, were mapped to the user attributes UniqueID and HomeDirectory in Directory Access. These steps are still not enough for the Mac OS X login to be successful.

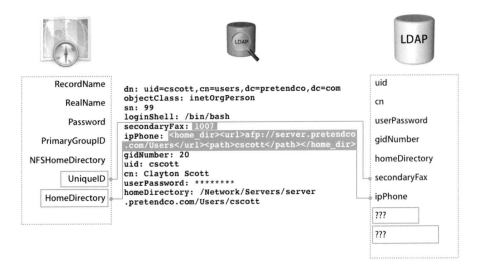

In this case, secondaryFax was populated with *1007* and ipPhone was populated with a value required for a user to have a network home folder:

<home_dir><url>afp://server.pretendco.com/Users</url><path>cscott</path></home_dir>

Notice that these values are unique to each user, and every Mac OS X user record will have to be populated prior to deploying Mac OS X.

Overall, repurposing is not flexible due to the limited number of attributes available, and can impact others with other applications and platforms.

Employ Local Static and Variable Mappings

When limitations with repurposing attributes are too restrictive for organizations, another option is to use *local mappings,* which are a convenient way, within Directory Access, to hard-code in directory data that would normally exist as an attribute in a user record. This is an attractive option for Mac OS X administrators who may not be able to make changes to the directory service, but still want to integrate into the existing infrastructure as best as possible. Plus, local mappings are quite flexible with variables and don't require any attention from the directory administrator.

Static mappings are effective when each user has an individual computer and when addressing universal mappings that may be the same for all users. Local mappings always begin with a number sign (#) as the first character of the mapping within Directory Access. Note that static mappings may require extra configuration after deploying with Network Install.

The first directory-service example in the following figure does not have an existing attribute populated with data suitable for mapping UniqueID. The solution maps UniqueID #1007 in Directory Access. So everyone who logs in to this computer will have a UID of 1007 with exactly the same access to local files and any files hosted by an NFS server.

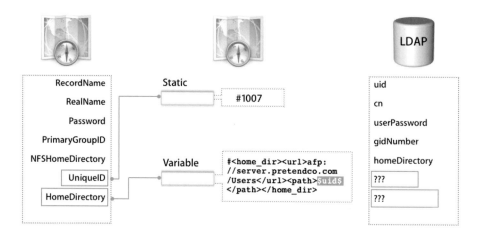

The second example in the figure addresses the missing attribute for HomeDirectory. In this case, the goal is for users to have separate home folders. A static value of

#<home_dir><url>afp://server.pretendco.com/Users</url><path>generic</path>
</home_dir>

will not work. Every user on this computer would have the same home folder called generic on mainserver.pretendco.com. To achieve separate home folders, a variable must be included in the static mapping.

In Mac OS X v10.3.3 and later, variables are included in the mapping by enclosing, or "wrapping," a valid LDAP attribute in dollar signs ($). For example:

#<home_dir><url>afp://server.pretendco.com/Users</url><path>uid</path>
</home_dir>

> **NOTE ►** Though we can't show it properly on the printed page, be sure to type each of these commands as a single line with no paragraph returns.

When a user logs in with this mapping in Directory Access, the home folder path will be dynamically constructed with the data stored in the attribute, uid, for that user. In this example, the user's short name was the data associated with the uid attribute in the directory. When each user logs in, Mac OS X looks for that user's home folder in a folder named with their short name on the server at mainserver.pretendco.com in a share point called Users, thus achieving the desired goal.

Local mappings are also used as a safety net to ensure that user logins are always successful by listing more than one attribute in a particular mapping and leaving the last entry as a local mapping. Mac OS X will search the directory for all of the listed attributes; if no matches are found, the local mapping will be applied. That's good news if your Mac OS X computers could be used by people outside of your immediate department.

Departmental users may have network home-folder information in their user records where nondepartmental users may not have specific Mac OS X home-folder information in their respective user records. They may still need access to your Macintosh lab with a valid LDAP login. To alleviate these two different needs, you could map HomeDirectory to both the valid attribute in the directory and a local mapping of #/tmp/uid.

The result is that nondepartmental employees have a functional home when they visit the lab and their data will be erased the next time the computer is restarted, while your departmental employees will still have functional network home folders.

Modify the Schema and Create New Attributes

The most significant step an administrator can take to integrate Mac OS X into an existing directory service infrastructure is to modify the schema on the LDAP server. Only the directory service administrator, who uses tools from the vendors of each directory service to add additional objects and attributes that accommodate the specific needs of Mac OS X user records, can modify the schema.

This is not a trivial task—it requires extensive knowledge of the existing LDAP schema and may be very difficult to undo. Changes should be scripted and tested thoroughly before rolling these changes into a production server. Keep in mind that user attributes are not the only attributes that can be added to the schema. Group account attributes, computer account attributes, managed account settings, and network view settings can also be added.

NOTE ▶ Do not attempt schema modification without consulting your LDAP server administrator!

In the following figure, the directory administrator has created two new attributes dedicated to host the missing Mac OS X user attributes. Specifically, the attribute unixid will host the value for UniqueID and macuserhome will host the value for the Network home folder.

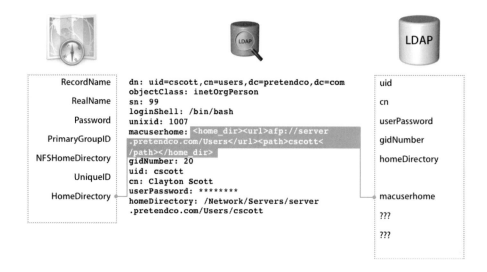

The newly created attributes still need to be populated with valid data for everyone using Mac OS X in your directory service environment. Verify this step has been completed with an LDAP browser prior to configuring Mac OS X to integrate.

> **MORE INFO** ▶ Apple has a set of Active Directory schema modifications that support most of the Apple attributes. More information can be found at www.apple.com/services/consulting.

Step 4: Integrating Mac OS X With LDAP Directory

Now that you have accounted for each user attribute required by Mac OS X, you can use Directory Access to configure Mac OS X to integrate with the LDAP directory. The process is similar to configuring Mac OS X to connect to an Open Directory server.

> **NOTE** ▶ While configuring an LDAP configuration may be simple, beware that a single typing mistake can render your configuration inoperable.

Directory Access has three presets for configuring the LDAP plug-in:

▶ Active Directory

▶ Open Directory Server

▶ RFC 2307 (UNIX)

When connecting to a third-party directory:

1 Use the LDAP plug-in in Directory Access to create a new LDAP connection.

2 Start with the RFC 2307 (UNIX) preset and then customize the mappings to your specific settings.

   First provide the default search base for your directory to find all records including users, groups, mounts, and other record types. If need be, you can edit the search base for each record type beyond this general setting.

3   Edit the configuration for your organization's specific needs.

If your LDAP browser required any connection configuration (such as a custom port, SSL encryption, or required user authentication), make sure to duplicate the working settings from the LDAP browser utility to Directory Access.

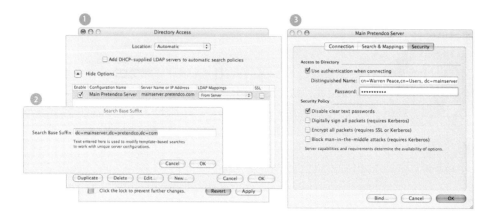

4   Now begin to assign your specific attribute mappings to match up with what you discovered with the LDAP browser utility

5   Make sure to incorporate mappings that will supplement the directory service

6   If multiple entries are entered for a particular mapping, Mac OS X will look for the data in the first mapping and work its way through the list of possible attributes until it has found a match.

TIP The RFC 2307 preset for Directory Access does not include the user attribute HomeDirectory. If your configuration is going to employ network-based home folders, you will need to add the HomeDirectory attribute for the user record mapping. Do not forget to configure the attribute once you have added it.

Step 5: Add Directories to the Authentication Path and Test

Now you need to add directories to the authentication path, as shown in the following figure:

1. Any directories that you want to use for authentication will be added to the search path within Directory Access.

2. You can sort the priority of different directories and Mac OS X will search each directory as they are listed within Directory Access.

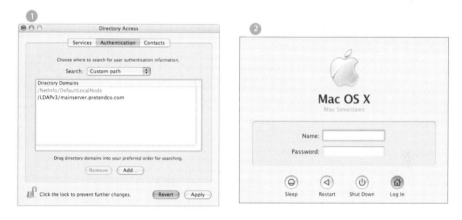

Once the LDAP configuration has been inserted into the authentication search path, you can begin to test the configuration. From the command line, you may use either lookupd -d or dscl to see if the configuration is working properly. If it is, you should get output that looks very similar to the output of the LDAP browser.

The final test is to see if your users can log in using the login window. If your users are going to have network home folders, expect an error message regarding the location of the home folder—a reboot may be required to initialize the supporting automount.

After you have tested the configuration, you can use the "Write to Server" button in the Search and Mappings pane of the LDAP plug-in to store the mappings in the LDAP directory so that it can supply them automatically to other Mac OS X computers.

Use a dn of an administrator or other user with write permission for the search base (for example, uid=diradmin,cn=users,dc=mainserver,dc=pretendco,dc=com) and the account's password. Also provide a search base to store the mappings. If you are writing mappings to an Open Directory server, the correct search base is

cn=config, *suffix*

where *suffix* is the server's search base suffix, such as

dc=mainserver,dc=pretendco,dc=com

So the full line would be

cn=config,dc=mainserver,dc=pretendco,dc=com

Integrating Specific Records With Third-Party LDAP Directories

There are certain characteristics of third-party directory services that require additional configurations when working with Mac OS X. The following figure compares how different directories can integrate Mac OS X by default. Attributes with "???" are deficiencies in the directory that must be addressed to successfully integrate.

Open Directory	Apple	Novell	Sun
RecordName	uid, cn	cn	cn
RealName	cn	fullname	cn
Password	userPassword		userPassword
PrimaryGroupID	gidNumber	gidNumber	gidNumber
NFSHomeDirectory	homeDirectory	homeDirectory	homeDirectory
UniqueID	uidNumber	uidNumber	uidNumber
HomeDirectory	apple-user-homeurl	???	???

Mac OS X Server integrates well because it provides all of the attributes required by Mac OS X. It takes some additional configuration to integrate Mac OS X with other servers as they are usually missing at least some key attributes.

A common deficiency amongst third-party directories is the HomeDirectory mapping. This mapping is an addition Apple applied to the RFC 2307 standard schema. It is a required attribute for users who will have a network home folder, and administrators should always plan to address this need when integrating into any directory not manufactured by Apple.

Integrating With eDirectory

eDirectory is a directory service offering from Novell that provides support for LDAP and can be configured to provide support for Mac OS X.

Open Directory	Novell
RecordName	cn
RealName	fullname
Password	
PrimaryGroupID	gidNumber
NFSHomeDirectory	homeDirectory
UniqueID	uidNumber
HomeDirectory	???

When configuring, be sure to leave the Password field blank so that authentication will occur over the LDAP Bind. Novell has provided the homeDirectory attribute as a UNIX-only attribute; using it will not conflict with native Novell clients. This was done to ensure compliance with RFC 2307.

By default the only missing user attribute is HomeDirectory; this will need to be addressed prior to integrating. Administrators interested in modifying the schema to better support Mac OS X can get functional unsupported LDIF files to automate modifying eDirectory's schema from www.macosxlabs.org.

Integrating With SunOne

SunOne directory service is an LDAP directory service provided by Sun Microsystems. Originally called iPlanet, it has a schema that is designed to ensure full compliance with RFC 2307. This leaves the schema ready for use with exception of the HomeDirectory mapping, which is not part of the RFC 2307 schema. Schema modification should be automated through the use of LDIF files.

Open Directory	Sun
RecordName	cn
RealName	cn
Password	userPassword
PrimaryGroupID	gidNumber
NFSHomeDirectory	homeDirectory
UniqueID	uidNumber
HomeDirectory	???

Although Sun has implemented a model RFC 2307 schema, administrators often make changes to meet the needs of an individual organization. A common change would be to not store the password in the directory as a user record attribute and use Kerberos instead. Be sure to follow the LDAP workflow and to use the above figure as a reference for your own integration.

Working With Home Folders and LDAP

Administrators need to decide where their Mac OS X users will store their home folders. Network authenticated users can have a home folder stored either locally on the workstation they are currently using or on a server over the network. Network home folders are an extension of simple automounts, and the data is spread out between user-specific data and generic mount data. Open Directory has built-in support for Mac OS X home folders and makes providing network home folders easy.

TIP ▶ A quick survey of any third-party directory server will reveal that the Apple implementation of network home folders is not part of the standard RFC 2307 LDAP schema and will need special attention to accommodate these specific requirements.

To get network home folders to function properly, you need to address the data for each user record and provide mount records with the associated mount attributes. If your directory does not have mount records as a part of your existing schema or the attributes necessary for mount records, administrators must provide valid mount records and their associated attributes in addition to the Mac OS X–specific user attributes covered previously.

	Open Directory	Mac OS X Server	Other LDAP
User record attributes	HomeDirectory	apple-user-homeurl	???
	NFSHomeDirectory	homeDirectory	RFC2307
Mount record attributes	RecordName	cn	???
	VFSLinkDir	mountDirectory	???
	VFSOpts	mountOption	???
	VFSType	mountType	???

Supplementing Mount Records

Supplementing your directory's lack of mount records and attributes is similar to the procedure for user records. You can mount records in the local NetInfo database, modify the schema to create new record types and attributes, or use secondary directory to supplement primary directory.

Here's a disadvantage to creating a mount record in the local NetInfo database, though: If the mount address changes, the administrator will have to change that information on each Mac OS X computer with local mount records.

An attractive third alternative may be to supplement one directory with another. This is done by configuring an Open Directory server to host mount records in its own directory. This server will not host any user records and will also be bound to the primary directory server. To configure Mac OS X to use both directories, add the Open Directory server to the custom authentication list in Directory Access. The resulting combination will allow Mac OS X to search both directories for user and mount records. It will find user records only in the primary directory and find mount records only in the Open Directory server.

Additional Concerns for Network Homes

Administrators who are planning to provide network home folders will also need to pick which protocol they prefer to use. The protocol you choose will depend on what features you need most.

> **NOTE ▶** Keep in mind how resource forks are handled by each protocol.

If you choose to use Apple Filing Protocol (AFP), you must be aware that to get full functionality out of Mac OS X you must use an AFP 3.x server. Version 3.x of AFP provides two critical features to Mac OS X:

▶ The ability to automatically reconnect; if a connection is lost or disconnected, the Mac OS X computer will attempt a reconnect when the network connection is resumed.

▶ The ability to write files with names over 31 characters in length, since many pieces of Mac OS X rely on being able to write files with long names

ByHost files are the most common type of file to have long names, as shown in the above figure. One of the most notable ByHost files is the com.apple.Classic. XXXXXXXXXXXX.plist file. If Mac OS X cannot access this file, the Classic environment will not be able to run. Administrators wanting to use their existing investment in Microsoft file servers will either need to give up these features or upgrade their AFP 2.x servers to 3.x with a product called Extreme Z-IP. This replaces Microsoft's Services for Macintosh with an AFP 3.x server. Currently there is no Microsoft Windows software that will share files over AFP 3.x.

An alternative to AFP would be to use NFS. NFS home folders are fully supported in Mac OS X, and most vendors support NFS. There are security concerns with NFS, as it does not rely on user authentication. In addition, NFS homes will exclude users still migrating from Mac OS 9.x.

Two Methods for Managed Mac OS X Clients

Most organizations would like to provide at least some basic amount of management, such as providing a default set of printers. Others prefer to fully lock down the box to ensure the highest level of computer uptime at the risk of hindering the user from being productive. An optimum solution would be to get these abilities while still integrating with a third-party directory.

To get these features, Apple chose to extend the standard RFC 2307 LDAP schema with over 50 new additions. All of these changes are listed in /etc/openldap/schema/apple. schema and can be applied to any directory service. For most directory administrators, this may be too daunting a task.

A simpler solution may be to supplement the primary directory with an Open Directory server. In the same way that you can use an Open Directory server to provide mounts for network home folders, the same server can provide Managed Client for X (MCX) settings for group and computer records. With this solution you can enjoy the ease of use of the Apple tools and their directory with built-in support for client management. When configured correctly, the Open Directory server is able to create and manage groups of users or groups of groups (new to Mac OS X Server v10.4) that exist only on the primary directory server.

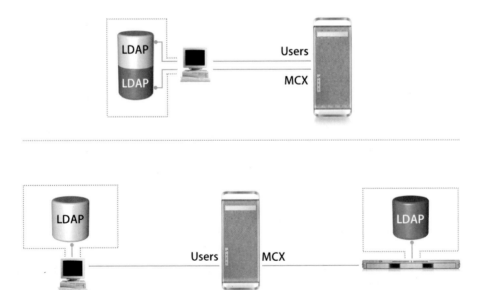

User Authentication With the LDAPv3 Plug-In

Having the additional directory servers bound to the Mac OS X computer to provide the array of services previously described raises some authentication questions. Depending on plug-in configuration, Mac OS X will attempt to authenticate the identity of the user using the following methods:

▶ Authentication authority: If the plug-in is configured to map the user attribute AuthenticationAuthority to a valid attribute in the user record, then Mac OS X will attempt to authenticate the identity with the associated value.

▶ Kerberos: Mac OS X will use this method if Kerberos is configured correctly with a valid edu.mit.Kerberos file (located in /Library/Preferences) and the login window is configured to use a modified right in the /etc/authorization file. A more flexible authentication authority permits the use of Kerberos for sshd, sudo, and chkpasswd, to name a few.

▶ Password User Attribute mapping: If mapped, Mac OS X will attempt to authenticate with the crypt user password in the directory stored in the mapped attribute.

▶ LDAP Bind: If the password mapping is left blank (as should be done with Microsoft and Novell), Mac OS X will use LDAP Bind to authenticate the identity. By default, this technique transmits the password in the clear. To avoid this security risk, LDAP plug-in should be configured to use SSL. LDAP binding will first try Generic Security Services Application Programming Interface (GSSAPI) and CRAM-MD5 before reverting to clear text.

▶ SSL: Permits all transactions to be encrypted using a certificate. The server and all client computers must have a copy of the certificate in order to communicate over SSL.

TIP ▶ Take time to coordinate with your directory administrator and other members of your IT/IS group to determine the risk and the appropriate steps you should take to authenticate your users securely. Administrators should be aware how and whether Mac OS X users will see administratively defined password policies. The LDAPv3 password policy support varies by vendor and currently does not work with either Novell or Microsoft directory servers.

Administrators may prefer a solution that does not provide supported server-based password policies so that they can enforce their own policies through mail and Web clients. This compromise gets the most features, such as AFP network home folders, allowing users to change their passwords in the Accounts pane of System Preferences.

Although this may be OK for some administrators, Kerberos would give password policy support while maintaining the functionality of the LDAPv3 plug-in. This combination of LDAP and Kerberos can give Mac OS X users a first-class experience with password policy support plus single sign-on (SSO) to all kerberized services. It must be understood that password policies will not work without a Kerberos authentication authority.

Troubleshooting Integration

When troubleshooting your directory integration, take a step back and observe the chain of events in a successful integration. Walking through this will help you troubleshoot issues that may crop up along the way.

Prior to rebooting, the Mac OS X computer was configured with Directory Access to use two different LDAP directory services for authentication. The primary directory is the third-party directory, where all user records exist. The second is an Apple Open Directory (Mac OS X Server) server that will supplement the third-party directory service by hosting Mac OS X–specific information outside of the user records, such as mounts and computer MCX records. This configuration is stored in two files:

▶ SearchNodeConfig.plist stores what order directories should be searched.

▶ DSLDAPv3PlugInConfig.plist has the specific mappings for each LDAP configuration.

1. On boot, these files are read and any available directories are searched for mount record information and computer-level MCX settings.

2. In the example in the following figure, the Open Directory Server has mount record information and computer MCX settings.

3. After those settings have been applied, the Login Window appears.

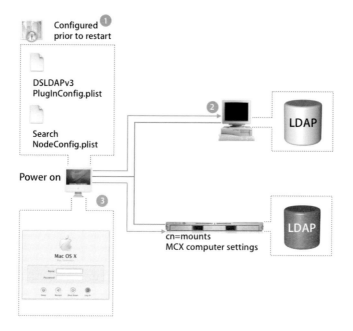

User Authentication

Once the Login Window appears, a user types in his or her user name and password, and the following occurs:

1. The Login Window process checks the local NetInfo database for the user record.

2. If no match is found, the Login Window process will query the first configured directory from Directory Access according to the Authentication list.

3. The listed directory server, bound correctly, will respond with the contents of the user's record.

4. Now that the Login Window process has found a matching user record, it will attempt to validate if the password entered was correct through LDAP bind.

5. If the password is correct, the user will be logged into the system with all the user attributes, such as User ID and home folder, applied to that user for this session.

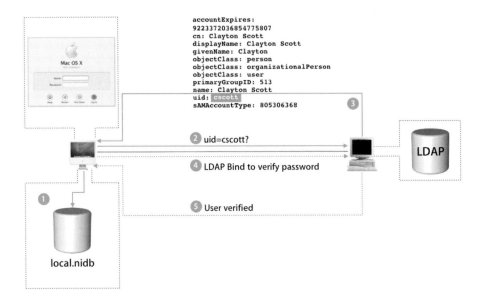

MCX Settings

After the user is verified, Mac OS X retrieves any available MCX records via the following process:

1. The user is verified.

2. Next, Mac OS X queries all available directories for MCX group records.

3. The Open Directory server, which is hosting MCX group records, responds with a list of groups and all of their MCX settings that are available to that user record, and the Login Window process presents the user with a list of groups from which to choose.

4. Once the user chooses a MCX group, the Login Window process resumes a traditional user login process and attempts to find the user's home folder.

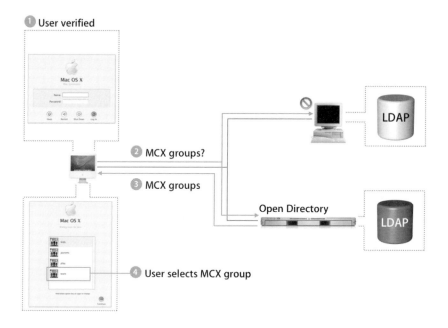

Home Directory

The Login Window process is designed to handle the listing of several groups; if more groups are found than can be shown, a scroll bar will appear on the right of the Login Window, allowing the user to scroll up and down to find the selected group. The following steps take place after the Login Window shows all available groups:

1. The user selects a managed group, and the process for mounting the home folder begins.

2. The home folder is automatically mounted by the automount binary located in /usr/sbin, which mounts remote file systems when they are first accessed.

    In the example in the figure below, the user's record in the directory had attributes that stated the home folder was on the Open Directory server.

3. Once the home folder is actually mounted on the remote server, the connection must be authenticated. The Open Directory server has no user names and does not directly know about the user who is attempting to connect. The local NetInfo database is searched first for valid criteria.

4. If no match is found, the server progresses through its own custom authentication path, configured in Directory Access on the server. In this case, the authentication moves up to the Open Directory directory service and then to the primary directory domain where the user actually exists. Now the user and password can be authenticated for the second time.

5. The home folder is successfully mounted.

6. The connection is allowed.

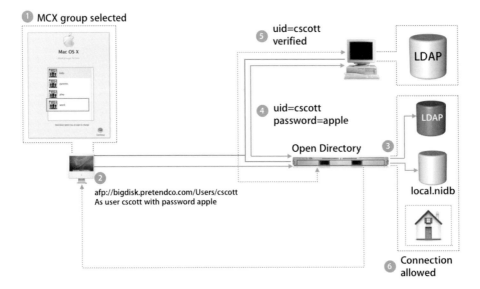

This complete process is essentially invisible to the user, which is the ultimate goal of spreading user data, home folders, and managed client settings on different servers.

What You've Learned

▶ Apple provides plug-ins for LDAPv3 and Active Directory and the option to integrate third-party custom plug-ins.

▶ When using the LDAPv3 plug-in, the requirements are the same as if Mac OS X were connecting to Open Directory.

▶ The key to integration is planning your approach to supplementing the existing directory. For the best results, start by connecting to the third-party directory service with an LDAP browser, and then follow the LDAP workflow outlined in this lesson.

▶ At login, Mac OS X needs to find user identification and to authenticate the identity.

▶ If using LDAP Bind, administrators need to use SSL to avoid exposing user passwords to the network.

▶ Kerberos can be used to securely authenticate identities, allow for password policies, or enable SSO to services.

References

Administration Guides

"Mac OS X Server Open Directory Administration": http://images.apple.com/server/pdfs/Open_Directory_v10.4.pdf

"Mac OS X Server Command-Line Administration": http://images.apple.com/server/pdfs/Command_Line_v10.4.pdf

Apple Knowledge Base Documents

The following Knowledge Base document (located at http://www.apple.com/support) provides further information about troubleshooting login problems with third-party LDAP directories.

Document 107523, "Mac OS X 10.2.5: Unable to Log In After Deleting NIS Server Entry"

Books

Carter, Gerald. *LDAP System Administration* (O'Reilly, 2003).

URLs

MacEnterprise.org: www.macosxlabs.org

Integrating Mac OS X in an NIS network: www.bresink.de/osx/nis.html

Novell eDirectory: www.novell.com/products/edirectory

Lesson Review

1. How can Open Directory be extended to communicate with alternate directory-service protocols?

2. What is the advantage of using an LDAP browser to test a connection to an LDAP server before using Directory Access?

3. What are three choices for supplementing missing directory-service data on a third-party server to successfully integrate Mac OS X?

4. What is a common deficiency when mapping Mac OS X to popular third-party directory services?

5. Which Open Directory attribute contains the address for the share point containing the home folder?

6. If the directory server does not provide mount records, how could you provide mount records for your client computers?

7. If you are unable to modify the schema on an LDAP server to support Mac OS X-specific records, what alternative method could you use?

Answers

1. A custom plug-in can be developed or purchased for use in an organization's network. One example of this is the ADmitMac plug-in available from Thursby.

2. An LDAP browser can confirm you have the correct settings and can establish a connection to the LDAP server. Once data can successfully be accessed, you can proceed with configuring Directory Access with the established settings.

3. Repurpose existing fields, modify the schema of the directory, use local mappings with static or variable attributes

4. Many directory servers do not provide a default attribute for HomeDirectory, which is required for a Mac OS X network home folder.

5. HomeDirectory

6. When a directory server is unable to provide mount records, the mount records could be created and stored in the NetInfo databases on the client computers.

7. Instead of modifying the schema on the main directory server, you could set up a Mac OS X Server computer to provide the additional records. The client computers would then be configured to retrieve data from both servers.

5

Time   This lesson takes approximately 2 hours to complete.

Goals   Understand basic Active Directory terms

Configure Mac OS X to use the Active Directory plug-in

Learn when the various advanced options available with the Active
Directory plug-in in Mac OS X should be considered

Use the Active Directory plug-in and Mac OS X Server to supplement an
Active Directory server

Use a Mac OS X Server to supplement directory services provided by an
Active Directory server

Use an Active Directory server for authentication and a Mac OS X server
for managed client information

Use a Mac OS X server to supplement an Active Directory server for
providing MCX information to Mac OS X computers

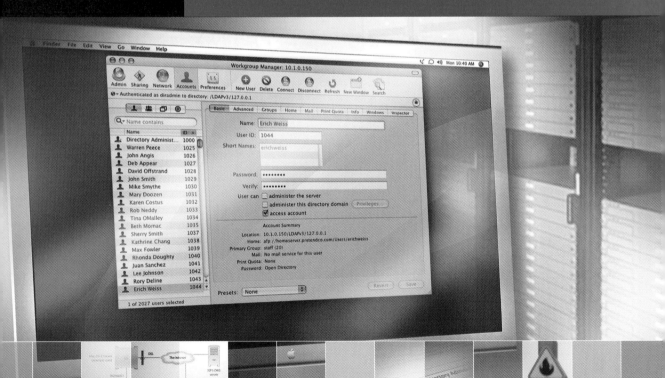

Lesson 5

Integrating Mac OS X With Active Directory

From Lesson 4, "Integrating Mac OS X With Third-Party Directory Services," you already know how to use the Lightweight Directory Access Protocol (LDAP) plug-in to bind a computer to an Active Directory server. Mac OS X also includes an Active Directory plug-in, which, when properly configured, allows your computer to access the same directory records as the Windows computers on the network.

With the Active Directory plug-in for Open Directory, configuring a Mac OS X computer to access an Active Directory server is fairly straightforward. If you prefer, though, you can override its default settings and specify how to map key user account attributes, where to store the home folder, and what accounts have admin access.

In this lesson, we will cover the many dynamics of integrating Mac OS X with Active Directory. Prior to Mac OS X version 10.3, the best way to integrate Mac OS X computers with Active Directory was through the LDAP plug-in, which is still a functional option. Today, the Active Directory plug-in facilitates easier configuration, a richer feature set, and a better user experience than that of the LDAP plug-in, which can still used for Active Directory integration. The focus of this lesson will be on the Active Directory plug-in with both Mac OS X and Mac OS X Server.

Understanding Mac OS X and Active Directory

Microsoft's Active Directory provides a standards-based LDAP directory service and various kerberized services. (Kerberos is covered in Lessons 6 and 9.)

Active Directory uses LDAP and provides Kerberos authentication.

Mac OS X supports LDAP and Kerberos authentication.

Active Directory has a unique schema with some standards compliance.

Mac OS X includes Active Directory plug-in to facilitate integration with Active Directory through the LDAP protocol.

Active Directory plug-in uses LDAP to communicate with the Active Directory server.

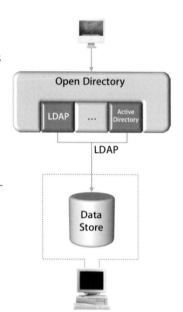

Open Directory, the Apple directory services architecture, also supports LDAP and Kerberos. It provides this support through a flexible and extensible plug-in architecture, as you have seen in previous lessons.

Active Directory Integration Configuration

Integrating Mac OS X with Active Directory requires the use of diverse tools, processes, and configuration files. All of these pieces work together to provide a flexible framework for integrating into an existing Active Directory deployment. Understanding these pieces and how they work together provides a proper picture for the modification, trouble-shooting, and migration of a configuration.

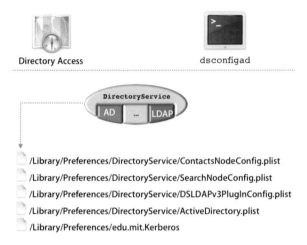

The Active Directory configuration process is the same for both Mac OS X and Mac OS X Server, depending on how the directory structure is configured on Mac OS X Server. If it is initially a standalone server, then the binding will be identical to that of Mac OS X. But if you are planning to turn the Mac OS X server into an Open Directory master, then the option of binding to an Active Directory domain must be made prior to this process, as a decision must be made on whether the Active Directory server or the Mac OS X server will be the Kerberos KDC.

> **MORE INFO** ▶ Kerberos is covered in Lessons 6 and 9, and Open Directory masters are covered in Lesson 7, "Hosting Open LDAP."

Using the Apple Active Directory Plug-In – Basic

Mac OS X includes an Open Directory plug-in to help administrators more effectively integrate Mac OS X with Active Directory's schema without making changes in the Windows world. The Active Directory plug-in is configured inside of the Directory Access application.

Before binding can begin, a better understanding of a few Active Directory terms is in order.

Key Active Directory Terms

▶ Active Directory forest: A *forest* is the first domain that is created in an organization. Because of this, no Active Directory deployment can be free of a forest. If your organization has only one domain, then the forest name is identical to the domain name. It is not necessary to fill out the name of the forest in the plug-in. When you fill out the domain name, it will correctly return the name of the forest.

▶ Active Directory domain: Similar to traditional Windows NT domains, Active Directory domains are used to store user and resource definitions and information. Active Directory domain names are in a domain name system (DNS) format and never include the host name of the server hosting the domain.

▶ Computer ID: The computer ID is used by the Active Directory domain to associate the Mac OS X computer to its computer account. Its name is limited to 16 characters and will truncate any characters over 16.

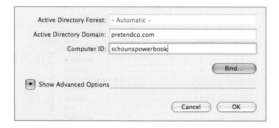

Initial Configuration

Basic binding to an Active Directory domain requires the name of the domain that you want to bind to (entered in the Network preferences pane of System Preferences) and a computer ID, which is how the Mac OS X computer will be recognized in the Active Directory domain. Even though the Active Directory plug-in sets the computer ID to the name of the computer, you can override the default if your organization has an established naming scheme. With both values, check with the Active Directory server administrator if you are unsure.

Binding

Once you are ready to implement the plug-in settings, click the Bind button and you will see another dialog, as shown in the figure below. After you've entered the user name and password of a user with the ability to add computer records to the Active Directory domain, the user's Mac OS X computer will join the specified domain.

NOTE ▶ You cannot configure the plug-in without entering the name and password of an account with the ability to add user names in the container (or ou) specified in the Computer OU field.

Similar to the LDAP plug-in, during the binding you can select the options to add the Active Directory domain to the Authentication and Contacts search paths with their two respective checkboxes. When the checkboxes are selected, the search paths will show up in the Authentication and Contacts tabs in Directory Access.

Once bound, the Mac OS X computer is fully configured to integrate with Active Directory, without a single modification to the Active Directory schema.

Default User Experience With the Active Directory Plug-In

With the Active Directory plug-in fully configured, users can now log in to Mac OS X with a user name and password in the bound Active Directory domain. There are several variations of the user name that can be used for login: long name, short name, email address, or domain principal. This allows Mac OS X users the same user name options that Windows users have when authenticating.

cscott@pretendco.com
cscott
Clayton Scott
PRETENDCO/cscott

After login, users can access certain network services without being continually prompted for a user name and password. Services like file and protected Web may no longer require reauthentication. This change occurs because a Kerberos ticket-granting ticket (TGT) is received from the Active Directory domain when the user logs in to Mac OS X with an Active Directory account.

Advanced Plug-in Configurations

Although the default configuration will suffice for many users, the Active Directory plug-in provides advanced options to configure the plug-in to meet your needs. The following figure shows the different user options.

Creating Mobile User Accounts

A mobile account caches the user's Active Directory identification data and authentication credentials on the bound Mac OS X computer, allowing the user to log in using the Active Directory name and password while the Mac OS X computer is disconnected from the Active Directory domain. A mobile account has a local home folder on the startup volume of the Mac OS X computer. You also have the choice of creating a notification when the user logs in for the first time.

Defining Home Folder Location

By default, the Active Directory plug-in creates a local home folder for each Active Directory user who logs in. Using a local home folder helps ensure that Mac OS X processes and applications have a place to store user-level preferences and resources, even during a network outage. Additionally, saving documents to a local drive is generally faster than saving to a remote volume.

By default, the plug-in is configured to create a local home folder named after the user's RecordName, as in SAMAccountName. When configured to create a local home folder, the plug-in also mounts the user's Windows network home folder (a native Active Directory HomeDirectory attribute, as specified in the User's Active Directory account) as a network volume, like a share point. To further assist the user's ability to access his or her data on the server, an alias to that user's network home folder is also placed in the Dock. The user can copy files between the Windows home folder network volume and the local home folder.

> **NOTE ▶** If a home folder already exists with the same short name as that of a new Active Directory user, Mac OS X will not know to create the new home folder and the logged-in user will be unable to access the pre-existing folder, due to a permission mismatch.

If you change the name of a user account in the Active Directory domain, the server will create a new home folder (and subfolders) for the user account the next time it is used for logging in to a Mac OS X computer. The user can navigate to the old home folder and see its contents in the Finder. You can prevent the creation of a new home folder by renaming the old folder before the user next logs in.

When someone logs in to Mac OS X with an Active Directory user account, the Active Directory plug-in can automatically mount the Windows network home folder that's specified in the Active Directory user account as the user's Mac OS X home folder. You can specify whether to use the network home specified by Active Directory's standard home directory attribute or by the Mac OS X Home Directory attribute, if the Active Directory schema has been extended to include it. The protocols that can be used for this are are Apple Filing Protocol (AFP) and Server Message Block (SMB), but not network file system (NFS).

Had the administrator chosen to use the LDAPv3 plug-in to support Active Directory users in a similar way, the Active Directory schema would have needed modification to map mount records and the two home folder user attributes. The Active Directory plug-in, on the other hand, dynamically creates these missing pieces for Mac OS X at login, thus obviating the need for schema modifications.

User Shell

Finally, you can set the command-line shell that users with Active Directory accounts will use when interacting with Mac OS X in the Terminal application. The default shell is also used for remote interaction via SSH (Secure Shell Protocol) or Telnet. Each user can override the default shell by changing a Terminal preference.

Mapping Options

When the "Map UID to attribute" option is not selected, the plug-in dynamically generates a unique user ID and a primary group ID based on the user account's globally unique ID (GUID) in the Active Directory domain. The generated user ID and primary group ID are always the same for each user account, even if the account is used to log in to different Mac OS X computers. When the "Map UID to attribute" option is selected, the Active Directory plug-in maps the user ID and primary group ID to the Active Directory attributes that have been previously repurposed or added to the AD schema to hold those user values. The user ID value is unique per user, but the Primary Group ID will generally be the same for most users.

The Active Directory plug-in also generates a group ID based on the Active Directory group account's GUID. Like the user ID, you can configure the plug-in to map the group ID for group accounts to a specified Active Directory attribute.

Administrative Options

You have a few additional options when binding to an Active Directory domain. These are found on the Administrative tab.

When you select the "Prefer this domain server" option, you tell Active Directory to first attempt a connection with a particular server rather than dynamically discovering the closest domain server. If the designated server is not found, Mac OS X will attempt to locate an alternate domain server at startup. If this option is not selected, the Active Directory plug-in automatically determines the closest Active Directory domain in the forest. This option is useful in situations where an older, slower Windows computer is being used as an Active Directory domain server within a given network. You may want to direct your requests to a faster, more powerful Active Directory server somewhere other than the server that is physically closest to your Mac OS X computers.

By selecting "Allow administration by," you can specify which groups of users within Active Directory have administration rights in Mac OS X. When logged in to Mac OS X, users who are members of these groups are treated as if they were members of the local admin group on the Mac OS X computer, meaning they have access to install applications and write to the local library folder. Some Active Directory administrators prefer to create a new group within the Active Directory domain called MacAdmins and place all Macintosh administrators within that group. You can then choose to allow only that MacAdmins group with this option.

If you select the "Allow authentication from any domain in the forest" option, Mac OS X will authenticate users who are members of domains outside of its own domain. After changing this setting, you need to change the custom search policy in the Authentication pane and/or Contacts pane to include the Active Directory forest or selected domains as appropriate. This could reduce the number of users who can log in to that Mac OS X computer.

You can also add the Active Directory forest to the computer's custom search policies for authentication and contacts. When adding to a custom search policy, the forest appears in the list of available directory domains as /Active Directory/All Domains (the default setting). Alternatively, you can add Active Directory domains individually to the computer's custom search policies for authentication and contacts. When adding to a custom search policy, each Active Directory domain appears separately in the list of available directory domains and can be rearranged just like any other directory service to which the Mac OS X computer is bound.

More Integration With Active Directory

Integration with Active Directory does not stop with simple login support; other, more subtle features are supported through the plug-in:

▶ Users who have successfully logged in to Mac OS X can change their password through System Preferences. If the Active Directory administrator has password policies in place, they are fully enforced.

▶ Depending on the plug-in configuration, members of Active Directory admin groups will be treated as administrators.

▶ Address Book and other applications that use Address Book for contact searches can now search Active Directory for contact information.

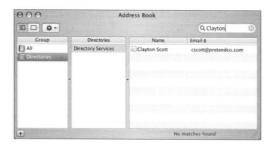

▶ The command-line tool dsconfigad can be used to set all Active Directory bind settings shown in the plug-in. Because it's a command-line tool, it can be used in shell scripts. And since AppleScripts can call shell scripts, dsconfigad can be used with AppleScript as well. A login hook shell script that binds a computer to an Active Directory domain the first time the computer is booted without user or administrator interaction can be very useful when doing mass deployment of Mac OS X systems within an Active Directory environment.

Exploring the Active Directory Plug-in

In this exercise, you will explore the various options of the Active Directory plug-in and its counterpart, dsconfigad.

1   Open Directory Access, located in /Applications/Utilities.

2   Select the Services tab, and double-click the Active Directory plug-in to open it.

3   Click the disclosure triangle on the left to show the advanced options.

4   Click each option to observe the various choices you have when binding to an Active Directory domain.

5   Close the plug-in, quit Directory Access, and open a Terminal window.

6   Type *man dsconfigad* and press the Return key to view the man page for dsconfigad.

7   Press the Space bar to view more of the man page.

The dsconfigad tool is well documented.

8   Quit the Terminal.

Behind the Scenes: Active Directory Bind

Now that you have seen the user experience with the Active Directory plug-in, let's go behind the scenes to understand how the plug-in makes integration so easy. Before users can log in, the plug-in must be configured. When an administrator clicks the Bind button and authenticates, the plug-in begins a sequence of events to appropriately configure Mac OS X.

1. The plug in uses _domain.tcp.domain.com to find the DNS server, which should return a list of hosts providing LDAP and Kerberos services.

2. It then uses LDAP to find out what domain it's currently in. The plug-in will attempt to authenticate to that domain to look for the closest domain controller.

3. Assuming a successful authentication, the domain controller will use another extension of DNS, which supports site records, and respond by supplying the host information for the nearest domain controller to the Mac OS X computer.

4. With a list of domain controllers now returned, the plug-in chooses one and builds an edu.mit.Kerberos configuration file based on it.

5. The plug-in will attempt to authenticate to the new domain controller and begin searching the domain and forest for a computer record with a computer ID that corresponds to the one specified for the plug-in.

6. If a match is found, the plug-in will use that computer record.

7. If a match is not found, the plug-in will create a new computer record with the plug-in's specified computer ID.

8. A password is then attached to the newly created computer ID or changed if the computer account already exists.

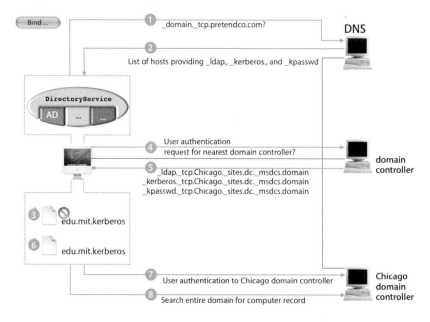

TIP The plug-in can create this record only if the user name and password provided belong to an account with the authority to add computer records to the domain.

At this point, Mac OS X is fully configured to integrate with Active Directory.

Encountering Errors

To cleanly unbind Mac OS X from an Active Directory domain, first connect the computer to the domain to ensure that the plug-in can remove the associated record. When you clicked the Bind button, it automatically changed to an Unbind button, so all you have to do now is click Unbind.

Administrators can forcefully remove the binding configuration information by deleting the ActiveDirectory.plist file. If you choose to do this, you will need to remove the computer record from the Active Directory domain manually, then remove the listing from the authentication path.

> **NOTE ▶** The ActiveDirectory.plist file is located at /Library/Preferences/ DirectoryService/.

However, several errors can occur when attempting to bind to Active Directory. Below are explanations of the more common errors:

▶ Invalid domain: This message refers to the plug-in's inability to find a domain controller or Global Catalog server with the existing Mac OS X network configuration. This is due to incorrect names being typed during plug-in configuration or because the Mac OS X computer is using a DNS server lacking the appropriate service records that would normally be populated through Dynamic DNS. For best results, Mac OS X computers should be using a Microsoft Dynamic DNS server or another DNS server that has been configured to allow Dynamic DNS updates from Active Directory servers.

▶ Active Directory time error: This error occurs because the plug-in depends on a functional Kerberos environment. Kerberos requires that all Kerberos host and client clocks be relatively in sync. In any Kerberos deployment, the use of a network time server is essential to reliable operation. In general, a 5-minute time difference is all that is permitted.

▶ Insufficient privileges: This error will occur when the user name and password supplied do not have permission to join a computer to the listed domain.

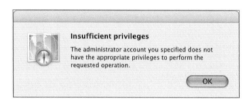

Troubleshooting

To troubleshoot Active Directory DNS issues, you can run nslookup in interactive mode:

    nslookup -sil

The prompt turns to >. To look at various service records associated with binding, type any of the following, depending on your query:

host -t SRV _ldap._tcp.domain.com

host -t SRV _kerberos._tcp.domain.com

host -t SRV _kpasswd._tcp.domain.com

NOTE ▶ For the word *domain,* substitute your Active Directory domain.

Each one of these will return information based on your lookup. If you do not see any results for the entries, then the entries are not valid domains.

You can also use nslookup to test reverse DNS lookups. To look up standard records, type *set type=A* and enter the server address, such as

    mainserver.pretendco.com

The results should look like the following:

    mainserver.pretendco.com = 10.1.0.1

Typing *10.1.0.1* should yield a result similar to this:

    10.1.0.1.in-addr.arpa PTR mainserver.pretendco.com

Also, when binding with the Active Directory plug-in, you can send DirectoryService a -USR1 message to request that it log to /Library/Logs/DirectoryService/ DirectoryService.debug.log.

    sudo killall -USR1 DirectoryService

This is a toggle switch command; running it again will turn off the debug log.

Plug-in Configuration Files
The Active Directory plug-in uses a collection of files to make Active Directory integration a reality:

▶ edu.mit.Kerberos: This is the primary Kerberos configuration file. It is chiefly responsible for identifying the Kerberos server used to facilitate password policies and single sign-on within the domain. This file is located in /Library/Preferences/.

▶ ActiveDirectory.plist: Contains all values for the plug-in's advanced options. Also contains the schema mappings being employed by default. Advanced users can make manual modifications to this file to further configure the plug-in. This file is located in /Library/Preferences/DirectoryService/.

▶ SearchNodeConfig.plist: Used by Directory Access to record which directories to search and in what order to search them. Administrators troubleshooting directory configurations may want to delete this file, thus resetting Mac OS X to a state in which no remote directories are searched. This file is located in /Library/ Preferences/DirectoryService/.

▶ ContactsNodeConfig.plist: Used by Directory Access to track which directories to use for contact lookups. Applications like Mail and Address Book use these directories to automatically locate contact information. This file is located in /Library/Preferences/DirectoryService/.

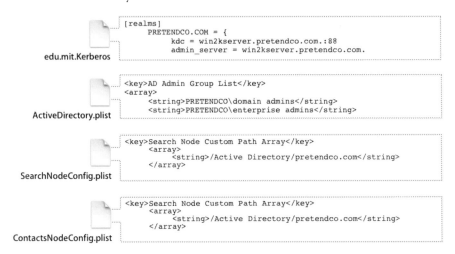

edu.mit.Kerberos
```
[realms]
        PRETENDCO.COM = {
                kdc = win2kserver.pretendco.com.:88
                admin_server = win2kserver.pretendco.com.
```

ActiveDirectory.plist
```
<key>AD Admin Group List</key>
<array>
        <string>PRETENDCO\domain admins</string>
        <string>PRETENDCO\enterprise admins</string>
```

SearchNodeConfig.plist
```
<key>Search Node Custom Path Array</key>
        <array>
                <string>/Active Directory/pretendco.com</string>
        </array>
```

ContactsNodeConfig.plist
```
<key>Search Node Custom Path Array</key>
        <array>
                <string>/Active Directory/pretendco.com</string>
        </array>
```

Supplementing Active Directory With Mac OS X Server

Like other third-party directory servers, an Active Directory does not include Mac OS X–specific attributes without modifying the schema. Through discussions with the server administrator, you need to determine the appropriate approach, either by modifying the Active Directory schema or by configuring a supplemental server.

MCX Records Can Be Stored in Active Directory

Being able to log in to Active Directory from Mac OS X is adequate integration for many organizations. However, others may also wish to use the Apple Managed Client for X (MCX) technology to further enhance their Active Directory user experience.

One way of supporting MCX on Mac OS X for Active Directory accounts is to modify the existing Active Directory schema so that it incorporates Apple's MCX schema attributes. Then the administrator will need to create and populate all the MCX user, group, and computer records with functional data.

MORE INFO ► Apple Professional Services has the ability to modify the Active Directory schema to include these and other Mac OS X–specific attributes. Please refer to the References at the end of this lesson.

Administrators using the Active Directory plug-in can deploy MCX in their Active Directory schema whenever they choose without thought to client configuration. If the Active Directory schema has been extended to include Mac OS X record types (object classes) and attributes, the Active Directory plug-in detects and accesses them automatically. This schema modification enables the Active Directory plug-in to support managed client settings (MCX) made using Workgroup Manager.

NOTE ► Mac OS X clients assume full read access to attributes that are added to the directory. Therefore, it may be necessary to modify the ACL of those attributes to allow computer lists to read these added attributes.

Integrating MCX, Active Directory, and Open Directory

Instead of merging the Apple schema with that of Active Directory, you can host MCX directory content on a separate Open Directory server. Configuring a Mac OS X computer to use this setup is relatively simple. In Directory Access, administrators just need to add an LDAP configuration for the Open Directory server in addition to their Active Directory configuration, which will work for both the Active Directory plug-in and the LDAPv3 plug-in. It also lets you use Workgroup Manager to create MCX workgroup and computer lists.

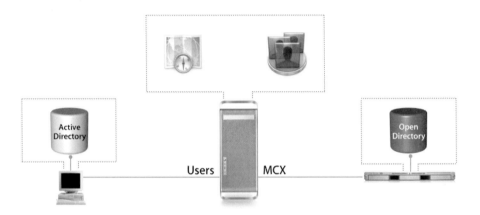

The biggest drawback is that administrators forfeit their ability to manage individual users; users will need to be managed by group or computer. Still, it's usually more than acceptable, since the more users you have, the more time consuming it is to manage them individually.

Startup

Understanding the big picture is an important part of being able to effectively troubleshoot a problem. In the following figure, you can see what happens at startup with a Mac OS X computer that has been configured to use the Active Directory plug-in for user records and the LDAPv3 plug-in for MCX settings.

1. All the appropriate plist files discussed earlier have been configured with Directory Access prior to restart.

2. At startup, the configured Mac OS X computer searches all configured directories for MCX computer records and applies the appropriate settings to itself.

3. After the MCX settings are applied to the Mac OS X computer, the login screen appears.

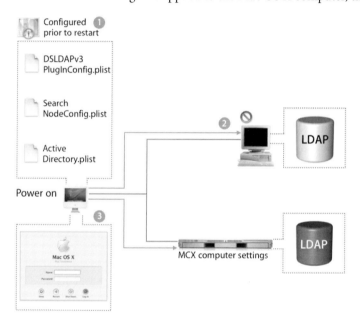

User Authentication

The following figure shows the process of user authentication:

1. The user now types a user name and password into the login screen and presses Return.

2. The loginwindow process checks the local NetInfo database for the user record and if no match is found, loginwindow will then query the first configured directory from the Directory Access authentication path list.

3. Assuming the directory server responds with the contents of the user's record, loginwindow will attempt to validate the user using the password.

4. The existing Kerberos server specified in the edu.mit.Kerberos file.

5. The user is issued a Kerberos TGT and is then logged in to the Mac OS X computer.

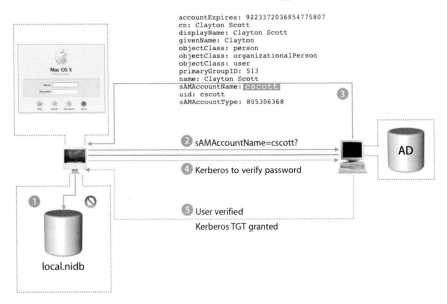

MCX and Home Directory

Now that the user has been verified, the following figure shows what happens next:

1. The user is verified.

2. Mac OS X searches all configured directories shown in the Directory Access authentication path list for MCX groups that are applicable to the current user.

3. The login screen presents the user with a choice of available groups.

4. The user chooses a group.

5. Mac OS X continues the login process with the MCX settings applied to the session.

6. If the user's record in Active Directory is configured with settings for an SMB home folder, Mac OS X attempts to mount the SMB home folder using Kerberos authentication. If the user's record in Active Directory is configured with settings for an AFP home folder, Mac OS X attempts to mount the AFP home folder.

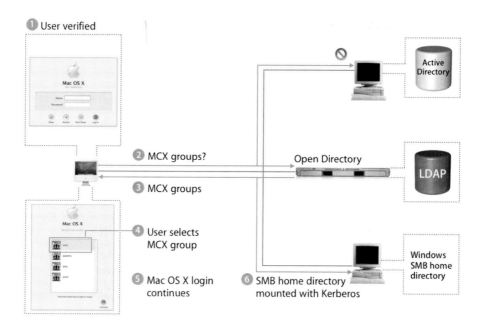

Other Binding Considerations

Administrators will want to consider some final details prior to deploying Mac OS X with the Active Directory plug-in:

▶ Currently, packet signing and packet encryption are not supported.

▶ Mac OS X attempts to mount SMB home folders using Kerberos for authentication. Domain controllers can be set up to allow various forms of authentication. If the server hosting the SMB home folder has been configured not to allow Kerberos, Mac OS X will attempt to connect with NTLMv2.

▶ The Active Directory plug-in is designed with the assumption that more than 40 user record attributes are readable by the computer record that the Mac OS X computer is configured to use. If these attributes are not readable, then Mac OS X may behave unexpectedly.

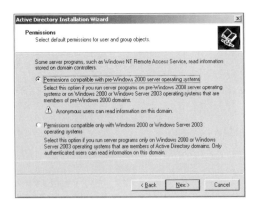

MORE INFO ▶ For a full list of user attributes used by the Active Directory plug-in, administrators should read the Knowledge Base document 107830, which is listed in the References section at the end of this lesson.

▶ The plug-in works best with Active Directory deployments that are set up with the pre–Windows 2000 permission style. If you are not sure which permission style was used when your organization's Active Directory deployment was set up, you should coordinate with the Active Directory administrator and inspect the permissions of the attributes the plug-in uses.

▶ The Active Directory plug-in makes Mac OS X computer integration with Active Directory a practical reality. The Active Directory plug-in greatly simplifies the work that administrators must perform to provide a full Active Directory experience for Mac OS X users. Some of the key Active Directory plug-in features are:

· LDAP and Kerberos support

· True SMB home folders

· MCX support

· No Active Directory schema modifications

What You've Learned

▶   The computer ID is limited to 16 characters and will truncate any characters over 16.

▶   The different methods a user can use to log in to a Mac OS X computer when bound to an Active Directory domain are: long name, short name, email address, and domain principal.

▶   When setting Active Directory administrative options, using "Allow administration by" specifies which groups of users within Active Directory have administration rights in Mac OS X.

▶   The majority of files connected with an Active Directory bind are located in /Library/Preferences/DirectoryService except the edu.mit.kerberos file, which is located in /Library/Preferences.

▶   Packet signing and packet encryption are not supported with the current Active Directory plug-in in Mac OS X v10.4.

References

Administration Guides

"Mac OS X Server Open Directory Administration": http://images.apple.com/server/pdfs/Open_Directory_v10.4.pdf

"Mac OS X Command-Line Administration": http://images.apple.com/server/pdfs/Command_Line_v10.4.pdf

Apple Knowledge Base Documents

The following Knowledge Base documents (located at www.apple.com/support) provide further information about Active Directory.

Document 107830, "Mac OS X Server 10.3 or later Active Directory: Using computer account attribute ACLs"

Document 301010, "Using the Active Directory plug-in in a multi-domain controller environment"

Books

Allen, Robbie, and Lowe-Norris, Alistair G. *Active Directory, 2nd Edition* (O'Reilly and Associates, 2003).

URLs

Open Directory and Active Directory: www.macdevcenter.com/pub/a/mac/2003/08/05/active_directory.html

Shukwit.com: www.shukwit.com

Windows Server 2003 Active Directory: www.microsoft.com/windowsserver2003/technologies/directory/activedirectory/default.mspx

Apple Professional Services: www.apple.com/services/consulting

Lesson Review

1. What protocol does the Active Directory plug-in use to retrieve directory data from an Active Directory server?

2. If an attribute is not specified, what Active Directory attribute does the Active Directory plug-in use to create the user ID?

3. If you do not configure the Active Directory plug-in other than binding to an Active Directory server, where is the user's home folder stored?

4. When binding to an Active Directory server, what information does the Active Directory plug-in require?

5. What are the server configuration options for implementing Managed Client for X (MCX) support for Active Directory users?

6. What is the possible danger of making changes to the schema of an Active Directory server?

7. What is an advantage to using an Open Directory server to supplement an Active Directory server?

8. If an Open Directory server is used to supplement an Active Directory server instead of modifying the Active Directory schema, can Workgroup Manager manage user account preferences?

Answers

1. LDAP

2. The Active Directory plug-in bases the user ID on the user account's globally unique ID (GUID).

3. A home folder for the user is created locally in /Users.

4. The Active Directory plug-in needs the Active Directory domain and a computer ID. It also requires the name and password of a domain administrator account on the server.

5. Modify the Active Directory schema or use an ancillary Open Directory server to store the MCX data for Active Directory users.

6. Erroneous schema changes on an Active Directory server are very difficult to correct. Great care should be taken when you make schema changes.

7. An Open Directory server can supplement an Active Directory server, providing Mac OS X computers with Mac OS X–specific records, such as MCX records.

8. No. In order to allow user preferences to be managed, the Active Directory schema must be modified to allow user records to store managed user preferences.

6

Time	This lesson takes approximately 2 hours to complete.
Goals	Understand the advantages and disadvantages of using Kerberos with Mac OS X
	Use Kerberos to verify passwords
	Edit the Kerberos configuration files on a Mac OS X computer
	Use klist, kinit, and kdestroy command-line tools to add, delete, and list Kerberos tickets on a Mac OS X computer
	List the contents of the edu.mit.Kerberos file on Mac OS X
	Learn how a user's kerberized authentication method is stored in an LDAP directory when using Mac OS X

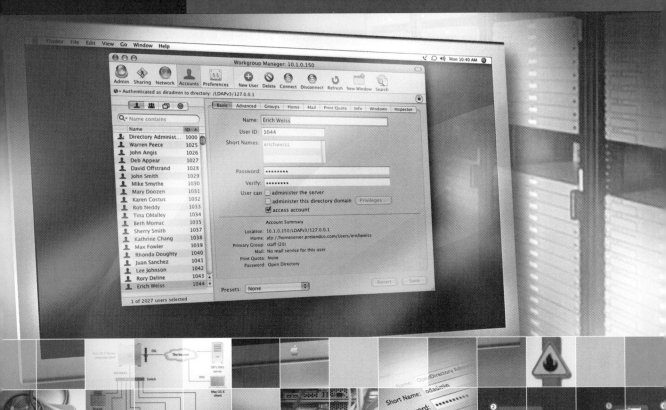

Kerberos Fundamentals

There's a famous *New Yorker* cartoon in which two dogs are sitting at a computer and one of them says, "On the Internet, no one knows you are a dog."

That's a big challenge on any network: identifying and authenticating who you are actually working with. Identification is the process of recognizing who the user says she is; authentication is the process of proving that the user is who she says she is. While subtle, the difference is important.

Kerberos provides authentication and secure, single sign-on (SSO) service for network services. This lesson shows how Kerberos works and how to integrate Mac OS X computers with Kerberos.

The most commonly used method to identify and authenticate a user is to assign the user a unique name and password. By providing their names (identity) and passwords (authentication), users can "prove" who they are to their network services—a Hypertext Transfer Protocol (HTTP) server, an Apple Filing Protocol (AFP) server, an SMB server, a mail server, and so on. You make many connections to network services when working with computers on a network—so many, in fact, that sometimes the aspect of identification and authentication are taken for granted.

Since each network service typically requires a separate name and password for each user, people often have to keep track of several different names and identities. That can obviously create a problem if you forget your password and are denied access, or can present a serious security risk if users track passwords in insecure ways. The risks associated with network security are covered in detail in Part 2, "Security," the next section of this book.

There are many technologies designed to address this issue, such as Keychain and Kerberos. Their basic premises are identical—that a user should be required to identify and authenticate only once to access all approved network services—but the methodology behind the two is vastly different. This lesson covers Kerberos in Mac OS X v10.4. Keychain is not directly related to Directory Services and is covered in Part 2.

Understanding Kerberos Basics

Kerberos provides secure authentication to a variety of network services. It also supports SSO, so users can access all of these resources by logging in just once. While extremely interesting, the background of Kerberos won't help you learn how to integrate Mac OS X with Kerberos and troubleshoot problems. Instead, let's take a look at how Kerberos works.

> **NOTE ▸** To further your background knowledge of Kerberos, refer to the "References" section, at the end of this lesson.

Meeting Requestor Needs

In a directory-services environment, servers on the network provide services; then clients request those services. Requestors like Login Window or the Mail application need to authenticate file or mail servers, authorize particular tasks, and centralize password management so that each person has to remember only a single password to access all network services. That provides a better user experience, but it still does not address the fact that the password may be used on each server to authenticate the user—something that is not in the best interest of keeping your network secure. But Kerberos addresses that issue, as well.

This figure illustrates how Mac OS X leverages identification information from one source while obtaining authentication information from another source. A third source can also be leveraged for additional information required by Mac OS X.

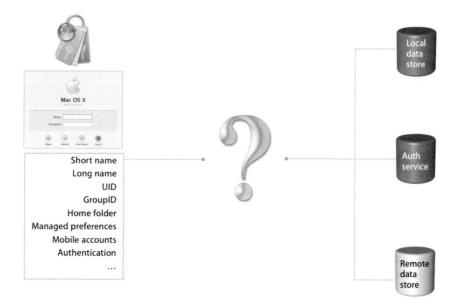

One comprehensive solution is to configure Mac OS X to use Kerberos for authentication. Kerberos provides secure authentication services using a ticket system, allowing for a seamless end-user experience. Also, Kerberos authentication works cross-platform, meaning that your Mac OS X computers can use existing Active Directory Kerberos services and vice versa, even if those services are served from another platform.

That provides a tremendous level of flexibility and compatibility when configuring various services that come from different servers on different platforms. The open architecture of Kerberos permits all this to take place, regardless of whether your users exist in the Mac OS X Server Lightweight Directory Access Protocol (LDAP) database or the

Active Directory domain. This piece of Kerberos, called cross-platform integration, will be explored in more detail in Lesson 9, "Integrating With Kerberos."

Defining Kerberos Terms

There are three main players in a complete Kerberos transaction:

▶ The user

▶ The service that the user is interested in accessing

▶ The key distribution center (KDC), which is responsible for creating and routing secure tickets and generally supplying the authentication mechanism

Within Kerberos there are different *realms,* specific databases or authentication domains. Each realm contains the authentication information for users and services, called Kerberos *principals.* For example, if you have a user with a long name of John Significant and a short name of johnsig on a KDC with the realm of PRETENDCO.COM, the user principal would be johnsig@pretendco.com@PRETENDCO.COM.

For a service to take advantage of Kerberos, it must be *kerberized,* which means that it can accept tokens from a client. While the service does not talk directly to the KDC, it is an integral part of the Kerberos structure. Not only can Mac OS X Server provide a KDC when configured to host a shared LDAP directory, but it can also provide a kerberized Login Window, HTTP, Mail, File Transfer Protocol (FTP), AFP, virtual private network (VPN), XGrid, Windows (SMB), and Secure Shell Protocol (SSH) services.

When a user account in the LDAP directory is configured to use the Open Directory password type (in Workgroup Manager), the keys pertaining to that user account exist solely on the KDC. Those keys are used to encrypt and decrypt any messages sent over the network. The Kerberos implementation in Mac OS X is based on Kerberos version 5 (Kerberosv5).

Using Kerberos

When a computer running Mac OS X binds to an LDAP directory on Mac OS X Server, it will, by default, also bind to the Mac OS X Server KDC. Then kerberosautoconfig (located in /sbin) uses the values found in the Config attribute in any LDAP directory in the directory search path to create the configuration file, edu.mit.Kerberos, on the Mac OS X computer. However, before a user can start using kerberized services, the account must receive a ticket-granting ticket (TGT) from the KDC.

When using Mac OS X Server as the KDC and using an account in the LDAP directory, the authentication process works as follows:

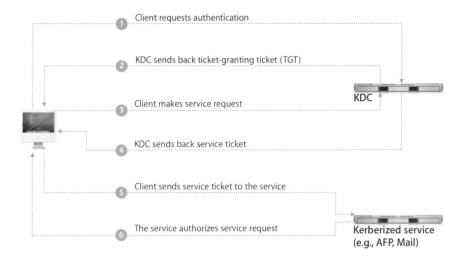

1. The client requests authentication from KDC:

   a. The user logs in (proposes a user name and password) with a user account on the LDAP directory configured to use a Kerberos password.

   b. Login Window requests and receives the identification information from the LDAP directory.

   c. If the identification includes Kerberosv5 as the AuthenticationAuthority, Mac OS X sends a KRB_AS_REQ message to the KDC. The message consists of the user name (so that the KDC knows which principal is attempting to authenticate), a timestamp, and the requested ticket lifetime.

2. The KDC generates a TGT:

   a. The TGT includes the user name, the name of the KDC, the current time and the time the ticket remains valid, the IP address of the Mac OS X computer, and a random session key generated by the KDC.

NOTE ▶ Most tickets are addressless (to accomodate Network Address Translation, or NAT) and therefore do not contain IPs.

b.   The KDC issues a KRB_AS_REP, in which the KDC combines the TGT with a copy of the random session key into a message. It then sends this back to the client in clear text because the TGT cannot be decrypted by the client; only the KDC can decrypt the TGT.

c.   Both the TGT and the session key are stored in the client's credentials cache, which is managed by the CCacheServer process. The Mac OS X version of Kerberos has a RAM-based credentials cache, making it more difficult for malicious parties to gain access to sensitive data, and ensuring that, should the machine quit unexpectedly or otherwise lose power, sensitive data will not be on the file system.

d.   The Mac OS X computer generates a user key using the proposed password. Using that generated user key, the requesting application (in this case, the Login Window) unlocks the message and extracts the TGT and session key.

e.   The user key is discarded. The TGT (in conjunction with authenticators generated with the initial session key) is used to authenticate the client to the TGT. A later service ticket and an authenticator generated with a second session key is used to authenticate (but not to identify) the user to kerberized services.

3.   The client makes a service request:

a.   When you want to access a kerberized service, in this case the AFP service running on mainserver.pretendco.com, you use the Connect to Server option under the Go menu in the Finder to specify the kerberized AFP server. Then the request is sent to the KDC. The negotiation for the use of Kerberos happens in the AFP protocol. Once the client and Mac OS X Server decide on Kerberos as the authentication method (as opposed to standard authentication), Kerberos on the server informs the client which service principal it should ask the KDC for. This is called KRB_TGS_REQ.

b.   The request message contains the TGT, the name of the service, and the host name of the server (Kerberos host principal).

4. The KDC sends back the TGT, which means:

    P• The KDC extracts and verifies the user based on the authenticator which was produced using the first session key and then sends a service ticket to the user for the requested service.

    •   The service ticket contains a version of the user's name that is encrypted with a service key, known only by the KDC and the service.

5. The user sends the service ticket to the service.

6. The service authorizes the request:

    a. The service unlocks the ticket with the service key, extracts the user's name, and determines if the user is authorized to use the service.

    b. If the user account is authorized to use the service, the client is given access to the service.

    c. All sensitive data exchanged between the client and the service is now encrypted is some fashion.

    NOTE ▶ Since Mac OS X Server can function as a KDC, it provides SSO authentication: As long as the user has a valid ticket, he or she is never prompted to authenticate when accessing kerberized services. One single password works for all kerberized services, and any user account in the shared LDAP directory that uses an Open Directory password is configured for Kerberos and takes advantage of the SSO feature. It is totally transparent to the user.

Configuring Kerberos on Mac OS X

To use Kerberos, a Mac OS X computer must be configured with the appropriate information about the Kerberos realm, the KDC, and the type of encryption being used.

Understanding Configuration Files

A kerberized principal needs to know the location of the KDC, the type of encryption to use, and the name of the Kerberos realm. In Mac OS X, this information is stored in a plaintext file called edu.mit.Kerberos. If your Mac OS X computer receives Kerberos information from a Dynamic Host Configuration Protocol (DHCP) or domain name system (DNS) server; or, if you had Kerberos already running on a previous version of Mac OS X, this file is created automatically.

The edu.mit.Kerberos file contains a libdefaults section and sections for realms and domain_realms. For compatibility, it also allows for Kerberosv4 realm settings. This file can be created using any text editor, as long as it is saved as plaintext.

The contents of the edu.mit.Kerberos file for the realm pretendco.com would be the following:

```
[domain_realm]
        .pretendco.com = MAINSERVER.PRETENDCO.COM
        pretendco.com = MAINSERVER.PRETENDCO.COM


[libdefaults]
        default_realm = MAINSERVER.PRETENDCO.COM
        dns_fallback = yes

[realms]
        MAINSERVER.PRETENDCO.COM = {
                admin_server = mainserver.pretendco.com:749
                kdc = mainserver.pretendco.com:88

        }


[v4 domain_realm]
        .pretendco.com = MAINSERVER.PRETENDCO.COM
        pretendco.com = MAINSERVER.PRETENDCO.COM
```

The libdefaults section describes the default behavior of the Kerberos libraries. The default_realm entry should be automatically entered correctly, so you do not need to edit it. The ticket_lifetime entry is not supported in this file. The value is set by the Kerberos application.

The realms and domain_realms sections refer to Kerberosv5 realms. These sections define the KDC and the admin server, as well as how the names are resolved. If your site includes Kerberosv4 realms, you must include the v4 realms and v4 domain_realms sections. Under these sections, you will define the Kerberos v4 KDCs, admin servers, and default domains. The domain_realm actually maps DNS domains to Kerberos realms, which is useful in authenticating using the host/principal (such as SSH).

A copy of the one edu.mit.Kerberos file is typically located in /Library/Preferences, and all users on the system use this file. However, user-specific realm and server information can also be stored in an edu.mit.Kerberos file stored at ~/Library/Preferences. If you are manually configuring an edu.mit.Kerberos file for a specific user account, avoid duplicate realm entries with the system edu.mit.Kerberos. The system edu.mit.Kerberos file can be edited with the Kerberos application (discussed in the next section).

Once the edu.mit.Kerberos file is created, it should be placed in /Library/Preferences (for system-wide settings) or in ~/Library/Preferences (for user-specific settings).

> **MORE INFO** ▶ For more information on configuring the Kerberos client manually, see the "References" section, at the end of this lesson.

In Mac OS X, the Kerberos login library preference and Kerberos management application preferences are stored in separate files: edu.mit.Kerberos.KerberosLogin.plist and edu.mit.KerberosApp.plist. The settings in these files are configured using the Kerberos application (located in /System/Library/CoreServices), and editing realms using the Kerberos application will write to both its preferences file and the edu.mit.Kerberos file. Mac OS X also provides UNIX compatibility allowing a krb5.conf file (which is formatted exactly like the edu.mit.Kerberos file) to reside in /etc, letting you use a standard Kerberos configuration file that comes from a UNIX workstation.

Configuration files for Kerberos are searched in the following order:

▶ /Library/Preferences/edu.mit.Kerberos

▶ ~/Library/Preferences/edut.mit.Kerberos

▶ /etc/krb5.conf

The realm values from these three files are merged and the libdefault values follow precedence (the first entry read is the first used). Mac OS X does not support a user configuration for Kerberos without a system configuration.

Using Kerberos Tools

Mac OS X has several tools to manage the Kerberos tickets. The command-line tool klist lists any credentials (tickets) stored locally in the cache. The -e option describes the encryption method used for each key, useful in determining whether the client has received tickets. When viewing the list of tickets, the krbtgt is the ticket-granting ticket.

But if you want to obtain a ticket from the command line, use kinit to request a ticket from a KDC. If you type *kinit sharon,* Mac OS X will request a ticket-granting ticket from the KDC for user account sharon. By using the -S option, kinit can be used to request a ticket for a particular service.

Finally, use the kdestroy command to remove tickets from the cache. If you run the command with no options, it will remove all tickets in the cache. Alternately, use the -p option to selectively remove tickets based on the principal name.

> **MORE INFO** ▶ For more information on the command-line Kerberos utilities, refer to the man pages for each utility.

Mac OS X also includes the Kerberos application that performs many of the same tasks as these command-line utilities. Located in the /System/Library/CoreServices folder, this application can be used to add, delete, and edit realms with the Edit Realms option under the Edit menu.

Receiving Kerberos Authentication

While you can get TGTs, obtain service tickets, and participate in SSO, you still need to know how your users can leverage the fact that a KDC can be used for that authentication. The authentication method for Kerberos is stored in the user's entry in the LDAP directory. If you use dscl to list the user accounts in the LDAP directory, you will see that user accounts with an Open Directory password (as configured in Workgroup Manager) have two authentication authority attributes. The value for a Kerberos authentication method will contain "Kerberosv5," a GUID, the principal name, the realm name, and a public key, as shown in the following figure.

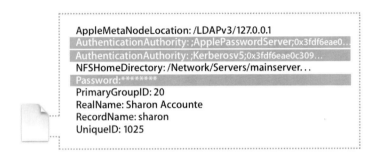

When the KDC attempts to identify the user principal, it will look for a principal entry first (*username@KDChostname*). If it cannot identify the principal based on that entry, or if the entry is not present, it will use the globally unique ID (GUID) and the realm name. If that does not work, it will find the short name to use. The public key is the same as that for ApplePasswordServer, but is not used for Kerberos. For example, this would be the Kerberos Authentication Authority for sharon:

;Kerberosv5;0x3fdf6eae0c3096df0000000600000009;sharon@MAINSERVER.PRETENDCO.COM;

MAINSERVER.PRETENDCO.COM;1024 35 1145578743083463835893899696524168101790707 9523

3023475948111304185096244575079064662043645069949051174748674690618626171556163371

6820513942592510402577124571207210754982210574570023051069011871542324730683479466

3830159086521568311947446273412496047754300427804383197071699373369259416693103774

9492941908043763 root@mainserver.pretendco.com

The ApplePasswordServer values reference the Simple Authentication and Security Layer (SASL) authentication method built in to Mac OS X Server. Password Server is covered in more detail in Lesson 8, "Providing Single Sign-on Authentication."

Troubleshooting Kerberos

When beginning to troubleshoot Kerberos issues, the most important is the TGT (krbtgt). If you do not have this ticket, you will not receive tickets for any other service.

If you are not receiving any tickets, verify that the date and time of the ticket is close to the date and time on your computer. Time is very important with Kerberos: If the client and the KDC are out of sync by more than 300 seconds (in default installations of both Mac OS X Server and Active Directory), the client will fail to achieve authentication with the KDC. It's a security measure to prevent any security breaches by people replaying packets at a later time. The date, time, and time zone information must be correct on the KDC server and clients, and they all should use the same network time service to keep their clocks in sync. TGTs also have a finite lifespan set by the KDC server administrator. All computers leveraging Kerberos—from the KDC to service servers to clients—can function properly in a Kerberos environment across multiple time zones.

If Login Window did not request the TGT, or if you destroyed all the tickets in the cache, you can use kinit to receive a new TGT. This will help isolate authentication problems to either Login Window or the KDC.

Identification and Authorization

Once you have configured your Mac OS X computer to bind to an LDAP directory on Mac OS X Server and authenticate using Kerberos, the following process takes place when a user logs in at the Login Window:

1. A user enters (or chooses) an account name, enters a password, and clicks Log In.

   By logging in, a user is proposing an identity and a means of authenticating that identity.

2. Login Window makes a request for the values of RecordName and AuthenticationAuthority through DirectoryService.

3. DirectoryService checks the local NetInfo database first (using the NetInfo plug-in).

   If the record is not found in the local NetInfo database, DirectoryService makes queries through the next configured plug-in—in this case, the LDAPv3 plug-in.

4. The LDAPv3 plug-in will make a request to the LDAP process on the server, remapping RecordName to uid and cn, and AuthenticationAuthority to authAuthority. This allows users to log in with their short name or long name.

5. If the entries are found, the values for uid and authAuthority are returned to Login Window.

   Since one of the values is ApplePasswordServer, DirectoryService will authenticate the user against the password server on Mac OS X Server.

6. Since the other value is Kerberosv5, Login Window verifies the entered password against the KDC so that a TGT will be sent back to the user.

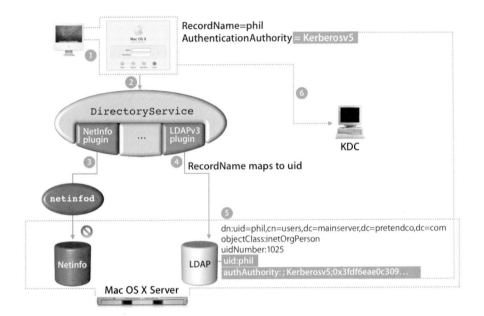

What You've Learned

▶ Kerberos uses principals, host, service, and user to define machines, services that can use Kerberos, and users who are allowed to obtain tickets from the KDC.

▶ The edu.mit.Kerberos file can be edited manually, edited with the Kerberos application, or created automatically from a bound LDAP server.

▶ The Login Window in Mac OS X can obtain a TGT from a KDC.

▶ Kerberos is very sensitive to time inconsistencies, so all machines relying on Kerberos in some fashion should get their time from the same time server.

▶ kinit, klist –e, and kdestroy are the command-line utilities to obtain a ticket, list all tickets, and destroy tickets, respectively.

References

Administration Guides

"Mac OS X Open Directory Administration": http://images.apple.com/server/pdfs/Open_Directory_v10.4.pdf

"Mac OS X Server Command-Line Administration": "http://images.apple.com/server/pdfs/Command_Line_v10.4.pdf

Apple Knowledge Base Documents

The following Knowledge Base documents (located at www.apple.com/support) provide further information about Kerberos and Mac OS X.

Document 107702, "Mac OS X Server 10.3: Kerberos Authentication May Not Work After Changing to LDAP Master or Replica, or Kerberizing a Particular Service"

Document 107875, "Mac OS X Server 10.3: Upgrading Password Server users to Kerberos and single sign-on"

Document 107543, "Mac OS X Server 10.2, 10.3: Password Authentication Options for Networked Environments"

Books

Garman, Jason. *Kerberos: The Definitive Guide* (O'Reilly, 2003).

URLs

Each of these URLs may help in your understanding of Kerberos. While they are slightly different in their delivery of the subject, they all basically explain Kerberos in more detail:

MIT's tutorial on Kerberos infrastructure and implementation: http://web.mit.edu/kerberos/www

http://web.mit.edu/macdev/www/kerberos.html

www.net.berkeley.edu/kerberos/k5concepts.html

www.net.berkeley.edu/kerberos

www.oit.duke.edu/~rob/kerberos

www.upenn.edu/computing/pennkey/sysadmin/d_install_unix/install_directions.html

www.afp548.com/Articles/Panther/kerberos1.html

www.afp548.com/Articles/Panther/kerberos2.html

www.isi.edu/~brian/security/kerberos.html

Editing the edu.mit.Kerberos file: http://web.mit.edu/macdev/KfM/Common/ Documentation/preferences-osx.html

Lesson Review

1. Instead of sending a password, what does Kerberos use for user authentication?

2. What are the benefits of using Kerberos for authentication?

3. What graphical user interface tool provides an interface for managing Kerberos tickets on a Mac OS X computer?

4. If a Mac OS X computer is unable to access kerberized services even though the user has a valid account, what should be one of the first things you check?

5. What Mac OS X configuration file contains the realm to be used by itself to access the KDC?

6. What does klist do?

Answers

1. The KDC sends a user a ticket-granting ticket, which is used for user authentication.

2. With Kerberos, the user's password is never sent across the network. Instead, Kerberos relies upon encrypted keys for authentication. Also, Kerberos provides a centralized authentication system, allowing users to authenticate once and then access different servers.

3. The Kerberos utility in /System/Library/CoreServices can be used to manage tickets.

4. Whenever a Mac OS X computer has problems accessing a kerberized service, you should verify that the client computer, the server, and the KDC computer are all set to the same time.

5. /Library/Preferences/edu.mit.Kerberos

6. The klist utility lists cached Kerberos tickets.

7

Time   This lesson takes approximately 2 hours to complete.

Goals   Understand the four roles of an Open Directory server and its
             functionality in standalone and Master mode

             Identify the OpenLDAP primary configuration files

             Use Server Admin to configure the maximum number of results returned
             by an Open Directory server

             Configure Mac OS X Server to host an LDAP directory domain

             Use the slapd process tools to manipulate data stored in the LDAP
             database on a Mac OS X Server computer

             Use Open Directory's Archive and Restore features on Mac OS X Server to
             back up and restore an Open Directory server

             Secure Open Directory connections between Mac OS X and
             Mac OS X Server

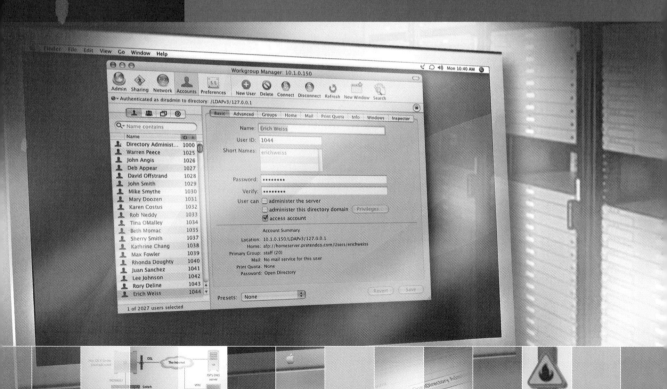

Hosting OpenLDAP

Using Open Directory services on Mac OS X Server enables system administrators to easily provide directory services. In previous lessons, you learned to connect Mac OS X computers as clients of a Mac OS X server, an Active Directory domain, and third-party directory services. Now you'll find out how to configure Mac OS X Server to be that directory service by hosting a Lightweight Directory Access Protocol (LDAP) directory domain, importing and managing the directory data on the server, and tuning the server for performance and security.

Open Directory Service Configuration

Configuring Mac OS X Server to provide directory data is a straightforward task. With just a couple of clicks, the Server Admin application creates an LDAP database and enables the Open Directory service to share the data.

Open Directory Overview

Open Directory relies on LDAP to provide access to directory service data on Mac OS X Server. As you've already learned, LDAP is provided by OpenLDAP, an open-source LDAP server. Apple has made very few changes to the stock distribution of OpenLDAP, and for most functions, you should be able to treat LDAP on Mac OS X Server as a normal OpenLDAP distribution.

The following figure shows the three main components of an Open Directory server.

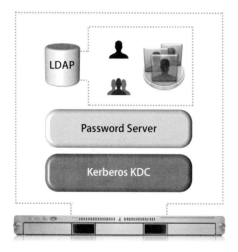

When working with Open Directory, the LDAP database maintains only the identification information for a user; the user's password is not kept in the LDAP database for obvious security reasons. Instead, the user will have an entry in the LDAP database that references a shadow password, an Apple Password Server password, or a Kerberos user principal. LDAP needs to work with these authentication services in order for Open Directory to truly be effective.

Roles for Open Directory Servers

An Open Directory service domain consists of a set of servers, each of which is configured to fill a specific role in the service domain. The role of each server is defined when the administrator sets it up, although the role can change if your service domain changes or you need to replace a machine that is out of service. The administrator has the option to choose a role during the initial configuration of the computer. However, the role of a system may be changed at any time after installation by using Server Admin.

The four Open Directory server roles are:

► Standalone Server: No LDAP database is running on the system. All users are local users and are located in the local NetInfo database. The Kerberos key distribution center (KDC) is not running.

► Open Directory Master: An LDAP database, a Password Server, and a KDC are on the system. Other Open Directory servers can connect to it and either share its network domain or replicate the network domain.

► Connected to a Directory System: Directory-service information for this system is received from another system. This may be over LDAP or an Active Directory connection. When connected to another system, this server will not be hosting its own LDAP database or Password Server. In addition, this server may join an existing Kerberos realm but will not be able to host its own directory.

You will need to connect to a directory server when you are trying to configure multiple servers to share a single identification and authentication system. These scenarios will be covered in Lesson 9, "Integrating With Kerberos."

► Open Directory Replica: Directory data and services are replicated from an existing Open Directory master server. It contains a copy of the master's LDAP database, the Password Server database, and the Kerberos principal database.

The following table lists the various roles for an Open Directory server.

	Standalone	Master	Connected to a Directory System	Replica
LDAP	●		+	⊕
Password Server	●		+	⊕
Kerberos	●		+	⊕
Replication	●			+

●	Provided by the server
+	Received by the server

Let's examine two of these roles, Standalone Server and Open Directory Master, in more detail.

Standalone Server

A standalone server has the simplest configuration of all the Open Directory roles. In effect, its directory-service structure is very similar to that of Mac OS X. A standalone server has user accounts separate from those on the Mac OS X computers on the network, as shown in the following figure.

Standalone server

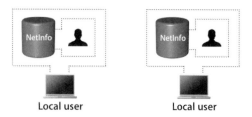

Local user   Local user

TIP ▶ It's a good idea to configure your server in a standalone role if you know that you will be changing its IP address before the final configuration.

When configured as an Open Directory standalone server, the server does not provide LDAP or Kerberos services. It is not precluded from joining a Kerberos realm, but it does not host one. The server may also provide other services, such as Web hosting, file sharing, and DNS. All of the users will be stored in the local NetInfo database, so they will not be visible to Mac OS X computers as network users.

A typical standalone typology might involve a small workgroup that does not require sharing user account information among a large number of computers. In this case, all Mac OS X computers are set up with local users and do not use the server for authentication. On the server, a corresponding server account has been set up for each user who wants to access services on the server. However, these server accounts are in no way synchronized with those of the local users being used on the Mac OS X computers.

TIP ▶ Standalone servers are also used to provide services that do not require advanced directory-service configuration, such as Dynamic Host Configuration Protocol (DHCP), domain name system (DNS), Network Address Translation (NAT), or Web services.

Open Directory Master

An Open Directory master adds a full LDAP server and a Kerberos KDC to a standalone server, as shown in the following figure. It can provide very robust network services—including the distribution of users, groups, and management information—to bound Mac OS X computers.

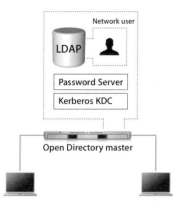

All network information can be stored in the Open Directory master and provided to the bound Mac OS X computers via LDAP. Administrators can create a combination of local Mac OS X computer users and policies, and network users and policies, to best fit their situation. Additionally, the LDAP server can be used to interact with other applications, like Address Book.

An Open Directory master can fully leverage all the best-of-breed technologies of Mac OS X Server, including Kerberos and subsequently single sign-on, secure authentication with Simple Authentication and Security Layer (SASL) Password Server, and replication for redundancy and load-sharing.

Creating an Open Directory Master

When you use Server Admin to promote a standalone server to an Open Directory master, you will be asked to provide a name and password for a new account to act as an LDAP directory administrator. (You will learn more about the Open Directory Master creation process is detailed in Lesson 8, "Providing Single Sign-on Authentication.")

TIP It's a good idea to use a name and password that differ from those of your initial administrator, because anyone who has the user name and password for the initial administrator account would then have access to manipulate the LDAP database, KDC, and Password Server as well.

You will also be asked for a Kerberos realm name. This field is preset to the server's fully qualified domain name, except it appears in capital letters, the standard convention for Kerberos realm names. You can enter a different name if your site has a different convention.

The search base field specifies the naming context of the LDAP database— the name that refers to the database itself. The search base in the figure above is dc=mainserver,dc=pretendco,dc=com, specifying that this database handles data under the dc=mainserver,dc=pretendco,dc=com container.

Much like the Kerberos realm name, the search base tends to be based on the server's DNS name. If you have a valid reverse DNS record for the server, you should see a default entry here. Again, if your organization has established different conventions for LDAP, you may enter a different search base here. If Mac OS X Server is the first LDAP server and the first Kerberos KDC on your network, the default values will serve you well.

Once you enter the information and click OK, the following actions take place, courtesy of slapconfig:

1. The file /etc/openldap/slapd_macosxserver.conf is created.

2. The LDAP database is created.

3. The directory administrator user is created in the LDAP database and added to the Password Server database as a Password Server administrator.

> **NOTE ▶** In versions of Mac OS X Server prior to 10.4, the initial administrator account was copied from the local NetInfo database to the LDAP database. With version 10.4, the LDAP database's initial administrator account is created with the user name and password provided for the Open Directory master server. You can have two different users with two different passwords, making it more difficult for attackers to gain access to both databases.

4. The local host is added to the search path in Directory Access (ldap://127.0.0.1).

5. OpenLDAP is configured to launch at system startup by editing /etc/hostconfig to contain the directive LDAPSERVER=–YES–.

6. The Launch Daemon for slapd is activated to automatically restart the slapd process, in case it abruptly quits.

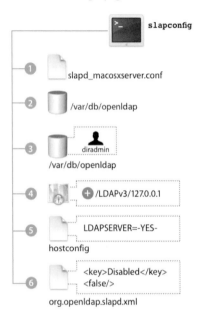

For a freshly created LDAP database, the new administrator user will be the only user account. You must authenticate as this user to make any changes to that LDAP database, since all other users will be in the local NetInfo database. Once the database is populated with users, you can designate other users to be administrators of the network directory domain with the same rights and privileges as the initial LDAP administrator. This process can be handled manually, should you wish to do so. However, it is best to rely on slapconfig.

The process of creating an Open Directory master is by no means over, as the Kerberos KDC has not yet been created. You will learn the rest of this process in Lesson 8.

TIP To learn exactly what takes place during the process of creating an Open Directory master, open the Terminal and type *tail –f /Library/Logs/slapconfig.log* to tail the slapconfig log file. This log file is an excellent resource.

OpenLDAP Configuration Files

The primary configuration files for the OpenLDAP system are kept in /etc/openldap/. There, you will find slapd.conf, the main configuration file for slapd, and some basic configuration information. Most of the configuration for Open Directory is kept in slapd_macosxserver.conf. An include statement in slapd.conf includes slapd_macosxserver.conf.

> **NOTE** ▶ Include statements are often used to let processes read more than one configuration file. At the end of the initial file, a line points to the location of the additional file(s). The process then reads that information as well.

The directives listed in these files can be modified from the GUI, so you should avoid adding custom configurations to these files unless you decide not to use the GUI administration tools. If you do use your own configuration file, add an include directive for it in the slapd.conf file.

When the slapd_macosxserver.conf file is created, it contains an entry for the root user of the LDAP database, the directive rootdn. This is not the same as the root user in the local NetInfo database; it's a user who has total control over all data inside the LDAP database, since access controls do not apply to the root user. An example value for rootdn is uid=root,cn=users,dc=mainserver,dc=pretendco,dc=com.

The entry for the root user in the slapd_macosxserver.conf file, by default, refers to the root user created in the LDAP database when you promote your server to an Open Directory master. Right below this entry is the rootpw directive containing an MD5-encrypted hash of the root user's password, which can be used to manage the LDAP server even when Password Server is not running.

Any user name and password can be used for the root LDAP user. In fact, this user doesn't even have to exist in the LDAP database itself, just here in the configuration file. An administrative user on the system can edit the slapd_macosxserver.conf file to add a new password hash, or plaintext password, into the file. Then that administrator user would be able to once again administer the LDAP database.

slapd will assume that a user who can authenticate to this name and password is the root user for the LDAP database and is not bound by any access controls to the database. That's useful when your LDAP database has reached a point where the user records are no longer readable. Without the LDAP root user, you wouldn't be able to edit the LDAP database. This technique can also be used when all passwords for users in the LDAP database have been lost or forgotten.

LDAP Protocol Settings

Some of the options from the Server Admin Protocols pane are written to slapd_macosxserver.conf. They are:

▶ Search base: An uneditable view of your LDAP server's current search base.

▶ Database: The location of the LDAP database files on your local disk. The default location of the LDAP database is /var/db/openldap. If you'd like to change the location of the database, shut down the LDAP server, copy over the database to the new location—ensuring that the permissions are the same—and then restart the LDAP server. This will not move an existing database to the new location; you need to do that by hand. Moving your LDAP database makes sense when you need to move to a larger capacity or more robust volume, such as a RAID array.

▶ Searching: Two other protocol settings change OpenLDAP configuration entries in slapd.conf:

• Maximum search results: The maximum results field limits the total records returned from an LDAP search. On publicly accessible LDAP servers, this is commonly done to prevent someone from "harvesting" the entire database. On Mac OS X Server, you might want to do this to increase response times for all LDAP servers.

• Search timeout: Represents the length of time before a search times out. You should need to worry about this only on very large databases. On a normal database of a few thousands users, all searches should return within a few seconds.

▶ SSL Certificates: Two options control security for your LDAP database:

• Enable Secure Sockets Layer (SSL): This enables SSL for encrypted communications between the Open Directory server's LDAP directory domain and the computers that access it.

- Certificate: This selects which certificates are used. You can use a self-assigned certificate or one obtained from a certificate authority.

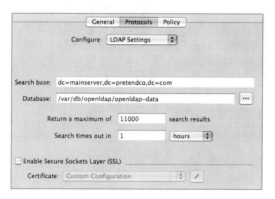

NetInfo Settings

Server Admin also provides an interface to modify NetInfo settings. NetInfo is being retired as a network directory, but Mac OS X Server still provides NetInfo access as backward compatibility for older clients.

The NetInfo service allows the data stored in the LDAP network domain to be accessed by NetInfo clients. This feature is enabled when you migrate a Mac OS X Server v10.2 NetInfo parent to a Mac OS X Server v10.4 Open Directory master. During the migration period, all Mac OS X v10.4 computers that were connecting over NetInfo will automatically be redirected to connect over LDAP. All other Mac OS X computers will need to be manually configured to use an LDAP connection to the server. Once the transition is complete, you can use the NetInfo Migration settings in Server Admin to permanently stop NetInfo.

Providing LDAP Connection Settings via DHCP

DHCP provides a standardized way to provide LDAP connection information through DHCP. As discussed in Lesson 6, "Kerberos Fundamentals," DHCP uses Option 95 to provide clients with connection information for the LDAP database, but not a description of the schema. Mac OS X supports a standard way to distribute the schema to all clients by keeping the schema mappings inside the directory itself. This is an incredibly efficient way of allowing clients access to the schema.

The following figure shows a DHCP server configured to send LDAP information along with the standard DHCP information.

Providing Schema Mappings

All Open Directory servers have a schema mapping configuration entry located in the LDAP database at cn=macosxodconfig,cn=Config. When a client connects to the LDAP database, the schema mappings are transferred to the client. If the client obtains LDAP server information via DHCP, the entire LDAP configuration process can be fully auto-mated on the client.

While this record is generated on an Open Directory server automatically, it can be saved to any LDAP server, as long as the configuration information is in the same place. If you have write access to your third-party LDAP server, you may be able to use the Write to Server button in Directory Access to generate the appropriate record on the server.

TIP ▶ Setting up a client to automatically trust a directory service that is provided through DHCP is potentially risky. While your client computers may be relatively secure on your LAN, using that computer on an untrusted network (for example, one at a hotel) may allow a nefarious system administrator to push out his or her own directory service over DHCP. Your client computer will trust this for authentication and thus allow other users to connect, unbeknownst to you.

You can also manually configure clients to use a particular schema:

▶ Use the generic Open Directory configuration in Directory Access on the client to map attributes to their common place on an Open Directory server.

▶ Specify on the client what mappings should occur. This method is commonly used when connecting a client computer to a third-party LDAP server.

Managing Directory-Service Data

Setting up an LDAP server is just the first step in providing directory data. Next you need to populate the server with data and then modify the data on an ongoing basis. This lesson will present different methods for populating the Open Directory server.

OpenLDAP Components

slapd, located in /usr/libexec, is started at boot time by launchd and implements the OpenLDAP server daemon. It must run as the root user and will listen for incoming LDAP connections on either port 389 for unencrypted connections or port 636 for SSL-enabled connections.

As the following figure shows, a number of different command-line utilities come with OpenLDAP. These tools can be separated into two types:

▶ Tools that begin with *slap* and operate directly on the LDAP databases

▶ Tools that begin with *ldap* and go through the LDAP protocol

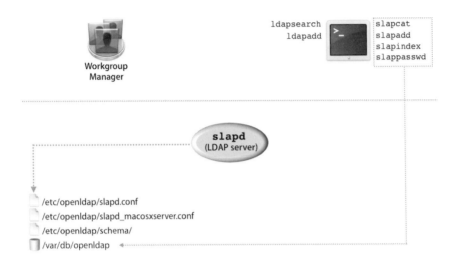

The slap tools must be run directly on the computer hosting the LDAP database. It is also advisable to shut down the LDAP server when using the slap tools or else your database may become out of sync. Keep in mind that two processes—the LDAP server itself and the slap utility—will be writing to it at the same time.

slapcat is primarily used to generate an LDAP Interchange Format (LDIF) file from a database, which can then be added to another database by using the slapadd command. This is typically how an LDAP replica is created by hand.

Other slap commands include slapindex, which will force a reindexing of your database, and slappasswd, which can generate password hashes to be stored in the LDAP database. Since passwords are primarily stored in Password Server on Mac OS X Server, and not directly in the LDAP database, you most likely will not need slappasswd.

The ldap tools interact with the LDAP server itself and can access the server over the network. The ldap tools are the best ones for troubleshooting your LDAP server, because they replicate the interactions the LDAP server would have with a Mac OS X computer.

A common LDAP tool is ldapsearch, which can be used to query the LDAP server for a particular entry or generate an LDIF file. When you use Mac OS X to authenticate to an LDAP server, your computer will do an ldapsearch against Open Directory's LDAP server to find out your user information. For example,

    ldapsearch -H ldap://127.0.0.1 -b cn=users,dc=mainserver,dc=pretendco,dc=com will dump all records in the users container of the server's LDAP database to your Terminal window.

You can use ldapadd to load an LDIF file into your LDAP server. For example,

> ldapadd -H ldap://mainserverserver.pretendco.com -f myusers.ldif

uploads the LDIF file myusers.ldif to the server once you have successfully authenticated as an administrator.

Apple LDAP Schema

The structure of the data stored in an LDAP database is defined not by the LDAP protocol but by a *schema,* a collection of files that define the types of records and attributes they might contain. The schema files used by Mac OS X Server are located in /etc/openldap/schema/.

The Open Directory LDAP server uses standard LDAP object classes whenever suitable. For example, accounts created with Workgroup Manager implement inetOrgPerson and posixAccount object classes. However, to support Apple-specific features, Apple has extended the schema to define auxiliary object classes so that user accounts can contain extra attributes that are not part of a defined LDAP standard. Similar object classes have been created for Apple-defined groups. These support features specific to Mac OS X:

▶   apple-user: Adds attributes that are part of an Apple user account but that are not supported by either the standard inetOrgPerson or posixAccount object classes. Examples include:

   •   URL of the home folder

   •   Home folder quotas

   •   Managed client settings (MCX settings)

▶   apple-group: Adds attributes that are part of an Apple group but that are not supported by the posixGroup object type. Examples include:

   •   URL of the group folder

   •   Managed client settings

This is just a small sample of the objects and attributes Apple added. All of the added objects and attributes are defined in the file /etc/openldap/schema/apple.schema.

```
/etc/openldap/schema/apple.schema

#
# User object class.
#
objectclass (
    1.3.6.1.4.1.63.1000.1.1.2.1
    NAME 'apple-user'
    SUP top
    AUXILIARY
    DESC 'apple user account'
    MAY ( apple-user-homeurl $ apple-user-class $
        apple-user-homequota $ apple-user-mailattribute $
        apple-user-printattribute $ apple-mcxflags $ apple-mcxsettings $
        apple-user-adminlimits $ apple-user-picture $
        apple-user-authenticationhint $ apple-user-homesoftquota $
        apple-user-passwordpolicy $ apple-keyword $ apple-generateduid $
        apple-imhandle $ apple-webloguri $ authAuthority $ acctFlags $
        pwdLastSet $ logonTime $ logoffTime $ kickoffTime $ homeDrive $
        scriptPath $ profilePath $ userWorkstations $ smbHome $ rid $
        primaryGroupID $ sambaSID $ sambaPrimaryGroupSID $
        userCertificate ) )

attributetype (
    1.3.6.1.4.1.63.1000.1.1.1.1.6
    NAME 'apple-user-homeurl'
    DESC 'home directory URL'
    EQUALITY caseExactIA5Match
    SUBSTR caseExactIA5SubstringsMatch
    SYNTAX 1.3.6.1.4.1.1466.115.121.1.26 SINGLE-VALUE )
```

LDIF

An LDIF file allows you to easily add the contents of one LDAP server to another. Any server that uses the standard LDAP protocol should be able to import and export an LDIF file.

The file is in plaintext, and each entry is specified by its distinguished name. An example of the contents of an LDIF file entry is as follows:

```
dn: uid=froosevelt,cn=users,dc=mainserver,dc=pretendco,dc=com
uid: froosevelt
objectClass: inetOrgPerson
objectClass: posixAccount
objectClass: shadowAccount
objectClass: apple-user
objectClass: extensibleObject
```

```
objectClass: organizationalPerson

objectClass: top

objectClass: person

sn: 99

cn: Franklin Roosevelt

uidNumber: 1025

apple-generateduid: 247E73B0-8339-11D8-B8CA-000A9585403C

apple-mcxflags:: PD94bWwgdmVyc2lvbj0iMS4wIiBlbmNvZGluZz0iVVRGLTgiPz4KPCFET0NUW

 ...

loginShell: /bin/bash

gidNumber: 20

authAuthority: ;ApplePasswordServer;0x406b01c33b4f78190000000a0000000a,1024 35

 ...

 09 root@mainserver.pretendco.com:10.1.0.1

authAuthority: ;Kerberosv5;0x406b01c33b4f78190000000a0000000a;froosevelt@SERVE

 ...

userPassword:: KioqKioqKio=

apple-user-mailattribute:: PD94bWwgdmVyc2lvbj0iMS4wIiBlbmNvZGluZz0iVVRGLTgiPz4

 ...

apple-user-homeurl:: PGhvbWVfZGlyPjx1cmw+YWZwOi8vc2VydmVyMTcucHJldGVuZGNvLmNvb

 ...

homeDirectory: /Network/Servers/mainserver.pretendco.com/Users/froosevelt
```

LDAP Contacts Database

Many large organizations will put all their contact or address book information into
an LDAP database. In fact, this was one of the original uses of an LDAP database. Most
modern email clients, including the Apple Mail and Microsoft Entourage applications,
have the ability to search for email and postal addresses over an LDAP connection.

The contact information can be located in a number of different locations. Which location your organization uses will depend on your LDAP configuration. Some administrators prefer to place contacts in the same container as the user accounts on the system.
This method has the benefit of allowing users to search for both employee information
and other contact information at the same time. However, mixing accounts and contacts
in the same container may cause confusion when administering your users, and user
accounts may contain sensitive information.

Another approach is to create an entirely new container especially for contacts. Common names for containers of this type are cn=People and cn=Contacts. This keeps the user information separate from the contact information but requires clients to either use the entire LDAP naming context as their search base or have two search entries.

A third approach, which is especially useful for organizations with a large amount of LDAP contact information, is to create an entirely separate LDAP database to hold contact information and to host it on the same computer. This "contacts" database would have a naming context unique from the other database and requires only another group of entries in the LDAP configuration files.

Workgroup Manager is a tool designed to manage account information for records specified by the Users search base in Directory Access. To edit attributes not exposed by Workgroup Manager, or if you wish to move your contact to a different container, you will have to find alternative tools to manage your contact information, such as the LDAP command-line tools discussed in the previous section.

Backing Up and Restoring Directory Data

With Server Admin, you can create an archive copy of the Open Directory master's directory and authentication data. After you select a location and click the Archive button, Server Admin creates a disk image containing the following:

- ▶ LDAP database and configuration files
- ▶ Password Server database
- ▶ Kerberos database and configuration files
- ▶ Local NetInfo database

To restore the data, enter the path to the archive image and click Restore. The data from the image will be merged with the existing master's data. If there are conflicts between the master's data and the image, the data in the master will take precedence and the conflict is recorded in the slapconfig log file.

If you have configured Open Directory replica servers to connect to Open Directory master, you will need to reconnect the replicas after restoring a server from an archive. Replica servers are covered in Lesson 10, "Replication."

> **NOTE ▸** It is better to promote a replica to a master than to restore a master from an archive.

Tuning the Open Directory Server

Part of configuring a directory server is tuning the server to provide secure yet responsive transactions.

LDAP Security Concerns

An LDAP database holds a lot of potentially sensitive account information. Mac OS X no longer requires that password hashes be stored in the directory; however, depending on your organization, you may still store contact information that should be restricted to legitimate members of your organization. For example, you probably wouldn't want a visitor on your network to get a list of all your employees or students. As you've seen with ldapsearch, it's a fairly straightforward task to query an LDAP server and dump the output to an LDIF file.

Another security concern is the vulnerability of the traffic on the network. You wouldn't want others to see the LDAP traffic as it passed along the network.

Disallow Anonymous Binding

A standard install of Mac OS X Server allows anyone to browse the contents of your LDAP database, making it easy for client computers to connect, especially when using DHCP to configure the clients.

To secure your LDAP server, there are two ways to control binding, as shown in the following figure.

Disallow anonymous binding

Enabling trusted binding

For better security, you can disable anonymous binding and limit access to authenticated users, requiring any connection to supply a valid user name and password for one of the users in the LDAP database. To disallow anonymous binding, add this line to /etc/openldap/slapd.conf:

    disallow bind_anon

Then restart the LDAP process, slapd, or reboot the server.

Using Trusted Binding

Using Server Admin, you can configure an Open Directory master to allow or require trusted binding between the LDAP directory and the computers that access it. Replicas of the Open Directory master automatically inherit its binding policy.

Trusted LDAP binding is mutually authenticated. The computer proves its identity by using an LDAP directory administrator's name and password to authenticate to the LDAP directory by means of an authenticated computer record created in the directory when you set up trusted binding.

Where authenticated binding proves the identity of the client computer, trusted binding proves the identity of both the client computer and the LDAP directory. Trusted binding is configured from the client computer using Directory Access

NOTE ▶ Clients need version 10.4 or later of Mac OS X or Mac OS X Server to use trusted LDAP binding. Clients using v10.3 or earlier won't be able to set up trusted binding.

Controlling Access to the Database

Access control lists (ACLs) are another way to secure your LDAP server. ACLs are specified in the AccessControls container in the LDAP directory. Each ACL specifies what a user can do to a specified container or object class in the LDAP database. Here's an example of a directory-service ACL:

1000:access to attr=userPassword by self write by sockurl="ldapi://%2Fvar%2Frun%2Fldapi" write

by group/posixGroup/memberUid="cn=admin,cn=groups,dc=mainserver,dc=pretendco,dc=com"

write by * read

Write access to the userPassword attribute is limited to either the specific owner of the attribute or any user in the admin group. The last line allows any user to read the value. (Remember, in this case this is not the password but the password attribute.)

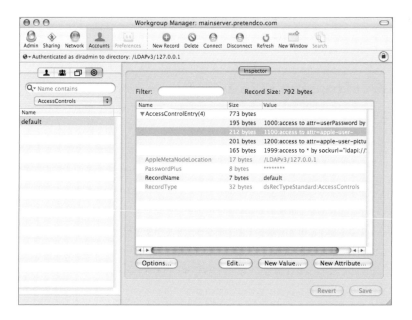

Alternatively, you can use Workgroup Manager to assign directory domain administrator privileges for an account stored in the LDAP directory of an Open Directory master or a NetInfo domain. A user with administrator privileges for a directory domain can make changes to user accounts, group accounts, and computer list accounts stored in that domain using Workgroup Manager. After enabling the domain administration option for the user account, you can specify the editing capabilities for each account type.

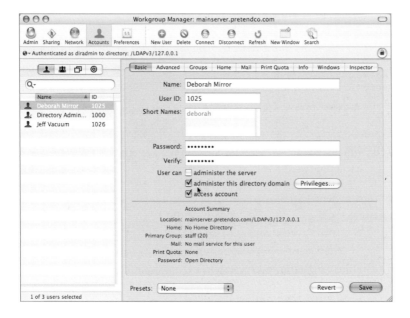

Preventing Eavesdropping With SSL

In Server Admin, you can enable SSL to provide encrypted communications between the Open Directory server and the client computers. SSL uses a digital certificate to provide a certified identity for the server. You can use a self-signed certificate or one obtained from a certificate authority, such as VeriSign or Thawte.

Once you have the certificate, you can store it anywhere you want, but it's best to put it somewhere accessible only by the root user. Also, remove any passphrase associated with the certificate, since OpenLDAP does not support passphrases.

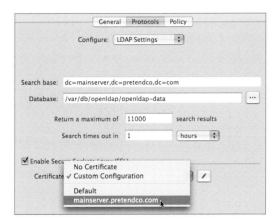

Enable SSL through Server Admin by choosing Enable Secure Sockets Layer (SSL) in the Protocols pane. After it has been enabled, choose the SSL certificate from the Certificate pop-up menu. To use a certificate not listed, choose Custom Configuration from the pop-up menu and supply the full path to the server's certificate and private key. If you created your own certificate, supply the one from the certificate authority.

To configure the LDAP server to listen only for SSL connections, you edit the launch arguments for slapd. The launch arguments are specified in /System/Library/ LaunchDaemons/org.openldap.slapd.xml. Delete the ldap:/// entry under ProgramArguments, but leave the ldaps:/// entry.

Once the server has been secured with SSL, you'll need to enable SSL on the client. In Directory Access on the client, choose SSL next to the LDAP entry for your server.

LDAP Indexing and Caching

Indexing increases the speed of queries by creating an indexed lookup table of attribute values, but it also increases the size of the LDAP database files on the server as well as the time of write operations.

```
/etc/openldap/slapd_macosxserver.conf

...
# Indices to maintain
index   cn,sn,uid          pres,eq,approx,sub
index   uidNumber,gidNumber          eq
index   objectClass        eq
```

The slapd_macosxserver.conf file specifies what attributes are cached by the server. By default, only a few attributes, such as user name and user ID, are indexed. However, if you have the space and need better responsiveness, you can index other attributes by editing the configuration file. The more attributes you index on, the slower the performance during writes, since the index needs to be updated for the added attributes.

Changing the Default BerkeleyDB Cache Size

In Mac OS X Server v10.4, the BerkeleyDB cache size depends on the amount of RAM installed on your computer when the LDAP master is created.

If your computer has 256 MB of RAM, the default BerkeleyDB cache size will be 16 MB. If your computer has more than 256 MB of RAM up to 512 MB, the cache size will be 32 MB. If your computer has more than 512 MB of RAM, the default cache size will be 64 MB.

If you've added more RAM to the server, you can manually increase the BerkeleyDB cache size, using the RAM to cache ratios described above as your guideline. This helps improve overall LDAP performance.

To change the BerkeleyDB cache size, edit the file /var/db/openldap/openldap-data/DB_CONFIG and change the set_cachesize entry to one of the following:

▶ For 4 MB: *set_cachesize 0 4194304 1*

▶ For 16 MB: *set_cachesize 0 16777216 1*

▶ For 32 MB: *set_cachesize 0 33554432 1*

▶ For 64 MB: *set_cachesize 0 67108864 1*

Save the file and restart the server to apply your change.

Troubleshooting LDAP Connections

As with most Mac OS X Server troubleshooting, you should start troubleshooting LDAP connections by reading the log files, specifically /var/log/system.log and the DirectoryServer logs in /Library/Logs/DirectoryServices.

Next run the LDAP server process, slapd, in debug mode. First stop the LDAP server by killing the slapd process. Then start it from the command line:

```
sudo /usr/libexec/slapd -d 99
```

This will now run the LDAP server and display all transactions and errors to the Terminal window. If you would like even more information, increase the value after -d.

You can also enable LDAP logging with

```
sudo slapconfig -enableslapdlog
```

which will allow slapd to log to /var/log/slapd.log.

You can also add logging options to the slapd.conf configuration file using the loglevel directive. Adding the numbers will add the output to the log file for that item.

loglevel <integer>

1	trace function calls
2	debug packet handling
4	heavy trace debugging
8	connection management
16	print out packets sent and received
32	search filter processing
64	configuration file processing
128	access control list processing
256	stats log connections/operations/results
512	stats log entries sent
1024	print communication with shell backends
2048	entry parsing

Another troubleshooting technique is to use an LDAP browser utility to view the contents of your LDAP database. If you do this from a client computer, you will be able to test all aspects of the client/server LDAP connection.

Also, keep in mind that the Inspector function of Workgroup Manager will also allow you to browse the LDAP database on the server and make changes as appropriate.

With Mac OS X Server, LDAP provides the advantages of industry standards, compatibility, and industry know-how. Apple has not merely taken OpenLDAP and added it to its list of features, but has gone the next step, integrating it into the entire Open Directory architecture. Additional tools, schema definitions, and configuration files have been added to make the management of an LDAP architecture as painless as possible. Mac OS X Server is a prominent player in the LDAP server arena.

What You've Learned

▶ Apple's implementation of LDAP is OpenLDAP.

▶ An Open Directory master consists of an LDAP database, a Password Server, and a KDC.

▶ Some basic LDAP configuration information is kept in slapd.conf; however, most of the configuration for Open Directory is kept in slapd_macosxserver.conf.

▶ OpenLDAP does not support passphrases in SSL certificates.

▶ slapcat is primarily used to generate an LDIF file from an LDAP database.

▶ The schema files used by Mac OS X Server are located in /etc/openldap/schema/.

References

Administration Guides

"Mac OS X Server Open Directory Administration": http://images.apple.com/server/pdfs/Open_Directory_v10.4.pdf

"Mac OS X Server Command-Line Administration": http://images.apple.com/server/pdfs/Command_Line_v10.4.pdf

Apple Knowledge Base Documents

The following Knowledge Base documents (located at www.apple.com/support) provide further information about the BerkeleyDB database and LDAP databases.

Document 301264, "Mac OS X Server: How to change the default BerkeleyDB cache size"

Document 301490, "Mac OS X Server 10.4: Open Directory LDAP databases must be migrated using Setup Assistant"

Books

Carter, Gerald. *LDAP System Administration* (O'Reilly, 2003).

URLs

Open Directory: www.apple.com/support/macosxserver/opendirectory

OpenLDAP: www.openldap.org

Lesson Review

1. What are the advantages of using a Mac OS X Server centralized directory store in a heterogeneous network?

2. What configuration file is used by the LDAP server process? Where is it located?

3. How do Mac OS X computers acquire the mappings when binding to an Open Directory server?

4. What is the schema and where is it stored?

5. In order for a client to work properly with Open Directory, what directory-service data items must be correctly mapped and populated?

6. What does adding disallow bind_anon to slapd.conf do?

7. What is the benefit of enabling SSL on the LDAP server?

8. When is the BerkeleyDB cache size set by Mac OS X Server, and how is its value determined?

Answers

1. a) There is only one directory store for ease of administration.

   b) Users can use the same account from disparate clients.

   c) The administrator has more control over the connection methods.

   d) As connection methods are secured, all clients take advantage of the increased security.

2. The LDAP server uses the /etc/openldap/slapd.conf file as its configuration file. The slapd.conf file includes a directive to include /etc/openldap/slapd_macosxserver.conf file, which is managed by Server Admin.

3. The mappings are provided as part of the configuration entry located in the LDAP database at cn=macosxodconfig,cn=Config.

4. The schema defines the types and format of records stored in the local LDAP database. The schema files are at /etc/openldap/schema.

5. In order for a client to work properly, the following data items must be correctly mapped and populated: RecordName, RealName, Password, UniqueID, PrimaryGroupID, NFSHomeDirectory, and HomeDirectory.

6. It configures the LDAP server to not respond to data requests without authentication.

7. When SSL is enabled on both the client and server computers, the LDAP data sent between the two computers is encrypted. This prevents attackers from eavesdropping on critical directory data.

8. Mac OS X Server sets the BerkeleyDB cache size when the server is promoted to be an Open Directory master. The size of the cache is based upon the amount of RAM installed on the server when it was promoted. The value can later be overridden to enhance performance.

8

Time

This lesson takes approximately 2 hours to complete.

Goals

Learn to identify the files used by the Kerberos service running on a Mac OS X server

Use the kdb5_util command to export and import data to and from the KDC database on a Mac OS X server

Use kadmin.local command-line utilities to manage Kerberos running on a Mac OS X server computer

Use klist to determine what encryption method was used to generate keytab files on a Mac OS X server

Use Workgroup Manager to configure password policies enforced by Password Server running on a Mac OS X server

Lesson **8**

Providing Single Sign-on Authentication

This lesson focuses on Mac OS X Server's single sign-on (SSO) architecture with an eye toward authentication—the process of proving you are who you say you are. Specifically, it looks at authentication as provided by MIT's Kerberos distribution and the Simple Authentication and Security Layer (SASL). These complex open-source components are simplified with Apple's configuration tools. Without harming their standards-compliant nature, these disparate systems are integrated into a smoothly functioning whole that's equally comfortable at the center of directory services and as a platform-specific component of a larger system.

The SSO architecture is made up of three open-source components:

- ▶ LDAPv3 (OpenLDAP)
- ▶ Kerberos (MIT key distribution center)
- ▶ SASL (via Password Server)

Open Directory offers these identification and authentication services to both Mac OS X and other heterogeneous clients. Building on the previous lesson dealing with Lightweight Directory Access Protocol (LDAP), this lesson focuses on Kerberos and Password Server.

Providing Kerberos Authentication

One of Mac OS X Server's key features is the Open Directory SSO infrastructure—a Kerberos-based set of services allowing authenticated users to securely access network resources, such as file and mail services, without having to reenter their passwords.

Adapting Kerberos

The following table shows the difficulties in implementing Kerberos and the Apple solution.

Difficulty	The Apple Answer
Complex server and client configuration	Automatic configuration
Directory-service integration	Complete directory-service integration
Lack of user-level account management	Server management tools' creation of user principals
Replica	Host and service registration
No support for legacy authentication protocols	Password Server's support of legacy protocols

Kerberos is designed from a model of mutual, initial distrust. This is well suited to today's network environment, and both Apple and Microsoft have chosen to incorporate Kerberos into their directory-service infrastructures. Before that, it was available for UNIX and Linux from MIT.

Integrating Kerberos into an existing infrastructure is not as well defined as some competing proprietary solutions are. In this sense, the open structure and flexible implementation of Kerberos has hindered widespread adoption. Apple built its Kerberos implementation to address these shortcomings with the following solutions:

▶ Automatic configuration: Kerberos, with its UNIX heritage, is typically difficult to configure in both its client and server forms, requiring a high level of architectural knowledge and a high proficiency in editing text-based configuration files. To circumvent this requirement, Apple provides a directory-based configuration mechanism, with several tools that automatically create a key distribution center (KDC) and configure clients to access it.

▶   Complete directory-service integration: Kerberos is an authentication mechanism, not a directory service. There's no standard way to determine which component of a user record should be assigned to that specific user's Kerberos principal name, much less to devise a solution for managing the finer points of integration. Apple has made some of those decisions and, among other things, has added a component to the user record in directory services that specifies how the user can be authenticated.

▶   Server management tools' creation of user principals: Kerberos doesn't have a standard method of user management, and various implementations use different technologies to manage user principals. Apple has adopted MIT's kadmin protocol and integrated it with the standard user creation process of Mac OS X Server, so that all new users in an Open Directory shared domain get Kerberos principals. This is a tremendous leap forward in permitting users to take advantage of the SSO methodology.

▶   Simplified host and service registration: Management of host and service principals can be especially difficult, given their distributed nature. For example, the encrypted service keys need to get to the kerberized services, which are generally hosted somewhere other than with the KDC. Apple has leveraged MIT's existing infrastructure and its built-in directory-based configuration architecture to provide a straightforward, graphical method for building SSO systems among several hosts again, making the process as seamless as possible.

▶   Password Server's support of legacy protocols: Not every service is kerberized, and as nice as Kerberos is from a security perspective, it is not a be-all and end-all answer to authentication. The Kerberos standard itself does not specify any method for integration with legacy protocols. Later in this lesson, you will learn about the Apple Password Server, an open-standard system for supporting legacy authentication methods. Integrated with the KDC, it rounds out and adds depth to the Apple authentication options.

It is important to note that Apple has made a solid investment toward integrating Kerberos into the structure of Mac OS X and Mac OS X Server. While some tools that manage Kerberos are command-line tools, others, such as the Kerberos utility discussed in Lesson 6, "Kerberos Fundamentals," are placed out of the user's normal view (located in /System/Library/CoreServices). Administrators may want to move this utility to the /Applications/Utilities folder if a significant portion of users may be accessing this utility from time to time. From a management standpoint, most administrators do not want their users poking around the /System/Library/CoreServices folder.

Kerberos Authentication Process

The Kerberos authentication process normally consists of several well-defined transactions:

1. When the client requests authentication, it sends a KRB_AS_REQ message to the KDC.

    This ticket-granting ticket (TGT) consists of the client's user name (so that the KDC knows which principal is attempting to authenticate), a timestamp, and the requested ticket lifetime.

    NOTE ▶ The TGT is really just a special kind of service, and so KRB_AS_REQ also includes the name of that service: krbtgt/pretendco.com@PRETENDCO.COM.

2. The KDC then responds with a KRB_AS_REP message.

    This consists of the TGT in clear text and a shared session key encrypted with a hash of the user's password. The TGT does not need to be encrypted again, because its contents are already encrypted with a key known only to the KDC. To the client, it looks like random data, but it actually contains the KDC's copy of the session key, the client's principal name, the ticket lifetime, a timestamp, and, optionally, the client's IP address.

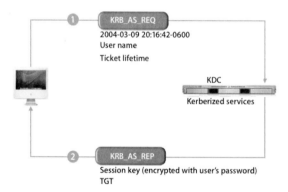

Both the TGT and the session key are stored in the client's credentials cache. The Mac OS X version of Kerberos has a RAM-based credentials cache, making it more difficult for malicious parties to gain access to sensitive data and ensuring that, should the machine quit unexpectedly or otherwise lose power, sensitive data will not be on the file system.

When the client wants to access a kerberized service, it must use the TGT and session key. These transactions are covered in Lesson 9, "Integrating With Kerberos."

Understanding KDC Architecture

The KDC process is called krb5kdc, which is located inside /usr/sbin, and is started and monitored by the kdcmond daemon, which is specified by the launchd XML property list /System/Library/LaunchDaemons/com.apple.kdcmond.xml. The configuration file, /var/db/krb5kdc/kdc.conf, specifies per-realm configuration data to be used by the KDC, and it also specifies the port (88 UDP and TCP/IP) over which the krb5kdc process communicates. As the following figure illustrates, krb5kdc is controlled by the command kdb5_util and reads from kdc.conf, .k5.YOURSERVER.YOURREALM.COM, and /var/db/krb5kdc/principal.

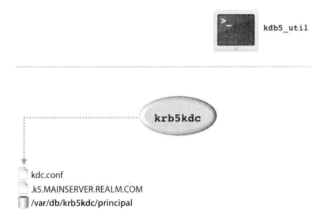

The KDC's user, host, and service principals are stored in /var/db/krb5kdc/principal. The principal database is encrypted with a key stored in a stash file called .k5.YOURSERVER.YOURREALM.COM (where YOURSERVER.YOURREALM.COM is the KDC's realm).

> **TIP** The files located in /var/db/krb5kdc are extremely sensitive and should be accessible only by root.

The Kerberos configuration files and data are backed up as part of the Open Directory Archive feature in Server Admin. You can back up just the KDC using kdb5_util, a utility for maintaining the Kerberos database. Like any database, it is problematic to back up the KDC while the krb5kdc process is running. Among other things, kdb5_util is useful for dumping the principal database to text to get a reliable backup. Keep in mind that the data in question is extremely sensitive; creating a copy of it, by definition, decreases your overall security. Generally this is an acceptable risk, given the improved redundancy that comes from a valid backup. Also keep in mind that these backups should be subject to the same security precautions as the other KDC files.

To dump the KDC's database, execute the following command:

    sudo kdb5_util dump > /path/to/secure/backup

To load KDC data from a dumped file, execute the following command:

    sudo kdb5_util load /path/to/secure/backup

Although these functions are not used regularly, the kdb5_util utility can be used to create and delete Kerberos databases and to manage the location of the stash file used to encrypt the database.

Kerberos Administration Architecture

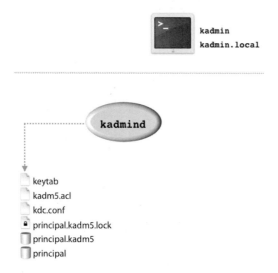

The krb5kdc process largely accesses its database in a read-only fashion—it doesn't make changes to Kerberos principals. For principal management, Apple has leveraged MIT's Kerberos administration architecture. The Kerberos administration daemon, kadmind, is responsible for making changes to the Kerberos database. Outside of Open Directory, kadmind is largely manipulated by the kadmin and kadmin.local command-line utilities. (These utilities will be covered in more depth in the next section.) Generally, in Mac OS X, the Apple tools are responsible for telling the kadmin tools what to do.

Several configuration files are used by kadmind, some of which can be modified for advanced customization but all of which are important for the sake of understanding the KDC's underlying structure. All of these files reside in /var/db/krb5kdc, because some are also used by the krb5kdc process. It can be confusing, but keep in mind that although krb5kdc reads the /var/db/krb5kdc/principal database, kadmind is primarily responsible for writing to it. The two processes are closely linked, and their configuration is intertwined. In reality, kadmind acts much like any other kerberized service required to have access to a secret key shared with the KDC. Typically keys are stored in /etc/krb5.keytab, but the key for kadmind is stored in /var/db/krb5kdc/keytab.

The kadm5.acl file is a list of Kerberos principals that have various administrative privileges. Kerberos's access controls are granular, as any principal may be granted one or more of a set of operations over any set of one or more other principals. However, in an out-of-the-box configuration, an Open Directory master has only two significant entries in kadm5.acl:

This file autogenerated by KDCSetup

*/admin@MAINSERVER.PRETENDCO.COM   *

diradmin   *

The first line is a comment. The second line specifies that any principal with the /admin suffix can access any kadmin function. The last line specifies the principal that has complete access to all principals in the database (the administrator created when the machine was promoted to the Open Directory master role, by default).

> **NOTE ▶** As of Mac OS X version 10.4, none of Apple's server management tools supports the /admin convention.

The database called principal.kadm5 is the kadmind process's policy database. It resides at /var/db/krb5kdc. While principals and their keys are stored in /var/db/krb5kdc/principal, policies that can be applied to principals are stored in principal.kadm5.

You would edit this file when user-specific policies, such as a 60-day password change policy, are necessary for a given organization.

Finally, principal.kadm5.lock is a lock file used by kadmind. It acts essentially in the opposite of most lock files, though, as kadmind will not write to either the policy or principal database unless it exists.

Kerberos Administration Utilities

Kerberos administration in Mac OS X Server is integrated to such a level that administrators will rarely need to administer Kerberos manually using the Kerberos command-line tools. All of the Apple tools work together to manage Kerberos authentication data.

The kadmin command-line tool is the native MIT administrative client to kadmind. When kadmin starts, it reads the Kerberos configuration file, edu.mit.kerberos, to discover the network location of the kadmind server. kadmin does not need to be run from the KDC because it can be run remotely, over port 749. kadmin authenticates as any principal listed in the kadm5.acl file and is bound by the access controls listed there. While that provides remote administration, it also opens up another port on the server, but you have another option when attempting to manage certain aspects of Kerberos.

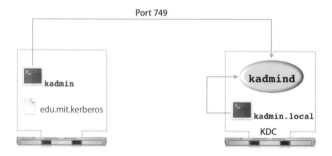

Unlike kadmin, kadmin.local cannot be run remotely, nor is it bound by the access controls of kadmind. Instead, it is a brute-force tool that is always run as root with full administrative privileges over the kadmind and KDC databases. This capability, as you will see later, is central to Apple's strategy to keep authentication data synchronized in Open Directory.

Both kadmin and kadmin.local can be run interactively or in query mode (using the -q flag). Despite the implication, "query" does not necessarily imply a read operation; query mode is useful for scripting changes to the Kerberos database.

The following are example applications of these tools:

▶ Add a principal:

sudo kadmin.local -q "add_principal johnisigna"

▶ Add an admin principal, specifying a password:

sudo kadmin.local -q "add_principal dave/admin -pw v3ryL8"

▶ Add a principal that expires tomorrow:

kadmin -p diradmin -q "add_principal -expire tomorrow temp0"

NOTE ▶ Use kadmin rather than kadmin.local. kadmin makes some assumptions that are incorrect on Mac OS X as of v10.3.3, so use the -p flag to specify the proper principal.

▶ Add a service principal:

sudo kadmin.local -q "add_principal afpserver/secondaryserver.pretendco.com"

▶ Delete a principal:

sudo kadmin.local -q "delete_principal johnsigna"

▶ Change the password on dave's admin principal:

sudo kadmin.local -q "change_password dave/admin"

▶ Get data about the principal tmp0:

sudo kadmin.local -q "get_principal tmp0"

▶ List all principals:

sudo kadmin.local -q list_principals

NOTE ▶ Policies are actually set up as an explicit set of requirements and then applied to a particular principal.

▶ Establish a policy named salesforce:

```
sudo kadmin.local -q "add_policy -minlength 8 -history 10 salesforce"
```

▶ Add the salesforce policy to the principal deborah:

```
sudo kadmin.local -q "modify_principal -policy salesforce deborah"
```

In general, a policy relates specifically to password requirements, such as history, length, and character restrictions. Other Kerberos settings, namely the password expiration date and change requirement, are stored in the principal, as seen in the output of the get_principal flag:

```
mainserver:~ nadmin$ sudo kadmin.local -q "get_principal deborah"
```

Here you are authenticating as principal: root/diradmin@MAINSERVER.PRETENDCO. COM so that you can view another user's principal.

```
Principal: deborah@MAINSERVER.PRETENDCO.COM
Expiration date: Sat Oct 1 00:00:00 PDT 2005
Last password change: Sat Sep 24 19:46:35 PDT 2005
Password expiration date: [none]
Maximum ticket life: 0 days 10:00:00
Maximum renewable life: 7 days 00:00:00
Last modified: Sat Sep 24 19:46:35 PDT 2005
(root/diradmin@MAINSERVER.PRETENDCO.COM)
Last successful authentication: [never]
Last failed authentication: [never]
Failed password attempts: 0
Number of keys: 4
Key: vno 2, Triple DES cbc mode with HMAC/sha1, no salt
Key: vno 2, ArcFour with HMAC/md5, no salt
Key: vno 2, DES cbc mode with CRC-32, no salt
Key: vno 2, DES cbc mode with CRC-32, Version 4
Attributes: REQUIRES_PRE_AUTH REQUIRES_PWCHANGE
Policy: policy11520min
```

Configuring the Open Directory Password Server

As we have seen, Kerberos handles authentication in Mac OS X and Mac OS X Server. But what if a service cannot utilize Kerberos? What if another authentication method must be used? Should Mac OS X Server revert to older clear-text passwords? That would be very insecure.

This section explains the fundamentals behind the use of and management surrounding Password Server. Mac OS X Server includes Password Server, which provides authentication for services that cannot use Kerberos.

Password Server Fundamentals

In a perfect world, every service would be kerberized. However, adopting Kerberos is a fairly complex and time-consuming process, and unfortunately, some widely adopted services such as Point-to-Point Tunneling Protocol (PPTP) are not easily kerberized. To support these legacy services, Apple includes a standards-based password server. The PasswordService process offers the following, all of which will be explained later in this section:

▶ Support for a broad range of authentication methods

▶ Simple Authentication and Security Layer (SASL) foundation

▶ Storage of credentials in an encrypted database separate from the LDAP directory

▶ A role as a centralized authorization server

▶ Global and per-user password policies

▶ KDC synchronization

▶ Secure multimaster replication

Password Server stores passwords in "slots" in an encrypted database separate from the user record. Because Password Server is available across the network, it can serve as a centralized authentication server when part of an Open Directory master. Password Server is always enabled when an Open Directory master is created, giving you the added benefit of protecting user credentials from a local attack and of supporting protocols like MS-CHAPv2 and CRAM-MD5, which are required by some Mac OS X Server services.

Password policies, in addition to being per-user policies, are represented in the graphical user interface and can be enforced on a global scale. (Policies will be discussed later in this lesson.) Furthermore, Password Server synchronizes with the Apple KDC to simplify user management and secure multimaster replication has been added to support improved redundancy in distributed organizations. In a nutshell, these two authentication services, Password Server and Kerberos, can use known command-line tools to stay synchronized with respect to users' passwords. The user policies however, do not synchronize.

Password Server Architecture

Password Server's daemon, PasswordService, is located in /usr/sbin and is started by launchd as specified by /System/Library/LaunchDaemons, which also monitors the process in case it needs to be restarted. Its primary database is located in /var/db/authserver/auth-servermain. This is a sensitive file, because it contains user secrets in their respective slots in that file. The authserverfree file, which resides in the same folder, contains a list of free slots in the database, and the authserverreplicas file, in the same folder, keeps track of all replicas. (Replicas are covered in Lesson 10, "Replication.")

The following figure shows how the PasswordService process reads from its main files, including com.apple.passwrodserver.plist. It shows the log files to which PasswordService writes, as well as two command-line tools, mkpassdb and pwpolicy, that can be used to work with PasswordService.

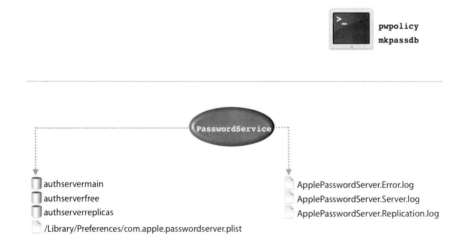

The PasswordService daemon logs fairly verbosely, mostly to the ApplePasswordServer. Error.log, ApplePasswordServer.Server.log, and ApplePasswordServer.Replication.log, all located in /Library/Logs/PasswordService. In some cases, it also logs to syslog.

By default, Password Server listens on ports 106 (3com-tsmux) and 3659 (apple-sasl). Pure Mac OS X v10.3 and later deployments should consider disabling port 106 for Password Server, because this port is generally used by other services. However, doing so will lock out Mac OS X v10.2 clients. You may disable Password Server from listening on port 106 by removing the 106 value from the ListenerPorts array in /Library/Preferences/ com.apple.passwordserver.plist.

Like many other text-based services, it is feasible to use the telnet command to issue commands on the Password Server's ports and gather a large amount of data. It's not necessarily a security risk, but a system administrator should be aware of what data is available.

Password Server uses a 128-bit hex ID to keep track of users in its database. The first administrator always has a value of 0x00000000000000000000000000000001, but if an administrator's short name is known, his or her ID can be obtained by issuing the GETIDBYNAME command to the Password Server port:

```
mainserver:~ diradmin$ telnet 127.0.0.1 apple-sasl
Trying 127.0.0.1...
Connected to localhost.
Escape character is '^]'.
+OK ApplePasswordServer 10.1.0.1 password server at mainserver.pretendco.com ready
GETIDBYNAME diradmin
+OK 0x403087be17ede7a50000000c0000000c
```

The Password Server ID is also part of the user's record in the authAuthority attribute. In a default configuration, a list of Password Server IDs can also be obtained by anonymously querying the Open Directory master with the following command:

```
ldapsearch -x -h serverhostname -b "dc=searchbase,dc=tld" objectclass=apple-user authAuthority
```

Simple Authentication and Security Layer (SASL)

SASL is a method for adding authentication support to connection-based protocols, such as LDAP. SASL provides a "pluggable authentication" architecture to Password Server.

Pluggable authentication means that the client and server may be configured to negotiate and use a variety of mechanisms for authentication (CRAM-MD5, Digest-MD5, NTLMv1, and so on). Clients can use different methods of authentication if Password Server is configured to support the desired protocols.

In addition to CRAM-MD5 and NTLMv1, which ship with the standard Carnegie-Mellon SASL distribution, Apple has added a number of other plug-ins to support applications:

▶ DHX: Used by the AppleFileServer process and also supports write operations initiated by the DirectoryService daemon

▶ WebDAV digest: Allows for secure WebDAV authentication

▶ APOP: Used for POP mail authentication

▶ LAN Manager: Enables older Windows clients to connect via Windows file service

▶ MS-CHAPv2: Allows Open Directory users to authenticate to the PPTP virtual private network (VPN) service

SASL methods are classified as strong or weak. Weak methods may be used only for authentication, while strong methods can be used to write data to the Password Server database. The mechanisms SMB-NT, SMB-LAN-MANAGER, and APOP are always considered weak.

Data regarding available authentication methods can be gathered by using the telnet command on the Password Server port and issuing the LIST command:

```
mainserver:~ diradmin$ telnet mainserver.pretendco.com apple-sasl
Trying 10.1.17.1...
Connected to mainserver.pretendco.com.
Escape character is '^]'.
+OK ApplePasswordServer 10.1.0.0 password server at 0.0.0.0 ready
LIST
+OK (SASL "SMB-NTLMv2" "SMB-NT" "SMB-LAN-MANAGER" "MS-CHAPv2" "OTP" "NTLM"
"GSSAPI" "DIGEST-MD5" "CRAM-MD5" "WEBDAV-DIGEST" "DHX" "APOP" )
```

Password Server Policies

Because Password Server acts as a central authentication authority, it is a convenient place to enforce password policies on a per-user basis. One way to do this is in the

Advanced pane of the user's record in Workgroup Manager. The Policy pane of Open Directory Settings in Server Admin lets you enforce global policies ranging from character restrictions to password aging. Although many policies can be configured on both a per-user and a global basis, some are limited to one or the other.

The following figure shows the global possibilities that exist when managing password policies with user accounts located on Mac OS X Server.

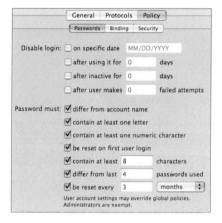

Global policy options are as follows:

▶ The password must differ from account name.

▶ The password must contain at least one numerical character.

▶ The password must contain at least one alphabetic character.

▶ The password must differ from the last n passwords used, where n is a number you can specify.

▶ The password must be changed periodically.

▶ The password must be mixed case (available only via pwpolicy as of Mac OS X Server v10.4.2).

Per-user policy options are:

▶ Allow the user to log in.

▶ Allow the user to change his or her password.

▶ Require a password change at the next login.

▶ Password must be changed every *n* days, where *n* is a number you can specify.

Global and per-user policy options are:

▶ Disable on date.

▶ Disable after a given number of days.

▶ Disable after a given number of inactive days.

▶ Disable after a given number of failed logins.

▶ The password must be a minimum of *n* characters, where *n* is a number you can specify.

When a global and a per-user policy have been set for the same parameter, the per-user policy takes precedence. To ensure that it has been recorded correctly, you can view the policy by using the telnet command to connect to Password Server and issuing the GETPOLICY and GETGLOBALPOLICY commands. GETPOLICY requires a user's Password Server ID as an argument:

```
mainserver:~ diradmin$ telnet 127.0.0.1 apple-sasl
Trying 127.0.0.1...
Connected to localhost.
Escape character is '^]'.
+OK ApplePasswordServer 10.1.0.0 password server at mainserver.pretendco.com ready
getpolicy 0x4284e8af3700c23a0000000200000002
+OK isDisabled=0 isAdminUser=1 newPasswordRequired=0 usingHistory=0 canModifyPassword
forSelf=1 usingExpirationDate=0 usingHardExpirationDate=0 requiresAlpha=0 requiresNumeric=0
expirationDateGMT=4294967295 hardExpireDateGMT=4294967295 maxMinutesUntilChangeP
assword=0 maxMinutesUntilDisabled=0 maxMinutesOfNonUse=0 maxFailedLoginAttempts=0
minChars=0 maxChars=0 passwordCannotBeName=0 requiresMixedCase=0 notGuessablePattern=0
isSessionKeyAgent=0
GETGLOBALPOLICY
+OK usingHistory=0 canModifyPasswordforSelf=1 usingExpirationDate=0 usingHardE
xpirationDate=0 requiresAlpha=0 requiresNumeric=0 expirationDateGMT=4294967295
hardExpireDateGMT=4294967295 maxMinutesUntilChangePassword=0 maxMinutesUntilD
isabled=0 maxMinutesOfNonUse=0 maxFailedLoginAttempts=3 minChars=0 maxChars=0
passwordCannotBeName=0 requiresMixedCase=0 newPasswordRequired=0 minutesUntilFailedLogin
Reset=0 notGuessablePattern=0
```

MORE INFO ▶ For an explanation of the output from GETPOLICY and GETGLOBALPOLICY, see the man page for pwpolicy.

Password Server Utilities

Apple provides several command-line utilities for managing Password Server data and configuration. Chief among them are pwpolicy, mkpassdb, and NeST. The pwpolicy command, among other things, can set either global or per-user policies in Password Server. The following table lists various flags for pwpolicy.

Flag	Usage	Comments
-getglobalpolicy	Sets global policies.	This is the same data that is available by using the telnet command on PasswordService and issuing GETGLOBALPOLICY.
-getpolicy	Gets policies for a user.	This is the same data that is available by using the telnet command on PasswordService and issuing GETPOLICY.
-setpolicy	Sets policies for a user.	
-setpolicyglobal	Sets a user account to use global policies.	
-setpassword	Sets a new password for a user.	Nonadministrators can use this command to change their own passwords.

NOTE ▶ pwpolicy can also be used on Mac OS X and Mac OS X Server, although not all policies will be effective.

▶ wpolicy: When specifying policies, pwpolicy uses the format "policy=value", where multiple policies are enclosed in quotation marks and separated by a space. For instance, to set a password expiration date for an account in the LDAPv3 database, you'd execute:

pwpolicy -a diradmin -n /LDAPv3/127.0.0.1 -u deborah -setpolicy "usingExpirationDate=1 expiration DateGMT=12/01/2005"

The -a flag is used to specify an administrator's short name. The pwpolicy utility has a very thorough -v (verbose) flag that provides a lot of information about the internal operation of Open Directory.

▶ mkpassdb: The mkpassdb utility can be used for everything from setting policies, for which its flags are identical to pwpolicy, to creating and managing replication intervals.

The following table lists various flags for mkpassdb.

Flag	Usage
-key	Outputs the RSA public key stored in the database.
-dump	Outputs all the Password Server IDs and their corresponding user names.
-getreplicationinterval	Gets the number of seconds between replication attempts.
-setreplicationinterval	Sets the number of seconds between replication attempts.
-b (The -b flag requires -a and -p)	Adds nonadministrators to the Password Server database.
-a	Outputs the Password Server administrator's short name.
-p	Prompts for a password.

▶ NeST: The NeST utility has been around in some form or another since Mac OS X v10.1. With every revision of Mac OS X, it gains additional functionality. It is a convenient way to stop and start the Password Server, verify the Password Server administrator, and confirm the address associated with the Password Server. However, its options are fairly broad, and some are no longer applicable. For example, NeST will allow you to easily create a NetInfo master, which has been deprecated in favor of an LDAP-based Open Directory master. To view the syntax and flags associated with NeST, simply type *man NeST* from the command line.

Password Server and KDC Synchronization

As you have seen, Mac OS X Server manages two authentication authorities: Kerberos and Password Server. These authentication authorities store their user secrets in different databases and different formats, making it necessary for the two authentication authorities to be transparent to the user. But when a user changes his or her password with the Kerberos utility, how does the Password Server know? If the user changes the password in the Password Server database, how does the KDC know? To provide a seamless experience for the user, Apple has instituted a two-way password synchronization process, so that passwords may be safely changed either in Password Server or in Kerberos.

Passwords and some policies changed in Password Server are written to the KDC automatically with the kadmin.local command. PasswordService executes kadmin.local, sending the modifications to the KDC using native Kerberos protocols securely so that user passwords cannot be seen in the process listing.

> **NOTE** ▶ While some password policies initiated in Password Server are synchronized with the KDC, password policies initiated in the KDC are not synchronized with Password Server.

When passwords are changed in Kerberos via the kpasswd command, kadmin, kadmin.local, or the Kerberos application, they are always sent to the kadmind process. In Mac OS X, kadmind is started, like krb5kdc and PasswordService, by launchd, with an Apple-specific -passwordserver flag. When run with the -passwordserver flag, kadmind knows to call the mkpassdb utility to update Password Server, similar to Password Server's use of kadmin. local except that the password policy and expiration data set with Kerberos tools are not propagated to Password Server.

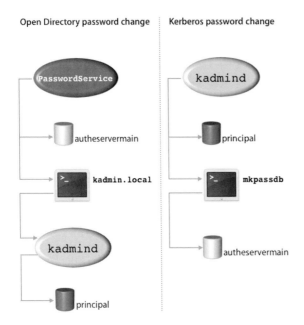

Open Directory password change   Kerberos password change

Configuring the KDC and Password Server

At the center of Open Directory's authentication capabilities is Apple's automated configuration architecture, which is responsible for setting up the LDAP, Password Server, and Kerberos functions for the server. In the previous lesson, you saw how changing the directory role of your Mac OS X Server to an Open Directory Master utilized a process called slapconfig to create the LDAP database, tweak a few configuration files, and create an LDAP administrator with the -createldapmasterdomain flag. slapconfig was not finished completing the process of changing the role of the server. After it finishes setting up the LDAP server, it sets up the KDC and configures it to work with Password Server.

The following is a detailed description of the Password Server and KDC configuration process:

1. The LDAP server setup is completed. (See Lesson 7, "Hosting OpenLDAP," for details.)

2. slapconfig calls kerberosautoconfig, which creates the edu.mit.Kerberos file.

3. slapconfig calls kdcsetup.

4. kdcsetup creates the required configuration and data files for KDC.

5. kdcsetup starts the krb5kdc and kadmind servers through launchd and adds kcmond and kadmin to the launchd configuration.

6. kdcsetup writes the KerberosKDC and KerberosClient configuration records to the Open Directory master in /config.

7. slapconfig copies the passwordserver configuration record from the local domain to the shared domain and starts Password Server.

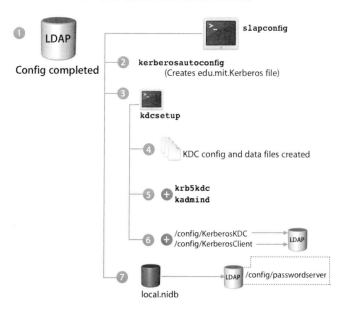

Open Directory Configuration Records

The KDC and Password portion of the Open Directory master creation process results in a number of configuration records stored in the /config directory:

▶   The KerberosKDC record is used when setting up Open Directory replicas.

▶   The kerberosautoconfig command uses the KerberosClient record to automatically produce an edu.mit.kerberos file for Open Directory clients in certain situations.

▶   The passwordserver value specifies which Password Server should be used with the domain, whether it allows replication, and which Password Server IDs the master is responsible for.

These records are useful in understanding the way Open Directory coordinates Kerberos and Password Server configuration and replication.

In the following figure showing the Workgroup Manager, click the bullseye on the All Records tab to display the Inspector tab and view all config records, including the KerberosClient, KerberosKDC, and passwordserver records.

apple-user authAuthority Attribute Contents

The authAuthority attribute defined by the apple-user object class tells Mac OS X how to authenticate Open Directory users. Users in an Open Directory master should have at least two authAuthority values: one for the KDC and one for Password Server. The loginwindow process has been modified to key off a Kerberos authentication authority in the user record. If Mac OS X sees a Kerberos authentication authority, it will attempt to autoconfigure (with the kerberosautoconfig utility) based on data in the /config/ KerberosClient record in that user's domain.

Password Server authAuthority values include the key ;ApplePasswordServer;, the user's Password Server ID, the RSA public key used to encrypt data sent to Password Server, and Password Server's IP address. A Kerberos authAuthority value also contains password server data. Additionally, it uses a ;Kerberosv5; key and includes the Kerberos principal and realm.

An example of a user's two authAuthority attribute values are as follows:

▶ Password Server:

;ApplePasswordServer;0x433becdf6c8f35760000000400000004,1024 35
1477574408453772116974069922318911980324467676138078592865772061 8699366555
5005634755080693023704392267029612215813689366929452131026016238136043569
6320627547176832253014986948227539724837833893755852543516295649694859 1320
7875438371321854093022080245906172565060077613272338368017569009432934246
100579129439333
root@mainserver.pretendco.com:10.1.0.1

▶ Kerberos:

;Kerberosv5;0x433becdf6c8f35760000000400000004;deborah@MAINSERVER.
PRETENDCO.COM;MAINSERVER.PRETENDCO.COM;1024 35
1477574408453772116974069922318911980324467676138078592865772061 86993665555
0056347550806930237043922670296122158136893669294521310260162381 3604356963
2062754717683225301498694822753972483783389375585254351629564969 4859132078
7543837132185409302208024590617256506007761327233836801756900943 2934246100
579129439333
root@mainserver.pretendco.com:10.1.0.1

> **NOTE** ▶ The bold part of the Kerberos authAuthority attribute value is the Kerberos portion, and the italicized part is the Password Server portion, even though both of these exist in the Kerberos attribute value.

Troubleshooting

Open Directory makes a fairly complex set of systems user-friendly. The goal of this lesson is to provide you with enough architectural knowledge that you will be able to successfully troubleshoot this environment.

One of the first steps in the analysis of any network infrastructure should be to employ a packet sniffer such as Ethereal or tcpdump. Both Password Server and Kerberos leave noncritical portions of their traffic unencrypted, and this data can be highly useful. Sniffing the network will often reveal error codes that are useful when debugging issues.

Log files are another useful tool. Logs are particularly useful in conjunction with a filter such as grep. For instance, to look for all KDC activity, you could execute the following:

    more /var/log/system.log | grep krb5kdc

You can also use kdcsetup with a –v n flag to enable verbose logging when manually setting up a KDC. The higher the number after the –v flag, the more verbose the logging.

For a Kerberos system to communicate securely, the KDC, the client, and all kerberized services must decide on a common encryption type. Because different vendors make different choices about Kerberos deployments, this is a common issue when building or maintaining kerberized infrastructures. A system administrator can tell what encryption is used by running klist -ke, which will show the encryption used to generate the keytab files.

Many of the pieces of the Kerberos protocol have a finite life span. For this reason, problems will occur in a Kerberos environment if various systems within the Kerberos infrastructure are not time-synchronized. Also, the clocks of all hosts involved (the KDC, the clients, and any service servers) must be synchronized. Typically, clock skews beyond 300 seconds (5 minutes) will prevent authentication from occurring using an otherwise valid ticket. The clock skew threshold is configurable on the KDC but should not be adjusted, as other issues may occur.

On occasion, Password Server and the KDC might become out of sync. Changing the user's password generally resyncs the authentication records. If this doesn't work, examine the system log for error conditions or processes quitting abruptly, as you may want to use the Kerberos application to change the Kerberos password and pwpolicy to change the Password Server password. If the lack of synchronization persists, checking the logs for both Kerberos and Password Server is in order.

Other common issues revolve around the promotion of standalone servers to Open Directory masters. If the domain name server (DNS) environment is not consistent with forward and reverse records that match, the KDC might not be created. The slapconfig process log should show useful information for tracking down this problem.

> **TIP** ▶ Unless DNS can be verified using the hostname and host commands to ensure that the Open Directory server resolves forward and reverse DNS names and addresses, you should not promote the server to an Open Directory master.

If an administrator cannot authenticate, create Password Server users, or change passwords, you can use NeST with its -NOpassworserver and -hostpasswordserver flags to re-create a Password Server administrator or promote an existing directory-service account to be a Password Server administrator.

To remove the Password Server entry from directory services, execute the command

> sudo NeST -NOpasswordserver

To create a Password Server administrator, execute the command

> sudo NeST -hostpasswordserver adminname password IPaddress_of_server

Finally, changing the IP address or hostname of an Open Directory master is not a trivial task. The changeip command does a complete, thorough, and safe job of updating every record that needs to be updated. Read the man pages for changeip for complete instructions on how to use this tool.

SSO is intended to make user authentication simple and secure. However, SSO, as implemented by Kerberos, is not as widespread as it could be. This is due in part to the slowness of various services becoming kerberized and the difficulty of integrating Kerberos realms at large. Apple has taken a significant step toward improving the adoption rate of Kerberos by combining the power and security of Kerberos with Mac OS X Server's ease of configuration and administration.

Where Kerberos is not supported, Mac OS X Server provides Password Server—a robust, multifeatured, Kerberos-integrated password service that provides SASL support, encryption, and password policies.

These two technologies, along with OpenLDAP, provide a robust, secure, and seamless identification and authentication architecture upon which all other services can be built.

What You've Learned

▶ Apple has addressed some of the major difficulties associated with creating a KDC on Mac OS X Server.

▶ The processes associated with the KDC are krb5kdc and kadmind.

▶ The role of Password Server is to permit authentication of non-Kerberized services.

▶ The main process for Password Server is PasswordService and is launched at startup by launchd.

▶ The main files used by Password Server are located in /private/var/db/authserver and are authservermain and authserverreplicas.

▶ You retrieve a user's Password Server ID from the user record.

▶ The slapconfig process logs verbosely to /Library/Logs/slapconfig.log.

References

Administration Guides
"Mac OS X Server Open Directory Administration": http://images.apple.com/server/pdfs/Open_Directory_v10.4.pdf

"Mac OS X Server Command-Line Administration": http://images.apple.com/server/pdfs/Command_Line_v10.4.pdf

Apple Knowledge Base Documents
The following Knowledge Base documents (located at www.apple.com/support) provide further information on Kerberos authentication.

Document 301339, "Mac OS X Server: Open Directory Master requires proper DNS for KDC to work"

Document 107702, "Mac OS X Server 10.3 or later: Kerberos authentication may not work after changing to LDAP master or replica, or Kerberizing a particular service"

Document 107289, "Mac OS X Server: Some Features Require Use of the Password Server"

Books
Carter, Gerald. *LDAP System Administration* (O'Reilly, 2003).

URLs
Kerberos: The Network Authentication Protocol: http://web.mit.edu/kerberos/www/

Kerberos: www.ietf.org/rfc/rfc1510.txt

SASL: www.ietf.org/rfc/rfc2222.txt

Lesson Review

1. What are the three types of Kerberos principals?

2. What is the KDC process on Mac OS X Server?

3. What process is responsible for making changes to the Kerberos database?

4. Why can the TGT be sent in clear text from the Kerberos client back to the KDC?

5. Why is it recommended that the /var/db/krb5kdc principal file be secured?

6. What is the name of the KDC's configuration file?

7. What is the name of the configuration file of kadmind?

8. What is SASL and how is it leveraged in Open Directory?

9. What tool does Password Server use to keep the KDC in sync? What tool does the KDC use?

10. Why might an administrator choose to disable some Password Server authentication methods?

Answers

1. User (user@REALM), host (host/fqdn@REALM), and service (service/fqdn@REALM)

2. The KDC process is krb5kdc.

3. kadmin

4. The TGT is already encrypted with a key known only to the KDC. The client may pass it around in the clear because it is useless without a session key, which is never passed over the wire unencrypted.

5. It contains all of the user keys.

6. kdc.conf

7. kdc.conf

8. The Simple Authentication and Security Layer (SASL) is a standard way of negotiating secure authentication- and transport-based protocols such as LDAP and IMAP. It is used by Password Server to provide legacy authentication protocols to Mac OS X Server services.

9. kadmin.local and mkpassdb

10. Some are more secure than others. Specifically, APOP requires that the user's password be stored in clear text.

9

Time   This lesson takes approximately 2 hours to complete.

Goals   Understand the four common ways that Mac OS X Server can participate in a Kerberos realm to authenticate user accounts

Use Workgroup Manager to add a Kerberos computer record to the Open Directory master server

Use Server Admin to configure a Mac OS X Server computer to join a Kerberos realm already established on an Open Directory master server

Use Server Admin to configure kerberized services running on Mac OS X Server to accept service tickets

Manage, install, and enable keytab files from a third-party Kerberos server on a Mac OS X server

Learn how to address the concern that Kerberos user keys are easily recoverable

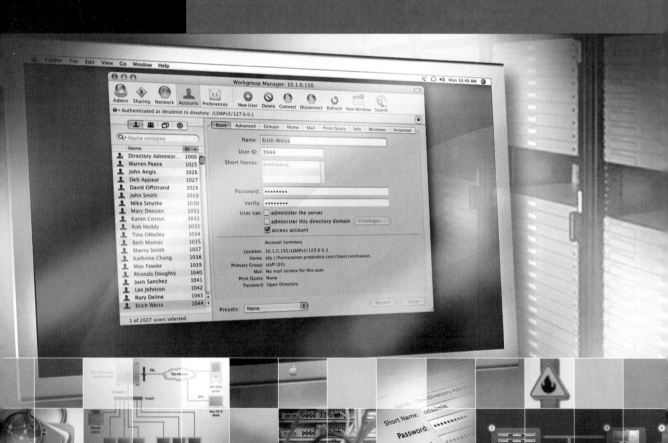

Lesson 9
Integrating With Kerberos

Now you'll learn about the basic strategies for combining multiple servers and services in a single Kerberos realm. Kerberos is only a piece of the overall puzzle because it handles only authentication, not identification. Integrating Kerberos usually requires a parallel plan for integrating a directory system to hold the user accounts that identify your users.

You can use Kerberos with multiple computers running Mac OS X Server, integrate third-party services with Kerberos provided by Mac OS X Server, or integrate services on Mac OS X Server with an existing Kerberos infrastructure. Common scenarios include integrating Kerberos with:

▶ Multiple servers running Mac OS X Server to provide a SSO environment for all your servers and services

▶ Mac OS X Server with an existing Active Directory server that provides Kerberos and directory service

If all your servers are running Mac OS X Server, identification and authorization are already integrated for you. Joining multiple servers to your Open Directory master is straightforward. Active Directory is a complex and sophisticated system similar to Open Directory, but it does provide a standard, predictable model for dealing with authentication and identification. Your biggest challenge will be accommodating nonstandard, customized systems that are unique to a given site, but luckily, Kerberos is flexible enough to be implemented in different ways and Mac OS X Server should provide all the tools you'll need.

Accessing Kerberized Services

To access a kerberized service running on a separate server, a client must first have a ticket-granting ticket (TGT) from the key distribution center (KDC), and the kerberized service running on the other server must be configured to accept service tickets from the KDC. The figure below shows the process of requesting a ticket, obtaining a TGT, and obtaining a ticket for a kerberized service on a separate server.

To access the service, the client uses the TGT to acquire a service ticket from the KDC in the following sequence:

1. The client sends the KDC a request, KRB_TGS_REQ. This request includes:

    •   The TGT in clear text

    •   The principal name of the service being requested (for example, afpserver/mainserver.pretendco.com@SECONDARYSERVER.PRETENDCO.COM)

2. Sent next is an authenticator, consisting of a timestamp encrypted with the secret session key the client originally obtained with the TGT in KRB_AS_REP.

3. The KDC decrypts the TGT and the authenticator (proving the client's identity) and prepares KRB_TGS_REP. This consists of:

    •   A new session key, for use between the client and the kerberized service, encrypted with the old session key to protect it as it is sent to the client

    •   A service ticket, otherwise unreadable to the client, containing the name of the client and a copy of the session key

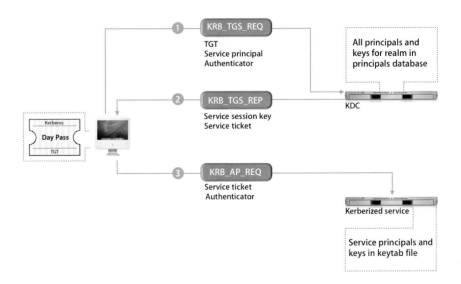

The session key and service ticket are encrypted with a secret password known only by the KDC and the kerberized service. The client sends the service ticket to the kerberized service, with an authenticator (now with a timestamp encrypted with the new session key). Because the service ticket is encrypted with the service's secret, the session key can be extracted from it only by a legitimate service. The service decrypts the service ticket and extracts the new session key to decrypt the client's authenticator. If the authenticator is decrypted successfully, the client is authenticated. This portion of the Kerberos exchange is called KRB_AP_REQ.

For successful Kerberos integration, make sure that:

▶ The KDC is configured with the proper service principal and key to issue a service ticket in step 2.

▶ The service has a copy of those principals and keys so it can validate that the service ticket came from the KDC.

Authentication Scenarios

When configuring multiple services to participate in a Kerberos realm, there are four basic scenarios, as shown in the following figure:

▶ Multiple Mac OS X Server computers: One Open Directory master provides the KDC. Additional servers are connected to a directory system and accept service tickets from the Open Directory master.

▶ KDC provided by a third-party server: This is typically an Active Directory KDC.

▶ Multiple KDCs (cross-realm authentication): Tickets issued by one KDC will be respected by a second KDC.

▶ KDC provided by Mac OS X Server supporting a third-party server.

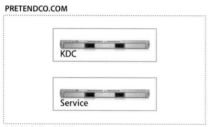

1. Multiple Mac OS X Server Computers

2. KDC Provided by a Third-party Server

3. Multiple KDCs (Cross-realm Authentication)

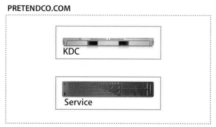

4. KDC Provided by Mac OS X Server Supporting a Third-party Server

Identification Scenarios

Two related but independent processes are involved in securely accessing resources on a server:

▶ The user must be identified: The service must know who is attempting to access the resource.

▶ The user must be authenticated: The service must be sure that the user is who he or she claims to be.

When the user has been identified and authenticated, the service can determine which resources the user has access to (authorization).

Kerberos provides only authentication; identifying the user is handled by separate processes and protocols. Because they are independent processes, identification and authentication can be implemented in a variety of ways, which makes for flexibility but also complexity.

The simplest scenario is for the authentication and identification to be integrated (as they are with Open Directory). A user named Tom is trying to log in. First, loginwindow attempts to locate Tom's user account. Tom has an Open Directory account that includes an AuthenticationAuthority attribute. Because Tom is on Mac OS X, his computer can interpret this attribute. The rules in /etc/authorization say that if the authentication process as defined in the AuthenticationAuthority succeeds, then Tom should be authorized to log in.

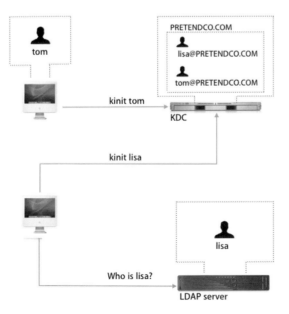

Because Tom's user account is in the local NetInfo database, he does not have an Authentication-Authority attribute spelled in the same fashion as the Lightweight Directory Access Protocol (LDAP) server's AuthenticationAuthority attribute or password data. (Refer to the table below for the attribute name listings.) His system is configured to authenticate with a KDC. The name in the directory, tom, matches the name of the Kerberos principal, tom@PRETENDCO.COM. The following table lists the various attribute names for authentication:

Database Type	Usage	Password Type
NetInfo	authentication_authority	Shadow hash
Open Directory	AuthenticationAuthority	Password Server Kerberos
OpenLDAP	authAuthority	Password Server Kerberos

Lisa's account is in a third-party LDAP directory and therefore does not have an AuthenticationAuthority attribute. The KDC and the LDAP directory containing Lisa's account do not have to be related. If Mac OS X is configured for Kerberos authentication, any user who can be identified from the LDAP directory can be authenticated with a separate KDC and can log in.

If there's a local user called lisa, she can log in with a Kerberos password specified in Active Directory. If there's an Open Directory user called lisa, she also will be able to log in with the Kerberos password specified in Active Directory. This leads to the feasibility of a loosely coupled integration strategy. Users stored in a Mac OS X directory—either locally or in a shared domain—can make use of the passwords stored in a Kerberos KDC, as long as their user names match.

Generally this implies some sort of synchronization process, or perhaps multiple synchronized directories relying on a single KDC.

Joining Multiple Mac OS X Servers

Single sign-on is a powerful feature of Mac OS X Server. It's enabled immediately for most of the services hosted on the Open Directory master when Kerberos is enabled. If you're hosting only one server, SSO requires no configuration beyond creating an Open Directory master.

However, it's more common for services to reside on a number of servers, thus spreading the load. SSO enables users to access all of these services with one user name and password. If all your servers use Mac OS X Server, Open Directory makes configuring this relatively simple.

> **NOTE ▶** Servers that are configured to use Kerberos provided by another server are members of the Kerberos realm, or member servers.

To participate in SSO by supporting Kerberos, member servers must first be authorized to access the KDC, and the services' secret keys (the shared secrets known only by the KDC and the services) must be established. Generally this involves obtaining a keytab file from the KDC, installing the keytab on the member server, and editing the Kerberos configuration file, edu.mit.Kerberos.

The following table lists the various services that can be kerberized:

LDAP	SSH	VPN
AFP	FTP	SMB
IMAP	POP	SMTP
HTTP	Xgrid	XMPP (Jabber)

Kerberos Configuration in Open Directory

Mac OS X Server includes utilities that streamline the process of joining multiple computers to a single Kerberos realm. To participate in a Kerberos realm, each member server must share a set of secret keys with the KDC. Joining a realm securely transfers the secret keys to the member server. In Mac OS X, as in any MIT Kerberos–based distribution, the secrets are stored in a keytab file: /etc/krb5.keytab. You can use the klist -ke command to view them.

> **TIP ▶** klist -ke can be useful for troubleshooting purposes. Sometimes authentication fails because the wrong keys get installed.

To transfer these keys, a number of processes need to occur:

1. An administrator on the Open Directory master must create a computer account for the member server. This is initially a standard computer account created using Workgroup Manager.

2. Server Admin modifies the account to contain additional Kerberos attributes containing the encrypted data (such as the keytab file) that the member server needs to join the directory domain hosted on the Open Directory master.

3. An administrator on the member server must use Server Admin to join the Kerberos realm established on the Open Directory master. The Kerberos data there is then decrypted and used for the local configuration files.

4. When the member server joins the Kerberos realm, it creates the local files necessary for the Kerberos configuration.

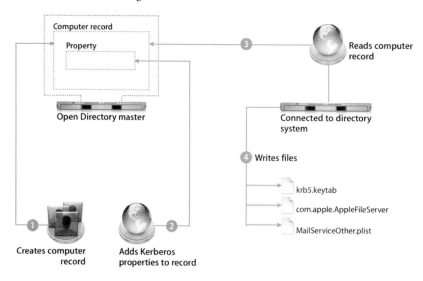

Creating a Kerberos Record on the Master

The first step to adding a kerberized server is to create a computer account for the member server by creating a computer record on the Open Directory master. When the computer account is created with Workgroup Manager, a basic computer record is stored in the shared domain.

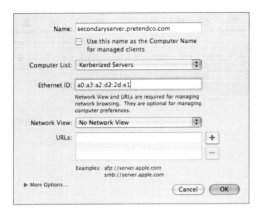

Example commands:

```
sso_util info -r /LDAPv3/127.0.0.1 -p
sso_util generateconfig -r SECONDARYSERVER.PRETENDCO.COM -R secondaryserver.pretendco.
com -f /LDAPv3/127.0.0.1 -U -a diradmin -p
```

The next step is to create the Kerberos record on the Open Directory master with Server
Admin. Click the Add Kerberos Record button in Server Admin's Open Directory
Settings pane and the dialog below will appear.

Authority to join the Kerberos realm must be delegated to a specific user, even if that user is already a domain administrator. This user name and password allow the member server to join the Kerberos realm. When you click Add to add the Kerberos records and then Save in Server Admin, the sso_util command performs the following actions:

▶ The default Kerberos realm is obtained using the sso_util info command.

▶ The service principals and keys are securely stored in the computer record using the sso_util generateconfig command.

> **NOTE** ▶ Server Admin does not indicate which computer accounts have Kerberos information added, and there is no easy way to delete the Kerberos information without manipulating the raw directory data (as with the inspector in Workgroup Manager). Be careful when entering information, and double-check your entry before you click Save.

Joining an Open Directory KDC

After you create the required Kerberos record on the Open Directory master, you can configure the member server to join the directory domain. To configure the member server as an Open Directory client to another server, click the Open Directory settings tab and choose Connected to a Directory System. Then configure Directory Access to search the LDAP server on the Open Directory master.

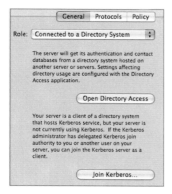

The member server queries the Open Directory master for directory information, including the Kerberos records you created previously. The process of binding the

Mac OS X server (the member server) to the Open Directory master is similar to that of binding a Mac OS X computer to an Open Directory master, covered in Lesson 3, "Accessing Mac OS X Server Directory Services."

The Open Directory master stores the Kerberos information in the computer record for the member server. Click the Join Kerberos button in Server Admin on the member server (see the preceding figure) and provide the user name and password of a delegated administrator. These credentials are used to authenticate to the directory and build a valid keytab file from the data that is stored in the server's computer record.

The resulting keytab contains the shared secret used to secure communication between the Open Directory master KDC and the member server. Once this secret is established, SSO is enabled.

When you save changes to the settings on the member server, sso_util useconfig produces a proper /etc/krb5.keytab, and it modifies both /Library/Preferences.com.apple. AppleFileServer and /etc/MailServiceOther.plist to reflect the service principals contained there.

This process occurs in the GUI and is very streamlined, giving the administrator freedom from manually managing the configuration files—a tremendous asset when using Mac OS X Server.

Integrating With Third-Party Kerberos Servers

In addition to integrating with Kerberos provided by another Mac OS X Server computer, you can integrate the services running on Mac OS X Server with a Kerberos realm provided by an Active Directory server or an MIT Kerberos server.

Using Third-Party KDCs

Creating service principals and keytabs in a UNIX-hosted KDC is similar to the process on Mac OS X without the Apple configuration mechanisms and infrastructures. The service principals must be created first, and then the process varies with the type of KDC being used.

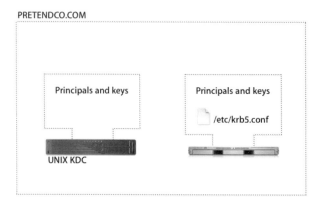

Keytabs—one for each service—should be extracted using a tool specific to the KDC. These keytabs would then be moved to Mac OS X Server for processing.

Installing Keytabs on Mac OS X Server

Once the keytabs have been produced, they can be transferred to Mac OS X Server. Use a secure method, such as physically transporting a drive or using an encrypted transport protocol such as Secure Shell Protocol (SSH).

TIP Keytab files are very sensitive, and in the wrong hands they could allow malicious parties to spoof the identity of your server. Securely copy the keytab files to the server using scp, or physically transfer them with a removable drive. Also delete any extra, unused keytab files so that unauthorized persons can't copy them.

Once the keytabs are on your Mac OS X server, they can be combined using the ktutil command, as demonstrated in the figure above. Optionally, the list command in ktutil may be used before the keytab is written out to verify that the principals were properly saved:

```
ktutil: list

slot   KVNO   Principal

----   ----   --------------------------------------------------------------

  1    1      afpserver/mainserver.pretendco.com@PRETENDCO.COM

  2    1      ssh/mainserver.pretendco.com@PRETENDCO.COM

  3    1      host/mainserver.pretendco.com@PRETENDCO.COM
```

The keytab must then be installed on Mac OS X Server at /etc/krb5.keytab and should be tested with the klist -ke command.

NOTE ▶ If the server will be hosting mail services, the mail group must have read rights on the keytab.

Finally, the service-specific configuration files must be edited to reflect their service principals:

▶   /Library/Preferences/com.apple.AppleFileServer.plist

Change the following keys:

<key>kerberosPrincipal</key>

<string>afpserver/mainserver.pretendco.com@PRETENDCO.COM</string>

▶ /etc/MailServiceOther.plist

Add the following keys in the <cyrus> dictionary:

<key>imap_principal</key>

<string>imap/mainserver.pretendco.com@PRETENDCO.COM</string>

<key>pop_principal</key>

<string>pop/mainserver.pretendco.com@PRETENDCO.COM</string>

Add the following keys in the <postfix> dictionary:

<key>smpt_principal</key>

<string>smtp/mainserver.pretendco.com@PRETENDCO.COM</string>

Kerberos authentication should now be enabled on the server.

Active Directory—Authentication and Identification

Like Open Directory, Active Directory provides both a directory of user records and a Kerberos KDC.

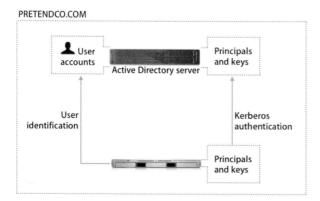

You can configure the Active Directory plug-in on a Mac OS X Server computer to allow a user to connect to services while authenticating as an Open Directory user. But what if your clients have already obtained a Kerberos TGT from the Active Directory server? Shouldn't they be able to access your kerberized services on Mac OS X Server using that TGT?

The first step is to join the Mac OS X server to the Active Directory domain. You can choose one of two methods to then have the Mac OS X server act as a member server to the Active Directory KDC:

▶ Click the Join Kerberos button and join the Active Directory KDC.

This is similar to having one Mac OS X server become a member server to another Mac OS X server.

▶ Use the command-line tool dsconfigad to join the Active Directory KDC:

sudo dsconfigad -enableSSO

At this point, the Mac OS X Server services that are kerberized—such as virtual private network (VPN), Apple Filing Protocol (AFP), and File Transfer Protocol (FTP)—are kerberized services of the Active Directory KDC. The one caveat is Server Message Block (SMB) sharing.

SMB Authentication With Active Directory

Windows file service (provided by Samba) is a special case of Kerberos integration. The SMB service works only with an Active Directory KDC, and its access method is different from the other Mac OS X Server services.

Mac OS X Server includes Samba 3, which acts as an Active Directory member server for Kerberos authentication. The shared secret is not stored in a keytab as it is with the other services on Mac OS X Server. Samba maintains the shared secret, and it's created when Mac OS X Server joins the Active Directory domain.

Although it's not enabled out-of-box, this feature brings tremendous value to Mac OS X Server. It provides an end-user experience and a level of authentication security that are equivalent to that of a Windows server.

> **NOTE** ▶ Mac OS X Server version 10.3 and later supports the NTLMv2 authentication method. Prior to Mac OS X v10.4, Mac OS X did not support NTLMv2, only NTLMv1, which is not as secure as NTLMv2. If your users are running Mac OS X v10.3 or earlier, they cannot use NTLMv2. If you connect Mac OS X Server v10.4 or later to a directory domain of Mac OS X Server v10.3 or earlier, users defined in the older directory domain cannot be authenticated with NTLMv2.

Apple has simplified the process of joining an Active Directory domain. When you join an Active Directory domain and kerberize the SMB service, the following additions and modifications are made to Samba's configuration file, /etc/smb.conf:

▶ spnego = yes

▶ realm = MYADDOMAIN.PRETENDCO.COM

▶ security = ads

▶ workgroup = MYADDOMAIN

The spnego entry already exists but is set to no; it's changed to yes. The realm property should be set to the name of the Kerberos realm your Active Directory server supports. Generally, this will be the capitalized DNS name of the Active Directory server. The security option is an internal Samba flag, alerting smbd that it should use Active Directory authentication (the ads flag). Finally, the workgroup should be set to the name of the NT domain emulated by Active Directory (although this is configurable in the graphical interface).

Modifying smb.conf was difficult in the previous version of Mac OS X Server, since sambadmind rewrote the configuration file every time it was restarted, and manual changes to the file were not preserved. In Mac OS X Server v10.4, the file is still rewritten every time Samba restarts, but manual changes are preserved.

Using Multiple Directories

Integration with Active Directory lets you take advantage of cross-platform directory standards. Because both Mac OS X Server and Active Directory support Kerberos and LDAP, a deep level of integration can be achieved with relatively little effort.

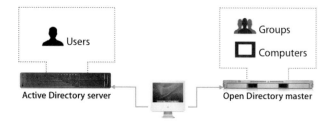

Unfortunately, the same cannot be said for many of the applications that rely on those directories. For instance, it would be unreasonable to expect Microsoft Exchange to work with Open Directory. Likewise, client management and group policy are features that tend to be proprietary and vendor-specific. The managed client data used by Mac OS X is not currently read or understood by other platforms. Similarly, Mac OS X servers are not going to enforce the policies defined by a Windows Group Policy object.

Because the format of the data is not standardized, Workgroup Manager is the only application capable of writing and maintaining it.

A common solution to this challenge is the deployment of a supplementary directory—one specifically for Mac OS X data, in addition to the Active Directory. User principals still reside in Active Directory, but management of Mac-specific data is delegated to the administrators of the Mac-specific domain. Mac OS X computers are then configured to access both domains and receive a combination of the data from both directories.

Here are two common scenarios describing how you can use both Open Directory and Active Directory to help manage your Mac OS X computers:

▶ User sadams logs in to workstation.pretendco.com. As a user account from Active Directory, sadams does not belong to any workgroups with managed preferences. However, the computer, named mac005, belongs to a group of computers (NY-office) defined in Open Directory. A set of preferences will be enforced for any user logging in to that group of computers, regardless of where the user record is stored: locally, in Active Directory, or in Open Directory. Mac-specific security policy is applied to Active Directory users without administrative impact on the enterprise directory.

▶ User jdoe logs in to workstation.pretendco.com. User jdoe exists only in Active Directory. However, mcx.loginplugin searches the authentication path of the computer named mac006 and determines that jdoe belongs to a workgroup with managed preferences. Because jdoe is logging in to a managed client (mac006 also belongs to the NY-office group), he will receive an aggregate of per-host and per-workgroup preferences.

Cross-Realm Authentication

A final Kerberos integration option involves a different kind of trust. Whereas in the last case of multiple directory integration, Mac OS X Server essentially trusted Active Directory, in this case Active Directory trusts Mac OS X Server. Cross-realm authentication is a standard built into the Kerberos v5 protocol, and it is widely deployed in organizations that had a well-developed pre-existing Kerberos infrastructure before their Active Directory rollout. Although user accounts still have to exist in both domains, a single authentication authority can be maintained.

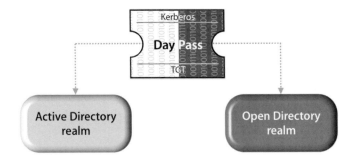

Once again, because cross-realm authentication is a feature of Kerberos, it can also be established with MIT (and Heimdal) KDCs. Active Directory is covered in depth, due to its ubiquitous nature and high impact on Mac OS X integration, but an MIT example is also included.

In cross-realm authentication, a TGT from the trusted domain is accepted in a second domain, and a shared secret is established so that data sent between the domains in question is secure.

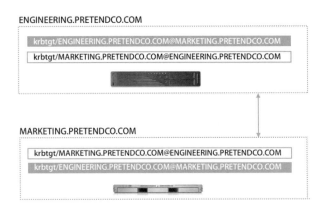

Setting up a trust with another MIT Kerberos realm is similar to integration with Active Directory. A cross-realm secret is established along with appropriate cross-realm tickets, but there are three primary differences:

▶ kadmin is used on both domain controllers, rather than just on the Open Directory master.

▶ More secure encryption types can be used.

▶ Service integration is site-specific. Active Directory offers a predictable model for integrating user and service principals with its KDC, as does Open Directory. This level of integration is not defined in the Kerberos standard, though, and the KDC you're establishing the trust with might follow a different model.

To create the cross-realm trust, use kadmin to add TGT principals to both KDCs.

```
kadmin.local -q "add_principal -pw password krbtgt/ENGINEERING.PRETENDCO.
COM@MARKETING.PRETENDCO.COM"
```

Use the same password on both KDCs when adding the principal.

```
kadmin.local -q "add_principal -pw password krbtgt/MARKETING.PRETENDCO.
COM@ENGINEERING.PRETENDCO.COM"
```

Again, use the same password on both KDCs when adding the principal.

Setting up cross-realm authentication with an Active Directory server involves using the Windows Active Directory Domain and Trusts utility and the New Trust Wizard. For details on establishing the trust, see "To create an external trust" in Windows Server Help.

The other half of the trust is established in the Open Directory domain using the
kadmin utility:

> kadmin.local -q "add_principal -e des-cbc-crc:normal -pw pass krbtgt/MAINADSERVER.
> PRETENDCO.COM@MAINSERVER.PRETENDCO.COM"
>
> kadmin.local -q "add_principal -e des-cbc-crc:normal -pw pass krbtgt/MAINSERVER.PRETENDCO.
> COM@MAINADSERVER.PRETENDCO.COM"

Note that the -pw flag should be used to specify the same password used in Active
Directory Domains and Trusts. If a more secure transaction is needed, don't specify the
-pw flag; kadmin.local will prompt you for it.

Next, mappings must be added to Active Directory users so that Open Directory principals can be used to authenticate them, and Windows clients must be set up to access the
Open Directory KDC.

Enabling Active Directory Users for Cross-Realm Authentication

Every Active Directory user who is going to be authenticated through Open Directory
needs to have a particular attribute added through his or her user record. Graphically,
this can be accomplished using the Active Directory Users and Groups MMC Snap-in
by enabling its Advanced Features option. After advanced features are enabled, you can
right-click the user in question and choose Name Mappings. In the resulting window,
shown in the following figure, choose Kerberos Mappings and add the user's Open
Directory Kerberos principal (the user's short name, followed by the @ symbol and
the name of the Open Directory Kerberos realm; for instance, dave@MAINSERVER.
PRETENDCO.COM).

However, in all but the smallest domains this will be scripted as part of the user creation process, so add the user's Open Directory Kerberos principal to the right attribute in their Active Directory user record. Having a standardized convention for the generation of user names lets you make assumptions when scripting, rather than querying a database or some other data source to determine the user's Open Directory user name.

Finally, Windows client computers must be alerted to the presence of the Open Directory KDC using ktpass, just as it was used on the domain controller. The Windows client must then be rebooted, and users should be able to choose the Open Directory KDC from the list of domains at the Windows login screen. On login, users will get an Open Directory TGT. To complete login, an Active Directory TGT will probably be needed (to access Active Directory resources such as home folder shares). Open Directory will grant a cross-realm TGT that will be respected by Active Directory due to the trust in place between the realms, and you've got true cross-realm integration.

Kerberos Security

Although Kerberos provides a reasonably secure authentication infrastructure, it's not perfect, and it's possible for a sufficiently sophisticated and motivated attacker to breach Kerberos security by attacking some of the weaker links in the Kerberos protocol. Luckily, most of these attacks are well understood, and much can be done to decrease the likelihood of their success.

The following table lists the various concerns when using Kerberos:

Concerns	Precautions
Keys are recoverable	Physically secure KDC
	Minimize services on KDC
Offline dictionary attack	Pre-authentication
	Password restrictions
	Network security
Man-in-the-middle attack	Mutual authentication
Replay	Address in ticket
	Finite authenticator lifetime
	Replay cache

Perhaps the most important security issue relating to Kerberos administration is that user keys are easily recovered, given root access to the KDC. For this reason, Open Directory master computers should run no other services if possible, and should be physically secured behind a locked door, through which access is thoroughly monitored. Note that even if the keys are recovered, an attacker could not extract the original passwords. The keys are created from the users' passwords via a hash. Still, uncontrolled access to the keys is a serious security breach that would compromise the security of the server.

A second concern is a dictionary attack. Specifically, certain Kerberos transactions encrypted with the user's secret are known to contain structured data. By sniffing an encrypted transaction off the network and applying a list of passwords against the encrypted data, the structured data may be decrypted. A number of measures can be used to foil dictionary attacks.

> **TIP** The risk of a successful dictionary attack can be greatly reduced by using sufficiently complex or non-English passwords. Policies can be put in place to help users choose safe passwords.

In Kerberos's default configuration, it is trivial to get Kerberos to send encrypted data across the network. To prevent such easy access to encrypted data, pre-authentication can be enabled. Pre-authentication forces the client to prove their identity before the KDC will send encrypted data and must be enabled on a per-principal basis. To enable pre-authentication for a principal, use the following command:

```
sudo kadmin.local -q "modify_principal +requires_preauth principalname"
```

And finally, malicious sniffing can be deterred though the use of Network Intrusion Detection Systems (NIDSs).

In a man-in-the-middle attack, a malicious party attempts to impersonate a kerberized service. Kerberos v5 minimizes the feasibility of this by using mutual authentication, which allows client-side software to require that the service prove it is legitimate by successfully using the shared session key.

Replay attacks harvest the authentication data that client software sends to a kerberized service. Although this data is encrypted, it can be reused later to gain access to the service. Several factors combine to make this sort of attack much more difficult.

One way Kerberos works to prevent replay attacks is by embedding the IP address of the client in the ticket, helping ensure that the ticket may be used only by a legitimate host. However, this is not entirely secure because IPs can be spoofed. Additionally, Network Address Translation NAT requires tickets that have no real address, since a nonroutable IP address generally has little meaning to the KDC.

Another way to prevent replay attacks is to add a timestamp to encrypted data. If the server's system clock differs by more than 5 minutes from the timestamp sent by the client, the user is not authenticated. Legitimate authentication data will probably be used shortly after it's obtained from the KDC.

Finally, the kerberized service caches the authentication data, disallowing the connection if it has seen the same data before. Ideally this would mean that a replay attack could not occur, because for a malicious party to harvest it, it would have to be sent to the server. It is feasible, though, that given a compromise of the network, the server could be subject to a Denial of Service (DoS) attack—meaning that the server would never receive the authentication data until the malicious party sent it.

NOTE ▶ This requires some very specific circumstances and is feasible only because of inadequacies in IPv4. (It relies on ARP spoofing.) If anything, it should indicate that no single tool is sufficient to secure a network. In this case, measures should have been taken to prevent ARP spoofing.

What You've Learned

- ▶ Open Directory provides a way to read directory data from most types of network directories.

- ▶ Mac OS X Server comes with all the standard Kerberos tools to deal with sharing and reading Kerberos service keys.

- ▶ Kerberos prevents a replay attack by containing the IP address in the ticket and having a finite ticket lifetime.

- ▶ Keytabs can be combined using the ktutil command.

- ▶ kadmin.local is used to configure the KDC in Mac OS X Server to support cross-realm authentication with a KDC running on a third-party server.

▶   You can use Server Admin to add a Kerberos record on an Open Directory master server and configure the SMB service running on Mac OS X Server to use authentication provided by an Active Directory KDC.

References

Administration Guides

"Mac OS X Open Directory Administration": http://images.apple.com/server/pdfs/Open_Directory_v10.4.pdf

"Mac OS X Server Command-Line Administration": http://images.apple.com/server/pdfs/Command_Line_v10.4.pdf

Apple Knowledge Base Documents

The following Knowledge Base document (located at www.apple.com/support) provides further information about Kerberos and cross-realm authentication.

Document 107702, "Mac OS X Server 10.3 or later: Kerberos authentication may not work after changing to LDAP master or replica, or kerberizing a particular service"

Books

Garman, Jason. *Kerberos: The Definitive Guide* (O'Reilly, 2003).

URLs

Developer Connection article on Kerberos: http://developer.apple.com/darwin/projects/kerberos

Kerberos: The Network Authentication Protocol: http://web.mit.edu/kerberos/www

Kerberos FAQs: http://web.mit.edu/macdev/Development/MITKerberos/Common/Documentation/faq-osx.html

Kerberos mailing lists: http://web.mit.edu/kerberos/www/mail-lists.html

NIDS and other security systems: www.honeypots.net

Lesson Review

1. What steps are involved in joining a Mac OS X Server to an existing Open Directory master?

2. Why are the keytab files sensitive?

3. Describe identification strategies that can be pursued in the context of kerberized authentication.

Answers

1. First create a computer record on the master, and then join the server to the Open Directory master.

2. The keytabs contain the secret shared between the KDC and the kerberized service. It is the basis of their cryptographic trust. A keytab file in the hands of a malicious user could compromise the security of your service.

3. An integrated user directory, such as Open Directory or Active Directory. A separate user directory that matches the Kerberos user principals. The separate user directory can still be a network directory, or a user in a local database.

10

This lesson takes approximately 2 hours to complete.

Goals

Use Server Admin to configure a Mac OS X server to act as an Open Directory replica

Configure a Mac OS X computer to connect to a replication system

Understand how LDAP data is replicated between an Open Directory master and replicas

Learn how passwords stored in Password Server are synchronized between an Open Directory master and replicas

Synchronize data between the master and replica servers

Identify entries in the Password Server and LDAP logs that indicate problems in replicating an Open Directory master server

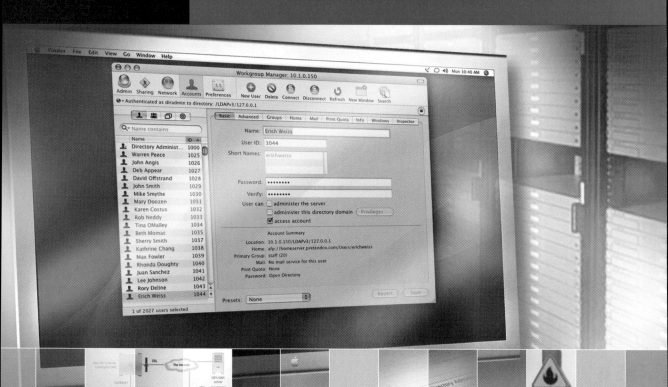

Lesson **10**
Replication

Because an Open Directory server provides data that is critical to the operation of your Mac OS X computers, you will need to set up more than just one server for redundancy and performance reasons. This is critical, because organizations must ensure availability in a directory-service environment. Understanding how replication works helps not only with planning and configuration, but also with troubleshooting.

In a Mac OS X Server replication system, one computer called the master is duplicated onto one or more computers called replicas, letting you move directory data closer to remote sites and provide data redundancy to eliminate service disruption. This lesson outlines the replication architecture. You will learn how to set up Open Directory replica servers and how the data—the contents of the Lightweight Directory Access Protocol (LDAP) server, Password Server, and the Kerberos key distribution center (KDC)—is synchronized between the master and replica servers.

Understanding Open Directory Replication

In a replication system, master and replica servers are dynamically and automatically synchronized to keep their contents identical. If computers go down, this ensures that services remain available and helps to avoid costly downtime. Mac OS X computers in your network can use either the master or any replica for authentication and other directory service functions. Any changes on a master or replica will be distributed to all replicas.

The process is described in the following figure:

1. The top Mac OS X computer is attempting to contact an Open Directory master whose LDAP database is not currently running.

2. Because it is configured to also look at a Replica of the Open Directory master, the Mac OS X computer can still access the LDAP information.

3. The second Mac OS X computer is simply configured to initially access the replica.

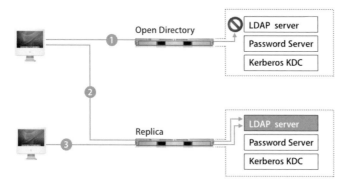

Replicas can greatly increase the robustness of your organization's network in two ways:

▶   Redundancy: Mac OS X computers will automatically use a replica system for authentication when the master system is down.

▶   Load sharing: Replication allows Open Directory servers to be load-shared. When a Mac OS X computer seeks authentication, it can query all known Open Directory systems. The Mac OS X computer will then use the first system to respond.

Essentially, an Open Directory replica is a server that contains a duplicate of the directory data stored on a master server. If you are configuring a Mac OS X computer to retrieve records from a replica server, you should add one replica to the Authentication and Contacts search paths. If a server failure should occur, Mac OS X will use other information to reconfigure itself to connect to another replica or master server. You'll learn more about this process later in this lesson.

Replication Topology

One Open Directory master can maintain several different replicas, and replicas can reside in the same local network as the master server or in remote networks, as illustrated in the following figure. Each replica is replicating the data from the Open Directory master with the IP address of 17.1.1.5.

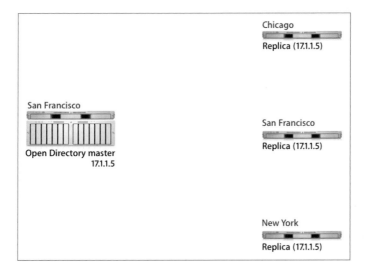

When designing a replication topology, consider the following needs:

▶   Redundancy: Redundancy dictates that every Open Directory master support at least one replica. If the master were to go offline for any reason, the replica would take over responsibilities until the master came back online.

▶   Performance: In a healthy network of even up to a few hundred computers, you should not need more than two or three replicas. If a remote location requires authentication services, you should install a replica at that remote location.

▶   Network bandwidth: Each replica adds to the amount of traffic on a network. Although there is no software limitation to the number of replicas you can create, don't burden the network unnecessarily.

TIP The actual number of replicas you need depends upon the needs of your network. As a rule of thumb, use 1 replica for every 250 computers, or 1 for every remote location. Effective planning will help you determine the right number for your organization.

Creating a Replica

Using the Open Directory module of Server Admin as seen in the following figure, you can define a Mac OS X server as a replica. The actual setup takes place on the computer you wish to assign as a replica, rather than on the existing master. You'll be asked for the IP address of the master Open Directory server, the system's root password on that server, and an LDAP directory administrator user name and password on that server. Because replication requires changes on the master server and to the master server's LDAP database, you need both the root and administrator passwords for the master. If replication is successful, you'll see the master server's address entered into the Master field on the replica.

Before creating a replica, make sure that your current Open Directory master is configured as you would like it to be, including that the KDC is running and that the naming context of your LDAP database is correct. Once you have established a replication system, it is a complex process to update existing replicas to be consistent with a significantly reconfigured Open Directory master. For example, if you did not have Kerberos enabled at the time replicas were created, and then you later enabled Kerberos on the master, you would need to create a Kerberos record for each of the replicas to allow them to fully participate in the Kerberos realm. This entails creating host keys for the replicas and entering the host principal into the KDC. This process would have already been done for you if the KDC was running on the master server before the replicas were created.

NOTE ► Each replica must have a serial number separate from that of the master, or replication will fail.

Replica Creation Process

As with establishing an Open Directory master, slapconfig is the engine that drives the replica creation process. Replica creation is logged in the /Library/Logs/slapconfig.log log file on both the master and the replica. These two logs, when viewed together, completely document the automated replica creation process, which is deceptively simple in design and well thought out.

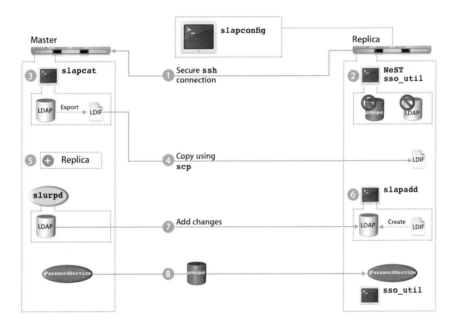

The following procedure details the replica creation process as driven by slapconfig and illustrated in the preceding figure.

1. Create a Secure Shell Protocol (SSH) connection between the replica and master computers.

   Before these steps can be initiated, an SSH connection must be created. On the replica, slapconfig initiates SSH connections to the master as the master's root user to check the supplied password for root and the LDAP administrator user on the master. If either the root or the domain administrator's password is wrong, or the supplied administrator user does not exist in the LDAP domain on the master, the replication process cannot continue. If there are any issues with the SSH keys between these two computers, the process will also fail. The server software serial numbers on the two computers are also checked at this time. If they are the same, the replication process will fail since the serial numbers are used to identify the servers during replication.

2. Destroy any LDAP and KDC databases.

   Any existing LDAP and KDC databases on the replica are destroyed and their servers are shut down.

   NOTE ▶ If you need any information stored in the replica's LDAP or KDC databases, export it before beginning the replication process and import it back in when the procedure is done.

   The Password Server's database on the replica is retained since this will contain passwords for local users on the replica computer in addition to the replicated network users.

3. Export the master computer's LDAP database.

   slapconfig stops the master computer's LDAP server and calls slapcat to dump the entire LDAP database to an LDAP Interchange Format (LDIF) file.

4. Copy the LDIF file to the replica computer using scp, which is called by slapconfig.

5. Update the master computer's configuration.

    The master adds the replica computer's IP address and a replication-specific user to a number of configuration files, including /etc/openldap/slapd_macosxserver.conf file, which correspond to an entry in the replica's copy of this file. All LDAP replication between the two servers is authenticated by this user, which is not listed in the actual LDAP database.

    Entries are also made in the LDAP database at cn=passwordserver,cn=config and cn =ldapreplicas,cn=config, which alert Mac OS X computers and other replicas to the existence of the replica. At this time, the master computer's LDAP server is restarted so that Mac OS X computers can continue to use the master for directory services while the replication process continues.

    NOTE ▸ The replication process for a large system of 30,000 users should take only a few minutes to complete over a LAN connection.

6. Generate a new LDAP database using the LDIF file.

    The LDIF file that was copied from the master computer is now used to generate a fresh LDAP database on the replica computer using slapadd. Once the LDAP database is created, the replica computer's LDAP database is started.

7. Start the replicator on the master computer.

    If slurpd is not already running on the master, it starts to read the change log generated by slapd. Then, using the replication user that is shared between the master computer and replica computer (created in step 5), it will add the changes into the replica computer's LDAP database.

8. Enable Password Server and KDC on the replica computer.

    The replica computer's Password Server is made aware that it is now in a multi-master situation. At this point, Password Server will attempt to contact the master Password Server in the replication system when any password change is initiated on this particular replica.

Password Server copies the KDC database on the Open Directory master in its entirety from the master to the replica. The sso_util command is then run to generate service keys for the services hosted on the local replica. This will also change the appropriate service configuration files to allow the master and replica computers to be fully integrated into the Kerberos realm.

After the KDC is created, the replica creation process is complete. Your next task is to configure replication settings on the master computer.

Replica Configuration

Once a replica has been established, you will see the server listed on the Open Directory master in Server Admin. In the General pane of the Open Directory module, you can force a replication to ensure that a replica is up-to-date, which is useful when a replica has been offline for a period of time and has just come back online.

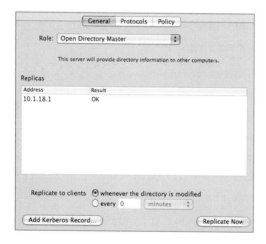

NOTE ▶ Clicking the Replicate Now button forces a replication to all replicas, not just the one you have selected in the list of replicas.

To customize the replication interval, services can either hold all changes and replicate once every interval or replicate whenever the directory is modified. If all your replicas are on the same local area network (LAN), you should probably set them to replicate when modified. However, if you have a number of remote networks, it is advisable to set the replication interval to a few hours to reduce traffic across wide area network (WAN) connections. Replication times set for under 60 minutes will not be recognized, and the replication will take place immediately.

> **NOTE ▶** Updates to the replication interval might not be recognized immediately by the replicas. Also, only major problems occurring during the replication process will be displayed in the Result column of the Server Admin interface. If the replica is offline, the interface status will display OK.

> **TIP ▶** A longer replication interval might cause some confusion because a changed password, for example, will not be immediately replicated to the other Password Servers.

Any confusion due to a longer replication interval will be mitigated by using single sign-on, since authentication is tied to a ticket instead of the user's password. The user can authenticate to the replica with the changed password and acquire a valid ticket that will be honored by all other servers in the Kerberos realm.

Connecting the Mac OS X Computer

In order for a Mac OS X version 10.4 computer to connect to a server in a replication system, the computer must have a search path listed in the Authentication pane of Directory Access. This allows the computer to discover the replication system and build its list of replicas.

As a general rule, a Mac OS X computer should not have more than one server from the same replication system listed in the Authentication pane of Directory Access, or that computer will search the same list of users multiple times, thus negating some of the benefits of actually having the replicas in the system.

When the Mac OS X computer first contacts a server in a replication system, it downloads a list of LDAP replicas from the LDAP server to the computer and stores it in /Library/Preferences/DirectoryService/DSLDAPv3PlugInConfig.plist. In addition, the Writable key identifies the Open Directory master in this file.

NOTE ▶ Mac OS X v10.2 computers and earlier are unable to automatically find a replica. However, you can sequentially list the replicas in Directory Access. Then the Mac OS X computer will try each server sequentially as necessary when attempting to authenticate a user.

The Mac OS X computer caches all known Password Servers in the replication system in /var/db/authserverreplicas.local. When the Mac OS X computer attempts to authenticate using Password Server, it looks at the Password Server public key that is stored in the user's authentication authority and references that key in this file to find out what Password Servers can be used for authentication.

The Mac OS X computer also keeps a cache of all known KDCs in the replication system in the edu.mit.kerberos file located in /Library/Preferences. Whenever a new KDC replica is added to the replication system, that server is automatically added to the default Kerberos config file stored in the Open Directory database. Mac OS X computers will check this serialized file to see if any changes have been made, and if so, the computers will download this modified file to /Library/Preferences/edu.mit.kerberos, thus giving them access to this new replica.

Once the Mac OS X computer has the listing of all servers in the replication system, it uses the server that is specified in the LDAP configuration plug-in. If that server is unresponsive, the Mac OS X computer will progressively contact all LDAP servers, Password Servers, and KDCs. The first of each type of server to respond is cached in memory and will be used for lookups and authentication. Ideally, this will result in the Mac OS X computer using the closest server—or servers, since it is entirely possible that you will use separate servers for LDAP, Password Server, and the KDC—to it in the replication system.

The Mac OS X computer will continue to use the servers cached in memory until it restarts, its network settings change, or a cached server becomes unresponsive. At this time, it will initiate the discovery process again. If the Mac OS X computer cannot contact any of the known Password Servers in its list, it will then search over Bonjour for any other servers that share the same public key. Failing that, the Mac OS X computer will attempt to connect to a Password Server running on local computer. This last step is of benefit only when the Mac OS X computer is actually a Mac OS X Server system that has had its IP address changed.

Maintaining a Replication System

Data, including passwords, are replicated between all of the servers in a replication system. The three services that take part in replication are the LDAP server, Password Server, and the Kerberos KDC.

A process called slurpd replicates the LDAP server; Apple has not changed the standard OpenLDAP replication process. The Open Directory master hosts a single master LDAP database. Since it's the only writable LDAP database in the replication system, all LDAP changes are pushed out by the master to the replicas.

Password Server is a multimaster system, so the version on the Open Directory master and on each replica can accept a password or a password change for a user. This change is then replicated from the originating server to the master server, and from the master server to the other replicas

Replication for the KDC is handled by the local Password Server. All changes are replicated through the normal Password Server replication process, which then updates the local KDC and reduces the potential for additional traffic on the LAN.

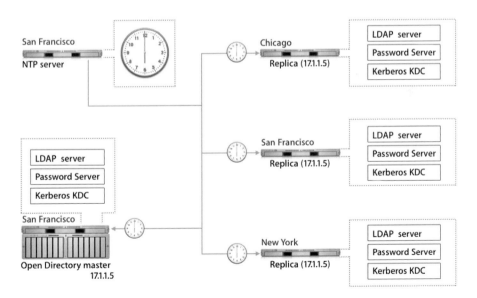

Because the replication architecture relies heavily on timestamps, it is good practice to keep the master and all replicas on the same Network Time Protocol (NTP) server. Mac OS X Server can act as an NTP server.

Replication Architecture

To implement a robust and complete Open Directory replication, Mac OS X Server relies on a diverse set of tools. Understanding which tools and files are used by the replication process enables the server administrator to track and troubleshoot replication problems. The following figure illustrates the processes, configuration files, and log files involved in the replication process.

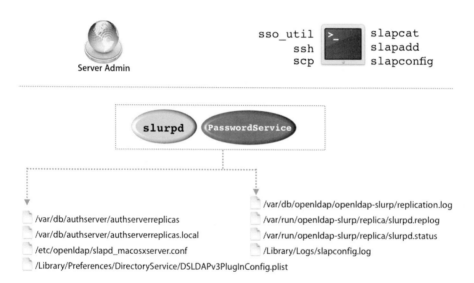

Some of the more commonly referenced files that concern the replication architecture are:

▶ /var/run/openldap-slurp/replica/slurpd.replog: A listing of replicated LDAP database changes that is kept on the master server. All changes are timestamped.

▶ /var/run/openldap-slurp/replica/slurpd.status: A listing of all replica servers and the last time that they were updated for any changes to the LDAP database.

▶ /var/db/authserver/authserverreplicas: A file that keeps a listing of all the currently known replica Password Servers and when they were last updated.

LDAP Replication

When a change is made to the LDAP server, that change is written to a log file named /var/db/openldap/openldap-slurp/replication.log, which contains an LDIF entry and a timestamp for every change made to the LDAP database.

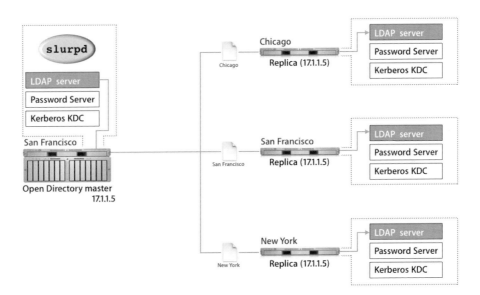

This log file is read by slurpd to acquire the changes pending replication. slurpd compares the timestamps of the log entries with the timestamp of the last successful replication with each replica. Replication status is kept in /var/run/openldap-slurp/replica/slurpd. status. slurpd then attempts to use standard LDAP commands to push changes out to the replicas. The master and the replicas share a user name and password, which ensures that only the master can propagate changes to the replicas.

If slurpd is unable to communicate with a replica, it will not increment the timestamp for that particular server in slurpd.status. During the next replication interval, slurpd will attempt to reconnect to the failed server and replay all changes since the last completed replication, which is useful if a server has been temporarily offline.

Only the master LDAP database can be changed. If the master server is offline, no changes to user records or other LDAP entries can be made until either the master has been brought online again, or one of the replicas has been promoted to a master.

If you attempt to connect using Workgroup Manager to a replica, you will be automatically redirected by an LDAP referral to the master server without any indication of being redirected. Similarly, if a user attempts to change the password hint or the picture for the user's account, the Mac OS X computer will be redirected by an LDAP referral to the master server. If the master's LDAP server is down, the Mac OS X computer will be unable to perform any changes.

Password Server Replication

Password Server engages in a multimaster replication scheme. Each server is capable of taking a change to a user's password or password policy. Using this system, password changes can be made even if the Open Directory master is extremely busy or offline.

The Password Server that took the change will contact the Password Server on the Open Directory master. The master Password Server then replicates the changes to the Password Servers on the replica servers.

The originating Password Server refers to a list of replicas in /var/db/authserver/ authserverreplicas, and also uses this file to track when it last synchronized with a replica and whether that synchronization was successful.

When Password Server replicates, it acts in a fashion similar to that of the LDAP server; Password Server checks the timestamp of the last synchronization of each replica and then looks in its database for all changes since that time. All conflicts are settled by using the most recent change based upon the timestamp. If the Password Servers' clocks are more than a few minutes out of sync, they will not be able to replicate. So if you are having trouble authenticating in a replication system, check the timestamp on each server.

The following figure shows how a password change is made between a replica and a master:

1. The password is passed from the replica back to the Open Directory master.
2. Password Server checks the password.
3. The Open Directory master pushes the change out to other replicas.

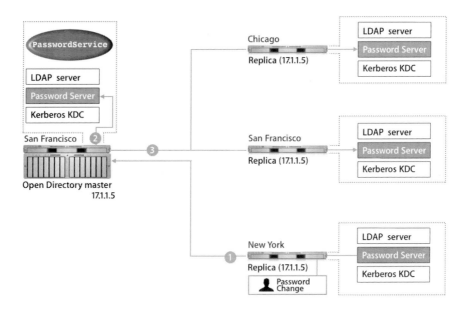

The security of the Password Server replication is entirely encrypted between each Password Server process. All share the same public/private key pair to both encrypt the actual database files on the local computer and also secure the communication between the servers.

> **NOTE** ▶ By default, each PasswordService process has a unique range of 500 slots or password IDs for storing passwords. The password IDs must be unique per PasswordService process in the replication system (between the master and all replicas). That way, Password Server can't use a password ID already in use by another PasswordService process in the replication system.

KDC Replication

The following figure shows how changing a Kerberos password is propogated to each Password Server:

1. Only the KDC on the Open Directory master runs kadmind, which is the process that accepts Kerberos password and password policy changes.

    All changes that are initiated from any of the Kerberos tools, such as kpasswd and the Kerberos application, will be redirected by the Kerberos realm to this server.

2. Once the changes are made on the master's KDC, the master's Password Server receives the changes and then attempts to replicate the changes to all other Password Servers in the replication system.

3. Once the changes are received, each updated Password Server will update its local KDC in turn.

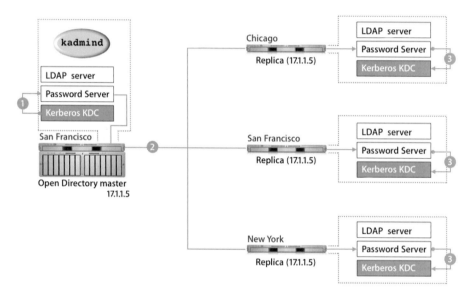

TIP ▶ Because password changes initiated with Kerberos must occur on the master server, no password changes initiated by Kerberos may take place when the master server is down.

Examples of Replication

This scenario shows the behavior of replication:

1. The Mac OS X computer starts up.

2. It attempts to use the server to which it was bound.

3. It stores the list of LDAP servers, Kerberos servers, and password servers from the replication system.

4. The LDAP server goes offline.

5. The Mac OS X computer consults its server list and attempts to connect to a new LDAP on that list.

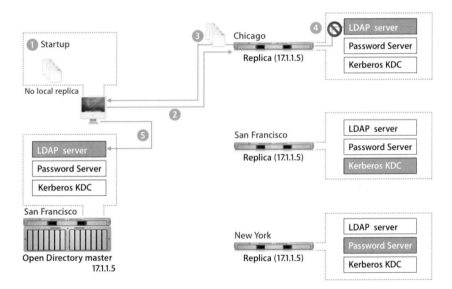

Replication Updates

This scenario illustrates the update behavior of replication:

1. The user successfully logs in and makes a change to his or her password. The new password is stored in the Password Server database of the replica that the Mac OS X computer is currently using for authentication.

2. Password Server will now begin the replication process via the master, which pushes this change out to all other Password Servers. Because the Chicago replica is down, the password update will fail there.

3. The Chicago replica comes back online.

4. After a secure connection is established with the replicas San Francisco master, the Chicago replica checks its logs to find the last time it was updated and requests updates from the San Francisco master. The San Francisco master plays back all entries in the database that have a timestamp more recent than the Chicago replica's last successful replication, thus synchronizing the Chicago replica with the rest of the replication system.

5. The Chicago replica comes back online.

6. The Open Directory master pushes the password change out to the Chicago replica.

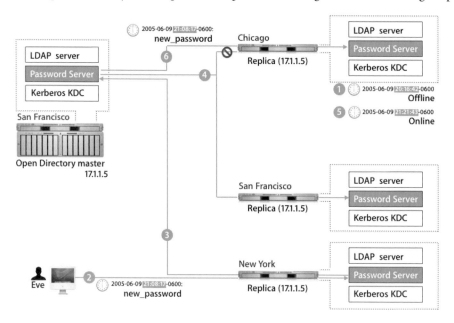

Promoting a Replica to an Open Directory Master

When your Open Directory master goes permanently offline, you can promote one of the replicas to be a master. Pick a replica—ideally a server that will be fast and robust enough to handle the demands of being the master server. The promotion process does not alter the data in the LDAP, Password Server, or Kerberos databases, but it does change the services' configuration files and causes Password Server to be rekeyed. A new public/private key pair is generated and the password database is reencrypted using the new key pair.

> **TIP** Never promote a replica that you do not want to permanently hold the position of master.

All of the new configuration information, including the Kerberos record and the list of available LDAP servers and Password Servers in the replication system, are uploaded into the server's LDAP database. When Mac OS X computers connect to a server in the replication system, they will update their configurations and their lists of replication servers.

Once you have created the new master, you will need to go to each replica in the domain and manually associate them with the new master as fast as possible. Otherwise, you might run into a situation where Mac OS X computers are using computers configured with the old replication data.

> **TIP** When you promote the replica, make sure that you use the same information for both the LDAP domain and the Kerberos realm as the previous master. Failure to do so will render your user records inaccessible.

Upgrading Mac OS X Server v10.3 to v10.4

In a replication system, you cannot have a mix of Mac OS X Server v10.3 and v10.4 computers. A Mac OS X Server v10.3 replica will not connect to a Mac OS X Server v10.4 master. If you upgrade your master server to Mac OS X Server v10.4, you must also upgrade the replicas.

The following figure shows four steps for upgrading a master/replica system from Mac OS X Server v10.3 to Mac OS X Server v10.4.

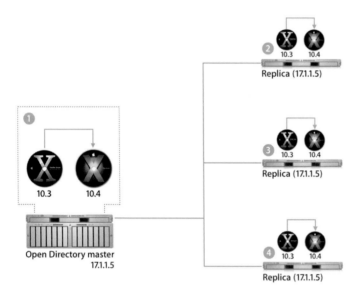

When upgrading, you should start with the master server; the installer will handle migrating the old databases into the new formats. After that, none of your replicas will be connected any longer. Do a clean install of Mac OS X Server v10.4 on each replica, and go through the process to configure it as a replica of your server and download the directory data to the replica.

During the migration process, the Mac OS X computers shouldn't experience any downtime. When a server is down while it is being upgraded, the Mac OS X computer will bind to a different server.

No data is lost during the upgrade, because the master server contains all the data and copies it to the upgraded replicas. The only potential issue is if a user upgraded his or her password while the servers were being upgraded—then the Password Servers on the replicas would accept and store changes.

After the master server has been upgraded and the replicas are disconnected, password changes can't be sent to the master Password Server. When Mac OS X Server v10.4 is installed on the replicas, the changed password will be lost, and the user's password will revert to the old password that was on the master server.

Replica Troubleshooting

The logs are very valuable when troubleshooting the replication process. The LDAP and Password Server logs will show any attempted replications and perhaps why the attempts failed.

You can try to force replication from Server Admin; even if it doesn't work, it might trigger errors to be written to the logs. You can also initiate replication manually from the command line with slapconfig to provide more error feedback than you get by using Server Admin.

For the initial replication to occur, you need to connect via SSH as the root user between the replica and the master server. Issues with SSH keys or other problems can prevent this from happening, so look at the SSH logs for errors.

Another common issue is time skew between the replicas or the Mac OS X computers and the authentication server. Point all of your computers to the same NTP server to ensure clock synchronization.

> **MORE INFO** ▶ The NTP service on Mac OS X Server should be synchronized to a Stratum 1, 2, or 3 NTP server. See http://ntp.isc.org/bin/view/Servers/WebHome for more information.

Directory service access control lists (ACLs) are also replicated as part of the Open Directory replication support. All nondefault ACLs will be copied to each replica each time they are updated.

Finally, as with all network services, make sure that the network is running correctly. Replication is a critical part of a robust and dependable Open Directory architecture. Apple has implemented its replication architecture using industry standard components and leveraging existing technologies. Understanding the way that replication works on Mac OS X Server is critical to planning, deploying, and supporting Open Directory in the workplace.

What You've Learned

▶ Open Directory replication applies to three primary technologies—LDAP, Password Server, and KDC—which are integrated to provide the best possible set of features while maintaining the Apple signature ease of use.

▶ Server Admin can promote an Open Directory replica to an Open Directory master to specify when data should be replicated to connected replicas.

▶ A Mac OS X computer goes through various steps during startup when it is bound to an Open Directory replica system.

▶ Custom directory-service ACLs are copied to each replica from the master in a replica system.

▶ When a user changes their password on a Mac OS X computer bound to a replica system, the password is changed on the bound replica and then passed to the master, which then updates all other replicas in the system.

References

Administration Guides

"Mac OS X Server Open Directory Administration": http://images.apple.com/server/pdfs/Open_Directory_v10.4.pdf

"Mac OS X Server Command-Line Administration": http://images.apple.com/server/pdfs/Command_Line_v10.4.pdf

"Mac OS X Server Upgrading and Migrating for Version 10.4 or Later": http://images.apple.com/server/pdfs/Migration_v10.4.pdf

Apple Knowledge Base Document

The following Knowledge Base document (located at www.apple.com/support) provides further information about Kerberos authentication.

Document 107702, "Mac OS X Server 10.3 or later: Kerberos authentication may not work after changing to LDAP master or replica, or Kerberizing a particular service"

Lesson Review

1. What information does Mac OS X Server require when creating a replica?

2. How does a Mac OS X computer choose the servers it will use for authentication once it has received its lists of replicas for each of the server types (LDAP, Password Server, and KDC)?

3. When does a Mac OS X computer reevaluate which Open Directory server to use?

4. What does /var/db/openldap/openldap-slurp/replication.log contain?

5. How does KDC replication work in a replication system?

6. When will changes to a user's record be propagated to the other servers in the replication system?

Answers

1. You must provide the IP address of the master, the root password for the master, and the directory domain administrator's name and password.

2. The Mac OS X computer uses the server specified by the LDAP plug-in configuration. If that server fails to respond, the client will choose the first responding server for LDAP, Password Server, and KDC, while progressively querying the servers on the lists.

3. A Mac OS X computer selects the server after the computer has restarted, the network settings have changed, or the directory server becomes unresponsive.

4. It lists the LDAP data that needs to be sent out to the replica servers.

5. All changes to the principals stored in the KDC on the Open Directory master will be pushed to Password Server, which will then update the member Passwords Servers. The member Password Servers will then update their local KDC.

6. All changes to both the LDAP database and Password Server are replicated based on the replication interval set on the Open Directory master.

11

Time   This lesson takes approximately 1 hour to complete.

Goals   Evaluate directory-service needs and use to determine how many replica servers, if any, are required

Construct a plan for deploying networked user accounts for a mix of Mac OS X and Windows computers

Construct a plan for providing Mac OS X–specific directory-service data to Mac OS X computers on a Windows-dominant network

Understand the security precautions you should take when setting up a directory server

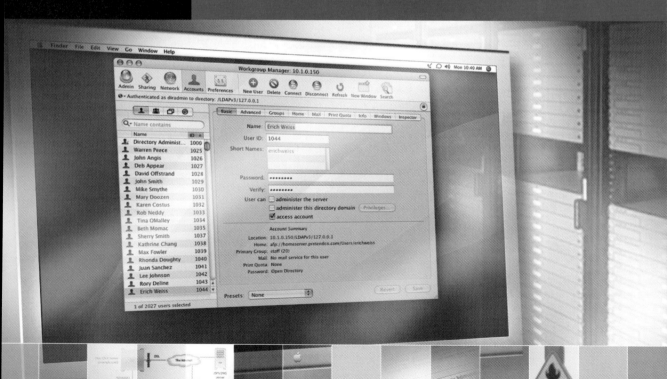

Planning and Deploying Directory Services

Because directory services constitute a critical component of modern operating systems, you need to create a directory-services plan before you deploy your client and server computers. In developing the plan, you will need to decide how many directory-servers you'll require, how they will be used, and where they will be deployed. As part of the deployment, you'll need to consider how to keep the servers secure while providing optimum performance.

Sharing Directory Data

If you don't need to share user and resource information among multiple Mac OS X computers, very little directory domain planning is necessary; you can gain access to everything from local directory domains. Just be sure that anyone who needs to use a particular Mac OS X computer has a user account residing in the local directory domain on the computer. Anyone who needs to use the Mac OS X Server file service, mail service, or other services that require authentication will also need a user account in the server's local directory domain. With this arrangement, each user has two accounts, one for logging in to a computer and one for accessing services of Mac OS X Server. The same short name cannot be used in this case, although the same password can.

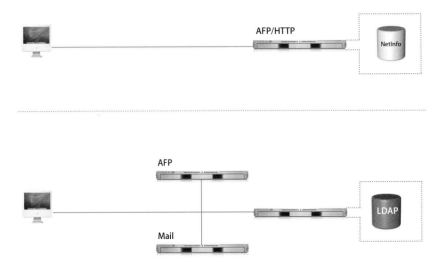

If you want to share information among Mac OS X computers and servers, you need to set up at least one shared directory domain with one account per user. With this account, the user can log in to Mac OS X on any computer and gain access to the services of any Mac OS X server configured to access the shared directory domain.

In many organizations, a single shared directory domain is completely adequate, allowing hundreds of thousands of users and thousands of computers sharing the same resources, such as printer queues, share points for home folders, share points for applications, and share points for documents. Replicating the shared directory domain can increase the capacity or performance of the directory system by allowing multiple servers to handle the directory system load for the network. Larger, more complex organizations can benefit from additional shared directory domains.

Configuring a Mixed Client/Server Environment

The simplest shared directory configuration is using Mac OS X Server to provide Open Directory services to Mac OS X computers.

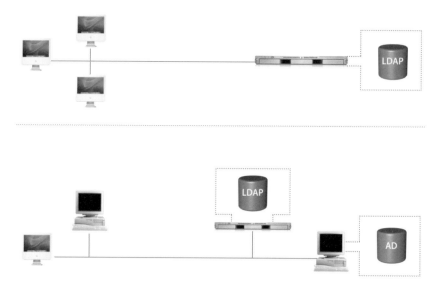

If you are adding Mac OS X computers to an environment that already has directory servers deployed, you'll need to determine whether the existing servers can provide the records and attributes Mac OS X requires. You may have to modify the schema on the server to create a custom Lightweight Directory Access Protocol (LDAP) configuration that the Mac OS X computers can utilize for the missing attributes not found in third-party directory servers.

You might find it easier to set up Open Directory servers to supplement existing directory servers, which can continue to provide user records that all of the computers can use. The Open Directory server can provide Mac OS X–specific information such as managed client and mount records, eliminating the need to modify the schema on the servers providing account information.

Improving Performance

You can improve the performance of Open Directory services by adding more memory to the server. To fully maximize the memory, you'll need to increase the BerkeleyDB cachesize directive.

You should minimize the number of other services running on the server. The more you can dedicate a server to Open Directory, the better its performance will be. Ideally, a server providing Open Directory services will not have any other services enabled. Also, by hosting services on servers other than the one providing directory services, you minimize the impact on directory services when you need to bring down other services for maintenance or upgrades.

You can also improve Open Directory server performance by storing the operating system and the logs on one disk and the LDAP database on another disk.

If your network will include replicas of an Open Directory master, you can improve the performance of the network by scheduling less frequent updates of replicas. Updating less frequently means the replicas' directory data is less up-to-date. You have to strike a balance between higher network performance and less accuracy in your replicas.

Configuring Replica Servers

As part of the deployment plan, you need to consider configuring replica servers to move directory information closer to users in a geographically distributed network. That will improve performance of directory and authentication services to these users. A replica also provides redundancy, so that users see little disruption in service if a directory system fails or becomes unreachable.

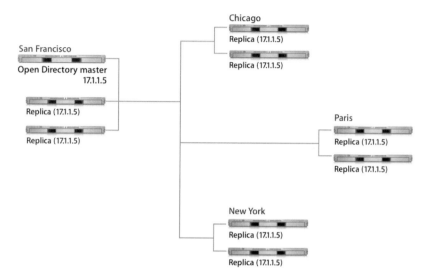

Avoid having only one replica on either side of a slow network link. If a replica is separated from all other replicas by a slow network link and that replica fails, clients of the replica will fail over to a replica on the other side of the slow network link. Their directory services may slow down markedly.

You should also have at least one replica at the same location as the master to allow the replica to act as a backup for the master. If the master server has a catastrophic failure, a replica can be promoted to master and quickly take its place.

Ensuring Security

Remember that Open Directory stores authentication data. This authentication data includes the Open Directory Password Server database and the Kerberos database, which is extraordinarily sensitive. Therefore, you need to make sure that an Open Directory master and all Open Directory replicas are secure by doing the following:

▶   Keep the server in a physically secure location.

▶   Always leave the server logged out.

▶   Secure the media you use to back up an Open Directory server.

▶   If possible, do not use a server that is an Open Directory master or replica to provide any other services. If you can't dedicate servers to be an Open Directory master and replicas, at least minimize the number of other services they provide. One of the other services could have a security breach that allows someone inadvertent access to the Kerberos or Open Directory Password Server databases. Dedicating servers to providing Open Directory services is an optimal practice but is not required.

▶   Set up Internet Protocol (IP) firewall service to block all ports except those used for directory, authentication, and administration protocols.

Open Directory Password Server uses ports 106 and 3659. The Kerberos KDC uses TCP/UDP port 88; TCP/UDP port 749 is used for Kerberos administration. The shared LDAP directory uses TCP port 389 for an ordinary connection and TCP port 636 for a Secure Sockets Layer (SSL) connection.

While creating an Open Directory replica, port 22 must be open between the master and prospective replica. This is the port used for Secure Shell Protocol (SSH) data transfer, which is used to transfer a complete, up-to-date copy of the LDAP database. After the initial setup of the replica, only the LDAP port (389 or 636) is used for replication.

Workgroup Manager uses TCP ports 311 and 625. Server Admin uses TCP port 311. SMB/CIFS uses TCP/UDP ports 137, 138, 139, and 445.

What You've Learned

▶   Directory services allow multiple processes to access common system data, such as user information.

▶   Data can be stored on a network server, allowing multiple computers to access the same data.

▶   With proper configuration, the same user account can be used to log into multiple computers on the network, rather than tying the user to a single computer.

▶   User records are the most frequently used record type and store information to uniquely identify a user.

▶   Group records define one or more users that should share certain system permissions.

▶ If a replica is separated from all other replicas by a slow network link and that replica fails, clients of the replica will fail over to a replica on the other side of the slow network link.

▶ You can increase the size of the BerkeleyDB cache to improve performance of the database.

▶ The Kerberos KDC uses TCP/UDP port 88; TCP/UDP port 749 is used for Kerberos administration.

References

Administration Guides

"Mac OS X Open Directory Administration": http://images.apple.com/server/pdfs/Open_Directory_v10.4.pdf

"Mac OS X Server Command-Line Administration": http://images.apple.com/server/pdfs/Command_Line_v10.4.pdf

Lesson Review

1. When deploying replicas, why should you set up at least two replicas at remote locations connected by a slow network connection?

2. Why should you set up a replica at the same location as master server?

3. Why should you avoid running other services, such as file services, on the same server that provides directory services?

Answers

1. Having a second replica provides a local (to the remote location) backup directory data source, should the first replica fail. Otherwise, computers at the remote location would be forced to connect over the slow network connection to retrieve directory data from the master or another replica.

2. If the master server should have a hardware failure, the replica can quickly be promoted to replace the master server.

3. The more services you run on the directory server, the greater the likelihood of a security breach. Also, running additional services on the same server decreases the performance of the directory server.

Part 2 Security Administration

12

Time   This lesson takes approximately 1 hour to complete.

Goals   Understand the purpose of the components of the Mac OS X security
architecture

Learn the Apple authorization philosophy

Identify the components of the security process

Produce an IT security policy document

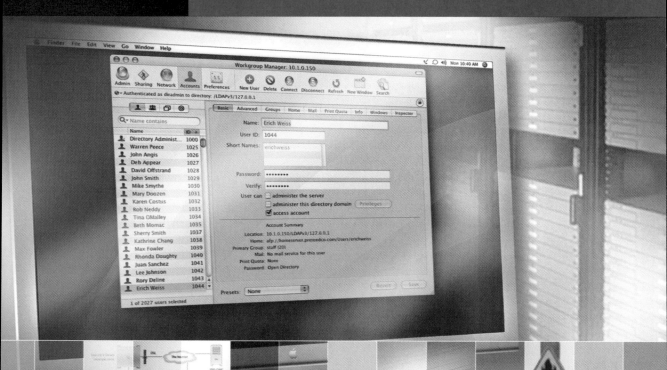

Lesson **12**

Mac OS X Security Overview

Security has never been a more important consideration when selecting a computer platform. Whether you're a home user with a broadband Internet connection, a professional with a mobile computer, or an IT manager with thousands of networked systems, you must safeguard the confidentiality of information and the integrity of your computers.

In Part 2: "Security Administration," you'll learn how to do just that. The lessons in this section will teach how to use the Apple security strategy, implementing the options that provide the best balance between protection and functionality. Beginning with this lesson on the underlying Common Data Security Architecture (CDSA), you will gain an understanding of the technical foundation of Mac OS X security features. Yet just as important is understanding and implementing appropriate security policies for your environment. This begins with a thorough risk analysis of your computers and data, assessing the likelihood and potential severity of individual threats and weighing them against the business costs and loss of productivity often introduced by highly protected computer systems.

With Mac OS X, Apple has implemented a security strategy that is central to the design of the operating system, ensuring that your Mac is safe and secure. Throughout the next ten lessons, you will learn all about that strategy, including the following elements:

▶   Open-source foundation: Using open-source methodology makes Mac OS X a more robust, secure operating system, as its core components have been subjected to peer review for decades. Problems can be immediately identified and fixed by Apple and the larger open-source community.

▶   Secure default settings: When you take a Mac out of the box, it is already configured in the most secure form—so you don't have to be a security expert to set it up. These secure settings make it very difficult for malicious software to infect your system.

▶   Modern security architecture: Mac OS X includes state-of-the-art, standards-based technologies that enable Apple and third-party developers to build secure software for the Mac. These technologies support all aspects of system, data, and networking security required by today's applications.

▶   Innovative security applications: Mac OS X includes features that take the worry out of using a computer: FileVault protects your documents using strong encryption, an integrated VPN client gives you secure access to networks over the Internet, and a powerful firewall secures your home network.

▶   Rapid response: Because the security of your system is so important, Apple responds rapidly to provide patches and updates. Apple works with worldwide partners, including the Computer Emergency Response Team (CERT), to notify users of any potential threats. Should vulnerabilities be discovered, the built-in Software Update tool automatically notifies users of security updates, which are made available for easy download and installation.

Understanding Common Data Security Architecture

Mac OS X security services are built on CDSA, with support for cryptography, certificate management, trust policy management, and key recovery. This layered security infrastructure makes it easy for Apple and Mac OS X developers to integrate leading-edge security features, such as authentication and encryption, into their applications.

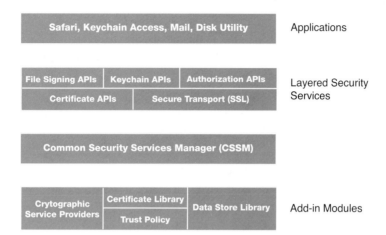

By using CDSA, Apple takes advantage of a well proven, flexible, extensible security architecture. That is in keeping with the open-source nature of the Darwin layer of Mac OS X. Apple then builds user-friendly front-end applications, such as Disk Utility and Keychain Access, that help the average user take advantage of the power of this cryptographic services toolkit. Anything in Mac OS X that is doing cryptography is doing it through the CDSA application programming interfaces (APIs).

CDSA was originally developed by Intel, in cooperation with other leading companies including Hewlett-Packard, IBM, JP Morgan, Motorola, Netscape, Trusted Information Systems, and Shell Companies. Apple has also been a major contributor to the standard and has greatly extended the functionality of CDSA.

Add-in Modules

The CDSA architecture uses plug-ins to allow additional services to be supported. The different types of plug-ins are Cryptographic Service Providers (CSPs), Data Library Modules (DLs), Certificate Library Modules (CLs), and Trust Policy Modules. To support Pretty Good Privacy (PGP) certificates, for example, a developer could write CL and TP Modules that know how to parse PGP certificates and the trust policies associated with them. The keychain is implemented as a combination CSP/DL. These are described in more detail in the CDSA reference.

Layered Services

Layered Services is the Apple terminology for convenience APIs built on top of the basic CDSA functionality. For example, most developers may have to save a password securely, and can do this through two APIs. Direct calls to CDSA might require thousands of lines of code. Apple chose to make security easy for third-party (and internal) developers as well, since most are not security experts. In addition, this gives the user a common experience.

Understanding Mac OS X Authorization Philosophy

Due to the mach microkernel, you will see some different behavior from standard UNIX, such as it is not separated from the standard UNIX kernel. You can get some things out of the system going the mach route that you wouldn't be able to get from a standard UNIX system. For example, there are ways to get root privilege by going through the mach passport facilities.

Authorization API

In this case the focus in on authorization, not capability (authentication), which is concerned only about whether to allow a privileged operation to proceed. The /etc/authorization file is where an administrator can set authorization rules.

The authorization APIs are extensible with plug-ins and can be two-way with Pluggable Authentication Modules (PAMs). Using this method, the applications never need to present anything unusual to the user. They all use these APIs to talk to the SecurityServer daemon, so the applications never see the administrator password. Finally the authorization APIs enable you to do single sign-on and selective single sign-on. That's why in certain instances you don't have to type your admin password if you have already done so in the last 5 minutes.

Keychains

Whether you know it or not, as a Mac OS X user you have at least one keychain, because the system makes one for you when you log in for the first time. The keychain is a file in your home folder where you can put secret information such as passwords, private and public keys, and sensitive notes. This information is encrypted and protected with CDSA access control lists (ACLs), and is stored in a database with extensible schemas. A system daemon, SecurityServer, manages the data in a secured memory space.

Administrative User Concepts

Mac OS X allows for three types of user accounts: standard user, administrator, and system administrator (root).

Standard Users

Standard, or nonadmin, users can use a basic set of applications and tools. They are limited to making configuration changes that affect only their own accounts, such as what applications and files are opened when the user logs in and what picture is displayed as the user's background pattern. A standard user cannot make changes to any systemwide settings, such as the Network, Date & Time, Sharing, Accounts, Security, Energy Saver, Startup Disk, or Print & Fax panes of System Preferences. A standard user is also restricted from using Directory Access and NetInfo Manager to change configurations.

If a standard user attempts to make a systemwide modification, the user will need to provide the user name and password of an admin user before the changes can be made.

Administrator

An administrator, or admin user, has basic use of the tools used to configure and customize Mac OS X. (The initial local account configured in Setup Assistant is an admin user.)

One of the most powerful attributes of an administrator is that this user type can change settings on any of the System Preferences panes. An administrator can make changes using certain utilities, such as NetInfo Manager, and can also install applications and resources that all users on the system can use.

System Administrator

A system administrator, also called superuser or root, has read/write access to all settings and files on the system, including hidden system files that a regular administrator user cannot modify.

By default, system administrator is disabled. The user exists, but you can't log in using that account. Mac OS X was configured this way to help secure the computer and avert unintentional deletion of important files and folders. System administrator can be enabled using NetInfo Manager, single-user mode, or the command line. When you view items owned by system administrator in the Finder, in the Info window, and with ls at the command line, you will see the owner as "system." When you view processes owned by system administrator in Activity Monitor, you will see the owner as "root."

Certificate and Trust Management

Mac OS X also embraces the X509 certificates and includes several of them by default. Additional certificates are added to the system keychain files. A default set of X509 anchors are also included and accessible by the keychain or by using the certtool and/or the security command-line tools.

Open Directory Authorization

Kerberos provides secure authentication services using a ticket system, allowing for a seamless end-user experience. Also, Kerberos authentication works cross-platform, meaning that your Mac OS X computers can use existing Active Directory Kerberos services, even if they are served from another platform. There are three main players in a complete Kerberos transaction: the user, the service that the user is interested in, and the key distribution center (KDC). The KDC is responsible for mediating between the user and the service, creating and routing secure tickets, and generally supplying the authentication mechanism.

Kerberos introduces the notion of a realm, which is a specific database or authentication domain. Each realm contains the authentication information for users and services. The users and services are called *Kerberos principals.*

For a service to take advantage of Kerberos, it must be *kerberized,* which means that it can defer authentication of its users to a KDC. Mac OS X Server not only provides a KDC when configured to host a shared Lightweight Directory Access Protocol (LDAP) directory, but it also provides a kerberized login window, Hypertext Transfer Protocol (HTTP), Mail, File Transfer Protocol (FTP), Apple Filing Protocol (AFP), virtual private network (VPN), XGrid, and Secure Shell Protocol (SSH) services.

The default edu.mit.Kerberos file does not include logging parameters. If the logging parameters are added, the log filenames are arbitrary and the files have to be manually created.

When a user account in the LDAP directory is configured to use the Open Directory password type (in Workgroup Manager), both the user account and the authentication server on the KDC hold a common user key. Keys are used to encrypt and decrypt any messages sent over the network.

NOTE ▶ The Kerberos implementation in Mac OS X is based on Kerberos version 5.

Developing an IT Security Risk Analysis

Security professionals recognize that the more secure a system is, the less functional it is likely to be. Security features often get in the way of quickly getting a task done, and strict policies can often have the opposite detrimental effect of causing users to seek ways to *bypass* security.

Security is an ongoing process, not an end product. Just like your immune system, your security process can never rest completely. Although you may face periods when new attacks are of little threat, you can never relax completely because you cannot predict when the next assault will occur or when a user will accidentally open up a previously closed hole.

The security process consists of the following steps:

1. Analyze your risks.

    Define how vulnerable your system is to attacks by assessing the threat level and the user's security skills.

2. Assess risk versus cost.

    Security is a compromise between an acceptable level of security and its associated cost. More security translates into more cost and vice versa.

3. Establish policies.

    Once you have gathered the necessary information in the previous two steps, write a security policy. This will be a balancing act. The most convenient access will often be the least secure. A large part of this effort will be defining the various levels of access that you want to allow and which users should be permitted into each level.

    Another large part of this effort will be user education. You'll have to develop a strategy for teaching users what they can do, what they can't do, and why certain things are not permitted. (Getting higher-level management backing on these issues is generally helpful.)

    Also important in the balance between security and convenience is *your own* convenience. You need to ensure that you are not making system administration so difficult that you are loathe to undertake the necessary tasks.

4. Implement solutions.

    Once policies are in place, the next step is to implement them. Set up the servers, firewalls, and user accounts. Get the users on your network using the servers.

5. Monitor the network.

   Security is an ongoing process. You must monitor your network constantly to ensure that your policies are effective and that someone hasn't inadvertently (or even deliberately) breached your security.

6. Formulate a response.

   You must develop a plan of action in advance for responding to a breach of security, a lack of conformance to policies and guidelines, or a change in user needs (for example, your company grows from 15 users to 200). You might have to repeat the entire cycle or make implementation changes and go back to monitoring.

The full cycle doesn't need to be completed each time you have a problem, but you should evaluate the full security picture with the full cycle in mind.

Assessing Threat Level

The first step in the problem space of the security process is to define vulnerabilities. To do so, you must assess threat level and user skills, which help determine the security needs of your organization.

The threat that has been popularized by mainstream media is that of an outside attacker accessing private information using a network connection. This is perhaps the least of the threats facing you in terms of security from the client side.

A more insidious attack is what is known as *social engineering,* which relies on people giving out information that they shouldn't. Someone may call a user claiming to be from the help desk in your organization and saying that they need to reset passwords on a system.

A more mundane attack is simple physical theft. In addition to the loss of equipment, you and your users face significant downtime while you replace equipment and figure out how to replace lost data. Even worse is a case where confidential data falls into the hands of your competitors.

An attacker may take advantage of multiple avenues. For instance, an attacker may use social engineering to discover a password, then steal a portable computer or security token to gain access to information.

Other forms of attack are viruses and Trojan horses. These pieces of code are the subtlest of the threats, infecting mail, hard drives, and networks. The effect of these attacks can range from inconvenient to devastating.

Perhaps the most dangerous and common threat comes from insiders who already have access to your information. Keeping this threat under control is beyond the scope of this book, but the key to lessening it is careful use of permissions.

Also when assessing threat level, try to assess how determined an attacker might be. For example, if you have a high-profile website that provides access to classified information that is sought by adversaries, it is highly likely that an attacker will try every possible way to get to the information, resulting in a high threat level.

Defining User Skills and Needs

Assess who needs to use a particular resource. What will users do to circumvent the security if it is too inconvenient? Examples of other issues to consider are that users may:

► Not use the service at all, which wastes money and time

► Not log out of the system, so password policy may be moot

► Leave passwords out in plain view

► Copy files to insecure areas

As mentioned, security is a compromise between how much risk you're willing to take and how much expense you're willing to incur. To assess risk versus cost, you must:

► Consider examples of compromise based on your experience.

► Assess user needs to help you determine how many of them you should address to maintain an appropriate level of security and the associated cost. Following are some examples:

  • Users access the network from outside the firewall using VPN.

  • Users can take their computers, which might contain sensitive information, with them wherever they go.

  • Users can share computers with other users.

▶ Assess organizational needs. Like user needs, an organization's computing and security needs help you determine where to draw the line between risk and cost. Following are some examples of organizational needs that affect the balance between security and cost:

- Back up computers daily.

- Monitor logs daily.

- Check computers for viruses on a regular basis.

▶ Perform regular security audits to evaluate the current state of security in your organization and determine how best to improve it.

Establishing Policies

When establishing policies, your challenge is to balance convenient user access to services with organizational security needs. An absolutely secure computer is one that is turned off, unplugged, and locked in a bank vault, but it is not very convenient. A computer placed in a public library with no individual user accounts is convenient for whomever comes into the library, but it is not very secure.

Providing a service always opens a potential breach in security. Think of a computer as a blank wall—every service is an additional gate through the wall. Even if the gate is well protected, it's still not as strong as a solid section of the wall.

Depending on the level of threat that your installation faces and the sophistication of your users, you will need to create a security policy that can keep your systems safe while still allowing for sufficient access.

Remember that convenience also includes the ease of system administration tasks. If you make system administration procedures too burdensome, someone will take a shortcut at some point that will potentially compromise security.

Keep in mind the phrase "obscurity is not security." You cannot and should not rely solely on keeping the configuration of your computer systems secret. Apart from the fact that there are many techniques available to probe your systems, some of the greatest threats to security come from colleagues who must know your systems because of job function and responsibility.

Documenting Policies

One of the most important things you can do is write down your security policy. This creates clear expectations for users, system administrators, and management. The policy should be written plainly, avoiding jargon. Following are some examples of the information it should contain:

▶ Allowable uses

▶ Resource access policy and limits

▶ Monitoring policy

▶ Anticipated threats and relative risks

▶ Implemented defenses against anticipated threats

▶ Best practices

▶ Escalation procedures

▶ Checklist for follow-up audit after an exploit

In addition, you should document threats that you have examined but consider of such low probability that they are not worth defending against, threats that are too costly to defend against, or threats that are possible but require the cooperation of other agencies, such as your Internet service provider, to develop a proper defense.

Writing down this information serves two very important purposes:

▶ You are forced to be clear and consistent with your thinking about security.

▶ Your written policy is an invaluable tool when it comes to the hardest part of security—educating your users.

Implementing Solutions: Creating a Secure System

Once you have defined policies, you move from the problem space to the solution space. This is where you implement policies through system architecture and design:

▶ Configure hardware: Set up hardware firewalls, servers, and computers to comply with the policies you have defined for your organization. This includes setting firmware passwords and physical security of equipment.

▶ Configure software: Server software, firewalls, and user accounts must be configured for security. The default configuration for Mac OS X leaves services off; an administrator must enable them. This means that at the beginning, there are no known holes in the Mac OS X security posture. Opening a hole requires an action by someone who should be knowledgeable about the operating system.

In addition, unlike older versions of Mac OS, Mac OS X is a true UNIX-based multiuser system. This means that access privileges are always enforced and cannot be bypassed except by the root user. It also means that, unlike AppleShare IP, the access privileges are available at the file level as well as the folder level, which enables you to configure privileges to allow a finer degree of access control.

▶ Define processes: Users and administrators need processes to follow when using computing resources. For example, you can define a process that administrators follow to report and respond to a breach of security.

Monitoring the Network

After implementing the solutions, you need to monitor computers and network activity in your organization to detect any attempt or actual breach of security (inadvertent or deliberate).

Examples of monitoring include:

▶ Using Console or Terminal to monitor logs

▶ Using virus-detection software to check systems for viruses

▶ Using packet sniffers such as tcpdump and Ethereal to monitor network traffic

Formulating a Security-Breach Response

When monitoring computers and network activity, you might detect or be alerted to an actual or attempted breach of security. You need to formulate an action plan that will enable you to respond to the potential threat based on the processes that you have in place.

The work involved in the formulation of the response will vary with the nature of the alert. If the alert is minor, you may not need to adjust your policies, but rather tighten your implementation of the policies or solutions and enter the monitoring phase again. If the alert is major, your threat level may have increased enough to warrant redefining vulnerabilities and starting the security process again from the beginning. In all cases, the alert should be documented and a follow-up audit should take place as part of the monitoring process to ensure that the response succeeded in addressing the issue.

In reality, formulation can lead you back to any point in the security process, keeping the process flowing and dynamic. This is good, as security is an ongoing and ever-changing challenge. There will always be attackers pushing the security envelope. The key to keeping them at bay is keeping your security process active and flexible.

What You've Learned

▶ Security is a process that should be continually reviewed.

▶ Organizations should consider the tradeoff between security and convenience when designing a security policy.

▶ User education is critical for a secure environment.

▶ Security audits enable you to monitor security environments in order to revise security policies as needed.

References

URLs

The Open Group, "Common Security: CDSA and CSSM, Version 2": www.opengroup.org/publications/catalog/c914.htm

Lesson Review

1. Mac OS X security services are built on what architecture?

2. What are the three user types in Mac OS X?

3. What is the single sign-on architecture used by Mac OS X?

Answers

1. Common Data Security Architecture (CDSA)

2. Standard user, administrative user, and system administrator (root)

3. Kerberos

13

Time   This lesson takes approximately 2 hours to complete.

Goals   Understand the four layers of Mac OS X local security

Set Open Firmware restrictions

Create secure Mac OS X installations

Use Disk Utility effectively

Understand Mac OS 9 (Classic) and security

Use the firewall in Mac OS X

Use FileVault

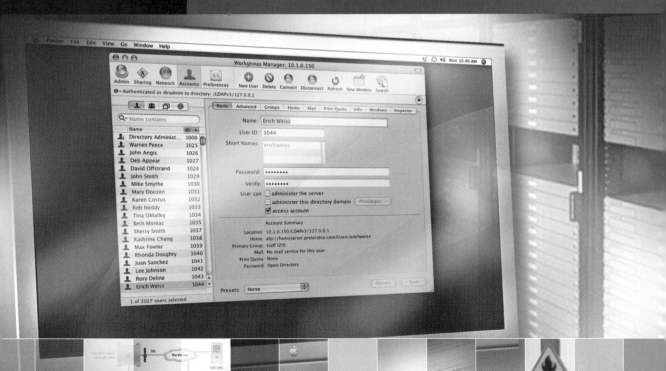

Lesson 13
Securing the Local System

The Mac OS X local security model has four layers. The layers are not independent; an attacker can use a weakness in one layer to bypass the protections provided by some or all of the other layers. So setting up a secure Mac OS X computer requires that all four be locked down properly. The four layers in the Mac OS X security model are:

▶ Physical security: An attacker who has physical access to the computer can bypass any firmware- or OS-based protection in any of the other layers.

▶ Open Firmware security: Open Firmware controls the boot process; unless this is secured (with an Open Firmware password), an attacker can use alternate boot modes to bypass normal access controls.

▶ Password-based user authentication: If attackers can steal or guess passwords, they can gain access by impersonating other users. (Some third-party solutions can augment this with pass-card or biometric authentication.)

▶ User account–based access controls: Access controls such as file permissions and administrative access regulate what a user can do. If these are set inappropriately, users may not only be able to access files they should be locked out of, but they may also reset other users' passwords or modify Open Firmware security settings.

If all four layers are secured, then the local system can be considered secure. The only exception to this rule is data security via encryption, such as that provided by the Mac OS X Keychain, FileVault, and encrypted disk image features. When securing all four layers is not practical (as with a PowerBook, where physical security is difficult), encryption may be the only option to reliably protect user data.

Ensuring Physical Security

If an attacker gains physical control of a computer, he can bypass any firmware- or OS-based security (such as an Open Firmware password, a login password, file permissions, and so on). With the actual hardware in hand, an attacker can remove the hard drive and attach it to another computer, then read or change any file on the drive. Less drastic attacks include changing the computer's RAM configuration and then resetting parameter RAM (PRAM), which removes the Open Firmware password.

To prevent this, Macintosh towers and minis have lock attachment points that control access to the hard drive and memory slots as well as prevent theft of the entire computer:

▶   In the Power Mac G5, the attachment point consists of a foldout padlock loop on the back panel. When a padlock or cable is connected to this loop, it prevents the access latch from being opened.

▶   In the Power Mac G4, a pullout padlock point on the back panel physically secures the hardware. When held out by a padlock or cable, the point locks the computer's side panel in a closed position.

▶   In the Macintosh mini and the iMac G5, installing a latch in the security slot in the back panel locks the computer's top and bottom cases together.

Physically locking the internals of many other Mac models is not possible. In many cases, you can gain some measure of protection by modifying the enclosure, or replacing the case screws with "security" screws.

Disconnecting or removing alternate boot devices (FireWire devices and CD drives, for example) will also limit an attacker's opportunities to take control of an incompletely secured computer. However, these measures should not be considered sufficient to protect critical computers and information.

If real data security is required when good physical security is not possible—particularly with PowerBook and iBook models, which have a high risk of theft or other loss—using data encryption (such as FileVault) in addition to the normal OS-based security is strongly recommended.

Implementing Open Firmware Security

The Open Firmware built into Macintosh computers supports a variety of startup options, many of which allow bypassing Mac OS X:

▶ Using FireWire Target Disk Mode: By pressing the T key as the computer starts up, an attacker can turn a computer into the equivalent of a FireWire hard drive. By plugging it into a computer under her control, the attacker can read or modify any file on the hard drive. The computer will display a moving icon (shown below) when it is in FireWire Target Disk Mode.

▶ Booting from other disks or partitions: By pressing the Option key at startup, an attacker can use Open Firmware's Startup Manager to select an alternate boot device such as a FireWire drive. If the attacker knows an administrator user name and password for that alternate boot device, she can take control of a computer booted from that device. If Mac OS 9 is installed on a separate partition, then booting from the Mac OS 9 partition allows total access to the Mac OS X partition.

▶ Booting from an installer CD: By pressing the C key at startup, an attacker can boot a computer from an installer CD and use its Reset Password option to change the passwords of accounts on any Mac OS X disk or partition.

▶ Booting from a NetBoot server: By pressing the N key at startup, an attacker can boot a computer from a NetBoot server. This may not be problem if you control the NetBoot server, but if the attacker provides his or her own NetBoot server, or if the default NetBoot image is actually a NetInstall or NetRestore image (which automatically log in to the root account), the attacker can gain control of the computer.

▶ Using Open Firmware command mode: By pressing Command-Option-O-F at startup, an attacker can enter Open Firmware mode and change boot parameters—enabling, for example, a startup from an alternate device.

▶ Booting in single-user mode: By pressing Command-S at startup, the attacker can halt the Mac OS X boot process before starting the minimum pieces of the operating system and gain access to a command-line interface with root access to the computer.

▶ Booting off any other device than the internal disk: By pressing Command-Option-Shift-Delete at startup, the attacker can force a bypass of the selected startup disk and boot off of another device.

Using an Open Firmware Password

To prevent attackers from selecting any of these alternate boot modes, you should enable an Open Firmware password. The easiest way to do this is with the Apple Open Firmware Password utility, provided on the Mac OS X version 10.4 (v10.4) installer DVD in the /Applications/Utilities folder.

The Open Firmware password feature is supported only by Open Firmware version 4.1.7 and later. You may need to update some older Macintosh models' firmware to use this feature. To determine which version of Open Firmware is installed on a computer, open the System Profiler located in /Applications/Utilities and click the Hardware option under the Contents pane. The BootROM version, which is also the computer's Open Firmware version, is displayed in the Hardware Overview window.

NOTE ▶ A list of the latest firmware updates for various models is available at http://docs.info.apple.com/article.html?artnum=86117. For some older Mac models, you may need to perform updates under Mac OS 9.

The following Apple computers can use the Open Firmware Password application:

- ▶ iBook: all models
- ▶ iMac G3: Slot Loading and later models
- ▶ iMac G4: all models
- ▶ iMac G5: all models
- ▶ eMac: all models
- ▶ PowerBook G3: FireWire model only
- ▶ PowerBook G4: all models
- ▶ Power Mac G4: AGP Graphics and later models
- ▶ Power Mac G4 Cube
- ▶ Power Mac G5: all models

When an Open Firmware password is enabled, it blocks the following boot modes by displaying a lock with an entry box for the Open Firmware password:

- ▶ CD-ROM (C key)
- ▶ NetBoot (N key)
- ▶ Target disk (T key)
- ▶ Verbose boot (Command-V)
- ▶ Single-user boot (Command-S)
- ▶ PRAM reset (Command-Option-P-R)
- ▶ Boot from any other device except the selected internal disk (Command-Option-Shift-Delete)

NOTE ▶ Target Disk Mode, NetBoot, and CD-ROMs may still be selected in the Startup Disk preferences pane; the Open Firmware password prevents them from being selected only at boot time.

Open Firmware mode also restricts the following modes, by requiring that the password be provided to use them:

▶ Startup Manager (Option key)

▶ Open Firmware (Command-Option-O-F)

Choosing an Open Firmware Password

Open Firmware does not support international or accented characters in passwords, so you must choose a password consisting only of the printing ASCII characters (character values 32 through 126). Also, to avoid a known-password issue, do not use the capital letter U in an Open Firmware password. Following are the allowed characters:

```
!"#$%&'()*+,-./0123456789:;<=>?
@ABCDEFGHIJKLMNOPQRSTVWXYZ[\]^_
'abcdefghijklmnopqrstuvwxyz{|}~
```

Be aware that Open Firmware stores its password in recoverable form. This means that if an attacker gains root access to a computer by other means, he can find out what the Open Firmware password is. For example, there are certain applications that will routinely collect the Open Firmware password from any computer on which they are installed. If multiple computers share the same Open Firmware password, the attacker can use that password to gain control of other computers with the same password.

Ideally, each computer should be given a unique password to prevent such cross-computer attacks. If completely individual passwords are impractical, at least split your computers into groups to limit the exposure. In particular, low-security computers (such as laptops and lab/general-access computers) should never be assigned the same Open Firmware password as high-security computers. Also, you should not use the Open Firmware password in any other context, such as a login password.

TIP ▶ You can use the command-line utility nvram to control firmware settings. Just type *man nvram* at the command line to see the arguments. To see a better set of options, type *nvram -p*.

Disabling an Open Firmware Password

You may find that you need to disable an Open Firmware password, either temporarily or permanently, to perform operations like installing a new version of Mac OS X from DVD. There are a number of ways to accomplish this:

▶ Run the Open Firmware Password utility again and deselect the "Require password" checkbox.

   This method requires that you authenticate as an administrator on the computer.

▶ Enter Open Firmware command mode (by pressing Command-Option-O-F during the boot process) and enter the following commands:

   setenv security-mode none

   setenv security-password

   reset-all

   This method requires that you know the current Open Firmware password. (You'll be prompted for it after you enter the first command.)

▶ Reset the computer's nonvolatile RAM (NVRAM, or PRAM) by changing its physical memory size (by adding or removing a DIMM) and then starting the system while pressing Command-Option-P-R until the system speaker has chimed four times. All PRAM settings (including the Open Firmware password) will be returned to factory defaults.

   This method requires that you have access to the computer's internals to change its RAM configuration.

Creating a Secure Mac OS X Installation

Securing Mac OS X begins with the initial setup of the computer, including the drive format and operating-system installation. Trying to go back and correct problems with the initial configuration can be difficult or even impossible, so it's important to plan out what you're going to do.

Considering Preinstallation Issues

Before installing Mac OS X, you should consider how the computer's hard drives will be formatted and partitioned. Several formatting and partitioning options have potential security implications.

Booting With Mac OS 9 Drivers

Each hard drive can optionally be formatted with Mac OS 9 drivers. Since the possibility of booting into Mac OS 9 is generally a security risk in a Mac OS X environment, you should omit this option whenever possible.

Macintoshes can ship with or without preinstalled Mac OS 9 drivers. If you have any doubt about the presence of Mac OS 9 drivers, open Disk Utility and click the Info button to check.

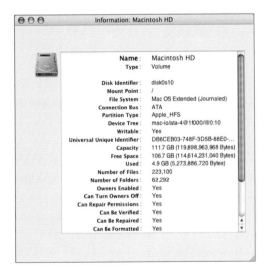

If the Mac OS 9 drivers are present, the only way to fully remove them is to erase or repartition the entire hard drive.

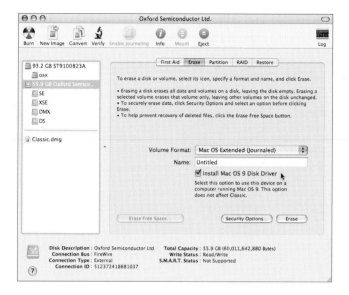

Note that the checkbox for installing Mac OS 9 drivers is available only when erasing an entire disk, not when erasing just a partition (even if it's the only partition on the disk). The presence or absence of a driver will not change per partition.

Disabling File Permissions

File permissions can be disabled on Mac OS Extended format (HFS Plus) volumes other than the boot volume.

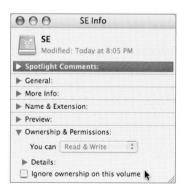

Disabling (or enabling) permissions requires administrator user access, but once permissions are disabled, all users will have the equivalent of owner access to all files on the volume. If you can't count on your administrators to avoid this, you can format additional volumes in Mac OS Standard format (hierarchical file system, or HFS) rather than Mac OS Extended format (which could lead to compatibility problems, especially with older Mac OS programs). Or you can periodically run the following CLI commands to audit the volume database:

```
sh
for V in /Volumes/*; do vsdbutil -c "$V"; done
exit
```

NOTE ▶ If you use sh or bash as your shell, the sh and exit commands can be skipped. If you don't know which shell you use, leave them in; they will not hurt anything.

If you see any local volumes listed as "disabled," you may have a problem.

Retaining Mac OS 9 Files

If the hard drive previously has been used with Mac OS 9 and contains files that need to be retained, consider copying the files temporarily to another disk, erasing the drive, and then copying the files back after installation. Files that Mac OS 9 created do not have ownership and permissions associated with them, and are readable by any user on the system. When the files are copied back under Mac OS X, they have ownership and permissions assigned based on the user who copied them.

Erasing Disks

When erasing a disk that has had important data stored on it, use one of the secure erasure features available in Disk Utility and the diskutil command-line tool, discussed in the next section.

By default, erasing a disk or volume does not actually erase the data that had been stored in files on the disk—it simply removes the catalog information that specified which files existed and which blocks of data belonged to those files. Even though the disk will appear blank after such an erasure, a disk editor or data recovery program may still be able to recover files from the disk.

If a disk or volume cannot be erased, it is a good idea to erase the free blocks on it (those not currently containing live files), as the free blocks will usually contain data from previously deleted files. You can do this with either Disk Utility or the diskutil command-line tool.

Choosing Secure Installation Options

There are two significant sets of choices in the process of installing Mac OS X v10.4: installation type and optional installation packages. Both sets of choices have security implications.

Selecting Installation Type

When the installer reaches the Select a Destination screen (which enables you to choose which volume to install on), there is an innocent-looking button labeled Options near the bottom of the screen. Depending on which (if any) operating system is already installed on the volume you select, you will be allowed to choose from the applicable installation types:

▶ Install: Available if there is no previous operating system to upgrade or replace. This option performs a from-scratch installation of Mac OS X v10.4. If you've already performed a secure erase of the volume (as recommended above), or if the volume contains documents that should be preserved, this is the preferred option.

▶ Upgrade: Available if there is an older operating system on the volume. This option merges the Mac OS X v10.4 into the older system. Since it is possible that some vestiges of the old version of Mac OS X may remain, as may older configuration settings that may no longer be optimal, you should avoid this option whenever possible. For example, user accounts created under Mac OS X v10.2 and earlier have their hashed passwords stored in the local NetInfo database, which is publicly readable. Accounts inherited from Mac OS X v10.2 will retain this password mode until the next time the password is changed.

> **NOTE** ▶ This warning does not apply to upgrading Mac OS 9 to Mac OS X. Because the two operating systems work very differently, Mac OS X will not reuse components from Mac OS 9. It will, however, use Mac OS 9 for the Classic compatibility environment. This has its own set of security implications, discussed later in this chapter.

▶ Archive and Install: Available if there is an operating system on the volume. This option moves parts of the old operating system to inactive locations, and replaces them with a relatively clean installation of the new operating system. This option is less likely to cause trouble than the upgrade option, but still has the potential to leave obsolete components and settings active (especially if the Preserve Users and Network Settings option is enabled).

▶ Erase and Install: Always available. This option is almost always the best way to ensure a clean installation of Mac OS X with no inherited glitches. The only exception is if a secure erasure has already been performed on the volume, in which case erasing it again is redundant.

Choosing Package Customization

The next screen will, by default, offer to perform an Easy Install on the selected volume. Normally you will want to click the Customize button so you can customize which optional system components will be installed. For Mac OS X v10.4.0, the only customizable components are print-driver collections, additional fonts, a variety of language localizations, and the X11 windowing system. The first three do not have significant security implications (although trimming them down to only the needed components is a good idea). X11, on the other hand, allows remote network access of some POSIX-layer programs. While you can configure X11 for a good level of security, doing so is beyond the scope of this book. Unless you know how to secure X11, you should not install the X11 component.

NOTE ▶ The default Easy Install includes all printers, fonts, and languages, but not the X11 component. As far as security is concerned, this is an acceptable combination, so customization is not necessary.

Using the Setup Assistant

After the installation completes, the computer will reboot and the Setup Assistant will
run to perform basic setup of the computer. For the most part you can simply follow the
prompts here, but there are a few security pitfalls that should be avoided:

▶   At the Do You Already Own a Mac? screen, you can opt to transfer information
    (documents, programs, user accounts, and system settings) from another volume
    or computer. This is a possible security risk, as you may not know exactly what is
    being transferred. As with performing an Archive and Install, it's possible to inherit
    a problem from the old configuration without realizing it.

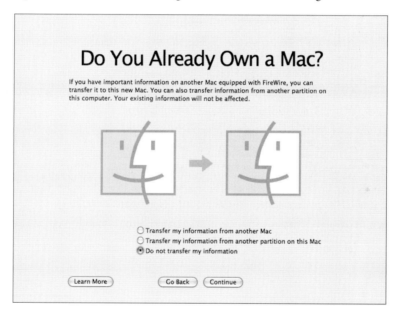

▶ At the Registration Information screen, you are asked to enter personal information for the computer's owner/user. This information will be submitted to Apple and possibly other companies.

Registration Information

Please enter your personal information. This information is used to register your Apple product. It's also used to create your user name and it will be stored in the Address Book as your personal contact information.

First Name

Last Name

Address

Email Address (if you have one)

City

Area Code   Phone Number

State

Zip Code

Company/School

Select

To learn how Apple safeguards your personal information, please review the Apple Customer Privacy Policy.

The warranty for your Apple product does not require you to register the product.

(Privacy Policy)   (Go Back) (Continue)

If you don't want to give away unnecessary information about your users, press Command-Q and you will be given the option to skip the registration and marketing screens.

You have not finished setting up Mac OS X.

Before you can use Mac OS X, you must create your login account. Click Skip to create your account and skip the remaining registration and setup process.

(Skip)   (Shut Down)   (Cancel)

▶ At the Create Your Account screen, you're asked to set up the initial local administrator account. Changing the account's short name later is not easy, so it's important to choose it right the first time. Since it is best to use a nonadministrator user account for day-to-day operation, this account should not be used as the primary user account on the computer, nor should it be named for the computer's primary user. Instead, create a separate (nonadministrator user) account for the primary user later.

Create Your Account

Every person who uses this computer can have a user account with their own settings and a place to keep their documents secure.

Set up your user account now. You can add accounts for others later.

Name:

Short Name:

This will be used as the name for your home folder and cannot be changed.

Password:

Verify:

Password Hint:
(optional)

Enter a word or phrase to help you remember your password.

Go Back   Continue

▶   When naming the initial account, avoid using a generic name like "admin" or "administrator," as these may conflict with other system or network names (such as the built-in "admin" group). If one particular administrator will use the account, combining the administrator's name with "admin" (for example, georgeadmin) is a good choice. If it will be a generic account, something like localadmin is okay.

▶   The initial account setup screen does not give you access to the Password Assistant to help you choose a strong password. If you want to use the Password Assistant, you can use the System Preferences Accounts pane (which does give access to the Password Assistant) to change the password later.

▶   Leave the Password Hint field blank.

▶   After the Setup Assistant finishes, it will place an alias to the Send Registration Assistant in the home folder of the initial administrator user account. If you don't want to submit registration information, simply delete this alias.

Securing Local Accounts

There are four basic categories of accounts available on a Mac OS X computer:

▶ Normal users: In the Mac OS X security model, normal (nonadministrator) users are more or less restricted to their own worlds within their accounts. They have full Finder access to the contents of their own home directories, and are permitted only read-only access to other users' Public folders and write-only access to others' Drop Boxes. They are also permitted read/write access only to items they own that are placed in the /Users/Shared directory and the /tmp directory. In general, normal users are fully subject to the limitations that the operating system and administrators choose to place on them.

▶ Administrator users: Administrator users have the power to control and configure the operating system. Administrator users are still subject to things like file permissions, but they have a variety of override mechanisms that allow them to get around these limitations. Directly or indirectly, administrators have complete control over the computer; as a result, administrative access should be given only to highly trusted users.

▶ Root (also known as System Administrator, System, or the superuser): Quite simply, the root user (there is only one) is not constrained by many of the normal limitations of the Mac OS X security model. For example, root ignores normal file permissions. Because of this, root is extremely dangerous to the computer's integrity. An administrator user can go beyond the normal system constraints, but must go through overrides that help make it clear that something unusual and potentially dangerous is being done. With the root account there are very few warnings (especially on the command line), and deleting something critical takes no more than one typo.

Because it is so dangerous, the root account is disabled by default on Mac OS X. It exists but does not have a password, and thus cannot be logged into directly.

▶ System accounts: These are identities used to keep track of and control various parts of the operating system (like www, used as the identity of the Apache Web server, and sshd, used for the remote login server). They are not full accounts in the sense that they do not have home folders or login passwords. They are used by programs, not by human users.

These system accounts are automatically configured as needed for the software included with Mac OS X. For most purposes, you can safely ignore them.

Many traditional UNIX administrators are used to logging into the root account to perform administrative duties; in Mac OS X this is strongly discouraged. The vast majority of administrative tasks can be performed from a standard administrator user account (or even a nonadministrator account) by using the padlock icon and its analogs to authenticate as an administrator for just the specific actions that require administrator access. If you have enabled the root account and decide later that you want to disable it, open NetInfo Manager and choose Security > Disable root.

Never log in as an Admin user for routine tasks such as checking mail and creating documents. Not only is there potential that you may forget to log out when you leave your desk or allow an intruder easy access to your computer, but viruses run as an administrative user are potentially much more destructive than those run as a normal user. If administrators have two accounts—one with administrator rights and one without—they can perform all necessary administrative functions but not accidentally invoke or give away that access when they're logged into their nonadministrator account.

For example, an administrator without special authentication can write to some parts of the file structure (like the Applications directory). If an administrator is tricked into running a malicious program (or one is launched through a security hole in a Web browser), that program will run as the administrative user and can modify or delete those administrator-accessible files. If the user were logged into a normal account instead, the damage would be limited to that one account.

Installing Updates and Security Patches

After initial installation, it is important that the operating system be brought up-to-date with all current system version and security updates. If the computer is connected to the Internet, it will automatically connect to Apple and check for available updates.

Software Update also provides a convenient way to check for applicable updates and the order in which they should be applied. Software Update runs through an SSL-secured connection, which is generally sufficient to ensure that the updates have not been tampered with. One thing to be aware of is that some of the required updates may be prerequisites for others (security updates often require that the operating system first be updated to the latest version first). As a result, Software Update may not be able to perform all updates in a single pass. So run Software Update, install the relevant updates it recommends, and then run it again. Keep running it until no updates appear.

In very high-security environments Software Update's security measures may not be considered sufficient, or it may be unacceptable to have configuration information sent to Apple. In these cases, manually downloading, verifying, and installing updates is the preferred method. You can download updates from https://www.apple.com/support/downloads.

> **NOTE ▸** This page is available over either HTTP or HTTPS. You are recommended to use the HTTPS URL to protect against spoofing and/or tampering.

Each available item will have a download link to the right and a description link to the left. Click the description link for detailed information on the update. This information will include system requirements to help you evaluate which updates are relevant to which configurations. For security-related updates, the information will also include an SHA1 hash that can be used to verify the integrity of the update after it is downloaded.

Download all relevant updates (usually in the form of disk images), and then verify each one by opening the Terminal utility and entering the command

```
/usr/bin/openssl sha1 /path/to/file.dmg
```

> **TIP ▸** To save entering the path to the file, you can enter the part of the command before the path, then drag the file from the finder into the Terminal window. The full path will be filled in automatically.

The openssl sha1 command will calculate the SHA1 hash of the file and should return something like this:

```
SHA1(/Users/localadmin/MacOSXUpdateCombo10.4.2.dmg)=
5149def0b79f030bdb2763283c376e4d87d085e9
```

Compare this SHA1 hash to the one listed on the update's webpage. If they match, the update is intact and can be used safely. If it does not match, something is wrong with the downloaded update and you should not use it.

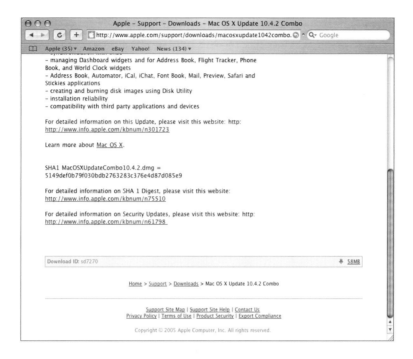

The main difficulty of using the manual method is that it is hard to figure out which updates need to be applied, and in which order. One way around this is with a hybrid method. Consult Software Update to check for relevant updates and their order of installation, and then download, verify, and install them manually. This provides the additional security of the verification step, but it does expose configuration information to the update server.

Even this can be solved by setting up a private update server on Mac OS X Server and downloading updates from that server instead of the Apple update server. This requires setting up an Open Directory server and binding the client to that server. Setting this up is nontrivial and beyond the scope of this book. If you haven't set up an Open Directory server for other reasons, the manual method is probably simpler; but if you're using Open Directory's client management anyway, adding the update server capability is an easy step.

Choosing Mac OS 9 (Classic) Security Options

Mac OS 9 can run in two different modes, both with undesirable security implications:

▶   In Native mode, the computer boots directly into Mac OS 9. In this mode, Mac OS 9 ignores all Mac OS X file permissions and most other security measures. Mac OS 9 has some user authentication capability of its own (using the Multiple Users Control Panel), but it is far more limited than the Mac OS X capabilities. As a result, Native-mode Mac OS 9 should be disabled in a secure environment.

▶   In Classic compatibility mode, Mac OS 9 runs as a process under Mac OS X control. In this mode, Mac OS 9 is constrained by the Mac OS X file permissions and other security features, but if multiple users share the same Mac OS 9 System Folder they may leak information that should be kept private. As a result, Classic mode should be disabled wherever possible. If it is required to run programs that cannot run natively under Mac OS X, special measures must be taken to prevent information leakage.

The simplest and most complete way to disable Mac OS 9 is to delete the operating system—or not install it in the first place. If access to the Classic compatibility environment is needed, there are several options available to retain Mac OS 9 but limit it to Classic mode:

▶   Mac OS 9 can be installed in (or copied into) a disk image. The Classic compatibility environment can run from an image, but Mac OS 9 cannot boot natively from an image, so this provides a robust way to limit Mac OS 9 availability. The Classic environment will automatically mount the image when it is needed, making this solution convenient for the user. Also, giving each user his or her own private image will avoid information leakage.

▶   The computer's hard drive can be formatted without Mac OS 9 drivers. Native-mode Mac OS 9 cannot read or boot from an ATA or SCSI hard drive that does not have appropriate drivers installed. This is not an absolute lockout, as the system can still read and boot from driverless disks over FireWire—thus, putting a Macintosh into FireWire Target Disk Mode will allow its hard drive to be read or even booted to Mac OS 9.

> **NOTE ▶** Enabling and disabling Mac OS 9 drivers can be done only when the hard drive is erased or partitioned—that is, when all data on the hard drive is being discarded. If this security measure is to be used, it must be configured before any other installation or setup of the computer is performed.

▶ The computer's hard drive can be formatted in UNIX File System (UFS) or Case-Sensitive HFS Plus. Mac OS 9 cannot read or boot from these volume formats natively, but it can read them in Classic mode (via the Mac OS X file manager). Note, however, that running Mac OS 9 on one of these volume formats may be subject to compatibility issues.

Finding Mac OS 9 Installations

The Mac OS 9 system files normally reside in the aptly named "System Folder" at the top level of the hard drive, but a bootable Mac OS 9 System Folder can actually have any name and reside anywhere on the hard drive. The first step in removing (or even just controlling) Mac OS 9 is to get a complete inventory of installed systems. You can use the System Preferences Classic pane to generate a list of Mac OS 9 systems, but it's not always complete. To make sure you find them all, use the command line.

1 Log in to a local administrator account and open Terminal.

2 Enter the command

```
sudo find -x / -iname System -exec mdls –name \
kMDItemFSTypeCode '{}' ';' | grep -B 1 ' 2054388083'
```

NOTE ▶ This is a single command split across two lines for the purposes of fitting on a book page. The backslash at the end of the first line tells the shell to treat the next line as a continuation.

3 Examine the command's output: It should list each system installation—both Mac OS 9 and Mac OS X—on the hard drive.

For example:

```
instructor:~ sregan$ sudo find -x / -iname System -exec mdls -name kMDItemFSTypeCode '{}' ';' | grep
 -B 1 ' 2054388083'
/System/Library/CoreServices/System -------------
kMDItemFSTypeCode = 2054388083
--
/System Folder/System -------------
kMDItemFSTypeCode = 2054388083
instructor:~ sregan$ ▮
```

This shows the Mac OS X system file (in /System/Library/CoreServices/System) and the Mac OS 9 system file (in /System Folder/System). The live Mac OS X system will always be in /System/Library/CoreServices/System; any other system files listed are either Mac OS 9 (or older) systems or previous Mac OS X systems that were archived by performing an Archive and Install of Mac OS X. Generally, all but the live Mac OS X system should generally be deleted.

4   If the computer has more than one volume mounted, search additional volumes with the command

```
sudo find /Volumes -iname System -exec mdls -name \
kMDItemFSTypeCode '{}' ';' | grep -B 1 ' 2054388083'
```

NOTE ▸ As with the command in step 2, this is a single command split between two lines.

Removing Mac OS 9

Deleting a Mac OS 9 system is easy enough. Discard the entire System Folder (or whatever it's named—in the example above, the two folders are /System Folder and /Previous Systems/System Folder 1) into the Trash and perform a Secure Empty Trash. (Secure Empty Trash is recommended to make sure security-related information, such as passwords in the Users & Groups Data File, is not recoverable.)

However, if Mac OS 9 has ever been used on the computer, it is likely to have created additional files that should either be moved to secure locations or deleted. Many of these files and folders are invisible, so the easiest way to deal with them is from the command line.

1   Log in to a local administrator account and launch the Terminal utility.

2   Open the Mac OS 9 Desktop Folder and Documents folder with the following command:

```
open '/Desktop Folder'; open '/Documents'
```

If this returns "no such file" errors, ignore them.

NOTE ▶ The single quotes shown in the command are very important. Omitting them could cause the accidental deletion of the Mac OS X Applications folder, which would require reinstallation to repair.

3   The Mac OS 9 Desktop Folder and Documents folder should be displayed in the Finder, if they exist. Any files or folders stored in them need to be deleted or moved to more secure locations, depending on local policy and the files' contents. If the determination cannot be made at this time, move the files and folders to a secure temporary location, as anything left in the folder will be deleted in the next step.

4   Purge leftover applications and data from Mac OS 9 with the following commands:

    sudo rm -rf '/Applications (Mac OS 9)'
    sudo srm -rf '/Documents'
    sudo srm -rf '/Desktop Folder'
    sudo srm -rf '/Trash'
    sudo srm -rf '/Network Trash Folder'
    sudo srm -rf '/Temporary Items'
    sudo srm -rf '/Cleanup At Startup'
    sudo srm -rf '/TheFindByContentFolder'
    sudo srm -rf '/TheVolumeSettingsFolder'
    sudo srm -rf '/VM Storage'
    sudo srm -rf '/AppleShare PDS'
    sudo rm -rf '/Shutdown Check'

If any of these commands give "no such file" errors, ignore them.

WARNING ▶ The single quotes shown in the command are very important; omitting them could cause the accidental deletion of the Mac OS X Applications folder, which would require reinstallation to repair.

NOTE ▶ The National Security Agency (NSA) has guidelines for installing and configuring Mac OS X. You may want to mirror some of their steps to secure your systems. You can find the NSA guidelines at www.nsa.gov/snac/downloads_macX. cfm?MenuID=scg10.3.1.1.

Deleting the Classic Environment

Even with all copies of Mac OS 9 purged from the computer, it is still possible for a user to copy in a Mac OS 9 System Folder and launch it in the Classic compatibility environment. Hopefully your users have more sense than that. If you don't want to count on that, it's possible to remove the components of Mac OS X that allow Mac OS 9 to run in Classic mode:

1   Log in to a local administrator user account and open Terminal.

2   Delete the Classic compatibility environment by entering the following commands:

```
cd '/System/Library'
sudo rm –rf 'CoreServices/Classic Startup.app'
sudo rm –rf 'PreferencePanes/Classic.prefPane'
sudo rm –rf 'UserTemplate/English.lproj/Desktop/Desktop (Mac OS 9)'
```

3   Restart the system.

Establishing Local Operating-System Security

Settings in Mac OS X fall into two general categories:

▶   System-wide settings apply to the computer as a whole and all users on it. Only administrators can change these settings.

▶   Personal settings are set separately for each user account. All users can change their own personal settings.

A preferences pane that includes system-wide settings will have a padlock icon in the lower-left corner; if the lock is unlocked, the user has been authenticated as an administrator.

Making system-wide changes does not require logging in as an administrator; it is sufficient to click the locked padlock and give the user name and password for an account with administrator rights. After making your changes, you can click the padlock again to cancel authentication and prevent further changes.

Some preferences panes contain a mix of system-wide and personal settings. These will have the padlock icon, but some settings (the personal ones) can be changed without authentication.

There are also a few idiosyncratic settings, such as parental controls. These are set by one user (an administrator user) but apply to specific other (nonadministrator) users.

Securing Unattended Computers

Users leaving themselves logged into their computers is a common source of operational insecurity. Teaching users to always log out can help, but logging out can be inconvenient enough that users will almost inevitably cheat sometimes. Mac OS X has three main options to help with this problem.

Require a Sleep/Screen Saver Password

The computer can be configured to require a password to wake from sleep or a screen saver. If the computer is configured to sleep and/or activate a screen saver after a certain amount of time, this will keep passersby from taking over a user's login session. The password requirement (enabled in the System Preferences Security pane) is a personal setting, meaning that it must be enabled separately for each user account; also, a user can disable it if desired.

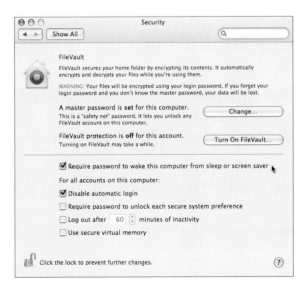

The activation settings for the screen saver are also personal settings, configured in the Desktop & Screen Saver pane. Configuring a Hot Corner to start the screen saver is recommended; this way the user can trigger the screen saver manually, eliminating the window of vulnerability between when the user leaves and when the screen saver activates.

Sleep timing is a system-wide setting, configured in the Energy Saver pane. Note that a password is required to wake the computer only from a full sleep, not screen sleep.

Enable Fast User Switching

Enabling Fast User Switching allows a user to quickly switch from a session to the login window (using the user menu near the right of the menu bar). Like the sleep/screen saver password, this prevents passersby from getting access to a user's session without supplying the correct password. Unlike the sleep/screen saver password, this protection can be activated only manually, not automatically after a period of inactivity. Enable this setting in the System Preferences Accounts pane, under Login Options.

> **NOTE ▶** Temporarily mounted volumes (such as FireWire drives or disk images) are (usually) fully accessible by all logged-in users, not just the user who mounted them. Using Fast User Switching may weaken FileVault protection on the user's home directory. As long as the FileVault user's session is running (even in the background), her home directory disk image will remain mounted. If another user logs in, the only thing keeping him out of the FileVault user's home directory will be the folder permissions on that directory. For maximum FileVault security, leave Fast User Switching disabled.

One security benefit of Fast User Switching is that it allows switching from a normal (nonadministrator) user account to an administrator user account when administrator access is needed, then immediately switching back to normal. This is actually safer than temporarily enabling administrator access from the nonadministrator account (by clicking a padlock and authenticating, for example). You can disable administrator access temporarily (by relocking a padlock icon), but it's easy to forget and leave it disabled (especially if multiple enables are needed). Switching to administrator and then logging out automatically disables all administrator access in a single step.

If both Fast User Switching and the sleep/screen saver are enabled, the option to switch users will be available from the sleep/screen saver password dialog box.

Log Out Users

You can configure the computer to log out users automatically after a period of inactivity. This is a system-wide setting, enabled in the System Preferences Security pane. This option does not provide much security protection, because any running application can (and often will) cancel the logout process. For example, if the user has any unsaved documents open, the Save dialog will cause the logout process to time out. Using this setting is not generally recommended.

Configuring the Login Process

The default settings for the login process are chosen more for the convenience of home users than for security. As a result, you should make a couple of changes to ensure a secure environment:

▶ Disable automatic login. By default, the computer will automatically log in to the initial administrator account every time the computer boots without requiring a password. You can disable this either in the System Preferences Security pane (by selecting Disable Automatic Login) or in the Accounts preferences pane's Login Options section (by deselecting "Automatically log in as").

▶ Turn off display of user names. By default, a list of users (names and pictures or icons) is displayed at the login window; this gives an attacker important hints about what logins are available on the computer. (The has to guess only passwords, not user names.) In the Accounts preferences pane's Login Options section, you can select the "Name and password" option, which causes the login window to display name and password fields; one must correctly enter both to log in.

▶ Keep "Show password hints" deselected. This check box is deselected by default and should not be selected. This login option makes the login window display a user-provided password hint after three unsuccessful login attempts. Users should not enter password hints in the first place, but if they do, the hints should not be displayed.

In some situations you may want the login window to display a warning message against unauthorized use of the computer. You can configure this by launching the Terminal utility and entering the following command (replace the example warning with whatever message you want displayed):

```
sudo defaults write /Library/Preferences/com.apple.loginwindow LoginwindowText "Example
Warning Message"
```

NOTE ▶ Although this command is reproduced here (and will display on screen) as several lines, it should be typed in as a single long command; do not press Return until you enter the entire command. If the message is particularly long, it may be easier to correct typos by entering the whole thing into a text editor and then pasting it into the Terminal window.

Using Other Security-Related Settings

There are other security-related settings that you can use. Here are some examples:

▶   Require a password to unlock each secure system preference (found in the Security preferences pane). By default, preference settings that affect all users (such as this setting) cannot be changed without first clicking the padlock in the bottom-left corner of

the preferences pane and authenticating as an administrator user. If this option is deselected, anyone logged in as an administrator may change system-wide settings without
specifically authenticating first. Keep this option enabled for higher security.

▶ Use secure virtual memory (in the Security preferences pane). This option enables
encryption of the virtual memory swap files. Since virtual memory can contain
important data (even including passwords), encrypting it is highly recommended.
See Lesson 14, "Optimizing Data Confidentiality," for more details. Note that changing this setting does not take effect until the next time the computer is rebooted.

▶ Add Dynamic Host Configuration Protocol (DHCP)–supplied Lightweight Directory
Access Protocol (LDAP) servers to automatic search policies. This option is automatically disabled if no LDAP server configuration is received from a DHCP server the first
time the computer boots. Nonetheless, it's a good idea to make sure this is disabled
and remains disabled. The risk of having it enabled is that an attacker could hook up
a specially configured DHCP/LDAP server, and the client would trust the information
in that server. This might include an administrator account with a password that the
attacker chose. This setting is not available in the System Preferences utility. To check
or change it, open the Directory Access utility, select the Services tab, click the padlock
icon, authenticate, select the LDAP line, and click the Configure button.

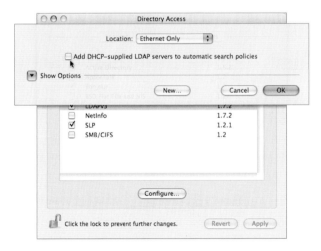

▶ Turn the authentication path option to "Local directory." This prevents any chance of remotely authenticating to a remote server by allowing authentication to only the local NetInfo database.

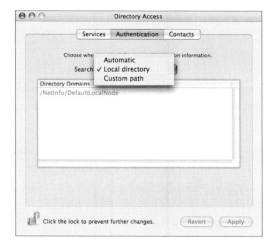

▶ Bluetooth is a wireless protocol intended for connecting relatively lightweight devices (cell phones, headphones, keyboards, mice, etc.) to each other or to computers. It has basic security built in, but its level of security is not adequate for critical situations. Disabling or limiting Bluetooth access will be discussed in Lesson 15, "Mobility Security Concerns."

Configuring a Client Network

The basic purpose of secure network configuration is to maximize security and minimize access. The default configuration of Mac OS X is already relatively minimal in terms of the network-accessible services it provides, but it tends to enable network access over all available interfaces (Ethernet, AirPort, modem, FireWire, and so on), and for both IP version 4 (IPv4) and version 6 (IPv6). To control network access, there are two main changes that you should make to the network settings:

▶ Disable unneeded network interfaces. In the Network preferences pane, review the network locations listed in the Location pop-up menu. For each location, select Network Port Configurations (these are actually network interfaces, not ports, but the interface calls them ports) from the Show pop-up menu, and deselect all ports (interfaces) that are not actually needed. This will limit unintended and unauthorized connections.

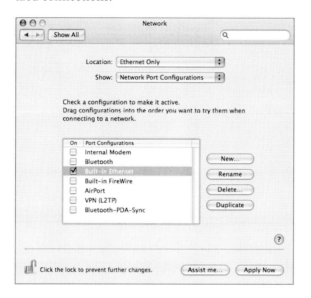

▶ Disable IPv6. IP version 6 is intended as a replacement for the currently popular IPv4 protocol; however, it is not yet widely supported in most organizations, or on the Internet. Because of this, it is rarely needed. Since support for securing it is also not universal—for example, the firewall built into Mac OS X does not filter it—you should disable it unless you actually need it.

IPv6 is controlled on a per-port (interface) configuration basis; as a result, disabling it requires reviewing each network location just as you did to limit the active ports. For each location, go through each active port (those listed in the Show pop-up menu) and, for each one, select the TCP/IP tab, click the Configure IPv6 button, and select Off in the Configure IPv6 pop-up menu. Then click OK and go on to the next active port.

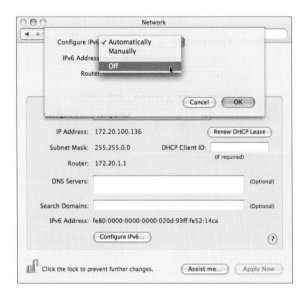

In addition to disabling these two settings, the System Preferences Sharing pane has a variety of options for enabling and controlling network access to Mac OS X. From a security perspective, less access is almost always better than more access. So the most secure sharing settings are:

▶ All services off

▶ Firewall on

▶ Internet Sharing off

But this is not always practical, so you should understand the implications of the available sharing options.

Services

On the Services tab in the Sharing preferences pane, you can enable a number of different network sharing protocols. As a general rule, each sharing protocol represents a potential security hole and should be enabled only if it is needed.

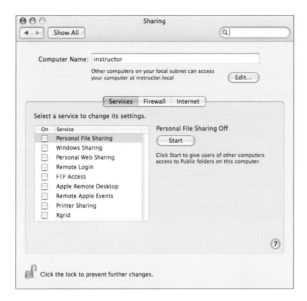

Personal File Sharing

This enables Apple Filing Protocol (AFP) serving from this computer. Enabling AFP raises a possible security issue: Since guest access is always enabled, a network attacker can easily connect and get a list of user accounts and users' Public folders.

Which folders are accessible over an AFP connection depend on the details of how the connection is made:

▶   Guest connections are allowed access to all users' Public folders.

▶   Connections that authenticate as a normal user are allowed access to the authenticated user's home folder and other users' Public folders.

▶   Connections that authenticate as admin users may be treated like normal users (above), or may be allowed to access to all volumes mounted on the computer with sharing enabled. In the default configuration, the difference is dependent on which version of AFP the client supports; older clients get access to entire volumes by default.

You can turn off guest access by changing the guestAccess key in the file com.apple. AppleFileServer.plist (located in /Library/Preferences) from Yes to No. Since most preference files are now saved as binary files, you will need an application called Property List Editor, which is installed with Apple Developer Tools.

You can also turn off the sharing of a user's Public folder by opening NetInfo Manager (located in /Applications/Utilities), selecting the "users" category, and clicking the user whose Public folder you want to stop sharing. Authenticate as a local administrator and select the value for the sharedDir attribute (NetInfo calls them properties) and remove it. Click another user to prompt NetInfo Manager to ask you to save the changes.

Windows Sharing

This enables Server Message Block/Common Internet File System (SMB/CIFS) serving from this computer. Doing so raises somewhat different issues than enabling AFP. First, since the password hashes that Mac OS X normally uses to authenticate users are not compatible with CIFS, accounts that will be accessed via Windows Sharing need to have their password hashes stored in additional formats. Unfortunately, one of these formats, known as NTLMv1, is particularly susceptible to dictionary attack; if an attacker manages to get a copy of the hashes (stored in /private/var/db/shadow/hash, which is readable only by root), the attacker has a good chance of recovering users' passwords. Only accounts that need Windows access should have their passwords stored this way.

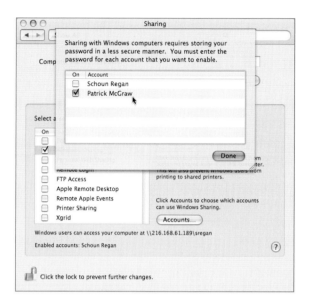

Also, Windows sharing does not just share the users' Public folders; it shares their entire home folders. This can lead to exposure of files that should not be network-accessible. Fortunately, this exposure is limited because guest access to the home folders is not allowed over SMB.

Personal Web Sharing

This enables the Apache Web server, serving the contents of the folder /Library/ WebServer/Documents as well as each user's Sites folder. By default, each of these contains a generic placeholder page, which generally doesn't represent much of a security risk, although it does allow an attacker to test what user names are in use on the system—a first step toward a password-guessing attack.

Replacing these documents with real content—adding CGI scripts to /Library/WebServer/ CGI-Executables or changing the config files for Apache—carries the same risks as running an Apache-based Web server on any other platform, with several notable additions:

▶   Since the standard Mac OS Extended file system is not case-sensitive, realm and other access restrictions can sometimes be bypassed by using nonstandard capitalization in a URL. This is mitigated in two ways in the default configuration file: the mod_hfs_apple module blocks nonstandard capitalization, and the built-in access restrictions (for example, to block reading of .htaccess files) use case-insensitive patterns like "^\.([Hh][Tt]|[Dd][Ss]_[Ss])".

▶ The Macintosh Finder creates files named .DS_Store throughout the file system with information about folder display formats, icon arrangement, and so on. If these files are served over the Web, they can leak information about the structure of files on the server to a Web client. The default config file includes a directive to block access to these files (see the example pattern above).

▶ The Mac OS X file system allows access to files' contents through unusual syntax, such as "filename/..namedfork/data" or "filename/rsrc," which might get past normal access restrictions. The default config file includes directives to block access via these tricks.

All of these possible problems are blocked by directives in the default httpd.conf file. If you modify or replace this file, take care to retain and/or extend these directives.

Remote Login

This enables remote shell access to the local computer over the Secure Shell Protocol (SSH). SSH is relatively secure and can be used to increase the security of other protocols (by tunneling them over an SSH connection); however, its power and flexibility make it a double-edged sword. Among the possible security problems SSH can raise are:

▶ SSH allows remote access to the entire file system (subject to standard authorization limitations) via just logging in and viewing files, or using the Secure Copy (SCP) or Secure File Transfer Protocol (SFTP) commands/subprotocols. Unlike other file sharing protocols, this access cannot be (easily) restricted to chosen share points.

▶ Since SSH can tunnel TCP/IP connections, it can provide a way to bypass firewall protection. For example, if a company's firewall is set to block all incoming AFP access, a user with SSH access to any computer behind the firewall can use that access to connect to any AFP server behind the firewall. The AFP connection will, as far as the company network and the AFP server can tell, appear to be originating from the computer the user has used SSH to log in to.

FTP Access

This enables File Transfer Protocol (FTP) serving from the local computer. FTP is a very old and insecure protocol; among its problems are:

▶   Passwords are normally passed in plaintext and are trivial for a network sniffer to capture.

▶   FTP gives access to the entire file system (subject to standard permissions limitations), not just selected share points as with AFP or SMB.

Some implementations (such as the one supplied with Mac OS X Server) include improved security features such as Kerberos authentication and the ability to control which folders are accessible via FTP. By default, the FTP server configuration included with Mac OS X does not do any of these things. Thus its use is not recommended in a secure environment.

Apple Remote Desktop

This enables remote control and monitoring of the computer from an Apple Remote Desktop (ARD) administrator workstation. ARD can be an extremely useful tool for remote administration, monitoring, and support, but it also carries its fair share of security risks.

To administer the computer, the administrator user must authenticate as one of the users on the computer. You can control which users are allowed to do this and which operations they may perform. Many of the operations have a high potential for misuse (for example, screen observing could be used to spy on a user), so access to these capabilities should be strictly limited.

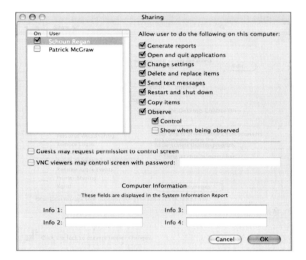

Remote Apple Events

This enables remote computers to send Apple events to the local computer (such as AppleScript events). This should not be enabled in a secure installation.

Printer Sharing

This enables access to the local computer's print queues via Internet Printing Protocol (IPP). Aside from the inherent risk of publishing unintended information about printers and their status, this also opens several possibilities for network-based attacks:

▶   Denial of Service (DoS) attacks can be launched by submitting large print jobs. (No doubt followed by spam that is advertising sales for replacement paper and ink!)

▶   Some printers can be configured via PostScript code; a malicious print job may be able to use this to cause problems with the printers themselves.

▶   Since some parts of job processing on the local computer takes place under the root identity, it might be possible for a malicious job to exploit a bug in a print driver to gain root access to the local computer.

Xgrid

This enables the local computer to act as an Xgrid agent, accepting jobs from an Xgrid controller. There are three main areas of security risk that this feature opens up:

▶ The risk of a malicious job being used to attack the local system. This risk is minimized by running jobs under a completely unprivileged identity (or user) named "nobody." Nonetheless, jobs still have the equivalent of guest access to files throughout the computer, as well as the ability to monitor local activity through unprivileged commands (for example, the ps command—and some programs use sudo in such a way that administrator passwords may be displayed by ps).

▶ The risk of running unauthorized jobs (such as those that have not been through the Xgrid controller's submission process). Xgrid has two features to limit this problem. It can be configured to accept jobs only from a specified controller (and since the agent initiates the connection to the controller, spoofing would be difficult). It can also require the controller to authenticate with either a password or a single sign-on (Kerberos) ticket. Since the password may be widely known—all agents use the same password—single sign-on is the more secure option.

> **NOTE** ▶ Single sign-on is available only if the agent and controller are members of an Open Directory master domain.

▶ The risk that the compute jobs themselves may be attacked, by having their data, results, or programs stolen or tampered with. Since jobs are run under the same identity used for other minimal-access processes, and because their data is stored in relatively accessible locations (such as the /tmp directory), there is relatively little protection against attack by nearly anyone with access to the local system (including even previously-executed Xgrid jobs).

Firewall

The Firewall tab provides a basic interface for configuring the firewall built into the Mac OS X kernel. When enabled, it blocks incoming TCP connections (except for specifically allowed services), but allows all outgoing, local, and (by default) UDP traffic. It also does not filter IPv6 traffic, so disabling IPv6 is recommended when the firewall is in use (as mentioned earlier in this section).

The default configuration of Mac OS X 10.4 does not provide any network services over TCP (except to itself), so this default configuration is not strictly necessary for network security. What it does do is provide protection against unintended network services, such as third-party or user-level programs that may open network ports and create security holes. The firewall blocks everything but the services you've explicitly allowed (or enabled on the Services tab), giving you a master-switch protection against such problems.

Services fall into four different categories, depending on how "built in" they are, and each is allowed by slightly different methods:

▶   Services that have been enabled on the Sharing tab are automatically allowed.

▶   Protocols enabled in other places (Network Time, iTunes, iPhoto, and iChat) are available in the Allow list. To allow access to them, simply select the box next to the protocol.

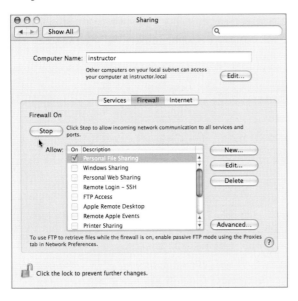

▶   Common services that may be added by third-party software (such as ICQ, Retrospect, and VNC) are preconfigured but not included in the standard list. To allow one of these, click the Add button, choose the service from the Port Name pop-up menu, and click OK. This adds the service to the main list and automatically allows it.

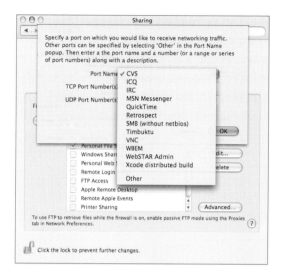

▶ You must manually add services that don't fall into any of the above categories. To do so, click the Add button, choose Other from the Port Name pop-up menu, enter the TCP and/or UDP port numbers that the service uses, and enter a short description (or name) for the service. Then click OK to add the service to the main list and allow access to it.

Click the Advanced button to make some additional changes to the firewall's behavior:

▶ Block UDP Traffic: Turns on filtering of UDP as well as TCP traffic. Unlike TCP traffic, the default for UDP is not to block all traffic other than what has explicitly been allowed; it implicitly allows access to ports 53 and 5353 (standard DNS and multicast DNS/Bonjour, respectively), 67 and 68 (DHCP and BootP requests and replies), 137 and 427 (SLP and SMB service advertisements, respectively), and 631 (IPP printer sharing advertisements). It also adds a keep-state rule to automatically allow replies to UDP packets sent from the local computer.

▶ Enable Firewall Logging: Logs blocked packets to /var/log/ipfw.log; click the Open Log button to launch the Console utility and view this log. In most normal circumstances, the firewall will block a lot of irrelevant packets (random chatter on a campus network and/or Windows-oriented worm attacks on the Internet), and this file can grow quite large. Generally, logging should be left disabled unless a significant network event or attack is in progress, or a network problem is being debugged.

▶ Enable Stealth Mode: Disables sending denials in response to blocked packets. Some attack programs use the replies they receive to profile a target computer. As a result, not replying at all can limit the information you leak. Unfortunately, this is not a panacea. Some information can be inferred from just the pattern of which probes get replies (even immediate rejection) and which get no reply.

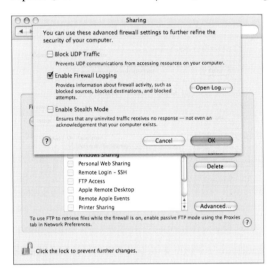

Internet Sharing

The Internet Sharing feature of Mac OS X allows a workstation to act as a NAT-enabled gateway router between two networks—much like the router/NAT capability of Mac OS X Server—but without the configurability or security controls. This feature can be very convenient for home users, allowing, for instance, a computer to share a DSL Internet connection with other computers over its AirPort interface. In a secure network, it is mainly a security risk. For instance, if the home computer is connected to a corporate network, it would become in effect a rogue wireless base station allowing access to the corporate network. In the default configuration, it will not even require a WEP password for access.

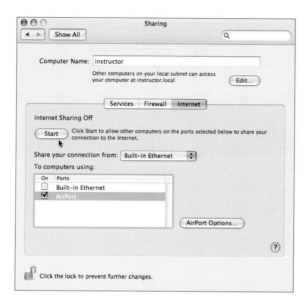

So the simple rule for Internet Sharing is: Don't enable it if you value your network integrity. Enabling it does require administrator rights, but since its implications extend so far beyond the integrity of the local desktop (the normal limits of what an administrator can mess up), you may want to take additional steps to make sure it does not get activated. One option is to delete or rename the program that implements sharing. To delete it, launch the Terminal utility and run the following command:

```
sudo rm /usr/libexec/InternetSharing
```

Note that this will not prevent Internet Sharing from being selected in System Preferences, but it will prevent it from actually functioning. Also, it is possible that a subsequent system update may replace (effectively reinstalling) the Internet Sharing program. Check after system updates (especially if they mention improvements to the Internet Sharing feature) and delete it again if necessary.

Enabling Temporary Administrative Access

Mac OS X provides several methods for a user to temporarily enable administrative access from a less-privileged starting point. These mechanisms allow users who need administrator access to do most of their work in an unprivileged account, and enable their privileges only when they're actually needed.

The most commonly used mechanism is the Authorization framework, which displays the standard Authenticate dialog whenever a padlock icon is unlocked, the installer is run, etc. The rules for how to authorize users for various operations are defined in the /etc/authorization file. Normally most operations require authentication with an administrator account, but do not require that operations be performed while logged in as an administrator. As long as you know the name and password for your admin-enabled identity, you can use this to perform administrative functions from within a nonadmin account.

The /etc/authorization file maintains both rights and rules. Rights are described by what you are attempting to do at the moment. Do you want to unlock a System Preference? Do you want to install software? Do you want to drag a file not owned by you (in a folder not owned by you) to the trash? These are rights.

Rules simply define whether certain conditions are met. For example, a rule might be to allow an owner of a file *or* any user with administrative privileges to permit the right to take place. The following table shows some examples of rights, rules, and comments extracted from the /etc/authorization file:

Rights	Associated Rules	Comments extracted from the authorization file
system.login.screensaver	authenticate-session-owner-or-admin	The owner, as well as any admin, can unlock the screensaver. Modify the group key to change this.
system.printingmanager	authenticate-admin	The associated right is checked for printing to locked printers.
system.install.admin.user	none	Used by installer tool: user installing in admin domain (/Applications)

Not all rights have associated rules. A right may look for a given user, permission, or an authentication mechanism. Whatever is associated with the class key will be used when attempting to comply with that right. An example of what is currently associated with a class:

▶ rule

▶ user

▶ allow

▶ deny

▶ evaluate-mechanisms

> **NOTE** ▶ Rights can also have their authentication credentials shared with other rights.

Fast User Switching

For operations that actually require being logged into an administrator account, Fast User Switching (if enabled) allows you to log in to an administrator account without shutting down your normal environment, doing what you need to do, then logging out the administrator identity and going back to normal. This is actually a good idea even for operations that could be done simply with the Authorization dialog, because once an Authorization right is enabled for a particular application, it remains active by default for 5 minutes (300 seconds) unless it is explicitly disabled (and it's not always easy to disable rights). If the right had been enabled from within an administrator account, switching back to a normal account would make the right inaccessible, removing the possibility that some other operation might sneak through on the coattails of the one you really wanted to authorize.

Command-Line Operations

For command-line operations, there are two commands—su and sudo—that allow you to either temporarily open a more privileged shell session, or perform specific commands with a higher privilege level. Their functions are similar, but different enough that it's important to understand and be able to use both.

su is the traditional UNIX command for switching user identities. Entering the command

```
su localadmin
```

will attempt to open a shell session with the user identity localadmin. It requires that the password for the localadmin account be entered. To go back to the normal account, use the exit command to close the shell that su opened under the alternate identity.

Using su to switch to the root user is not possible in a standard Mac OS X configuration for two reasons:

▶ Root does not have a password and, even if it did, su has a special security restriction that allows only members of the wheel group to su to root.

▶ By default, root is the only member of the wheel group.

This command is useful, however, to switch from a nonadministrator account to an administrator user account.

sudo is a newer program intended to provide a more flexible capability to run single commands from a different user identity (especially root). Unlike su, it does not open a session in its default mode; instead, it switches identities, runs the specified command, then switches back to normal (or at least, back to the identity you were using before). Also, unlike su, sudo requires the password for the account you're switching from, not the account you're switching to. (To save typing, it also caches credentials. Once you provide your password, you will not be asked for it again for the next 5 minutes.

> **NOTE** ▶ Each time you use sudo, the credential is renewed; so this is really a 5-minute timeout between invocations.

The file /etc/sudoers defines which accounts are allowed to perform which operations using which temporary identities. By default, only members of the admin group are allowed to do anything—and they are allowed to do virtually anything.

For example, consider the command

```
sudo srm -rf '/Trash'
```

What this command does is attempt to execute the command

```
srm -rf '/Trash'
```

under the root identity. If the command is run from an administrator user account, and the administrator's password is provided correctly, it will succeed.

You can also use sudo to open a shell session, rather than just execute a single command. Using its -s flag invokes this mode:

```
sudo -s
```

Because this -s option leaves the privileged session open and possibly available for misuse, this is not recommended. The safest way to use root is to get in, do exactly what you need to do, and get right back out; this is exactly what sudo does in its normal (single-command) mode.

Because using sudo to get root access does not require either a root password or wheel membership, it is the preferred tool for getting root access on the command line in Mac OS X.

You can use su and sudo together to get root access while logged in as a normal (non-admin) user: First use su to switch to an administrator identity, then from there use sudo to perform commands as root. Both commands will require the same administrator password to authorize their operations. This may seem redundant, but the two-step process provides protection against things like misuse of cached sudo credentials. For example, if you run sudo while logged into an administrator account and then run a malicious program, the program could use the cached credentials to gain full root access.

A weakness in the Secure Empty Trash or srm approach is that programmers often utilize a technique called a "safe save." When an application needs to save changes to a file, it does not write out the changes to the original file. Instead, it renames the original file to a temporary name, so for example, it might rename Myfile.doc to Myfile.doc~. Then it writes the new content to a new file which has the same name as the original and deletes the renamed original file. This ensures that the old content is not deleted until after the new content has safely been written to disk.

However, the deletion of the renamed original file does not go through the Secure Empty Trash or srm process and leaves a copy of the document on the disk in unallocated free space, which is precisely the vulnerability that Secure Empty Trash or srm seeks to avoid. To prevent this problem you can use one of two approaches. The first is to regularly run the Erase Free Space tool from Disk Utility on your volume on a regular basis, but that can take a long time if you have a large amount free space on your drive. The second approach is to store your documents on an encrypted disk image, whether through FileVault or a stand-alone disk image. By using an encrypted disk image, any erased files are still left on the disk in encrypted form, making them unrecoverable to an attacker.

> **MORE INFO ▶** For more information on creating encrypted disk images, see Lesson 14, "Optimizing Data Confidentiality."

Using FileVault

The Mac OS X FileVault feature converts a user's home folder to a disk image encrypted with that user's login password. FileVault images are encrypted with the Advanced Encryption Standard using a 128-bit key (AES-128). When a user logs in, the home folder is automatically mounted and the login password is used to decrypt and encrypt home folder contents as they are used, so files can be accessed normally. When the user is not logged in, the contents of the folder are inaccessible, even through mechanisms (such as root mode) that can normally bypass file protections. Because of this, FileVault is the preferred method to secure a user's files when Mac OS X integrity cannot be guaranteed (especially when proper physical security is not possible, as with laptops).

When the user is not logged in, the disk image of the home folder is stored in /Users/username/username.sparseimage. When the user logs in, the /Users/username folder is renamed to /Users/.username (which makes it invisible), a new folder named /Users/username is created, and the disk image is mounted over the /Users/username folder. When the user logs out, the mount folder is deleted and the folder that contains the disk image is renamed.

If the computer should happen to crash, this leads to a scary-looking situation where the user's disk image appears to have vanished into thin air. Don't panic. The disk image is still there, it's just hidden in the invisible /Users/.username folder. The next time the user logs in, everything should be restored automatically.

NOTE ▶ Encrypted disk images can also be created and mounted manually. These can be used in addition to or instead of FileVault to provide additional control over the security level of files. Using a manually created disk image with a different password (not the user's login password) would be appropriate for storing extremely sensitive files because they would be available only when the disk image is specifically mounted, not whenever the user is logged in. Using a manual disk image instead of FileVault would be appropriate if only certain files need to be stored securely, and those files can be stored in a user-defined location (not preference files or other files that are automatically stored in the user's Library folder).

FileVault has several limitations that you should consider before enabling it for any user account:

▶ The contents of an encrypted disk image are vulnerable to corruption. Normally, file corruption is only likely to render individual files unusable. Since the user's entire home folder is stored by FileVault as a single disk image, corruption of that image may render the entire contents of the home folder inaccessible. This makes backups particularly important to protect FileVault users against data loss.

▶ Forgetting the password to a FileVault-protected account is a more serious problem than with a normal account. The master password (discussed in the next section) can be used to reset FileVault-protected account's passwords, but if both the normal account password and the master password are lost or forgotten, you won't be able to recover the contents of the FileVault account.

▶ FileVault-protected home folders can be difficult to integrate into a backup strategy. When the user is not logged in, only the disk image will be accessible, not the files in the home folder. Since this file will be modified at least slightly every time the user logs in, an incremental or differential backup strategy that backs up only files that have changed since the previous backup will need to back up the entire image every time. On the other hand, if the user is logged in, the disk image may be inaccessible (hidden behind the mounted home folder).

▶ Because FileVault protects all of the contents of the home folder—even folders that are intended to be publicly available—FileVault users cannot publish files using their Public folder (Personal File Sharing) or Sites folder (Personal Web Sharing).

▶ Because Windows Sharing requires storing low-security hashed user passwords, FileVault accounts should not be enabled for Windows sharing. (See "Configuring a Client Network," earlier in this lesson.)

▶ Passwords—including those used to protect FileVault accounts—sometimes get paged out to the virtual memory swap files. To avoid leaking the password by this path, you should enable encrypted virtual memory on all computers on which FileVault will be used.

▶ Access to FileVault-protected files will be slower than normal, due to the need to encrypt and decrypt then as they are used.

Setting a Master Password for FileVault

Before you can enable FileVault for any user accounts, you must set a master password for FileVault. This password provides an emergency safety net for FileVault-protected accounts; without it, losing the user's login password would result in the loss of all data in the user's home directory. The master password is used to encrypt a Keychain, which secures an encryption backdoor that can be used to reset access to FileVault accounts if their passwords are lost.

The password assistant gives you suggestions for different types of passwords:

▶ Memorable

The Memorable passwords are still secure, since they include a word from the local dictionary, followed by a number 1 to 3 digits long, followed by a punctuation mark, followed by another word from the local dictionary.

▶ Letters & Numbers

▶ Numbers Only

▶ Random

▶ FIPS-181 compliant

To set a master password for FileVault:

1 Open System Preferences and choose the Security pane.

2 Click the Set Master Password button.

3   Authenticate as an administrator by entering an administrator user name and password.

4   Enter the master password you have chosen in the Master Password and Verify fields, or click the ? button to open the Password Assistant.

   NOTE ► Since the master password provides backdoor access to all FileVault-protected accounts, choosing a strong password is very important. The recommended procedure is to use the Password Assistant to generate a long random-type password, write it on a slip of paper, seal the paper in an envelope (so you can tell if it has been opened and used), label the envelope clearly (remember to include information to identify which computer this master password applies to), and store the envelope in a secure location.

5   Leave the Hint field blank.

6   Click the OK button.

Using the Master Password to Reset a Lost Account Password

If the password for a FileVault-protected account is lost, the only way to properly reset it is with the master password. Normal password reset options (using the System Preferences Account pane) do not work. Some reset methods, such as running the Password Reset utility from the Install DVD, may appear to work, but at most they will reset the user's login password, not the FileVault encryption password. If these passwords do not match, the user still will not be able to log in.

To reset a FileVault account's password, use the login window to attempt to log in to the account three times, entering a wrong password each time. After the third unsuccessful attempt, LoginWindow will ask for the master password. If it is provided successfully, you can provide a new password for the account. Both the account's login password and the disk image's encryption password will be switched.

One password that will not be switched is the encryption password for the account's login Keychain. This password will remain set to the old (lost) password. During the reset process, LoginWindow claims that it will create a new (blank) Keychain and move the old one aside, but it may not actually do this.

To create a new (blank) login Keychain with a password that matches the login and disk image passwords, navigate to ~/Library/Keychains and rename or delete the login.keychain file. Then log out of and back into the account; a new Keychain will be created automatically. Since the FileVault recovery mechanism does not handle the Keychain's encryption, there will be no way to recover the contents of the old Keychain unless its password can be found or recovered. Instead, the user will have to reenter her various service passwords into the new Keychain.

Enabling FileVault

The FileVault conversion process is started within the account to be converted. The conversion should be the only thing happening on the computer. No other users may be logged in, and no other programs may be running. Since the conversion process can take time, plan the conversion for a time when the computer can sit effectively idle until it is done. Last-minute conversions (just before the user leaves with his PowerBook to catch a flight) are a recipe for trouble.

To enable FileVault:

1 If Fast User Switching is enabled, log out all active user sessions.

2 Log in to the account to be converted to FileVault protection.

3 Open System Preferences and choose the Security pane.

4 Click the Turn On FileVault button.

5 If necessary, authenticate as an administrator by entering an administrator user name and password.

6 Enter the current account's password.

7 If there is currently any important information stored in the account's home directory, select the "Use secure erase" checkbox.

If the account has just been created and has not been used yet, it's acceptable to leave this box deselected.

8 Click the "Turn on FileVault" button.

You will be automatically logged out, and the FileVault conversion process will proceed automatically.

If there is much data in the user's home folder, encrypting it and securely erasing it may take a while; do not attempt to use the computer while this process takes place.

What You've Learned

▶ When using Open Firmware Password, all startup keys are disabled except the Option key.

▶ Fast User Switching back to the Login Window is an excellent way to increase security.

▶ By default in Mac OS X, every time the computer boots, it automatically logs in to the initial administrator account without requiring a password; use the Accounts preferences pane.

▶ Enabling Stealth Mode disables sending denials in response to blocked packets.

▶ When a user with a FileVault home folder is not logged in, the disk image of that home folder is stored in /Users/username/ username.sparseimage.

References

Apple Knowledge Base Documents

The following Knowledge Base documents (located at www.apple.com/support) provide further information about using the command-line interface:

Document 106482, "Setting up Open Firmware Password Protection in Mac OS X 10.1 or later"

Document 301416, "Mac OS X 10.4: If FileVault "secure erase" is interrupted, data loss may occur"

Document 25695, "Mac OS X 10.3, 10.4: FileVault—How to verify or repair a home directory image"

Document 25614, "Mac OS X 10.3, 10.4: FileVault—Home directory, Public folder unavailable while logged out"

URLs

Open Firmware commands: www.firmworks.com/QuickRef.html

Apple security: www.apple.com/macosx/features/security

Mac OS X v10.4 Security Help: http://docs.info.apple.com/article.html?path=Mac/10.4/ en/cdb_scr.html

Lesson Review

1. Open Firmware Password requires what version of the Firmware?

2. Open Firmware Password disables what?

3. What command line utilities are used to manage disk images?

4. Using Secure Virtual Memory secures what files from being read?

Answers

1. 4.1.7

2. All keys except the option key on the keyboard

3. diskutil and hdutil

4. virtual memory swap files

14

Time   This lesson takes approximately 2 hours to complete.

Goals   Review standard UNIX permissions

Configure appropriate file-system permissions and ACLs to provide data security

Determine when to use SUID and GUID permissions

Audit for inappropriate SUID and GUID permissions

Restrict the administrator's home folder permissions so that other users cannot browse it

Learn the location and function of file-system access control lists

Configure Mac OS X computers for optimum data confidentiality by encrypting sensitive data on the local file system

Understand the encryption features of FileVault

Create a secure documents folder by encrypting a disk image

Disable possible data leaks by encrypting the swap space, wiping clean free space, and using secure empty trash

Optimizing Data Confidentiality

In a collaborative, networked computing environment, the ability to share your information with others benefits group productivity. However, controlling access to that data is of incredible importance; information accidentally made available to the wrong person can seriously compromise the success of your project or company.

In this lesson, you will work with several security techniques to ensure that only intended recipients see the data you want to share.

Securing File Systems Permissions

Mac OS X is built on a foundation of UNIX, which includes advanced features such as file and folder-level permissions and, new to Mac OS X 10.4, access control lists (ACLs). Permissions ensure that the owner of the file or folder controls is authorized (and who isn't authorized) to have access to that file or folder.

Here are the folders included in a typical Mac OS X user's home folder. In this case the user, osxuser1, opened Terminal (/Applications/Utilities) and entered *ls -l ~osxuser1* on the command line to view this output:

```
powerbook:~ osxuser1$ ls -l
total 0
drwx------     7    osxuser1    osxuser1    238    18 Mar 00:03    Desktop
drwx------    12    osxuser1    osxuser1    408    24 Mar 10:50    Documents
drwx------    25    osxuser1    osxuser1    850    15 Feb 12:17    Library
drwx------     3    osxuser1    osxuser1    102    24 Feb 2004     Movies
drwx------     3    osxuser1    osxuser1    102    24 Feb 2004     Music
drwx------     5    osxuser1    osxuser1    170    24 Feb 2004     Pictures
drwxr-xr-x     5    osxuser1    osxuser1    170    24 Mar 10:50    Public
drwxr-xr-x     5    osxuser1    osxuser1    170    24 Feb 2004     Sites
```

By reviewing the UNIX permissions, you see that each folder—"d" for directory in UNIX parlance—is owned by user osxuser1, and associated with the group osxuser1. Before Mac OS X 10.3, the group may have appeared as "staff" (or, occasionally, "wheel"), but beginning with Mac OS X 10.3, for increased security, when a new user is added to the system, a group is automatically created with the same name as the user's short name.

Except for the Public and Sites folders, only user osxuser1 has access to the remaining folder contents. Permissions for Group and Others are all "-".

For the Public, Sites, and other folders, user osxuser1 has full rwx (read, write, and execute) permissions, but the Group also has the permissions r-x (a read-only folder), and Others also have r-x permissions.

By default, a home directory for a Mac OS X user has no access to anyone but the owner for most of the folders, with exceptions being made for the Public and Sites folders.

The Sites folder (intended to be used for an individual's website) is accessible by others. Only information intended to be accessible to all users should be placed in the Sites folder. This folder is not intended to be a location for a secure website, but for a user's "personal" website. The Public folder allows its owner to share information with everyone in a controlled manner. All users can view the contents of the Public folder, but they cannot modify or add any contents, except through the Drop Box folder (which will be explained later).

Here are the contents of user osxuser1's Public folder:

```
powerbook:~/Public osxuser1$ ls -l
total 12536
drwx-wx-wx    4    osxuser1    osxuser1    136        3 Jul 12:10     DropBox
-rw-r--r--    1    osxuser1    osxuser1    29637      7 Nov 2004      GremInterior.jpg
drwxr-xr-x    3    osxuser1    osxuser1    102        3 Jul 12:13     Misc
-rw-r--r--    1    osxuser1    osxuser1    64512      27 May 2004     Quarterly05.xls
-rw-r--r--    1    osxuser1    osxuser1    711734     1 Jul 11:34     Scott.tiff
-rw-r--r--    1    osxuser1    osxuser1    5605250    25 Aug 2003     cowbell.mp3
```

Every file and folder is readable by everyone (-rw), yet only the owner, osxuser1, has write access to the files and folders contained in the Public folder, so these files cannot be modified by others. And since the Public folder can be modified only by the owner, the files and folders cannot be deleted or renamed.

The Drop Box allows others to "drop something off" in the Public folder, but only the owner of the folder can see what has been left there. Think of placing a letter into a public mailbox. Once you leave the letter and close the door, only the postal carrier has access to that letter (not even you can retrieve it). This is because user osxuser1 has full rwx access, but the Group and Others access is only -wx, meaning a write-only folder.

Let's say that a user named deborah wants to grab a copy of the file Quarterly05.xls, make modifications to it, and drop that file in osxuser1's Public folder. Deborah (or anyone else with access to the system) can use the Finder to navigate to osxuser1's Public folder and copy (not move) the file into her home directory. She can then modify that file and drop it in the Drop Box folder in osxuser1's Public folder. User deborah cannot replace the file that existed in the Public folder because she does not have write permission into that folder, thus the Drop Box is the alternative.

Setting Access Rights for Files and Folders

What if you have a file that you want only a certain user or group of users to be able to read? The default Public folder setup is not sufficient for this, and you will need to go a little further to control the granularity of access.

A user can create a folder or file with more granular permission control from either the Finder (which refers to the three levels of granularity as Owner, Group, or Others) or from the CLI (User, Group, or Others). The user can (if authenticated) also change the User/Owner of the file or folder or Group associated with the file or folder.

Note that the Finder allows only certain permissions options, whereas the command-line interface (CLI) allows all eight possible permutations of rwx to apply to each of the three levels of granularity.

Also note that there is no way from the Finder to control Group membership—you can select from preexisting Groups, but cannot create your own, or modify who is (or isn't) in either new or preexisting groups.

The Sticky Bit

The Public folder/Drop Box system employed by Mac OS X is very powerful and, as you have seen, extensible into even more granular control by you. Another powerful aspect of the UNIX permissions system is something called the "sticky bit."

The sticky bit solves the problem of how to control permissions on a single collaborative folder in such a way that you can create your own new folders and files for other to have access to (with a granularity which you control) without fear of those same others being able to delete or modify your files (which would be annoying, to say the least).

Without the sticky bit, it might seem intuitive to create a collaborative folder called Collaborate with rwx permission enabled for each user who wants to collaborate (whether that's everyone, or it is controlled via a specific group). Sure enough, users who have write access to that folder will be able to create their own folders and files, but there is a problem: The same power that enables users to create files and folders in the Collaborate folder also allows them to delete or rename *any* file or folder within that folder—*nothing* prevents them from deleting or renaming *other* collaborative users' files or folders!

The sticky bit ensures that this cannot happen. When the sticky bit is enabled on a folder (it cannot be enabled on a file), each user can create his or her own files and folders, but others are *not* allowed to delete, rename, or modify those files or folders (since they are not the owner).

The sticky bit is already utilized in a default Mac OS X installation on the Shared folder, as seen by using the CLI to view the permissions on the /Users folder:

```
powerbook:/Users osxuser1$ ls -l /Users
total 0
drwxrwxrwt    9    root      wheel      306    26 Jun 14:54    Shared
drwxr-xr-x   18    deborah   deborah    612    24 Dec 2004     deborah
drwxr-xr-x   21    local     local      714    25 Jun 00:57    local
drwxr-xr-x   15    preso     preso      510    22 Aug 2004     preso
drwxr-xr-x   24    osxuser1  osxuser1   816    26 Jun 14:55    osxuser1
```

Notice the "t" in the permissions for the Shared folder; this delineates a folder that has the sticky bit set.

To set the sticky bit on another folder, you must use the CLI. (This option is not available in the Finder.)

You can create your Collaborate folder within the /Users/Shared folder, and make it usable only by the owner of the folder (you will use the administrative user local for this example) and members of the group users (a group designed for all nonadmin users, and automatically created and populated on Mac OS X).

1   Log in to the CLI as the admin user local.

2   Navigate to the /Users/Shared folder:

```
powerbook:~ local$ cd /Users/Shared
```

3 Make the Collaborate folder:

```
powerbook:/Users/Shared local$ mkdir Collaborate
powerbook:/Users/Shared local$ ls -l
total 0
```

drwxrwxrwx	6	root	wheel	204	9 May 2004	Adobe PDF 6.0
drwxr-xr-x	2	local	wheel	68	11 Jul 10:57	Collaborate
drwxrwxr-x	2	root	wheel	68	19 Nov 2003	Faxes
drwxrwxrwx	3	osxuser1	wheel	102	20 Jun 2004	SC Info

```
drwxr-xr-x 7 osxuser1 wheel 238 21 Apr 20:58 WO
```

4 Change the group of the Collaborate folder to users:

```
powerbook:/Users/Shared local$ sudo chown :users Collaborate
Password:
```

5 Set the permissions to User rwx, Group rwx, Other "---":

```
powerbook:/Users/Shared local$ chmod 770 Collaborate
powerbook:/Users/Shared local$ ls -l
total 0
```

drwxrwxrwx	6	root	wheel	204	9 May 2004	Adobe PDF 6.0
drwxrwx---	2	local	users	68	11 Jul 10:57	Collaborate
drwxrwxr-x	2	root	wheel	68	19 Nov 2003	Faxes
drwxrwxrwx	3	osxuser1	wheel	102	20 Jun 2004	SC Info

```
drwxr-xr-x 7 osxuser1    wheel 238 21 Apr 20:58 WO
```

6 Set the sticky bit:

```
powerbook:/Users/Shared local$ chmod +t Collaborate
powerbook:/Users/Shared local$ ls -l
total 0
```

drwxrwxrwx	6	root	wheel	204	9 May 2004	Adobe PDF 6.0
drwxrwx--t	2	local	users	68	11 Jul 10:57	Collaborate
drwxrwxr-x	2	root	wheel	68	19 Nov 2003	Faxes
drwxrwxrwx	3	osxuser1	wheel	102	20 Jun 2004	SC Info
drwxr-xr-x	7	osxuser1	wheel	238	21 Apr 20:58	WO

You have successfully created your Collaborate folder! Now take it for a test drive. First, the admin user local will create a folder within the Collaborate folder, and then a normal user (osxuser1 as an example) will also create a folder within the Collaborate folder. (osxuser1 is in the users group).

1   Make a folder in Collaborate called localshare:

```
powerbook:/Users/Shared local$ cd Collaborate
powerbook:/Users/Shared/Collaborate local$ mkdir localshare
powerbook:/Users/Shared/Collaborate local$ ls -l
total 0
drwxr-xr-x 2 local users 68 11 Jul 11:12 localshare
```

2   Log in as osxuser1 and create a folder:

```
powerbook:~ osxuser1$ cd /Users/Shared/Collaborate
powerbook:/Users/Shared/Collaborate osxuser1$ mkdir osxuser1share
powerbook:/Users/Shared/Collaborate osxuser1$ ls -l
total 0
```

| drwxr-xr-x | 2 | local | users | 68 | 11 Jul 11:12 | localshare |
| drwxr-xr-x | 2 | osxuser1 | users | 68 | 11 Jul 11:51 | osxuser1share |

3   As the normal user, try to delete the localshare folder:

```
powerbook:/Users/Shared/Collaborate osxuser1$ rm -rf localshare
rm: localshare: Operation not permitted
```

4   As the normal user, try to delete your own newly created folder:

```
powerbook:/Users/Shared/Collaborate osxuser1$ rm -rf osxuser1share
```

You are able to make and remove your own folder, but you are not able to remove the one created by local.

Working With Access Control Lists

The standard UNIX permissions model has some limitations that prevent it from allowing as much granular access control as a user may desire. For example, imagine a college English class with a teacher and students, and a workflow that allows each student to do certain things (like get homework assignments and submit them when they are finished) but does not allow anyone but the teacher to populate the "assignments" folder or be able to read each student's submitted assignment.

One way to solve this problem is to create a folder called ENG_101_Assign, owned by eng101teacher, who would have rwx privileges. A group could be created called eng101, which would contain all of the students in English 101 (and, optionally, also the teacher). The ENG_101_Assign folder could be assigned to the eng101 group, and Group privileges could be r-x (read only). Permission for Others would be "---" (no access), ensuring that only students registered in the class have access.

You would also put in a Drop Box for submission of homework assignments, owned by eng101teacher with rwx privileges, Group ownership by eng101 with -wx (write only) privileges, and Other privileges of "---". Students would use an enforced nomenclature for submitting their assignments (such as Eng101Assign5_studentinitials), and because of the time stamping of the UNIX file system, the teacher would know when the assignments were submitted.

This is one way to accomplish this task. It of course has its limitations and might not be as expandable and adaptable as one would like.

You might want to add some more granularity and features. First, you would like to allow not only the teacher to have "admin" access to the assignments (be able to put them into the ENG_101_Assign folder and view the contents of the Drop Box folder), but also allow a teacher's assistant to do the same. Also, you want to allow tutors to have specific access to certain student's assignments to assist them. You also want an automated school records system to have limited access to the ENG_101_Assign folder so the submissions and tracking can be done over the Internet. And, of course, the district superintendent wants to have visible access to *everything*. (But as a Mac OS X system admin, you are smart enough to *not* give out total access.)

How would you solve this problem? Given the limitations of the standard UNIX permissions system, you would have a very difficult time doing this by finagling folder ownership and group access, and you would have to basically "trick" the file structure to do what you want with potentially a multitude of folders and groups.

Thankfully, in Mac OS X 10.4, a system called access control lists (ACLs) was incorporated, which allows much more granular control of access to files and folders.

Understanding ACL Attributes

ACLs consist of individual access control entries (ACEs). These entries are specific to a file-system volume and are set on individual files or folders. Each ACE contains the user or group associated with the entry, and permission information to control granularity, some of which is applicable only for folders, some of which is applicable only for files, and some of which is applicable to both.

The attributes that apply to all file-system objects (folders and files) include the following:

- delete: Allow deletion.
- readattr: Allow reading of an object's basic attributes (implicitly granted if object can be looked up).
- writeattr: Allow writing of an object's basic attributes.
- chown: Allow changing the ownership of the object.

The attributes that apply only to folder objects include the following:

- list: Allow listing of the entry.
- search: Allow the folder to be looked up by name.
- add_file: Allow adding of files.

The attributes that apply only to nonfolder objects include the following:

- read: Allow read access (like an "r" permission).
- write: Allow write access (like a "w" permission).
- execute: Allow execute access (like an "x" permission).
- append: Allow write access, but only for appending to the file, not overwriting what already exists.

Folders also allow ACL inheritance, meaning that files within the folder, or subfolders, can inherit the rules that apply to their parent folder:

▶   file_inherit: Allow ACL inheritance to files within the folder.

▶   directory_inherit: Allow ACL inheritance to subfolders within the folder.

▶   only_inherit: ACL properties of the folder apply *only* to items within the folder (files and subfolders), but do *not* apply to the folder itself.

Creating ACLs Using the CLI

In Mac OS X, there is no GUI to create ACL entries. (Mac OS X Server does provide a very nice GUI interface via Workgroup Manager.) So, in order to create your ACL entries, you need to first enable ACLs for the volume (they are turned off by default) with the following command:

```
powerbook:~ local$ sudo /usr/sbin/fsaclctl -p / -e
```

This enables ACLs on the root volume / (this can be any mounted volume), and -e means "enable." (You could also give -d to "disable.")

Once ACLs are enabled on a volume, you can apply ACLs to any file or folder on that volume. In order to do this, use the same chmod command that controls standard UNIX permissions, but with the new ACL arguments, some of which you will now look at.

> **MORE INFO ▶** For more complete information on the new ACL arguments, including all of the available options for ACLs, please refer to the man page for chmod.

To view ACLs, add the argument -e to the ls –l command:

```
powerbook:~ local$ ls -le
-rw-r--r--+ 1 osxuser1 osxuser1 0 Apr 28 14:06 file1
```

Notice the + after the set of standard permissions, but you haven't added any ACE entries to this file, so there's nothing else to see yet. To change that to allow all members of the admin group to write to file1, execute the following command:

```
powerbook:~ local$ sudo chmod +a "admin allow write" file1
```

To view your handiwork, look again:

```
powerbook:~ local$ ls -le
    -rw-r--r--+ 1 osxuser1 osxuser1 0 Apr 28 14:06 file1
    owner: osxuser1
    1: admin allow write
```

Notice the additional ACL information for the file, and the one ACE that allows members of the admin group to write to this file.

To deny read access to the guest group for file1:

```
powerbook:~ local$ sudo chmod +a "guest deny read" file1
powerbook:~ local$ ls -le
-rw-r--r--+ 1 osxuser1 osxuser1 0 Apr 28 14:06 file1
    owner: osxuser1
    1: guest deny read
    2: admin allow write
```

ACEs are numbered from 1 to n (for n ACEs in the ACL). The order of entries is important—lists are evaluated top to bottom (rule 1 to n), with new entries usually being added to the top of the list. (The exact explanation of this ordering is explained later in this section.)

Note that Allow and Deny matches work differently for ACLs. Allow matches are cumulative for *all* matches that apply to a user, whether from user or group ACE matches. Deny matches apply upon the first ACE match.

It is possible to specify which rule number you would like to use when adding your ACE. To override the default ordering when adding an ACE, use the +a# *rulenum* syntax:

```
powerbook:~ local$ sudo chmod +a# 2 "others deny read" file1
powerbook:~ local$ ls -le
-rw-r--r--+ 1 osxuser1 osxuser1 0 Apr 28 14:06 file1
    owner: osxuser1
    1: guest deny read
    2: others deny read
    3: admin allow write
```

To rewrite a specific ACE, use the =a# *rulenum* syntax:

```
powerbook:~ local$ sudo chmod =a# 2 "others deny read,execute" file1
powerbook:~ local$ ls -le
-rw-r--r--+ 1 osxuser1 osxuser1 0 Apr 28 14:06 file1
    owner: osxuser1
    1: guest deny read
    2: others deny read,execute
    3: admin allow write
```

To delete an ACE, use the -a# *rulenum* syntax:

```
powerbook:~ local$ sudo chmod -a# 2 file1
powerbook:~ local$ ls -le
-rw-r--r--+ 1 osxuser1 osxuser1 0 Apr 28 14:06 file1
    owner: osxuser1
    1: guest deny read
    2: admin allow write
```

To create an ACE inheritance rule, use the +ai or +ai# *rulenum* syntax:

```
powerbook:~ local$ sudo chmod +ai "others allow read" file1
powerbook:~ local$ ls -le
-rw-r--r--+ 1 osxuser1 osxuser1 0 Apr 28 14:06 file1
    owner: osxuser1
    1: guest deny read
    2: admin allow write
    3: others inherited allow read
```

Notice that the just-added inheritance rule did not get placed at position 1, but was instead placed at the end. When new ACEs are added to an ACL, each entry is sorted into one of the following four categories:

▶ Local deny

▶ Local allow

▶ Inherited deny

▶ Inherited allow

Unless overridden with the +a# *rulenum* or +ai# *rulenum* syntax, new rules will be placed in the first position available within their category. In this case, you already had one local deny rule (category 1), one local allow rule (category 2), and no inherited deny (category 3) or inherited allow (category 4) rules, so the first inherited allow, a category 4 rule, gets placed after all category 1 through 3 rules.

> **MORE INFO** ► See the man page for chmod to see a more complicated example that includes all ACE categories.

> **NOTE** ► In addition to directly navigating to a home folder using the Finder, a user may also obtain access to your home folder via AFP (enabled in the System Preferences Sharing pane by allowing Personal File Sharing), SMB (enabled in the System Preferences Sharing pane by allowing Windows Sharing), and FTP.

Understanding SUID/SGID

In addition to access permissions, there is another permission-related aspect for files (it does not apply to folders) known as set user ID on execution (SUID) or set group ID on execution (SGID). This is a powerful, but potentially dangerous, attribute for a file, so understanding its purpose is crucial, because only certain files should have this bit set (and you should flag those files that should *not* have it set).

By setting the SUID bit on an executable file, you are telling the file system that, no matter who launches the executable file, the file will execute as though it was launched by the assigned owner of the file. For instance, the command passwd allows any user to change his or her own password. However, this program needs to run with the privileges of root (so it can appropriately modify the Open Directory password), which a user probably does not have the ability to do otherwise. So, when any user runs /usr/bin/passwd, it needs to run as though it was executed by the root user, since you don't want to give admin or root access to all users.

The SUID bit is set for /usr/bin/passwd as follows:

```
powerbook:/ local$ ls -l /usr/bin/passwd
-r-sr-xr-x  1 root wheel 35092 Mar 20 16:26 /usr/bin/passwd
```

Instead of the user x bit being set, it is shown as s. Since SUID is set, whenever *anyone* runs /usr/bin/passwd, it will run as though it was run by root (since root owns the file). Note that an executable does not necessarily need to be owned by root, it could be another owner, but if the SUID bit is set, the file will execute as though launched by the owner of the file, not by the user who actually launched the file.

The same logic applies to SGID, except instead of the file executing as though it was launched by the owner of the file, it will execute as though the person who executed it belongs to the group associated with the file (even if he or she doesn't). For instance, the lsof command needs access to attributes of the UNIX system that require membership in the kmem group, so its SGID bit is set:

```
powerbook:/usr local$ ls -l ./sbin/lsof
-rwxr-sr-x  1 root kmem 111356 Mar 26 14:04 ./sbin/lsof
```

Finding Files With SUID/SGID

As part of your regular security audit, it is important to identify files that have either the SUID or SGID bit set, because these could be potential security breaches if exploited. To find all of the files on your file system that have the SUID bit set, execute the following command:

```
sudo find / -perm +4000 -print
```

To identify all files with SGID, execute the following:

```
sudo find / -perm +2000 -print
```

To identify all files with both SUID and SGID, execute the following:

```
sudo find / -perm +6000 -print
```

As mentioned earlier, it is necessary for a healthy and happy UNIX that some files have either SUID or SGID. However, you need to proactively ensure that the files with these bits set are actually the correct versions of the executable, and not surreptitiously placed clones that give an attacker inappropriate access to your system.

One good way to ensure that your files are correct is to do a regular MD5 audit on the files you know have either SUID or SGID (as discovered with the find commands just listed). An MD5 checksum ensures that the files on your hard disk(s) have not been changed—if the checksum is different, you have a potential replacement, and this could be an issue. (Or it could just be an updated version of the command, but you need to be proactive to decide which it is.)

Understanding Keychain Security

The Mac OS X Keychain mechanism is an often-misunderstood, underutilized component of security. The Keychain infrastructure allows a user to store passwords in a 3DES-encrypted, OS-level password database, so that users do not have to enter passwords each time they are needed. Instead, the OS will, for Keychain-aware applications, search through the user's keychains to see if the password already exists.

Keychain-aware applications utilize the Apple-provided Keychain Services, provided in the Security Framework. The Security Framework is maintained by Apple to provide convenience wrappers around the CDSA (www.opengroup.org/security/cdsa.htm) library included with MacOS X, facilities for manipulating keychains, and more. Programmers who include support for Keychain Services in their applications can then leverage the power of Mac OS X security.

Keychain-aware applications that are included in Mac OS X include Safari, iTunes, Mail, and the Finder's Go > Connect to Server command. If a Keychain-aware application finds a valid keychain entry in any of the keychains in the search path, it will then attempt to use that password automatically to authenticate the user. If the password is correct, the user will be automatically logged in; if it is not correct, or if no keychain entry exists for that password, the user will be given the opportunity to enter the password (and, optionally, save that password in the keychain to prevent having to enter it again).

The application Keychain Access allows a user to manipulate his or her keychains (as you shall see in a later example) and also create new keychains (both on a per-user and global basis).

Mac OS X has a set of core OS keychains it uses to store SSL certificate authority information (located in /System/Library/Keychains) and also global keychains that apply to all users on the system (in /Library/Keychains). Each individual user's keychain is stored in his or her home folder (~/Library/Keychain) with the name login.keychain.

> **NOTE** ▶ In the version of Mac OS X prior to 10.3, each user's personal keychain would be named with his or her associated short name, for instance osxuser1. keychain. You may run across this naming convention for accounts that have been updated from older version of Mac OS X.

A default installation of Mac OS X would show the following keychains in those locations:

```
powerbook:~ local$ ls /System/Library/Keychains/
X509Anchors X509Certificates
powerbook:~ local$ ls /Library/Keychains/
System.keychain
powerbook:~ local$ ls ~/Library/Keychains/
login.keychain
```

Each keychain is password-protected and must be unlocked by the OS before the entries contained within can be used. The OS will attempt to unlock the keychains it uses automatically if it knows the password (which it does for the System and X509 keychains).

When a new account is created, the login keychain is created and password-protected with the exact same password as used for the user's login. So, when the OS attempts to utilize an entry within a user's login.keychain, it will attempt to unlock it with the user's login password (entered at the login window). If the user has not changed the password on the keychain, the OS will be able to unlock it without user intervention; if the user *has* changed the keychain password, the user will be asked to enter the keychain password to unlock the keychain.

A user may add other keychains, both global and local. A custom global keychain can be used to store passwords for all users on the system, but it can be password-protected so that it is not automatically unlocked like the default System.keychain is. A custom local keychain can be used for more sensitive information that the user does not want to have in his or her default local.keychain, because it will not be unlocked automatically by the OS.

A system administrator can prepopulate a global or local keychain, and then place it into the correct place for usage: /Library/Keychains for global keychains and ~/Library/Keychains for user-specific ones.

Keychain-Aware Applications in Action

When a Keychain-aware application wants to search for keychain entries that are appropriate to it, it will follow this flow:

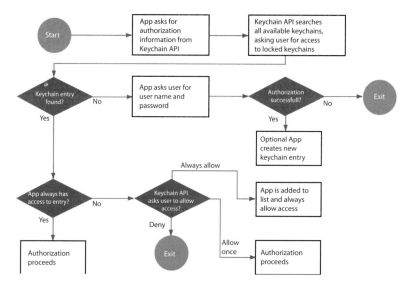

Assuming that an entry does not previously exist in any keychain, the user will hit the section of the flowchart that states "App asks user for user name and password." If the user enters the correct password, the entry is now stored in the user's login.keychain.

Look at the diagram again, knowing that there *is* a valid keychain entry. At the "Keychain entry found?" question, we now have a Yes, and proceed to the next question: "App always has access to entry?" The first time through this flow, this will *not* be the case, so you can proceed to "Keychain API asks user to allow access?", which appears as a dialog to the user.

If the user clicks Deny, the keychain entry, even though it exists, will not be utilized. If the user clicks Allow Once, the keychain entry is used this one time, and the next time through the flowchart, the user will be presented with this dialog again. If the user clicks Always Allow, that keychain entry will be marked as always available in a Keychain ACL list.

Modifying Keychain ACLs

Each keychain entry has a separate access control list with three possible levels of strictness:

▶ Always allow access: Applications can always read this item without any additional authentication or warning. This setting is generally not recommended.

▶ Confirm before allowing access: Before an application can read this item, the user will be presented with a dialog that asks whether the application should be denied access to the item, given access to the item once, or always given access to the item. Recommended for lower security passwords where convenience is more important than high security, such as a server in another department that the user may access once in a while.

▶ Confirm before allowing access and ask for keychain password: In addition to asking the user to deny, allow access once, or always allow access to the item, the user will also be asked for the keychain's password. This is the most secure option and is recommended for most uses.

In addition, applications may be given access to an item without requiring user interaction on an application-by-application basis. When a user clicks the Always Allow button in the access confirmation dialog, that application requesting access is added to the item's "Always allow access" list automatically. Once this is done, it is as though the item had the "Always allow access" option selected for that particular application, but any other applications still need to ask for confirmation before they can access the item. You can also add and remove applications from this list by using the Keychain Access application.

Controlling Keychains With Keychain Access

To control how your keychains function, use the Keychain Access application (located in /Applications/Utilities/Keychain Access).

View and Modify Keychain Entries

You can add as many keychains as you like and move items from one keychain to another to increase security. These keychains can all have different passwords and contain different items. For example, you can have one keychain for your Web forms, one for your certificates, one for servers, email, VPN, and so on. Each keychain will have a different password and can be locked separately. Use the Keychain Access application to create each keychain.

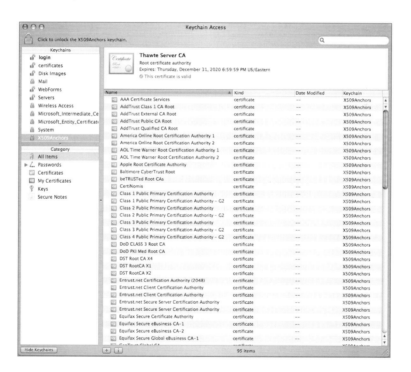

Perform Keychain First Aid

Sometimes keychains can start acting crazy and they need to be repaired. Corrupted keychains reveal themselves in many ways, including you being naggingly asked to use or store an entry in a keychain, even though you know you have done it at least once already. Another potential problem is a keychain password for local.keychain getting out of sync with the login password, and then forgetting the original local.keychain password (which prevents you from changing it).

Within Keychain Access is a menu item called Keychain First Aid (which was formerly a separate application), which can be used to repair keychains gone awry. In Keychain Access, choose Window > Keychain First Aid to enable this repair.

Using Encrypted Disk Images

If you have downloaded software for Mac OS X from the Internet, you may have noticed that the file format of choice for storing installer packages ends with the suffix .dmg. This type of file is known as a *disk image*—a very powerful method of storing multi-folder and multifile hierarchies in a single, Internet-friendly file.

Disk images appear to the Mac OS X file system as though they are mounted drives—if you've mounted one by double-clicking it, you notice that a disk-like image shows up on your desktop and in the Finder (and, for those who prefer the CLI, it gets mounted in the standard location /Volumes). A disk image may be read-only or read/write; it may be fixed in size or resizable as its contents grow; and it may be one of many file-system types: HFS+ (aka Mac OS Extended) and its journaled or case-sensitive varieties, UFS (UNIX File System), or the MS-DOS file system.

When you are done with a disk image, you "eject" it. The disk image will then be unmounted, and all contents are reconstituted back into the original .dmg file. In other words, with a read/write disk image, you can modify the contents of the mounted disk image as though it was a virtual drive. When you "eject" that disk image, all of your changes are folded back into the original .dmg file, so when it is reopened, it will be as though you mounted the disk again with your changes intact.

So how can you leverage these single-file-based virtual drives for security? Disk images can be password-protected (double-clicking the disk image to open it will require the user to enter a password) and encrypted (so if the disk image falls into the wrong hands, its contents cannot be easily obtained). You can create as many password-protected, encrypted disk images as you want, with different passwords for different users (whether they are meant to be shared or not), and you can populate each disk image as though it was its own very secure virtual drive (which, basically, it is).

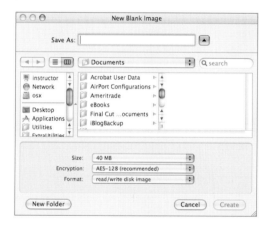

Password-protected, encrypted disk images ensure that your highly sensitive data can be safely packaged up in an easy-to-use and very secure file, which you can then share with selected recipients or keep to yourself.

You can use Disk Utility to create encrypted disk images. Like any other disk image file, an encrypted disk image can be copies or created on network volumes or removable media, including USB flash media and FireWire drives. You can also burn encrypted disk images onto a CD-R or DVD-R disk for archival purposes. Each encrypted disk image is protected by a password, which may be composed of 7-bit ASCII characters and can be 1 to 255 characters in length.

Creating Encrypted Disk Images

You can create disk images using either the GUI Disk Utility tool or the CLI hdiutil:

```
hdiutil create sizespec [options] imagepath
```

hdiutil provides much more power and granularity in creating disk images than Disk Utility does, including the ability to create MS-DOS file-system images and unformatted disk images.

> **MORE INFO** ▶ For more information, see the man page for hdiutil.

To create an encrypted disk image, do the following:

1   Open Disk Utility (/Applications/Disk Utility).

2   Click New Image.

3   From the Encryption pop-up menu, choose AES-128 (recommended).

4   From the Size and Format pop-up menus, choose a size and format.

5   Click Create.

> **NOTE** ▶ Because Disk Utility uses 128-bit encryption, your data will be irretriev-ably lost if you forget the password.

Enabling FileVault

The Mac OS X FileVault system leverages the power of the disk image by providing OS-level support to turn a user's entire home folder into an encrypted, password-protected disk image. FileVault is an all-or-nothing system for a user's home folder, so it's best to understand some of the issues involved—a lost password can make the contents of the folder irretrievable.

Setting Master Password

Mac OS X features an important security feature called the *master password,* which is set from the Security pane of System Preferences. When set, it should not be shared with *anyone.* This master password allows you to log in as any user on the system.

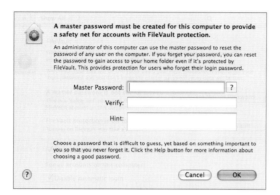

As a system administrator, it is *very* important that you set a Mac OS X master password before any of your users use FileVault for their home directories. This master password is the only potential emergency backdoor to unlock a user's home folder if he or she has forgotten his or her own password (or if the user has been specifically locked out of his or her home folder due to job termination or a security breach). If another administrative user creates the master password before you, it is possible you do not know that password.

Turning On FileVault

FileVault is enabled on a per-user basis from the Security pane of System Preferences.

Besides the very real problem of accidentally losing access to *all* of a user's data in his or her home folder, there are some other caveats when using FileVault. First, the ability to share information through the Public and Sites folder is no longer possible, since those folders are now password-protected and encrypted along with the rest of the home folder.

Second, backups will potentially be much larger, because it's harder to track incremental changes from an encrypted image than to look at the files and folders themselves.

One key issue when using a FileVault home directory is resetting user passwords. If a user should forget his or her password, the user's entire home directory would be irretrievably lost if not for the Master Password mechanism. This allows a system administrator who knows the master password to recover the user's home directory.

> **NOTE ▸** The master password is not related to any administrator user's password, and in fact should not be the same as any user's password.

When you set a master password on a machine, the system creates a new keychain file at /Library/Keychains/FileVaultMaster.keychain. The password for the new keychain file is the master password. The system then generates a X.509 private key and certificate. It stores the certificate in /Library/Keychains/FileVaultMaster.cer, and the private key in the newly created keychain.

> **NOTE ▸** For enterprise deployments, you can copy the two files FilevaultMaster.cer and FileVaultMaster.keychain to /Library/Keychains on another machine and it will automatically use the same master password.

When a user's home directory is converted to a FileVault home directory, the system generates a 128-bit random encryption key, which is used to encrypt the disk image. Two copies of this key are then encrypted and stored along with the disk image—the first is encrypted using the user's password, the second is encrypted using the FileVaultMaster. cer certificate. When the user logs in normally, the password that he or she enters is used to decrypt the first copy of the disk image's encryption key so the user can mount and access the disk image.

However, if an administrator needs to reset the user's password, he or she can enter the master password for the machine to unlock the FileVaultMaster.keychain file and retrieve the private key. This private key then decrypts the second copy of the disk image's encryption key, letting the administrator recover the contents of the user's home directory. However, that does not allow the administrator to recover the user's original password since it only retrieves the underlying encryption key for the disk image, not the password for the first copy.

Performing Additional Data Security Measures

There are other ways an attacker can obtain information that should be secret from your system, and Mac OS X is proactive in plugging these holes.

Securely Erasing Disks

Disk Utility and the diskutil command-line utility can erase either an entire volume or just the free (unused) space, with several different levels of security. Simply writing over the old data with zeros or random data might seem sufficient, but it can actually leave behind traces of magnetization from what used to be on the disk. These traces are very difficult to extract, but for security-critical data it's best to use a multipass erase to make sure all traces have been overwritten.

> **NOTE ▶** Overwriting the disk takes time proportional to the number of times the disk is overwritten. If the disk is large and/or slow, it could take several hours per pass, so budget your time accordingly.

Under Disk Utility's Erase tab, clicking the Security Options button gives you the options shown in the following figure.

▶ Don't Erase Data: This is the default setting. It leaves the disk's previous contents vulnerable to recovery.

► Zero Out Data: This option writes zeros over the entire disk, rendering its previous contents safe from normal disk editing and data recovery tools. However, it may still be possible to recover data from the drive by removing the platters from the drive and using a highly sensitive read mechanism to pick up residual magnetism that the erasure did not completely wipe out.

► 7-Pass Erase: This option writes data over the entire disk seven times, thus masking any residual magnetism behind multiple layers of new data, and making recovery extremely difficult. This mode is designed to comply with the United States Department of Defense's National Industrial Security Program Operating Manual (NISPOM, aka 5220.22-M).

► 35-Pass Erase: This option writes data over the entire disk 35 times, making recovery even more difficult than with the 7-Pass option. This uses a sequence of patterns known as the Gutmann algorithm.

MORE INFO ► For additional information on the Gutmann algorithm, visit www.cs.auckland.ac.nz/~pgut001/pubs/secure_del.html.

If you are using diskutil to erase a disk or volume, the following command-line options are available:

► sudo diskutil zeroDisk diskname: Equivalent to the Disk Utility Zero Out Data option, this writes zeros over the entire disk.

► sudo diskutil secureErase 1 diskname: Writes random data over the disk once.

► sudo diskutil secureErase 2 diskname: Equivalent to the Disk Utility 7-Pass Erase option.

► sudo diskutil secureErase 3 diskname: Equivalent to the Disk Utility 35-Pass Erase option.

► sudo diskutil randomDisk [times] diskname: Writes random data over the entire disk the specified number of times. Note that for the same number of passes, this will provide less security than the 7-pass or 35-pass options, as these use include patterns designed to make sure each bit gets thoroughly erased; the random data might or might not contain good patterns for every bit.

If you want to be doubly sure that all data has been erased, use the diskutil randomDisk or secureErase option, followed by the diskutil eraseDisk option, followed by the command

```
sudo od /dev/disk4s7
```

You will change the number (in this case, 4) and the slice (in this case, 7) to reflect the appropriate device you want to erase.

If the disk was zeroed successfully, the output should look something like this:

```
localhost:~ george$ sudo od /dev/disk1
0000000  000000 000000 000000 000000 000000 000000 000000 000000
*
356000000
localhost:~ george$
```

After verifying that the volume is truly zeroed, you can use Disk Utility or diskutil to partition it and create volumes.

Erasing Free Space

Erasing free space with either Disk Utility or diskutil is very similar to erasing an entire volume (although diskutil has fewer erasure options).

Under Disk Utility's Erase tab, the Erase Free Space button enables you to overwrite free space with zeros, perform a 7-Pass Erase, or perform a 35-Pass Erase. These are directly analogous to the options for full erasure listed in the previous section.

With diskutil's secureErase option, adding the freespace option restricts the erasure to just free blocks:

```
sudo diskutil secureErase freespace 1 diskname
sudo diskutil secureErase freespace 2 diskname
sudo diskutil secureErase freespace 3 diskname
```

NOTE ► When using Disk Utility or diskutil, free space can be erased only from a mounted volume, not an entire disk.

Using Secure Empty Trash

When files are removed from a volume, either by taking out the Trash or by using the CLI rm command, the blocks on the volume are freed up for use by other files by unlinking the blocks. However, the content of those blocks is *not* modified, so potentially secret data may still be contained on the volume (and easily obtained by scouring the volume).

To prevent this from happening, a secure version of rm, called srm, may be used to not only free up the blocks by unlinking, but also overwrite those blocks with either all 0s, using seven U.S. DoD–compliant passes, or with a single pass of random data.

MORE INFO ► See the man page for srm to see how to enable these different options.

The Mac OS X Finder now has a GUI menu option called Secure Empty Trash, which uses srm to remove the Trash instead of using the default rm. To empty the Trash securely, choose Finder > Secure Empty Trash.

Using Encrypted Swap File

The built-in virtual memory system on Mac OS X functions by swapping out currently unused RAM memory to a file on the boot volume called a *swap file.* So, at least temporarily, memory that would otherwise be inaccessible if it was in RAM is stored on the boot volume in a well-known place that could be easily copied and then analyzed. Passwords, financial data from an Excel spreadsheet, or anything that the OS decides to temporarily swap out of RAM and onto the boot volume can potentially be stored here.

If you want this to happen in a secure way (it is not possible to disable virtual memory, and you really wouldn't want to), you can tell the operating system that you would like it to use an encrypted swap file. To do this, run System Preferences and navigate to the Security pane. Select the "Use secure virtual memory" box (if it is not already), and you will then have an encrypted swap file.

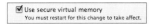

This may cause minor slowdowns in the swapping of virtual memory (since everything needs to be encrypted and decrypted now), so decide how important this is to you.

If you want to make a backward check of your swap files, you can boot into single-user mode and erase all of those older swap files (they may not be cleared automatically after crashes) by using the srm command on the swap files:

```
# srm /var/vm/swapfile*
```

What You've Learned

► When the sticky bit is placed on a folder, only the owner of an item within that folder can delete or edit that item.

► You can use fsaclctl to work with Access Control Lists on Mac OS X and Mac OS X Server.

► By setting the SUID bit on an executable file, you are telling the file system that, no matter who launches the executable file, the file will execute as though it was launched by the assigned owner of the file.

► Mac OS X has a set of core OS keychains it uses to store SSL certificate authority information; the keychains are located in /System/ Library/Keychains.

► The command line srm uses seven U.S. DoD–compliant passes, or a single pass of random data to erase data.

References

Administration Guides

"Mac OS X Server Getting Started": http://images.apple.com/server/pdfs/
Getting_Started_v10.4.pdf

"Mac OS X Server File Services Administration for Version 10.4 or Later":
http://images.apple.com/server/pdfs/File_Services_v10.4.pdf

"Mac OS X Server Windows Services Administration for Version 10.4 or Later":
http://images.apple.com/server/pdfs/Windows_Services_v10.4.pdf

"Mac OS X Server Command-Line Administration for Version 10.4 or Later":
http://images.apple.com/server/pdfs/Command_Line_v10.4.pdf)

Lesson Review

1. What folders are read access by others in every user's home folder?

2. What three levels of granularity can be set when using standard UNIX permissions?

3. What is the command to set the sticky bit for a folder?

4. How do you enable ACLs on the local volume using Mac OS X?

5. Name four attributes permitted on all objects.

6. How do you find all items on your local hard disk that have both SUID and GUID set on them?

7. What is the command-line utility that permits the creation and management of disk images?

Answers

1. Public and Sites

2. Read, write, and execute

3. chmod +t /path/to/folder

4. sudo /usr/sbin/fsaclctl -p / -e

5. delete, readattr, writeattr, chown

6. sudo find / -perm +6000 -print

7. hdiutil

15

Time   This lesson takes approximately 1 hour to complete.

Goals   Understand the features and security risks of Bluetooth and 802.11 WLANs

Configure Mac OS X Bluetooth for security

Compare the features and level of security provided by WEP, 802.1X/WEP, WPA Enterprise, and WPA Personal

Configure Mac OS X for WEP, 802.1X/WEP, WPA Enterprise, and WPA Personal

Mobility Security Concerns

Macintosh users are on the move. They expect to get work done at home, at school, at work, in their cars, in meeting rooms, in the company cafeteria, and even in the local coffee shop. Now that notebook computers really are the size of notebooks, mobility is here to stay. Employers and IT departments recognize the increases in productivity and employee satisfaction when workers have reliable mobile connectivity. They also recognize the challenges of providing safe and secure mobile connectivity. Fortunately, Mac OS X has many features that support mobile technologies.

In this lesson, you will become familiar with mobile technologies and the security risks associated with them. Then, you'll learn how to implement Mac OS X security features for these technologies.

Choosing Mobile Technologies

The computer industry has addressed users' demand for mobility in many ways. Users can read e-mail, surf the Web, and conduct business over the Internet using notebook computers, cell phones, personal digital assistants (PDAs), and even wearable technology built into clothing.

Two technologies have emerged as the leaders in connecting devices and networks while on the move: Bluetooth, a short-range radio technology for connecting devices, and 802.11, a set of IEEE standards for radio frequency wireless local area networks (WLANs).

Understanding Bluetooth

Bluetooth is a technology for connecting devices within a short range (about 10 meters) using a radio link between the devices. Bluetooth-enabled devices, including Macintosh systems, keyboards, mice, and cell phones, can pair with each other in a manner that is user friendly and doesn't require cables. The Bluetooth Special Interest Group hopes that Bluetooth will one day replace the cables that currently connect one device to another.

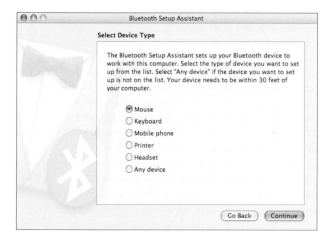

Other benefits of Bluetooth include simplicity, low cost, low power usage, and robustness.

NOTE ▶ Bluetooth is standardized by an industry consortium called the Bluetooth Special Interest Group. The founding members of this group include Ericsson, IBM, Intel, Nokia, and Toshiba. Apple Computer is an associate member.

Bluetooth radio modules operate in the unlicensed Industrial Scientific Medical (ISM) frequency band at 2.4 GHz, which is a band used by many technologies. Bluetooth radios avoid interference from other signals by hopping to a new frequency after transmitting or receiving a packet. Compared with other systems in the same frequency band, including 802.11b and 802.11g wireless LANs, a Bluetooth radio hops faster and uses shorter packets. This means that Bluetooth operates well in environments with a lot of radio frequency activity.

When connected, Bluetooth devices allow users to upload and download files, access peripherals such as printers without using cables, listen to music on wireless headphones, and automatically synchronize contact and calendar information.

Mac OS X includes a Bluetooth File Exchange application that allows remote users to browse, upload, and download files from a specified directory on a Bluetooth-enabled Macintosh. Bluetooth File Exchange also lets a Macintosh user send files to other Bluetooth devices. Setting up Bluetooth connectivity and applications is easy to do, but there are security concerns, as discussed later in this lesson in the "Identifying the Security Risks of Mobility" and "Implementing Bluetooth Security in Mac OS X" sections.

Understanding 802.11 Wireless LANs

Whereas Bluetooth pairs two short-range devices so they can share information, 802.11 technology creates a WLAN permitting multiple devices to communicate over a distance of up to 50 meters. With the addition of a wireless access point, such as the Apple AirPort Extreme Base Station, devices can access the wired network and often the Internet, assuming that the wired network (or the access point itself) includes a router with Internet connectivity. Although 802.11 protocols support users communicating in an "ad-hoc mode" in a computer-to-computer network, it is more common to use an access point, which IEEE calls *infrastructure mode*.

> **NOTE ▶** The distance listed here is 50 meters, but could be further under certain circumstances. It's best to simply assume that all wireless connection methods should be secured.

Like Bluetooth, 802.11 WLANs use radio frequency. The IEEE 802.11 Working Group has standardized the following WLAN technologies:

▶ IEEE 802.11 operates in the 2.4 GHz frequency band, supports 1 to 2 Mbps, and uses direct-sequence spread spectrum (DSSS) or frequency-hopping spread spectrum (FHSS).

▶ IEEE 802.11a operates in the 5 GHz frequency band, supports 54 Mbps, and uses orthogonal frequency division multiplexing (OFDM).

▶ IEEE 802.11b operates in the 2.4 GHz frequency band, supports 1, 2, 5.5, and 11 Mbps, and uses high-rate DSSS (HR/DSSS).

▶ IEEE 802.11g operates in the 2.4 GHz frequency band, supports 54 Mbps, and uses OFDM, but is not compatible with 802.11a, which also uses OFDM. (802.11g is compatible with 802.11b.)

Today, most WLANs use 802.11b or 802.11g. 802.11g is preferred by most users because it has a faster data rate. The IEEE is also working on a new standard, called 802.11n. The promise of 802.11n is longer range and even higher data rates. Whereas most WLANs today offer a maximum speed of 54 Mbps, 802.11n will approximately double that transmission speed to about 100 Mbps.

Identifying the Security Risks of Mobility

Without proper configuration, data on wireless networks and devices can be intercepted, analyzed, changed, or deleted, resulting in compromised data confidentiality and integrity.

Network services can also be compromised. Bad routing or naming information can be injected into a network. User passwords can be compromised and used for further intrusions. The configuration of devices can be changed to allow unauthorized connections or to disallow connections that should be allowed.

Mobile computers are vulnerable to worms, Trojan horses, and viruses. A compromised computer can be used to launch a Denial of Service (DoS) attack on a user's home or business network, when the user returns from roaming. Security measures are necessary to avoid these problems.

Basic networking classes teach that networks are structured in bus, ring, or star topologies. Although this may be true for very simple wired networks, it's not true for wireless networks. Even the simplest wireless network is amorphous, with radio waves emanating in many directions. Wireless users and wireless network signals can wander to unexpected places, where ordinary security protections may not be in place. That can compound this risk when mobile computers are taken off the main network and placed on a wireless network, where they are exposed to attacks, viruses, and Trojan horses. There's also the danger that they'll bring those risks back to the wired network. This means that users, and the IT representatives who support those users, must be even more vigilant about mobile security than they are with wired connectivity.

The previous section mentioned that 802.11 networks can span about 50 meters. With good antennas and favorable physical conditions that limit signal degradation, 802.11 networks can actually extend to much wider areas. A problem for network administrators is that networks can sometimes spread into parking lots or areas outside a building. Network attackers have been known to sit in the parking lots of companies and break into the wireless network and from there into the wired network. In August 2004, three Michigan men reached separate plea bargain agreements with the U.S. federal government in connection with a case in which they hacked into the national network of a retail store chain from one store's parking lot.

Other unscrupulous individuals have used wireless bandwidth without authorization to send huge amounts of spam or other objectionable material. In September 2004, a Southern California man pled guilty under the federal CAN Spam Act to driving around Venice, California, searching for unprotected wireless hot spots and exploiting them to distribute unsolicited e-mail that advertised adult websites.

In addition to the possibility that unauthorized users might exploit unsecured wireless bandwidth to launch attacks or send spam, there's also an increased risk to individual wireless devices, including notebook computers, on wireless networks. One reason for this is that wireless users can roam to unprotected networks, such as Internet cafés, hotels, and airports. Without proper protection, these users are vulnerable to DoS attacks and virus infections.

Wireless networks use shared bandwidth and therefore are more vulnerable to spying than wired networks. Wireless networks are analogous to legacy wired Ethernet networks that were designed using hubs or shared coaxial cable. In these older, nonswitched networks, every user on the network saw every other user's network traffic. Wireless networks still work that way today. Without added security features, both Bluetooth and 802.11 networks are vulnerable to *sniffing,* whereby an attacker monitors data being transmitted over a network. The confidentiality of data is at risk, as is the integrity of data if the attacker has the ability to change or remove data.

Tools are readily available for sniffing an unencrypted or weakly encrypted WLAN. They include Kismet, AirSnort, Ethereal, and WildPackets' AiroPeek. Network managers have legitimate uses for these tools, but attackers also can use them to peek at confidential data transmitted wirelessly.

Bluetooth networks that don't use encryption are also vulnerable to sniffing, although the tools are not as readily available as they are with WLANs. Without proper configuration, Bluetooth devices are also vulnerable to *Bluesnarfing,* where attackers gain unauthorized access to data stored on Bluetooth devices, and *Bluejacking,* where tricksters send bogus (often silly or flirtatious) business cards to Bluetooth devices. In early versions of Mac OS X, Bluetooth support allowed files to be shared without properly notifying the user. This has been addressed in Mac OS X 10.4.

NOTE ▸ Never underestimate the potential for attackers to send malicious applications that the user may execute.

Despite these security risks, and others that are beyond the scope of this lesson, users demand mobility. They won't go back to being tethered to their desks. To meet the need for secure mobility, Apple Computer supports numerous industry standards for protecting Bluetooth and 802.11 networks.

Using the security features discussed in this lesson, you can control which users have access to mobile devices and networks, and what those users can do while they have access. You can also enable strong encryption that will make it virtually impossible for attackers to understand confidential data transmitted over wireless networks. The wireless genie is out of the bottle and surfing a radio wave near you, but that doesn't mean your security has to go up in smoke.

Implementing Bluetooth Security in Mac OS X

Because Bluetooth is used by consumer devices such as cell phones, headphones, keyboards, mice, and laptop computers, an important goal is that Bluetooth users should be able to effortlessly and quickly pair devices to work together and share information. However, ease-of-use is a tradeoff with security. If pairing devices and sharing information is made too easy, attackers will take advantage. Security options are necessary to make Bluetooth acceptably safe for most environments.

In its "Mac OS X v10.3.x Panther Security Configuration Guideline," the National Security Agency (NSA) of the U.S. federal government recommends completely disabling Bluetooth. (As of this writing, a newer version of the document isn't available, but the next version will likely make the same recommendation.) The NSA document has detailed recommendations on how to completely disable Bluetooth for all Macintosh users. IT professionals and users in environments with stringent security requirements should read the NSA document and implement the recommendations in it, where appropriate.

Bluetooth should be disabled by default and enabled as necessary. Less rigorous and restrictive approaches can be taken in environments in which users regularly connect wireless keyboards, mice, and other devices, or share files between Bluetooth-enabled laptops, cell phones, and PDAs. Some aspects of Bluetooth (such as using it for Internet connectivity) can be disabled, while others can be allowed, depending on your specific security requirements and policies. You can completely disable Bluetooth by removing the Bluetooth kernel extensions (IOBluetoothFamily.kext and IOBluetoothHIDDriver. kext) located in /System/Library/Extensions/. Keep in mind that these drivers can be replaced with a software update, so you still need to perform regular preventative measures. That means, for example, creating a launchd item to watch the Extensions directory for the Bluetooth kernel extensions and remove them as necessary. And before installing Bluetooth on your production computers, it's a good idea to test software updates on another computer.

Securing Bluetooth Internet Access

Bluetooth users have the ability to pair their Macintosh computers with a Bluetooth-enabled cell phone that has Internet access, and access the Internet using that link. This should be discouraged. Although the speed of the link is so slow that most attacks would not succeed, slow speed is not a good excuse for lax security measures. Attackers are persistent.

> **NOTE ▶** There are actually two links in this example that are vulnerable to sniffing and other attacks: the Bluetooth link and the cellular Internet link.

A network administrator or IT professional who distributes laptops to mobile users can configure the laptops so that users who don't have the administrator password can't use Bluetooth for network connectivity and Internet access.

1   In the System Preferences window, click the Network icon.

2   Choose Network Port Configurations from the Show pull-down menu.

3   Select the Bluetooth port configuration check box and then click Delete.

4   Click Apply Now and then click the lock icon to prevent further changes.

Controlling Bluetooth Discoverability

Bluetooth discoverability allows devices on a Bluetooth network to easily find each other. Configuring a device to be nondiscoverable makes it harder to find. To prevent attackers from discovering a Bluetooth device, especially a Bluetooth-enabled Macintosh, configure the device to be nondiscoverable. In Mac OS X, you can do this in the Bluetooth System Preferences by deselecting Discoverable in the Bluetooth Status menu.

Another Bluetooth device can still connect to your computer even if you make your computer nondiscoverable. One way to accomplish this is for you to initiate the connection.

Another possible security weakness is that your computer was once configured as discoverable and another device still "remembers" how to access your computer with Bluetooth. In other words, making your computer nondiscoverable doesn't make it completely inaccessible via Bluetooth; other devices just have a harder time finding it, which enhances security.

Using Bluetooth File Transfer Security Options

Bluetooth file transfer allows other devices to browse files on your computer, but your computer must be discoverable for this to work. Beginning with Mac OS X 10.4.1, Bluetooth file transfer is not turned on by default, which is good from a security point of view.

In some situations, however, allowing other users to browse your files could come in handy. For example, some cell phones can share files with a Macintosh, which can be useful for getting contact information onto a cell phone. In situations like this, you can temporarily make your computer discoverable. Then temporarily enable file transfer and specify a folder that other devices can browse and drop files into. Other users can also retrieve files from this folder. Make sure you require pairing for file transfer. You can enable file transfer options by opening the Bluetooth System Preferences and clicking Sharing.

> **NOTE** ▶ Use caution when attempting to pair Bluetooth devices in a public place, since attackers can harvest the passkey for later use.

When you require pairing for security with Bluetooth file transfer, if another user wants to browse your files, you will be warned and given the opportunity to enter a passkey. Because Bluetooth has limited range, you should be able to physically look around and see who wants to browse your files. If it's a coworker, friend, or other legitimate user, enter a passkey and tell the person what it is. That person will also enter the passkey on his device. If you don't see anyone other than some shadowy figure in the dark looking at you with a sneaky, anticipatory smirk, then simply reject the invitation to pair. A Pairing Request dialog box appears when another user tries to browse the files in your public folder.

Using Bluetooth File Exchange Security Options

Mac OS X Bluetooth preferences also include options for securing the Bluetooth File Exchange utility. Bluetooth File Exchange is on by default. You should turn it off until you need it.

To maximize the security of file exchange, configure Mac OS X to prompt for each file that it receives, and to ask before accepting Personal Information Management (PIM) or other types of files. Also, be sure to select "Require pairing for security."

Using Bluetooth PDA Sync Security Options

Under the Bluetooth Sharing preferences, best security practices dictate not turning on the serial port, not showing the serial port in Network preferences, and requiring pairing for security.

Implementing WLAN Security in Mac OS X

Security on 802.11 wireless networks is even more important than on Bluetooth networks. Whereas Bluetooth is a nice feature that some users appreciate for connecting wireless devices and sharing information, 802.11 technology has become a mainstream method for connecting computers in businesses, homes, colleges, hotels, coffee shops, stores, airports, and so on. Extensive enterprise networks based on 802.11 are much more prevalent than the smaller, personal networks that connect Bluetooth devices, and they must be protected with the security measures discussed in this lesson.

> **NOTE** ▶ Using a Virtual Private Network (VPN) connection, especially over a wireless network, is an excellent way to combine a tunneled connection to your network with relatively strong encryption.

Before discussing detailed recommendations, it's worth exploring a few general guidelines for WLAN security:

▶ Protect each Macintosh that roams to other networks with firewall and antivirus software, and appropriate user authentication and authorization measures, as covered elsewhere in this book.

▶ Lock down or turn off file sharing.

▶ Users who roam to insecure places, such as hotel lobbies or coffee shops, should be vigilant about maintaining physical security.

▶ Use screensaver passwords so that if a computer is stolen, the thief will have a hard time accessing data on the computer.

▶ For extremely sensitive information, use FileVault to encrypt data on the hard drive.

▶ Require mobile users to use virtual private networking (VPN) software to remotely access their "home" network, whether the home network is really at home, or in a business or educational institution.

To ensure mobile users don't stumble into insecure wireless networks, configure Mac OS X systems to ask the user before the computer automatically joins a network. For corporate environments with stringent security requirements, you can also require an administrator password when a user wishes to move to a new network or to create a computer-to-computer network. To enable these options, do the following:

1   In the System Preferences window, click the Network icon.

2   Choose AirPort from the Show pop-up menu.

3   Click the Options button to configure the security features for AirPort.

For those peripatetic users who roam to hotels, airports, coffee shops, and so on, requiring firewall and antivirus software is essential, but requiring authentication and encryption to use the wireless networks where they end up is usually not appropriate. Can you imagine a mobile user stumbling into the local coffee shop at 7 A.M., laptop under her arm, craving some caffeine, and having to ask the barista for the 128-bit encryption key to access the coffee shop's wireless network? That's not how most coffee shop networks work.

When the user accesses her "enterprise" wireless network, however, whether that network is at home or at a business or school, requiring the authentication and encryption methods discussed in the next sections are absolutely appropriate.

Implementing Wired Equivalent Privacy

Wired Equivalent Privacy (WEP) was the first authentication and encryption standard built into the original 802.11 specification, which IEEE standardized in June 1997. You shouldn't use WEP unless your network must carry traffic for older devices that don't support newer security mechanisms. WEP isn't secure. Without much effort, attackers can derive the WEP encryption key and compromise a network that is supported only by WEP.

If possible, upgrade any older devices that only support WEP right away. If upgrading isn't possible, try to use WEP in conjunction with 802.1X user authentication. This lesson discusses WEP in case you need to use it to support older devices that can't be upgraded and because it provides good background information to help understand newer security mechanisms. But keep in mind that WEP is not secure and should be avoided if possible.

In wired networks, a device must physically plug into the network to have access. This provides some security. An attacker has to have physical access to a port on a hub or switch, or a live jack in a wall, to gain access.

This isn't possible on a wireless network. There's nothing to plug in and there aren't any ports or jacks. IEEE recognized this issue in the early development of 802.11 and built authentication capability into the standard. IEEE specified both open authentication (which is essentially no authentication) and shared key authentication using WEP. WEP requires that a device send a key to log on to the network. From that point, the key is also used to encrypt data sent on the network. This shared key must be configured on the wireless access point and on any devices that join the network.

WEP supports two lengths for the shared key: 64 bits and 128 bits. Both of these key lengths include a 24-bit initialization vector. The 64-bit key is often called a 40-bit key, which represents the key length minus the 24-bit initialization vector. The 128-bit key is rarely referred to as a 104-bit key, even though that is technically accurate and would match the terminology used for 64-bit keys.

As part of the encryption process, WEP concatenates the shared key with the randomly-generated 24-bit initialization vector. WEP includes the initialization vector in the clear (unencrypted) in the first few bytes of a packet. The receiving station uses the initialization vector along with the shared key to decrypt the payload portion of a packet.

The 24-bit initialization vector is one of the sources of WEP's infamous vulnerabilities. WEP eventually uses the same initialization vector for different data packets. If an attacker collects enough packets based on the same initialization vector, the attacker can eventually discover the shared key. For high-usage WLANs, an attacker can capture traffic for a few hours and discover the key. This allows the attacker full access to the network and to any confidential data being transmitted on the network.

Note that the IEEE knew they weren't providing strong privacy with WEP, but the same amount of privacy found on wired networks. As Sun Microsystems Inc. chairman and CEO Scott McNealy said, "You have no privacy. Get over it." Wired networks don't have much privacy, and neither do WLANs that use WEP.

Configuring WEP

Because WEP is reasonably easy to crack, don't use it unless it's the only option. Apple supports other options, but you may need to configure WEP for compatibility with non-Apple devices or Macintosh computers running older system software.

To configure WEP, you need to know the shared key that is configured on the access point. You should enter the key in the exact format that the administrator for the access point specifies.

A WEP key can be a plain-language password, an exact number of ASCII characters, or an exact number of hexadecimal digits. Access points that permit a plain-language password don't require the network administrator to create a key of an exact length. Instead, the access point handles the "heavy lifting" for the user and hashes the password to a key of the right length.

Unfortunately, the hashing used on one vendor's access point may not match the hashing used by other vendors' wireless network interface cards (NICs), resulting in a multi-platform compatibility problem. In this case, you may need to enter a precise number of characters or digits for the key.

For a 40-bit WEP key, you may have to enter precisely 5 ASCII characters or precisely 10 hex characters. Each ASCII character is 1 byte or 8 bits. Five of them add up to the 40 bits in the 40-bit key, which some access points may call a 64-bit key (because they include the length of the 24-bit initialization vector). For a hex-based key, you need to enter exactly 10 hex digits because each hex digit is 4 bits. Valid hex digits are 0 through 9 and A through F.

For a 128-bit WEP key, you may need to enter precisely 13 ASCII characters or precisely 26 hex digits. Thirteen multiplied by 8 adds up to the 104 bits in the 128-bit key, not counting the 24-bit initialization vector. Twenty-six multiplied by 4 also adds up to 104. Again, this is only if you need to use WEP for compatibility with older machines.

When your Macintosh tries to join a network that uses WEP, you will be prompted to enter a WEP key. You can also enter a WEP key by using the menu from the AirPort status icon in the menu bar. (If the AirPort status icon isn't visible in the menu bar, go to System Preferences and select the Network pane to make it visible.) Choose Other from the menu and enter the name of the network.

After you enter the name of the network, use the Wireless Security pop-up menu to choose the right type of password. If the network you are joining is already up and running, you will see only the options that are allowed by the administrator of the access point for that network.

Understanding 802.1X Authentication

WEP uses a shared key for authentication and encryption that is configured on all clients and the access point. Management of this key can be difficult. How does the administrator securely let everyone know that the key has changed? If a laptop gets stolen, how does the administrator lock out the thief from the wireless network? What does the administrator do if an attacker captures enough packets to recover the supposedly secret WEP key?

Wireless vendors realized during the early days of WEP deployment that a better method for authentication was necessary. Fortunately, the IEEE already had an authentication protocol that was gaining popularity in the wired world. That protocol is 802.1X, standardized in IEEE's "802.1X Port-Based Network Access Control" document. The IEEE adopted 802.1X as a standard in August 2001.

IEEE 802.1X specifies a method for authenticating a user who attaches a device to a LAN port. It is used on both wired switches and on wireless access points (where the "attachment" is not purely physical). 802.1X can be used with an authentication server, such as a Remote Authentication Dial-In User Service (RADIUS) server, which is good practice for larger enterprises. The Apple Wi-Fi Protected Access (WPA) Enterprise security feature, for example, works with a RADIUS server and is described later in this lesson in the "Using WPA Enterprise" section. For older environments that still use WEP due to legacy NICs or access points, WEP security can be enhanced by requiring 802.1X.

802.1X supports many authentication algorithms. The most common are varieties of the Extensible Authentication Protocol (EAP), which is an Internet Engineering Task Force (IETF) standard, documented in Request For Comments (RFC) 2284. With 802.1X and EAP, devices take on one of three roles:

▶   A *supplicant* resides on a wireless LAN client device.

▶   An *authenticator* resides on an access point.

▶   An *authentication server* resides on a RADIUS server.

When 802.1X and EAP are implemented, a client device that associates with a wireless access point cannot use the wireless network until the user is authenticated. An EAP supplicant on the client obtains credentials from the user, which could be a user name and password, a user name and one-time password, or a digital certificate. The credentials are passed to the authenticator and then to the authentication server where a session key is developed.

With 802.1X, the heavy lifting is done on the supplicant (the wireless client) and the authentication server, and the access point has very little work to do. Configuring 802.1X on most access points is as simple as enabling the option to use 802.1X and then point-ing the access point at a RADIUS server that supports 802.1X. Some access points are even easier to set up because they support a built-in authentication server. This can make deployment much faster, especially if setting up a RADIUS server is a bit daunting for novice network administrators.

When using 802.1X and EAP, session timeouts force a client to reauthenticate to main-tain network connectivity. This causes a WEP key to be regenerated. This feature miti-gates statistical key derivation attacks and is a critical WEP enhancement.

> **NOTE ▶** Reauthentication can cause some delay, when compared to using a static WEP key. This may cause a problem for users who roam with delay-sensitive devices, such as 802.11 phones.

Note that 802.1X and EAP authenticate users, whereas basic WEP authentication is device-based. A WEP shared key is entered into wireless devices and the access point. If a thief steals a laptop computer using a static WEP key, the thief can access the wireless network which would probably require the network administrator to change the WEP key on the affected access points and all clients. 802.1X and EAP, on the other hand, generate a unique key for each user. This relieves network administrators from the burden of managing static keys. EAP also supports mutual authentication, which allows a client to be certain that it is communicating with the intended authentication server and not an attacker posing as a server.

EAP supports the use of digital certificates. A *digital certificate* is a special kind of data structure that contains information about who it belongs to, who it was issued by, a unique serial number or other unique identification, valid dates, and an encrypted "fingerprint" that can be used to verify the contents of the certificate. Digital certificates are issued by trusted third parties known as *certificate authorities*. A wireless user's digital certificate can include a user name and password, a one-time password provided by a smart card, or any other identity credentials that the IT administrator is comfortable using.

Selecting EAP Types

When setting up wireless clients, access points, and authentication servers, you need to choose the right EAP standard to match your users' needs and security policies. Selecting the right EAP type can be challenging because there are so many options and because they go by funny names, such as LEAP and PEAP. You need to get this right though. The supplicant, authenticator, and authentication server must all be configured for the same variety of EAP, which is mostly likely one of the following:

► EAP Transport Layer Security (EAP-TLS): Supports mutual authentication and dynamically generated user and session keys. Because EAP-TLS requires certificates on both the client and server, some experts consider EAP-TLS more secure than other EAP types. However, for a large WLAN installation, managing certificates can be cumbersome, especially if the need arises to revoke certificates after an attack occurs. EAP-TLS is often used to support Windows clients. Note that Microsoft developed EAP-TLS (and documented it in RFC 2716).

► EAP Tunneled Transport Layer Security (EAP-TTLS): An extension of EAP-TLS that provides for certificate-based, mutual authentication through an encrypted tunnel, as well as a means to derive dynamic, per-user, per-session keys. Unlike EAP-TLS, EAP-TTLS requires a certificate only on the server. Organizations can avoid installing digital certificates on every client machine.

► Protected EAP (PEAP): Supports mutual authentication and dynamic per-user and per-session keys. PEAP uses a certificate for the client to authenticate the server. The server uses a one-time password or a user name and password to authenticate the client. Once the client validates the server's certificate, it builds an encrypted tunnel and then uses EAP in the tunnel to authenticate. PEAP tunnels provide a method to securely transport authentication data, including legacy password-based protocols. Like EAP-TTLS, PEAP authenticates wireless LAN clients using only server-side certificates, thereby simplifying management.

► Lightweight EAP (LEAP): Developed by Cisco, but is licensed to other vendors, including Apple Computer and Intel. LEAP supports dynamic per-user and per-session keys. LEAP is popular in Windows environments because user authentication is based on a user's Windows logon, which means the user does not have to supply additional logon information to access the wireless network. Like the other EAP types covered, LEAP supports mutual authentication whereby the client authenticates the server and the server authenticates the client.

The following table summarizes features of the various EAP types:

Type	TLS	TTLS	PEAP	LEAP
Client-side certificate required	Yes	No	No	No
Server-side certificate required	Yes	Yes	Yes	Yes
Key management	Yes	Yes	Yes	Yes
Mutual authentication	Yes	Yes	Yes	Yes
Setup difficulty	Very	Moderate	Moderate	Moderate
Security	Highest	High	High	High

Combining 802.1X With WEP

For networks with legacy equipment that don't support newer wireless security standards such as WPA, 802.1X can be used to enhance the security of WEP.

Although WEP encryption is still crackable in theory, 802.1X means every connection authenticated with 802.1X gets its own WEP key, which can be changed as often as the network administrator controlling the WLAN desires.

A second benefit with 802.1X is that the administrator actually knows who is on the network. Bandwidth thieves and other attackers can't get on without getting authenticated and that requires going through a true authentication dialog where a user name and password must be entered.

Understanding Wi-Fi Protected Access

The IEEE started working on enhancements to WEP as soon as its problems became known, and in June 2004, the IEEE 802.11i Working Group ratified a new security standard called 802.11i. Because there was quite a long gap between the time that WEP vulnerabilities were proven (2001) and the release of 802.11i, vendors started implementing parts of 802.11i long before 2004, under the auspices of an industry consortium known as the Wi-Fi Alliance.

In 2003, the Wi-Fi Alliance finalized WPA. WPA is a subset of 802.11i, leaving out the more complicated aspects of 802.11i which would require a hardware upgrade on some vendors' equipment, including a requirement to use the Advanced Encryption Standard (AES). WPA includes the following features:

▶ 802.1X and EAP can be used to authenticate users of a wireless network.

▶ The Temporal Key Integrity Protocol (TKIP) implements per-packet keying, which provides every packet with a new and unique key to mitigate WEP key derivation attacks.

▶ A Message Integrity Check (MIC) provides a mathematical function that senders and receivers apply to packets to ensure their authenticity and to mitigate man-in-the-middle attacks. The MIC is designed to prevent an attacker from capturing data packets, altering them, and resending them.

In September 2004, the Wi-Fi Alliance introduced WPA2. With WPA2, the entire IEEE 802.11i specification is supported. Like WPA, WPA2 supports IEEE 802.1X/EAP authentication or preshared keys. It also includes support for AES, which is newer and stronger than WEP or TKIP. AES satisfies U.S. government security requirements. It has been adopted as an official government standard by the U.S. Department of Commerce and the National Institute of Standards and Technology (NIST).

Apple added support for WPA2 in Mac OS X 10.4.2. Unlike some vendors, Apple equipment does not require a hardware upgrade because Apple base stations and cards already have an AES chip built in.

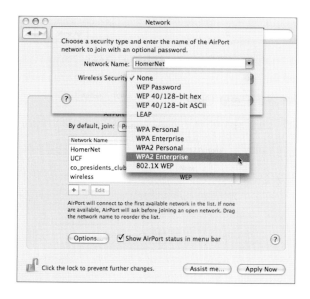

Apple offers two modes for both WPA versions:

▶ Enterprise mode, which uses a RADIUS server for user authentication

▶ Personal mode, which relies on the capabilities of TKIP without requiring a RADIUS server

Using WPA Enterprise

WPA Enterprise is intended for large organizations, such as businesses and educational institutions, with rigorous security requirements and sizeable wireless installations. WPA Enterprise leverages the IEEE 802.1X authentication framework, which uses an EAP type with an authentication server to provide strong mutual authentication between a client and authentication server via an access point. (See "Understanding 802.1X Authentication," earlier in this lesson.)

The authentication server is a RADIUS server, which could be running on Mac OS X Server or any other server that supports RADIUS. Each user is assigned a unique user name and password for access to the WLAN. This affords a high level of individual privacy.

As with WPA Personal, WPA Enterprise uses TKIP encryption. TKIP issues a new encryption key for each data packet sent for each session of each user, making the encryption extremely difficult to break. What distinguishes Apple WPA Enterprise from WPA Personal is that WPA Enterprise requires a RADIUS server whereas WPA Personal does not.

Large institutions with many mobile users often have numerous wireless access points. Users roam from one access point to another. With a good network design, which access point their computers have associated with is transparent to users. To make this secure, all access points must have knowledge of user authentication information.

Here's where the benefits of a RADIUS server come into play. Network administrators could configure authentication information in each access point, but that is cumbersome. Instead, authentication information can be configured in one RADIUS server (which is optionally backed up by a secondary server).

Livingston, Inc. developed the RADIUS protocol to authenticate dial-up users back in the early 1990s. It was formalized by the IETF and is currently standardized in RFC 2865. It has become a de facto standard for authenticating users of all types, not just dial-up modem users. RADIUS gives an administrator the option of having a centralized database of user information. The database can include user names and passwords, configuration information, and the type of services permitted by a user. RADIUS is a client/server protocol. In a wireless network, an access point acts as a client of a RADIUS server.

RADIUS uses User Datagram Protocol (UDP) for its underlying transport. The registered UDP port number for RADIUS is 1812. More advanced versions of RADIUS can also use ports 2083 and 3799. Early implementations of RADIUS used port 1645. Because of these multiple port numbers, most access points let you configure which port number to use to reach the RADIUS primary and secondary servers.

Several companies offer RADIUS server implementations for Mac OS X Server. Setting up a RADIUS server is not difficult; refer to the documentation that came with the RADIUS server.

An access point must be configured with the Internet Protocol (IP) address of the RADIUS server (and optionally the address of a secondary server). For Apple AirPort Extreme Base Station, you can use the AirPort Admin Utility to configure the addresses of the RADIUS servers.

1   Open AirPort Admin Utility (/Applications/Utilities).

2   Select your base station.

3   Click AirPort if it's not already selected.

4   Click the Change Wireless Security button.

5   From the Wireless Security pop-up menu, choose WPA Enterprise.

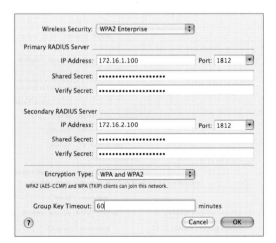

6 In the IP Address field, type the IP address for the primary RADIUS server.

7 In the Port field, type the port number that your primary RADIUS server uses (or choose the port number from the menu).

8 In the Shared Secret field, type a shared secret.

This secret is shared between the base station and the RADIUS server. You should type it here exactly the way it was typed when configuring the RADIUS server.

9 In the Verify Secret field, retype the shared secret.

10 Repeat steps 6 through 9 if you have a secondary RADIUS server.

11 Click OK.

12 Click the Update button to save the base station settings.

Setting up Mac OS X clients to use WPA Enterprise is reasonably straightforward. To make it even simpler, Apple supports a feature whereby the administrator can save a configuration file that can be placed on each user device. Follow these steps to create such a file:

1 Open Internet Connect (/Applications).

2 If there is no 802.1X icon visible, choose File > New 802.1X Connection.

3 Click the 802.1X icon.

4   From the Configuration pop-up menu, choose Edit Configurations.

5   In the Description field, type a name for the configuration.

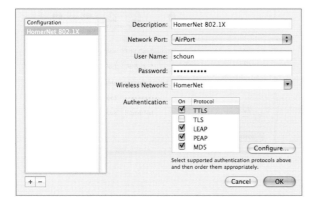

6   Click the Wireless Network pop-up menu and choose the network.

7   Select the EAP authentication protocol of the RADIUS server.

See the documentation that came with the server for more information.

8   Configure the protocol, if necessary.

Some authentication protocols require additional settings, such as an outer identity or a digital certificate. See the documentation that came with the server for more information.

9   Click OK to save the connection settings.

10 Choose File > Export Configurations to create a file you can distribute to network users.

To join a WPA network, users can double-click the configuration file to open it in Internet Connect. When prompted, the users should then enter the user name and password they were given for the network and, if necessary, choose the network from the Wireless Network pop-up menu.

Using WPA Personal

In small and home offices, WPA Personal allows the use of a single, shared password. A RADIUS server is not required. The user enters the password (also called a key) into the access point and each client. WPA takes over from there. The password ensures that only devices and users with proper credentials can join the network. Entering a correct password starts the TKIP encryption process. TKIP derives its encryption keys mathematically from the password and regularly changes and rotates the key so that the same key is never used twice.

WPA Personal supports two types of passwords:

▶   A text-based password between 8 and 63 ASCII characters

▶   A preshared key that is exactly 64 hex digits

TKIP makes it extremely difficult for attackers to derive the key simply by capturing network traffic (as they could with WEP). To increase security, though, it's still a good idea to follow standard password security practices with the key and make sure it's a complicated, somewhat long word or phrase with lowercase and uppercase letters, numbers, and symbols.

Also, note that although the key changes (it's temporal), the starting key is a shared key that is configured on the access points and on users' computers. Users are notorious for not keeping secrets. They have a tendency to write passwords on sticky notes. They tell passwords to friends or send them in e-mails, or they type passwords into files stored on their computers. For this reason, WPA Enterprise, which uses a unique password for each user, is preferable.

Other than entering the password, the network administrator and users aren't required to do anything to make WPA Personal work, which is beneficial for small businesses and home users where the expertise for setting up a RADIUS server may not exist. For larger networks, however, the added security and the economies of scale associated with having one RADIUS server manage all user credentials for all wireless access points outweigh the disadvantages associated with the need for expertise. If you have more than about five users, WPA Enterprise is recommended over WPA Personal.

Comparing WLAN Security Mechanisms

The previous sections covered WEP, WEP with 802.1X, WPA Enterprise, and WPA Personal. Each of these mechanisms has a place in configuring WLAN security (although WEP's place should be strictly limited to networks that must support older devices). This table summarizes the features, benefits, and liabilities of the security options covered in the lesson.

Type	WEP	WEP with 802.1x	WPA Enterprise	WPA Personal
Security	Lowest	Low	High	Moderate
Setup difficulty	Low	Moderate	Moderate	Low
Authenticates users, not just devices	No	Yes	Yes	No
Uses shared key	Yes	No	No	Yes
Supports EAP	No	Yes	Yes	No
Supports TKIP	No	No	Yes	Yes
Appropriate for large installations	No	No	Yes	No
Upgradeable to WPA2 with AES	No	No	Yes	Yes

What You've Learned

▶ Mobile users present unique challenges to network administrators because they roam to unprotected networks where standard security precautions may not be in place.

▶ Wireless networks also present a challenge because the wireless radio frequency signal can migrate beyond walls, into parking lots for example, and because wireless networks use shared bandwidth that is visible to attackers. Attackers can intercept and analyze traffic on wireless networks, and possibly even change data on wireless networks and devices.

▶ To protect Bluetooth users, Macintoshes should not be discoverable, Internet access via Bluetooth should be avoided, and Bluetooth file transfer and exchange capabilities should be disabled until they are needed. Pairing should be required to start any sort of file transfer or exchange.

▶ To protect WLAN networks and users, the best option is WPA Enterprise. WPA Enterprise requires the configuration of a RADIUS server, which may not be appropriate for home and small business networks that support five or fewer users.

▶ WPA Personal does not require a RADIUS server but is still more secure than WEP because it uses TKIP. With TKIP, the encryption key is changed with every packet, thus thwarting key-derivation attempts.

▶ Mobility is one of the most sought-after features of laptop users. These users expect to be "plugged in" at all times, communicating with coworkers, friends, and family members wherever they are. However, mobile users, and the IT professionals who support them, should be especially vigilant when using Bluetooth and WLAN technologies to ensure a successful computing experience, unhampered by security problems.

References

Books

Gast, M. *802.11 Wireless Networks: The Definitive Guide,* 2nd ed. (O'Reilly & Associates, 2005).

Negrino, Tom and Smith, D. *Mac OS X Unwired* (O'Reilly & Associates, 2003).

URLs

Apple Computer, "Choosing a password for networks that use Wired Equivalent Privacy (WEP)": http://docs.info.apple.com/article.html?artnum=108058

Apple Computer, "Designing AirPort Networks": http://manuals.info.apple.com/en/DesigningAirPortNetworks.pdf

Apple Computer, "Managing AirPort Extreme Networks": http://manuals.info.apple.com/en/Managing_AirPort_Extreme_Networks_v3.4.pdf

Bluetooth Special Interest Group, "Wireless Security": www.bluetooth.com/help/security.asp

Institute of Electrical and Electronics Engineers (IEEE), "802.1X: Port-Based Network Access Control": http://standards.ieee.org/getieee802

Lee, Wei-Meng, "Securing AirPort Extreme Networks with WPA": www.oreillynet.com/pub/a/wireless/2003/12/18/wap.html?page=last&x-maxdepth=0Lesson Review

Lesson Review

1. Why are wireless networks susceptible to sniffing?
2. List the most important steps to secure Bluetooth.
3. Compare WPA Enterprise and WPA Personal in terms of their level of security and their target markets.

Answers

1. Wireless networks are susceptible to sniffing because they use shared bandwidth. Every user can "see" every other user's network traffic. This is different from a wired Ethernet network where a switch directs traffic to a specific device. Wireless networks are also susceptible to sniffing because the wireless signal can travel relatively long distances to areas that may be outside the perimeter of a wired network (to a parking lot, for example). Wireless sniffing tools such as Ethereal and Kismet are readily available. Networks that use WEP are susceptible to sniffing because the encryption key is crackable. Newer security standards use strong encryption and can require user authentication; thus, they aren't as susceptible to sniffing.

2. For really paranoid users, you can completely disable Bluetooth. Assuming that this solution is not desirable, the other options for Bluetooth security are to disable discoverability and Internet access via Bluetooth, and to disable Bluetooth file transfer and exchange until they are needed. You should also require pairing for file transfer and exchange.

3. WPA Enterprise and WPA Personal both offer good security because they support strong encryption with TKIP. WPA Enterprise offers better security, however, because every user has a unique user name and password. WPA Personal uses a shared key that attackers could learn by asking users or by stealing a laptop. WPA Enterprise offers better management for large wireless installations. For enterprises with many access points and users who roam from one access point to another, a centralized database of users, which is possible with WPA Enterprise, simplifies management. The major downside of WPA Enterprise is that the user database resides on a RADIUS server. Configuring and managing a RADIUS server is too complicated for most home users and small business network administrators. For that reason, the market for WPA Enterprise is enterprises and companies with five or more wireless users.

16

Time   This lesson takes approximately 2 hours to complete.

Goals   Understand open ports

Implement ssh, scp, and sftp

Set up a VPN client

Lesson **16**

Secure Network Connections

One of the Achilles heels of computing security is the network itself. It provides the connectivity users need to collaborate, but also provides potential "stealing" points for attackers. You may use encrypted disk images, encrypted swap space, ACLs controlling access to files and folders, and myriad other proactive techniques to prevent security breaches, but as soon as you transfer a file over the network without precaution, you may leak your information.

In this lesson, you'll see how to prevent attackers from "sniffing" out secret information on a network, ensuring that the network does not become the "weakest link" in the security chain. If you assume that *every* network is being sniffed for secrets, you can actively ensure that your network communication will not be breached.

Understanding Network Services

Services on computers generally run on assigned network ports. A computer running services ensures that the services are available on these standard assigned ports, and "listens" for incoming requests from other computers.

So, if a computer is running the Apache Web server (httpd) on the default port of 80, a client machine can access Web pages through port 80, as long as there are no firewall rules preventing access to a client machine. Similarly, port 25 is the standard port used for SMTP mail access, port 143 is standard for IMAP mail, and so on.

> **TIP** ▶ For a complete list of services that OS X is familiar with, refer to the file /private/etc/services.

Since a service's communication protocol is well-defined, the only information one computer needs to start communicating with another computer is that computer's IP address (or hostname, which is resolved into an IP address by DNS), along with the port through which it would like to communicate. The combination of an IP address and a port is called a *socket*.

In the early days of networking, when trust was implied because very few had access to what was the beginning of the Internet, it was fine for network services to communicate over the network through unprotected sockets, since the only people who had access to (or understood) the network usually were trustworthy system administrators.

The commands that were developed to serve users include the following:

▶ telnet, for remote logins to other computers, and to test access to a socket when an optional port is specified

▶ rcp, for remote copy, to copy files to a local drive from a remote host

▶ login, also used to log in to remote computers (but does not provide socket access test capabilities)

▶ ftp (File Transfer Protocol), a common method of transferring files

Each of these protocols does its job, but without protecting the information as it's transferred. Worse, each of these protocols sends authentication passwords to the remote system in clear text, making it very easy for an attacker to grab passwords and use them. Fortunately, there are improved versions of these tools, which you'll learn about in this lesson, that are designed to ensure that information is secure as it is sent over a network. There are now more secure ways to transfer your data from one computer to another device over a network.

Using Telnet to Test Socket Connectivity

Although Telnet should not be used as a remote login protocol, it is very useful as a technique for testing the ability for your machine to communicate successfully with a remote computer socket. You are, in essence, mimicking the exact communication that computers use to communicate with each other across sockets.

For instance, if you can Telnet from your machine to a remote machine on port 80, you can send HTTP commands to verify that your machine has unencumbered access (no network or firewall blocks) to that Web server.

The syntax for adding a port to the hostname/IP address when using Telnet is

```
Telnet remote-hostname-or-IP remote-port-number-or-service-name
```

For the optional second argument, either a port number or the name specified in /etc/services can be used.

Both of the following would be equivalent:

```
Telnet www.apple.com 80
Telnet www.apple.com http
```

If you are successful in reaching the remote socket, you will see something like this:

```
albook:~ smn$ Telnet www.apple.com http
Trying 17.254.0.91...
Connected to www.apple.com.
Escape character is '^]'.
```

Quit the Telnet session by typing the characters in the line Escape character is '^]'., in this case Ctrl-]. You will then be back at the Telnet prompt, and can enter *q* and press Return to quit. If you take too long, the remote server may automatically disconnect you.

Common protocols that communicate in this manner include HTTP, SMTP, POP, IMAP, and so on.

Note that Telnet does not work with SSL-encrypted sockets, but there is an equivalent— see man s_client (part of OpenSSL), specifically the –connect option.

Understanding SSH

In its simplest sense, SSH (Secure Shell), is a secure login replacement for rlogin, ensuring that the remote connection is completely encrypted, and that the password used for authentication is not sent in clear text.

However, SSH is much more than a replacement for Telnet, although it does not duplicate the non-SSL socket access tests, for which Telnet is still very useful.

On Mac OS X and Mac OS X Server, SSH is implemented using the open-source implementation OpenSSH.

Enabling the sshd Daemon

The daemon that enables SSH functionality is sshd, which must be running on the remote host that you would like to log in to. The sshd daemon listens on port 22, so this port must be available (not blocked by a firewall) for those clients that wish to connect.

The current protocol version for SSH is version 2. Version 1 has some known security holes and should be avoided. Note that, by default, an SSH client attempting to connect to an sshd remote host will attempt to use version 2, but if it is unsuccessful (because the remote host does not support version 1), the client will then attempt a connection using protocol version 1. As a result, for best security, you should force SSH to only use version 2. (See "Advanced SSH" in this lesson.).

To enable sshd on Mac OS X (it is automatically enabled when you install Mac OS X Server) using System Preferences, follow these steps:

1 In System Preferences, open the Sharing pane.

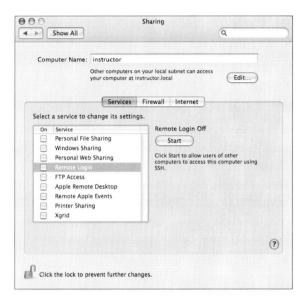

2 If the padlock is locked, click it and authenticate.

3 Verify that Remote Login is selected.

Note that if you have a firewall enabled, Mac OS X automatically will open port 22 through the firewall, but this is not the case on Mac OS X Server.

On Mac OS X Server, you can also enable sshd through the Server Admin application:

1 Launch Server Admin.

2 In the Computers & Services list on the left, click the hostname of the server.

3 Click the Settings button.

4   Click the General button.

5   Select the SSH checkbox in the Protocols section and click Save.

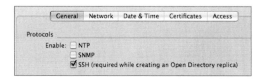

Note that there is no way to enable Telnet access into a Mac OS X or Mac OS X Server machine using the GUI. This is intentional, because Telnet access into your machine should not be enabled.

Using SSH in Place of Telnet

When used as a replacement for the remote login capabilities of Telnet, SSH has a very similar syntax, requiring a remote hostname or IP address, and an optional user name. With Telnet syntax, which is very straightforward, a user can specify the remote hostname that he or she wishes to log in to, and optionally the remote user name:

Telnet *remotehost*

or

Telnet *remotehost –I username*

If the user name is omitted, you will be prompted to enter a user name.

If you authenticate successfully, you will then have a login shell on the remote machine. However, as mentioned earlier, not only is your entire session unencrypted and easily snooped, both the user name and the password are sent across the network to *remotehost* in clear text!

Now compare this with SSH syntax:

ssh *remotehost*

With this syntax, the user name is not explicitly specified, and unlike Telnet, you will not be prompted for a user name. SSH will assume you want to log in to the remote computer using the same login name that is currently used for your local login (which may or may not be a correct assumption).

To specify the user name explicitly, use the following syntax:

ssh *remotehost* -l *username*

or

ssh *username@remotehost*

Both syntax versions are equivalent in functionality; you may use whichever syntax you prefer: "Telnet-style" with the -l, or "email-style" with the @.

Let's assume that you have SSH access to a remote host called host.pretendco.com as the user scott for the following exercise:

1   Enter a command-line shell and type the following:

ssh scott@host.pretendco.com

2   Enter the password (it will not be echoed to the screen).

Upon initial installation of SSH, or upon your first usage of it, a hidden folder is created in your home folder called .ssh. This folder is used by your client SSH process to access information it needs, which you will learn later in this section.

When you attempt to log in to a remote computer with SSH for the first time, a warning appears:

The authenticity of host 'host.pretendco.com (10.1.0.1)' can't be established.

RSA key fingerprint is aa:06:48:3d:d3:d3:1a:c2:d3:de:de:72:97:d3:90:d3.

Are you sure you want to continue connecting (yes/no)?

This indicates that your client has never connected to the remote host before. If you answer "yes," a copy of the remote host's public key is placed into ~/.ssh/known_hosts.

At your next login attempt using SSH, you won't be asked this question again because SSH sees that host key in the known_hosts file.

At a later time, when connecting to a familiar host (a host you've previously used with its host key previously placed into the known_hosts file ~/.ssh/known_hosts), you may see a warning that they keys are different.

This indicates that the host key returned by the remote host is not the same as the one that is stored in your known_hosts file. Ordinarily, this could simply mean that the remote host now has a different property (such as a new IP address). In the worst case, you may be the victim of a "sshmitm" or "ettercap" man-in-the-middle attack, and this warning should be taken *very* seriously.

```
powerbook:~ local$ ssh scott@host.pretendco.com
@@@@@@@@@@@@@@@@@@@@@@@@@@@@@@@@@@@@@@@@@@@@@@@@@@@@@@@@@@@@@@@@
@ WARNING: REMOTE HOST IDENTIFICATION HAS CHANGED! @
@@@@@@@@@@@@@@@@@@@@@@@@@@@@@@@@@@@@@@@@@@@@@@@@@@@@@@@@@@@@@@@@
IT IS POSSIBLE THAT SOMEONE IS DOING SOMETHING NASTY!
Someone could be eavesdropping on you right now (man-in-the-middle attack)!
It is also possible that the RSA host key has just been changed.
The fingerprint for the RSA key sent by the remote host is
34:84:47:e9:8d:1d:43:1e:dc:4c:e1:14:61:15:2a:1a.
Please contact your system administrator.
Add correct host key in /Users/local/.ssh/known_hosts to get rid of this message.
Offending key in /Users/local/.ssh/known_hosts:1
RSA host key for host.pretendco.com has changed and you have requested strict checking.
Host key verification failed.
powerbook:~ local$
```

The SSH protocol comes in two versions, ssh1 and ssh2. ssh1 has known cryptographic weaknesses: Tools like Cain & Abel or Ettercap can decrypt ssh1 connections in real time, so you should use ssh2 only when connecting to another computer. However, by default, OpenSSH uses ssh2 but falls back on ssh1 if the client or server understands only ssh1. Attack tools can conduct a protocol downgrade attack and trick a client into thinking a server understands only ssh1, thus opening up the connection to snooping.

There are several ways to force OpenSSH to use only ssh2, depending on how much control you have over the target computer.

For a Mac OS X Server where you have admin privileges:

▶ In the file /etc/sshd_config, uncomment (or add) the line

#Protocol 2,1 to read Protocol 2

and restart ssh. This will force any computers to connect using the ssh2 protocol. The server will not accept ssh1-based connections.

On a Mac OS X computer where you have admin privileges:

▶ In the file /etc/ssh_config, uncomment (or add) the line

#Protocol 2,1 to read Protocol 2

This will make any connections from the Mac OS X computer use the ssh2 protocol only. If the server does not understand the ssh2 protocol, the Mac OS X computer will not make a connection.

On a Mac OS X computer where you do not have admin privileges but can change your own SSH preferences:

▶ In the file ~/.ssh/ssh_config, uncomment (or add) the line

#Protocol 2,1 to read Protocol 2

This will make any connections from the Mac OS X computer initiated by the current user ssh2 only. If the server does not understand the ssh2 protocol, the Mac OS X computer will not make a connection.

On a Mac OS X computer where you cannot or should not make changes to the user's SSH preferences (perhaps because you are using someone else's system):

▶ When you type in the ssh command line, add the -2 flag

ssh -2 *...other arguments to ssh*

This will make this connection attempt ssh2 only. It will not affect other connections by this user or those from other users.

NOTE ▶ You can ssh into Mac OS X Server from any SSH client on any type of operating system. These steps can be applied to any configuration file of OpenSSH to disable ssh1 and use only ssh2.

Using SCP

With the Secure Copy (SCP) program, a replacement for RCP, a user can copy any file from a local host to a remote one, or vice versa, over a secure, encrypted SSH connection.

For instance, to copy a file from our local machine to a remote host that has SSH enabled, use the following syntax:

scp *local_filename user@hostname:remote_path*

where *local_filename* is the name of the local file you wish to copy, *user@hostname* is the SSH syntax for logging in to a remote host, and *remote_path* is the path on the remote server where you want to place the file.

If a connection is allowed, you will be prompted for your password (unless you have enabled public/private key authentication, discussed later).

Try this out with the following exercise:

1   Enter a command-line shell and navigate to your home folder:

cd ~

2   Create a file using a text editor called myfile.txt:

vi myfile.txt

3   Securely copy myfile.txt to the remote server host.pretendco.com as the user scott to scott's desktop:

scp myfile.txt scott@host.pretendco.com:~/Desktop

Using sftp

Quite a bit of Internet file transfer is done using FTP, which has been around for a long time. FTP is available on just about every Internet-connected host, but since the authentication password is sent in clear text, you should avoid using FTP. (This is not such an issue for public FTP sites, where the password may be nonexistent or known by many users. However, any clear text password is insecure, and publicly-known passwords are worse.)

To allow sftp access, a host must be running only the sshd daemon, and port 22 (SSH) must be accessible through any firewall to the clients.

Fugu is an application from the University of Michigan that permits only SCP and sftp connections to be made to remote servers.

Advanced SSH

The ability to log in to a remote host over a secure connection using a login/password isn't only one way to use SSH. In this section, you will see advanced SSH techniques.

> **MORE INFO** ▶ See the man page for SSH for more information or clarification.

Forcing SSH to Use Only Version 2 of the Protocol

In order to force SSH to connect using only protocol version 2, include the -2 argument by entering

```
ssh -2 username@remotehost
```

You can also choose Connect to Server from the File menu in the Terminal application to discover local computers that can be connected to via the following:

- ▶ SSH
- ▶ SFTP
- ▶ FTP
- ▶ Telnet

The only secure connections, of course, would be SSH and SFTP.

Using SSH Authentication with Public/Private Keys

In addition to standard login/password authentication, you can set up a public/private (also known as asymmetric) key authentication mechanism with SSH that allows a user to create a SSH connection without entering his or her password for each login. Through the .rhost file, Telnet and rlogin users are able to semi-automate their login processes, but there are major security risks in using that method, because it is host-based, not public/private key-based (see man hosts.equiv).

One of the main benefits of using the command-line interface is the ability to automate tasks through scripting. Often, it is desirable to have a script log in remotely to a system and perform a task (such as installing software or software updates, or performing security audits). If you want to use SSH, you need a means for the script to log in to a remote host without providing a password, because SSH does not allow scripts to send passwords via a command-line argument. (This is a good feature because you should not store passwords in scripts unless it is otherwise unavoidable.)

With public/private key authentication with SSH, users and scripts (which all run as users) can remotely access a computer without having to enter a password. In order to use public/private key authentication, you must create a public/private key pair. This is done with the OpenSSH ssh-keygen program. Once the keys are generated, you need to move them to the correct places.

Move your private key into the location where SSH needs to find it, but only on your local machine. *Never* share your private key—if someone obtains a copy of your private key, he or she can log in to the remote machine with your matching public key without having to enter a password!

When you think of encryption, you usually think of encrypting a message with a key, and then using that same key to decrypt a message, kind of like putting messages in a diary with a lock on it, mailing the diary, and having someone else unlock it with a copy of the key. So to send encrypted messages to a friend, each person has to have a copy of the same key. But how do you get that key to the other person without a third person making a copy of the key and also using it to decrypt messages?

Through the miracle of mathematics, it is possible to generate two different—but related—keys: one that can encrypt and one that can decrypt. It is not possible to use the same key to both encrypt and decrypt a message—in other words, if one person locks the diary with one key, the same key cannot be used to unlock it—only the other key can be used. This may be counterintuitive, but the fact that this type of technology exists is very important.

In public/private key encryption, as the title states, two keys are generated—one shared with the public and one kept private. To send a person an encrypted message, lock it up with his or her public key, and send the message. Since only his or her private key, and not the public key, can unlock the message, it is safe—only the recipient of the message has the private key.

MORE INFO ▶ For more information on Public/Private key encryption, see http://www.webopedia.com/TERM/P/public_key_cryptography.html.

The first part of this exercise involves generating the two keys:

1   Enter a command-line shell and type

ssh-keygen –t dsa

2   When asked where to save the file, press Return.

This will save the two generated keys in ~/.ssh.

3   Enter a passphrase, which can further help prevent users from gaining access to your computer: Even if they get the private key, they will need your passphrase.

Two files are generated: ~/.ssh/id_dsa.pub (your public key) and ~/.ssh/id_dsa (your private key).

The next thing to do is copy your public key to the account and host you want to be able to log in to. An easy and secure way to do this is to use the SCP command:

1   Move the public key to the home directory of the user (scott, in this example) on the server you want to be able to log in to using SCP (place it on the desktop for now, and then move it into the right place later):

scp ~/.ssh/id_dsa.pub scott@host.pretendco.com:~/Desktop/local_dsakey.pub

Make sure you are copying the public key (ending in .pub), *not* the private key (with no file extension).

2   Log in to the remote server:

ssh scott@host.pretendco.com

3   Make sure that the .ssh folder exists in the user's home folder. If not, create an empty one.

4   Append the key just copied up into the user's ~/.ssh/ authorized_keys files (or create it if it doesn't exist):

cat ~/Desktop/ local_dsakey.pub >> ~/.ssh/authorized_keys

5   Log out of the remote server:

exit

If all went well, you will now be able to log in to the remote account without having to enter a password; however, if you used a passphrase, you will still need to enter that passphrase.

Disabling Root SSH Logins

By default, if SSH is enabled on Mac OS X or Mac OS X Server, root SSH login is also enabled. Many consider this to be a *huge* security risk. In this exercise, you will learn how to disable root logins from an SSH-enabled machine:

1   Using a text editor, open the file /etc/sshd_config.

2   Find the following line:

#PermitRootLogin yes

3   Uncomment the line by removing the # sign.

4   Replace the word yes with no.

5   Save the file.

6   Restart sshd.

Note that certain services in Mac OS X and Mac OS X Server, such as Open Directory Replication, require root SSH login access, so you may want to consider whether or not you want to do this on your host.

Using SSH Tunneling

In addition to superceding the abilities and security of Telnet, SSH also has the ability to create an *SSH tunnel*, which is a way of forwarding information from one port to another, on different hosts, over a secure, encrypted SSH connection.

One limitation of SSH tunneling is that only the TCP protocol is supported. Other protocols, such as UDP, ICMP, and so on, are not.

Local-to-Remote SSH Tunneling

Sending email outside of your normal network is a common use of an SSH tunnel. For example, a frequent traveler, concerned that the local ISP connection is not trustworthy, may not want to risk using his or her SMTP server for outgoing mail. He or she may have a trustworthy SMTP server on the home office network, but may not wish to expose that SMTP server to the world (port 25 is blocked by a firewall rule). If sshd is running on the home office server, he or she can create an SSH tunnel to utilize that SMTP service, even if it is not externally available, by linking a local port (which a local service can easily communicate with) to a remote port through an encrypted SSH connection.

This type of tunnel is referred to as a *local-to-remote tunnel,* since you are creating a port on your local computer, which will be forwarding requests (and responses) to (and from) a remote port on another computer. You then configure your local applications to communicate not with a remote port directly, but with the local port that has been assigned a connection to the remote port via the SSH tunnel.

Because you are creating a local port connection to a remote port, you need to ensure that the local port you decide to use is not already assigned for local services. (Refer to /etc/services for a list of well-known ports, or use the netstat –an command to see what ports are currently being used on your machine.)

In the following exercise, you will set up a local-to-remote SSH tunnel between your machine and a remote mail server in order to use the remote mail server's SMTP services.

The remote mail server hostname is mail.pretendco.com, and its SMTP service is not accessible via the public Internet because a firewall is blocking port 25. In fact, it is an internal server and has no connection to the public Internet—it is *not* running sshd.

A gateway server exists, which has access to the public Internet and also to the internal network. This gateway host, named gateway.pretendco.com, is running sshd and is accessible through the firewall since port 22 is open. You have a login account on the gateway host called scott. (Any account can be used.)

First create the SSH tunnel connecting your local host's port 2525 (currently unused) to the remote mail server host's port 25 (where it is listening for SMTP requests).

Then configure your mail client application to not use SMTP service from a remote host as you normally would, but to instead link to local port 2525 by using the hostname localhost (which always refers to your local machine) and specify the local port that you used when creating the SSH tunnel.

Refer to the following figure for an illustration of this exercise. (The exercise steps do not correlate directly to the steps in the diagram.)

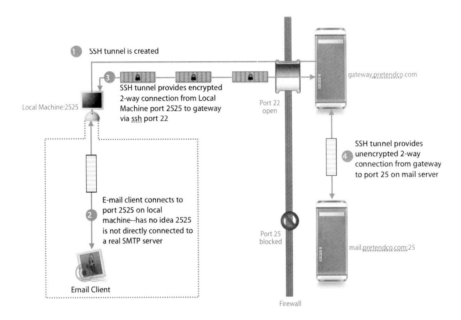

1   Open a command-line shell on the local machine and execute the following command:

ssh –L 2525:mail.pretendco.com:25 scott@gateway.pretendco.com

This will create the SSH tunnel, as shown in step 1 of the figure.

–L creates a local-to-remote tunnel.

2525 refers to the local port you wish to assign to the remote host port:

mail.pretendco.com:25.

scott@gateway.pretendco.com is the machine that will be used to create the SSH tunnel; it is running an sshd that you have access to from the external network, and it has access to the host mail.pretendco.com internally.

NOTE ▸ You can make this tunnel persistent and work in the background. (See the man page for SSH, specifically the –f option.)

2 Configure your email program to use port 2525 on localhost for SMTP services (step 2 in the figure).

Steps 3 and 4 in the figure illustrate the flow of information once the tunnel has been created.

By merely substituting some port numbers, you can apply the preceding exercise to not only other mail services such as POP (on port 110) or IMAP (port 143), but to *any* service that is running on a port on an internal host. And remember, even though your local applications believe they are communicating with a local port, each request/response is actually sent to/from a remote host over an encrypted connection.

Remote-to-Local SSH Tunneling

In addition to creating a tunnel from your Mac to another computer, you can also create a tunnel in reverse. You can forward information intended for a remote socket over a secure SSH connection to your local system.

Why might it be useful to create a tunnel in reverse? Perhaps your consulting company is working on a top-secret website for PretendCo, and you wish to share your latest version with them. They are unable to visit you, and for security reasons, you do *not* want to open up a connection through your firewall to allow them access (since you would also be allowing access to others, and there will be upcoming product announcements that you do not want to leak to the press). No problem—a remote-to-local SSH tunnel is just what you need to allow them access remotely to your local site through an encrypted SSH tunnel.

In the following exercise, you will create a tunnel at your consulting firm, which shares the internal Web host internal.vendor.com with the remote host gateway.pretendco.com. Upon execution of the remote-to-local SSH command, port 8080 on gateway.pretendco.com (the remote host) will actually be a reference to an SSH tunnel to port 80 on internal.vendor.com (the local host), utilizing the SSH process running on your local machine and the sshd process running on gateway.pretendco.com.

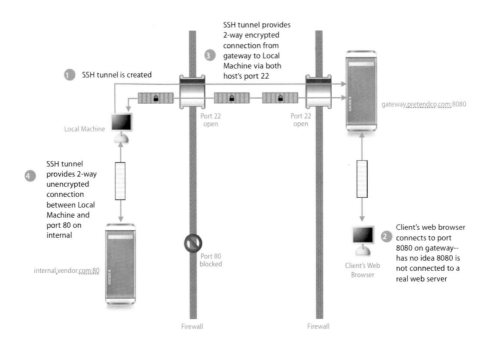

▶   Open a command-line shell on the local machine and execute the following command:

ssh –R 8080:internal.vendor.com:80 scott@gateway.pretendco.com

This will create the SSH tunnel, as shown in step 1 of the figure.

–R creates a remote-to-local tunnel.

8080 refers to the remote port you want to assign to the local host port:

internal.vendor.com:80.

scott@gateway.pretendco.com is the machine that will be used to create the SSH tunnel—it is running an sshd that the local machine's SSH process has access to from the external network, and it can be accessed by internal hosts at PretendCo.

NOTE ▶ You can make this tunnel persistent and work in the background. (See the man page for SSH, specifically the –f option.)

Any internal client on the PretendCo network can now access gateway.pretendco.com:8080 to send requests (and get responses) from internal.vendor.com:80 through an encrypted SSH tunnel (step 2 in the figure).

Steps 3 and 4 in the figure illustrate the flow of information once the tunnel has been created.

As in a local-to-remote tunnel, you can apply the technique shown in this exercise to other ports for similar results.

SSH Tunneling of AFP

The Mac OS X Finder supports creating SSH tunnels for Apple Filing Protocol (AFP), ensuring that your AFP traffic is sent encrypted over the network.

When making a connection to an AFP server using the Finder's Connect To Server menu option, a request can be made to create an SSH tunnel for that connection using the Options pane, as shown in the following exercise:

1   From the Finder, choose Go > Connect To Server.

2   Select an AFP site to connect to.

3   When presented with the Authentication dialog, instead of immediately authenticating, click Options.

4   Select the "Allow secure connections using SSH" checkbox to use an SSH tunnel.

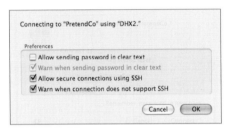

If the remote server supports an AFP SSH tunnel, you will be connected automatically. If the tunnel cannot be created for some reason, a dialog will appear asking you if you would like to use a non-SSH tunnel.

> **NOTE** ▸ There isn't really an slogin program; it is a symbolic link to the standard SSH command, for those who are migrating from using rlogin and prefer to use the name slogin.

Understanding VPN

You have seen SSH in action, providing a secure, encrypted connection over an insecure, visible network. You can also take the next step and ensure that the entire network connection is secure and encrypted, thus allowing any type of access to be safe, even insecure protocols such as Telnet and standard FTP.

This process is known as creating a virtual private network (VPN). A VPN can consist of a single host connecting to a private network, or an entire remote site connecting into a private network, in both cases using VPN security protocols over an insecure network (such as the Internet). The following figure shows a VPN connection from a client computer to an internal corporate network using NAT for IP addressing (shown at the bottom). The client machine has both a public IP address 17.187.175.4 (provided by an ISP, either at home, or at a hotel, or at a remote site) and a private VPN address 10.1.1.100 on the internal network (provided by the VPN server after authentication). Note that transactions to the internal network go through the VPN pipe, but non-VPN connections get blocked at the VPN/firewall server and are not allowed internal access.

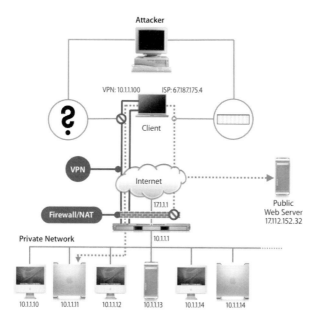

An attacker can snoop the non-VPN network transactions but will see only encrypted gibberish while observing the VPN connection. You will see later that when you create a VPN connection, you have full control over which packets get sent over the VPN and which get sent over the public network.

VPN comes in a variety of flavors and textures, featuring various authentication schemes and transport protocols.

VPN Transport Protocols

Mac OS X and Mac OS X Server support two transport protocols:

▶ Layer 2 Tunneling Protocol (L2TP)

▶ Point-to-Point Tunneling Protocol (PPTP)

A Mac OS X system may have multiple connection profiles to different VPN servers (which may or not be using Mac OS X Server), each using either one or the other of these transport protocol for connectivity.

Mac OS X Server can provide VPN services using one or both of these protocols.

Before you learn how to implement VPN connectivity in Mac OS X and Mac OS X Server, let's take a look at each transport protocol in detail.

L2TP

L2TP is the more secure of the two protocols. The default configuration is L2TP/IPSec, which supports a shared secret mechanism. You can also use certificates instead of shared secrets, which you will find out how to do later in this lesson.

PPTP

PPTP, which was developed by Microsoft, provides more compatibility with older Windows clients. It supports both 40-bit and 128-bit encryption, but unless you need to support older Windows clients, it is best to stick with 128-bit, because 40-bit is very susceptible to security breaches.

> **NOTE** ▶ Regardless of the protocol used to connect to the VPN server, you should enable all traffic to go over the VPN. In the Internet Connect application, choose Connect > Options and select the "Send all traffic over the VPN connection" checkbox.

Authentication Methods

Because different organizations require different levels of authentication security, VPN supports several authentication schemes. On Mac OS X Server, the default authentication protocol is MS-CHAPv2.

MS-CHAPv2

MS-CHAPv2 is a fairly simple user name/password authentication model using a password hash.

Kerberos

Beginning with Mac OS X 10.4, Kerberos VPN authentication is supported with L2TP.

Two-Factor

A two-factor authentication protocol utilizes a user name, but instead of a fixed password, a token (which can change) is combined with a password. The most common example is the RSA SecurID system, where the user carries a device that generates tokens dynamically. This SecurID device is either a keychain, or credit-card sized device (for easy placement in a wallet or planner). Each SecurID device is usually specifically coordinated to a user—in other words, one SecurID device cannot be used by another person, even if he or she is in the same system.

Providing VPN Service With Mac OS X Server

Mac OS X Server provides a graphical interface for VPN configuration using the Server Admin program. Most popular VPN configuration options are easily configured through the GUI, but other configuration options are configurable only via the command line.

Mac OS X Server can provide both L2TP and PPTP VPN service concurrently, or you can enable just one of the types.

VPN configuration information for OS X Server is stored in /Library/Preferences/ SystemConfiguration/com.apple.RemoteAccessServers.plist.

L2TP Configuration

After enabling L2TP, which you will do in the next exercise, you must first select a block of IP addresses that the VPN system will vend to clients as they attach, similar to what a DHCP server does. Speaking of DHCP servers, it is very important that the IP address range you select is not already assigned statically or allocated to a DHCP server.

Next, you must select PPP authentication type. Mac OS X Server defaults to MS-CHAPv2 authentication, but you can also choose to use Kerberos authentication instead (from the pop-up menu, new to Mac OS X Server v10.4). To enable two-factor protocols such as RSA SecurID, a trip to the command line is necessary.

Also new to the Mac OS X Server v10.4 Server Admin GUI is the ability to use a certificate instead of a shared secret for client-server host authentication. You must already have generated a certificate. You could do this from the command line in previous versions of Mac OS X Server, but it is now a welcome addition to the GUI.

Here, you will configure L2TP over IPSec to use MS-CHAPv2 PPP authentication and use a client/server host shared secret:

1 On Mac OS X Server, launch Server Admin and authenticate.

2 From the Computers & Services list, select VPN.

3 Click the Settings button.

4 Click the L2TP tab.

5 Select the "Enable L2TP over IPSec" checkbox.

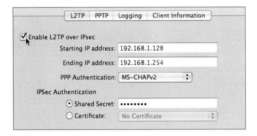

6 Select Starting IP address and Ending IP address blocks.

7 Make sure the PPP Authentication pop-up menu is set to MS-CHAPv2.

8 Make sure the Shared Secret radio button is selected.

9 Enter a shared secret—this should be an extremely-difficult-to-guess password. (It will be entered only once on the client side, as shown in a later exercise.)

10 Click Save.

You are not done setting up VPN yet, but if this is the only configuration you want, skip ahead to the exercise on setting up client information.

In this exercise, you will configure L2TP over IPSec to instead use Kerberos for PPP authentication and use a certificate for IPSec authentication:

1 Execute steps 1 through 6 from the previous exercise.

2 For PPP Authentication, choose Kerberos.

3 For IPSec Authentication, select the Certification radio button.

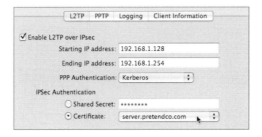

4 Choose a pre-existing certificate from the pop-up menu.

5 Click Save.

PPTP Configuration

PPTP configuration is straightforward in Mac OS X Server, because Server Admin offers only a few simple configuration options. As with L2TP, you must first select a block of IP addresses that the VPN system will vend to clients as they attach, similar to what a DHCP server does. Again, it is very important that the IP address range you select is not already assigned statically or allocated to a DHCP, VPN, or other type of server elsewhere.

1 On Mac OS X Server, launch Server Admin and authenticate.

2 From the Computers & Services list, select VPN.

3 Click the Settings button.

4 Click the PPTP tab.

5 Select Enable PPTP.

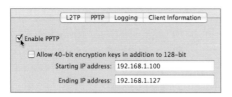

6 Enter a Starting IP address and Ending IP address block.

Again, these addresses must not already be allocated elsewhere.

7 Optionally, select the checkbox allowing for 40-bit encryption keys.

This is a security breach, but it may be required for older VPN clients.

8 Click Save.

Configuration for Two-Factor Authentication

As mentioned earlier, you can configure VPN on OS X Server to support two-factor authentication.

In this exercise, you will add support for SecurID:

1 Launch a command-line shell on Mac OS X Server.

2 Create the folder /var/ace:

```
cd /
sudo mkdir var/ace
```

3 Copy the SecurID configuration file sdconf.rec from your SecurID server to the /var/ace folder.

4   Enable EAP-SecurID authentication by typing in the following commands, one
at a time, all on one line without paragraph breaks:

serveradmin settings vpn:Servers:com.apple.ppp.l2tp:PPP:AuthenticatorEAPPlugins:_array_index:0 =
"EAP-RSA"

serveradmin settings vpn:Servers:com.apple.ppp.l2tp:PPP:AuthenticatorProtocol:_array_index:0 =
"EAP")

5   Exit your command-line shell.

Client Information: "DHCP"-like

With Server Admin, you can configure your clients to receive not only an IP address, but
also default DNS server and search domain info. If this sounds like the type of information a DHCP server would provide for non-VPN clients, you are correct.

To configure VPN to provide a default DNS server of 10.1.1.1 and a default search
domain of pretendco.com, perform these steps:

1   On Mac OS X Server, launch Server Admin and authenticate.

2   From the Computers & Services list, select VPN.

3   Click the Settings button.

4   Click the Client Information tab.

5   In the "DNS servers" text box, enter PretendCo's default VPN DNS server of *10.1.1.1*.

6   In the "Search domains" text box, enter *pretendco.com*.

7   Click Save.

This information will be provided to all clients who connect via VPN, whether through L2TP or PPTP.

Client Information: Public/Private Network Routing

With Server Admin, you can also configure public and private routing for VPN users. This ensures that public IP address routing, which does not require a VPN tunnel, does not waste VPN resources, and also that private network traffic is required to be on the private VPN network.

When packets are sent through a VPN tunnel, this results in a load on the VPN server for encrypting/decrypting packets. For connection to internal hosts, as shown in the connection from the client machine to the internal host 10.1.1.11, this is the exact behavior you want. However, if the client machine wants to contact a public Web server at 17.112.152.32, is it necessary to burden the VPN server with this request? If you don't think so you may configure public and private network routing within your VPN client information to control this behavior.

In this exercise, you will configure the network so that packets destined for 10.1.1/24 go through the VPN server, and packets destined for 17/8 do not:

1   On Mac OS X Server, launch Server Admin and authenticate.

2   From the Computers & Services list, select VPN.

3   Click the Settings button.

4   Click the Client Information tab.

5   Click the plus sign under the Network Routing Definitions table.

6 In the sheet that appears, enter *10.1.1.0* for the address and *255.255.255.0* for the subnet mask; then choose Private from the Type pop-up menu.

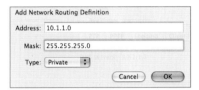

7 Click OK.

8 Again, click the plus sign under the Network Routing Definitions table.

9 In the sheet that appears, enter *17.254.0.0* for the address and *255.255.0.0* for the subnet mask; then choose Public from the Type pop-up menu.

10 Click OK.

11 Click Save and start the VPN service.

Connecting to VPN Service

Mac OS X and Mac OS X Server users connect to VPN servers using the Internet Connect program located in /Applications.

In this exercise, you will connect to a VPN server:

1 Launch Internet Connect (located in /Applications).

2 Click the VPN icon.

3   In the sheet that appears, select "L2TP over IPSec" and click Continue.

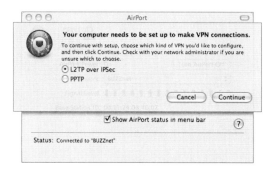

4   In the sheet that appears, choose Edit Configurations from the Configuration pop-up menu.

5   In the sheet that appears, enter a new description, something like *L2TP host.pretendco.com*.

6 Enter the following:

Server Address: *host.pretendco.com*

Account Name: *scott*

User Authentication: Password *<scott's password>*

Machine Authentication: Shared Secret: *<your shared secret>*

7 Click OK.

8 Click Connect.

What You've Learned

▶ Unless it's a Kerberized service, File Transfer Protocol is not secure under any circumstances because the password is passed in clear text.

▶ To force SSH to use version 2 of the protocol, type *ssh -2 username@hostname* when connecting to the SSH server.

▶ You can use ssh-keygen –t dsa or rsa to create the key pair used to augment or replace password authentication with SSH.

▶ The Apple VPN solution supports both L2TP and PPTP protocols.

▶ You can force all traffic to go over the VPN connection.

References

Administration Guides

"Mac OS X Server Getting Started": http://images.apple.com/server/pdfs/Getting_Started_v10.4.pdf

"Mac OS X Server Command-Line Administration for Version 10.4 or Later": http://images.apple.com/server/pdfs/Command_Line_v10.4.pdf

URLs

RSA Security: http://rsasecurity.agora.com/rsasecured/guides/imp_pdfs/MacOSX_ACE_51.pdf

OpenSSH: http://www.openssh.org

Lesson Review

1. Why is Telnet an insecure connection protocol?
2. What is the command-line executable to create SSH key pairs?
3. Does an FTP server need to be running to connect via SFTP?
4. What two protocols does the Mac OS X Server VPN server support?

Answers

1. Because all information, including the user name and password are passed in clear text.
2. ssh-keygen
3. No
4. L2TP over IPSec and PPTP

17

Time   This lesson takes approximately 2 hours to complete.

Goal   Understand the concepts behind authentication

Use Mac OS X Server to provide SASL-based encryption

Understand the role Kerberos plays in Mac OS X and Mac OS X Server

Lesson **17**

Secure Authentication

Authentication is the process of proving your identity. This is a concept that is of great interest to anyone in charge of a server or a network providing services like Apple File Protocol (AFP) or email. Historically, this meant entering separate user IDs and passwords for every service you needed to use (and sometimes every server), even if you entered the same user ID and password each time. However, by integrating technologies such as single sign-on (SSO) via Kerberos, and supporting multifactor authentication via smart cards, thumbprint scanners, RSA keys, and so on, Apple has made the authentication process more secure *and* easier to use.

But, even with things like smart cards and the rest, we still secure our access to networks via the password, and it is the password that can be either a strong part of your security chain or the weakest link. By definition, a good password is difficult to remember.

In general, a good password should:

▶   Consist of more than just a few characters. Although versions of Mac OS X and
      Mac OS X Server prior to Mac OS X 10.3 cared only about the first eight characters
      in a password, as of Mac OS X 10.3, passwords can now be longer than eight charac-
      ters. Every additional character in a password increases the potential complexity of
      the password on a near exponential scale.

▶   Consist of a mix of uppercase and lowercase letters, numbers, and special characters.
      Since passwords on Mac OS X and Mac OS X Server are case-sensitive, even just two
      or three changes in case increase the complexity by a fairly large number. Add in
      numbers, and special characters, and you can easily create a complex password.

▶   Not be based on real words or your identity. Even an older G4-based Mac can search
      an extremely large database of words and names in multiple languages quite fast,
      and execute a dictionary attack on your password.

▶   Be unique for each service, if you aren't able to use a proper SSO implementation,
      a la Mac OS X Server's kerberized SSO infrastructure.

Because remembering multiple passwords can be difficult, Mac OS X and Mac OS X
Server help users manage their passwords with the Keychain, provided as a standard part
of every Mac OS X and Mac OS X Server installation. Mac OS X also provides Password
Assistant to help with the selection of high-quality passwords.

Although an essential part of any security implementation, even the best password can
be broken or circumvented. Someone might look over your shoulder and see you type
the keys, or it might be breakable via a number of attacks, including brute force. To help
keep the password from becoming a single point of failure, Mac OS X and Mac OS X
Server support multifactor authentication, best described as a combination of something
you know (a password or PIN), something you have (such as a smart card), and what
you are (biometrics). Multifactor doesn't mean you use all of these. The most common
implementation is a smart card of some kind used with a password/passphrase/PIN.
ATM/debit cards are the most common form of multifactor authentication.

This lesson ventures beyond passwords. When you are just dealing with your own controlled environment, setting up shared secrets such as passwords is easy. You set a password and tell the user what it is. For situations where a shared secret or predetermined
password is not possible, Mac OS X and Mac OS X Server can use certificates, which

require that all parties involved trust a third party, also known as a certificate authority (CA). Mac OS X Server makes it easy for you to generate your own certificates (also called "self-signed certificates"), so you can provide authentication for everything you use, from your email address to your Web server.

Once authentication is out of the way, the next step is usually authorization, or the granting of rights or privileges to a resource, based on the authenticated identity of the requestor. One of the best features of the current version of Mac OS X Server (10.4, or Tiger) is its support for access control lists (ACLs), which give you greater flexibility in both the rights you can assign (or deny) and the users and groups you apply those rights to.

> **NOTE ▶** A discussion of ACLs is outside the scope of this lesson.

Configuring Secure Client Authentication

When you configure a Mac OS X Server as an Open Directory master, you enable both a SASL-based (simple authentication and security layer) Password Server and a Kerberos key distribution center (KDC). Once a client participates in that server's Open Directory domain, client users and computers can take advantage of these secure authentication services.

When you create a network user in an Open Directory domain, that user will have a password type of Open Directory, and will be able to use the Password Server and Kerberos. However, if you import lists of users, or migrate users from previous versions of Mac OS X Server, these users may have a password type of Shadow. However, once you change a shadow password for an Open Directory network user, the password is automatically upgraded to an Open Directory password.

Historically, UNIX passwords used the *crypt* function to generate encrypted passwords. A password or string, when "crypted," would result in an encrypted version of the password, which looks like random characters. There is no known function that can directly reverse the encryption back into its original text. However, because using the crypt function on a given password will always result in the same random encryption, no matter which computer you use to perform the encryption, it is possible to crack passwords via brute force. You just use the crypt function on random strings (or lists of words) and compare the result to the original encrypted password(s).

Early versions of UNIX stored user records in places readable to all users. Although this made managing user information much easier for system administrators, it also made it much easier for those with malicious intent to subvert the user records for their own uses. Since attackers could copy the entire contents of the user database, including the encrypted passwords, they could transport this information offsite (or for the really bold, just use local computing resources) and use brute force to crack passwords at their leisure.

Early versions of Mac OS X did this as well, storing the encrypted version of user passwords in semi-public locations. In the following example, user1's password was side042walk, and the encrypted version of that was stored right there along with the rest of the user information:

```
nidump passwd / | grep user1
user1:Ro8wktYdhRWYI:505:505::0:0:UserOne:/Users/user1:/bin/bash
```

As of version 10.3, Mac OS X and Mac OS X Server store the encrypted passwords of local users in locations that only the system (and the system administrator) can access, making it much more difficult to do offline brute force attacks. Also, various encryption methods more modern than crypt are used.

Using Shadow Passwords

As of version 10.3, both Mac OS X and Mac OS X Server store encrypted versions of each local user's password in /var/db/shadow/hash.

With shadow passwords:

▶ Files are stored in /var/db/shadow/hash.

▶ Files are readable only by root and the system.

▶ Each user gets his or her own file.

▶ Each user's filename is not based on user name, rather based on his or her GUID (generated user ID—automatically generated).

▶ Each file contains the password encrypted or hashed in possibly several different ways.

▶ There may be a .state file for each user, which contains information such as date and time the file was created, a count of failed logins, the last login date, and whether the password needs to be changed. This is stored in XML format.

This is a sample listing of the contents of the shadow directory:

```
client1:~ root# ls /var/db/shadow/hash/
09A5DB08-FEF3-425D-BC6C-D6D66C690795
09A5DB08-FEF3-425D-BC6C-D6D66C690795.state
3DE5A4DB-7219-40B0-A6FF-8D8ED12B3869
3DE5A4DB-7219-40B0-A6FF-8D8ED12B3869.state
53503B45-BCA2-4AE5-AB4D-C63CAC9832D0
53503B45-BCA2-4AE5-AB4D-C63CAC9832D0.state
65CD47D9-EE4B-451E-93A5-C5ACA4697CF0
65CD47D9-EE4B-451E-93A5-C5ACA4697CF0.state
C0B6905F-1D79-4A61-8FB2-E6E9C1C81FB8
C0B6905F-1D79-4A61-8FB2-E6E9C1C81FB8.state
```

The pwpolicy utility (in /usr/bin) shows that there are several types of hashes stored in Mac OS X. Note that later we will look at the same command on Mac OS X Server, which supports more hash types.

```
client1:~ root# pwpolicy -getglobalhashtypes
SALTED-SHA1
SMB-LAN-MANAGER
SMB-NT
```

SHA-1 is considered to be fairly strong and secure, and is on by default. Once you enable Windows Sharing, the other two hash types, SMB-LAN-MANAGER and SMB-NT, will be enabled only on a per-user basis after you enable Windows Sharing for each user.

SHA-1 is a function in the SHA (secure hash algorithm) family of cryptographic hash functions. SHA-1 produces a 160-bit digest of its input, which can contain a maximum of 264 bits. Because it is salted, the same password will have a different SHA1 hash each time it is set or changed; two users with the same password will have different hashes, making it that much more difficult for an offline attack.

A one-way hash function should have two characteristics. It should be one way; it should be impossible to apply any functions on the hash to recover the original text. It should also be collision free; no two inputs should result in the same hash. For more information about revelations that the SHA-1 hash function may not be collision-free, and what that means in practical terms, see Bruce Schneier's "Cryptanalysis of SHA-1" at http://www.schneier.com/blog/archives/2005/02/cryptanalysis_o.html.

To illustrate the use of various hashes, examine this user2's shadow hash file before and after windows services is enabled. Here is the hash file before enabling Windows Sharing. dscl was used to find the GUID of user2 (because the shadow hash file is based on the GUID):

    dscl localhost read /Search/Users/user2 GeneratedUID

The next step is to use that GUID to find the specific user hash in /var/db/shadow/hash/:

    more /var/db/shadow/hash/09A5DB08-FEF3-425D-BC6C-D6D66C690795

This shows us the shadow password for user2. The pwpolicy command returns the type of hash stored in the user's shadow hash file:

    pwpolicy –u user2 -gethashtypes

In this case, user2's hash uses the SALTED-SHA1 encryption method, which is considered fairly strong and secure.

```
client1:~ root# dscl localhost read /Search/Users/user2 GeneratedUID
GeneratedUID: 09A5DB08-FEF3-425D-BC6C-D6D66C690795
client1:~ root# more /var/db/shadow/hash/09A5DB08-FEF3-425D-BC6C-D6D66C690795
00000000000000000000000000000000000000000000000000000000000000000000000000000000
00000000000000000000000000000000000000000000000000000000000000000000000000000000
000000002C1490A07062DCD09DFD1D4D38845FFC6F48F9013C29EA6C0000000000000000000000000
00000000000000000000000000000000000000000000000000000000000000000000000000000000
00000000000000000000000000000000000000000000000000000000000000000000000000000000
00000000000000000000000000000000000000000000000000000000000000000000000000000000
00000000000000000000000000000000000000000000000000000000000000000000000000000000
00000000000000000000000000000000000000000000000000000000000000000000000000000000
00000000000000000000000000000000000000000000000000000000000000000000000000000000
00000000000000000000000000000000000000000000000000000000000000000000000000000000
00000000000000000000000000000000000000000000000000000000000000000000000000000000
00000000000000000000000000000000000000000000000000000000000000000000000000000000
00000000000000000000000000000000000000000000000000000000000000000000000000000000
00000000000000000000000000000000000000000000000000000000000000000000000000000000
00000000000000000000000000000000000000000000000000000000000000000000000000000000
000000000000000000000000000000000000000000
client1:~ root# pwpolicy –u user2 -gethashtypes
SALTED-SHA1
```

Because the password is stored in a nonrecoverable form, if you want to store a differently encrypted hash of the password, you have to give the operating system the user's password to generate the new hash. In the following figure, the OS is asking for the user's password when enabling Windows Sharing.

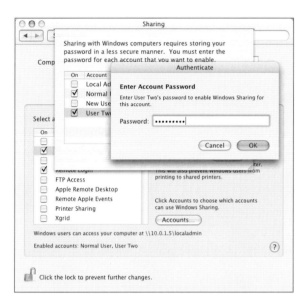

The following figure shows the updated contents of user2's shadow hash file. Note the new strings at the beginning of the file, which represent the new hashes SMB-NT (also known as NTLMv1) and SMB-LAN-MANAGER (sometimes known as "lanman"). The pwpolicy command shows that user2's shadow hash file contains three hashes: SALTED-SHA1, SMB-NT, and SMB-LAN-MANAGER.

```
client1:~ root# more /var/db/shadow/hash/09A5DB08-FEF3-425D-BC6C-D6D66C690795
FB55149C3B7614E259C13D131ABA6A860E22818FA7E00983B75E0C8D76954A50000000000000000
00000000000000000000000000000000000000000000000000000000000000000000000000000000
000000002C1490A07062DCD09DFD1D4D38845FFC6F48F9013C29EA6C00000000000000000000000
00000000000000000000000000000000000000000000000000000000000000000000000000000000
00000000000000000000000000000000000000000000000000000000000000000000000000000000
00000000000000000000000000000000000000000000000000000000000000000000000000000000
00000000000000000000000000000000000000000000000000000000000000000000000000000000
00000000000000000000000000000000000000000000000000000000000000000000000000000000
00000000000000000000000000000000000000000000000000000000000000000000000000000000
00000000000000000000000000000000000000000000000000000000000000000000000000000000
00000000000000000000000000000000000000000000000000000000000000000000000000000000
00000000000000000000000000000000000000000000000000000000000000000000000000000000
00000000000000000000000000000000000000000000000000000000000000000000000000000000
00000000000000000000000000000000000000000000000000000000000000000000000000000000
00000000000000000000000000000000000000000000000000000000000000000000000000000000
00000000000000000000000000
client1:~ root# pwpolicy -u user2 -gethashtypes
SALTED-SHA1
SMB-NT
SMB-LAN-MANAGER
client1:~ root# 
```

The man page for pwpolicy reveals the purpose for all of the hash types, in the section "Stored Hash Types." The following table contains information about the hashes supported by Mac OS X.

Hash Types for Windows Sharing in Mac OS X

Hash Type	Also Called	Used for Compatibility with
SMB-LAN-MANAGER	lanman	Windows 9.x file sharing
SMB-NT	NTLMv1	Windows NT/XP file sharing

Many authentication protocols use a challenge-response mechanism. Just as it is no good to transmit the password over the network in the clear because eavesdroppers could capture and reuse the information, the same problem exists if you send the hashes over the network. If you used a hash of the password instead of the clear-text password and sent that over the network, eavesdroppers could simply reuse that hash. Instead, the authentication protocols require the client and server to compare their results of complex calculations on the hash, hopefully combined with some randomness; if the calculated results are the same, the server can assume the client knows the password. Again, the password is not sent over the network, and the hash is not sent over the network; rather, the result of calculations using the hash is sent over the network. The strength of the authentication protocol is affected by the strength of the hash itself, as well as the strength of the calculations involved.

Identifying NTLM Hash Vulnerabilities

One problem with the SMB-LAN-MANAGER hash type is that it is a fairly weak encryption type. If someone obtains a shadow hash file (by obtaining root access somehow), he or she can generate the password from the hash. Third-party (and unsupported by Apple) programs such as John the Ripper can break this hash in a matter of days. The SMB-LAN-MANAGER protocol, or LM, was introduced with Windows 3.11, and it is considered very weak.

NOTE ▶ To generate and store the LM hash, all characters in the original password are converted to uppercase before hashing, resulting a much more limited keyspace to begin with. Because LM uses the Data Encryption Standard (DES) to generate the hash, and DES requires a fixed key size for its input, the password is either truncated to 14 bytes or padded with null bytes to make it 14 bytes. Those 14 bytes are split into two 7-byte keys. Each of these two keys is used to DES-encrypt the characters in the constant string "KGS!@#$%". The result of each DES encryption is 8 bytes of output. These two 8-byte outputs are concatenated, resulting in a 16-byte hash, which is stored. For more details, see www.ubiqx.org/cifs/SMB.html#SMB.8.

The SMB-NT authentication protocol, also referred to as NTLM, was introduced with Windows NT 3.1. It is similar to LM, with some improvements. The hash of the password is stronger, for example.

NOTE ▶ To generate and store the SMB-NT hash, the original password is not converted to uppercase, which allows for a much larger keyspace to begin with. The password is hashed with the MD4 message digest method instead of DES. MD4 can use an arbitrarily-sized input, so the password does not need to be truncated nor padded. The result is a 16-byte hash that is much better than the LM 16-byte hash.

Though the NTLM protocol uses a stronger hash, it uses the same challenge-response algorithm, which provides only 56-bit encryption.

NOTE ▶ Unless you specifically configure your Windows clients otherwise, it is likely that they will start with the worst possible authentication protocol, even though they can support better levels protocols, with the goal of being able to connect to older servers.

If someone obtains a shadow hash file (by obtaining root access physically or logically), he or she can generate the password from the hash pretty trivially. Third-party programs such as John the Ripper can break weak passwords with this hash in a matter of days.

> **MORE INFO** ▸ See http://support.Microsoft.com/kb/147706/ for more informa-
> tion about the weaknesses of SMB-LAN-MANAGER and SMB-NT. For instance,
> the article claims that "hardware accelerators costing $250,000 have been built that
> can find either the LM or NTLM password-derived key in 3 to 6 days no matter how
> long the password is. These numbers change as technology gets better…Having the
> password-derived key of a user does not allow an attacker to log on interactively but,
> with special software, it is sufficient to access network resources as that user."

In order to remove the SMB-LAN-MANAGER and SMB-NT hashes, it is not enough to
simply disable Windows Sharing. You must disable Windows Sharing for each user, and
you need to enter each user's password in order to do this.

This brings up the importance of physical as well as logical security. If someone manages
to get root access to your computer (by physical or logical means), he or she has access to
your hash files and can crack your passwords in a matter of hours or days.

Removing NTLM Hashes

In version 10.3, Mac OS X Server automatically ran a Password Server; however, in version 10.4, the Password Server is not turned on until you configure a server as an Open
Directory master.

When you create local users with the Accounts pane of System Preferences, or even with
Workgroup Manager, you are creating users with shadow hashes. Mac OS X Server supports a few more types of hashes for local users. The following is an illustration of the
hashes supported for local users under Mac OS X Server (note that the –getglobalhashtypes
works only in Mac OS X 10.4).

```
mainserver:~ localadmin$ pwpolicy -getglobalhashtypes
CRAM-MD5
RECOVERABLE
SALTED-SHA1
SMB-LAN-MANAGER
SMB-NT
mainserver:~ localadmin$ 
```

When you create a new local user, the CRAM-MD5, RECOVERABLE, SALTED-SHA1,
SMB-LAN-MANAGER, and SMB-NT hashes will all be stored in that local user's hash file.

Some services, such as WebDAV, require a hash that is recoverable. If you are not using such services, you can disable the storing of various hashes with pwpolicy:

```
mainserver:~ root# pwpolicy -setglobalhashtypes SMB-LAN-MANAGER off SMB-NT off R
ECOVERABLE off
mainserver:~ root# pwpolicy -getglobalhashtypes
CRAM-MD5
SALTED-SHA1
mainserver:~ root# █
```

Here are the contents of a shadow hash file for a local user in Mac OS X Server. Please note that the number of characters in the hash does not reflect the security of the hash method. The most secure hash method, SALTED-SHA1, uses only 64 characters.

Contents of a Shadow Hash File for a Local User

Column	Contains Password Hash Type
1–32	NTLM and NTLMv2
33–64	SMB-LAN-MANAGER
105–168	CRAM-MD5
169–216	SALTED-SHA1
217–1240	RECOVERABLE

Some services, such as WebDAV and APOP, require recoverable hash methods, which need the clear-text version of the password to generate the necessary hashes. If you will not need certain hashes to be stored, disabling them is a good idea. The following screen shot shows how to do this with the pwpolicy command:

```
mainserver:~ root# pwpolicy -setglobalhashtypes SMB-LAN-MANAGER off SMB-NT off R
ECOVERABLE off
mainserver:~ root# pwpolicy -getglobalhashtypes
CRAM-MD5
SALTED-SHA1
mainserver:~ root# █
```

The pwpolicy command will affect only newly created local users. For existing local users, you can use Workgroup Manager to disable storing various hashes. However, in order for the hash change to take effect, you will have to either assign a new password or have the user change his or her password.

The Password Server in Mac OS X Server supports a larger group of password hashes than Mac OS X client does. If the Password Server is running, you can use telnet to communicate directly with the Password Server running on port 3659, also known as apple-sasl in /etc/services. (Note that the "Connection refused" is because IPv6 is enabled; you can safely ignore this refusal, and in fact, it will be handled for you automatically.) As you can see, there are more hashes supported by the Password Server, such as MS-CHAPv2, which is used for the VPN service.

```
mainserver:~ localadmin$ telnet localhost apple-sasl
Trying ::1...
telnet: connect to address ::1: Connection refused
Trying 127.0.0.1...
Connected to localhost.
Escape character is '^]'.
+OK ApplePasswordServer 10.1.0.0 password server at 0.0.0.0 ready
LIST
+OK (SASL "SMB-NTLMv2" "SMB-NT" "SMB-LAN-MANAGER" "MS-CHAPv2" "OTP" "NTLM" "GSSA
PI" "DIGEST-MD5" "CRAM-MD5" "WEBDAV-DIGEST" "DHX" "APOP" )
QUIT
+OK password server signing off.
Connection closed by foreign host.
mainserver:~ localadmin$ []
```

Again, the Password Server is enabled when you configure a server to be an Open Directory master. When you create network users in the Open Directory domain, those users will have the password type of Open Directory. When you inspect the user record, the user should have two values for the AuthenticationAuthority attribute: one for Password Server and one for Kerberos.

In the following figure, the Workgroup Manager Inspector is used to examine the AuthenticationAuthority attribute of a network user, and there are two values. One starts with ;ApplePasswordServer; and the other starts with ;Kerberosv5;. Although you may not be able to see them in the line, you can copy and paste the full attribute into a text file and examine it.

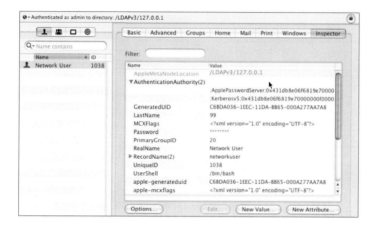

In comparison, here is what Workgroup Manager shows for a local user that has been migrated from an earlier version of Mac OS X Server and still has the user password type of Crypt Password. Note that you can click the menu and migrate the user to a Shadow Password type.

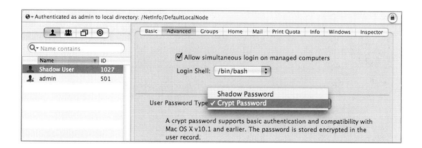

Here is an example of a local account that has a user password type of Shadow Password. Note the Security and Options buttons.

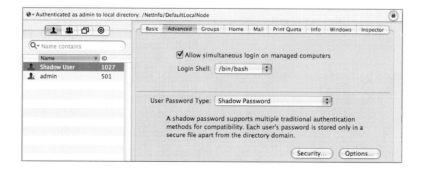

Clicking the Security button will give you a GUI equivalent to the pwpolicy command to enable or disable the storing of various hashes in the user's shadow hash file.

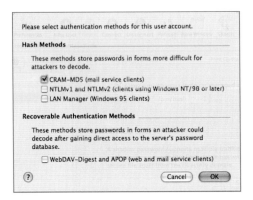

Note that you cannot change NTLMv1 without also changing NTLMv2. Also note that NTLMv1/NTLMv2 are not listed separately as available authentication methods when you use pwpolicy. Although they are available, they both use the same root SMB-NT hash, and therefore do not have their own listing.

> **NOTE** ▶ For a user, if you use Workgroup Manager, click the Advanced button, and click the Security button to disable or enable an authentication method, the changes do not take effect until the user authenticates (or you specify a password for that user).

While you are examining user password settings with Workgroup Manager, you should also check out the password policy options, accessed via the Options button.

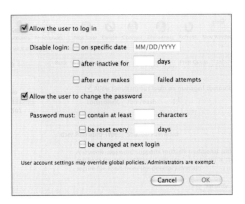

Finally, here is what Workgroup Manager has in the Advanced tab for an Open Directory network user. Note that the globe in the upper-left corner shows that you are looking at the /LDAPv3/127.0.0.1 domain, rather than /NetInfo/DefaultLocalNode. The User Password Type is Open Directory, and the user's PasswordID is displayed. The PasswordID is completely separate from the GeneratedUID, from which a local user's shadow hash filename is generated.

> **NOTE** ▶ pwpolicy is a utility that was originally written to be used on Mac OS X Server, but now can also create a limited set of password policies for local users. One of the primary uses of this utility is to require a minimum password length. The following command will force users on local computers to create passwords of at least 12 characters, whether or not they are connected to a directory server:

pwpolicy -n /NetInfo/DefaultLocalNode –a administrator –setglobalpolicy minChars=12

Defining Kerberos Pre-Authentication

An additional improvement in authentication security in Tiger Server is Kerberos pre-authentication, which you could implement in Panther Server, but only by modifying the user principal via the command line. Pre-authentication requires a potential client to prove that it is making a legitimate request of the KDC in order to prevent brute force attempts at cracking the session key.

In order to obtain a ticket granting ticket (TGT), a potential client contacts the KDC with a KRB_AS_REQ (Kerberos authentication service request). The KRB_AS_REQ contains a user principal name, but in Tiger, it also contains an authenticator: a time-stamp encrypted with the user's password. A potential cracker will not have the user's password with which to encrypt the authenticator, the KDC will reject the request, and the transaction will stop there.

Authenticating via a Trusted Third Party

When you need to authenticate yourself to another person or service, yet you do not have a predetermined password set up to use for authentication, you can use mutually trusted third parties.

We'll look at managing mail resources using Web of Trust systems such as Pretty Good Privacy (PGP) and GNU Privacy Guard (GPG), and show you what you need to know about certificates, CAs, and public key infrastructure (PKI). Both Web of Trust and certificates use some combination of public and private keys.

Using Cryptography

The primary way to prevent transaction attacks is to select secure protocols that use cryptography to protect the messages. Cryptography relies on large keys that are used to encrypt data. The larger the key, the more secure and less likely it can be broken. There are two types of cryptography: symmetric and asymmetric.

In *symmetric cryptography,* two parties agree on an algorithm to use and on a shared session key based on the specified algorithm. The session key is used to both encrypt and decrypt the message. It is kept private between the two sides and as long as it remains private the two sides can send messages back and forth securely. This method is referred to as symmetric because the same key is used to both encrypt and decrypt messages. Although the symmetric method is fast, it can be less secure than other methods.

Asymmetric cryptography (also known as Public Key Infrastructure or PKI) uses a pair of keys for secure communication. It is asymmetric because is uses two different keys, one to encrypt (public key) and another to decrypt (private key). The public key can be distributed freely, but the private key is always kept secret. Messages that are encrypted with the public key can be decrypted only with the private key. For example, if you wanted to send a message privately, you would encrypt the message with the public key. Only the holder of the private key would be able to read the message. Conversely, if you encrypted the message with the private key, it could be decrypted only with the public key, thus assuring your identity. Asymmetric cryptography is very secure as long as the private key is not compromised. However, this method is slower than symmetric cryptography and has additional overhead. The S/MIME (Secure Multipurpose Internet Mail Extensions) protocol is an example of asymmetric cryptography (www.imc.org/ietf-smime/index.html).

Public and Private Keys

A public key can be available to everyone, and it has a corresponding private key, which should be kept secret. When someone encrypts data or a message with your public key, only your private key can decrypt the message. Keep this in mind through the rest of the lesson.

Web of Trust

A Web of Trust system is decentralized and is mostly useful with email programs. In a Web of Trust, you may not know someone, but if that person is trusted by someone you know, you can trust that person. For example:

▶   Alice knows and trusts Bob, but does not know Charles.

▶   Bob knows and trusts Charles.

▶   Alice can trust Charles because she trusts Bob, who trusts Charles.

There are a few drawbacks to the Web of Trust system. The exchange of trust information should take place in person, and although there are organized events such PGP signing parties, it can be cumbersome to get connected into a sizeable Web of Trust without implementing directory-based solutions, such as provided by PGP. Furthermore, the presence of PGP/GPG in an OS is not guaranteed; it must be manually checked for and, if not present, installed and configured.

> **MORE INFO** ▶ For more information about PKI, including a list of relevant RFCs, see the IETF's PKI working group's site at www.ietf.org/html.charters/pkix-charter.html.

Managing Certificates on Mac OS X

Mac OS X and Mac OS X Server have built-in support for public key certificates, referred to as simply "certificates."

> **MORE INFO** ▶ Apple documentation for certificates is published as an appendix to the "Mail Service Administration" document available at www.apple.com/server/documentation.

This system relies on trusting one or more CAs, such as VeriSign. CAs sign other certificates, vouching for the identity of the certificate holders. Apple distributes the OS with a list of CAs (in /System/Library/Keychains/X509Anchors), which Apple asserts you should trust. In the following illustration, the Keychain Access application displays the partial contents of the X509Anchors keychain. The bottom of the window indicates "98 items," indicating that there are 98 CAs in this X509Anchors keychain preloaded by Apple.

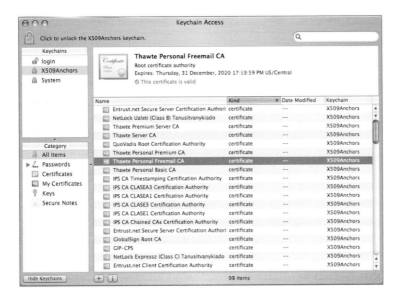

Any application using the Mac OS X certificate infrastructure will automatically trust and use a certificate if it is issued or signed by a CA in X509Anchors. Likewise, the application should notify the user if the application encounters a certificate that is not issued or signed by a trusted CA.

Different applications have various ways of signaling that a certificate is in use. Safari will display a lock in the upper-right corner of the browser window. Mail will indicate if a message is signed or encrypted with a small icon and text right in the message header.

To view a secure website certificate from within Safari, click the lock in the upper-right corner of the Safari window.

According the to the following figure, the certificate for the Apple training site (https://train.apple.com) is issued by the VeriSign CA.

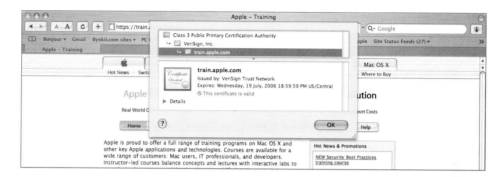

Even though Mail uses certificates for signing and encrypting messages, you cannot directly examine the certificate from within Mail. When Mail processes a message signed or encrypted with a certificate, Mail automatically imports the certificate into the default keychain, as well as the intermediate issuing CA if necessary.

You can view a certificate used for email with Keychain Access. In the following figure, the top part of the window shows that the certificate for ldennison@apple.com was issued by the Thawte Personal Freemail Issuing CA.

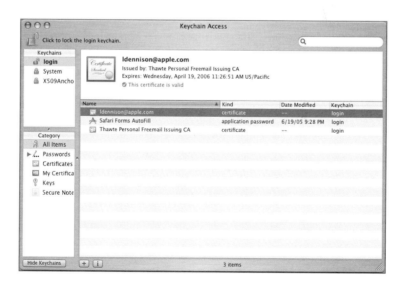

TIP ▶ New to Keychain Access in Tiger is the search feature; you can enter an email address in the search field to highlight its certificate. This search is case-sensitive, which matters if you're searching for something with capital letters like "VeriSign" or "Thawte." You can get a free email certificate at www.thawte.com/email/index.html.

Remember, it is up to the application to notify the user if it encounters a certificate that is not signed by a trusted CA. You may run into self-signed certificates like the one shown in the following figure. You have the option to go ahead and trust the certificate anyway, or to stop browsing that site. The default in this dialog is Continue, and unfortunately, some users just go with whatever the default is whenever a window pops up. Train your users to not exchange sensitive information, such as credit card information, with a site that does not have a trusted certificate.

If you are using internal sites with certificates signed by an internal CA, prevent the verification hassle by importing the internal CA certificate into the X509Anchors keychain.

One way to import a certificate is to double-click the certificate file. Keychain Access will launch and ask if you want to import the certificate into a keychain. Be sure to select the X509Anchors keychain. Because this affects all users on a computer, you will be challenged to authenticate as an administrator before the item will be added to X509Anchors.

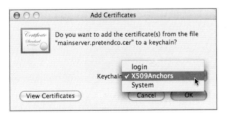

Using Certificates to Offer Secure Services

If you want to use SSL to protect the services you offer, you first need a certificate for each service. To obtain a certificate, you have some flexibility:

▶ You can pay a trusted CA that is already in your X509Anchors keychain to sign a certificate for you.

▶ You can create your own self-signed CA, distribute the self-signed CA certificate to your organization's computers, and sign certificates with your self-signed CA.

▶ Although it is technically feasible to get a trusted CA to sign your CA, to sign certificates with your CA, and have those certificates trusted around the world, this is prohibitively expensive and cumbersome for most organizations.

Although the command-line openssl tools are still available to create CAs, certificates, and certificate requests, Mac OS X Server comes with several GUI tools to help you manage certificates.

With Certificate Assistant, you can:

▶ Create a self-signed certificate

▶ Create a certificate to be signed by your self-signed CA

▶ Create a self-signed CA

▶ Create a CA to be signed by your self-signed CA

▶ Use your CA to create a certificate

▶ Request a certificate from an existing CA (generate a certificate signing request [CSR])

▶ View and evaluate certificates (similar to what you can do with Keychain Access, but you can also use this interface to ask remote hosts for their certificates to evaluate them)

> **NOTE** ▶ Apple documentation claims that Certificate Assistant resides in /Applications/Utilities, but it is actually in /System/Library/CoreServices.

Apple documentation refers to Server Admin's Certificate Manager. To get to the Certificate Manager, open Server Admin, select the computer (as opposed to any of its services), click the Settings button, then click the Certificates button. This interface displays a list of certificates in /etc/certificates. From this interface, you can:

▶ Generate a self-signed certificate

▶ Generate a CSR and send it via the Mail program to a CA

▶ Add a signed certificate from a CA

▶ Import a certificate (if you can have the certificate), the private key, the CA certificate, and optional private key passphrase.

> **NOTE** ▶ Each fresh installation of Mac OS X Server will come with a default certificate, which is used to enable SSL communications for tools such as Server Admin. This certificate, the private key, and the public key are all in the System keychain. Do not use the default certificate for services like Web services, because it is just a self-signed certificate, and your users should be trained to not trust self-signed certificates.

Although you can ask outsiders to download and trust your self-signed CA, they really have no assurance that you are who you say you are and that your CA is trustworthy.

Getting a CA to Sign Your Certificate

There are a number of certificate authorities that you can work with to get your CA on the "chain of authorities" so that when users access your site, they are not warned that OS X cannot verify your certificate. The largest of these is VeriSign, at www.verisign.com. Services such as VeriSign will work with you to get your CA added to the various chains of authorities that Web browsers use by default, although not for free, and the cost is based on your needs.

Strong Authentication

To help overcome some of the weaknesses of authenticating with only a user name and password, Mac OS X and Mac OS X Server support strong multifactor authentication.

Typical sources of multifactor authentication are the following:

▶ What you know: These are things like passwords, passphrases, PINs, and so on. Your ATM PIN is an example of this.

▶ What you have: The authenticator device itself. This can be anything from a USB dongle, to a keychain fob that creates passkeys for you automatically, to a card, like your ATM card.

▶ Who you are: This is a physical characteristic, such as your facial structure, a fingerprint, the physical characteristics of your retina, and so on.

Mac OS X also ships with support for smart cards you can use to make your login more secure. With a smart card, you need the physical card and a password or PIN to log into your Mac. There are many different types and manufacturers of smart cards, including:

▶ Chip card interface devices

▶ USB readers: Athena, CRYPTOCard, GemPlus, SCM

▶ PC card readers: CRYPTOCard, SCM, OmniKey

▶ USB dongle readers: OmniKey

▶ Smart cards (lots of different kinds):

  • CAC—U.S. federal government

  • BELPIC—Belgian personal ID card

  • JPKI—Japanese ID card

▶ Bind to user account

Biometrics are automated methods of recognizing a person based on a physiological or behavioral characteristic, such as the following:

▶ Face, iris, retina

▶ Fingerprint, hand geometry, vein pattern

▶ Handwriting, voice, or typing

With biometrics, you have no password to lose or forget—you have a single sign-on without need for Kerberos or PKI infrastructure, and they are difficult to duplicate.

The challenges, however, are that they're not yet widely implemented, people have been able to duplicate supposedly unique features, and they have a relatively high cost.

Open Directory Security

In the first part of this lesson, you learned about the password methods and hash files for local users. Now you'll examine the situation after you promote a server to be an Open Directory master and the LDAP, Password Server, and Kerberos services are all running. This section examines Password Server security before moving on to the new Directory ACLs.

Password Server

As noted before, the Password Server in Mac OS X Server supports a larger group of authentication methods than Mac OS X client does. The following tables note these:

Hashes, Authentication Methods, and Services for Local Node and ShadowHash

Hash Name	Hash Type	SASL Method	Service
CRAM-MD5	MD5	CRAM-MD5	IMAP, SMTP, LDAP, iChat
RECOVERABLE	AES with fixed key		APOP, WEBDAV-DIGESTPOP, Web
SALTED-SHA1	SHA1	DIGEST-MD5	loginwindow
SHA1	SHA1	DIGEST-MD5	loginwindow (deprecated)
SMB-LAN-MANAGER	LM	SMB-LAN-MANAGER	Windows95
SMB-NT	NT	SMB-NT, MS-CHAPv2, NTLMv2	VPN, All other Windows clients

Hashes, Authentication Methods, and Services for Password Server

SASL Method	Hash Stored	Service
SMB-NTLMv2	NT	Windows 2000, XP, 2003
SMB-NT	NT	Windows 98, 2000, NT, ME
SMB-LAN-MANAGER	LM	Windows 95
MS-CHAPv2	NT	VPN
OTP	None	Not used
NTLM	None	Not used
GSSAPI	None	Not used
DIGEST-MD5	MD5 with digest encoding	Login window
CRAM-MD5	MD5 with CRAM encoding	IMAP, SMTP, LDAP, iChat
WEBDAV-DIGEST	Obfuscated plaintext	Web
DHX	CRAM-MD5	Apple change password/ administration tools
APOP	Obfuscated plaintext	POP

Authentication Methods Available with Password Server

Method	Used For
SMB-NTLMv2	Windows 2000, XP, and 2003 clients
SMB-NT	
SMB-LAN-MANAGER	Windows 95, 98, and ME
MS-CHAPv2	VPN
OTP	One-time password, not really used
NTLM	NTLMv1 for pre NTSP4
GSSAPI	Kerberos
DIGEST-MD5	
CRAM-MD5	
WEBDAV-DIGEST	
DHX	Used to generate a symmetric key for exchanging private information
APOP	Authenticated POP

The Password Server is turned on only after you configure a server to be an Open Directory master.

When you create network users in the Open Directory domain, those users will have the password type of Open Directory. When you inspect the user record, this user should have two values for the AuthenticationAuthority attribute: one for Password Server, and one for Kerberos.

In the following figure, the Workgroup Manager inspector is used to examine the AuthenticationAuthority attribute of a network user (in the shared domain), and there are two values. One starts with ;ApplePasswordServer;, and the other starts with ;Kerberosv5;.

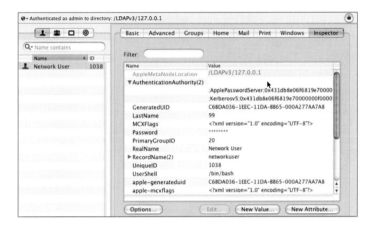

Here is what Workgroup Manager has in the Advanced sheet for an Open Directory network user.

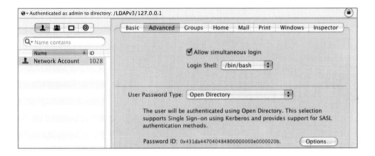

NOTE ▶ The Password Server and Kerberos services do not have a GUI tool; for the most part, they just work. /Library/Logs/slapconfig.log is a good place to look if you run into problems when you promote a server to become an Open Directory master. The mkpassdb and kadmin.local commands are not designed to be used on a daily basis, but can be useful for troubleshooting. Before trying them out for the first time on a production system, practice using these tools on a test system. sudo mkpassdb –dump will display each Password Server slot with its corresponding Password ID and short name. With the kadmin.local command, you can examine and manipulate Kerberos principals, policies (which are not normally used), keytabs, and privileges. These tools are not normally used directly.

New in Mac OS X v10.4 is *LDAP trusted binding*, in which the client authenticates itself to the server, and the server authenticates itself to the client. Trusted binding does not by itself provide encryption—simply mutual authentication. This is critical to prevent a client from authenticating and binding to a rogue directory server that happens to have the same name as the proper one.

Setting up a trusted bind from the client is fairly straightforward: Open Directory Access, configure LDAPv3, click the New button, and enter the server name. (It is best practice to use the FQDN, not the IP address.)

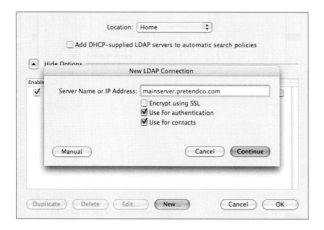

After you click Continue, Directory Access will attempt to discover information about that LDAP server. If the discovery is successful, the dialog box will change, and you can set up trusted binding. To continue with setting up trusted binding, you must specify the computer name of the client (which should be auto-populated) and an LDAP domain administrator and password.

After you successfully configure trusted binding, the client computer now has a Kerberos principal, a Password Server entry, and a computer record in Open Directory's LDAP database. The computer record has two AuthenticationAuthority values, for the Kerberos and Password Server services. This allows the client and the Open Directory master or replica to mutually authenticate each other. You cannot use DHCP-supplied LDAP server information when you implement trusted binding.

> **NOTE ▶** Because there are now entries for this client, if you need to change the computer name, or replace the client, you may need to manually remove the entries from LDAP in order to bind another client with that computer name. It is best practice to use Directory Access to unbind a client computer before removing it from service. In Directory Access, configure LDAPv3, select the configuration for the LDAP server, and click Delete. You will be prompted to unbind with a domain administrator user name and password.

Trusted binding is available only to Mac OS X 10.4 clients and Mac OS X 10.4 servers. In fact, the binding options in Server Admin are advisory only to the directory services of other Tiger clients. The "Require clients to bind to directory" option will not disallow access by clients who have not bound. It does not affect Panther clients, Windows clients, or command-line or third-party LDAP search tools. It does not prevent a Tiger client from manually specifying an LDAP connection. You would set this option to help ensure that client computers are bound correctly, not only to ensure a good user experience, but also to add a degree of security because client and server will mutually authenticate each other.

NOTE ▶ If a client is not running Mac OS X 10.4, these options are essentially ignored; all the Security checkboxes and those for requiring trusted binding are advisory only to directory services of Tiger clients.

Here are the Open Directory > Policy > Binding options in Server Admin. Note that the checkbox to "Require clients to bind to directory" is selected.

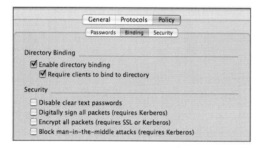

Once that option is enabled, a Tiger client using Directory Access to set up a new LDAP server hosted by a Tiger Open Directory master will be prompted to supply a directory administrator user name and password. Notice that the Manual button is dimmed (but the Cancel button is not).

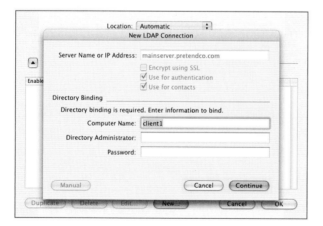

After successfully authenticating, the computer will now bind to the directory using the distinguished name of the computer record that was created in the LDAP directory during the process of setting up the trusted bind. Note that all of the Security Policy options are left unselected by default. These options are useful only if the server supports them.

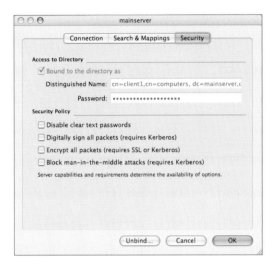

Keeping Your Backed-Up Information Secure

Mac OS X Tiger makes it easy to back up your Open Directory master with Server Admin. You specify the location, and Server Admin creates a disk image with all the files necessary to back up your Open Directory master information.

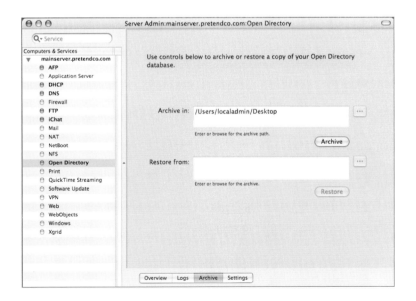

It is best practice to specify a password for the archive to keep it secret.

This archive contains hashes of passwords from the Password Server and Kerberos, and it contains the hashed password of the rootdn for the LDAP database (in slapd_macosxserver.conf). Treat these files with care. Multiple backups of these files are probably a good idea.

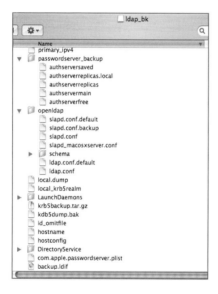

Prevent Anonymous Access to Your Directory

By default, the LDAP server will answer all queries it sees. This can be a security concern in some environments; In general, you might not want to allow everyone to harvest information from your shared domain. Although neither passwords nor even hashes of passwords are stored in the LDAP directory, other information is there, such as short names, group membership, and possibly email addresses. Furthermore, new to Tiger is the ability to use Workgroup Manager to store information such as phone number and address—information that can be used for social engineering.

In previous versions of Mac OS X Server, one way to increase directory security was to add the line disallow bind_anon to /etc/openldap/slapd.conf, use Directory Access at the client to specify a user name for LDAP requests, and enable LDAP over SSL. The disallow bind_anon line is not recommended for use with Mac OS X Server 10.4, because trusted binding requires an initial anonymous access to the LDAP directory. Though it is not supported in the GUI, a better approach is to implement directory access control lists (DACLs).

DACLs are a new feature in Tiger server. The implementation of DACLs introduces the ability to store ACLs right in the LDAP directory itself. One big advantage of this method is that the ACLs can easily be replicated to Open Directory replicas; previously, you would have had to edit config files at each server if you wanted to make any change in access. Another advantage is that since the information is in the LDAP directory, it's easy to export and import DACLs via LDIF files.

> **MORE INFO ▶** For more info on access control lists with OpenLDAP, see www.openldap.org/doc/admin22/slapdconfig.html#Access%20Control.

> **NOTE ▶** Tiger's implementation of OpenLDAP is 2.2; make sure you consult the correct documentation.

This section of /etc/openldap/slapd_macosxserver.conf points to the location of the default DACL:

```
# This file should NOT be world readable.
# This file is maintained by Server Admin.
#
# Access Controls
access specified-in-directory apple-acl "cn=default,cn=accesscontrols,dc=mainserver,
dc=pretendco,dc=com"
```

> **NOTE ▶** Though we can't show it properly on the printed page, you should type the last part of the previous command as one line without a paragraph break.

Here is an Inspector view in Workgroup Manager of the default DACL. The AccessControlEntry attribute in this example has four entries. Each entry consists of a number, a colon, and the rule itself. This example controls access to userPassword, apple-user-authenticationhint, apple-user-picture, and * for everything else not specified.

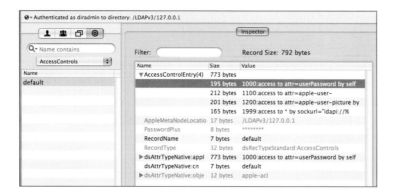

In order to better view an attribute's entry, you can highlight that entry and click the Edit button.

Here are the general steps to disable anonymous binding and queries to your LDAP server, yet allow enough access for regular operation:

1   Use Workgroup Manager to update the config > default > AccessControlEntry entries.

2   On the Open Directory master, use Directory Access to specify "Use authentication when connecting."

3   Make sure that all replicas and clients are using trusted binding or specify "Use authentication when connecting."

To disable most anonymous queries to the LDAP database, here are some suggested AccessControlEntry values to add to enable anonymous access where necessary:

> **NOTE ▸** Again, for each command shown here, type one line of text without paragraph breaks.

```
1300:access to dn.base="" by * read
1310:access to dn.subtree="cn=config,dc=diradmin,dc=mainserver,dc=pretendco,dc=com" by
sockurl="ldapi://%2Fvar%2Frun%2Fldapi" write by group/posixGroup/memberUid="cn=admin,
cn=groups,dc=mainserver,dc=pretendco,dc=com" write by * read

1320:access to dn.subtree="uid=diradmin,cn=users,dc=diradmin,dc=mainserver,dc=pretendco,
dc=com" by sockurl="ldapi://%2Fvar%2Frun%2Fldapi" write by group/posixGroup/memberUid=
"cn=admin,cn=groups,dc=mainserver,dc=pretendco,dc=com" write by * read

1330:access to attr=authAuthority by self write by sockurl="ldapi://%2Fvar%2Frun%2Fldapi" write
by group/posixGroup/memberUid="cn=admin,cn=groups,dc=diradmin,dc=mainserver,dc=pretendco,
dc=com" write by users read by anonymous

1999:access to * by sockurl="ldapi://%2Fvar%2Frun%2Fldapi" write by group/posixGroup/
memberUid="cn=admin,cn=groups,dc=diradmin,dc=mainserver,dc=pretendco,dc=com" write by
users read by anonymous auth
```

After you update an AccessControlEntry, the LDAP server will automatically use the new settings.

To test whether or not your updated DACLs prevent anonymous access to your LDAP Directory, use ldapsearch with the –x flag:

```
ldapsearch -x -h mainserver.pretendco.com -b cn=users,dc=www,dc=ssh22,dc=com uid=diradmin
```

Update Directory Access on the Open Directory Master

The Open Directory master must be updated to no longer access itself anonymously:

1   Open Directory Access.

2   Configure LDAPv3.

3   Highlight the entry for the server, and click Edit.

As you can see, the server will try to anonymously authenticate to itself.

4   Click the Security button, and enter a name and password for authenticating.

   NOTE ▶ The distinguished name should be in the form of
   uid=diradmin,cn=users,dc=mainserver,dc=pretendco,dc=com.

What You've Learned

▶ Complex passwords play a very important role in a secure computing environment.

▶ The various types of passwords used by Mac OS X and Mac OS X Server include shadowhash and Open Directory.

▶ Use the Password Assistant to identify insecure password types.

▶ Because you can leverage both SASL and Kerberos implementations, it is important to have more than one password type when using an Open Directory master.

▶ You can use the AccessControls records to restrict access to your OpenLDAP directory data.

▶ Use the Keychain application or its command-line equivilants, security and certtool, to manage certificates in Mac OS X.

References

Administration Guides

"Mac OS X Server Getting Started": http://images.apple.com/server/pdfs/Getting_Started_v10.4.pdf

"Upgrading and Migrating to Mac OS X Server v10.4 Tiger": http://images.apple.com/server/pdfs/Migration_v10.4.pdf

"Open Directory Administration": http://images.apple.com/server/pdfs/Open_Directory_v10.4.pdf

"Mac OS X Server Command-Line Administration": http://images.apple.com/server/pdfs/Command_Line_v10.4.pdf

Apple Knowledge Base Documents

The following Knowledge Base documents (located at www.apple.com/support) provide further information about secure authentication.

LDAP

Document 107242: "Mac OS X Server: How to Get More Than 500 Returns from LDAP Server."

Authentication

Document 107543: "Mac OS X Server 10.2, 10.3: Password Authentication Options for Networked Environments."

Document 107875: "Mac OS X Server 10.3: Upgrading Password Server Users to Kerberos and Single Sign-On."

Kerberos

Document 107702: "Mac OS X Server 10.3: Kerberos Authentication May Not Work After Changing to LDAP Master or Replica, or Kerberizing a Particular Service."

Books

Carter, Gerald. *LDAP System Administration* (O'Reilly, 2003).

Garman, Jason. *Kerberos: The Definitive Guide* (O'Reilly, 2003).

URLs

Massachusetts Institute of Technology Kerberos release: http://web.mit.edu/kerberos/www

"Designing an Authentication System: a Dialogue in Four Scenes": http://web.mit.edu/kerberos/www/dialogue.html

Lesson Review

1. Where are the user passwords stored on Mac OS X?
2. What types of password hash methods can be enabled/disabled using Server Admin?
3. What application is used to manage certificates in Mac OS X and Mac OS X Server?

Answers

1. /private/var/db/shadow/hash/
2. CRAM-MD5, NTLMv1 and NTLMv2, LAN Manager, APOP, and WebDAV
3. Keychain Access

18

Time   This lesson takes approximately 2 hours to complete.

Goals   Understand network security design principles

Learn methods for implementing a secure network design, including NAT, VPNs, and firewalls

Use the Mac OS X Gateway Setup Assistant to enable and configure routing, NAT, and VPN services

Use the Mac OS X Server Admin application to configure the firewall service

Create firewall rules to lock down traffic to and through a Mac OS X server, including remote administration traffic, Web and e-mail traffic, DNS zone transfers, pings, and ping replies

Configure Mac OS X firewall service for stealth mode

Analyze firewall rules with the UNIX ipfw show command

Monitor network security with logging

Lesson 18
Secure Network Configuration

Mac OS X Server can handle advanced network security tasks that were once the specialized job of expensive, hard-to-use hardware devices. With the Mac OS X Gateway Setup Assistant and Server Admin applications, you can easily configure a Mac OS X server to act as a router, a Network Address Translation (NAT) gateway, a virtual private network (VPN) server, and a firewall.

Configuring a server to act as a router enables you to connect multiple networks to the server and route Internet Protocol (IP) traffic between the networks. Once you have multiple networks set up, NAT lets you use private addresses on the internal networks. VPNs allow remote users to connect securely to a private network and appear as if they are connected directly to the private network. The Mac OS X Server firewall helps you secure the server and implement policies regarding services that your internal and external users can reach.

Designing a Secure Network

A basic explanation of design principles is always a good start in any security discussion. Design starts with requirements analysis, so the first step for getting security right on Mac OS X Server is to understand requirements. You should talk to users, managers, and technical staff to find out what security concerns must be addressed. Before implementing security mechanisms, you need to know if you are securing services that run on the server, protecting internal servers on a private network connected to the server, controlling which outside services your internal users can reach, or all of these.

One basic aspect of requirements analysis is to find out who the users are, where they are located, and what resources they use. Designers sometimes use the concept of a user community to help them recognize requirements. A *user community* is a set of users with similar application and security requirements. This can be a corporate department, a set of outside users, a set of business partners, or a single user who has unique requirements. You should document user-community names, sizes, locations, and applications. Also document the names and addresses of servers, their locations and applications, and which user communities depend on them. With that documentation in hand, you can begin to understand what needs to be secured.

Next, to ensure system and data availability, you must understand the direction of network traffic flow to and from services. Talk to your users, examine network diagrams, study network traffic with a protocol analyzer, and review network logs to help you understand the direction of network traffic flow and how your security measures can filter this flow to implement user requirements.

Analyzing Network Security Threats

An important step in network security design is analyzing threats, their likelihood and severity, and the dangers associated with not taking action to prevent and mitigate these threats. Network devices—such as servers, routers, and firewalls—are attractive targets for attackers.

If an attacker undermines the security of a network device, the following problems arise:

▶ Data flowing through the device and the networks it connects can be intercepted, analyzed, altered, or deleted, compromising confidentiality and integrity.

▶ The device's configuration can be changed to block legitimate access and allow future attacks.

▶ User passwords can be compromised.

▶ Configuration and management data can be monitored, showing the attacker other devices that are reachable from the device.

Tools for intercepting and analyzing data on a network are readily available. Ethereal, for example, is a free and easy-to-use protocol analysis tool that runs on almost every platform. Ethereal captures network traffic and displays each packet in human-readable format, which makes it a useful network management tool as well as a powerful tool for network attackers. The following output from Ethereal shows a Telnet packet. Notice that the output is helpful for analyzing packet headers while troubleshooting a problem, but it's also helpful for attackers, who can easily see in the Telnet data section at the end of the output that the user typed *co* followed by a carriage return (\r).

```
Frame 27 (58 bytes on wire, 58 bytes captured)
Ethernet II
    Destination: 00:00:0c:00:2e:75 (Cisco_00:2e:75)
    Source: 00:0d:93:28:c9:f6 (AppleCom_28:c9:f6)
    Type: IP (0x0800)
Internet Protocol
    Version: 4
    Header length: 20 bytes
    Differentiated Services Field: 0x10
    Total Length: 44
    Identification: 0x22fe (8958)
    Flags: 0x04
        .1.. = Don't fragment: Set
        ..0. = More fragments: Not set
    Fragment offset: 0
    Time to live: 64
    Protocol: TCP (0x06)
    Header checksum: 0x02d8 (correct)
    Source: 10.10.0.209 (10.10.0.209)
    Destination: 10.10.0.2 (10.10.0.2)
Transmission Control Protocol
    Source port: 51854 (51854)
    Destination port: telnet (23)
```

```
Sequence number: 2722440935
Acknowledgement number: 3672130357
Header length: 20 bytes
Flags
    0... .... = Congestion Window Reduced (CWR): Not set
    .0.. .... = ECN-Echo: Not set
    ..0. .... = Urgent: Not set
    ...1 .... = Acknowledgment: Set
    .... 1... = Push: Set
    .... .0.. = Reset: Not set
    .... ..0. = Syn: Not set
    .... ...0 = Fin: Not set
Window size: 65535
Checksum: 0x788a (correct)
Telnet
    Data: co\r
```

From output such as this, an attacker can gain information about Ethernet addresses (in the Ethernet II section of the example, see Destination: 00:00:0c:00:2e:75 (Cisco_00:2e:75) and Source: 00:0d:93:28:c9:f6 (AppleCom_28:c9:f6)) and IP addresses (in the Internet Protocol section, see Source: 10.10.0.209 (10.10.0.209) and Destination: 10.10.0.2 (10.10.0.2)). This knowledge of addresses helps an attacker find targets.

An attacker can also gain information about the identifiers used for IP datagrams and the sequence numbers used for Transport Control Protocol (TCP) segments. (In the Internet Protocol section, see Identification: 0x22fe (8958); in the Transmission Control Protocol section, see Sequence number: 2722440935.) This type of information could be used to craft an attack packet.

Finally, as mentioned, the attacker can see that the user typed *co* followed by a carriage return. These were the last two characters in the Telnet password, which was Cisco.

Reconnaissance Attacks

An attacker launches a *reconnaissance attack* to learn about potential targets and their weaknesses in preparation for a more focused attack. Reconnaissance attackers use tools to discover the reachability of computers, networks, services, and applications. While on a reconnaissance mission, an attacker might try to gather the following information:

▶   The existence of and names of servers configured in a domain name system (DNS) server

▶   Configuration information listed in a Simple Network Management Protocol (SNMP) server

▶   The reachability of servers and end-user systems via ping and port scans

▶   Operating system and application versions

One tool that attackers use to test the reachability and vulnerabilities of a network server is the UNIX nmap utility. nmap sends traffic to the target for numerous TCP and User Datagram Protocol (UDP) ports and examines the results to discover open ports, application and operating system versions, and vulnerabilities.

By default, Mac OS X Server has very few ports open. In this example using nmap on the Mac OS X Server with the IP address of 192.168.3.1, some default ports have been closed while others have been opened:

```
Pretendcos-Computer:~ Pretendco$ nmap 192.168.3.1
Starting nmap V. 3.00 ( www.insecure.org/nmap/ )
Interesting ports on  (192.168.3.1):
(The 1592 ports scanned but not shown below are in state: closed)
Port      State    Service
25/tcp    open     smtp
53/tcp    open     domain
80/tcp    open     http
110/tcp   open     pop-3
311/tcp   open     asip-webadmin
407/tcp   open     timbuktu
427/tcp   open     svrloc
548/tcp   open     afpovertcp
625/tcp   open     unknown
Nmap run completed -- 1 IP address (1 host up) scanned in 10 seconds
```

NOTE ▶ The nmap utility has nefarious as well as reputable qualities. You can use it to test the security of your own network devices, for example. This testing method should be used sparingly and with caution, however. nmap sends a huge number of packets to the target in a short period of time.

Denial of Service Attacks

Denial of Service (DoS) attacks target networks, servers, or applications, making it impossible for legitimate users to gain access. DoS attacks usually result from the inability of a network, computer, or application to handle a huge load, which crashes the system or halts the system's services. These attacks pose a significant risk because they can interrupt business processes and are reasonably easy to conduct, even by an unskilled attacker.

DoS attacks include:

▶   Flooding servers with huge numbers of connection requests

▶   Sending so many pings that a device gets so busy replying that it can't handle legitimate traffic

▶   Flooding network paths with so much traffic that all bandwidth is consumed

Preventing DoS attacks is best handled by dedicated hardware firewalls and intrusion detection systems (IDSs) that have built-in software that recognizes and mitigates attacks. For example, some dedicated firewalls have advanced software that can recognize and deflect a flood of TCP connection requests, also known as a TCP SYN flood attack.

Dealing with DoS attacks may also require help from network administrators of upstream networks. For example, if the Internet pipe into your company is being flooded with huge amounts of traffic, consuming all available bandwidth, this must be stopped at your Internet service provider (ISP).

In the case of Mac OS X Server, simple DoS attacks are stoppable by disallowing Internet Control Message Protocol (ICMP) echoes (pings) and echo replies, and by disallowing all traffic from a known attacker—both of which are relatively easy to do with Mac OS X Server firewall service.

Using Network Security Mechanisms

Network security mechanisms protect servers, facilitate packet filtering with firewalls, and enable the use of private addresses with NAT. VPN is another security mechanism that provides secure, encrypted remote access to an internal network from computers on the Internet. This section discusses these mechanisms.

Network servers are valuable assets that should be protected with physical security and hardened (strengthened) against intrusions. To harden a server, you should enable only the services that you absolutely need. If the server has network interfaces that you aren't using, you should disable those interfaces. You should also carefully maintain software and apply security patches when necessary.

Avoid using nonsecure protocols such as Telnet to administer a network server. Firewall rules can establish which computers can connect to servers using safer remote administration methods such as Secure Shell Protocol (SSH), SNMP, Apple Server Admin, or Netopia's Timbuktu.

When a server is compromised, attackers may try to use that server to attack other servers. Although network security usually focuses on what traffic is allowed into servers, you may also want to develop firewall rules that restrict applications that a server can go to, in case the server gets compromised.

Finally, one last general point is that you must read logs. Firewall logs are especially important for recognizing impending (or possibly already successful) attacks.

Setting Up Firewalls

A *firewall* is software or hardware that guards the entrance to a network or computer and keeps out unwanted network traffic. It creates a protected environment "behind" or "inside" the firewall that is distinct from the risky world that lies "beyond" or "outside" it. A firewall can run on a router, a server (such as a Mac OS X server), a dedicated hardware box, or an individual Macintosh or PC.

Security experts often make a distinction between a host firewall and a network firewall:

▶   A host firewall protects the computer on which it runs. Personal host firewall software is essential for protecting individual computers, especially mobile computers. Server host firewall software is essential for protecting a server.

▶   A network firewall enforces security policies at the boundary between two or more networks. The Mac OS X Server firewall can be both a server host firewall and a network firewall.

A firewall has a set of rules that specify whether network traffic should be accepted, denied, or handled in some other way. As part of your network security design, you must decide if you want to configure firewall rules that protect the server or rules that protect the networks connected by the server, or both.

Firewall rules specify criteria that are applied to a packet to determine if the packet should be accepted or denied. Typical criteria are the packet source address, the packet destination address, the protocol type in the IP header, or the source or destination port numbers in the TCP or UDP header.

Some firewalls, including Mac OS X Server, have more advanced capabilities. For example, to allow all TCP traffic back in for a connection that an inside user initiated, you can allow all packets with the TCP ACK or RST (reset) bits set. This avoids traffic with only the SYN bit set, which would indicate traffic initiated by an outsider rather than an inside user. Allowing traffic with the ACK or RST bit set is called "allowing established traffic."

For each packet, a firewall reads the list of rules in order. If a rule applies to the packet, the action specified in the rule is taken (for example, accept or deny) and the reading of further entries in the list usually ends.

Because firewall software tests a packet against each criterion in the list of rules until a match is found, you should design rules with care to avoid problems and to provide good performance. It won't work, for example, to deny all TCP packets from a network before you allow TCP from one host on that network. You would have to do it the other way around.

On the other hand, to optimize performance, when possible you should design the list so that most packets match the earliest conditions. Fewer conditions to check per packet means better throughput. To optimize security, the last statement should be a general deny-all statement.

A *stateless firewall* looks at packets as individual events. A *stateful firewall*, on the other hand, can track multipacket communication sessions and more intelligently accept or deny traffic. For example, a stateful firewall can remember that a protected client initiated a request to download data from an Internet server and allow data back in for that connection.

Mac OS X Server can do both stateless and stateful processing. To use stateful processing, Mac OS X Server adds the keep-state keyword to rules.

Set Up Mac OS X Server Firewall Service

The Mac OS X Server firewall is built on the standard, open-source ipfw software from FreeBSD UNIX. Like most firewalls, the Mac OS X Server firewall scans incoming packets and accepts or denies them based on the packet-filtering rules that you configure. You can restrict access to any service running on the server, and you can customize filters for all internal clients or for a range of internal IP addresses. You can also allow or disallow traffic from the server to implement advanced security policies.

Although you can add and delete rules with the UNIX ipfw tool using Terminal, usually you don't need to do this; Server Admin provides a sophisticated and easy-to-use interface to ipfw. The one ipfw command that you will use regularly, however, is sudo ipfw show, which displays the rules that ipfw is using. It shows you exactly what the underlying ipfw service is doing and helps you verify that the configuration you set up with Server Admin is correct.

Create Firewall Address Groups

To simplify configuring firewall rules, Server Admin enables you to set up address groups. An address group can be a single address, such as 192.168.3.1, or a range of addresses, such as 192.168.3.0–192.168.3.255. You can set up a range of addresses using subnet mask notation (192.168.3.0: 255.255.255.0) or Classless Interdomain Routing (CIDR) notation (192.168.3.0/24). Mac OS X Server has three preset firewall groups:

▶ any

▶ 10-net (10.0.0.0/8)

▶ 192.168-net (192.168.0.0/16).

As part of your network security design process, you should have identified the user communities in your environment that need security. These user communities can become address groups. Because you will probably have many rules that apply to addresses, configuring address groups as your first step will save you much typing when configuring rules. By default, the Mac OS X Server firewall includes an address group for "any" (meaning any IP address) and may include other defaults, depending on your configuration.

To create an address group:

1   Launch Server Admin and choose Firewall from the Computers & Services list.

2   Click Settings.

3   Click Address Groups.

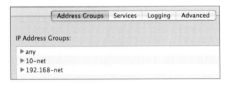

4   Click the Add (+) button to add a group.

5   Enter a group name.

6   Click the Add (+) button to configure addresses for this group.

7   Enter the addresses you want rules to affect.

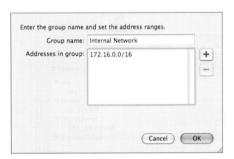

8   Remove the default "any" if it doesn't apply by clicking the Delete (-) button.

9   Click OK.

10 Click Save.

As an example, you could configure an address group for the network manager. Later, you could use this address group when setting up rules to specify what the network manager can do (remote server administration, SSH, and so on.)

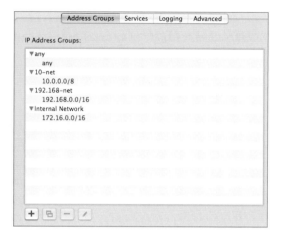

Use the Services and Advanced Panes

Once you have some address groups configured, you can configure rules using the Services and Advanced panes in Server Admin. The Services pane is quite user-friendly, whereas the Advanced pane is optimized for a finer degree of control.

In the Services pane, you can configure rules that will apply to traffic into the server. For example, one of your first configuration steps should be to specify which services the any group can reach on the server. To do this, you enable (select) or disable (deselect) services for any.

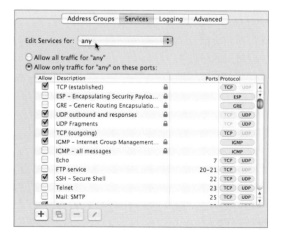

The wording in the Services pane can be confusing. When the pane says "edit services for any," for example, it actually configures rules to allow traffic *from* any address to the services checked. For example, by checking Mail: SMTP, the following rules are added to ipfw:

▶   12305 allow tcp from any to any dst-port 25

▶   12305 allow udp from any to any dst-port 25

The 12305 is a rule number. (The firewall can have more than one rule with the same number. It reads and obeys the rules in the order that they appear in the list.) The first "any" in the rule means any source IP address. The second "any" means any destination IP address. Port 25 is the well-known port for Simple Mail Transfer Protocol (SMTP). When using the Services pane to add rules, the firewall automatically allows traffic destined to both UDP and TCP ports 25, even though SMTP doesn't use UDP.

To configure more advanced rules, use the Advanced pane. The Advanced pane is also useful for displaying default rules. The firewall adds low-numbered rules (1000-1030) to cover well-known vulnerabilities and high-numbered rules (63200-65534) to cover typical default policies. The most important default policy is covered by rule 65534, which denies all IP traffic not covered by lower-numbered rules.

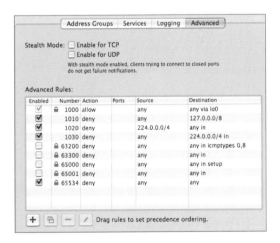

Generate and Review ipfw show Output

You can see the rules that your firewall has enabled by clicking Active Rules in the Server Admin application or by opening Terminal (Applications/Utilities) and entering *sudo ipfw show.* The following table explains the rules in use on a typical server that connects an "outside" Ethernet network that goes to the wide area network (WAN) and the Internet, and an "inside" Ethernet interface that connects a private local area network (LAN). The outside interface is en0 and the inside interface is en1. The inside network is 192.168.3.0/24. The server is providing NAT for this private address range.

Rule Number	Rule	Default	Explanation
00001	allow udp from any 626 to any dst-port 626	Yes	Serial number management for Mac OS X Server.
00010	divert 8668 ip from any to any via en0	No	NAT rule.
01000	allow ip from any to any via lo0	Yes	Allow internal traffic using the loopback interface.
01010	deny ip from any to 127.0.0.0/8	Yes	Deny traffic to the loopback IP address.
01020	deny ip from 224.0.0.0/4 to any in	Yes	Deny incoming traffic from multicast.
01030	deny tcp from any to 224.0.0.0/4 in	Yes	Deny incoming TCP traffic to multicast.
01040	allow tcp from 192.168.3.2 to any dst-port 311	No	Allow 192.168.3.2 to send to port 311 (Server Admin).
01050	deny tcp from 192.168.3.0/24 to any dst-port 311	No	Deny 192.168.3.0/24 from sending to port 311.
12300	allow tcp from any to any established	No	Allow TCP traffic with the ACK or RST bits set.
12301	allow tcp from any to any out	No	Allow outbound TCP.
12302	allow udp from any to any out keep-state	No	Allow outbound UDP and keep state so that replies are allowed.
12303	allow icmp from any to any icmptypes 8	No	Allow pings.

Rule Number	Rule	Default	Explanation
12304	allow icmp from any to any icmptypes 0	No	Allow ping replies.
12305	allow tcp from any to any dst-port 25	No	Allow SMTP using TCP.
12305	allow udp from any to any dst-port 25	No	Allow SMTP using UDP.
12306	allow tcp from any to any dst-port 80	No	Allow HTTP (Web).
12307	allow ip from 192.168.3.0/24 to any via en1 keep-state	No	Allow traffic initiated by inside users and keep state to allow replies.
12308	allow udp from any 68 to any	No	Allow Dynamic Host Configuration Protocol (DHCP) requests from inside users.
65534	deny 1000 ip from any to any dst-port 67 via en1	Yes	Deny all other ip traffic.
65535	allow ip from any to any	Yes	ipfw default; won't be used because of Mac OS X default rule 65534.

Understanding Network Address Translation

NAT converts addresses that are used on an inside network to addresses that are appropriate for an outside network, and vice versa. NAT is useful when computers that need access to the Internet have private addresses.

Private IP addresses are addresses that a network administrator assigns to internal networks without any coordination from an ISP or one of the regional registries for IP addressing, such as the American Registry for Internet Numbers (ARIN). An ISP or registry provides public addresses for Web servers or other servers that external users access, but public addresses aren't required for internal computers.

The Internet Engineering Task Force (IETF) reserves the following numbers for private networks:

▶   10.0.0.0 through 10.255.255.255

▶   172.16.0.0 through 172.31.255.255

▶   192.168.0.0 through 192.168.255.255

With NAT, when an internal computer sends a packet, a NAT gateway (such as Mac OS X Server) dynamically translates the private source address in the packet to a public address. The gateway keeps track of this translation and converts the destination address on return packets to the correct private address.

Private addressing offers some security, although it could be considered merely security by obscurity. Private network numbers are never advertised to the Internet because they aren't globally unique. Not advertising internal network numbers provides some privacy.

Of course, additional security—including firewalls, IDSs, and antivirus software—should also be deployed. NAT sometimes gives people a false sense of security, but keep in mind that a privately addressed computer is actually still reachable from the Internet if the NAT gateway is functioning correctly, but a firewall is not in place and configured correctly to protect the computer.

Mac OS X Server NAT Services

Mac OS X Server makes an excellent NAT gateway, especially when used with Gateway Setup Assistant (added in Mac OS X version 10.4), which makes setting up NAT even easier than it was in previous versions of Mac OS X. When Mac OS X Server provides NAT services, it translates internal addresses to the address assigned to the external address. It also keeps state information so that traffic coming back in can be translated and sent to the right internal address.

When you enable NAT, the natd process is started and a rule is added to the firewall to divert packets that come in via the outside interface to the natd process. For example, the previous table showed the following rule, where 8668 is the process ID for natd and en0 is the outside interface:

00010 divert 8668 ip from any to any via en0

Enabling NAT also adds a rule to allow traffic initiated by inside users and to keep state so that return traffic is allowed. For example, the following rule is added to support internal users on the 192.168.3.0/24 network, reachable via the server's inside interface en1:

12307 allow ip from 192.168.3.0/24 to any via en1 keep-state

Note that if you enable the NAT service, you are also required to enable the firewall service. Otherwise packets won't be diverted to the natd process and NAT service will not take effect.

Mac OS X Server Gateway Setup Assistant

The Gateway Setup Assistant helps you quickly and easily set up Mac OS X Server for routing and NAT. It also enables the firewall and adds some default firewall rules. Depending on your configuration choices, the assistant will do the following when it is finished:

▶ Assign the server a static IP address for each internal network interface. The address assigned is 192.168.x.1. The number used for x is determined by the network interface's order in System Preferences > Network. For example, for the first interface, x is 0, and for the second interface, x is 1.

▶ Enable DHCP to allocate addresses on the internal networks.

▶ Set aside internal (192.168.x.x) addresses for DHCP to use. Without VPN enabled, each interface can allocate 192.168.x.2 through 192.168.x.254.

▶ Optionally enable VPN to allow authorized external clients to connect to the local network.

▶ Set aside addresses for VPN to use. If VPN is selected, half of the allotted IP addresses in the DHCP range are reserved for VPN connections. The addresses 192.168.x.128 through 192.168.x.254 are allotted to VPN connections.

▶ Enable the firewall to help secure the internal networks. Address groups are added for each internal network interface, with all traffic allowed from the newly created DHCP address ranges to any destination address.

▶ Enable NAT on the internal network and add a NAT divert rule to the firewall to direct network traffic to the appropriate computer.

▶ Enable DNS on the server.

To use the Gateway Setup Assistant, you can open the Gateway Setup Assistant application from the Applications/Server directory on the server, or you can select View > Gateway Setup while in Server Admin. Follow the directions in the assistant and click Continue after each page. Read the final output carefully, and make sure you approve of the configuration before finalizing the settings.

Before running Gateway Setup Assistant, you should have planned which interface will connect the outside network, which interfaces will connect the inside networks, and whether you want to enable VPN. The first interface that Gateway Setup Assistant asks about is the outside interface that connects to the Internet. The assistant calls this the WAN interface, even though the interface probably uses a classic LAN technology such as Ethernet.

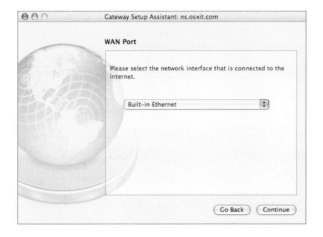

NOTE ▶ Gateway Setup Assistant assumes that the outside "WAN port" gets its address via DHCP. A DHCP address for an outside interface is typical in home networks but not in enterprise networks. On an enterprise network, it's more common for the outside interface to have a public address or an address assigned by a corporate network manager. You may need to use System Preferences > Network to reenter the correct address for your outside WAN interface after running Gateway Setup Assistant.

Understanding Virtual Private Networking

VPN supports mobile users, telecommuters, and business partners who may not physically be on a private network but want to virtually appear as if they are. Users run VPN client software that lets them connect to the private network in a secure fashion. Because the users might be on a public, insecure network, such as the Internet, all their traffic to the private network is sent in an encrypted tunnel. This allows users to travel outside the physical boundaries of the private network, but still have access to the network.

LAN-to-LAN VPNs are also possible. In this case, two private networks are connected via a public network, such as the Internet. Security is maintained because all traffic between the LANs is sent in an encrypted tunnel.

Mac OS X Server VPN Services

The built-in VPN server on Mac OS X Server supports Mac, Windows, and Linux systems running standards-based VPN client software. Both the Layer Two Tunneling Protocol (L2TP) and the Point-to-Point Tunneling Protocol (PPTP) are supported.

L2TP runs on top of IPSec, which is an IETF set of standards for Network-layer encryption and authentication. You can also use MS-CHAPv2 or Kerberos for authentication. IPSec uses security certificates (either self-signed or from a certificate authority such as VeriSign) or a predefined shared secret. The shared secret must be entered on the server as well as on the clients.

L2TP is a better choice than PPTP because it uses strong IPSec encryption and supports both IPSec and Kerberos for authentication. PPTP is still commonly used, however, to support older Windows computers and Mac OS X v10.2 clients. PPTP offers good encryption (provided strong passwords are used) and supports a number of authentication schemes. With PPTP, you can allow 40-bit encryption in addition to the default 128-bit encryption if needed by your VPN clients, but note that 40-bit encryption is weaker.

NOTE ▶ PPTP has known weaknesses, so you should use L2TP whenever possible.

VPN requires firewall configuration. The firewall must be able to pass network traffic from external IP addresses through the firewall to the private network. This can be as open or restricted as you deem necessary. For example, if the VPN clients travel a lot and may come in via a large range of IP addresses, you may need to open the "any" firewall address group to VPN connections. If you know where your users will be coming in from, you can narrow access to a small range of IP addresses. You can create an address group that reflects that smaller range and only enable VPN traffic originating from that list.

Configuring Network Security

So far in this lesson, you learned about security concepts and basic configuration. In this section, you will learn configuration guidelines for using the firewall to lock down traffic to the server and through the server, and for setting up VPN services.

When locking down traffic to the server, it's important to consider remote administration. For example, which computers should be allowed to access the server via various remote management ports?

It's also important to consider which computers should be allowed access to the services running on the server, which can include Web, e-mail, file, print, and other services.

When locking down traffic through the server, the goal is to control the traffic that your inside users are allowed to send.

Locking Down Remote Administration

Before locking down remote administration of the server, determine which computers should be allowed to remotely administer the server and which applications they use. Once you have identified the applications in use, you should also determine whether the applications run on TCP or UDP and which port numbers they access. In general, you probably will be working with the following TCP port numbers when configuring remote administration:

22	Remote Login or Secure Shell (SSH)
311	Mac OS X Server Admin
407	Timbuktu
687	Mac OS X Server Monitor
1417–19	Timbuktu (old versions)
5500	Virtual Network Computing (VNC)
5800	VNC
5900	Apple Remote Desktop (ARD) & VNC
5901	VNC
5988	ARD and Web-Based Enterprise Management

> **NOTE** ▶ You may also work with UDP ports 161 and 162 for SNMP.

The TCP port for Telnet (23) isn't in this list because you shouldn't use it. It sends the user's password and all other data in clear text (unencrypted). A sniffer user could snoop the commands being sent to the server and gather useful information. The Telnet service is not enabled by default on the server, but for extra precaution, if no other rule is already covering Telnet, then you should add the following rule:

deny tcp from any to any dst-port 23

To configure rules that allow legitimate computers to remotely administer the server, use the Advanced pane in Server Admin. The Advanced pane lets you add specific, low-numbered rules to your list that override higher-numbered general-purpose rules.

Carefully plan the order of your rules to avoid logic mistakes. For example, it's easy to end up with a low-numbered rule allowing all traffic from 192.168.3.0/24 that precedes a higher-numbered rule that allows Server Admin (port 311) traffic from the network manager at address 192.168.3.2. The first rule allows other users on the private network access to 311 also, which is probably not what you intended.

Another possible logic mistake is to deny all users on network 192.168.3.0/24 access to port 311 before allowing the network manager at address 192.168.3.2 access to port 311. The first rule overrides the second rule. Your network manager never gets to port 311 because the first rule blocks the network traffic.

So, how would you allow only the network manager at 192.168.3.2 access to port 311? The first step is to set up an address group for the 192.168.3.2 address and call it something like "Network manager."

To create the address group:

1 Launch Server Admin and choose Firewall from the Computers & Services list.

2 Click Settings.

3 Click Address Groups.

4 Click the Add (+) button to add a group.

5 Enter *network manager* for the group name.

6 Click the Add (+) button to configure the network manager's IP address.

7 Enter *192.168.3.2.*

8 Remove the default "any" by clicking the Delete (-) button.

9 Click OK.

10 Click Save.

Next, follow these steps to create a rule for the network manager that allows the manager access to port 311 (Server Admin):

1 Launch Server Admin and choose Firewall from the Computers & Services list.

2 Click Settings.

3 Click Advanced.

4 Click the Add (+) button to add a rule.

5 Click the Action pop-up menu and choose Allow.

6 Click the Protocol pop-up menu and choose TCP.

7 Click the Service menu and choose "Server Admin SSL, also Web-ASIP."

8 Click the Address menu and choose "Network manager."

9 Click the Destination menu and choose the address of the server (or "any" to allow management of all servers).

10 Click OK.

11 Click Save.

The following output from sudo ipfw show displays the firewall rule list after rules were successfully added to allow only a local manager (192.168.3.2) and a remote manager (17.17.17.17) access to port 311. Similar rules could be configured to allow other types of remote management, such as Timbuktu or ARD.

```
pretendco:~ mgr$ sudo ipfw show
00010    312175   225883045    divert 8668 ip from any to any via en0
01000   1385552   757262930    allow ip from any to any via lo0
01040         0           0    allow tcp from 192.168.3.2 to any dst-port 311
01050         0           0    deny log logamount 1000 tcp from 192.168.3.0/24 to any dst-port 311
01060    103104    28060328    allow tcp from 17.17.17.17 to 17.17.17.1 dst-port 311
12300    152335   187847220    allow tcp from any to any established
12301         0           0    allow tcp from any to any out
12302     13771     1663284    allow udp from any to any out keep-state
12307         0           0    allow ip from 192.168.3.0/24 to any via en1 keep-state
12308         0           0    allow udp from any 68 to any dst-port 67 via en1
65534     16641     6223176    deny log logamount 1000 ip from any to any
65535      3038      475990    allow ip from any to any
```

Notice from the sudo ipfw show output that logging has been enabled. For example, rule 01050 denies users on network 192.168.3.0/24 (other than 192.168.3.2, which is permitted by rule 01040) access to port 311 and logs their attempts up to 1000 packets. Note also that this output has two columns past the rule number column that weren't shown before. The first of these columns is a count of the number of packets that have matched the rule. The second is the number of bytes for those packets. For example, notice that 16,641 packets and about 6.2 MB bytes have been denied by rule 65534.

> **NOTE ▶** It may surprise you to see that any packets have been allowed by the default rule 65535, since rule 65534 should override it. Packets allowed by rule 65535 were allowed before rule 65534 was configured.

Locking Down Access to Public Servers

Before locking down any services on a server, you must complete a network security design that will help you know which services to lock down and for whom to lock them. You need to know if the server is a public server that outsiders can reach or a private server only for internal users.

You also must find out which specific services are public. Typically Web and e-mail services are public, whereas file and print services are not. On the other hand, you may have outside business partners who need to reach files on the server. In that case, you need to know if they use Apple Filing Protocol (AFP), network file system (NFS), or the Windows standard Server Message Block (SMB) and Common Internet File System (CIFS) protocols. Locking down Windows file protocols is especially important because they are vulnerable to viruses, worms, and Trojan horses.

A public server usually allows incoming Web traffic that uses the Hypertext Transfer Protocol (HTTP), port 80. If the public server is an e-mail server, it should also allow SMTP, port 25. A mail server should accept mail from its internal users as well as any public servers.

SMTP is used between Internet mail servers as well as between mail clients and servers. You can't predict which Internet e-mail servers will need to send SMTP traffic, so you should allow traffic from any server. (You can configure mail services for protection from junk mail with tools such as SpamAssassin. Usually this isn't done with a firewall rule, although if necessary you could configure rules to deny SMTP from known spammer IP addresses. Spammers can move to a different address, however, and thwart that measure.)

To support a public Web and mail server, configure rules to allow all traffic from any to ports 80 and 25, as follows:

1 Launch Server Admin and choose Firewall from the Computers & Services list.

2 Click Settings.

3 Click Services.

4 Choose the "any" address group.

5 Choose "Mail: SMTP."

This adds two rules to your firewall:

▶ 12305 allow tcp from any to any dst-port 25

▶ 12305 allow udp from any to any dst-port 25

6 Choose "HTTP – Web service."

This adds one rule to your firewall:

▶ 12306 allow tcp from any to any dst-port 80

7 Click Save.

All other ports are locked down because of the default rule 65534, which says to deny IP from any to any.

To support users reading e-mail, you should allow Post Office Protocol version 3 (POP3, port 110). Usually, you don't need to allow access from any address. POP users are generally local. However, if you want to allow mobile users to read e-mail from anywhere, than you might want to open up POP3 to any address.

> **NOTE** ▶ Mail protocols other than SMTP and POP are possible, such as the Internet Message Access Protocol (IMAP, port 143). Follow the directions mentioned for SMTP, except choose a different protocol from the Services menu or enter the appropriate port number.

Locking Down Access to Services From a Private Network

If you use the Gateway Assistant Setup, your private, internal network will be allowed to send traffic to all addresses and services. Traffic will also be allowed back in because the assistant adds a firewall rule with the keep-state keyword. For example, if the private network is 192.168.30.0/24 and it's reachable via en1, the assistant adds the following rule:

allow ip from 192.168.3.0/24 to any via en1 keep-state

If you want better control of which services your internal users can reach, you can add an address group for the internal network and then enable only the services you really want in the Services pane.

The following rules run on a typical server that allows access to only specific, commonly-used services from the private 192.168.3.0/24 network. SMTP, DNS, HTTP, POP, and DHCP are allowed.

```
00010        divert 8668 ip from any to any via en0
01000        allow ip from any to any via lo0
12307        allow tcp from 192.168.3.0/24 to any established
12308        allow udp from 192.168.3.0/24 to any out keep-state
12310        allow tcp from 192.168.3.0/24 to any dst-port 25
12310        allow udp from 192.168.3.0/24 to any dst-port 25
12311        allow tcp from 192.168.3.0/24 to any dst-port 53 out keep-state
12311        allow udp from 192.168.3.0/24 to any dst-port 53 out keep-state
12312        allow tcp from 192.168.3.0/24 to any dst-port 80
12313        allow tcp from 192.168.3.0/24 to any dst-port 53
12313        allow udp from 192.168.3.0/24 to any dst-port 53
12314        allow udp from 192.168.3.0/24 to any dst-port 67
12315        allow tcp from 192.168.3.0/24 to any dst-port 110
12315        allow udp from 192.168.3.0/24 to any dst-port 110
65534        deny log logamount 1000 ip from any to any
65535        allow ip from any to any
```

Locking Down and Logging Traffic Through the Server From a Private Network

Notice from the rules displayed in the previous section that locking down services for an internal network controls access to servers at any address. (See the "any" in this rule; for example, 12310 allow tcp from 192.168.3.0/24 to any dst-port 25). In other words, the rules allow access to services on the Mac OS X server as well as services running on other servers.

Since the Mac OS X server is also acting as a router and forwarding traffic, if you allow traffic from the internal network to a service (TCP or UDP port number), the server can either accept the traffic for itself or forward it out its external interface to an external server. The choice depends on the destination IP address in the packets. If you want to be more precise, you must use the Advanced pane in the Server Admin firewall configuration.

First make sure you aren't allowing all traffic in the Services pane. Instead you should allow only established TCP traffic (traffic with the ACK or RST bits set—in other words, return packets for traffic initiated locally). While still in the Services pane, also be sure to allow outgoing TCP and UDP traffic from the server so it can send replies.

In the Advanced pane, configure precise rules to allow traffic to the server. Follow this with rules that allow traffic to any for the services you want to allow users to reach on any server. To log traffic, be sure to click the log button. For example, you might want to log all traffic to HTTP so you can record the IP addresses for websites that your users go to.

The following rules resulted from a typical policy that allows only SMTP and POP3 traffic into the server from the internal network, and allows and logs only DNS, HTTP, and HTTP over Secure Socket Layer (HTTPS, port 443) traffic to external sites:

Rule Number	Rule
00010	divert 8668 ip from any to any via en0
01000	allow ip from any to any via lo0
01020	allow tcp from 192.168.3.0/24 to 192.168.3.1 dst-port 25
01030	allow tcp from 192.168.3.0/24 to 192.168.3.1 dst-port 110
01040	allow log logamount 1000 tcp from 192.168.3.0/24 to any dst-port 80
01050	allow log logamount 1000 tcp from 192.168.3.0/24 to any dst-port 443

Rule Number	Rule
01060	allow log logamount 1000 udp from 192.168.3.0/24 to any dst-port 53
01070	allow tcp from any to 17.17.17.1 dst-port 25
12300	allow tcp from any to any established
12303	allow tcp from 192.168.3.1 to any out
12304	allow udp from 192.168.3.1 to any out keep-state
65534	deny log logamount 1000 ip from any to any
65535	allow ip from any to any

SMTP and POP3 are allowed from the internal 192.168.30.0/24 network into the server's internal 192.168.3.1 address. SMTP is also allowed into the external address of the server, 17.17.17.1, so that Internet mail servers can send messages to the server. These rules were configured in the Services and Advanced panes, using the steps mentioned in this section and in "Locking Down Access to Services From a Private Network," above.

Locking Down DNS Zone Transfers

A DNS zone is a database of all name-to-address and address-to-name mappings that a DNS server controls. DNS supports both a primary and a secondary server. All changes to the database records for a zone are made in the primary server. The secondary server can acquire the zone data by setting up a TCP connection and transferring the data using TCP packets destined to TCP port 53.

In the DNS server configuration (in Server Admin), you can enable or disable zone transfers. Disabling zone transfers breaks the ability of DNS to have a secondary (backup) server: It makes the secondary server unable to acquire the zone data. So, if you have a legitimate secondary server but you don't want to transfer zones to just anyone, you can set up firewall rules rather than selecting the Server Admin box to completely disable zone transfers. For example, to allow only the secondary server at address 192.168.3.5 to acquire zone data from your server whose address is 192.168.3.1, use the following rules:

allow tcp from 192.168.3.5 to 192.168.3.1 dst-port 53

deny tcp from any to 192.168.3.1 dst-port 53

NOTE ▶ Normal client/server DNS transactions use UDP, so these rules don't break typical DNS usage. These rules do, however, give you some protection from server mining, which is a type of reconnaissance attack in which an attacker pretends to be a secondary server and requests a copy of the primary server's records. With a copy of the primary zone data, the attacker can learn the IP addresses of named devices. The attacker can then try specific attacks on those devices.

Locking Down Pings and Ping Replies

One type of DoS attack involves an attacker sending a flood of ICMP echo messages, commonly known as pings. Another, less common type involves a server receiving a flood of echo replies (ping replies). This can happen if an attacker is spoofing the server's address and sending a flood of pings. The replies are routed to the legitimate owner of the address: the server. (IP address spoofing is rare these days, because most firewalls are set up to allow out only traffic that uses a legitimate address, which hampers an attacker's ability to use a spoofed address.)

To mitigate the effects of a ping DoS attack, you can configure the firewall to deny echo requests or echo replies:

1   Launch Server Admin and choose Firewall from the Computers & Services list.

2   Click Settings.

3   Click Services.

4   Choose the "any" address group.

5   Deselect "ICMP – echo request messages."

6   Deselect "ICMP – echo reply messages."

7   Click Save.

If you prefer, you can use the Advanced pane to enable the default rule:

63200 deny log logamount 1000 icmp from any to any in icmptypes 0,8

> **TIP** ▶ Ping-based DoS attacks are somewhat rare, so you should deny ICMP echoes and echo replies only if you think your server may be vulnerable to an attack. If you deny ICMP echo messages, network managers can't ping the server to tests its reachability, which is a problem. Also, services that use ping to locate network services will be unable to detect the server.

Enabling Stealth Mode

Stealth mode makes a server less visible to attacks, especially reconnaissance attacks. You can configure stealth mode for both UDP and TCP. In the case of UDP, stealth mode causes a server not to send back an ICMP Destination Unreachable, Port Unreachable message (ICMP message type 3, code 3) when a sender tries to reach a closed UDP port on the server.

Although a determined attacker can still learn a lot about a server in other ways, stealth mode offers some deterrence. For example, if the attacker uses nmap, the nmap software takes a long time to time out and declare that UDP ports are filtered. An impatient attacker might give up.

Note from the following output that nmap took 163 seconds when stealth mode was configured (whereas usually it takes only a few seconds):

```
Pretendcos-Computer:~ Pretendco$ sudo nmap -sU 192.168.3.1
Starting nmap V. 3.00 ( www.insecure.org/nmap/ )
All 1468 scanned ports on  (192.168.3.1) are: filtered
Nmap run completed -- 1 IP address (1 host up) scanned in 163 seconds
```

In the case of TCP, stealth mode causes the server not to send back an RST message when a sender tries to reach a closed port. Note that Mac OS X Server doesn't send back an RST message anyway if you have a deny rule to deny traffic to the port. The underlying ipfw software prevents the sender's SYN packet from ever getting to the protocol stack, which is responsible for sending back a RST. The ipfw deny rule is designed to avoid RST messages, whereas the ipfw reset rule sends back resets. Normally reset rules aren't used, and Mac OS X Server doesn't use them when you configure rules with Server Admin.

TCP traffic that ipfw allows, on the other hand, is passed to the protocol stack, which sends back a RST if the port is closed, unless you enable stealth mode.

To enable stealth mode:

1   Launch Server Admin and choose Firewall from the Computers & Services list.

2   Click Settings.

3   Click Advanced.

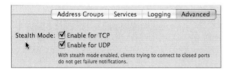

4   Select "Enable for TCP" and/or "Enable for UDP" as desired.

5   Click Save.

Logging Firewall Activity

Logging firewall activity is an essential component of network security. You should establish policies and procedures that specify how much data is logged and how it is stored and analyzed. For enterprise networks, you should err on the side of logging too much data rather than too little. This will ensure that network managers and security analysts have sufficient data to catch attacks as they occur, analyze trends, and conduct forensics analysis for use in criminal or civil court cases. For small and home offices, it's not as imperative to log lots of data, but it's still important.

During the network security design process, decisions should be made about the trade-offs associated with logging a huge volume of data. Is there disk space available to save the data? (Huge hard drives are inexpensive these days, though, so that's generally not a good reason to limit the amount of log data.) Is it possible an attacker could conduct a DoS attack by causing a server to fail because it has filled a hard drive with log data? Good server software helps avoid such a problem. With the exception of a busy Web server, where allowing all traffic to port 80 would result in an unmanageable volume of data, logging all allowed and denied packets is recommended.

TIP Save firewall logs in a protected place that attackers can't reach. Attackers can gather useful data from firewall logs and use that data in future attacks.

With Mac OS X Server Admin, you can enable logging for individual rules in the Advanced pane. You can also control logging in a more general sense in the Logging pane. You can log only the packets that are allowed by the rules you set, only the packets that are denied, or both.

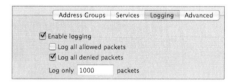

By default, Mac OS X Server logs only 1000 packets for each rule. This isn't sufficient if you plan to use the data for trend analysis or forensics. A server can easily receive 1000 packets in just a few minutes. Because it's difficult to predict the exact number of packets that a server will handle (and because hard drive capacity is inexpensive these days), you should log all packets by entering *0* in the "Log only N packets" field in the Logging pane. Doing so removes the logamount 1000 words from the ipfw rules that you create.

Mac OS X Server saves the log in the /var/log/ipfw.log file. Every 7 days, the server archives the log and starts a new log. The server saves only four archives and deletes older ones. To ensure that data doesn't disappear, use scripts or third-party software to save older log data to a different directory than /var/log.

Studying the firewall log is as important as setting it up. You should check the log regularly. You can view the current log within Server Admin. You also can view the log and the log archives using UNIX commands or third-party software.

If the number of entries is overwhelming, you can filter which entries are displayed using the Server Admin text filter box. For example, to view denied packets to help you identify attack attempts and troubleshoot your firewall rules:

1 Launch Server Admin and choose Firewall from the Computers & Services list.

```
Aug 26 00:17:48 xserve servermgrd: servermgr_ipfilter:ipfw config:Info:Finished generating rules in
9 ms
Aug 26 00:17:48 xserve servermgrd: servermgr_ipfilter:ipfw config:Notice:Flushed rules
Aug 26 00:17:49 xserve servermgrd: servermgr_ipfilter:ipfw config:Info:Finished applying generated
rules in 980 ms
Aug 26 00:17:49 xserve servermgrd: servermgr_ipfilter:ipfw config:Info:Timing: Finished applying
NAT rules
Aug 26 00:17:50 xserve servermgrd: servermgr_ipfilter:ipfw config:Info:Timing: Finished applying
local rules
Aug 26 00:17:50 xserve servermgrd: servermgr_ipfilter:ipfw config:Notice:Enabled firewall
Aug 26 00:17:54 xserve ipfw: 65534 Deny UDP 69.44.14.30:137 69.44.14.31:137 in via en0
Aug 26 00:17:54 xserve ipfw: 65534 Deny UDP 69.44.14.30:137 69.44.14.31:137 in via en0
Aug 26 00:17:55 xserve ipfw: 65534 Deny UDP 69.44.14.30:137 69.44.14.31:137 in via en0
Aug 26 00:17:58 xserve ipfw: 65534 Deny UDP 69.44.14.29:137 69.44.14.31:137 in via en0
Aug 26 00:17:59 xserve ipfw: 65534 Deny UDP 69.44.14.29:137 69.44.14.31:137 in via en0
Aug 26 00:18:00 xserve ipfw: 65534 Deny UDP 69.44.14.29:137 69.44.14.31:137 in via en0
Aug 26 00:18:00 xserve ipfw: 65534 Deny UDP 69.44.168.234:65067 224.0.0.251:5353 in via en0
Aug 26 00:18:00 xserve ipfw: 65534 Deny UDP 69.44.168.234:65068 224.0.0.251:5353 in via en0
Aug 26 00:18:00 xserve ipfw: 65534 Deny UDP 69.44.168.234:5353 224.0.0.251:5353 in via en0
Aug 26 00:18:02 xserve ipfw: 65534 Deny UDP 69.44.168.235:64702 224.0.0.251:5353 in via en0
Aug 26 00:18:02 xserve ipfw: 65534 Deny UDP 69.44.168.235:5353 224.0.0.251:5353 in via en0
Aug 26 00:18:12 xserve ipfw: 65534 Deny UDP 69.44.14.30:137 69.44.14.31:137 in via en0
Aug 26 00:18:13 xserve ipfw: 65534 Deny UDP 69.44.14.30:137 69.44.14.31:137 in via en0
Aug 26 00:18:13 xserve ipfw: 65534 Deny UDP 69.44.14.30:137 69.44.14.31:137 in via en0
Aug 26 00:18:16 xserve ipfw: 65534 Deny UDP 69.44.14.29:137 69.44.14.31:137 in via en0
Aug 26 00:18:17 xserve ipfw: 65534 Deny UDP 69.44.14.29:137 69.44.14.31:137 in via en0
Aug 26 00:18:18 xserve ipfw: 65534 Deny UDP 69.44.14.29:137 69.44.14.31:137 in via en0
Aug 26 00:18:22 xserve ipfw: 65534 Deny UDP 69.44.14.30:137 69.44.14.31:137 in via en0
Aug 26 00:18:23 xserve ipfw: 65534 Deny UDP 69.44.14.30:137 69.44.14.31:137 in via en0
```

2   Click Log.

3   Enter *deny* in the text filter box.

4   Press Return.

Enabling and Configuring the VPN Server

The easiest way to get VPN going is to use the Gateway Setup Assistant. The assistant asks if you want to allow VPN and, if you say yes, configures VPN to use L2TP with IPSec. The assistant also asks you to enter a shared secret. The assistant automatically divides internal IP addresses so that half are used for users who physically reside on the internal network and the other half are used for the virtual users connecting in from external networks, including the Internet. These virtual users can now appear as if they are on the internal network, and use the resources of that network and any networks it connects to, assuming no firewall rules deny them access.

If you don't use the Gateway Setup Assistant, you can still configure VPN services from Server Admin. In that case, you have the option of using L2TP or PPTP. PPTP is appropriate for older Windows clients and Mac OS X v10.2 clients.

To configure VPN:

1   Launch Server Admin and choose VPN from the Computers & Services list.

2   Click Settings.

3   Click L2TP or PPTP and configure the IP addresses that the server can give out to the VPN clients.

When configuring VPN with Server Admin, be sure to first release some addresses from the DHCP pool for VPN to use. If you don't, Server Admin displays an error message stating the address ranges are not valid.

In the Client Information tab, you should also configure a DNS server that the VPN clients can use. The Client Information tab is also useful for specifying that users can reach some networks using the routing that's available where they are currently, rather than the routing they would use as virtual clients of the internal network.

For example, perhaps a traveling salesperson needs to access nonsensitive data on the Internet while visiting customers. Assuming the customer can provide the salesperson with Internet access, there's no need for the salesperson to use the VPN tunnel to reach public websites. You can improve performance for the salesperson if nonsensitive network traffic relies on the customer's network, and only traffic back to the headquarters (HQ) private network is encrypted over the VPN tunnel. This makes more sense than requiring nonsensitive traffic to travel from the customer site, over the Internet in an encrypted tunnel to the VPN server at HQ, back out the server across any networks to the HQ Internet connection, and out to the Internet.

To configure which traffic uses the tunnel and which doesn't, you can set up VPN network routing definitions using the Client Information tab. Any routes you specify as private go over the VPN connection; any routes you specify as public do not go over the VPN connection, nor do all others not specified.

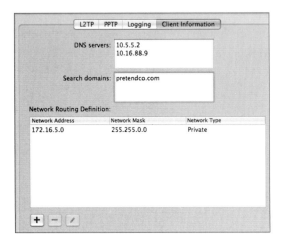

What You've Learned

▶ Network security configuration should be preceded by network security design in which you analyze requirements, identify user communities and traffic flow, and analyze typical threats.

▶ Security threats include reconnaissance attacks and DoS attacks.

▶ Methods for implementing your secure network design include NAT, VPN, and firewalls—all of which you can implement on Mac OS X Server.

▶ The easiest way to configure NAT on Mac OS X Server is to use the Gateway Setup Assistant, which starts the NAT process, enables DHCP, sets aside addresses for DHCP to use, enables the firewall, and adds a divert firewall rule to direct traffic to the correct, privately addressed computer.

▶ The easiest way to configure VPN is to use the Gateway Setup Assistant, which starts the VPN process, assigns addresses for use by VPN clients, and configures VPN to use L2TP with IPSec.

▶ The Mac OS X firewall is configured using Server Admin. You can also directly manipulate the firewall with the ipfw UNIX feature (although usually that's not necessary, with the exception of the ipfw show command).

▶ You should configure firewall rules to lock down traffic to the server, including remote administration and Web, mail, file, and DNS traffic. You should also configure firewall rules to lock down traffic through the server to control what traffic is allowed in and out of the connected networks.

▶ Logging firewall data is advisable so that you can confirm that your rules are working and keeping out unwanted network traffic.

References

Apple Knowledge Base Documents

The following Knowledge Base documents (located at www.apple.com/support) provide further information about firewalls:

Document 107846, "Mac OS X Server 10.3, 10.4: About firewall settings and logging"

Document 106439, "Well Known TCP and UDP Ports Used By Apple Software Products"

Books

Greenberg, Eric. *Mission-Critical Security Planner* (Wiley & Sons, 2003).

Hines, Annlee A. *Planning for Survivable Networks* (Wiley & Sons, 2003).

Kaeo, Merike. *Designing Network Security,* 2nd ed. (Cisco Press, 2003).

Oppenheimer, Alan B., and Whitaker, Charles H. *Internet Security for Your Macintosh* (Peachpit Press, 2001).

Oppenheimer, Priscilla. *Top-Down Network Design,* 2nd ed. (Cisco Press, 2004).

Oppenheimer, Priscilla, et al. *Troubleshooting Campus Networks* (Wiley & Sons, 2002).

URLs

Apple "Mac OS X Network Services Administration": http://manuals.info.apple.com/en/ MacOSXSrvr10.3_NetworkServicesAdmin.pdf

Peter Hickman, "Exploring the Mac OS X Firewall": www.macdevcenter.com/pub/a/ mac/2005/03/15/firewall.html

National Institute of Standards and Technology, Computer Security Resource Center: http://csrc.nist.gov/index.html

Lesson Review

1. Compare a reconnaissance attack to a Denial of Service (DoS) attack. Which is a more serious problem?

2. What are the best applications to configure network security on Mac OS X Server?

3. Firewalls fall into two broad categories: host firewalls and network firewalls. Which is the firewall on Mac OX Server, or is it both? Defend your answer.

Answers

1. A reconnaissance attack is used to learn about potential targets and their weaknesses in preparation for a more major attack. A DoS attack, on the other hand, is a major attack. With a reconnaissance attack, an attacker sends packets (using nmap, ping, and other utilities) and captures packets (using a protocol analyzer such as Ethereal) to learn about target systems. With a DoS attack, an attacker sends a huge volume of packets or sends specially crafted packets to crash or halt services on a target system. Although reconnaissance attacks can generate a lot of traffic, they aren't nearly as serious as DoS attacks, which can render network devices inoperable.

2. The easiest way to configure NAT and VPN is to use Gateway Setup Assistant. You can also use Server Admin. Gateway Setup Assistant enables the firewall, but most configuration of the firewall is best accomplished with the Server Admin application. The Unix ipfw utility can also be used to configure the firewall, but usually that isn't necessary.

3. The Mac OS X Server firewall is both a host firewall and a network firewall. You can configure rules to accept and deny traffic to the server itself, which matches the behavior of a host firewall. When you have routing enabled on the server, you can configure rules to accept or deny traffic forwarded by the server. This behavior matches the behavior of a network firewall.

19

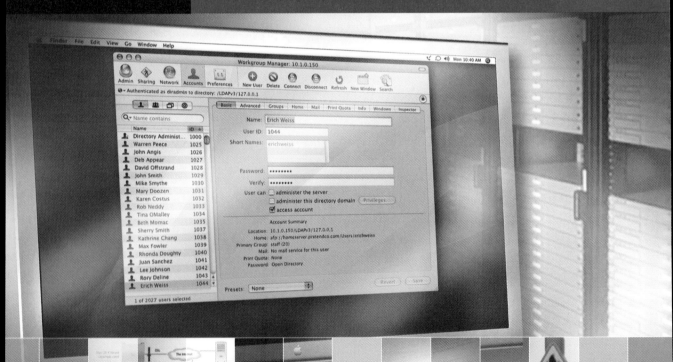

Mail Security

Email is one of the world's most popular methods of communication today. Speed and simplicity are the big reasons for this, but they are also why you must exercise caution when using email and configuring an email service. Although email is a relatively simple system, securing it involves actions taken in numerous areas, each making email slightly more secure in its own way. In this lesson, you'll learn how to reduce the risks associated with the email you send and receive through your email client software, as well as how to reduce risks associated with email transferred through an email server.

The bad guys are coming up with new and innovative ways to violate your security every day, so no technology will ever provide a 100 per-cent complete solution for securing your email. The cheapest and sim-plest solution for secure email lies between the chair and the keyboard. You've heard these things already, but they're worth stressing again: Never send extremely confidential data via email unless it's encrypted, and never open attachments unless you're expecting them, and they're from a trusted source.

Although technology can't provide guaranteed protection for email, numerous tools can reduce your risk.

Protecting Your Email Client

The first thing to look at in the realm of email protection is what's available in your email client—the program you use to read your email.

Filtering Junk Mail

If your client has built-in junk mail detection and filtering, turn it on. In the case of the Apple Mail application, choose Mail > Preferences, and look at the options available on the Junk Mail tab.

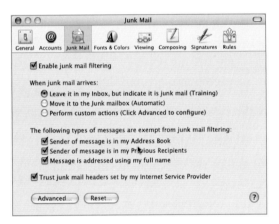

First check that "Enable junk mail filtering" is selected. Then, for a period of time (which will vary depending on the amount of mail, and spam, you receive), train your junk mail filter by having it leave all mail in your inbox, but indicate any messages it considers junk mail. You can then verify that a message is junk mail, or you can mark it as acceptable. Eventually, the junk mail filter will become more accurate.

> **TIP** ▶ To reduce the amount of spam you receive, create two email addresses. Give one email address to only people you know, and use the other email address as a "throwaway" address given to companies when you make online orders, postings to message boards, and other less direct communication.

Protecting Your Company Email

The Apple Mail application also provides a unique layer of security that can protect you from sending confidential information outside of your company.

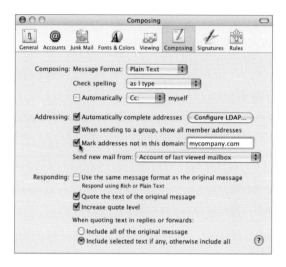

In the Composing tab, by selecting "Mark addresses not in this domain," any time you're composing a message with a recipient outside of your company's domain name, the recipient's address will be flagged with a different color.

Using Parental Controls

Apple also includes a feature geared toward protecting children by providing a list of approved email addresses with which the child can exchange messages. To access this feature, open System Preferences, click the Accounts pane, and select a user. Inside the Parental Controls tab for that user, click Configure, which brings up a window containing a list of approved email addresses, along with a permissions email address where unapproved email is sent first.

Although this feature is intended for parents managing their children's activities, a small company may also utilize this feature for limiting email communications to a small group of individuals necessary for those people to fulfill the duties of their jobs.

Protecting Email From Prying Eyes

When it comes to the security provided by your mail client, there are many different options you can set. Each option increases the security of your email communications through different means of password hashing and encryption. This is especially important if you are reading and sending email over a wireless or any other unsecure link. Email Internet traffic, like most Internet traffic, is, by default, unencrypted and easily monitored by anyone on the same wireless or insecure network.

Keep in mind that there are two separate communication channels used by email: one for retrieving messages, and one for sending messages. These two channels are configured separately, and also offer differing levels of security. One thing that is often confused with respect to mail client security is what you're actually trying to protect. It's important to draw the distinction between protecting your password and protecting the content of the email message body. Ideally, you'd want everything encrypted, but some email service providers don't offer a fully encrypted service.

When you're setting up a new email account in Apple's Mail application, you're given the option to set your incoming mail security.

The best thing you can do is to use Secure Sockets Layer (SSL) if your email service provider supports it. This is the same strong encryption used by secure websites for protecting your credit card information during an online purchase. The use of SSL for your incoming mail will encrypt both the password you send when logging into your email and the email messages themselves as they are downloaded from the mail server.

The Apple Mail application also provides alternative ways to authenticate to the email service. Although Mail supports many different types, your email service provider may not. These options range from simple password authentication where your password is sent directly to the email server, to various forms of hashed passwords, to Kerberos authentication, which uses a number of two-way ticket exchanges to authenticate you without ever sending your password to the server.

As mentioned before, this protects only one side of your email communication—retrieving messages from the server. You'll also want to protect the email being sent from your computer. Unfortunately, many email providers don't support using SSL encryption for your outgoing mail, but if it is available, use it. The Apple Mail application doesn't offer you the option to enable SSL for outgoing mail when creating your account, but you can get to it by choosing Mail > Preferences and looking at the Accounts tab.

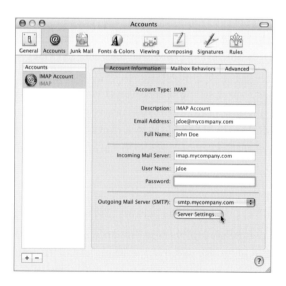

Select your account in the left frame and click the Server Settings button. After the new window appears, select the Use Secure Sockets Layer (SSL) checkbox, assuming your email provider supports it. Some email providers also require you to authenticate yourself when sending messages through their servers. If this is required, your account information is entered in the same window.

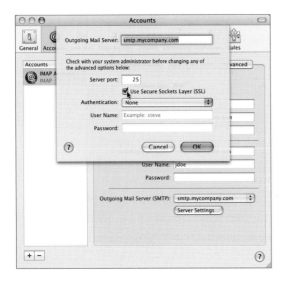

TIP Not all email providers support SSL. Often, however, an email provider supports SSL but doesn't tell you about it in fear of increased support costs. If you're not already using SSL, try turning it on. If you're still able to connect to your inbox, your email and account information will be much safer now that they're encrypted. If you can no longer connect to your inbox, then your email provider probably doesn't support SSL, so simply deselect the Use Secure Sockets Layer (SSL) box and everything will be working again.

Using Mail Certificates

Many computer viruses spread because people generally trust that an email is from the person it says it's from. In reality, it's incredibly easy to forge the From line of an email through a practice known as *spoofing*. There is, however, a nearly fail-safe method for you to prove to others that your email actually came from you: by using *certificates*. In order to use certificates, you create what is known as a certificate-key pair, comprised of private and public keys and a public certificate. Next, you send your certificate to all of your friends, coworkers, your website, online directory entries, and so on. When you create an email message with The Apple Mail application, it will be digitally signed using your certificate key pair. When the recipient opens your message, his or her computer will use the certificate you sent earlier to verify the integrity of the digital signature, which not only proves that you sent the message, but that the message has not been modified by a third party.

Certificate transactions involve at least two pieces—a public part, which everyone sees, and a private part, which you should keep very secure. A matching public certificate and private key are created at the same time. They are created using a complex mathematical method that yields a product with very unique properties. Something encrypted with the private key can be decrypted only using the corresponding public certificate. Likewise, and much more common, something encrypted with the public certificate can be decrypted only using the private key. This one-way encryption/decryption is what makes certificates, and SSL in general, very secure. Anyone can encrypt something for you with your public certificate, but only you can decrypt it since only you have the matching private key. Since you must be in possession of the private key to decrypt it, and since that private key is often encrypted itself by a password, certificate-based encryption is one of the best methods for highly secure transactions.

Using SSL Certificates With Mac OS X Server

Mac OS X Server can use certificates to send and receive mail. The mail services look for the certificates in the following locations:

▶ Cyrus: /var/imap/server.pem
▶ Postfix: /etc/postfix/server.pem

Further SSL configuration is possible through the config files for Cyrus and Postfix, /etc/imap.conf and /etc/postfix/main.cf, respectively.

> **NOTE ▶** Postfix requires that the key and the certificate are both in the same file. Additionally, Cyrus requires that the server certificate be accessible to the mail user. Permissions have to be modified to allow user mail access to the file. Both Cyrus and Postfix require passphrase free certificates.

SSL allows you to encrypt your data so that it's passed securely. Keep in mind, though, that if you encrypt everything, SSL adds a performance hit to your server and client. The server will have to encrypt the data and the client will have to decrypt. Depending on the size of the encryption key, that process can add to your server and client load.

Whether to use SSL with IMAP vs. POP is a performance consideration. POP downloads all of the user's email at once and thus will require heavy usage of the CPU for a short period. IMAP, on the other hand, maintains a constant connection to the server and will thus place a steady load on the server. It's best to analyze the server load using log analysis tools combined with CPU usage to understand the implications of enabling SSL for POP and IMAP on your server.

Certificate Renewal

If you choose to obtain a certificate from VeriSign and use that certificate for your email server, you will go through the following steps:

1. Contact VeriSign an obtain a certificate.

2. Create a Certificate Authority on your computer.

3. Store the CA Certificate in your login keychain.

4. Store your VeriSign certificate in your login keychain.

    This allows users to benefit from a valid certificate when checking their email.

    NOTE ▶ Certificates are generally renewed on a yearly basis. If your users do not update their public key, they may be unable to read mail sent by users who have updated their public key. Conversely, if users delete their older public key, they may not be able to read older mail.

Create a Certificate

In order for a certificate to be valid, it must be signed. Normally this is done by generating a certificate signing request (CSR) after you've created your key pair and sending it to a recognized certificate authority (CA). The certificate backing that CA is present on every computer, and once your certificate is signed by that CA, it will be recognized as valid on everyone's computer as well. Getting an officially signed certificate often costs money, but because the market is constantly changing, visit the websites of popular certificate authorities—they may offer personal email certificates for free or at a very low cost for noncommercial uses.

For the purposes of this exercise, we'll show you how to create and sign a certificate that, although it won't be officially signed, will demonstrate the processes involved.

1   Open /Applications/Utilities/Keychain Access.

2   Choose Keychain Access > Certificate Assistant.

3   Select Create a Certificate Authority (CA).

4   Leave the box selected to indicate that the certificate will be self-signed (root). Enter your email address and in the Common Name field, type *My Little CA*. If you were doing this in a production environment, you'd also fill in the other fields.

5   Leave the Key Size at its default of 2048 bits.

Larger keys are more secure than smaller keys, but require more computational power and are often not even supported by other computers. The algorithm shouldn't matter, although RSA tends to be more popular.

6   The next pane looks similar to the previous one, but specifies the key pair information for others that use this CA. Again, just leave them at their defaults of 2048 bits / RSA.

7   Leave the Key Usage Extension For This CA settings at their defaults.

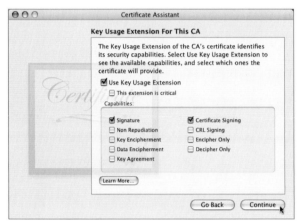

8   Leave the Key Usage Extension For Users Of This CA checkbox deselected.

9   Leave the Miscellaneous Extensions For This CA settings at their defaults.

10   Leave the Miscellaneous Extensions For Users Of This CA settings at their defaults (all deselected).

11   Store this certificate in your login Keychain. In a tighter security environment, you may wish to save your certificate in another Keychain that automatically locks, or even in a Keychain on an external device for extra security.

12   Leave the CA Configuration File Name at its default, and be sure that the "Make this CA the default" checkbox is checked.

13   Quit Certificate Assistant.

Now that you've created your certificate authority for the computer, you'll use it to sign a certificate that's associated with you directly.

1   In Keychain Access, choose Keychain Access > Certificate Assistant to open the assistant again.

2   Select the option to create a certificate for yourself.

3   Deselect "Certificate will be 'self-signed'" and fill out the Certificate Information form with your information. Be sure that the user email address matches the Apple Mail email address. The serial number will be 1 for the first certificate you create, but it will increment any time you create another certificate in the future.

4   When you choose an issuer, you will see My Little CA, which you created in the first half of this exercise. Select it and click Continue.

5   Leave the Key Pair Information at their defaults of 2048 bits / RSA.

6   Leave the Use Key Usage Extension box deselected.

7   Do not include basic constraints extension or subject alternate name extension.

8   Store this certificate in your login Keychain. In a tighter security environment, you may wish to save your certificate in another Keychain that automatically locks, or even in a Keychain on an external device for extra security.

After your certificate has been created, it will be saved to your Keychain.

9   Back in the Keychain Access application, you will see new entries: a private key, public key, and certificate for yourself and for your CA.

10   Click the certificate bearing your name, and notice that it has a red X and a warning about it not being trusted.

You need to make your unofficial certificate authority into a CA your machine trusts.

11   Select the My Little CA certificate in the list. At the top of the window, you will see a larger certificate icon. Drag that icon to your desktop where it'll be saved as My Little CA.cer. You'll be using it in a few moments.

12 At the bottom of the window, click the Show Keychains button.

13 Drag the My Little CA.cer file you just created onto the X509Anchors Keychain. You'll probably be prompted to enter an administrator username and password to unlock the X509Anchors Keychain.

14 Select the X509Anchors Keychain on the left side, then find the My Little CA certificate in the main frame of the window amongst all of the other official certificate authorities.

15 Double-click the My Little CA entry in the list, which will display the details of that certificate.

16 At the bottom of the window, click the triangle to reveal the trust settings.

17 Change the first option so that "When using this certificate: Always Trust" is selected.

18 Close the window, then quit Keychain Access.

19 Reopen Keychain Access. (You quit and restarted because Keychain Access caches its old trust settings.)

20 Locate the certificate bearing your name in the login Keychain.

It should now bear a green checkmark indicating that the certificate is valid.

Now, to see if it all worked:

1 Open Apple Mail.

2 Compose a new message (File > New Message).

If everything went as planned, you will see a star icon with a checkmark inside indicating that the message you're about to send is signed.

3   Send a message to someone else.

When the person receives the message, Mail will indicate that it is unable to verify the message signature. This is because you're using a self-signed certificate. The recipient can click the Show Details button, which will display your certificate. Clicking OK will add your certificate to their Keychain. Subsequent messages sent to that same person will indicate that the message is signed.

Encrypting Email

After someone has your certificate, he or she can use Apple Mail to encrypt future email to you. This is a secure method of passing email because when the sender uses your certificate (which he or she received previously via a signed message or other technique) to encrypt email to you, that message can then be decrypted only using the corresponding private key stored on your computer. This ensures that nobody else can see the body of the message (or its attachments), regardless of the security settings of any email server. This level of security is achieved because the email body is encrypted before leaving the sender's computer, and it isn't decrypted until it's opened on your computer. It's important to note that the message header is not encrypted (necessary for the servers to deliver the message), so don't include any confidential information in the subject of the message.

Encrypting email is as simple as signing it. You'll know this very quickly when composing a new message. If the lock icon is not present or is disabled, you don't have a certificate for that person and can't send encrypted email to him or her.

However, if you do have a certificate for the recipient of the email, as well as a certificate for yourself, the lock icon will be enabled. Just click it (so the lock is closed) to encrypt the message.

TIP Using self-signed certificates is OK for situations where you may not need that level of authenticity, or if you can guarantee the authenticity of the certificate by physically handing it to someone on CD or other similar media.

Protecting Your Email Servers

So far, we've talked about what any user can do to protect his or her personal email. For the rest of this lesson, we'll discuss what you can do if you're a system administrator responsible for your own email service. As you've already seen, many small techniques play a part in email security. It's best to configure your email service to offer as many of these as you can. If you're running services already, you know that there's always a fine line between security and usability. On one hand, it would be nice to force users to utilize more secure methods of email communication, such as requiring SSL or more robust authentication methods. But on the other side, one must keep usability in mind. Some people may have email clients that aren't capable of those higher levels of security, or may be prohibitively complex to configure that way.

If you're new to the world of email server administration, fear not. Maintaining an email server today is far simpler than it was in years past thanks to the creation of user-friendly graphical configuration environments. Although we'll be talking about how to secure an email server in this lesson, many email services topics are beyond the scope of this book. Be sure to read, at a minimum, Apple's online documentation about Mail Service Administration.

As we discussed in the first half of this lesson, there are two parts to email. Sending and receiving messages with other servers is done via the Simple Mail Transfer Protocol (SMTP). The other major mail subsystem allows users to retrieve messages from their inboxes using either the Post Office Protocol (POP) or the Internet Message Access Protocol (IMAP). Although these are very separate aspects of email, they are all configured via the same service in the Apple Server Admin tool.

Setting Up a Secure Email Service

In this exercise, you'll set up an email server to demonstrate many forms of mail server security. As was mentioned earlier, however, this is not an exhaustive lesson on setting up an email server. There are other tasks, particularly with DNS, that won't be covered here.

1   Install the Server Admin utilities (included with Mac OS X Server, or downloadable from Apple).

2   Open /Applications/Server/Server Admin and connect to your server.

3   Select the mail service in the left frame, and click the Settings tab.

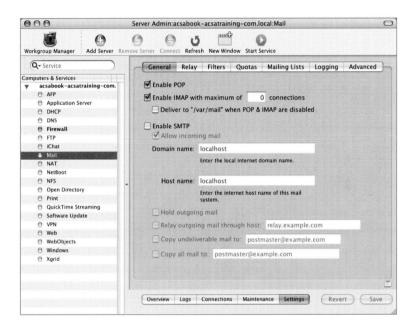

4   In the General tab, disable the POP service by deselecting the Enable POP checkbox.

POP and IMAP can both be used to access email. They both have advantages and disadvantages, but if you won't be using both of them, your server will be more secure with fewer services enabled. POP is more friendly for your network and server load, but it's best used only when users are always connecting from the same computers. IMAP, on the other hand, keeps everything on the server, and thus works great for users accessing their email from multiple computers. The downside to IMAP is that users who are connected to the email server will maintain a connection to the server, increasing the load on both the server and the network.

5   Leave IMAP enabled.

6 Enable the SMTP service—which will allow users to send email out through this server—by selecting the Enable SMPT checkbox. Since you'll be setting up a general-purpose email server, leave the "Allow incoming mail" option enabled.

In a high-usage environment, you might have different servers handling your domain's incoming and outgoing mail. This would be better for the server load and more secure, but it would be practical only if you have multiple servers.

7 On the Relay tab, leave the "Accept SMTP relays only from these hosts and networks" option selected. The 127.0.0.1/32 host in the list indicates that this SMTP server will relay mail only from itself. If this host were acting as the SMTP server handling all outbound email for your organization, you would add more entries to this list, indicating all of the IP address ranges or domain names allowed to send email through this server.

This setting affects only mail *relaying*, not mail *acceptance*. The mail server will always accept mail destined for users that exist on that machine. What you want to limit are the hosts that are allowed to pass messages through your server to another server. Generally, this is just people in your organization. If you don't set this option appropriately, you may inadvertently allow anyone to relay through your server—a situation known as an *open relay*. This is good for spammers, but bad for you.

8 Click the Advanced tab, followed by the Security tab.

9 The quickest and biggest win for security is to enable SSL. From *both* the SMTP SSL and IMAP/POP SSL pop-up menus, choose Require.

If you have older mail clients on your network that can't do SSL, choose Use instead.

10 For both entries, choose Default from the next pull-down menu.

This menu controls which SSL certificate will be used to protect this service. This is similar to the public/private key pair used to sign and encrypt email in the first half of this lesson. Normally, when you obtain an officially signed SSL certificate, you will have created it in (or added it to) the server's Settings tab that contains the Certificates tab. Every Mac OS X server comes preconfigured with a default SSL key pair that is self-signed, appropriately named Default. Although the use of this certificate will show a warning on every client that connects to it, it's free, and you can use it to test the encryption of your service. If desired, you can even set each client to trust this certificate if you'd like to continue using it.

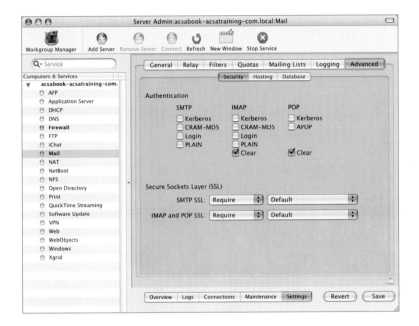

11 Click Save.

12 Click the green Start Service button at the top of the window.

13 Open /Applications/Server/Workgroup Manager.

14 Select all users (or at least yourself).

15 Click the Mail tab.

16 Change the Mail setting to Enabled. Leave all of the other options at their defaults and click Save.

17 Quit Workgroup Manager.

Everything is configured correctly now. If you'd like to test the configuration, do the following:

1 Open Apple Mail and create a new IMAP account to connect to the server localhost. Use localhost as your SMTP server as well. Don't forget that you must enable SSL for both the IMAP server and the SMTP server since you required them in the preceding exercise—you'll have to do this by selecting Mail > Preferences and then clicking the Accounts tab.

2 Choose Mail > Go Online. You'll see a certificate warning since you're using a self-signed certificate. Click OK to close the warning, and enter your password when prompted.

3 Send a new message to yourself.

4 Click the Get Mail button, and you will see the message you just sent.

5 Quit the Mail application.

6 Back in the Server Admin application, click the Logs tab for the Mail service, and click Refresh. Examine the SMTP and IMAP logs.

Tightening Authentication Requirements

One of the easiest ways to balance security and usability is to offer email clients their choice of all available authentication schemes. Many modern-day clients are smart enough to choose the most secure method automatically.

1 In Server Admin, select Mail in the left frame, and click Settings tab.

2 Click the Advanced tab.

3 For the IMAP column, select every box (Kerberos, CRAM-MD5, Login, PLAIN, Clear).

4 For the POP column, select every box (Kerberos, APOP, Clear).

5 For the SMTP column, select every box (Kerberos, CRAM-MD5, Login, PLAIN).

NOTE ▶ PLAIN is plaintext passwords on the wire. At a minimum, administrators should disable PLAIN authentication.

Choosing these settings means that *anyone* sending messages through your server will have to authenticate. Normally SMTP is an anonymous service that doesn't require authentication. Anonymous SMTP is the default because a number of email clients can't do authenticated SMTP. Automated scripts are also unable to authenticate when sending status emails since there's no user present to type in a password.

6   Click Save.

Now you have an email server that *offers* higher security. This allows mail clients the option of using higher security if they choose to. You may, however, want to *require* users to use a higher security method. If this is the case, you need to disable some of the less-secure methods:

▶   For the IMAP column, deselect Login, PLAIN, and Clear.

▶   For the POP column, deselect Clear.

▶   For the SMTP column, deselect Login and PLAIN.

7   Click Save.

To support Kerberos authentication, you must either be using an Open Directory system or have your mail server tied into an existing Kerberos infrastructure. To support CRAM-MD5 and APOP, each user's account must have the supporting password type enabled. You can verify this with these steps:

8   If your server is a member (or master) of an Open Directory system:

a   In Server Admin, select the Open Directory service in the left frame.

b   Click the Settings tab.

c   Click the Policy tab.

d   Click the Security tab.

Otherwise, if you're just using a dtandalone directory service (not an Open Directory system):

a   Open Workgroup Manager and connect to your server.

b   Select a user.

c   Click the Advanced tab.

d   Click the Security button.

A window appears listing all of the supported password types for that user.

9   If a password type you're using isn't enabled, click the box to enable it, and change that user's password.

As the following figure indicates, you should use caution in enabling the APOP method because all of your users' passwords can be determined if your server is ever compromised. For this reason, many mail server administrators choose to not enable POP access at all.

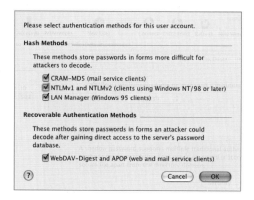

Controlling Spam at the Server

We spoke earlier of open relays through which a spammer can anonymously send large quantities of mail. Let's pretend that a mail server at openrelay.example.com was one such open relay, and you were getting bombarded with spam from that host.

1   Return to the Server Admin application if you are no longer in it.

2 Select Mail in the left pane, click the Settings tab, and click the Relay tab.

3 Add *openrelay.example.com* to the second box, and select the "Refuse all messages from these hosts and networks" box.

You can also reduce spam by the use of real-time blacklists (RBLs). This works by having a remote server tracking a dynamic list of open relays. Although this is usually more effective than maintaining such a list by hand (as in the previous step), you should use caution because it's possible for legitimate mail sources to be mistakenly added to RBLs, which would result in missed messages for your users.

4 Click the Filters tab.

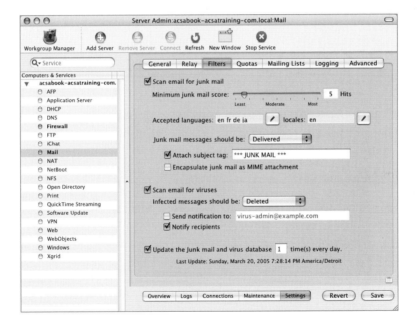

5 Select the "Scan email for junk mail" checkbox.

This option turns on the Spam Assassin junk mail filter. This is the server's way of detecting spam based on a weighted set of tests on the message, such as certain patterns of words, HTML usage common to spam, obviously forged email headers, and much more.

6   Leave the "Minimum junk mail score" set to its default of 5 hits.

Every message that is scanned by Spam Assassin on the server will be assigned a score. The higher the score, the more likely it is to be spam. There are, however, two things to watch out for:

▶   False negatives are messages that are actually spam, but are missed by the spam filter. Although annoying for users, this isn't an important concern—the user is just getting extra mail. If you set your minimum junk mail score too high, you will get more false negatives, but the quantity will decrease over time as your junk mail filters become better trained.

▶   False positives are messages that are not spam but are mistagged as spam. These messages are more problematic since users may never see legitimate messages intended for them if a junk mail filter automatically deletes the messages thinking they're spam. If you set your minimum junk mail score too low, you will get more false positives, and more upset users.

Remember, it's always better for users to get a few extra messages that they didn't want than to not get messages they did want. Leaving the minimum score at the default of 5 is generally a good starting point.

7   Click the pencil icons next to the "Accepted languages" and "locales" fields.

If, for example, you wanted all non-English messages to be marked as spam, you could deselect the other languages. However, if someone corresponds with a pen pal in a foreign country, getting messages in a different language may be normal, so use this feature with care.

8   Take a look at the "Junk mail messages should be" menu. Leave it set to Delivered so that users can decide on their own what they want to do with their spam.

If spam becomes a huge problem at your organization, you may want to just bounce spam, which hopefully will make the spammers think they have an invalid email address. Be sure to keep in mind though the possibility of false positives getting bounced if you change this option.

9 You can optionally change the subject of any messages by using the "Attach subject tag" option.

This is generally a good thing to do because it allows users to quickly identify messages the server thinks are spam.

10 Click Save.

Just like with the Apple Mail application, Spam Assassin must learn the difference between spam and non-spam (or "ham" as Spam Assassin refers to it). There are two methods to teach Spam Assassin:

▶ Have users of your mail system bounce, or redirect, any messages that are spam to junkmail@your.email.domain.

▶ Bounce any messages that are not spam to notjunkmail@your.email.domain.

Be sure to empty those mailboxes every day. Spam Assassin scans the messages in those mailboxes during the night, but won't delete them for you.

Hopefully, you have a folder or mailbox already stuffed with spam, and another mailbox or folder that contains only non-spam. An outbox, or sent-mail folder, is a great example of the latter. Save all the messages from each category to two distinct folders. Be sure to use at least 200 messages for each to sufficiently train Spam Assassin. From a Terminal window, type the following two commands:

```
sa-learn –spam NameOfFolderContainingJunkMail/*
sa-learn –ham NameOfFolderContainingNonJunkMail/*
```

These two commands will take some time to run, so be patient. If you prefer to have visual feedback, add the –showdots option to each of the commands.

As you can see, setting up spam filtering at the server is both simple and powerful. There are many other options you can use to further configure Spam Assassin directly from its configuration files, but those are beyond the scope of this book.

Protecting Everyone from Viruses

Although today there are few (if any) viruses that can affect Macs, it should be remembered that an email virus will still affect others even if it passes through a Mac.

Also, since a Mac OS X email server uses standard email protocols, it's possible that some of your users may be accessing their email from a PC or other platform, and thus would be susceptible to viruses.

Every email-server administrator should implement virus-scanning software for the good of the entire Internet. Here's how simple it is on a Mac OS X server:

1   In Server Admin, select Mail in the left pane, and click the Settings tab.

2   Click the Filters tab.

3   Select the "Scan email for viruses" checkbox.

This will scan each message with a popular Open Source antivirus scanner known as ClamAV.

4   From the "Infected messages should be" pop-up menu, choose Deleted.

You have a number of different options here, each with their own advantages:

▶   Bounced: Lets the sender know that they've probably been infected by a virus.

▶   Deleted: Lets the message get through to the recipient.

▶   Quarantined: Saves the message in case the recipient needs to get something out of it, or if the virus needs further examination. This can also be useful for examining the infected email headers and manually notifying the infected users if desired.

5   Select the "Send notification to" box and type in your email address.

It's a good idea for the mail system administrator to know if there's a virus storm in progress because you may need to tighten up security briefly at that time.

6   Select the "Notify recipients" box.

This will send a message to the original recipients letting them know why they may not have gotten the message they might have been expecting.

7 Select the "Update the junk mail and virus database" box. Given the speed at which email viruses spread and the frequency in which new ones are born, you should set the number of times per day to at least 2, but 8 might be a better number.

8 Click Save.

Ensuring Physical Security

One aspect of security that is often forgotten is protecting the physical pieces related to your servers. This includes restricting access to the room containing your servers to only those essential people who need access. Remember—if someone has physical access to the hardware, that person has access to everything stored on that machine, no matter what software settings are in place.

A related item that also needs to be protected is any backup copy that you make of the mail data. It makes sense to store any backup media offsite to remain safe during a fire or other disaster. Remember, though, that all of your users' confidential data is stored on those backups, and so they should be treated with the same high level of physical protection that you establish for the server itself.

What You've Learned

▶ Use SSL wherever possible when setting up a mail server.

▶ Use Certificate Assistant to create your own certificate.

▶ Once a certificate has been added to your keychain, you can start using it with the Apple Mail application.

▶ The Apple Mail service permits many authentication methods, such as Kerberos and CRAM-MD5.

▶ Requiring the use of certificates when checking e-mail decreases the risk someone else will view your e-mail in transit.

▶ Enable virus and spam detection on your e-mail servers to reduce the number of potential attacks and unwanted e-mail traffic.

References

Apple Knowledge Base Documents

Document 25555, "How to Use a Secure Email Signing Certificate (Digital ID)":
http://docs.info.apple.com/article.html?artnum_25555

URLs

Apple Collaboration Services Administration: http://images.apple.com/server/pdfs/
Collaboration_Services_v10.4.pdf

Apple Mail Service Administration: http://images.apple.com/server/pdfs/
Mail_Service_v10.4.pdf

Lesson Review

1.   True or false: SSL encryption is only important if you're connected to the Internet
     with a wireless network.

2.   What is a certificate authority?

3.   How is Apple Mail more secure with the use of certificates?

4.   What programs are used by an administrator to maintain certificates on Mac OS X
     and on Mac OS X Server?

5.   What is an open relay?

6.   What open-source software is used for spam and virus protection in Mac OS X Server?

Answers

1.   False. You have no idea how secure the networks are between your computer and the
     other end of the connection. There may even be a wireless link at the other end that
     you don't know about. SSL will encrypt your session from end to end.

2.   A certificate authority, or CA, is a trusted organization that digitally signs a certifi-
     cate and guarantees through a number of checks that the person or organization
     using that certificate is genuine.

3.   Certificates can be used in mail to digitally sign and/or encrypt a message. Certificates
     are also a necessary component for SSL encryption between the mail client and server.

4.   Mac OS X: Keychain Access; Mac OS X Server: Server Admin

5.   An open relay is an email SMTP server that permits anyone on the Internet to route messages anonymously through it. These are often abused by spammers.

6.   Spam is detected with Spam Assassin. Viruses are detected with ClamAV.

20

Time   This lesson takes approximately 2 hours to complete.

Goals   Configure Safari security features

Establish a secure website using SSL

Redirect from an HTTP site to an HTTPS site

Set up WebMail securely with SSL

Set up WebDAV securely with SSL

Set up a proxy server to block selected sites

Lesson 20
Web Security

The most secure you can make your computer (short of not powering it on in the first place) is to not connect it to the Internet. The very thing that makes the Information Age what it is also comprises your computer's greatest security risk. Nonetheless, being connected to the Internet is the essence of modern computing.

The World Wide Web is the first thing most people think of when they envision the Internet—and then they think of pop-ups, viruses, cookies, identify theft, their kids getting into pornography sites…

System administrators think of these things too, but their list also includes getting hacked, downtime, and the never-ending balancing act of providing more and better services versus reducing vulnerabilities and risk. You can configure Safari, the Apple browser, for yourself and your users to increase security, and if you provide Web services, you can reduce the vulnerabilities of your servers while providing the services you want.

Securing the Web Client

The browser that Apple provides with Mac OS X 10.4, Safari 2.0, provides a number of security features that make it relatively simple to set up a safe browsing environment for you and your users. One of the main concerns is a site that executes malicious code upon loading the webpage or that tricks the user into activating the code. A common example is a site that pops up additional windows, often masquerading as Windows alert boxes or games, deceiving the user into clicking them, and then executing more malicious code. Even though most malicious software, or "malware," out there is written targeting Windows, Java and JavaScript are cross-platform, as are many plug-ins. It is a good practice to enable services only when you get to a *trusted* site that requires them—and then turn them back off again.

Setting Security Preferences

Most of the Security options are available by opening Safari preferences and selecting the Security tab.

The Security tab offers these options:

▶ Browser plug-ins are programs that extend the capability of your browser. The QuickTime and Flash plug-ins are perfect examples—they let you play QuickTime and Flash content, such as movies or sounds, that are embedded in the webpage. To see the plug-ins that Safari has installed, go to Safari's Help menu and select Installed Plug-ins.

▶ Java is a software platform and programming language that allows highly portable programs to be run in many different environments, including browsers. Because there are malicious programmers out there, there is a way to turn off Java.

▶ JavaScript is a scripting language that can be used in webpages and run by browsers, or used in server-based applications, similar to Common Gateway Interface (CGI) programs. It is often used to create menus, validate forms before submitting them, track user history, and provide interactive effects.

▶ In addition to being an annoyance, pop-up windows are often used for "phishing," or attempting to trick users into providing sensitive information or executing additional malicious code. However, as with plug-ins, Java, and JavaScript, there are legitimate uses for pop-up windows. This feature is also accessible through the Safari application menu.

▶ Cookies are files that websites store on your computer to save user information such as shopping preferences and shopping carts, and to gather accurate statistics on their visitors—total number of new versus repeat visitors, for example. But the information that cookies gather can be sold for marketing, and some infrastructure providers gather information about you across multiple sites. Safari lets you decide how to handle cookies and to view the individual cookies.

▶ If you select the "Ask before sending a non-secure form to a secure website" checkbox, Safari will ask for approval before sending unencrypted form information to a secure site.

When you enter a secure website (HTTPS), the data transferred between the client and the server is encrypted with the Secure Sockets Layer (SSL) protocol. Aside from the URL beginning with "https," your secure connection is signified by a padlock icon in the upper-right corner of the browser window. The SSL encryption algorithm is generated in conjunction with a digital certificate, which also helps establish the website as authentic. By clicking that padlock, you can view the credentials of the certificate and evaluate its authenticity.

▶ Selecting the "Enable parental controls" checkbox does two things: It restricts the ability of the current account to modify the "New windows open with" and "Home page" settings under Safari's general preferences, and it requires an administrator to add each allowed website. You do this by navigating to a site, clicking the Add Website button, and providing an administrator name and password. The site is added to the browser's Bookmarks bar.

NOTE ▶ The website restriction becomes active as soon as you select "Enable parental control," but the "New windows open with" and "Home page" restrictions do not—you must quit and restart Safari for that change to be in effect.

"Enable parental control" is also available through System Preferences > Accounts > Parental Controls.

TIP ▶ All of the websites that were in the Bookmarks bar before you turned on parental control will be allowed sites. If you have a long list of sites you want to add, add them to the Bookmarks bar before you turn on parental controls.

NOTE ▶ "Enable parental control" will be grayed out if you are logged in as an administrator. You must be logged in as the user being "controlled."

Using Safari on a Public Access Mac

If the computers you maintain are set up securely, there should be little need for this feature, but what if you are using a public access computer, or a computer with a questionable security configuration? In the Safari application menu, there are three methods (in addition to Block Pop-Up Windows) to make sure you don't leave sensitive information from your browsing session behind.

▶ If you select Private Browsing, the sites you've visited are not being added to the history, the Downloads window is cleared when you quit Safari, no information—including names and passwords—is saved in AutoFill, and searches are not added to the Google search box. While browsing, you can still use the Back and Forward buttons to navigate sites, but when you close the window, that information is gone.

> **NOTE** ▶ Do not confuse Private Browsing with Anonymous Browsing, which is concerned with your browsing being monitored from outside the computer. Internet service providers (ISPs) can monitor your browsing, including what file types you are downloading, and commercial sites collect information such as your Internet Protocol (IP), what Web browser you are using, and who your ISP is. Consequently, there are Anonymous Browsing services that offer various degrees of "anonymization." These vary from simple proxy servers that retrieve webpages for you, without your information being sent to the remote site, to services that also encrypt your browsing transaction from end to end.

▶ Reset Safari erases your browsing history, empties the cache, clears the Downloads window and Google search entries, and removes cookies and AutoFill text.

▶ Empty Cache deletes webpage contents that were stored locally. The reason for caching files in the first place is to speed the browsing of sites that you have already visited, as those files can now be accessed from your hard drive rather that waiting for them to download every time you visit the page—especially sites you visit frequently, like your home page. It is a good idea to empty the cache on public computers when you are done using them, as the cache files may contain personal or sensitive information such as passwords or credit card numbers.

> **NOTE** ▶ Private Browsing performs essentially the same function as Reset Safari, but you turn it on when you start your browsing (as opposed to resetting Safari and emptying the cache when you finish browsing).

Using a Proxy Server

You can go one step further to control the content that reaches your client computers, and that is to filter them through a *proxy server*. Originally, proxy servers were utilized to speed Web access—it was much faster to grab cached content from your local server than to reload it over a slow Internet connection. Yet with current access speeds, it is usually not worth the effort of maintaining the service. However, proxy servers do allow you to easily block access to specific sites, and optionally import free or commercial blacklist files. This is less restrictive—and less precise—than Safari's built-in "allowed sites" mechanism. It has an advantage in that it scales well—you can have a great number of clients using the server as a proxy.

Setting up a proxy server will be covered later in this lesson. To configure Safari as a *proxy client:*

1   From Safari's application menu, select Preferences and click the Advanced tab.

2   Click the Proxies: Change Settings button.

This will open System Preferences > Network.

3   Open System Preferences > Built-in Ethernet and click the Proxies tab.

NOTE ▶ You must configure proxy settings for each network interface that has Internet access. Potentially this includes Ethernet, AirPort, Modem, Bluetooth, Built-in FireWire, and VPN.

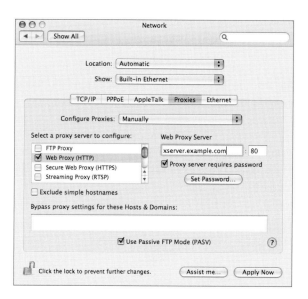

4   Select the proxy server you want to configure—in this case, Web Proxy (HTTP).

5   Enter the address or DNS name of your Web proxy server.

6   Enter a user name and password for the proxy server, if necessary.

7   Click the Apply Now button.

From this point on, all of your client's Web traffic will be funneled through the proxy server, including its site-blocking filter.

Web Security

Websites present many security risks. Without protection, anyone can read private information that you post on a website as long as they have the URL to the site. Also, when users send private information, such as a credit card number, to the server through a form, anyone with a packet sniffer can read the information because it is sent in clear text.

Included with the standard installation of Apache on Mac OS X Server is mod_ssl, an open source, freely-distributed add-on module to Apache. This module lets Apache use OpenSSL, enabling cryptographically-protected connections to Web servers via the SSL and Transport Layer Security.

Enabling SSL for Apache allows encrypted access to your Web services. SSL lets Web applications access your server in a secure way, hides passwords passed to your server in Web-based forms from packet sniffers, and encrypts data transmitted to a browser.

The mod_ssl package is not merely another module in Apache: It goes to the core of Apache by implementing its Extended Apache Programming Interface (EAPI). In addition, mod_ssl interfaces with the OpenSSL libraries for encryption, decryption, and other services.

SSL in Apache (HTTPS) typically runs on port 443, the standard HTTP-SSL port registered with IANA. However, you can configure it to run on any other port. by creating a virtual host to handle the HTTPS content.

TIP ▶ To enable mod_ssl, select ssl_module in the Modules pane in Server Admin, click Save and then restart the Web service.

MORE INFO ▶ You can find documentation for mod_ssl on your Mac OS X Server computer at /Library/Documentation/Services/apache_mod_ssl/index.html.

Setting Up Secure Web Services

Perhaps the three most universal guidelines for keeping a server secure are:

▶ Don't turn on more services than you need to provide.

▶ Keep up-to-date on vulnerabilities and patches.

▶ Read your log files.

The reasoning of the first guideline is simple: The more exposure to the outside world, the more potential vulnerability and the possibility that an exploit of one service could compromise another service. Also, the more services running, the more there is to maintain and monitor. Apple respects this guideline by providing a secure default configuration: All native services are off, and all communications ports are closed.

Keeping up-to-date is obvious enough, but it becomes increasingly difficult to balance with the other demands on our time. Apple helps ease this load by working with security watchdog organizations such as CERT and FIRST, as well as tapping into the rapid development pace and diligence of the open software community. Apple passes the benefit of this effort along by way of the Software Update utility; set it to update daily, and you can reap disproportionate rewards of Apple's frequent security (and other) updates with almost no effort.

"Did you look at the log files?" This constant inquiry from the UNIX sages is a good indicator of the usefulness of this technique. Regularly checking logs helps you with not only the obvious problems, but also with things that *aren't* obvious but may well *be* problems. The Apple Console utility consolidates all of the system's logs into a searchable, dynamic log viewer.

Establishing a Secure Website Using SSL

Most of the information on the Web is not sensitive; in fact, accessibility is perhaps the biggest single basis for its incredible popularity. But the Web is also increasingly serving private and sensitive information, including e-commerce, medical records, filing taxes, and Web-based e-mail. In the vast majority of cases, these transactions are encrypted with a protocol called Secure Sockets Layer (SSL).

Secure websites rely on certificates to provide two central tenets of their security:

▶   That your server can be trusted because it has an authentic certificate

▶   For the encryption of the interaction

Viewing Certificates

Unencrypted Hypertext Transfer Protocol (HTTP) traffic typically travels over port 80: When you type in an HTTPS URL, you are telling your browser to initiate a secure (SSL) connection to port 443 of the Web server. The browser and server negotiate the strongest cipher they have in common, and then the server sends the browser its X.509 certificate. If the browser can't verify the identity of the secure website, it will display a dialog allowing you to examine the certificate. To view the certificate, click the Show Certificate button.

If it is a server you trust (your own, for example), you can select the "Always trust these certificates" checkbox, after which you'll need to authenticate to add the certificate to your keychain. The next time you go to that site, the certificate will be trusted. Your browser then uses the certificate as an encryption key for the secure connection.

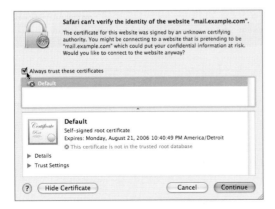

Setting Up a Secure Website

The following steps walk you through setting up a secure Web mail server site. If you'd like to have WebMail running on your server, you must have the IMAP mail server set up and running properly. Basically, there is just a one-checkbox difference between Web-serving mail and not!

1 Install the Server Admin utilities (included with Mac OS X Server, or downloadable from the Apple website).

2 Launch /Applications/Server/Server Admin and connect to your server.

3 Select the Web service in the left frame and open the Settings tab using the button at the bottom of the main window.

4 Click the Sites tab in the top of the main window and click the "Add a new website" (+) button.

5 Enter the domain name of your server, select its IP address from the drop-down menu, and click the Options button.

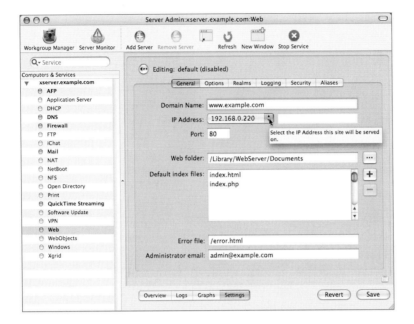

6 Turn off the Performance Cache, turn on WebMail, and click the Security tab.

7 Select the Enable Secure Sockets Layer (SSL) checkbox and click OK.

8 In the Certificate drop-down menu, select Custom to configure your certificate (we're using the server's default certificate in this example).

9 In the upper-left corner of the frame, click the button to return to the list of sites.

10 Click the Enabled button next to your new secure website (the one on port 443).

11 Select the unencrypted site (the one on port 80), click the "Edit selected website" (/) button, and click the Aliases tab.

12 Click the "Add new alias or redirect" (+) button.

13 Select Redirect from the drop-down menu, then enter */webmail* for the pattern and *https://www.example.com/webmail* for the path. Click OK.

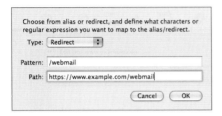

14 Click the Return button to return to the list of sites.

15 Click the Save button in the lower-right corner of the window.

16 If the Web service was running when you added your new secure site, the following dialog will come up. Click Restart to restart the Web service.

Alternately, if the Web service was not running, you can start it now by clicking the Start Service button.

17 To check your work, open a browser and type *www.example.com* into the URL field.

The browser should take you to your unencrypted site.

18 In the URL field, type in *www.example.com/webmail*.

The redirect that you created in steps 11 through 14 should redirect you to the secure WebMail site.

NOTE ▶ Redirects must follow particular formatting requirements. The Pattern field cannot contain the http://domain_name portion of the URL—it must be a search term such as a file or directory (for example. anything you might type in after the domain name of the site). The path must be a fully qualified domain name, such as a complete URL.

We've seen in other lessons the usefulness of certificates and encryption, and we put them to use here in our exercise. If you are serving a lot of static pages, the performance cache (step 6) can improve how quickly pages are served by keeping them stored in RAM. With pages that are created dynamically, this can cause problems or incompatibilities, as the content would not all fit into RAM. Therefore, we disabled it in order to use WebMail.

Is WebMail really as simple as one checkbox? Well, yes and no. After mail services are deployed in a compatible mode, yes. WebMail simply ties in with the IMAP mail services already running on your server, and gets its user account information from Directory Services, just as the mail services do. The compatible mode is as follows:

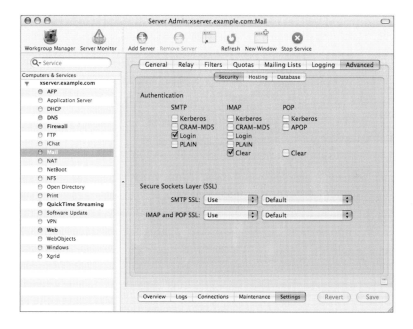

Look in Server Admin > Mail > Settings > Advanced > Security. At the minimum, you must choose the following settings:

▶ Login for SMTP

▶ Clear for IMAP

▶ Use for both SMTP SSL and "IMAP and POP SSL."

WebMail's default configuration uses these settings, and does not use SSL. Because we are serving WebMail from a secure site, all traffic between the browser and the server is encrypted with SSL.

You can (and should!) have more secure authentications options selected for your mail client users. For example, you might have Kerberos, CRAM_MDS, and Clear all selected for IMAP authentication methods. The weakness of this is that you are now relying on your users to configure their mail clients securely; with this configuration, nothing is requiring them to use SSL, or preventing them from using Clear authentication.

The final requirement for one-click WebMail is that your Web service is running on the same server as your mail service. That way, no unencrypted data is passing between two servers.

> **NOTE** ▶ Though it *is* possible to configure WebMail to use SSL (thereby allowing you to *require* SSL for mail clients), the PHP implementation on Mac OS X was compiled without the necessary openssl PHP extension.

Configuring Secure WebDAV

Web Distributed Authoring and Versioning (WebDAV) was originally conceived of as a way to allow Web authors to access website files and make changes to them using HTTP, all on a live website. Since then, it has become a much more widely used method of file sharing because of its ease of use, much of which comes from the fact that it uses HTTP and because it runs over the same ports as the Web—so firewalls are seldom a barrier to use.

Since Web serving is typically about read-only access for everyone, configuring WebDAV requires that you:

▶ Define realms (folders) to restrict access to WebDAV users (via Server Admin > Web > Settings > Realms).

▶ Define User & Group access to those realms (via Server Admin > Web > Settings > Realms).

▶ Allow file system-level Read & Write file permissions to the www user and group for each realm folder (via Workgroup Manager).

Creating Realms and Adding Access

The following procedure will add WebDAV to the services you are offering via SSL. This will be an "employees only" area of the website.

1 Launch /Applications/Server/Server Admin and connect to your server.

2 Select the Web service in the left frame, open the Settings tab using the button at the bottom of the main window, and click the Sites tab at the top of the frame.

3 Select the secure site you created in the previous exercise, and click the "Edit selected website" (/) button.

4 Click the Options tab and select WebDAV, then click the Realms tab.

5 Click the "Add a new realm" (+) button.

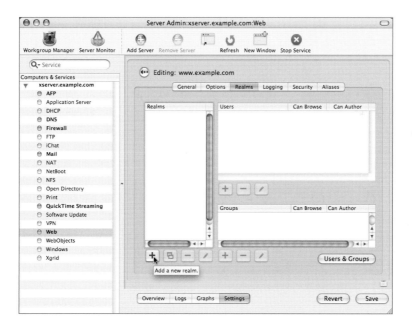

6 Either type in the path to the folder you want to make accessible, or navigate to it by clicking the path button (...) and selecting the folder you want. Click OK.

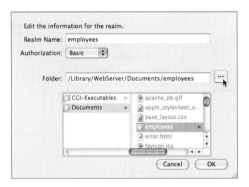

7 Click the "Add a new group to the currently selected realm" button.

Note that there is a typo in the pop-up note—it should be *user,* not *group*.

8 Enter the user short name, and select the access privileges you want the user to have.

Alternatively, you can click the Users & Groups button, drag in the users, and set their permissions by selecting the appropriate checkboxes.

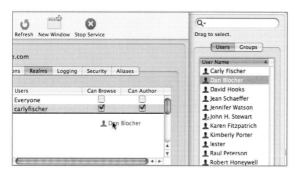

9   Add the groups you'd like to have access to realm the same way, either by clicking "Add a new group to the currently selected realm" button or by clicking the Users & Groups button, selecting the Groups tab, and dragging the appropriate Groups to the Groups box. Select the appropriate permissions.

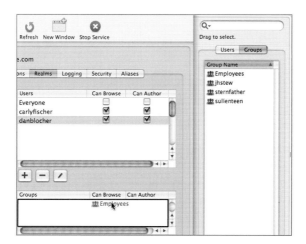

10 When you are finished adding the users and groups you want and assigning their access privileges, click Save.

11 As in the previous exercise, add a Redirect to your unencrypted site to redirect users from the unencrypted site to the encrypted site.

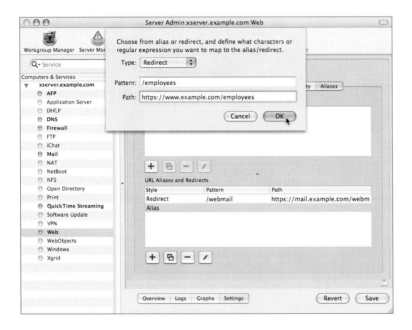

12 If necessary, restart the Web service to make the changes take effect.

Setting File Permissions

The last part of getting WebDAV going is setting the proper file permissions. The default location of the Web directory is /Library/WebServer/Documents; it and its contents owner is root, and its group is admin. For Web folders, the owner and group (root and admin) have read, write, and execute privileges, and others have read and execute privileges (775, in UNIX parlance). For Web documents, the owner and group have read and write privileges, and others have read privileges (664). You simply need to change the both the owner and group of the directories you are making available via WebDAV to www and www, respectively. This may seem like it's setting quite unrestricted privileges, but remember that the users, groups, and permissions you set up in realms are what restrict access via the Web.

1   Launch /Applications/Server/Workgroup Manager and connect to your server.

2   Click the Accounts icon in the toolbar at the top of the window, and then click the
Groups tab beneath it.

3   Click the New Group button in the toolbar at the top of the window, and type a
name for the group.

4   Click the "Add group members" (+) button and drag users (and optionally groups)
to the Members area of the new group window.

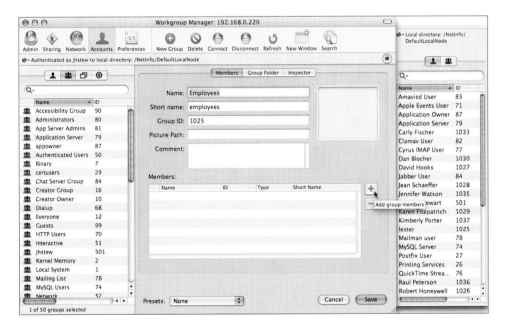

5   When you are finished populating your members list, click Save.

6   Click the Sharing icon in the upper left of the toolbar, and then click the All tab underneath.

7   Select the folder you want to share out via WebDAV.

The example folder, employees, is inside /Library/WebServer/Documents.

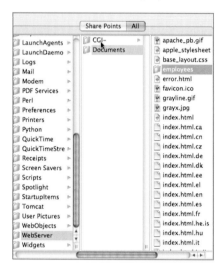

8   In the right frame, click the Access tab at the top, and click the Users & Groups button at the bottom to reveal the Users & Groups drawer.

9   Drag the World Wide Web Server user (whose short name is www) to the Owner field, then click the Groups tab in the Users & Group drawer.

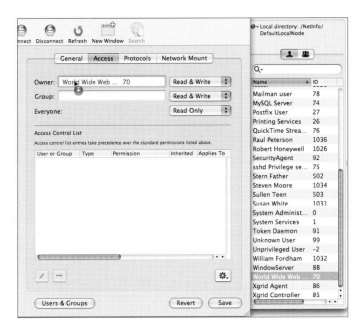

10 Drag the HTTP Users group to the Group field.

11 Click the Save button and quit Workgroup Manager.

In this configuration, you used Basic authentication, because you are running WebDAV in an SSL-encrypted site, so all communication between the browser and the Web server is encrypted. You should either encrypt your sessions in SSL or use Kerberos authentication (or both)—the other methods alone give a false sense of security to users, and their account passwords can easily be compromised.

So how do you access the site? With a browser, it works the same way getting to WebMail does: type *www.example.com/employees* into the URL field of Safari, and you will be redirected to https://www.example.com/employees and asked to authenticate. Notice that the lock icon is in the upper-right corner of your browser window, indicating a secure session.

In the Finder's Go menu, select Connect to Server and type in the entire URL—the Finder does not follow Redirects.

A WebDAV authentication dialog will open—log in with your name and password.

A Finder window will appear with your WebDAV share mounted:

Setting Up a Filtering Proxy Server

Setting up a proxy server is actually a very simple process. The more involved part is maintaining the blocked hosts list.

1   Launch /Applications/Server/Server Admin and connect to your server.

2   Select the Web service in the left frame, open the Settings tab using the button at the bottom of the main window, and click the Proxy tab at the top of the frame.

3   Select the Enable Proxy and Control Access To Proxy checkboxes.

4   Click the "Add a new host to the list" (+) button to type individual hosts into the "Blocked hosts" list box.

You can also drag a comma-delimited (csv) or tab-delimited (tsv) text file of addresses into the "Blocked hosts" list box.

5   Click the Save button.

Those clients you configure to use this proxy server will now be filtered through it, allowing you to restrict access to specific Web hosts. It's also strongly recommended that you restrict your proxy server usage to just your domain, as it is a security risk. When the cache space fills up, the oldest information will be dumped. You may need to adjust this setting, but if your primary reason for using proxy caching is to filter incoming traffic, you can probably leave the size quite small.

> **NOTE ▶** There are both commercial and free block lists available; they are what make proxy filtering worthwhile. The results, though, will only be as good as the block lists, and won't be perfect, either.

What You've Learned

▶ A proxy server is used to block access to various websites and is configured using the Web services section of Server Admin.

▶ Websites configured to use SSL default to port 443.

▶ Redirects are an excellent way to automatically send a request for one page to another page.

▶ Realms are an excellent way to restrict access to portions of a website.

▶ The performance cache should not be used with secure websites.

References

URLs

Apache HTTP Server: http://httpd.apache.org

Apple Computer, Mac OS X 10.4 Security Help: http://docs.info.apple.com/article.html?path=Mac/10.4/en/cdb_scr.html

Apple Computer, Mac OS X 10.4 Server Documentation: www.apple.com/server/documentation

Apple Computer, Mac OS X 10.4 Server Web Technologies Support: www.apple.com/support/macosxserver/webtechnologies

Apple Computer security: www.apple.com/macosx/features/security

CERT® Coordination Center: www.cert.org

Forum of Incident Response and Security Teams (FIRST): www.first.org

OpenSSL: www.openssl.org

SquirrelMail Web Mail Server: www.squirrelmail.org

WebDAV: www.webdav.org

Lesson Review

1. Name three types of Web content that Safari can block.

2. What does Reset Safari do? How is this different from Private Browsing?

3. Describe Redirects.

4. How do you secure WebMail?

5. Who are the default owner and group for websites? Who do they need to be changed to in order to be made available via WebDAV?

6. Name a security drawback of proxy server filtering.

Answers

1. Plug-in–based content, Java content, JavaScript content, pop-up windows, cookies, and sites not allowed by parental controls

2. Reset Safari erases your browsing history, empties the cache, clears the Downloads history and Google search entries, and removes cookies and AutoFill text. Private Browsing is essentially the same but it is activated on public machines before using them to prevent the data from being written in the first place.

3. A Redirect is a function of the Apache module mod_alias that enables you to search an incoming URL string for a particular directory or file path, and forward it to a complete URL.

4. Host it in an HTTPS SSL–encrypted site. Though SquirrelMail itself is capable of SSL, it requires a PHP extension that Mac OS X Server configuration lacks.

5. The default for owner is root, and for group is admin. They both must be reset to www.

6. The security is only as good as your "Blocked hosts" list, and the Web is always changing. Maintaining the "Blocked hosts" list can be very involved.

21

Time This lesson takes approximately 2 hours to complete.

Goals Understand which files to watch for modification

Detect malicious software

Use virus protection software

Use rootkit safely

Maintenance, Intrusion Detection, and Auditing

When it comes to Mac OS X security, it is crucial to regularly monitor your system for changes in software, look for signs of intruders, and detect malicious software. We hope that you already have a clear understanding of the way your system works every day. The more familiar you are with your system when it is running properly, the more obvious it will be when something unauthorized is happening. Although Trojan horses, viruses, worms, and other malicious software are less common in the UNIX and Mac OS X world than on other platforms, they should be taken very seriously.

In this lesson, you will learn how to maintain the security of your Mac OS X computers through proper maintenance and auditing, how to detect malicious software and deal with it appropriately, and how to constantly monitor your system to ensure you are aware of any changes.

Differentiating Between Types of Malicious Software

There's a wide variety of malware types and technologies out there, all waiting to attack—and possibly damage—your network and individual computers on that network. To effectively diagnose and resist malware attacks, you must learn the differences between, for example, a Trojan horse, a virus, a worm, and other types of malicious software.

Trojan Horses

Just as in the classic Homer legend, Trojan horse software seems like something you can use, but actually conceals something that can cause as much destruction to data as an entire legion of soldiers.

It is extremely unlikely that well-known, shrink-wrapped software will contain a Trojan horse. The main concern here is that shareware, freeware, or other software distributed through nonretail channels can easily be modified by a malicious attacker. A well-written Trojan horse, however, can install itself on top of shrink-wrapped software to disguise its actual source—so it may not be have originated in the application you purchased or downloaded, but from another source entirely.

Viruses

A virus attaches itself to a good program and can not only attack its host computer, but, like a biological virus, can replicate itself and spread to other computers. Viruses can be triggered only when an infected program is opened, so human "cooperation" is required—most commonly by inadvertently opening an attachment from an email. If a virus-infected program is not opened or executed, the virus will not infect a system.

> **NOTE** ▶ Currently, Microsoft Office Macros can adversely affect your Microsoft Office documents, depending on the type of virus.

Worms

Worms are similar to viruses, with one important exception: Worms can spread to other computers without human involvement. A worm will take advantage of a transport mechanism on a single computer and automatically spread itself to other computers.

The most common worm is an email-address bookworm, which obtains all of the email addresses stored on a single computer and sends a copy of itself to each addressee.

The email attachment that it sends is often a virus that installs a worm that repeats the process, infecting all of the computers in the recipient's address book.

> **NOTE** ▶ Microsoft Outlook e-mail worms can spread to other computers if you forward e-mails that have not been checked for Outlook worms.

Spyware

Spyware is very insidious. A system may seem like it is running normally, but a spyware is running in the background, secretly sending private information to an unauthorized recipient. A spyware-infected computer may be transmitting anything from address book contacts to passwords to confidential client information without the user even being aware that unauthorized data-sharing is happening.

> **NOTE** ▶ Spyware can also masquerade in the form of Microsoft Internet Explorer helper objects.

Understanding the Opener Rootkit

A rootkit is a hacker term for a software package whose intent is to provide the hacker with access to a system's root account. In UNIX systems, the root account has superuser capabilities and can make changes anywhere in the system. In other words, if you have root access, you control the system and can have it do anything that you would like. Rootkits are used to extend the attacker's capabilities once he already has root access, often by introducing backdoors into the system that the attacker can use at a later date.

Mac OS X and Mac OS X Server are UNIX-based and therefore do have root accounts. By default, the root account is disabled on Mac OS X but not Mac OS X Server. Even though the account itself is disabled, the support for the superuser account still exists. It is possible for an application to take on the superuser privileges to accomplish some task. This ability is important and is often used by trusted applications to effect changes within the operating system itself. A prime example of this legitimate usage is within the programs that make up the Systems Preferences panel.

Since there is this vulnerability, an attacker can use a rootkit to create additional, unauthorized programs that run as the superuser. With a rootkit installed, the hacker can execute any program with superuser privileges. This allows the hacker to make the system do anything he or she wants. Of course, even with root access the attacker still needs access to the system.

Most rootkits include additional programs that support remote access of the system and, as part of the rootkit installation, make configuration changes that enable the remote access programs. For example, most rootkits will enable the secure shell, ssh, that listens on Transmission Control Protocol (TCP) port 22 as well as adding a separate, "backdoor" application that is listening on another known TCP port. Either of these access points can be used to gain control over the system.

Because of the nefarious nature of most rootkits, additional work is performed during the installation to help hide the fact that the rootkit has been installed. This "hiding" process typically involves the installation of custom versions of many programs that are used to determine the status of a server. Some examples include ls and du, which are modified to not "see" the rootkit directory in the location that it has been installed; netstat, which is modified to not "see" the TCP ports that the backdoor programs are using; and ps, which is modified to not "see" any background processes that the rootkit has installed. Additional configuration changes will also be made to facilitate this "hiding" as well as to enable the continued operation of the rootkit. For example, changes will be made to the firewall configuration to open the backdoor TCP ports as well as the addition or modification of startup scripts to start up the rootkit programs whenever the system is restarted.

The installation of a rootkit on a system can lead to significant issues. Many rootkits are used to enable costly or destructive services such as anonymous email relays, file sharing, game servers, port scanners, Denial of Service (DoS) agents, IRC bots, and so forth. These services can cause the system or the local Internet connection to slow down to a crawl and impact their use for legitimate work. Even if a rootkit is not being used to implement a costly service, there can be other detrimental problems. If the rootkit installed was not built for the exact version of the operating system that it is installed on, there can be conflicts with the system libraries or event the kernel itself. This can cause the programs to behave erratically or even not work at all. Since these programs are often used either directly by users or by scripts and programs running on the system, this can cause significant problems.

Since the rootkits make many changes to a system, it is often very difficult to remove the rootkit and still have a working system. Because of this, if a system is ever compromised by a rootkit, recovery often requires a complete reinstallation the operating system from scratch.

It is important to note that the installation of a rootkit requires the use of superuser privileges. On Mac OS X (not Mac OS X Server), the root account is disabled by default. System administrators must use the sudo command to execute an application as the superuser. This significantly lessens—but does not eliminate—the possibility of a rootkit being installed. In addition to a user explicitly executing a program as the superuser, there are those legitimate programs that also operate with superuser privileges. The system's package installation program is a prime area of risk for a rootkit installation. By necessity the package installation program has to operate with superuser privileges to be able to install legitimate programs. This can be abused to install a rootkit as well. If you have administration access to the system, it is important that you know exactly what applications are being installed when you are prompted to enter the administrator password.

Even with all of the negative aspects of rootkits, they can have a noble use. In certain situations, it may be desirable to have backdoor access to a system. For example, you may have systems that have been deployed in a semipublic venue and you want to minimize the administration access to the systems. In that case, you may either disable the administration account or provide a random password to the administration account. This effectively locks out administration of the system. In this case, having undocumented, backdoor, superuser access can be beneficial.

If you do intend to install a rootkit on a system, it is important that you configure a system to be exactly the same as the system on which you want to install the rootkit. You will then need to build the rootkit on that system so that all of the versions of the rootkit programs and the libraries will match. Also, you will need to build an updated rootkit and reinstall the updated rootkit after each software update.

Currently, there were only three known rootkits for Mac OS X— osxrk, WeaponX, and jworm (known as Opener or SH/Renepo)—and all of them are out of date. They will work only on Jaguar or Panther systems. Opener is a simple shell script that is a rootkit only in that it opens a system for someone to access that system as root. It does not have any provisions for the typical rootkit hiding. It should also be noted that even though Opener is labeled a worm, it has not been seen replicating in the wild.

Understanding Infection Effects

Malware produces a wide variety of results, from relatively innocuous to devastatingly destructive. In learning how to repel or repair the results of malware, it is important to understand what can happen to a system once you have been infected.

"Cute"

Some infections are meant as a "joke" for the recipient. An infected computer may have its screen reversed, have all of its windows move about randomly, or display the message "You Have Been Infected" on the screen. These infections may be considered harmless by the author (who is often just trying to show off), but they can be very annoying to the recipient.

"Cute" infections may also be used by its creator or programmer to verify a new security hole that allows the infection to spread. Therefore, a so-called harmless "cute" infection may portend a more serious infection.

Identity Theft

Some frightening statistics bring to light the overall costs of identity theft. According to the Identity Theft Resource Center, approximately 20,000 people per day are victims of identity theft; each of them spends an average of 600 hours over a period of years recovering from this crime. Some studies estimate that up to $92,000 per name is lost to the business community in fraudulent charges, and victims spend an average of $1,400 clearing their records. All it takes to get the ball rolling is for someone to capture an unencrypted password.

> **MORE INFO** ▶ For more on identify theft, go to www.idtheftcenter.org/facts.shtml.

Destructive

The worst type of infection is the one that actually causes your computer to no longer function properly. Destructive infections may cause permanent loss of your data or require you to reinstall the operating system.

Protecting Against Malicious Software

It's true on the sports field and it's true when you're facing off against malware: The best offense is a good defense. By responsibly using preventative procedures and implementing protective features built into Mac OS X, you can avoid malware attacks and improve your chances of total recovery if a system or network does become infected.

Backing Up Data and Testing the Backup

The first line of defense and a sure way to prevent an extreme crisis if a computer is infected is to back up data! Be extremely proactive in regularly backing up important data on all the computer systems that fall under your responsibility. Just as important is to test the integrity of those backups and your ability to restore that data from that backup.

The goal of performing a backup isn't to archive data—it is to actually restore the original data. If you cannot take your backup to that last step of full restoration, your backup efforts are worthless.

Using Virus Protection Software

You now know how bad malicious software can be, including the damage that it can do to your machine and how it can be transmitted to other machines. Although there are few (if any) Mac OS X viruses today, there likely will be in the future, and you'll be better off if you're prepared before it happens rather than scrambling to figure out what to do after it happens. Lesson 19, "Mail Security," talked about what you, as an email server administrator, can do to quickly add antivirus protection to the users of your email service. But what can end users do to protect their machines?

You no doubt know that there are a number of popular antivirus programs available for other popular operating systems. A number of those are even available on Mac OS X. But as it turns out, there's a free program available called Clam AntiVirus, or ClamAV. This is the same software that the Mac OS X Server mail server uses, and it can protect your workstation too.

Obtain ClamAV

ClamAV is normally distributed as source from www.clamav.net, which you have to download and compile on your machine. After compiling, you must configure and run ClamAV from the command line. Thankfully, Mark Allan has developed a free port called ClamXav, which includes an easy way to use GUI. Here's what to do:

1   Download ClamXav from www.clamXav.com.

2   Open the disk image and drag the ClamXav application to your Applications folder.

3   Open the ClamXav application.

4   When prompted to install the ClamAV engine, click the Install button, and proceed through the prompts to complete the installation.

5   After the installation of the engine is complete, you'll probably have to relaunch ClamXav.

6   Click the "Update virus definitions" button.

You'll want to do this every time you run ClamXav to ensure that your computer always knows about the most recent viruses.

7   Click the "Choose what to scan" button.

Scanning your whole drive is optimal but can take some time, so you may need to scan only your home directory.

8   Click the Preferences button.

9   On the Internet tab, you probably want to check the boxes at the bottom to automatically check for ClamXav, ClamAV, and virus definitions updates.

10   The rest of the tabs in the preferences window contain a number of options that you may want to set, particularly the ones that enable automatic scheduled virus scans. For now, just click the OK button to close the preferences window.

11   Click the Start Scan button in the main ClamXav window.

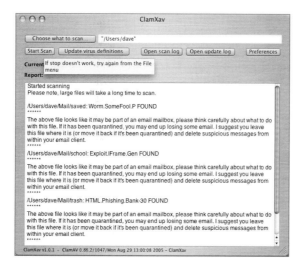

Understanding Maintenance

Maintenance on Mac OS X all comes down to doing your homework through updates to your applications, operating system, and security safeguards. Checking Apple-specific security sites is an excellent way to stay on top of events that may have an impact on computers within your organization. Here are some websites that provide information relevant to Macintosh computers:

▶   Apple product security: www.apple.com/support/security/index.html

▶   Apple security mailing list: http://lists.apple.com/mailman/listinfo/ security-announce

▶   SecureMac: www.securemac.com

▶   Macintosh Security: www.macintoshsecurity.com

You should also have an arsenal of general security websites as resources to find information about potential threats to your computers and your system. The following offer late-breaking information on other security matters, such as network security, security standards, and potential threats:

▶   U.S. Department of Energy Computer Incident Advisory Capability: www.ciac.org/ciac

▶   Carnegie Mellon Software Engineering Institute: www.cert.org

▶   U.S. National Institute of Standards and Technology Computer Security Resource Center: http://csrc.nist.gov

▶   The Center for Education and Research in Information Assurance and Security: www.cerias.purdue.edu

▶   SANS Institute: www.sans.org/aboutsans.php

What if you have already been the victim of an attack? AFP548.com is a website devoted to Mac OS X Server, but in recent years it has become a premier site for all things Mac OS X. You'll find discussions of security issues, as well as articles devoted to locking down and monitoring your system, and what to do if you've experienced an attack. You can find more information about this at www.afp548.com/Articles/security/postmortem.html.

Developing a good security policy is the best way to manage your users and systems. Coming up with that policy can be a daunting task, as you balance personal freedom with company policy, outside threats, inside threats, and legal repercussions. You should add these websites—devoted to guiding administrators into these waters—to your list of frequently visited places:

▶ National Security Agency: www.nsa.gov

Security Guidance for Mac OS X 10.3, Mac OS X 10.3 Server, and Mac OS X 10.4 (forthcoming)

▶ Defense Information Systems Agency: www.disa.mil

▶ Center for Internet Security: www.cisecurity.org

▶ National Institute of Standards and Technology, Computer Security Resource Center: http://csrc.nist.gov

▶ National Institute of Standards and Technology, Common Criteria Evaluation and Validation Scheme: http://niap.nist.gov/cc-scheme/index.html

No matter where you get your information, be aware of how Apple institutes its policies regarding certain vulnerabilities and security updates. Apple is a member of the Forum of Incident Response and Security Teams (FIRST), www.first.org, which handles security incidents as a group. When Apple posts a security notice, CERT distributes it simultaneously.

Performing Security Updates

Software Update allows Apple to send the latest security updates to the operating system and system software, and install them. Run Software Update regularly so that every computer checks with the Apple servers for all available updates to the system software, applications, and utilities installed on each system. Software Update can be run manually, or you can configure it to open on a set schedule.

> **NOTE ▶** Using Software Update may require an active connection to the Internet if a Software Update server is not available.

You can also proactively check for security updates from Apple by visiting http://docs.info.apple.com/article.html?artnum=61798.

Software Update updates only those programs that Apple publishes or supports. Since any given system probably has an array of third-party programs also in use, it is important to check individual third-party websites for any security or version updates available for their programs.

Detecting Intrusions

With intrusion detection, vigilance is the name of the game, —but when you're trying to figure out whether someone has been on your network or computer, others are likely to accuse you of attempting to get into their system.

To help you watch your network, you can turn to several tools, such as a network intrusion detection system (NIDS), intrusion detection system (IDS), or heuristic packet sniffer. Attack tools send out known patterns of packets; an IDS listening silently on the network can detect these patterns and warn the administrator. However, these tools cannot warn of brand-new types of attacks until the library of known patterns is updated. Still, intrusion detection software will often point out weaknesses in the entire system.

Let's take a look at two of the detection tools available for Mac OS X: Network Mapper (nmap) and HenwWen. Both systems rely on the network administrators of the network to be aware of the detection methods in progress, so that they are not mistaken for additional attacks.

Using nmap

Open ports are often the first casualties in the assault against systems, since open ports and the associated processes that run on them are open doors and thus vulnerable to attacks. An attacker can send packets to your open FTP port (port 21) and possibly trick the process into accepting it. One tool for watching these ports is Network Mapper (nmap), an open-source application designed to detect various types of information about systems on your network. While nmap can be considered attack software, it is a useful tool when the administrator uses it to discover holes in a network. It's important to be careful when using nmap with an organization's network, because some NIDS tools will see nmap activity as an attack and report it thusly.

Using HenWen

Another detection tool is HenWen, a GUI for the Mac OS X that is derived from the popular open -source tool is Snort, which has a GUI version available for Mac OS X called HenWen. HenWen is based on rules and can be used in various modes, such as:

▶ Sniffer mode: This is the basic mode that collects packets on the network and continually displays them in the window. Similar to the basic tcpdump.

▶ Inline mode: A more advanced mode, this mode collects packets from iptables.

▶ Packet-logger mode: Logs all packets to the disk of your choice.

▶ NIDS mode: The most advanced mode, NIDS allows you to capture traffic and filter it based on rules you've set up. Post-capture macros or scripts can manipulate and compare the data captured.

Like nmap, HenWen is often considered attack software, as it can show passwords sent in the clear, unauthorized access attempts to servers, and open ports on systems. Use caution when rolling out HenWen on a network.

Monitoring the System Using UNIX Commands

It is important to familiarize yourself with the list of processes that commonly run on Mac OS X and Mac OS X Server to be able to identify those processes that do not belong to a normal Mac OS X configuration. UNIX has a wealth of command-line features and utilities that show you what is currently running on a system. In addition to the command line, Mac OS X and Mac OS X Server provide an excellent graphical tool, the Activity Monitor, to access those same powerful resources.

> **NOTE** ▶ Some of the UNIX techniques explained in this lesson assume your prior knowledge of the UNIX command-line interface.

Using ps

The ps command enables you to identify processes that are running and processes that other users are running. When it is executed, ps takes a snapshot of the running processes at that moment in time.

If you don't add any arguments to the command, ps returns all of the processes that you are running within the current shell. For example:

```
powerbook:~ localuser$ ps
  PID   TT   STAT   TIME     COMMAND
  575   p1   S+     0:00.05   -bash
 1471   p4   S      0:00.03   -bash
```

In this example, you don't receive much information. All you see is that the localuser user is running two interactive CLI bash shells. You know that more processes are running, but using ps doesn't display that—you need more information!

Adding arguments to the ps command will provide more information about what is actually running on the system. There are many arguments available to ps, but an excerpt from the output from one of the most popular sets of arguments, -auxww, can be seen here:

```
powerbook:~ localuser$ ps -auxww
```

USER	PID	%CPU	%MEM	VSZ	RSS	TT	STAT	STARTED	TIME	COMMAND
localuser	1799	12.8	7.2	289696	75636	??	S	5:35AM	14:18.54	/Applications local/Microsoft Office X/Microsoft Word /Applications/ local/Microsoft Office X/Microsoft Word -psn_0_17694721
localuser	184	6.6	11.4	327132	119880	??	Ss	Sat07PM	46:59.47	/System/ library/Frameworks/ApplicationServices.framework/Frameworks/ CoreGraphics.framework/Resources/WindowServer -daemon
localuser	1394	4.9	6.1	248684	64336	??	S	Sun08PM	16:44.85	/Applications local/Acrobat 6.0 Professional/Acrobat 6.0.1 Professional.app/Contents/ MacOS/Acrobat /Applications/local/Acrobat 6.0 Professional/ Acrobat 6.0.1 Professional.app/Contents/MacOS/Acrobat -psn_0_10485761
localuser	698	4.5	2.4	233192	25496	??	S	Sat08PM	39:26.15	/Applications iTunes.app/Contents/MacOS/iTunes -psn_0_2752513
localuser	811	1.1	1.6	174020	17188	??	S	Sat11PM	3:03.64	/Applications local/RBrowser.app/Contents/MacOS/RBrowser -psn_0_3538945
localuser	573	0.6	0.9	160232	9288	??	S	Sat08PM	2:20.93	/Applications Utilities/Terminal.app/Contents/MacOS/Terminal -psn_0_2097153
localuser	1296	0.3	9.0	308440	94860	??	S	Sun04PM	17:15.86	/Applications iWork/Keynote.app/Contents/MacOS/Keynote -psn_0_8781825
root	117	0.0	0.0	27672	352	??	Ss	Sat07PM	0:01.40	netinfod -s local
root	119	0.0	0.0	18056	100	??	Ss	Sat07PM	0:22.11	update
root	122	0.0	0.0	18080	108	??	Ss	Sat07PM	0:00.03	dynamic_pager -F /private/var/vm/swapfile

This set of arguments tells ps to output *all* processes (in this case, you see the processes run by users root and localuser), to include the full path to the executable, and to not truncate the output of the line (that's what the ww does). The columns show the owner of the process, the process ID, the percentage of the CPU processing currently being used by that process, some memory statistics, the time the process was started, and the full path to the command that was executed to start the process.

If you don't need the entire path to the executable, which saves a lot of screen real estate and scrolling, you may give the argument -aucxww to ps and receive a result that looks like this:

```
powerbook:~ localuser$ ps -aucxww
```

USER	PID	%CPU	%MEM	VSZ	RSS	TT	STAT	STARTED	TIME	COMMAND
localuser	1394	16.5	6.1	248684	64316	??	S	Sun08PM	17:17.06	Acrobat
localuser	1799	16.1	7.6	290892	79284	??	S	5:35AM	15:46.90	Microsoft Word
localuser	1296	9.9	9.0	308440	94860	??	S	Sun04PM	18:12.78	Keynote
localuser	184	6.5	11.5	328504	120952	??	Ss	Sat07PM	47:43.31	WindowServer
localuser	698	4.1	2.5	233224	25948	??	S	Sat08PM	40:38.55	iTunes
localuser	338	0.7	2.7	264472	27872	??	S	Sat07PM	18:55.44	Finder
root	93	0.0	0.0	18676	232	??	Ss	Sat07PM	0:00.67	notifyd
root	117	0.0	0.0	27672	352	??	Ss	Sat07PM	0:01.40	netinfod
root	119	0.0	0.0	18056	100	??	Ss	Sat07PM	0:22.17	update
root	122	0.0	0.0	18080	108	??	Ss	Sat07PM	0:00.03	dynamic_pager

It will take a little time, but do some research on each of the processes using man pages or a Web-based search engine. It's good to learn more about what your Mac OS X is doing. After you've familiarized yourself with typical processes running on your system, it will be easier to spot rogue processes.

> **NOTE** ▶ To view all the arguments that can be used with ps, open Terminal and enter *man ps.*

Using ps and grep

Sometimes seeing all the information available from ps is a little overwhelming. A common technique used to search for specific processes without scrolling through them is to use a UNIX pipe to combine the ps command with grep –i (this finds matches that are not case-sensitive).

```
powerbook:~ localuser$ ps -auxww | grep –i httpd
root       2003 0.0     0.3     31456 2844   ??   Ss   9:00AM   0:00.04   /usr/sbin/httpd
www        2012 0.0     0.0     31456 320    ??   S    9:00AM   0:00.01   /usr/sbin/httpd
localuser  2024 0.0     0.0     18644 100    std  R+   9:00AM   0:00.00   grep httpd
```

Notice how you not only found the two Apache (httpd) Web-server processes, but you also found the process running your grep search. (It was running as you ran ps!)

If you are looking for a specific rogue process (for instance, seen on a security page that you actively peruse), you can enter that process name instead. Below is a search for a process called trojanhorse:

```
powerbook:~ localuser$ ps -auxww | grep –i trojanhorse
localuser  2024 0.0     0.0     18644 100    std  R+   9:00AM   0:00.00   grep trojanhorse
```

In this example, you see only the grep itself, so you know that trojanhorse is not running.

Using top

The top command is similar to the ps command, but instead of taking a "process snapshot" in time, top checks the running processes and dynamically outputs their names to the screen.

Without any arguments, top sorts its output based on process ID (PID), with the highest process ID (the most recently launched process) listed first:

```
powerbook:~ localuser$ top
Processes: 95 total, 2 running, 93 sleeping... 283 threads       09:10:36
Load Avg: 0.65, 0.94, 0.77   CPU usage: 36.6% user, 16.8% sys, 46.6% idle
SharedLibs: num = 123, resident = 50.9M code, 3.02M data, 13.4M LinkEdit
MemRegions: num = 14690, resident = 369M + 17.8M private, 292M shared
PhysMem:  106M wired, 579M active, 304M inactive, 990M used, 33.6M free
VM: 7.68G + 85.2M  108983(0) pageins, 72106(0) pageouts
```

PID	COMMAND	%CPU	TIME	#TH	#PRTS	#MREGS	RPRVT	RSHRD	RSIZE	VSIZE
2164	top	11.7%	0:08.12	1	16	26	420K	440K	796K	27.1M
1817	QuickTime	0.0%	0:20.05	3	276	249	3.34M	23.0M	11.2M	169M
1800	Microsoft	0.0%	0:07.26	1	65	134	1.86M	8.76M	4.41M	138M
1799	Microsoft	14.8%	18:11.02	1	92	445	62.0M	64.1M	83.4M	287M
1689	lookupd	0.0%	0:00.32	2	34	60	356K	884K	1.12M	28.5M
1681	Mail	0.0%	2:35.43	6	128	292	10.1M	29.0M	29.6M	177M
1475	bash	0.0%	0:00.18	1	12	19	172K	836K	812K	18.2M
1474	su	0.0%	0:00.01	1	14	41	84K	732K	636K	27.2M
1471	bash	0.0%	0:00.03	1	12	19	120K	864K	804K	18.2M
1470	login	0.0%	0:00.02	1	13	38	124K	440K	488K	26.9M
1394	Acrobat	0.6%	17:41.50	4	81	354	31.4M	57.8M	62.5M	242M
1353	RealPlayer	0.0%	28:58.16	9	398	611	15.7M	28.9M	23.1M	216M
1296	Keynote	5.5%	19:50.65	5	325	563	90.4M	47.5M	92.5M	301M
1177	writeconfi	0.0%	0:00.30	1	26	31	348K	784K	1.58M	27.6M
1148	NetCfgTool	0.0%	0:00.28	1	22	25	424K	660K	1016K	27.4M
1146	System Pre	0.0%	1:27.43	7	457	472	10.1M	31.1M	17.1M	232M

When using top, it is usually more useful to sort the output based on percentage of CPU being utilized by each process, rather than process ID. You can do this by adding the argument -u.

```
powerbook:~ localuserlocal$ top -u
Processes: 95 total, 2 running, 93 sleeping... 283 threads     09:12:31
Load Avg: 1.08, 0.96, 0.79   CPU usage: 62.3% user, 31.4% sys, 6.3% idle
SharedLibs: num = 123, resident = 50.9M code, 3.02M data, 13.4M LinkEdit
MemRegions: num = 14686, resident = 370M + 17.8M private, 292M shared
PhysMem:  106M wired, 579M active, 305M inactive, 992M used, 31.8M free
VM: 7.68G + 85.2M  109013(30) pageins, 72106(0) pageouts
```

PID	COMMAND	%CPU	TIME	#TH	#PRTS	#MREGS	RPRVT	RSHRD	RSIZE	VSIZE
573	Terminal	28.0%	2:50.25	7	96	270	7.38M-	17.5M	11.8M-	160M
1799	Microsoft	12.6%	18:29.13	1	92	447	62.8M	64.2M	84.3M	287M
0	kernel_tas	9.7%	28:22.48	43	2	2784	20.9M	0K	91.3M	846M
2165	top	6.5%	0:01.04	1	16	26	420K	440K	796K	27.1M

184	WindowServ	6.1%	48:37.69	2	489	1281	15.3M+	126M-	121M+	322M+
1296	Keynote	6.1%	19:59.78	5	325	563	90.4M	47.5M	92.5M	301M
698	iTunes	4.0%	42:27.73	8	252	692	16.0M	34.9M	25.0M	227M
1394	Acrobat	1.6%	17:42.39	4	81	354	31.4M	57.8M	62.5M	242M
338	Finder	0.8%	19:48.39	6	318	520	18.2M	43.0M	26.8M	258M
467	UniversalA	0.4%	3:18.68	1	58	96	804K	4.88M	2.25M	143M
189	loginwindo	0.4%	2:23.07	5	224	166	1.67M	8.06M	3.70M	136M
1048	TextEdit	0.4%	1:48.07	2	119	207	5.12M+	17.7M	9.14M+	167M
119	update	0.4%	0:22.41	1	9	16	40K	336K	100K	17.6M
1353	RealPlayer	0.0%	28:58.59	9	398	611	15.7M	28.9M	23.1M	216M
937	Safari	0.0%	12:25.63	9	279	374	14.7M	35.4M	29.7M	258M
811	RBrowser	0.0%	3:06.65	5	234	257	4.23M	23.8M	16.8M	169M

MORE INFO ▶ For more information on top and its arguments, open Terminal and enter *man top*.

Auditing Mac OS X

Auditing involves checking your Mac from time to time to make sure that nothing has happened to make it less secure. There are several ways to do this, including checking that the actual files on your computer have not been tampered with, monitoring your log files, and using a standard set of tools to determine whether your computer is as safe as other systems.

Monitoring Log Files

It may seem a bit academic, but watching log files is an excellent way to monitor the health of your computer. Inside Mac OS X are dozens of log files, all of which are important in one way or another. With respect to security, however, the following two log files, located in /var/log, stand out from the rest.

secure.log

secure.log relays information about users' attempts at accessing rights in the /etc/ authorization file, such as whether the screen saver has been invoked and a password is needed to unlock the screen, whether Fast User Switching is being used, whether there has been an attempt to use su or sudo from the command line, and whether there has been any attempt at unlocking a System Preferences pane.

Like the wtmp file, whether the user has logged in via the Login Window or remotely (usually via SSH), secure.log will show all logins and logouts. secure.log is extremely useful when watching attempts to access rights that may not be granted to the user. You can search for the word *failed* in the log; conversely, an administrator whose account may have been compromised can search for the word *succeeded*, which will indicate the acceptance of authentication to a given right. If attackers gain access to your system, the first thing they do is doctor or delete the log files in an attempt to hide their presence. So if you are an administrator, you may want to look for any absence of normal day-to-day authorization, as well.

wtmp

wtmp keeps a listing of restarts, shutdowns, logins, and logouts, both from the login window and via remote access (SSH). wtmp is a powerful log file that can show you who logged in to your computer, when it was shut down or restarted, whether anyone else has a hidden account on your machine, and whether he or she is using that account to access your computer. You cannot view the wtmp file directly; you must use the last command to view the contents of the file.

Using a Centralized Log Server

Reading log files to monitor the security health of your computer may seem like a good idea, and most of the time it is. But what if you have been attacked and your computer has been compromised? Remember, the first thing an attacker will do is doctor the log files to disguise their presence.

Therefore, you may want to create a centralized log server whose only job is to accept log files from another server (such as a Mac OS X Server running file services). If that file server is compromised, the attacker has no way to doctor the log files. You have a better chance to discover what happened and trace it back if your log files are safe from editing or deletion. When doing this, you must open up additional ports. It's not always possible to secure the log server against spoofing.

Apple Certification Compliance

Apple has augmented its commitment to security by becoming Common Criteria—certified for both Mac OS X and Mac OS X Server for version 10.3.6 and later. Achieving Common Criteria certification, a standard method of evaluating the security capabilities of information technology products, provides for a safer, more user-centered computing experience. Along those lines, Apple is working to comply with various security standards that many software companies, organizations, governments, and even nations are using. Among the certifications Apple adheres to are the following:

▶ Controlled Access Protection Profile/Evaluation Assurance Level (CAPP/EAL3): This is set forth by the National Security Agency to ensure security requirements and baselines for IT infrastructure with the U.S. government. EAL3 is the common denominator among assurance levels with respect to operating systems.

▶ National Institute of Standards and Technology, Federal Information Processing Standards (FIPS 140-2): Used to set security standards for cryptographic modules.

▶ Common Criteria: This internationally approved set of security standards provides a clear and reliable evaluation of products' security capabilities. By furnishing an independent assessment of a product's ability to meet security standards, Common Criteria gives customers more confidence in the product's security and leads to more informed decisions. Security-conscious customers, such as the U.S. government, are requiring Common Criteria certification as a determining factor in their purchasing decisions. Because the requirements for certification are clearly established, vendors can target very specific security needs with a broad range of offerings.

A protection profile defines a standard set of security requirements for a specific type of product. Common Criteria rates these as Evaluation Assurance Levels (EALs) numbering 1 to 7.

Common Criteria Tools

The Common Criteria tools available from Apple let administrators audit their systems. Running Common Criteria tools does not make an operating system inherently more secure, but it offers stellar event reporting via auditing, and a manageable way to benchmark one system against another. Keep in mind that a higher EAL level does not necessarily mean the system is more secure. The profile from Common Criteria must be matched against the EAL and measured against others in its category. In this manner, a more realistic view of the level of security can be established.

Common Criteria tools allow administrators to review results based on how secure the operating system environment is compared with the CCAP standard. Once the tools are installed, you configure the line AUDIT=–*ABC*– in the /etc/hostconfig file, where *ABC* can be one of four options:

▶ AUDIT=–YES–

 Enable auditing and ignore failure.

▶ AUDIT=–FAILSTOP–

 Enable auditing and allow processes to quit or halt if failures occur.

▶ AUDIT=–FAILHALT–

 Enable auditing and allow the operating system to halt if a failure occurs.

▶ AUDIT=–NO–

 No audits are run.

Once an audit option has been chosen, it will add records of certain events to a log file whose name is based on the date and time the file was created and stopped. For example, a log named 20051017060025.20051017113047 indicates that the log was started on October 17, 2005, at 6:00 A.M. and 25 seconds and stopped on October 17, 2005, at 11:30 A.M. and 47 seconds. If an audit is still in progress, the ending date and time will not be shown. Instead, the text not_terminated will appear in the log file name.

By using commands, you can force the rotation of log files (audit –n) and reload the criteria settings (audit –s), which will also automatically rotate the log file for you. The audit command has several other flags, all of which should be explored more thoroughly by reviewing the man page for audit.Once you have logged your audits, you can begin to make some sense of them. The auditreduce command lets you select only those topics relevant to you from the records. For example, you may want to see only those entries that exist when you log in as an administrator, rather than logging in as a regular user. In that case, you would use:

```
auditreduce –e shortnameofuser /var/audit/20051017060025.20051017113047
```

to view only audited items pertaining to that user from that particular log file. The praudit tool allows you to print audit records.

Several files (audit_class, audit_control, audit_event, and audit_user) let you manage the breadth and scope of your auditing. Another part of auditing is the ability to configure the auditing subsystem to handle audit events. The file audit_class shows a list of those audit events and can configure the auditing subsystem based on your criteria. For example, a line in the audit_class file could be 0x00000000:fr:file read, indicating that the event file read is a recordable event.

The file audit_control can be edited to change where the log files are stored, specify which event classes are audited for all users and which are to be audited when a user cannot be identified, and set a limit on the amount of free space that must exist before warnings are issued and logging is potentially halted.

You use the audit_event file to view events indicated by number, name, description, and class.

Edit the audit_user file to specify which audit event classes are recorded for a given user. This is very useful when attempting to audit one user out of ten on a given machine. For example, you would add +lo to log events performed by a specific user or users.

Finally, audit_warn—which is not really a file but a script—will send messages to the audit_messages file, such as whether the system is running, a given directory is out of space, or errors have occurred in the shutdown of the auditd process.

Auditing Software Using Checksums

A very sneaky technique to breach security is to replace known programs on a system with new versions of those programs that seem to operate like the normal versions, but allow easy access to an attacker.

Most likely replaced by a Trojan horse program, any common program can be replaced by an evil version, including UNIX daemons (such as ftpd, sshd, httpd, and so on) or, less likely but still possible, desktop applications.

Using mathematical calculation done in a predictable way, it is possible for auditing software to create a specific "number" for any file on the file system. If anything about that file is changed, even one byte of it, the number that is generated will be changed. This number is called a *checksum*. It is nearly impossible for two very different (or even very similar) files to generate the same checksum value.

Since programs on a computer are merely executable files in the file system, you can utilize auditing software to generate checksum values for some, or all, of the programs on a computer. Often, software developers will include the associated checksum with their software, either in the associated Read Me file, or on a webpage that contains the download link.

You can use the checksum mechanism to pre-audit the "correct" versions of the software, and then proactively check those checksums during regular security audits of the system. If the checksum has changed, either a new, legitimate version of software has been installed (which you can verify), or an unauthorized attacker has modified the program, perhaps with the intention of breaching the security of the system. There are existing utilities that permit this method of detection.

One type of checksum generator utilizes the Method Digest 5 (MD5) technique. To generate MD5 checksums, Mac OS X includes a program called md5.

Detecting UNIX Hacks

Virus scanners are great for detecting known viruses, particularly those popular with email. The downside, though, is that they often don't know about UNIX hacks. The UNIX hacks mentioned at the beginning of this lesson usually involve modifying a script, or completely replacing a system binary with one that has malicious intent. Virus scanners may not always know about or be able to detect these types of infections. This is where intrusion detection comes in.

Some tools used for intrusion detection compare binary checksums of the known good system and important files with current files. Tripwire is a well-known example. Tripwire detection involves scanning the entire file system of a computer and saving that snapshot. Later (usually once every day), you rescan the entire file system and compare this scan with the snapshot you saved earlier. If there are new files, or files that have changed, you should be suspect as to why they changed. The changed files could be totally normal. Maybe someone installed a new version of some software on the computer, or an administrator updated a configuration file. But if you didn't modify your computer and files are showing up as changed in a tripwire report, you should use some extra caution until you can rule out the possibility that they may now be malicious files.

There are a number of popular intrusion detection packages available:

▶ Commercial and open-source products named Tripwire (www.tripwire.com, http://sourceforge.net/projects/tripwire)

▶ FSLogger (www.kernelthread.com/software/fslogger)

▶ fsdiff, part of the radmind project (http://eq.rsug.itd.umich.edu/software/radmind)

▶ logGen (www.lsa.umich.edu/lsait/admin/mac/software/index.asp)

These products range in levels of sophistication from complex to simple. For example, Tripwire lets you decide if you want to omit certain directories, flag what signifies a change of a given file or directory (timestamps, file hash, file size, etc.), and specify options useful in special directories (like log file directories) to tell you only if a file has appeared or disappeared but to ignore changes to existing files. On the other end of the spectrum, logGen can ignore directories, but lacks other customization. logGen does offer a much more compressed set of output, however, in that it compresses the output down to show only the top level of a directory as changed rather than all of the files inside it. This is particularly useful if you're using logGen to create packages:

1 Take a snapshot of the system with logGen.

2 Install the software you want to package.

3 Run logGen again to see what files or directories were created, modified, or deleted.

   These are the files or directories you need to include in your package.

Tripwire

You must have the Apple Developer Tools (Xcode) installed to build Tripwire from scratch. Although there is a precompiled version available from www.macguru.net/~frodo/Tripwire-osx.html, compiling it from source is fairly simple, as shown in the following steps. The site www.macguru.net/~frodo/Tripwire-osx.html does have some good documentation, and is worth the read.

1 Download Tripwire from www.frenchfries.net/paul/tripwire.

   This is an updated port of the open-source Tripwire software that has been fixed up a bit to be easier to compile and use on Mac OS X.

2   Type the following:

```
tar –zxf tripwire-portable-0.9.tar.gz
cd tripwire-portable-0.9
 ./configure
make (this will take a while…)
sudo make install
```

3   When prompted for the keyfile pass-phrases, enter something that you'll remember but that's secure.

4   Examine the twpol.txt and twcfg.txt files.

Their locations should be indicated in the last few lines of output from the installation, and may vary for your site. These files control how much Tripwire will scan. You may need to modify them to accommodate your specific configuration, but just leave the files alone for now. If you do make changes, use the twadmin command to create new signed versions of these files that Tripwire will actually use.

5   Type *sudo /usr/local/sbin/tripwire –init* and enter your passphrase when prompted.

This will initialize your tripwire database. This process takes a snapshot of what your system should look like, and will take a while to run.

6   Type *sudo touch /etc/testfile.*

7   Type *sudo /usr/local/sbin/tripwire –check* (you won't have to enter your passphrase this time).

You'll see output that contains something similar to the following:

```
-----------------------------------------------------
Rule Name: OS Boot and Configuration Files (/private/etc)
Severity Level: 100
-----------------------------------------------------
Added:
"/private/etc/testfile"
```

Modified:

"/private/etc"

Rule Name: Variable System Files (/private/var/db)

Severity Level: 60

Modified:

"/private/var/db/shadow/hash/A90B4CDD-8696-11D9-9221-000D93BFA322.state"

Rule Name: Variable System Files (/private/var/tmp)

Severity Level: 60

Modified:

"/private/var/tmp"

As you can see, even though you made only one tiny change, there are many other files being changed automatically in the background. This is why customizing the configuration of Tripwire is important.

logGen

Once you install logGen on your computer, you'll want to test it by creating new files, modifying those files, and comparing the initial state with the older state looking for differences.

1   Create some new files on your system by entering the following:

```
sudo mkdir /etc/tripdemo
sudo chmod 777 /etc/tripdemo
cp /etc/hosts /etc/tripdemo/hosts
cp /etc/motd /etc/tripdemo/motd
```

2   Download logGen from www.lsa.umich.edu/lsait/admin/macenv.asp.

3   Double-click the package to install logGen.

4   Type *sudo /usr/local/sbin/logGen /var/db/logGen-baseline.*

This process takes a snapshot of what your system should look like, and will take a while to run:

```
logGen -- version 1.5
Copyright 2005 - The Regents of the University of Michigan
All Rights Reserved
 Checking File: 237202
---------------
/
---------------
0 changed files
0 deleted files
```

5   Create some new files on your system by entering the following:

```
touch /etc/tripdemo/file1
mkdir /etc/tripdemo/testdir
touch /etc/tripdemo/testdir/file2
touch /etc/tripdemo/testdir/file3
```

6   Modify a file on your system by entering the following:

```
echo "changing..." >> /etc/tripdemo/hosts
```

7   Delete a file on your system by entering the following:

```
rm /etc/tripdemo/motd
```

8   Compare what's currently on the file system with the baseline, and output the difference by entering the following:

```
sudo /usr/local/sbin/logGen /var/db/logGen-current /var/db/logGen-baseline
```

This command also outputs a new file (logGen-current) as a snapshot of how it currently looks. You can either move that into place (replacing the baseline file) if you want it to be the new baseline, or just ignore it.

```
logGen -- version 1.5
Copyright 2005 - The Regents of the University of Michigan
All Rights Reserved
```

```
Checking File: 237202 of 237202 (100%)
4 new files:
---------------
/private/etc/tripdemo/file1
/private/etc/tripdemo/testdir/
---------------
1 changed files:
---------------
/private/etc/tripdemo/hosts
---------------
1 deleted files:
---------------
/private/etc/tripdemo/motd
---------------
```

Notice that logGen reported all of the changed, deleted, and new files, and that even though both file2 and file3 were new, it didn't list them individually because the entire directory that contains them is new.

9   If your files were legitimately updated, you may want to move the current logGen snapshot to the location of your baseline with this command:

```
sudo cp /var/db/logGen-current /var/db/logGen-baseline
```

Detecting Mac OS X Intrusions

Older installation packages created in Mac OS X v10.3 and earlier and those created by third-party software vendors may ask for *prebinding,* a process to speed up application launch times and generally improve the user experience. It accomplishes this, however, through some changes to each application's executable file. The side effect of this is that a simple prebinding action (the step you see when you install software and at the end where it optimizes your system performance) can literally cause all of the executables to be shown as changed. Because of this, you may need to take a new baseline snapshot of your system every time you install new software.

You should also take some time to configure your intrusion detection application to your specific system. Both Tripwire and logGen offer ways to customize the directories that are searched or ignored.

As with any intrusion detection system, you'll want to keep a copy of your baseline snapshot file on a CD-R outside of your computer. The whole point of intrusion detection software is to detect if your computer has been compromised and your files have been changed. If that's happened, the attacker could quickly modify your baseline snapshot to hide the changes they made. However, if you keep your snapshot on read-only media or completely off your computer, you always have a picture of what your computer looked like while it was clean.

Intrusion detection is really effective only if you regularly run reports to detect any differences. Mac OS X offers a number of different options for regularly running software, but the easiest method is to simply create a shell script containing the commands you want to run every night and drop it in /etc/periodic/daily.

What You've Learned

▶   Vigilance is paramount when watching for any sort of malicious software.

▶   Intrusion detection software such as logGen should be run on a regular basis if operating a computer as administrator.

▶   The auditd process creates files that use the date and time they were created as the name of the file.

▶   You can use the audit_event file to view events indicated by number, name, description, and class.

References

Administration Guides
Mac OS X Server Getting Started: http://images.apple.com/server/pdfs/Getting_Started_v10.4.pdf

Mac OS X Server Command-Line Administration: http://images.apple.com/server/pdfs/Command_Line_v10.4.pdf

URLs
Rootkits explained: http://channels.lockergnome.com/windows/archives/20050630_sorry_rootkits_have_nothing_to_do_with_cheerleaders.phtml

MD5 Instructions: www.cert.org/security-improvement/implementations/i002.01.html

Lesson Review

1. What does a Trojan horse application do?

2. What binary does a checksum on a file?

3. What commands can you use to indicate whether processes are running?

Answers

1. Hides inside another application.

2. md5

3. top, ps

Part 3   Networking and File Services

22

Time   This lesson takes approximately 1 hour to complete.

Goals   Understand the purpose and advantages of address assignment, naming, and browsing (service discovery) on a network

Learn how AppleTalk and Bonjour function as service discovery protocols, and discover their advantages and disadvantages in a mixed platform environment

Use Bonjour to locate services

Unmanaged Networking

Welcome to Part 3, "Networking and File Services." The first four lessons in this section cover Mac OS X networking topics, such as IP networks and services and advanced configurations, while the last four are devoted to file services.

In this lesson you will learn about the need for unmanaged networking and get a historical perspective on how AppleTalk led the way in ease of network configuration. To gain a more complete knowledge of similarities and differences between managed and unmanaged networking, the lesson includes detailed information about Bonjour, and some overview information about managed networking concepts. At the end, you will learn how to troubleshoot and monitor Bonjour activity.

Understanding Unmanaged and Managed Networking

Unmanaged or ad-hoc networking allows you to create a network without performing any configuration. This type of networking is ideal in situations where access to a managed network is not possible, such as at home or in an airport. The following figure shows some of the issues with unmanaged networks.

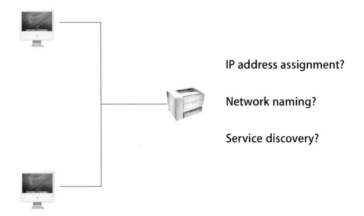

For an unmanaged network to function, it must fulfill the following main requirements:

▶   Assign IP addresses automatically

▶   Assign network names automatically

▶   Discover services automatically

Other considerations for unmanaged networking are:

▶   Plug-and-play networking

▶   No assumed user technical skills

▶   No assumed system administrator role

In this lesson, you'll learn how Bonjour technology fulfills these requirements and lets you create an instant network of computers and smart devices just by connecting them together.

To understand how Bonjour works and to appreciate its role in simplifying networking, it's worthwhile to see how managed networks deal with IP address and network name assignment. As shown in the following figure, traditional methods of network management included a DNS server, DHCP server, and static addressing.

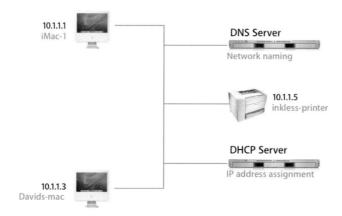

In a managed network, IP addresses are assigned either automatically by a DHCP server or manually by a system administrator. In addition, network names are assigned by an administrator who must edit DNS files to map every assigned name to its corresponding IP address. Furthermore, an administrator needs to provide the information necessary for users to access services on the network.

So unlike an unmanaged network, a managed network not only requires skilled personnel, but also additional software and hardware resources, making it impractical in small offices, homes, and on the road.

A Look Back at AppleTalk

While Bonjour technology for creating instant networks is fairly new, Apple had long ago pioneered AppleTalk, which enabled instant networking without any configuration but was limited to the Apple platform. To connect a printer to a network, all you had to do was connect it to the network. Then, you could open the Chooser on your Mac OS 9 or earlier computer, select the printer from the list of available printers, and print to it. You typically didn't need special knowledge to configure the printer.

Similarly, connecting Macintosh computers to a network and sharing files was easy: Just enable file sharing on one computer and look in the Chooser on the other computers to find the shared system on the network.

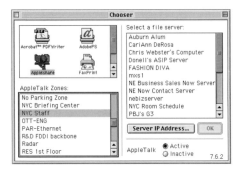

AppleTalk made simple plug-and-play configuration and network browsing possible, allowing Macintosh computers to thrive in locations where traditionally a network administrator was not available, such as K–12 schools and small businesses.

Mac OS X still supports AppleTalk to allow you to connect and access AppleTalk devices in a network, although this support is slowly being phased out. For example, as of Mac OS X version 10.4, Apple file-sharing services can be discovered via AppleTalk, but the connection itself must be made using TCP/IP.

Introducing Bonjour

Although AppleTalk excelled in ease of network configuration, a new IP-based protocol that provides the same ease of use and cross-platform flexibility was needed. So Apple engineered Bonjour, an implementation of Zeroconf, an open protocol built on other standards such as Internet Protocol (IP), domain name system (DNS), and Address Resolution Protocol (ARP).

The following figure shows the simple steps for requesting and discovering devices with Bonjour area request (1) and receiving a reply (2).

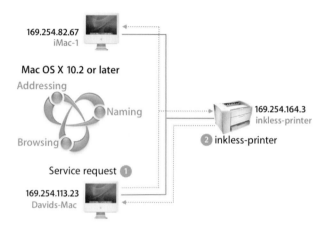

MORE INFO ▶ Zeroconf is a working group of the Internet Engineering Task Force (IETF). This group was chartered in September 1999 to create a standard for IP networking without configuration. A Zeroconf solution must allocate addresses without a DHCP server; translate between names and IP addresses without a DNS server; find services, such as printers, without a directory server; and coexist gracefully with large configured networks without damaging the network when a Zeroconf machine is added. For more information about Zeroconf, visit www.zeroconf.org.

With Bonjour, which is available in Mac OS X v10.2 and later, you can create unmanaged networks that are plug and play. Bonjour configures each device's IP settings automatically and then makes the services available on each device easily accessed by all the devices on the network.

Bonjour works on a network subnet, making it ideal for ad-hoc local area networking. Simply bring your Macintosh computer running Mac OS X v10.2 or later into range of another AirPort-enabled Macintosh computer running Mac OS X v10.2 or later—or plug in an Ethernet cable—and Bonjour configures your computer and accesses the services and capabilities of other computers available on the network. Bonjour does this over the worldwide standard IP networking protocol.

NOTE ▶ Examples of ad-hoc local area networking include sharing computers in conference rooms, airports, hotels, and homes.

When you connect two or more devices that implement Bonjour, they can do the following, without needing a dedicated DNS server, DHCP server, or directory server:

▶ Addressing: Automatic network address assignment

▶ Naming: Automatic network name assignment and translation between names and IP addresses

▶ Browsing: Service discovery without a directory server

Bonjour is part of Apple's open-source Darwin effort. Developers wishing to incorporate Bonjour into their products can access implementations for Mac OS 9, Mac OS X v10.1, POSIX (such as Linux), and Windows.

Assigning Addresses

When a computer is first connected to a network, it needs an address so other devices can access it. To do this, Bonjour devices use the industry standard IPv4 link-local addressing. When configured to use DHCP and DHCP isn't available, the device randomly assigns itself an IP address in the 169.254/16 range (169.254.1.0 to 169.254.254.255) and checks to make sure no other device is using that address on the subnet. It continues checking for conflicts during the lifetime of the link.

Two subnets on the same physical network using the same interface (en0)

192.168.1.1

169.254.164.3
inkless-printer.local

```
> netstat -nr
Destination        Gateway            Flags    Refs      Use   Netif Expire
default            192.168.1.1        UGSc        6       10     en0
127                127.0.0.1          UCS         0        0     lo0
127.0.0.1          127.0.0.1          UH         55   357676     lo0
169.254            link#4             UCS         0        0     en0
192.168.1          link#4             UCS         8        0     en0
192.168.1.1        0:a0:c5:49:32:a5   UHLW        7        0     en0   1125
```

A Mac OS X computer with a link-local address can access all other devices on the subnet, and they can all access it. When accessing devices outside the subnet, our computer is dealing with a larger managed network and it needs a managed IP address, such as one from the DHCP server or one that's been manually entered. The ability to start with a link-local address and later substitute a valid IP address when a DHCP server is configured shows how link-local addressing can be complementary when reaching beyond the local subnet.

Link-local addressing first appeared in Mac OS 8.5 and Windows 98. Mac OS X and the extension protocol for IPv4, called IPv6, includes link-local addressing. Before Mac OS X v10.2, you could not access a link-local address from a machine with a static address or vice versa, but that restriction was lifted starting with Mac OS X v10.2 and later.

Naming Your Network

If an IP address is randomly assigned, networking is available but not user friendly. Others must know your random IP address to access your Bonjour host. Because people remember names better than numbers, DNS is used for mapping IP addresses to domain names. Bonjour provides domain-name-to-IP-address resolution using multicast DNS. Multicast DNS is especially helpful because the computer's randomly picked IP address may change over time, but the service should still be accessible via its Bonjour name.

In the past, if you needed to log in to a computer on your local subnet via the secure shell command ssh, you would have to know the computer's IP address. When using DHCP, the IP address often changes. In a multicast DNS environment, if you set the computer's Bonjour name to "powermac," you could open Terminal and type

ssh powermac.local

to log in to it without ever needing to know its IP address. You could also open the Terminal application and choose Connect to Server from the File menu.

> **NOTE** ▶ This guide refers to a Bonjour "service" instead of a Bonjour computer. A single computer may have multiple Bonjour services running and available, such as Personal File Sharing, iChat, Windows File Sharing, and so on.

Every Bonjour host contains a small DNS responder to respond with the service's IP address when another client requests a lookup of the hostname. Whereas a typical DNS lookup is pointed at a single DNS server, Bonjour allows multicast DNS requests that are visible to all Bonjour DNS responders on the local link. These DNS responders ensure name-to-address lookups get resolved, even without having a centrally managed DNS server or if computer IP addresses change over time. The following figure shows how a Bonjour multicast query is answered by an mDNS responder—in this case, a printer.

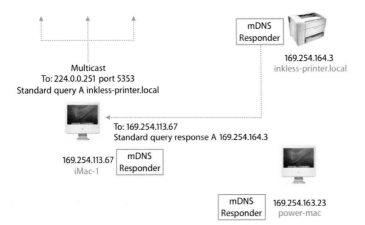

A computer has three names, which can be different or identical:

▶ Computer name: You can define the computer name in the Sharing pane of System Preferences. This name, which supports Unicode characters (including mixed case, spaces, and non-Roman languages), is the name you will see when you use Connect to Server to browse for servers. It also is the name of the folder that contains all mounted partitions. The computer name can contain any Unicode characters (up to 63 bytes of UTF-8). AppleTalk also uses the computer name, however the computer name is available only to machines in the same local link.

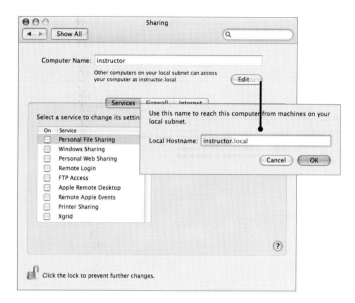

► Bonjour name: You can define the Bonjour name, which is also referred to as the local host name in the Sharing pane of System Preferences. Unlike the computer name, the Bonjour name is limited to the same restrictions of DNS: Roman characters, no spaces, almost no punctuation, and cannot start with a number. The Bonjour name is for AFP (Apple Filing Protocol) URLs, SMB (Server Message Block) URLs, SSH (Secure Shell), FTP (File Transfer Protocol), and HTTP (Hypertext Transfer Protocol) and is available only to other machines on the same subnet. By default, the Bonjour name is the same as the computer name, with spaces replaced by dashes, symbols removed, and the suffix .local appended to the end. However, you can change the Bonjour name (but not the suffix .local) using the Edit button in the Sharing pane of System Preferences.

TIP ► If you change the Bonjour name, keep it as similar to your computer name as possible to avoid confusion.

You can use the Bonjour name with command-line tools such as ftp, ssh, telnet, and ping. Your Bonjour name is also the name that will appear to Windows users in the Network Neighborhood.

NOTE ▸ The computer name is the default name used for Bonjour service registrations. In addition, the computer name provides a suggested default for applications to use. However, you can use any name as long as it is up to 63 bytes of UTF-8 character (unlike the Bonjour name of the computer, which has more stringent requirements). For example, you can use iTunes to advertise a network service that shares music files and call it "Dave Pugh's Party Music Mix."

▸ Hostname: The hostname is defined in the hostconfig file, which is discussed in more detail later. The hostname is used by scripts and services such as ftp and telnet that run from the command line. By default, the host name is set to the word AUTOMATIC. The hostname is defined by the following set of rules, in order:

1. If defined, hostname is the hard-coded name in the /etc/hostconfig file.
2. If available, hostname is the name returned by the DHCP or BOOTP server.
3. If available, hostname is the DNS name associated with the system's primary address.
4. If defined, hostname is the Bonjour Name.
5. If none of the above rules are met, hostname is defined as localhost.

Network Browsing—DNS Service Discovery

Link-local addressing (IP address assignment) and multicast DNS (name-to-address lookups) provide access to services only if the service name is previously known. To find services or device names, Bonjour supports *service discovery*, or *browsing*. Service discovery has been available to Macintosh users via AppleTalk and SLP, but traditionally not to the larger IP community because IP did not have built-in support for discovery. The Zeroconf Working Group solution to this limitation is *DNS Service Discovery*.

Presented with the same process of request and reply, the following figure shows that Davids-mac (1) is requesting an Internet Printing Protocol (IPP) service (2). The IPP protocol is commonly used in printing.

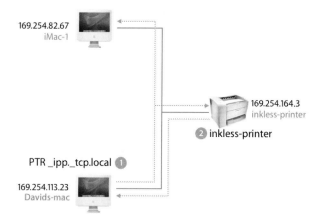

DNS Service Discovery relies on the DNS ability to do a *key-value lookup*. Whereas DNS traditionally uses a domain name key to look up an IP address value, DNS Service Discovery extends the meaning of *key* to include a *service type* and the *value* to be the service type's name. Because DNS supports multiple responses, DNS Service Discovery allows you to see all available services of a specific type on the local subnet.

> **NOTE ▶** DNS Service Discovery looks for services, while DNS looks for devices. This distinction is key to how network protocols really work, such as where an IPP client is looking for "things that speak IPP." In this case, the search for IPP services might return a list of IPP printers. It could also include an IPP archival storage device used in document management situations where IPP is the protocol used to archive (print) documents to an offline storage management system.

For example, to search for an IPP printer, your computer sends IPP requests to the local subnet, which might look like the following:

    PTR _ipp._tcp

Bonjour-compatible IPP printers would respond with their Bonjour name, such as inkless-printer. When the computer displays the list of available printers, you can select inkless-printer and print to it.

DNS Service Discovery complements link-local addressing and multicast DNS by completing the networking requirements of assigning IP addresses, matching names to IP addresses, and browsing for services.

A main limitation of browsing protocols is the level of additional traffic generated to support them. Although AppleTalk is easy to use, it is a browsing protocol. Every browsing protocol generates additional network traffic; Bonjour takes a number of steps to reduce traffic to a minimum, thereby making it an excellent method for local browsing.

Caching

The multicast DNS responder running on Mac OS X maintains a cache of multicast packets to prevent requesting information that it already has. For example, when one host requests a list of LPR print spoolers, the list of printers comes back multicasted, so it is visible to all local hosts. The next time a host needs a list of print spoolers, it already has the list in its cache and does not need to reissue the query. The following figure shows how only a new device connected to the network will respond to a request for services.

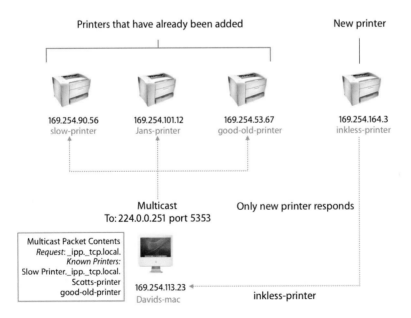

Printers that have already been added · New printer

169.254.90.56 slow-printer   ·   169.254.101.12 Jans-printer   ·   169.254.53.67 good-old-printer   ·   169.254.164.3 inkless-printer

Multicast
To: 224.0.0.251 port 5353 · Only new printer responds

Multicast Packet Contents
Request: _ipp._tcp.local.
Known Printers:
Slow Printer._ipp._tcp.local.
Scotts-printer
good-old-printer

169.254.113.23 Davids-mac · inkless-printer

Suppressing Duplicate Responses

To prevent repeated answers to the same query, service queries include a list of valid responses. For example, if a host is browsing for printers, the first query includes no print services and gets ten available print services. The next time the host queries for print services, the query includes the ten known print services. Only hosts that provide print services but are not listed in the query respond.

Exponential Back-Off and Service Announcement

When a host is browsing for services for an extended period, it reduces the query traffic sent over time. The host issues an initial query, and subsequent queries are sent exponentially less often: after 1 second, 2 seconds, 4 seconds, 8 seconds, and so on, up to a maximum delay of 1 hour.

This does not mean that it takes over an hour for a service browser to identify new services. When a service starts up on the network, it announces its presence with the same exponential back-off delay. This way, the background noise is kept to a minimum, but new services are seen very quickly.

> **NOTE** ▶ Some network administrators would argue that any additional traffic on their network is cause for concern, no matter what the level of "chattiness." Unfortunately, the tradeoff for not providing functionality such as service discovery would typically require someone to manually configure the system for novice users. With today's level of built-in 100/1000BASE-T Ethernet, it is much less costly to send a few packets across the network than to send an administrator to configure each user's workstation, especially as new Internet-enabled devices get added to existing networks.

Adopting Bonjour

As mentioned earlier, Bonjour and Zeroconf implement IP networking without configuration for existing devices as well as new classes of devices or services. Bonjour support in Mac OS X provides simple configuration for home or cafe computing scenarios (where people need to network computers in a coffee shop or bookstore). Examples of applications that take advantage of Bonjour are iChat, iTunes, and iPhoto.

Today, most early Bonjour adoption outside of Apple has focused on network printer support. Before Bonjour, network printer manufacturers had to decide whether to include legacy support for AppleTalk to allow easy network configuration, in addition to the expected IP printing support. By supporting Bonjour, printer manufacturers have an alternative way to allow easy network operation.

Brother, Canon, Epson, Hewlett-Packard, Lexmark, and Xerox support Bonjour, often called Zeroconf (on older printers you may also see the name Rendezvous, which is what Apple called it in Mac OS X v10.2 and Mac OS X v10.3).

Other manufacturers that have announced Bonjour support are:

▶ Sybase: Sybase's Adaptive Server Enterprise 12.5

▶ World Book, Inc.: World Book's 2003 Mac OS X edition allows students to automatically share their World Book research and bookmarks

▶ Philips: Future electronics products

▶ TiVo: To listen to shared music or view shared photos on a TV

▶ Aspyr: Networked games

Bonjour is ideal for accessing devices that do not include a monitor or keyboard and where the only option for configuration is first accessing the device over a network. Because the manufacturer must provide some initial configuration option, a Bonjour address that is dynamically assigned when the device joins the network would be preferable to a static address that might be incompatible with the network or conflict with an existing network device. Bonjour-enabled devices have the advantage of working on both configured and unconfigured networks because a Bonjour-enabled device can choose an appropriate address and advertise its services to the local subnet. Because many new devices include embedded servers for accessing or updating their software, such as HTTP, FTP, or SSH servers, Bonjour is excellent for locating these devices on the network.

Troubleshooting Bonjour

Even though Bonjour is meant to address zero configuration scenarios and requires no management, there might be situations where you will need to troubleshoot Bonjour-enabled networks. Here are a few troubleshooting tips that can help you understand what is happening on a network where Bonjour is used. It is helpful to remember that Bonjour is associated with services, not devices. A single device (for example, a Macintosh computer) might have multiple Bonjour services running concurrently (for example, Personal File Sharing, iChat, and iTunes).

Name Conflict Resolution

The Bonjour name is based on the initial installation assistant values entered for First Name and Last Name, and you can modify the Bonjour name in the Sharing pane of System Preferences anytime after the initial configuration. You can type any valid name into this field and Bonjour will map the name to a valid link-local name, as well as check for duplicate name conflicts on the local subnet. If a duplicate name is found, Bonjour will increment the current Bonjour name until a unique name is found. If two users have the Bonjour name jan on the same subnet, one machine may end up with the Bonjour name jan-2.local. To avoid any confusion that might arise from having duplicate names, use names that are most likely to be unique.

Packet Sniffing

Bonjour uses a standard DNS packet format, but on UDP Port 5353 instead of 53. You can use the tcpdump, ethereal, tethereal, or other packet-sniffing tools to monitor Bonjour activity and detect abnormalities. For example, to capture Bonjour packets only using tcpdump, use the following commands:

▶ sudo tcpdump -i en0 dst port 5353

▶ sudo tcpdump -i en0 | grep mdns

Log Monitoring

Use Console to view the system log and look for mDNS entries to detect errors or other types of problems. You can also view the mDNS entries in the system log using the following command:

grep mDNS /var/log/system.log

What You've Learned

▶   Zeroconf is an IETF working group whose purpose is to enable IP networking without configuration.

▶   Apple's implementation of Zeroconf is called Bonjour.

▶   Zeroconf and Bonjour have three main areas of work: addressing, naming, and service discovery (browsing).

▶   Address assignment is implemented using IPv4 link-local addressing.

▶   Naming is handled by multicast DNS.

▶   Service discovery is handled by DNS Service Discovery.

▶   To troubleshoot Bonjour-enabled networks, you can use packet sniffers, logs, and third party utilities to determine the problem, as long as you're using unique Bonjour names.

References

URLs

Bonjour information: http://developer.apple.com/networking/bonjour

Zeroconf Working Group information: www.zeroconf.org

Apple Service and Support page: www.apple.com/support

Bonjour Browser provides a convenient GUI interface to explore what devices are responding to each Bonjour-enabled service: www.tildesoft.com/Programs.html

Multicast DNS: www.multicastdns.org

Lesson Review

1.   Describe how Mac OS X is designed to support networking without requiring configuration.

2.   What are the three key networking issues addressed by Bonjour?

3.   What is IPv4 link-local addressing? Describe its use in Bonjour?

4.   What is multicast DNS? Describe its use in Bonjour?

5.   What is DNS Service Discovery? Describe its use in Bonjour.

6.   What is the difference between a computer name and a Bonjour name?

Answers

1.   Mac OS X includes support for work based on the IETF's Zeroconf Working Group for Zero Network IP Configuration. The Apple implementation is called Bonjour. Bonjour configures Mac OS X for network support without requiring the user or network administrator to do any configuration.

2.   IP address assignment, naming, and service discovery (browsing)

3.   Link-local addressing allows a computer to self-assign an IP address when the computer is configured to use DHCP but no DHCP server is available. With link-local addressing, a computer randomly selects an address from the 169.254/16 range and checks to make sure no other device is using this address throughout the lifetime of the link. This is referred to as link-local since the address is valid only on the local link, or subnet.

4.   Every Bonjour host contains a small DNS responder. This DNS responder can respond with the service's IP address when it sees another client requesting a lookup of its host name. Whereas a typical DNS lookup is pointed at a single DNS server, Bonjour allows multicast DNS requests that are seen by all Bonjour DNS responders running on the local link. The DNS responder ensures name-to-address lookups happen, despite not having a centrally managed DNS server, as well as when IP addresses change over time.

5.   DNS Service Discovery relies on the DNS capability of doing a key-value lookup. Whereas DNS traditionally uses a domain name key to lookup an IP address value, DNS Service Discovery extends the meaning of key to include a service type and the value to be the service type's name. DNS supports multiple responses, which allows someone looking for a specific type of service to see all services of that type on the local subnet.

6.   The Bonjour name is your link-local multicast DNS host name, which you can use with command-line tools like FTP, ssh, Telnet, and ping, as well as Mac OS X Windows File Sharing. The computer name is the default name that Bonjour uses for DNS Service Discovery.

23

This lesson takes approximately 1 hour to complete.

Configure Mac OS X to use IPv6 and IP over FireWire

Configure DHCP and DNS in Mac OS X

Identify network monitoring tools to check packet transfer from the client to other clients on the network

Use ipconfig to find rogue DHCP servers

Learn how xinetd and launchd work in Mac OS X

Understand how Mac OS X implements single-link and multilink multihoming

IP Networks and Services

In this lesson, you'll learn how to configure a Mac OS X computer to run in a managed network. We'll start with an overview of IP addressing basics and then cover advanced IP addressing topics, including IP over FireWire, IPv6, 6 to 4, and advanced Ethernet options. You'll also learn how the DHCP and IP services work in Mac OS X, how launchd and xinetd work to control access to services, and how Mac OS X implements multihoming.

Understanding IP Addressing

The Internet Protocol (IP) is the cornerstone of modern networking and is used in most networks, including the biggest of all, the Internet. Here is a quick review of the most important concepts in IP networking:

▶ IP address assignment: Two strategies exist for IP addressing. The first is manually assigning static addresses, and the second is using a server to assign IP address information dynamically to devices on the network. A common example of dynamic assignment is using a Dynamic Host Configuration Protocol (DHCP) server to provide IP addresses.

▶ Subnet mask: After a computer is assigned its IP address information, the computer belongs to the subnet defined by the subnet mask and network address. The subnet mask is used to determine which IP addresses are on the same subnet as your computer.

▶ Router: The router address is where traffic destined to go outside the local subnet is directed. A computer keeps a routing table to determine how to pass packets outside the local subnet. If the routing table does not know where to send a specific packet, it hands it off to the default gateway. Technically, routers and gateways are two different types of devices. However, the terms router and gateway are often used interchangeably to mean a device or interface where packets are sent when the packets are destined for outside the local network. You can see a computer's routing table with the command netstat -nr. The arp -a command will show known hosts in the local subnet.

▶ DNS server: Domain Name System (DNS) servers provide domain name lookup information that allows you to translate domain names to IP addresses. This lookup ability allows you to reach computers on an IP network through their more human-friendly host names. Mac OS X allows you to define multiple DNS servers.

Defining a valid IP address, subnet mask, router, and DNS servers allows you to perform other networking services, such as discovering available services on your network. The following figure shows the Network preferences pane and the options associated with configuring an IP address.

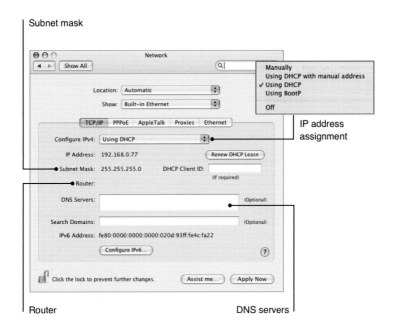

IP Addressing Pros and Cons

DHCP is easier for the user to configure because it assigns the IP addresses automatically so you don't have to specify an IP address on each machine. Furthermore, the DHCP server handles all IP address assignment for you, so you don't need to keep track of your IP addresses as they become available or are assigned.

Manual IP addressing, on the other hand, gives a machine a permanent IP address, which is useful if your machine is accessed by its domain name. For example, your system administrator can assign you the domain name imac-17.sales.pretendco.com and map it to your static IP address. In this way, any requests for your domain name are always routed to your computer.

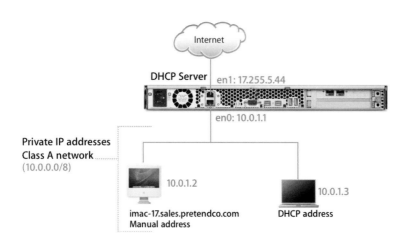

Some TCP/IP networks are set up with the intent that they will never be connected to the Internet and, therefore, do not need specific Internet addresses assigned from IANA (the Internet Assigned Numbers Authority). Examples would be home users, corporations that have secure needs, and training situations. Because of concerns over the growing shortage of IP addresses, a special range of IP addresses called private IP addresses was set aside for these scenarios:

▶ 10.0.0.0–10.255.255.255 (also referred to as 10/8)

▶ 172.16.0.0–172.31.255.255 (also referred to as 172.16/12)

▶ 192.168.0.0–192.168.255.255 (also referred to as 192.168/16)

Private IP addresses are sometimes referred to as *non-routable IP addresses* because the addresses are not routed on the Internet by an Internet service provider (ISP) or Internet routers. The name is misleading because these addresses can be routed by standard routing equipment within private networks and intranets or in conjunction with Network Address Translation (NAT) to connect a private network to the Internet through a valid IP address.

Advanced IP Addressing

Basic IPv4 over Ethernet is the main staple of the network today. However, for growth, Mac OS X allows for other forms of networking.

Using IP Over FireWire

You can set up your computer to connect to other computers over FireWire using IP. Because FireWire allows data transfer speeds of 400 Mbit/s and 800 Mbit/s that are faster than what most networks offer (most IP networks run at 10 or 100 Mbit/s), IP over FireWire is suitable for networking and clustering solutions that involve the transfer of large files, as well as temporary connections to the Internet using Internet Sharing.

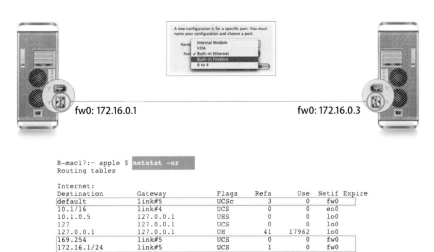

If you run the ifconfig command in Terminal after enabling an IP over FireWire configuration, you should see an entry like this:

```
fw0: flags=8863UP,BROADCAST,SMART,RUNNING,SIMPLEX,MULTICAST mtu 2030
    lladdr 00:03:93:ff:fe:44:75:00
    media: autoselect full-duplex status: inactive
    supported media: autoselect full-duplex
```

Also, if you run the netstat -nr command in Terminal, you'll notice that the routing table forwards packets to the FireWire interface (fw0).

Using IPv6

IPv6 is short for Internet Protocol Version 6. IPv6 is the Internet's next-generation proto-col designed to replace the current Internet Protocol, IP Version 4 (IPv4, or just IP). The current IP is beginning to have problems coping with the growth and popularity of the Internet, so here are some of the drawbacks to IPv4:

▶ Limited IP addressing: IPv4 addresses are 32 bits, meaning there can be only around 4,300,000,000 network addresses.

▶ Increased routing and configuration burden: The amount of network overhead, memory, and time to route IPv4 information is rapidly increasing with each new computer connected to the Internet.

▶ End-to-end communication is routinely circumvented: This point is actually an outgrowth from the IPv4 addressing problem. As the number of computers increases and the address shortages become more acute, another addressing and routing ser-vice has been developed, NAT, which mediates and separates the two network end points. This limits a number of network services.

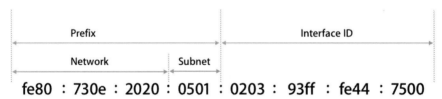

IPv6 fixes some of these problems and helps others. It adds improvements in areas such as routing and network auto-configuration. It has increased the number of network addresses to a maximum of 4 billion x 4 billion x 4 billion x 4 billion, which is an astro-nomical number, and eliminates the need for NAT. IPv6 is expected to gradually replace IPv4 over a number of years, with the two coexisting during the transition.

> **NOTE ▶** At present, IPv6 is used primarily by some research institutions. Most computers do not need to set up or use IPv6.

IPv6 Addressing Model

IPv6 addresses are assigned to interfaces (for example, your Ethernet card), and not nodes (for example, your computer). A single interface can be assigned multiple IPv6 addresses. Also, a single IPv6 address can be assigned to several interfaces for load balancing. Finally, routers don't need an IPv6 address, eliminating the need to configure the routers for point to point unicast transmission. Additionally, IPv6 doesn't use IPv4 address classes.

IPv6 Address Architecture

An IPv6 address consists of two main parts:

▶ Prefix: The prefix consists of a network address and a subnet address where the target device is located. Network routers use the information in the prefix to route packets to the subnet in which the target device (for example, a computer or a printer) is located.

▶ Interface ID: The interface ID consists of the address of the target device's network interface. Once a packet reaches the subnet in which the target device is located, the device's network interface picks up the packet addressed to it using the information in the interface ID.

IPv6 Address Notation

IPv4 addresses are 4 bytes long and expressed in decimals. IPv6 addresses are 16 bytes long and can be expressed a number of ways. Pairs of IPv6 bytes are separated by a colon and each byte is represented as a pair of hexadecimal numbers, as in the following example:

E3C5:0000:0000:0000:0000:4AC8:C0A8:6420

or

E3C5:0:0:0:0:4AC8:C0A8:6420

IPv6 addresses often contain many bytes with a zero value, so a shorthand notation is available that removes the zero values from the text representation and puts the colons next to each other, as follows:

E3C5::4AC8:C0A8:6420

NOTE ▶ Double colons (::) can be used only once per string.

The final notation type includes IPv4 addresses. Because many IPv6 addresses are extensions of IPv4 addresses, the far right 4 bytes of an IPv6 address (the far right 2-byte pairs) can be rewritten in the IPv4 notation. This mixed notation (from the previous example) could be expressed as

E3C5::4AC8:192.168.100.32

Using IPv6, a computer can assign itself a unique address to communicate with other computers on the local subnet or with other networks. In automatic address mode, a computer's interface can assign itself a unique address in two ways:

▶ Define prefix: If the computer is connected to other networks through a router, the computer starts by querying the router to determine its address and whether to use automatic configuration or DHCP. In the case of automatic configuration, the network interface creates a routable network address based on the router's address.

▶ Define interface ID: The network interface creates a unique address that consists of an IPv6 link-local address prefix, a link-local address valid in the local subnet, and a unique address (possibly the Ethernet ID of the network interface).

Not only has Apple placed IPv6 into the Mac OS X infrastructure, but file sharing over AFP (whether the share point is on Mac OS X or Mac OS X Server) will attempt to connect over IPv6 before it tries IPv4. If you do not want Mac OS X or Mac OS X Server to attempt IPv6 connections, you can turn off IPv6 in the Network preferences pane or in the Server Assistant during initial setup on Mac OS X Server.

> **MORE INFO** ▶ For more technical details about the structure of an IPv6 address, go to www.ipv6.org.

Using 6 to 4

The 6 to 4 port configuration allows you to connect to IPv6 networks if you have access to only an IPv4 connection, such as a modem. The 6 to 4 port configuration assigns your computer an IPv6 address based on your current IPv4 address, encapsulates IPv6 traffic in IPv4 packets, and routes them to a 6 to 4 gateway that is connected to an IPv6 network.

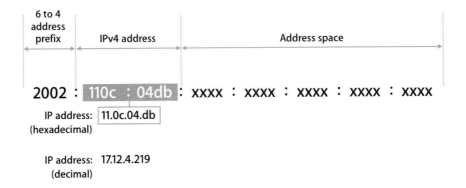

You can connect to an IPv6 address from a computer using IPv4 by setting up a 6 to 4 network port configuration:

1   Open System Preferences and click Network.

2   Choose Network Port Configurations from the Show pop-up menu and click New.

3   Choose 6 to 4 from the Port pop-up menu and give the configuration a name.

4   If you were given a relay address, choose Manually from the Configure pop-up menu and enter it. Otherwise, leave the Configure pop-up menu set to Automatic.

> **MORE INFO** ► For more information about 6 to 4 addressing, refer to the man page of the ip6config command (man ip6config).

Advanced Ethernet Options

You can configure advanced Ethernet settings if you have specific requirements for the network you are connected to. Usually, the settings that are configured automatically are correct. In some network environments, you may need to set advanced options. For example, you might need to change the Duplex setting to match a switch that has been set to half-duplex. Also you may discover that changing MTU to 1491 improves performance for some DSL providers.

Your network administrator or ISP can give you the settings specific to the network and help you determine if you need to adjust them. The following figure shows the options available when manually choosing the speed of your network connection.

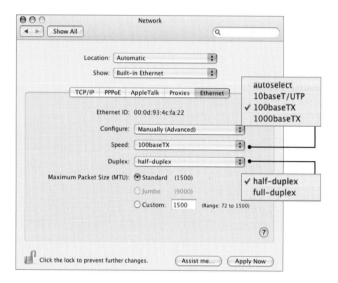

NOTE ▶ These advanced settings affect the way your computer interacts with your network. Unless your network administrator has given you specific settings, use the automatic settings. Entering the wrong settings can adversely affect network performance.

To set advanced Ethernet options:

1 Open System Preferences and click Network.

2 Choose your Ethernet port configuration (named Built-in Ethernet unless you created another) from the Show pop-up menu.

3 Click Ethernet and then choose Manually (Advanced) from the Configure pop-up menu.

4 Choose a speed from the Speed pop-up menu, and "half-duplex" or "full-duplex" from the Duplex pop-up menu.

5 Select a maximum packet size.

6 Click Apple Now when finished.

Working With DHCP in Mac OS X

The following describes the DHCP process Mac OS X uses to obtain a valid IP address from a DHCP server:

1. The client sends a DHCPDISCOVER broadcast message to locate available servers and let the servers know that the client is looking for configuration information.

    Any DHCP server can receive the message and prepare to lease the client an IP address.

2. The DHCP server prepares an offer message, which contains:

    • The IP address that the server is offering to lease

    • Additional DHCP options requested by the client, such as the subnet mask

    • The IP address of the server

    • The time period of the lease

    The offered address is marked as reserved. The DHCP server then broadcasts the DHCPOFFER message over the network. If there are multiple DHCP servers, the client will receive multiple messages.

3. After receiving the DHCPOFFER messages, the client chooses one server from which to request configuration parameters. The client then broadcasts a DHCPREQUEST message that includes the selected server's IP address and the client's leased IP address. Other options specifying various configuration parameters might also be included. This broadcast message is received by all DHCP servers. This message lets those servers not selected by the client know that the client has declined their offers.

4. The server selected in the DHCPREQUEST message responds with a DHCPACK message containing the configuration parameters for the requesting client. These parameters include some of the same information that was provided in the DHCPOFFER:

    • The IP address of the selected server

    • The committed IP address for the client

    The DHCPACK message might include other options specifying additional configuration parameters.

NOTE ▸ If there is a problem (such as the client has moved to a different subnet or the requested address has been allocated) and the selected server is unable to satisfy the DHCPREQUEST, the server sends a DHCPNAK message.

5. When the client receives the DHCPACK message, it uses Address Resolution Protocol (ARP) to perform a final check on the parameters. The client notes the duration of the lease specified in the DHCPACK message. The client is configured at this time.

NOTE ▸ If the client detects that the address is currently in use, the client then sends a DHCPDECLINE message to the server and restarts the configuration process.

6. Mac OS X sends a release only if the user de-configures the DHCP service, such as by turning off the IP settings in the Network pane of System Preferences or by performing a graceful shutdown.

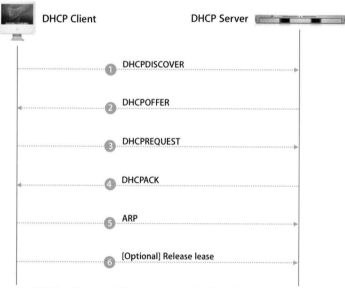

DORA = Discover, Offer, Request, and Acknowledgment

Renewing DHCP With an Existing Lease

A computer configured to acquire a DHCP address always attempts to reuse its last assigned IP address on subsequent connections. When a computer reconnects to a network with a DHCP server, because it has already received an address, it uses the following abbreviated lease renewal process (which takes half of the lease time):

1. The Mac OS X computer reconnects to the network and broadcasts a DHCPREQUEST message. This message includes the computer's last assigned IP address in the "requested IP address" field. The request asks for an extension of that DHCP lease. A DHCP lease is the process by which a DHCP server guarantees, within a specific lease time, not to reallocate that address.

    NOTE ▶ The computer broadcasts the DHCPREQUEST message on the network until it receives a DHCPACK response from a server. Your network may have one or more DHCP servers providing addresses.

2. The DHCP server verifies that the computer is located on the correct network and is eligible to receive an address. If the client's network address is verified, a DHCP server responds with a DHCPACK message and renews the lease.

    If the client's network address is not verified, the server will either generate a new lease or deny an IP address to the client.

    The computer also stops sending DHCPREQUEST messages when it receives a DHCPNAK (not acknowledged) message from a server. This DHCP server feature is designed to eliminate undesirable network traffic from unverified requestors. To start a new DHCPREQUEST cycle, you can click Renew DHCP Lease in the Network pane of System Preferences.

3. When the client receives the DHCPACK message, it performs a final conflict check on the parameters using ARP. If the address is not in use by another machine, the client notes the duration of the lease specified in the DHCPACK message. The client is configured at this time.

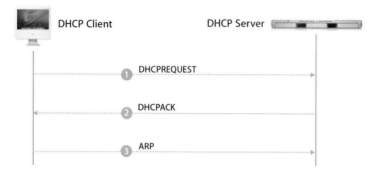

Finding DHCP Servers on a Subnet

Mac OS X includes the ipconfig and arp commands, which you can use to locate a DHCP server on your local subnet. These commands are useful when trying to track a rogue DHCP server that is wreaking havoc in your network.

To find a rogue DHCP server, do the following:

1   Use the getpacket option with ipconfig to get the last DHCP or BOOTP offer packet received on a given interface. For example, to get the last DHCP received on the interface en0, enter the following command:

ipconfig getpacket en0

In the output, the following fields display basic information from the DHCP server:

▶   server_identifier: The IP address of the DHCP server

▶   yiaddr: The IP address the DHCP server assigns to your computer

▶   subnet_mask: The subnet mask the DHCP server assigns to your computer

▶   router: The IP address of the default gateway

▶   lease_time: The amount of time before the DHCP server can reclaim the IP address it assigned to the computer

In addition, the DHCP server can provide additional information such as LDAP information, DNS servers, and search domains.

Although some of the output generated by ipconfig can be gathered elsewhere, it is the only command that shows the IP address of the DHCP server that your computer uses.

2   Use the arp command to discover the MAC address associated with the DHCP server you found in the previous step.

arp *ip_address*

where *ip_address* is the IP address of the DHCP server.

This command displays the MAC address and interface of the specified IP address.

3   Find the port that is connected to that MAC address and disconnect the cable connected to the port.

Alternatively you could look up the vendor prefix for the MAC address and look for equipment made by that manufacturer to discover the rogue DHCP server.

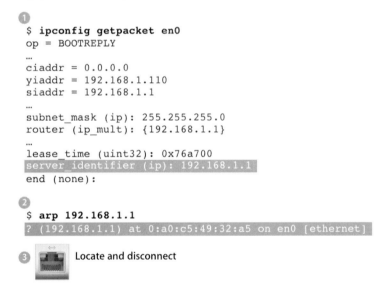

```
$ ipconfig getpacket en0
op = BOOTREPLY
...
ciaddr = 0.0.0.0
yiaddr = 192.168.1.110
siaddr = 192.168.1.1
...
subnet_mask (ip): 255.255.255.0
router (ip_mult): {192.168.1.1}
...
lease_time (uint32): 0x76a700
server_identifier (ip): 192.168.1.1
end (none):
```

```
$ arp 192.168.1.1
? (192.168.1.1) at 0:a0:c5:49:32:a5 on en0 [ethernet]
```

Locate and disconnect

Using Mac OS X as a DNS Client

There are a variety of processes on Mac OS X that require DNS services. These processes communicate with the DNS resolver on the DNS client computer via the gethostby() routine (standard C library routine modified to resolve addresses via lookupd).

In Mac OS X, the DNS resolver is a process called lookupd. This process also performs other lookup functions for Mac OS X. In Mac OS X the name of the current domain and the IP address or addresses of the DNS server or servers are stored in /etc/resolv.conf. This configuration file is provided by Mac OS X for processes that depend on the information in the file, but is not used to configure the DNS server, as is the case in other UNIX-based systems.

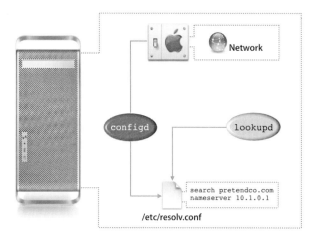

The DNS client configuration is either entered manually or derived automatically via DHCP. When DNS client configuration is modified, the configd daemon (described in more detail in Lesson 24, "Mac OS X Network Architecture") modifies the resolv.conf file accordingly.

If the name server has the authority (names and IP addresses are stored on it for the resolution requested) it responds to the request by the DNS client. If it does not have the authority, it checks its cache to see whether the name was resolved recently. If the name was resolved recently, the server reports the caching information to the client. If the resolver does not have the authority for the name or have it stored in its cache, it directs the request to the root server of the global DNS system for a top-down search.

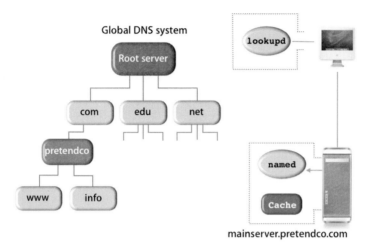

The file /etc/resolv.conf is a symbolic link to /var/run/resolv.conf. If this link gets broken, the system behaves in unexpected ways. The configd daemon creates and maintains /var/run/resolv.conf, the contents of which are dynamic. If your network or location changes, the IP Configuration Agent might rewrite this file with new contents.

In Mac OS X, processes like Apache and sendmail also use DNS name resolution. If some functions—such as logging in, Internet communication, and direct Web access—seem to take an unusually long time to complete or don't work at all, check the domain and subdomain name servers for correct configuration. An excessive delay logging in when using Mac OS X Server administration applications can also indicate invalid DNS settings.

Providing Network Services

It is important to understand the role that processes play in providing network services in Mac OS X and how to provide more than one IP address per computer, a process known as multihoming. Now let's examine both the processes responsible for networking and adding more than one IP address.

Working With launchd

New in Mac OS X version 10.4 is launchd, which replaces PID 1 as the top-level master process, init, found on most UNIX systems. As such, launchd is the parent process for most of the system daemons and manages most of the incoming network traffic.

The configuration files for launchd can be found in at /System/Library/LaunchDaemons/ and are XML property lists. These property lists offer many new options for configuring a daemon that weren't available with xinetd. You can see numerous examples of different options in the launchd configuration directory, or open the Terminal and type *man launchd* and *man launchd.plist* to view the documentation. One thing worth noting is that xinetd is now started by launchd.

All of these configuration files are updated when you change the service setting in the Sharing preferences pane. Also, the configuration files are updated when you use the /sbin/service command, which allows you to start and stop services (for example, sudo service ftp start and sudo service ftp stop).

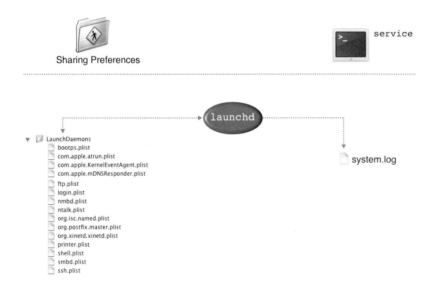

The launchd daemon listens to service requests and forwards the requests to the appropriate daemon. The following process illustrates how launchd works:

1. At startup, launchd reads the configuration files from /System/Library/LaunchDaemons/.

    In addition to reading configuration files at startup, launchd can be signaled to start or stop other services via the launchctl program.

2. launchd sets up listeners for the services that are enabled.

3. Whenever a listener receives a service request from the network, it forwards the request to launchd.

4. launchd forwards the request to the appropriate daemon.

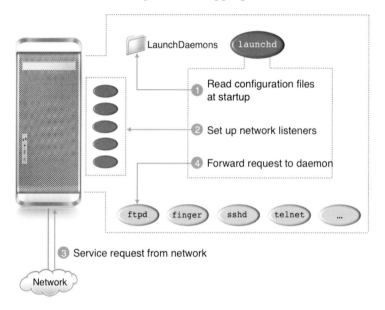

For example, if launchd receives an FTP service request, it forwards the request to ftpd.

The configuration files for launchd (in /System/Library/LaunchDaemons/) map services to the executable that should be run to handle a request for a given service. If you enable FTP file sharing, the ftpd process is not started immediately. Instead, the configuration file is updated to reflect that launchd should listen for FTP requests, and when it receives one, it should launch ftpd to service the request. When the first FTP request arrives, launchd receives the request, then launches ftpd to handle it. In this way, launchd can keep the number of services running on a particular machine lower by launching only those that are requested by a client.

NOTE ▶ The inetd, xinetd, and launchd processes have different configuration files. The inetd process uses one file, inetd.conf, to map a given service to its executable. All standard services that inetd handles are already listed in the file. The xinetd and launchd processes, on the other hand, use a different configuration for each service it provides. The /etc/xinetd.d folder contains configuration files for each of the services that xinetd handles, while the launchd configuration files are kept in /System/Library/LaunchDaemons/. When you enable FTP sharing, Mac OS X modifies the configuration file /System/Library/LaunchDaemons/ftp.plist.

launchd also has a number of other locations for configuration files that it reads from for services that aren't provided by Apple. Some of the places launchd reads its configurations from include:

▶   /System/Library/LaunchDaemons/

▶   /System/Library/LaunchAgents/

▶   /Library/LaunchDaemons/

▶   /Library/LaunchAgents/

▶   ~/Library/LaunchAgents/

Consult the man page (man launchd) for details regarding the purpose of each of these directories.

Comparing xinetd and inetd

Although used much less in Mac OS X v10.4, the xinetd process is sometimes referred to as the super server. This process, which is a secure replacement for inetd, replaces and extends the capabilities of TCP wrappers and cohabit combined. However, because xinetd does not handle RPC services very well, both inetd and xinetd are included with Mac OS X and both of them can successfully coexist.

The xinetd process does the exact same things as inetd with the added security benefits of:

▶   Access control based on source address, destination address, and time

▶   Extensive logging (system.log)

► Efficient containment of Denial of Service attacks

► Ability to bind services to specific interfaces

NOTE ► The configuration files for xinetd are located in /etc/xinetd.d/.

Multihoming

According to RFC 1122, a multihomed host has multiple IP addresses, which you can think of as logical interfaces. These logical interfaces might be associated with one or more physical interfaces, and these physical interfaces might be connected to the same or different networks.

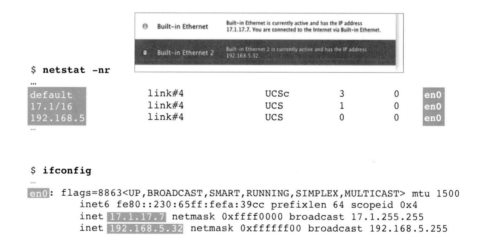

As many as 64 IPs can be associated with a single interface. An effective use of multihoming is in conjunction with port forwarding. If you have one firewall server but want to provide two separate AFP services, you use multihoming to assign two IP addresses to the same interface and forward requests to each of the IP addresses to different internal servers.

Another example of multihoming is a system configured for both AirPort and Built-in Ethernet at the same time. This system shown in the following figure has more than one IP address.

To assign different IP addresses to the same interface:

1   Open the Network pane of System Preferences and select Network Port Configurations from the Show menu.

2   Click New and create another configuration on the same interface.

3   Fill in the information associated with this virtual interface and it will be bound to the same interface as the original configuration.

4   Click Apply Now.

As it does on a single defined IP address on an interface, the xinetd process will be listening on multiple defined IP addresses on the same interface and passing service requests to the appropriate daemon.

Troubleshooting Networks

The following are tips for troubleshooting network issues:

▶ Check network status: The first step you may want to perform when troubleshooting network issues is to check the Network Status pane of the Network pane of System Preferences. Network Status indicates whether port configurations are active and provides a brief description of their status.

▶ Check network settings: In many cases, networking issues can be fixed by modifying the network settings in the Network pane of System Preferences.

▶ Use Console: You can use Console to view log entries in the lookupd.log and ipfw.log files.

▶ Use ifconfig: You can use ifconfig to get a bird's-eye view of your network settings, which is crucial when troubleshooting network issues.

▶ Use ipconfig: If you want to find a rogue DHCP server in your local subnet, you can use the getpacket option of ipconfig to get the last DHCP or BOOTP offer packet received on a given interface. The packet includes the address of the DHCP server that is providing your computer with its IP address.

What You've Learned

▶ The Internet Protocol (IP) provides manual and dynamic addressing strategies.

▶ IP over FireWire allows you to connect to other computers using IP, and is ideal for clustering solutions and as a failover option.

▶ The extra bandwidth available with IP over FireWire allows you to transfer large amounts of data to a backup system without impacting your other network activity.

▶ Mac OS X supports IPv6 and automatically assigns an IPv6 address, but does not use it as the primary address except when operating in an IPv6 environment.

▶ You can provide for special networking requirements by using the Ethernet pane of the Network pane of System Preferences to define advanced Ethernet settings.

▶ The Mac OS X DNS resolver is lookupd.

▶ The launchd and xinetd daemons listen to service requests and forwards them to the appropriate daemon.

▶ Mac OS X implements multihoming by allowing you to define multiple IP addresses for your computer.

References

Administration Guides

Mac OS X Server Network Services Administration: http://images.apple.com/server/pdfs/Network_Services_v10.4.pdf

Apple Knowledge Base Documents

The following Knowledge Base document (located at www.apple.com/support) provides further information about IP networks and services.

Document 18237, "DHCP: What Is It?"

Books

Hunt, Craig. TCP/IP Network Administration, 3rd ed. (O'Reilly, 2002).

Hagen, Silvia. *IPv6 Essentials,* 1st ed. (O'Reilly, 2002).

URLs

"Getting Started with launchd": http://developer.apple.com/macosx/launchd.html

Resources for DHCP: www.dhcp.org

IPv6: The Next Generation Internet: www.ipv6.org

Lesson Review

1. What does an IPv6 address consist of?

2. What is IP over FireWire suitable for?

3. What is the purpose of the Domain Name System (DNS)?

4. Describe a DNS lookup process.

5. List three advantages of using a DHCP server on your network.

6. How do you find a rogue DHCP server on your local subnet?

7. If your users require more than one IP address, what would you do?

Answers

1. An IPv6 address consists of eight 16-bit numbers (128 bits). The first four numbers contain network and subnet information. The last four numbers form the address of the network interface on a network device.

2. IP over FireWire is suitable for networking and clustering solutions.

3. The purpose of DNS is to perform IP address-to-name and name-to-IP address resolution for computers on the Internet.

4. A computer running Mac OS X uses lookupd to locate the name of its own domain and the IP address of its name server. The computer makes a system call to named on the DNS name server to perform the IP address-to-name translation. If the name server has the authority (names and IP addresses are stored on it for the resolution requested), it responds to the request by the DNS client. If it does not have the authority, it checks its cache to see whether the name was resolved recently. If the name was resolved recently, the server reports the caching information to the client. If the resolver does not have the authority for the name or have it stored in its cache, it directs the request to the root server of the global DNS system for a top-down search.

5. Automatic IP address assignment, reclaims unused addresses, and avoids UIP address conflicts.

6. To find a rogue DHCP server on your local subnet, use the getpacket option of the ipconfig command to get the IP address of the rogue DHCP server. Then use the arp -a command to find the MAC address that corresponds to the IP address of the rogue server.

7. Use multihoming to configure more than one IP address for each network interface. In the Network pane of System Preferences, you can choose active ports, add a new port, and configure a port with a new IP address.

24

Time   This lesson takes approximately 1 hour to complete.

Goals   Understand the content of hostconfig, NetworkInterfaces.plist, and preferences.plist files

Understand the architecture of configd and the different plug-ins associated with it, and identify their functions

Use ifconfig to identify the computer's network interfaces and their attributes

Understand the importance of lookupd and how it impacts networking

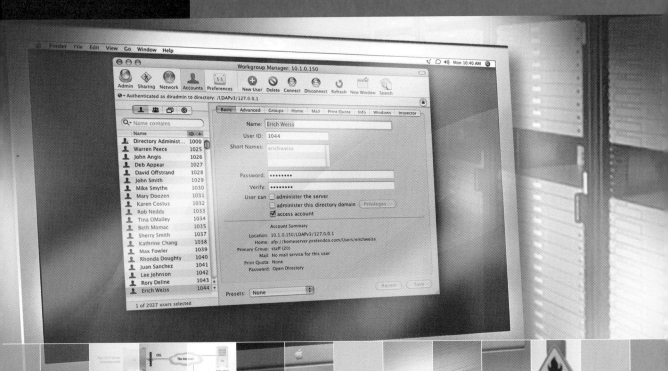

Mac OS X Network Architecture

To be an effective system administrator, you need to effectively configure, administer, and troubleshoot Mac OS X on a network. This lesson presents the underlying network architecture of Mac OS X, which is the foundational to everything else you will do with a Mac OS X computer.

In Lesson 22, "Unmanaged Networking," you saw how various processes such as Bonjour handle networking without management. And in Lesson 23, "IP Networks and Services," you reviewed domain name system (DNS), Dynamic Host Configuration Protocol (DHCP), and Internet Protocol version 6 (IPv6) to understand how managed networking works in Mac OS X. With this lesson, you'll go behind the scenes of Mac OS X to gain a deeper understanding of how networking works.

Networking in Mac OS X

Networking in Mac OS X is designed to be robust, dynamic, and easy to configure, primarily through the Network pane of System Preferences.

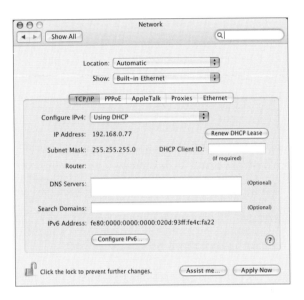

Users can configure multiple IP addresses per interface, as well as multiple protocols per interface, from the Network preferences pane without any command-line intervention. The infrastructure allows a user to switch between sets of configuration settings stored as locations. In addition, the infrastructure senses changes (such as an Ethernet link becoming inactive) and provides for an automatic mechanism to use another interface (such as an AirPort connection). All of these changes can be made without rebooting, and most occur with little or no user intervention.

These features make network configuration in Mac OS X easy, and they manage much of the complexity for users. System administrators, however, need a deeper level of understanding. What occurs when you make changes and click the Apply Now button? Where is network configuration information stored? What mechanisms are in place that provide the dynamic configuration infrastructure?

In traditional UNIX-based operating systems, ifconfig is used to configure interfaces, and calls to ifconfig are present in the system's startup script to configure the interfaces at boot time. Although ifconfig is present and operative in Mac OS X, it is not advisable to use it to configure a network interface because Mac OS X provides a more dynamic configuration infrastructure. Further, ifconfig should be used only to view network information and not to edit that information.

Understanding Networking Architecture

Although the System preferences pane provides a simple interface for a user to make changes to Mac OS X, configuration elements appear throughout the file system.

The Mac OS X kernel provides the hardware interaction with drivers that allow the computer to communicate with network interface cards, such as an Ethernet adapter or an AirPort card. In addition, the kernel allows a Mac OS X computer to communicate using standard TCP/IP, with support for various low-level features, such as IP addressing and IP packet filtering and forwarding.

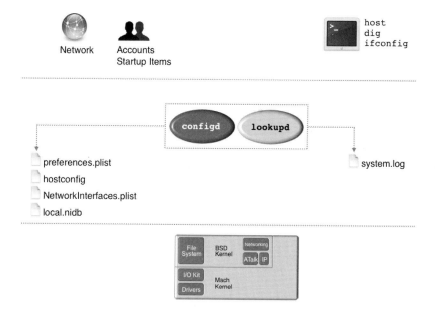

Key processes serve to dynamically configure the system and to perform DNS name service for name-to–IP address and IP address–to-name resolutions. This DNS name service is critical on a TCP/IP network.

Text-based configuration files and the local NetInfo database are used by Mac OS X to store its configuration information. The system.log log file holds records of the activity of daemons such as configd.

Finally, several scripts help keep preferred network settings consistent across reboots. These scripts are used to start services and can be found in /System/Library/StartupItems/ and /System/Library/LaunchDaemons/. launchd uses the configuration files found in the LaunchDaemons directory to start network services such as sshd for remote access to your computer. The files in the StartupItems directory provide an alternative way to start certain services. One such startup item is AppleShare for starting Apple File Sharing services.

The Kernel's Role in Networking

The kernel in Mac OS X is Darwin. Network Kernel Extensions (NKEs) have been added to the BSD Kernel component to implement additional capabilities beyond the basic TCP/IP stack. The Mach Kernel component of Darwin contains the I/O Kit to control network interface access.

NKEs provide a way to extend and modify the networking infrastructure of Mac OS X dynamically, without recompiling or relinking the kernel. The effect is immediate and does not require rebooting the kernel.

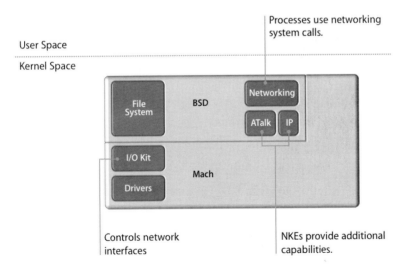

Use System Profiler and kextstat to view kernel extensions currently loaded in the kernel. Use kextload to load a new kernel extension. This command loads and starts a kernel file by loading moduleﬁle into the kernel and starting its execution. Use kextunload to stop and unload a kernel module previously loaded with kextload.

Networking system calls access the kernel through the networking level. Mac OS X supports both TCP/IP and AppleTalk. The Mac OS X IP stack implementation includes the following implementation and tuning parameters:

▶ Transmission Control Protocol (TCP)

▶ User Datagram Protocol (UDP)

▶ Address Resolution Protocol (ARP)

▶ Internet Protocol (IP), including packet forwarding over multiple network interfaces

▶ Internet Control Message Protocol (ICMP), for network maintenance and debugging TCP

Functionality such as IP forwarding, IP filtering, and multihoming is supported in the TCP/IP networking stack.

IP Address Resolution

Once the system has a valid network configuration, users will want to get the most out of their connection. Users often rely on name-to-IP address resolution to make access to network resources such as mail, Web, and file servers simple and convenient. lookupd is Mac OS X's primary DNS resolver. Applications such as Safari and Mail rely on the operating system for name-to-IP address resolution, and lookupd provides the resolution the applications and the operating system need.

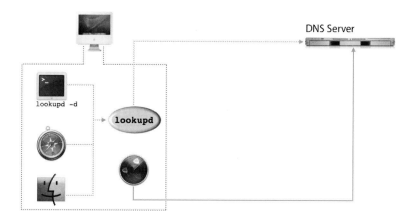

host and dig bypass both the operating system and lookupd, and query the configured DNS server directly. Keep this in mind as you employ either of these tools. Their output is invaluable, as they show how the configured DNS server is responding to a specific request. However, their output does not show how the operating system is resolving the lookup.

Only lookupd can show you how the operating system and running applications are resolving lookups. The system may be configured to use additional sources for host-names outside a traditional external DNS server, such as a local hosts file or dynamic hostnames populated by Bonjour.

To query lookupd, start with the command lookupd –d. This will begin an interactive session with lookupd. To look up hosts, use this command:

    hostWithName: *domain_name*

where *domain_name* is the domain address you want to look up.

Dynamic Network Configuration

To get a better understanding of the Mac OS X network architecture, you need to see how the pieces fit together. Look at what happens when you make a network setting change.

1. You make a change to the TCP/IP settings of the default Ethernet port in the Network preferences pane, and click Apply.

2. System Preferences writes to the preferences.plist file at /Library/Preferences/SystemConfiguration/preferences.plist.

3. System Preferences also notifies configd's Preference Monitor that preferences.plist has changed.

4. Preferences Monitor reads the current set and determines the changes. It then changes the information stored in configd. (configd is a daemon, and therefore is always running.)

5. The IP Configuration Agent receives the notification of the changes from configd and adjusts the configuration of any interface (starting DHCP, probing for an IP address collision, and so forth).

> **NOTE** ▶ Although these agents exist in bundles, they are hard coded into configd.

6. If you had changed settings for the built-in modem, the PPP Controller would have been notified of changes relevant to PPP connections.

7. If the order or availability of interfaces changes, the IP Monitor reevaluates which interface should be set as the primary interface and makes a change if necessary.

8. Finally, configd will restart lookupd so that changes in the DNS settings are applied to the entire operating system.

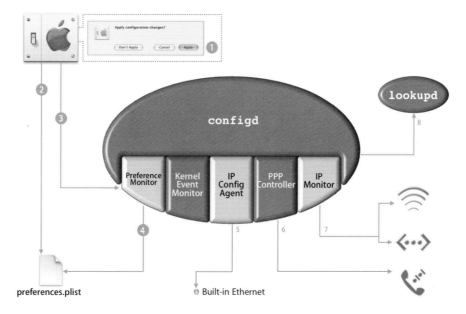

Adapting to External Changes

Networking is dynamic in nature. Let's look at an example of how Mac OS X adapts to an external change.

1. Someone unplugs the Ethernet cable.

2. configd's Kernel Event Monitor notices the interface's link has changed—in this case, it has gone down—and notifies configd of the change in state.

3. configd notifies the IP Configuration Agent of the change, and the IP Configuration Agent takes the interface offline. If the modem connection had been terminated, the PPP Controller would have been notified.

4. Because the availability of an interface has changed, the IP Monitor reevaluates which interface should be set as the primary interface and makes a change to the routing table, if warranted.

5. Finally, configd will restart lookupd to ensure that the correct DNS settings are now in place for the current network configuration.

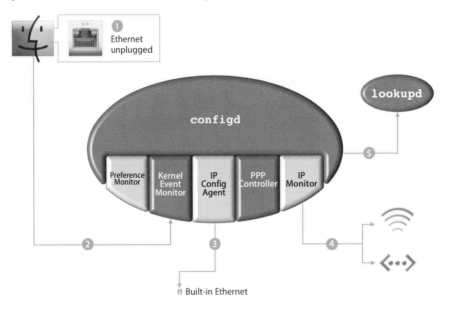

Using ifconfig

Mac OS X includes the standard UNIX tool for configuring network interfaces, ifconfig. Both ifconfig and System Preferences make system calls to change the interface configuration. However, ifconfig and System Preferences do not communicate with each other.

```
en0: flags=8863<UP,BROADCAST,SMART,RUNNING,SIMPLEX,MULTICAST> mtu 1500
        inet6 fe80::203:93ff:fed4:d816 prefixlen 64 scopeid 0x4
        inet 17.197.35.196 netmask 0xfffffc00 broadcast 17.197.35.255
        ether 00:03:93:d4:d8:16
        media: autoselect (100baseTX <half-duplex>) status: active
        supported media: none autoselect 10baseT/UTP <half-duplex> 10baseT/
UTP <full-duplex> 10baseT/UTP <full-duplex,hw-loopback> 100baseTX <half-duplex>
100baseTX <full-duplex> 100baseTX
```

WARNING ▶ ifconfig changes the network interface settings. If you use ifconfig, your system will be out of sync and will revert back to the contents of preferences.plist after a reboot. Also, while the terminal may be able to communicate with the network after editing with ifconfig, GUI applications may not work. This is why ifconfig should not be used to edit network configurations.

In early versions of Mac OS X, ifconfig was the only way to set the speed and duplex of a particular interface manually. As you learned in the previous lesson, users can now adjust their speed and duplex settings directly within System Preferences. These changes are written to preferences.plist and incorporated as a variable in a network location.

This new feature does not make ifconfig obsolete. ifconfig is the only way to view the entire interface configuration in one place, allowing easy examination of the current duplex state, speed, and MTU settings. This is particularly beneficial when your system is using an auto-negotiated Ethernet connection.

NOTE ▶ Duplex mismatches are a common cause of poor network performance and connectivity issues. When troubleshooting network issues, make sure to run ifconfig and verify that the problem is not auto-negotiation.

Configuration Data

The majority of network configuration information is stored in preferences.plist. This file contains the various sets of configuration information that a user creates, such as different locations and interface configurations. NetworkInterfaces.plist is a database that gives persistent names to network interfaces. Both of these configuration files are unique to Mac OS X and are located in /Library/Preferences/SystemConfiguration.

One important note about hostconfig: Not all the information in hostconfig is useful, as some parameters are no longer used. In particular, the ROUTER property is still present yet has no function. It's a legacy attribute.

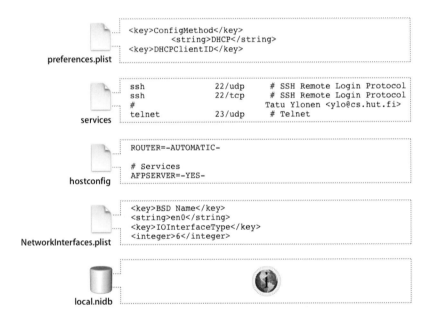

```
preferences.plist
          <key>ConfigMethod</key>
                    <string>DHCP</string>
          <key>DHCPClientID</key>
```

```
services
          ssh          22/udp      # SSH Remote Login Protocol
          ssh          22/tcp      # SSH Remote Login Protocol
          #                        Tatu Ylonen <ylo@cs.hut.fi>
          telnet       23/udp      # Telnet
```

```
hostconfig
          ROUTER=-AUTOMATIC-

          # Services
          AFPSERVER=-YES-
```

```
NetworkInterfaces.plist
          <key>BSD Name</key>
          <string>en0</string>
          <key>IOInterfaceType</key>
          <integer>6</integer>
```

```
local.nidb
```

The /etc/hostconfig file is a standard UNIX configuration file and contains information about the status of some services. In addition, the /etc/hostconfig file contains network configuration information. The /etc/services file is a text file that contains the default port numbers designated to different services registered with the Internet Assigned Numbers Authority (IANA).

Some network configuration information is stored in the local NetInfo database, local.nidb. Note that the contents are not plaintext, so you need a tool such as NetInfo Manager or one of the NetInfo command-line tools to edit the local NetInfo database, such as nicl or dscl. It is important to back up the local NetInfo database along with the other configuration files. The local.nidb database is located in /var/db/netinfo.

> **WARNING** ▶ It is best to maintain these files through System Preferences. If you make mistakes when you edit the configuration files manually, it may cause your system to be unstable and will be difficult to troubleshoot.

What You've Learned

▶ The Mac OS X network architecture is one of its unique aspects compared with other UNIX-like operating systems.

▶ The Mac OS X Darwin kernel provides low-level networking support.

▶ Users maintain the configuration of network settings in Mac OS X using System Preferences.

▶ configd is a daemon that facilitates the dynamic nature of Mac OS X networking.

▶ Most configuration information is stored in preferences.plist.

▶ lookupd is the DNS resolver for Mac OS X.

▶ ifconfig can be useful when troubleshooting or checking current settings.

References

Books

Albitz, Paul, and Liu, Cricket. *DNS and BIND,* 4th ed. (O'Reilly, 2001).

URLs

"Introduction to System Configuration Programming Guidelines": http://developer. apple.com/documentation/Networking/Conceptual/SystemConfigFrameworks

Lesson Review

1.   What files contain the network configuration information for your Mac OS X computer?

2.   What daemon maintains dynamic network configuration information?

3.   Describe the function of the IP Configuration Agent.

4.   What is the purpose of lookupd?

Answers

1.   preferences.plist, hostconfig, NetworkInterfaces.plist, and local.nidb

2.   configd

3.   The IP Configuration Agent asks configd to notify it of any changes to IP-related settings. When such a change occurs, the IP Configuration Agent gets the changed information from configd and uses system calls to update the interface configuration information in the kernel.

4.   lookupd is the primary DNS resolver for Mac OS X.

25

Time	This lesson takes approximately 1 hour to complete.
Goals	Understand which aspects of the system processes to monitor on a regular basis
	Monitor and troubleshoot the system with Mac OS X applications and command-line applications
	Use cron to automate log monitoring
	Use startup scripts to monitor systems
	Build a startup script

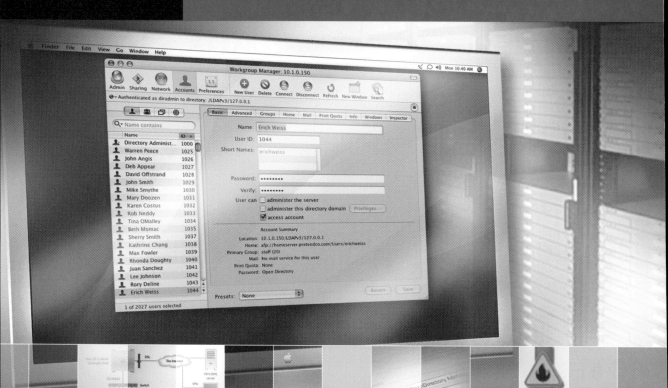

Lesson **25**

Resolving Network System Issues

In an enterprise environment, network reliability and maintenance determine how effectively your end users can work without network downtime. Your skill at monitoring and troubleshooting network issues will serve as a primary factor in sustaining the overall health of your enterprise computing environment. In other words, you troubleshoot situations as they arise, and monitor your network to catch them before they spiral out of control.

In this lesson, you'll learn to use a particular methodology and set of tools to troubleshoot Mac OS X–related issues. In addition, you'll learn to use Mac OS X utilities and command-line tools to monitor network activity. While this lesson focuses on monitoring and troubleshooting network issues, many of the concepts also apply to other issues, such as local file services, printing, and directory services.

Troubleshooting a Network

The following figure shows a network that has several problems: Computers on the network can't access the Internet; the domain name system (DNS) server is down; some computers can't see the other computers on the network because they are getting their Internet Protocol (IP) addresses and DNS information from an unsanctioned Dynamic Host Configuration Protocol (DHCP) server; and a Mac OS X computer (in this case, the iMac) has some services like File Transfer Protocol (FTP) and remote login turned on. In this lesson, you'll learn how to troubleshoot these issues.

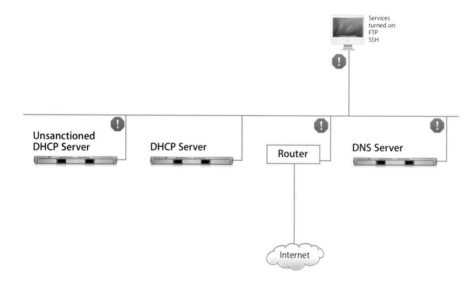

Establishing a Methodology

The following flowchart, which provides a framework for the network troubleshooting process, is a condensed version of the Apple General Troubleshooting Flowchart.

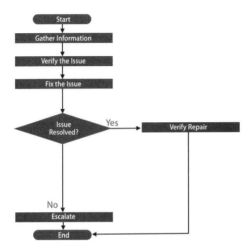

Gather Information

The first step in this process is to gather information about the issue. You're trying to establish its exact nature by getting as much information as possible. For example, you may find that the symptom the end user is reporting has stopped the user but has nothing to do with the underlying issue. Initial reports may be misleading. "I can't connect to the Internet" is meaningless until you have more information.

To ensure that you have the best possible understanding of the report, ask a mix of open-ended and yes/no questions. Keep in mind that your end user may not have an understanding of networking in general and almost certainly does not know your network architecture. The following questions are useful:

▶ Did things work at one point but suddenly stop working, or is this the first time you've tried to do this?

▶ Do you know if anything changed recently on your system or in your settings? What is that?

▶ Have you installed all current updates from Software Update (particularly any security updates)?

▶ When did the issue first appear?

▶ Is anyone else in the area having a similar issue?

▶ Is the issue constant or intermittent?

▶   Does it occur in only one application?

▶   Does it persist if you restart?

You should resist jumping to conclusions or making suggestions based only on the answer to one or two questions. While these suggestions might keep your users at bay for a short time or even temporarily cure the symptom, you still have not identified the cause.

When you are gathering information, don't hesitate to request logs or System Profiler reports. You can also log in to the remote computer to view relevant log entries or run System Profiler remotely.

Verify the Issue

The next step is to verify the issue. Ask yourself if you recognize the issue, log in to the remote computer, and try to reproduce it there. Walk your end user through the process and see if you can identify where the issue recurs. Use Apple Knowledge Base documents at www.apple.com/support as a reference.

When you have completed the information-gathering and verification steps, you should have enough information to try a fix. Evaluate the nature of the issue: Is it local to this machine, specific to the network, or specific to a particular server?

> **NOTE** ▶ Fixing the issue may involve network configuration on servers that you do not control, so you'll want to discuss the issue with other system administrators in your organization.

When you are ready to try a fix, start by isolating as much as possible. Eliminate possible sources. Narrow your scope from general topics ("the network is slow") to specifics ("the network is slow when browsing specific websites using specific machines"). Often the answer will reveal itself without your having to make major changes to the network. In any case, before making any changes, consult with your network architect or a senior system administrator to double-check your reasoning.

Fix the Issue

Once you have established and verified the issue and have a solution in mind, apply the appropriate fix. Evaluate the fix to see whether it resolves the issue, and pay special attention to ensure that you have not introduced network instability or new issues for other end users. Give yourself a time frame for evaluating the results: In most cases, if the issue goes away for more than 24 hours, it is resolved.

Finally, if you reach the point where you have evaluated several solutions and none of your fixes have worked, reevaluate your reasoning. If you can't find a flaw in your approach, or you don't find a fresh approach, escalate the issue to a senior system administrator or your network architect.

Troubleshooting Network Access

When a computer cannot access other computers on the network, first check the physical connection. Many network problems stem from loose or incorrectly wired cables. To thoroughly check the physical connection between two machines, you may need to check a series of switches for activation lights.

If the physical connection is active and you are working in a DHCP network environment, see whether the computer received a valid IP address and subnet mask from the DHCP server. Also check whether the computer can use Bonjour connections to servers.

You can also use several command-line tools to troubleshoot connectivity, as illustrated in the following figure.

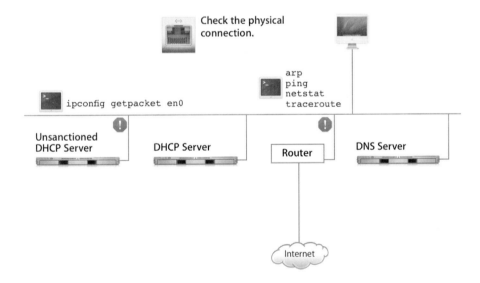

Here are detailed descriptions of the command-line tools you can use to troubleshoot connectivity:

▶ ping: Use this command to send packets to hosts on the network and receive an answer in response. If you ping a host and don't receive packets back, ping another host that you know is up and running to determine whether the issue is limited to the host in question. When using ping, remember that firewalls might not allow the traffic that is generated by the ping command. If you suspect a firewall is causing a computer not to answer, use telnet or another command that may penetrate firewalls.

▶ traceroute: Use this command to determine whether you have a routing problem. You trace the route to a particular host to determine at what point the route stops functioning. In addition, use this command to determine whether you have a deadlock that causes packets to go back to the original host. Using this command, you can also determine whether there is congestion on the network by looking at how long it takes packets to get through.

▶ arp: Use this command to show what hosts in the local subnet are known and verify that there are no duplicate entries. The arp –a command displays a table that lists the addresses of the computers on your local subnet and their corresponding MAC addresses. If the arp output lists the other systems on your network, it means that your network card is functioning properly but you might have a routing problem.

▶ netstat –nr: Use this command to display the routing table. You want to make sure that the default destination defined in your routing table points to a gateway and that the gateway is accessible.

In the following example, the default destination points to the 192.168.1.1 gateway:

```
>netstat –nr
Routing tables
Internet:
Destination   Gateway       Flags    Refs    Use    Netif Expire
default       192.168.1.1   UGSc     9       3      en0
```

▶ scutil and ipconfig: Use these commands to show the state of your network configuration. You can also examine NetworkInterfaces.xml to look for any discrepancies. If you suspect that the source of the issue is an unsanctioned DHCP server, you can use the ipconfig –getpacket *interface* command (where *interface* is your network interface, such as en0) to display the last packet received from the DHCP server on your computer.

NOTE ▶ Some sites do not allow Internet Control Message Protocol (ICMP) traffic. This can hamper the troubleshooting effectiveness of ping and traceroute on those networks.

Troubleshooting DNS and Domain Names

If you determine that you have no problems accessing other computers on the network, but you cannot connect to hosts using their domain names, it is likely that the error lies with the domain name lookup process. The following figure illustrates that the problem likely lies with the DNS server.

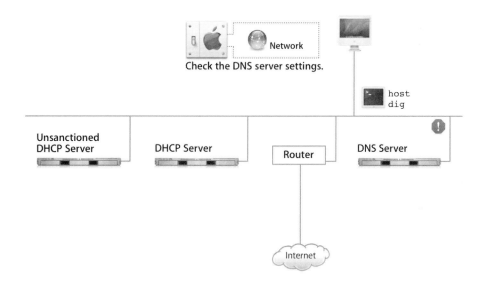

Make sure that the DNS server is properly set on the Network pane of System Preferences. Then use the following commands to figure out the issue:

▶ host: Use this command to perform a domain name lookup. If the command fails, it means either that the host you're trying to connect to doesn't have a valid DNS entry in the DNS zone files maintained by the DNS server, or that the DNS server is down. You can use the –a or –v option to get the entire DNS record.

▶ dig: This command performs a domain name lookup like host. In addition, this command displays the responses returned by the queried DNS servers. Analyzing the responses helps you determine whether the issue is the result of an error in the domain name's DNS entry or a missing entry for the domain.

▶ nslookup: This command is deprecated. Use host or dig instead.

Another useful tool to resolve names is lookupd –d (used with options hostWithname: or hostWithInternet Address:). Lesson 11, "Planning and Deploying Directory Services," covers lookupd in more detail.

> **NOTE ▶** You can also use the Lookup pane of the Network Utility tool to perform domain name lookups.

Troubleshooting Network Services

If you are running services on your computer, and other computers are having difficulty reaching your machine, as shown in the following figure, you should ensure that the services are configured properly. Check the configuration files for each process; in this case, you would first examine the /System/Library/LaunchDaemons directory. Try to connect to these services locally from your own machine, such as ssh *yourusername*@127.0.0.1. If the service does not allow you to connect, then there is an issue with the service running locally on your computer.

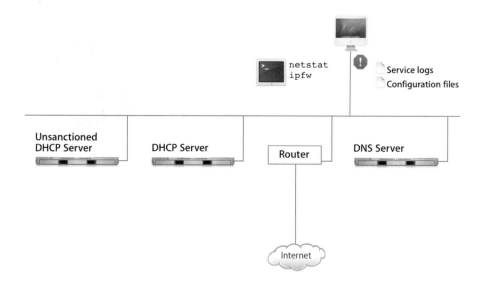

You can also use tools such as netstat, which allow you to see network statistics as well as the different sockets and ports that you have open on your machine. For example, the netstat –an command displays the state of the ports that are currently being used.

In the output, entries can contain one of the following keywords:

- ▶ LISTEN: Indicates that the port on your computer is listening for requests.
- ▶ ESTABLISHED: Indicates an established connection and shows the address of the connected system.
- ▶ CLOSED: Indicates that the port is closed and might explain why other systems can't access a particular service on your computer.
- ▶ CLOSE-WAIT: Indicates that a port is closed and is waiting for a defined period of time before returning to a LISTEN state (may indicate a Denial of Service attack).

When looking at the output of the netstat –an command, check for patterns that might indicate an issue. For example, if you notice that port 22 is being used by an unknown system when you know that only systems with certain IP addresses should be using the port, it is a sign of intrusion into your system. Also, if you notice that port 139 is closed when it's supposed to be open, it'll explain why Windows machines can't access your computer.

One way to quickly check the status of ports is to use the following command:

```
netstat –an | grep LISTEN
```

Another command to use to list processes listening for Internet connections is the following:

```
sudo lsof –i | grep LISTEN
```

This command lists all open Internet files. Each entry lists the process that has opened the file and the port on which it's listening.

Another thing to check when troubleshooting access to services is the firewall. Make sure that the firewall is not preventing other machines from connecting to you. You can use sudo ipfw list to see firewall rules or use the Firewall pane of System Preferences' Sharing preference pane.

Use grep to filter output to show rules based on whether they allow access or deny it:

```
sudo ipfw list |    grep allow
sudo ipfw list |    grep deny
```

You should also check service-specific log files and run any service in question in the foreground or in debug mode. Most log files are found in either /var/log/ or /Library/Logs/.

Monitoring a Network

As system administrator, you must monitor the use of the machines you administer to make sure that their performance is acceptable and detect issues early on.

To monitor network activity, you can use the tcpdump command, which returns information contained in packets sent and received by network interfaces on your computer, as illustrated in the following figure. In other words, tcpdump lets you monitor the network traffic going in and out of your computer.

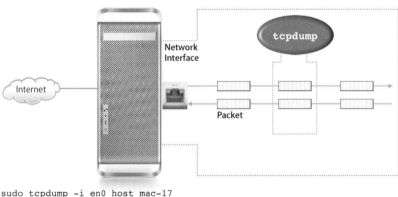

```
sudo tcpdump -i en0 host mac-17
sudo tcpdump -i en0 dst port 80
sudo tcpdump -i en0 -w DumpFile.dmp
tcpdump -r DumpFile.dmp
```

To run tcpdump, Mac OS X requires that you run the command as root using sudo. This requirement prevents unauthorized users from running tcpdump on your computer. Remember, packets can contain sensitive information, such as passwords and confidential information contained in email.

To use tcpdump effectively, you should determine what you're looking for to avoid having to sift through tons of irrelevant packets. To that end, tcpdump provides many options and allows you to use Boolean expressions. For example, to print all packets arriving at or departing from mac–17.pretendco.com, use the following command:

```
sudo tcpdump –i en0 host mac–17
```

Monitoring network traffic using tcpdump is useful in cases of Denial of Service attacks. For instance, you can use the following command to monitor all incoming traffic destined to port 80 on your computer:

```
sudo tcpdump –i en0 dst port 80
```

If you detect an unusual number of requests coming from the same source, you can use the firewall rules on your computer to block all traffic coming from that source.

> **NOTE ▶** You can create a script that takes output from tcpdump and analyzes it to detect attack patterns and alert the system administrator.

tcpdump is also useful when trying to determine whether packets are sent to the correct IP address and port.

When you run tcpdump, it will keep running until you stop it by pressing Control-C, using the kill command, or closing the Terminal window. If you stop tcpdump and close the Terminal window, you lose the packets that were captured. To store the packets in a file, use the –w option when running the command. For example:

```
sudo tcpdump –i en0 –w bonjour.dmp dst port 5297 or 5298
```

After you capture traffic, use the –r option to read the packets from the file:

```
sudo tcpdump –r bonjour.dmp
```

> **MORE INFO ▶** For more information about tcpdump, refer to its man page.

Using Ethereal

Ethereal is an open-source packet-sniffing tool that runs on an X Window system. This tool has a graphical user interface that lets you monitor packets in a user-friendly manner and offers features such as the ability to trace a set of related packets. In addition, it provides an easy way for creating filters (Boolean expressions) that you can use to display packets of interest.

To use Ethereal, you have to first install X11 for Mac OS X on your computer using the third Mac OS X installation DVD or the X11 package, which you can download from the Apple support website, www.apple.com/support. Once you have installed X11, locate, download, and install Ethereal from www.ethereal.com/download.html.

In addition to displaying packets, Ethereal has powerful analytical tools that display protocol hierarchy and capture options/output statistics, as shown in the following figures.

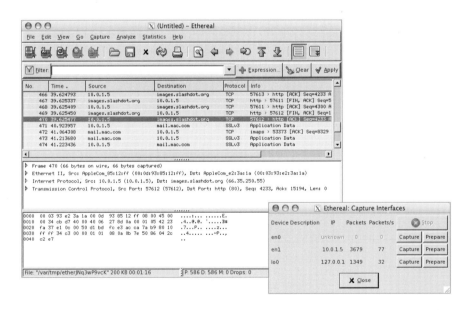

Monitoring Remotely

There will be times when you'll need to do remote monitoring. When a computer is physically remote (such as in a data center or another building) or simply inaccessible for some reason (they must be network accessible, of course), you will rely upon remote monitoring tools. Two of those tools are ssh, for remote login from the command line, and Apple Remote Desktop (ARD), for remote management through a Mac OS X application.

ARD has three features that are useful for remote monitoring. As shown in the following figure, it allows you to observe and control the remote computer to run monitoring tools, it can pass commands from the administration software to selected machines, and it can check network performance to get a more qualitative report from a remote computer. One issue with ARD is that it currently doesn't provide secure encrypted communications between computers, so it will be most useful within a corporate firewall.

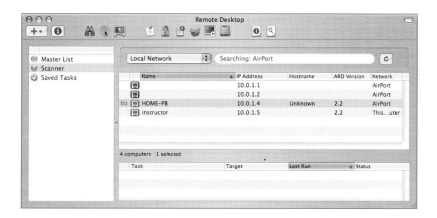

ssh, on the other hand, is a command-line tool that provides secure encrypted login, making it suitable for connections to computers located anywhere. Using ssh, you can run any command-line tool or script on any computer to which you have administration access, including useful tools such as system_profiler, tcpdump, and netstat.

Remote access to a Mac OS X computer using ARD and ssh is disabled by default. To enable remote access using these two methods, you must enable ARD and Remote Login in the Services pane of System Preferences' Sharing pane.

To start ARD via ssh, use the kickstart command. The following example shows how to activate ARD access for the user david and restart the processes:

```
$ sudo /System/Library/CoreServices/RemoteManagement/ARDAgent.app/Contents/Resources/
kickstart -activate -configure -access -on -users david -privs -all -restart -agent -menu
```

Monitoring With Log Files

Log files are an excellent source of information for troubleshooting and monitoring system and network activity. Log files might contain:

▶   More detailed information than what you see in error messages

▶   Informative messages that are not displayed anywhere else

▶   Progress messages

▶   Messages useful to a developer or technician assisting you with an issue

Commands and Tools

To monitor log activity, use Console, which provides a powerful search feature and allows you to add markers (log entries containing a timestamp) to separate log entries and make it easier to browse the log. You can also view logs using a text editor, however as shown in the following figure, Console makes it easy to view multiple log files while they are still being written to.

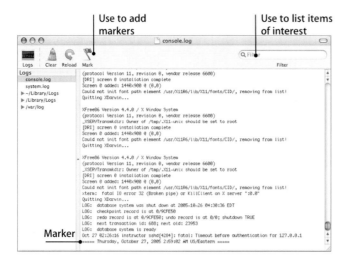

In addition to Console, you can use the tail –f command, which displays the contents of a log file. The command keeps running while it waits for additional entries, which the command displays as they are added to the log file. To stop the execution of tail –f, press Control-C or close the Terminal window in which the command is running.

When troubleshooting, you can use Console to log the sequence of events as you re-create the issue. The resulting log file can be useful in determining the cause of the issue.

To log a sequence of events:

1 Open the Console application, located in Applications/Utilities.

2 Click Logs in the toolbar.

3 Click the disclosure triangle next to a log to see more available logs.

4 Select the appropriate log and click Clear.

5 Perform the actions that produced the issue you are troubleshooting.

6 Read the messages that appear in the Console window.

> **NOTE ▶** If you don't understand the messages recorded in the log, you can still save the log file for a developer or technician helping you troubleshoot the issue.

When monitoring an activity, it's essential that you keep an eye on logs related to the activity. For example, if you've enabled FTP access to your computer and want to keep potential attackers from using it as a network storage device for illegal material, monitor the /var/log/ftp.log file regularly. You might detect that a host is continuously trying to access your computer at very short intervals (for example, every minute). In such a case, you would use the information in the FTP log to determine the source of the request and block it.

The following is a list of logs that you might want to monitor:

▶ /Library/Logs/console.log and /var/log/system.log: Use to monitor general system activity.

▶ /Library/Logs/Software Update.log: Use to determine whether important software updates have been performed.

▶ /var/log/daily.out: Use to get a daily synopsis of the state of a computer.

▶ /var/log/ftp.log: Use to monitor FTP activity.

▶ /var/log/httpd/access_log: Use to monitor personal Web sharing access activity.

▶   /var/log/httpd/error_log: Use to monitor failed Web sharing access attempts.

▶   /var/log/install.log: Use to monitor software installation activity.

▶   /var/log/ipfw.log: Use to monitor firewall activity.

▶   /var/log/mail.log: Use to monitor email activity.

▶   /Library/logs/panic.log: Use to monitor kernel panics.

The /etc/syslog.conf has information for the location of different log files.

Automation

One way to automate the process of log monitoring is to schedule commands or scripts that monitor log files to be executed automatically when a certain condition is met.

To automate the process of log monitoring:

1   Determine what you're looking for in a particular log file.

In almost all cases, you'll be looking for string patterns in log entries. For example, you might want to be notified every time the string "failed" appears in a log entry. The built-in command to use for finding patterns is grep. When searching a log file, grep returns the log entries that match the search criteria.

2   Determine the actions that must be performed when a certain condition is met.

For example, you might want an email sent to you every time the string "failed" appears in a log entry. You also might want to be emailed whenever a Denial of Service attack is detected.

3   Define the commands or scripts to run.

For example, if you want to be emailed whenever the string "failed" appears in an entry in system.log, use the following commands:

grep –i "failed" /var/log/system.log | mail –s "failed" david@pretendco.com

Here, the grep command finds the entries or lines in the log file that contain the string "failed login attempt." Then the output from the grep command is redirected as input to the mail command, which you use to send an email via postfix, the built-in program that Mail uses to send and receive email.

4   Schedule the running of commands or scripts.

The following is an example of a useful command combination to monitor the system profile to detect whether hardware components such as memory have been removed:

```
system_profiler SPHardwareDataType | grep –i memory
Memory: 256 MB
```

This command combination searches the output generated by system_profiler SPHardwareDataType, which returns only core hardware data, for the word *memory*, and displays the results. Using a data type with system_profiler, such as SPHardwareDataType, is more efficient because system_profiler fetches only the relevant data instead of all system data, which can take a long time. To get a list of all available data types, enter the following:

```
system_profiler –listDataTypes
```

Using Other Third-Party Tools

In addition to the built-in tools mentioned earlier such as tcpdump, Ethereal, tethereal, and Console, you can use a host of third-party tools to monitor network and log activity. These include:

▶ Little Snitch: This customizable tool notifies you when an application is attempting to connect to the network and/or the Internet. For more information, go to www.obdev.at/products/littlesnitch.

▶ MacSniffer: This packet-sniffing tool acts as a front end or graphical user interface for tcpdump. MacSniffer displays the information in an easy-to-read form and lets you filter through packets using a library of filters that you can customize. For more information about MacSniffer, go to http://personalpages.tds.net/~brian_hill/macsniffer.html.

Adding Monitoring to Startup Items

System startup items are folders containing scripts or other programs that prepare a Mac OS X computer for normal operation. While launchd has taken over much of the role of starting most services, startup items still have a place in Mac OS X. Some of the system startup items provided by Apple are located in /System/Library/StartupItems. You should not modify the items in this folder, however, you can define your own custom startup items and store them in /Library/StartupItems.

You can add specialized behavior to the booting sequence using startup items. To create a startup item, make a subdirectory named to describe the behavior you are providing, create a shell script or program that has the same name as the subdirectory, and create a file containing a property list and having the name StartupParameters.plist, as illustrated in the following figure.

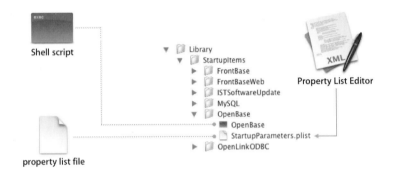

The StartupParameters.plist file must contain a set of key-value pairs that defines the startup item's provided services and its dependency relationships to other services. The name of the startup item (the folder and executable name) does not necessarily have to be the same as that of a provided service. For example, the script Apache in the folder Apache provides the service HTTP.

When SystemStarter processes a startup item, it looks for an executable file with the name of the containing folder and runs that file with the argument start during system startup. Currently, the start argument is always supplied, because startup items are executed only at system startup. Apple reserves the right to modify SystemStarter to invoke startup items at other times with other arguments. For example, startup items could be executed at system shutdown with an argument of stop.

If you have installed the Developer Tools package, you can use the Property List Editor application in /Developer/Applications/Utilities/ to create an XML-style property list for StartupParameters.plist.

Incorporating Login Hooks

The preferred way to set a login or logout hook is through use of the defaults command with the key LoginHook or LogoutHook and the path of a script as the value. For example:

```
sudo defaults write com.apple.loginwindow LoginHook /User/david/myscript
```

Alternatively, you can change the line in the /etc/ttys file that tells the system to launch loginwindow on the Console Terminal.

You can modify that line to add the following options to loginwindow:

Parameter	Description of value
–LoginHook	Path of the program to run when a user logs in
–LogoutHook	Path of the program to run when a user logs out
–HostName	Alternative name to display in the login window (can be empty)
–PowerOffDisabled	Disables the Shutdown and Restart buttons; same as Login preferences setting

Here is an example of a loginwindow line from the ttys file that uses the –LoginHook option to invoke a program whenever a user logs in:

```
console "/System/Library/CoreServices/loginwindow.app/Contents/MacOS/loginwindow –LoginHook
/Users/David/Scripts/mailLoginToAdmin" vt100 on secure onoption="/usr/libexec/getty std.9600"
```

What You've Learned

▶ The Apple General Troubleshooting Flowchart is an example of a well-defined troubleshooting methodology to use whenever you diagnose issues.

▶ Pick the tools that are most appropriate for the issue you are troubleshooting, whether they are network tools, system tools, or file-system tools.

▶ Early detection of suspicious activity or issues can eliminate or reduce the damage that might be incurred if things go undetected.

▶ Scripts are powerful tools you can use to automate functions you want performed on a regular basis, as well as to monitor your computer. Scripts are an integral part of any system administrator's repertoire.

▶ Mac OS X allows you to customize startup using startup items, which are scripts invoked at system startup, and through login hooks, which are scripts invoked when a user logs in from the login window.

References

Apple Knowledge Base Documents

The following Knowledge Base document (located at www.apple.com/support) provides further information about network issues.

Document 106796, "Mac OS X: Connect to the Internet, troubleshoot your Internet connection, and set up a small network"

Books

Orebaugh, Angela D. *Ethereal Packet Sniffing* (Syngress, 2004).

Sloan, Joseph. *Network Troubleshooting Tools,* 1st ed. (O'Reilly, 2001).

URLs

Mac OS X Downloads: www.apple.com/downloads/macosx

RFC 3164 (Syslog): www.faqs.org/rfcs/rfc3164.html

Network Troubleshooting Guide: http://support.3com.com/infodeli/tools/netmgt/tncsunix/product/091500/c1ovrvw.htm

Network Troubleshooting: http://compnetworking.about.com/cs/troubleshooting

Troubleshooting 101: "Lesson 7, Internet Issues": www.apple.com/support/mac101/help/7

Syslog—all about it: www.monitorware.com/en/topics/syslog

Syslog Discussion and Help Forum: www.syslog.org

Ethereal: www.ethereal.com

MacSniffer: http://personalpages.tds.net/~brian_hill/macsniffer.html

Logwatch: http://www.logwatch.org

"Introduction to System Startup Programming Topics": http://developer.apple.com/documentation/MacOSX/Conceptual/BPSystemStartup

Lesson Review

1. What's the importance of following a methodology when troubleshooting?

2. What are some tools or configuration files you can use to view the current network state and configuration for the Ethernet card?

3. One of your users is having performance issues logging in to her machine. What questions do you ask to help troubleshoot the situation?

4. What are the most important log files, and where are they located?

5. What's one way to automate log monitoring?

6. What are login hooks?

Answers

1. Following a methodology ensures that you ask the right questions at the right time and that you're able to troubleshoot in an effective and efficient manner.

2. A few are scutil, System Preferences, ipconfig, NetworkInterfaces.plist, and Network Utility.

3. Were you able to log on before, or is this the first time you've tried?

   Do you know if anything changed recently on your system or in your settings? What is that?

   Have you installed all current updates from Software Update (particularly any security updates)?

   Is anyone else in the area having a similar issue?

   Does the issue persist if you restart?

4. The system log found in /var/log/system.log; the console log found in /var/tmp/console.log; the panic log found in /Library/Logs/panic.log; and the install log found in /Library/Receipts/Mac OS X Log.txt.

5. Create a script that uses grep to detect patterns in logs and emails the results to you. Then, add an entry to the crontab file to run the script at a specific time interval.

6. Login hooks are used to customize login procedure. You can write scripts that can be run at login or logout.

26

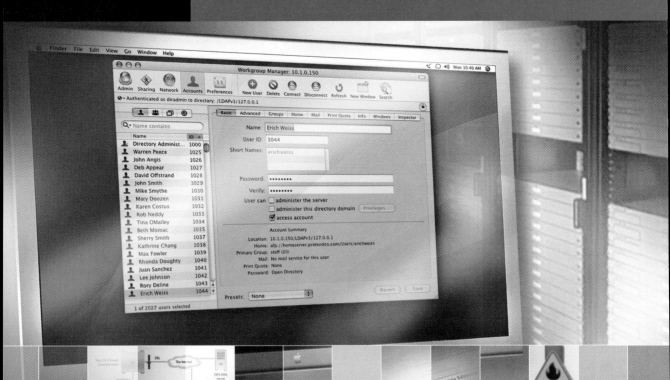

Maintaining Local Volumes and Files

Mac OS X supports several file-system types. In this lesson, the first of four focusing on file services, you will learn how the differences between these types can affect the experience of users and system administrators. For example, Mac OS X stores metadata differently on different file-system types, which affects the appearance and behavior of files.

Mac OS X has inherited features from UNIX, as well as from earlier versions of the operating system. Sometimes the UNIX features and Apple features are similar in purpose but different in behavior. This lesson covers symbolic links and aliases, which are also similar in purpose yet are different enough to possibly cause confusion.

Mac OS X keeps track of mounted volumes by means of disk arbitration, another topic focused on in this lesson, and you'll learn to update that information from the command line. You will also learn several command-line tools for monitoring and troubleshooting file systems.

Understanding File-System Formats

Mac OS X supports several file-system formats, whose characteristics are outlined in the following table.

	HFS Plus	UFS	MS-DOS
Compatible OS	Mac OS	UNIX	Windows
Case treatment	Case preserving by default Case sensitive available	Sensitive	Preserving
Forked file support	Yes	No	No
Journaling	Yes by default May be disabled	No	No
OK as Mac OS X Server boot volume	Yes	No	No
Visible to Mac OS 9	Yes, if not case sensitive or journaled	No	No

▶   Hierarchical File System Plus (HFS Plus): This is the file-system type used on Mac OS 9 and earlier systems. It is also known as Mac OS Extended File System. In Mac OS X version 10.2, you could enable journaling on new or existing HFS Plus volumes using Disk Util. As of Mac OS X v10.3 and going forward, newly created HFS Plus file systems have journaling enabled by default.

Occasionally, HFS Plus causes problems with UNIX programs and shell scripts that assume case sensitivity. You can format a new HFS Plus volume as case-sensitive by using Disk Utility or diskutil from Terminal. Many third-party Mac applications do not work correctly with case-sensitive file systems, however, so you generally don't want to use a case-sensitive file system, especially on a Mac OS X boot volume.

▶ UNIX File System (UFS): This is similar to other UNIX file systems in that it is case-sensitive. The problem with UFS on Mac OS X is that it does not support forked files. For that reason, UFS is not recommended as the root volume on Mac OS X. Another feature of UFS is that Mac OS 9 cannot see UFS file systems. This can be an advantage because Mac OS 9 is less secure.

▶ MS-DOS: Mac OS X v10.3 and up also support the Windows disk format, MS-DOS (FAT). This feature allows you to use an external drive or flash memory device that was formatted for a Windows computer on your Mac OS X computer. Another Windows disk format, NTFS, is supported in read-only mode. Like UFS, Windows file systems do not support forked files.

▶ Other formats: Mac OS X supports the Andrew File System (AFS), a common networked file system that is particularly popular among educational institutions, with the help of a package available from openafs.org. It also supports the standard ISO 9660 format for CDs and DVDs.

Identifying Resource and Data Forks

Files on Mac OS X can be composed of two distinct halves called *forks*. Much more popular in the OS 9 days, resource forks were used to contain objectlike information such as icons, strings, and small chunks of code, while the data fork was used for unclassified raw data such as that involved in composing an image file. In Mac OS X, most files keep their data exclusively in the data fork, but resource forks are still used by older applications, and even by Mac OS X to store elements such as custom file icons.

Copying Forked Files on HFS Plus

When you use the graphical user interface to move files around, the File Manager built in to Mac OS X handles forked files automatically.

As of Mac OS X v10.4, most command-line utilities, such as cp, mv, and tar, now handle forked files properly. Previous versions of Mac OS X required command-line utilities that were designed for use with forked files. Two such commands—ditto (with the –rsrcFork option) and CpMac—were specifically written to handle forked files correctly. Though it is no longer necessary to use these utilities, ditto is still included on all Mac OS X systems. You must install the Developer Tools package to get CpMac, which will then be placed in the /Developer/Tools/ directory.

The following figure shows what happens when you copy files within an HFS Plus file system or between two such file systems using cp, tar, ditto –rsrcFork, or CpMac.

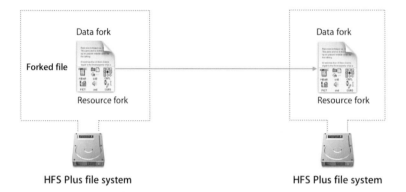

You can use a number of commands to check whether a file has a resource fork. If you need to check only for the existence of a resource fork, you can simply use the ls command. Normally you look at a long file listing with the –l option:

```
ls –l MyFile
–rw–r––r–– 1 david david 3624 Oct 20 22:02 MyFile
```

In the line above, the data fork is 3,624 bytes. You can examine the resource fork by looking at what acts like a hidden object inside the file, as follows:

```
ls –l MyFile/..namedfork/rsrc
–rw–r––r–– 1 david david 9928 Oct 20 22:02 MyFile/..namedfork/rsrc
```

Although it's redundant, you can also use this method to look specifically at the data fork, like this:

```
ls –l MyFile/..namedfork/data
–rw–r––r–– 1 david david 3624 Oct 20 22:02 MyFile/..namedfork/data
```

You can dump the contents of a resource fork by using the developer tool DeRez. Note that the Mac OS 9 application program SimpleText appears to be empty when you look at it with ls. All the content of this file is in the resource fork. Note that the output of DeRez is the same whether the file has a resource fork or a shadow file (shadow files are discussed in the next section).

Copying Forked Files to Other File Systems

When you use the Finder to move forked files to a file system that does not support forks, such as UFS, the File Manager puts the resource fork information into shadow files. A *shadow file* has the same name as the original file, with ._ prepended to its name. When you copy the file back to an HFS Plus file system, the File Manager re-creates the specific file forks.

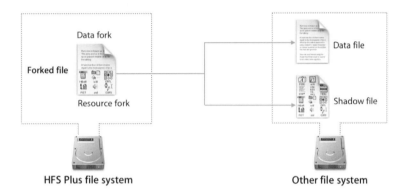

The same happens when you use ditto –rsrcFork or CpMac to copy files to and from a non–HFS Plus file system.

Copying Forked Files With Non-Mac Applications

In Mac OS X versions prior to v10.4, ordinary UNIX command-line utilities, such as cp and mv, were not designed to handle file forks or shadow files. When you used cp to copy forked files or files with shadow files, you lost the resource fork or shadow file. This was true whether the destination was HFS Plus or another file system. DeRez will also report that the copy has no resource fork and ls lists no shadow files.

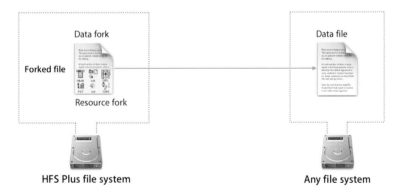

Similarly, applications on Windows computers were not designed to handle file forks or shadow files. This can be an issue if, for example, you transfer files back and forth between your Mac OS X computer and a Windows computer using a flash memory storage device. If you use the Finder or CpMac to copy the files to the device, the files will preserve their shadow files. But if you rename the files or move them around while the device is connected to the Windows computer, the shadow files are lost.

In some cases, you won't notice any problems if the resource fork is missing. In other cases, however, you may notice missing file information. Fonts may be absent from a document. Mac OS X might not know what application to use to open the file. In most cases, a file's custom icon will be replaced with a more generic icon.

Aliases and Symbolic Links

Sometimes you want users to be able to access a file by a different name, or from a different file-system location than the one in which it actually resides. You may have a script or program that depends on a file-system hierarchy that's different from what you have. You may have multiple versions of a document or folder and want a link called Latest to always point to the most current one.

You can use two types of files on Mac OS X to access files and folders indirectly. One is an alias, which you create in the Finder. The other is a symbolic link, which you create using the command line. Symbolic links are common on UNIX systems. Classic applications handle symbolic links correctly.

Some examples of symbolic links in Mac OS X exist because of an extra folder, called private, which was held over from NEXTSTEP. private contains other directories like etc, var, tmp, and Network. Mac OS X uses symbolic links for each of these folders and so the operating system thinks these folders actually exist at the root level of the boot volume, not one level deep inside private, where they actually exist.

Mac OS X makes liberal use of symbolic links. You can locate links using the find command:

```
find / –type l –ls
```

Aliases and symbolic links both act as pointers to files and folders, but their behavior is different. At the very basic level, the Finder understands both aliases and symbolic links but UNIX via the Terminal has no concept of aliases so they show up as a zero byte length file.

Using Aliases

You create an alias to a file or folder using Make Alias from the Finder's File menu. The following figure shows an alias to the folder AFP548. The arrow on the folder icon indicates it is an alias. If you use Get Info to display more information about the alias, you see that Kind is listed as Alias and that Original shows the location of the folder to which it points.

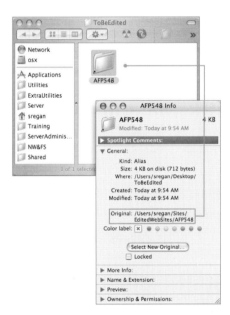

Move Original Files

If you move the original folder somewhere else—in this case, into the folder called EditedWebSites—and use Get Info to display information about the alias again, you'll see that the information has changed. Now Original shows the new location of the original folder. Mac OS X automatically updates aliases when the original file or folder is moved. Keep in mind that dragging a file or folder to the Trash is not deleting—it's moving it to the Trash. The file still exists, and an alias will continue to point to it.

Alias data is stored in the resource fork of a file. You can use the techniques discussed earlier to look at the resource fork of an alias. To see the raw data stored about an alias, issue the following command:

> /Developer/Tools/DeRez *YourAliasFile* –only alias

You can also get data using the strings command:

> strings *YourAliasFile*/..namedfork/rsrc

You'll see some of the path information in the output.

Delete and Replace Original Files

If, instead of moving the original folder, you delete it from the computer completely (for example, by using rm from Terminal), Get Info will show that the alias no longer points to anything. If you re-create the folder in the original location, the alias will point to the new folder.

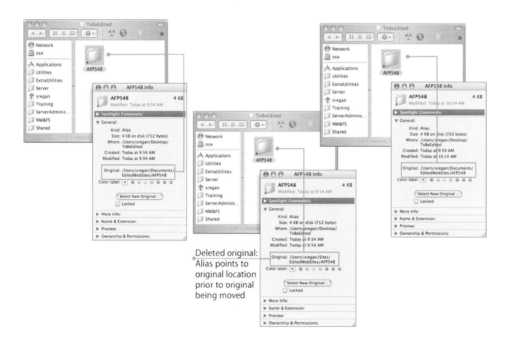

Deleted original: Alias points to original location prior to original being moved

In Mac OS X v10.1, alias resolution was based upon an HFS Plus identifier called the file ID. Starting with Mac OS X v10.2, alias resolution attempts to resolve the file pathname before attempting to resolve the alias using the file ID. This behavior corrects a problem in Mac OS X v10.1 that prevented aliases from working as expected on volumes restored from a backup copy.

Creating Symbolic Links

Symbolic links originated in the UNIX world. You create a symbolic link using ln with the –s option. In the following figure, a symbolic link is created to AFP548Site. A long listing shows what the link points to. Note that the file mode begins with the lowercase letter l.

```
$ ln -s AFP584Site AFP548Site_link
```

```
$ ls -l
drwxr-xr-x 2 david david 68 13 Jan 10:10 AFP584Site
lrwx------ 1 david david  8 13 Jan 10:12 AFP548Site_link -> AFP584Site
```

NOTE ▶ The above text is all on one line when viewed in the Terminal. We are unable to display it all on one line here.

```
$ ls -l AFP548Site/
total 56
-rw-r--r-- 1 david david   722 13 Jan 10:16 MyDoc.rtf
-rw-r--r-- 1 david david 21190 13 Jan 10:17 MyPhoto.jpg
$ ls -l AFP548Site_link/
total 56
-rw-r--r-- 1 david david   722 13 Jan 10:16 MyDoc.rtf
-rw-r--r-- 1 david david 21190 13 Jan 10:17 MyPhoto.jpg
```

Move Original Files

When you look at a symbolic link in the Finder, it looks just like an alias. In fact, if you use Get Info to display more information, you will see that Kind is listed as Alias and that Original shows the location of the original folder. But something different happens when you move the original file somewhere else, as illustrated by the following figure.

First of all, the link's icon changes (it may take a Finder refresh or a log out to see the icon change). Additionally, when you use Get Info, you see that it still points to a file that does not exist and it cannot be reassociated with another original here, as the button Select New Original cannot be chosen.

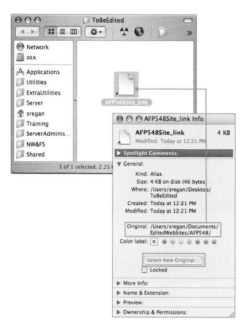

Symbolic links are not updated when you move the original file or folder. A symbolic link that no longer points to anything is called a *dangling symbolic link*.

> **NOTE** ▶ If you try to change folders from a dangling symbolic link using cd from the command line, you will get an error.

Re-create an Original Path

A symbolic link is set to a fixed path when it is created. If you move or delete the original file and then place another file at the original location, the symbolic link will point to the new file. This can be useful, because you do not have to re-create the link when you replace the file. This is very useful when you update the files upon which the links rely.

Comparing Alias and Symbolic Links

The following table summarizes the differences between aliases and symbolic links. It lists how each one is created, how it appears in the Finder and the command line, and what happens when you move the file or directory pointed to.

	Alias	Symbolic Link
Create with	Finder File Menu	ln –s
Finder shows	Icon with arrow Kind=Alias	Icon with arrow Kind=Alias
ln –s shows	Empty file	Leftmost letter = l link > original
Move original	Still points to original	After log out and log in dangling symbolic link
Move original and create new file in original location	Still points to original	Points to new file
Delete original	Dangling Alias	Dangling Symbolic Link
Delete original and create new file in original location	Points to new file	Points to new file

Mounting and Disk Arbitration

The disk arbitration daemon, diskarbitrationd, monitors disk connections and maintains a *disk arbitration table,* which is a list of disks available to graphical user interface applications such as the Finder. When you insert a disk or mount a file system from the Finder, diskarbitrationd probes the disk to determine its file-system format, checks the disk for issues, mounts the file system, and updates the disk arbitration table.

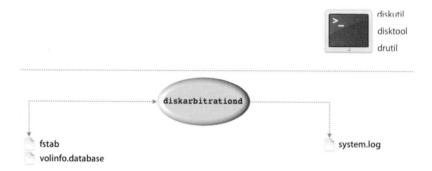

Using Commands

There are several commands that permit you to manage disk mounts and troubleshoot mounting issues.

disktool

Sometimes you need to update the disk arbitration table manually by using the command disktool –r. Although disktool is deprecated for most of its uses, it is still useful for refreshing the disk arbitration daemon. Use this command after mounting a disk drive or disk image from the command line. Although you can use disktool for much more, it's best to use diskutil for most features. Most features of disktool require root access to the volume. The disktool command has no man page. For more information, type *disktool* with no options.

diskutil

The diskutil command provides functionality similar to that of the Mac OS X application Disk Utility. You can use diskutil to mount and diskutil to unmount local disk volumes from the command line, so they disappear and reappear in the Finder. It can also be used for many other disk-related operations such as partitioning and erasing disks, conducting RAID maintenance, ejecting media, and much more. For more information, type *man diskutil.*

drutil

The drutil command lets you interact with attached CD and DVD burners. For example, you can use the tray command to open, close, and eject media. The command

```
drutil tray close –drive 1
```

closes the tray of the first burning device seen, if possible. The man page for drutil explains each of its options in great detail.

mount and umount

If you mount or unmount a local volume using the mount and umount commands, diskarbitrationd does not detect the disk. You typically use the mount and umount commands only for network volumes. In some cases, however, you might need to mount a local volume with mount to pass mount options that are not available with diskutil or disktool. For example, when you boot into single-user mode, you type */sbin/mount –uw /* to mount the root volume read-write. You should refresh disk arbitration with disktool –r after using the mount or umount command. You can use mount with no options to obtain a list of mounted volumes.

For more information, see the man pages for mount, mount_afp, mount_ftp, mount_hfs, mount_msdos, mount_nfs, mount_ntfs, mount_smbfs, mount_webdav, and umount.

Mounting With Files

Command-line tools are not the only way to deal with local mounts, though. Next we'll look at a couple of files that deal with mounted volumes.

volinfo.database

Mac OS X distinguishes between native HFS Plus volumes, which are present at startup, and removable volumes. The system keeps a list of native volumes in the file /var/db/ volinfo.database. Each volume in the list has a unique 64-bit volume identifier.

fstab

Mac OS X supports an fstab file so that you can mount file systems in particular locations at system startup. The format of the Mac OS X fstab file, however, is slightly different from that of other UNIX systems. Because of disk arbitration, the device files on Mac OS X are not static. You cannot create an fstab file to mount /dev/disk0s1 at /, because you have no guarantee that the mounted disk will be disk0s1 the next time the computer reboots. Instead, use the device label; for example:

LABEL=Disk2 /Disk2 hfs rw 0 0

Monitoring and Troubleshooting

This section describes some techniques for monitoring file systems and for correcting problems related to file systems. You will learn some techniques for dealing with dot files in folders you copy to Windows computers. You will learn how to use fsck to check a file system for issues and how to determine why a mounted local volume cannot be ejected. You will also learn two command-line utilities for determining file space utilization.

Dot Files in Windows

As you learned earlier in this lesson, Mac OS X folders sometimes contain shadow files. In addition, they often contain .DS_Store files. The Finder creates a file called .DS_Store in every folder it visits. The Finder uses the .DS_Store files to keep track of folder view options, icon positions, and other visual information about folders. You can safely delete these files.

When you copy a folder from your Mac OS X computer to a Windows computer, shadow files and .DS_Store files become visible, as the following figure illustrates, because the Windows graphical user interface does not hide filenames that begin with a period (dot).

If you want to delete the .DS_Store files before you transfer folders to a Windows computer, you can use a command in Terminal. For example, you could run the command

```
sudo find / –name ".DS_Store" –depth –exec rm {} \;
```

You could substitute –name "._*" in the command line to delete shadow files, but remember that you might want the shadow files if you copy the folder back to a Mac OS X computer.

Sometimes when you copy files back and forth between Mac OS X and Windows, files lose their custom icons. You can restore a file's custom icon if you have another file that has the same icon. Just copy and paste the icon from one Get Info window to another.

If you do not want these files to show up, add the following line to the Global section of the /etc/smb.conf file:

hide dot files = yes

The next time you start the computer or restart Windows file sharing, these files will not appear to Windows users.

Check for File-System Issues With fsck

A crash, power failure, or other sudden shutdown can render a nonjournaled file system unusable. The startup script, rc, runs fsck during system startup to repair such a situation.

If the volume is HFS or HFS Plus, the fsck command invokes fsck_hfs. By default, the fsck_hfs command does not check journaled HFS Plus file systems. Occasionally, however, a journaled HFS Plus file system becomes unusable during normal usage. You can use fsck_hfs –f to force the command to check and repair a journaled HFS Plus file system with the following commands:

```
$ sudo fsck_hfs /dev/disk0s2

fsck_hfs: Volume is journaled.  No checking performed.

fsck_hfs: Use the -f option to force checking.

$ sudo fsck_hfs -f /dev/disk0s2

** Checking HFS Plus volume.

** Checking Extents Overflow file.
```

To get fsck_msdos to run on a flash memory device, connect the device, then use the umount command to unmount it.

```
$ sudo fsck_msdos /dev/disk2s1

** Phase 1 - Read FAT

** Phase 2 - Check Cluster Chains

** Phase 3 - Checking Directories

** Phase 4 - Checking for Lost Files
```

The fsck command invokes fsck_msdos on MS-DOS file systems.

Getting Information About Open Files

Sometimes when you try to eject a disk, you get an error message such as "The disk 'Data' is in use and could not be ejected," as shown in the following figure. The best way to resolve this problem is to determine whether a file on the disk is open and, if so, close the file from the application or utility that opened it. If you don't know which application or utility is using a file on the disk, you can find out by using the lsof command.

daves-mac:~ david$ lsof /dev/disk1s2

COMMAND	PID	USER	FD	TYPE	DEVICE	SIZE/OFF	NODE	NAME
Finder	145	david	14r	VDIR	14,5	68	351	/Volumes/Data/ .Trashes/501
Finder	145	david	16r	VDIR	14,5	4182	35	/Volumes/Data/ com.apple.iChat .plist
Finder	145	david	18r	VDIR	14,5	714	2	/Volumes/Data

Run lsof as root (using sudo) to see processes you do not own. You can use grep to find processes using files on a specific volume. For example, if Preview is using file /Volume/Data/MyDir/MyFile.pdf, the output of

    sudo lsof | grep "/Volumes/Data"

might contain the following line:

    Preview 721 student17 54r VREG 14,15 448581 559 26 /Volumes/Data –– MyDir/MyFile.pdf

The command fs_usage is useful for showing which files an application uses. Type

sudo fs_usage | grep Application

where *Application* is the name of the application you are interested in. You will see all file-system activity related to that application, including the pathnames of files while they are being read or written.

Alternatively, to show files used by a specific process, use ps or Activity Monitor to get the process identifier (PID) of an executing application. Then type

sudo fs_usage pid

where *pid* is the PID of that application.

Getting Disk Usage Information

Use the df command to view disk capacity and the amount of free and available disk space on file systems. By default, values display in 512-byte blocks. Use the –h option to display values in a format that is easier to read, with unit suffixes such as kilobytes and megabytes instead of 512-byte blocks. Use the –l option to restrict output to local disks.

```
$ df -lh
Filesystem     Size    Used    Avail    Capacity    Mounted on
/dev/disk0s2   37G     13G     24G      36%         /
/dev/disk2s2   88G     44G     44G      50%         /Volumes/HD2
```

Use the du command to view the file-system block usage for each file specified as an argument. By default, every file in the hierarchy is listed under each folder argument. Use the –s option to get summary totals for folders. Use the –h option to display values in a format that is easier to read.

```
$ du -sh *
660K    Documents
108M    Library
8.0K    Movies
```

Disk space needs vary, depending on the types of files users store on disk. Movies, for example, can consume much more disk space than other types of files.

Computers shared by multiple users need more home folder space if home folders are local. You can use shared volumes for home folders. You can also use shared volumes for files that are accessed by multiple users instead of providing individual copies to each user.

Some jobs or businesses require more work space. Video files, for instance, might require more disk space.

What You've Learned

▶ The HFS Plus Mac OS X volume type differs from UFS and other supported types, particularly with respect to the handling of file forks.

▶ Mac OS X supports both aliases and symbolic links.

▶ The disk arbitration daemon keeps track of available disks.

▶ Use the find command to remove dot files that would show up on Windows machines connected to your file share.

▶ lsof will show you what processes are using currently open files.

▶ du and df are important tools for determining disk utilization.

References

Apple Knowledge Base Documents

The following Knowledge Base documents (located at www.apple.com/support) provide further information about local volumes and files.

Document 8647, "File System Specifications and Terms"

Document 25557, "Mac OS X: Mac OS Extended Format - Volume and File Limits"

Lesson Review

1. List some important differences between HFS Plus and UFS.

2. Is it safe to delete all of those dot files Windows users see when you save a file on a Windows file server?

3. What does diskarbitrationd do when you connect a USB storage device?

4. What is the main difference between an alias and a symbolic link?

5. What does the df command do?

Answers

1. HFS Plus is normally case-preserving but not case-sensitive. (A case-sensitive version is available.) HFS Plus provides native support for files with resource and data forks, and it is journaled by default on Mac OS X v10.3 and later. UFS is case-sensitive. It provides no native support for forked files. Journaling is not available for UFS.

2. No. Windows does not hide dot files the way most UNIX systems do. If the files are .DS_Store files, they are safe to delete as they contain only the icon position and other layout information for the Finder. However, resource fork shadow files (those that begin with ._) may not be safe to delete, as they may contain data belonging to the other half of that file.

3. diskarbitrationd probes the disk to determine its file-system format, checks the disk for unusable files, mounts the file system, and updates the disk arbitration table.

4. When you move the original file, the alias is updated to point to the new location. The symbolic link is not updated and is left dangling.

5. The df command displays disk capacity and the amount of free and available disk space on file systems.

27

Time

This lesson takes approximately 1 hour to complete.

Goals

Learn how file modes other than read and write can be used to implement file usage policies

Set and remove execute permissions on a script or program, and understand that the program cannot be run without the execute bit set

Set and remove execute (search) permission on a folder, and demonstrate the effect on a user's ability to list the contents of that folder

Use chmod to set the sticky bit on a folder, and understand that a user cannot delete or rename files owned by others in that folder

Use chflags to set flags

Understand what a umask is and what role it has in setting permissions policy for new files

Lesson **27**
File Permissions and Flags

By now you have learned how to set basic file and folder permissions. In this lesson, you will learn to set additional permissions from the command line, as well as how to set and clear a file lock using the Finder and the command line. You will also learn some monitoring and troubleshooting techniques, such as finding locked files or files with specific permissions, and using Disk Utility to repair permissions.

Understanding Permissions

On Mac OS X and other UNIX-based operating systems, files and folders have an attribute known as the *file permission mode*. This mode determines how the file's owner, group, and others may access the file. You can view the mode in a long ls listing. For example:

```
% ls -l
lrwxr-xr-x   1    david    david    5      7 Jan 09:57    DirLink -> MyDir
lrwxr-xr-x   1    david    david    6      7 Jan 09:57    FileLink -> MyFile
drwxr-xr-x   2    david    david    68     7 Jan 09:56    MyDir
-rw-r--r--   1    david    david    6      7 Jan 09:57    MyFile
-rw-rw-r--   1    david    david    498    7 Jan 09:58    NewFile
-rwxr-xr-x   1    david    david    369    7 Jan 09:59    Script
```

In a long ls listing, the leftmost character indicates the type of file: d for directory or folder, l for symbolic link, and - for a regular file. The next nine characters represent the file mode, which consists of three sets of three bits. The three sets correspond with Owner, Group, and Other permissions. The three bits in each set correspond with read (r), write (w), and execute (x) permission. A hyphen (-) replaces the r, w, or x character for permissions that are not set.

The following figure shows the correspondence between the information you see in the Finder's Get Info window and the information you see in a long ls listing.

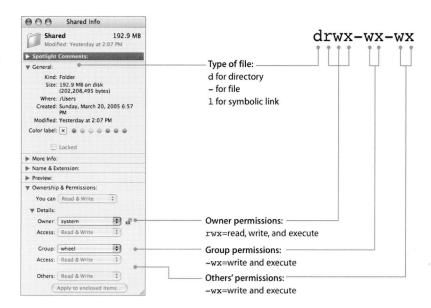

The Finder's Get Info window enables you to choose from three types of access permission on a file and four on a folder. The figure shows the available Finder permission choices and how they appear at the command line. Note that the Finder automatically sets x permission on a folder whenever you choose "Read only," "Read & Write," or "Write only" from the Finder.

File

Finder	Command Line
Read only	`r—`
Read & Write	`rw—`
No access	`———`

Directory

Finder	Command Line
Read only	`r—x`
Read & Write	`rwx`
Write only (Drop Box)	`—wx`
No access	`———`

If you use the command line to set permissions, other permission combinations are available.

> **NOTE** ▶ Copying files using the Finder may change their permissions, as viewed from the command line. When you create a new file from the command line on Mac OS X, the file's group is set to the group of the parent folder, even if the user who creates the file is not a member of that group. In some versions of UNIX, a file's group is set to the group of the user who creates the file.

Setting Permissions With chmod

You use the chmod (change mode) command to set the permission mode from the command line. Because "owner" and "other" both begin with the letter *o*, you use u (user) for owner permission.

The symbolic mode argument shown in the following figure consists of three characters, one from each table.

u	User
g	Group
o	Other
a	All three

+	Add
−	Remove
=	Equals

r	read
w	write
x	execute or search
s	setuid/setgid
t	sticky

You will learn about the setUID, setGID, and sticky bits later in this lesson. You will also learn about numeric and absolute arguments to the chmod command.

Why Set or Clear x Permission?

There are three cases in which you might find it useful to set or clear the x permission from the command line. You can:

▶ Allow or restrict execution of a program or script

▶ Restrict long listing of a folder while allowing short listing

▶ Restrict display of folder contents while allowing access to contents

To grant or deny program execution, set or clear the x permission:

```
student17$ ls -l Ascript;   ./Ascript
-rwxr--r--  1 david  david  29 14 Jan 11:15 Script
bash: ./AScript: Permission denied
```

To deny long but grant short directory listing, set r and clear x permission:

```
student17 $ ls -ld ADir;   ls -l ADir
drwxrw-r--  3 david  david  102 27 Jan 18:48 ADir
ls: Information.txt: Permission denied
```

To deny directory listing but grant file access by name, clear r and set x permission:

```
student17$ ls -ld ADir;    ls ADir;   cat ADir/Docz.txt
drwx--x--x  4 david david 106 28 Jan 14:42 ADir
ls: ADir: Permission denied
This is the contents of Docz.txt.
```

Grant or Deny x Permission on a File

To execute a program or shell script, you must have both r and x permission to it. When a programmer creates an application or command-line utility, the software that builds the program sets x permission automatically. When you create a script, you must set x permission on it with the chmod command.

As an administrator, you can deny x permission to restrict execution of a command to the file's owner or group. For example:

```
david$ ls -l shutdown
-r-sr-xr-- 1 root operator 20636 16 Nov 09:19 shutdown
david$ /sbin/shutdown
/sbin/shutdown: Permission denied.
```

Deny x and Grant r Permission on a Folder

Execute permission on a folder is sometimes called *search permission*. Without search permission, you cannot perform a long listing of the folder's contents. You can perform a short ls listing (as long as you have r permission to the folder), so you can view the file-names and copy the files.

As an administrator, you can prevent users from seeing the other information fields in the long listing by denying x permission. For example:

```
david$ ls -ld modetest
drwxrw-r--  3 root david 102 27 Oct 48 12:20 modetest
david$ ls modetest
Information.txt
david$ ls -l modetest
ls: Information.txt: Permission denied
```

Grant x and Deny r Permission on a Folder

A user who has x but not r permission on a folder cannot display the contents of that folder at all. The user can, however, access a file in that folder by name (if the user has r permission to the file).

This might be useful when an administrator wants to provide quick selective access to a file, without changing permissions on server folders, as opposed to a long-term strategy for providing selective access to files.

Granting x and denying r on a folder can be useful when you want to make a file available to a limited set of users—for example, to limit file access over FTP. Users who know the name of the file can get it, but other users cannot see the name in a folder listing. For example:

▶ I have x but not r permission to the folder:

```
david$ ls -ld noreaddir
drwx--x--x  4 root david 26 136 Sep 14:42 noreaddir
```

▶ I cannot list the folder contents:

```
david$ ls noreaddir
ls: noreaddir: Permission denied
```

▶ I can cat a file in the folder if I know its name:

```
david$ cat noreaddir/Documentxyz.txt
This is the contents of Documentxyz.txt.
```

Controlling File Deletion From a Folder

Users need write permission to a folder in order to add, delete, or rename a file. By denying w permission to a folder, you can prevent users from deleting files or adding files.

If you grant a user w permission to a folder:

▶ The user can create files in that folder.

▶ The user can delete files—even files owned by other users—in that folder.

Using the Sticky Bit

What if you want finer control than just one owner of a folder being able to delete everything? How do you allow users to add files to a folder, but prevent users from deleting each other's files from the folder? You set the *sticky* bit on the folder using chmod:

```
$ chmod +t MyDir
$ ls -ld MyDir
drwxrwxrwt 3 david david  102  Oct 28 16:27 MyDir/
```

NOTE ▶ You omit the u, g, and o when you set the sticky bit.

In the following example, user david owns a folder with the sticky bit set. Owner, group, and other all have rwx permission. User laura cannot delete user david's file.

```
laura$ ls -ld nodeldir
drwxrwxrwt 3 david david 102 28 Oct 16:27 nodeldir/
laura$ rm nodeldir/efile
override rw-r--r--  david/david for nodeldir/efile? y
rm: nodeldir/lfile: Operation not permitted
```

A user can remove or rename a file in a folder with the sticky bit set only if both of these statements are true:

▶ The user has write permission to the folder.

▶ The user is the owner of the file, the owner of the folder, or a system administrator.

Note that the sticky bit does not prevent a user from changing or overwriting another user's file. A user who has write permission to a file can change the contents of that file, even if the sticky bit is set on the folder. To prevent overwriting, users must deny write access to group and other on files they create.

NOTE ▶ On some versions of UNIX, new folders inherit the sticky bit from their parent folder. This is not true on Darwin/Mac OS X.

Starting a Process As a Different User

When a program has the setUID (set user ID on execution) bit set, that program always executes with the user ID of the owner of the file, regardless of who actually executes the program. In a long ls listing, a file with the setUID bit set has an s in place of an x in the owner (user) permissions.

A program with the setGID (set group ID on execution) bit set executes with the group ID of the file's group. In a long ls listing, a file with the setGID bit set has an s in place of an x in the group permissions.

In early UNIX, someone added a feature to mail so users could mail a file, but that person forgot that mail ran setUID to root. As a result, you could read any file, regardless of its permissions, by mailing it to yourself!

Modern programming techniques for eliminating flaws in setUID programs include privilege bracketing: Programmers use a system call to make some sections of the code run as root and other sections run as an unprivileged user.

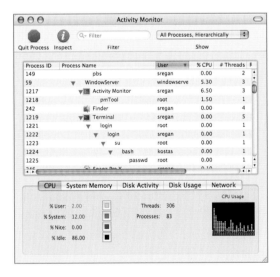

The setUID and setGID bits are important because some commands installed on your computer must run with the user or group ID of an administrator in order to perform their function. For example, the passwd command must execute as root to modify your user information when you change your password.

> **NOTE** ▶ If a program is installed with the setUID or setGID bit set, do not clear it!

If a program that runs as root contains a security flaw, a malicious user might be able to obtain root access to a computer by exploiting that flaw. Programmers try to eliminate vulnerabilities, but they don't always succeed. You can find examples of setUID-related security vulnerabilities by searching for setUID on the CERT webpage, www.cert.org. Mac OS X does not honor the setUID or setGID bit on shell scripts.

> **WARNING** ▶ Utilities on your computer rely on file permissions to prevent users from causing inadvertent or malicious damage. To avoid exposing your computer to malicious or inadvertent damage, do not set the setUID or setGID bit on utilities installed on your computer.

Set the SetUID and SetGID Bits

You set the setUID bit using the command chmod u+s *filename*. Clear the setUID bit using the command chmod u-s *filename*. Use g in place of u to set and clear the setGID bit.

A long ls listing shows the letter s in place of x in the owner bits for setUID. For example:

    -rwsr-xr-x 1 david david 60 20 Nov 17:52 myprogram

A long ls listing shows the letter s in place of x in the group bits for setUID. For example:

    -rwxr-sr-x 1 david david 60 20 Nov 17:52 myprogram

Using Numeric Arguments to chmod

You can set the mode of a file or folder by using numeric arguments to chmod. Numeric arguments enable you to set exactly the mode you want with just one command.

NOTE ▶ Don't recursively use chmod with numerical arguments on home directories. Use the textual method when you want to operate only on specific permissions categories (user, group, and other). The numerical method always sets all three categories, which is not appropriate for home directories.

In the following figure, the first table shows that the r, w, and x bits correspond with the values 4, 2, and 1. The second table shows the value of each triplet.

```
$ chmod 754 ~/bin
$ ls -ld ~/bin
drwxr-xr—  2 david david 68 Oct 28 17:01 bin
```

		Symbolic	Numeric
r	4	rwx	4+2+1=7
w	2	rw-	4+2=6
x	1	r-x	4+1=5
		r—	4
		-wx	2+1=3
		-w-	2
		—x	1
		—-	0

You can set the sticky bit on a folder by adding 1000 to the mode. For example,

```
$ chmod 1755 mydir
```

will set the permissions to

```
-rwxr-xr-t 1 david  david 68 Nov 20 20:28 mydir
```

You can set the setUID bit by adding 4000 to the mode. For example,

```
$ chmod 4755 myprog
```

will set the permissions to

```
-rwsr-xr-x  1 david  david 102 Nov 20 20:28 myprog
```

You can set the setGID bit by adding 2000 to the mode.

> **NOTE** ▶ Before you use numeric arguments to chmod, look at the current mode of the file or folder to be sure you do not inadvertently clear the sticky, setUID, or setGID bit.

Setting Permission Policy Within the Session: umask

The *umask* (user mask) masks the mode bits when you create a file or folder. The umask enables you to set a permission policy within a Terminal session.

For folder creation, subtract the umask from a maximum of 777 to see what the folder creation mode will be.

For file creation, subtract the umask from a maximum of 666 to see what the file creation mode will be.

For example, when the umask is 022, folders are created with mode 755 (drwxr-xr-x), and files are created with mode 644 (-rw-r--r--).

The umask command with no arguments lists the current umask. The default umask in Terminal is 022.

Use the umask command to set the umask within a session. You can omit leading zeros, so 22 is equivalent to 022 and 2 is equivalent to 002.

When the umask is 002, new folders you create have mode 775 (drwxrwxr-x), and new files have mode 664 (-rw-rw-r--). For example:

```
$ umask 002
$ umask
2
$ echo Test > testfile
$ mkdir testdir
$ ls -l
drwxrwxr-x    2     david     david     68     28 Oct 17:06     testdir
-rw-rw-r--    1     david     david     16     28 Oct 17:06     testfile
```

When you set the umask in Terminal, it is effective only for the session in which it is set. You can set the umask for all of your Terminal sessions by setting the umask in your .profile, .login, or .cshrc files.

Unfortunately, the defaults command uses decimal numbers, and umask values are octal numbers. To set a umask of 22, you would use the argument -int 18, not -int 22.

As administrator, you can set a global, systemwide umask by adding an umask command to the script /etc/rc. The umask will apply to the Finder and other graphical user interface programs, as well as the Terminal interface.

A user can set a per-user umask that applies to the Finder and other Utilities, as well as the Terminal interface, by using the defaults command. For example,

```
defaults write -g NSUmask -int 2
```

will set the umask to 002.

Understanding Access Control Lists

Access control lists (ACLs) are a new feature in Mac OS X v10.4. File-system ACLs provide a much more granular set of permissions options than the traditional UNIX permissions explained so far. In addition to more granular permissions, now you can also assign different permissions to different users or groups, where with traditional UNIX permissions, you were limited to setting permissions to only one user and one group. By default, file-system ACLs are disabled on volumes in Mac OS X. Before you can use ACLs, you must turn them on for that particular volume:

```
fsaclctl -p /Volumes/MyACLedDrive -e
```

To determine first if ACLs are already enabled on a volume, type *fsaclctl -p /Volumes/ MyACLedDrive*. If you're using Mac OS X Server, you can also use Workgroup Manager to turn on file-system ACLs, as seen in the following figure.

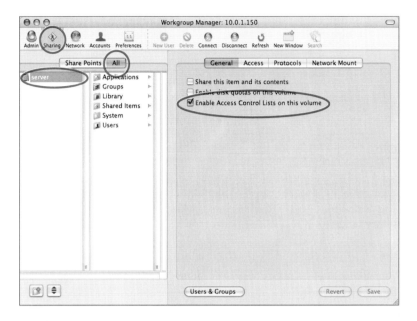

Once you've enabled ACLs for the volume, you must assign specific rights to a file. As with traditional UNIX permissions, you use the chmod command to do this, but you must add the +a argument.

Some examples include:

```
chmod +a "admin allow write" file1
chmod +a "guest deny read" file1
chmod +a "admin allow delete" file1
```

When you need to see what ACLs are attached to a given file, you use ls with the -le options:

```
ls -le file1
-rw-r--r--+ 1 juser  wheel  0 Apr 28 14:06 file1
owner: juser
1: guest deny read
2: admin allow write,delete
```

Workgroup Manager also makes the task of assigning and viewing ACLs easier, as shown in the following figure.

As you can imagine, ACLs get very confusing very quickly. Again, Workgroup Manager comes to the rescue with the Effective Permissions Inspector. Just select a file or folder in Workgroup Manager, pull down the gear menu in the lower-right corner, and select Show Effective Permissions Inspector. With this tool, you can type in any user name, and it will parse through all of the ACL entries—many of which may be overlapping—and show you quickly which permissions that specific user will have on that file or folder.

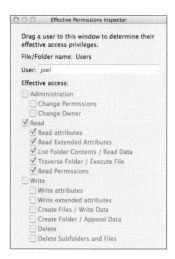

WARNING ▶ File-system ACLs are very complex and you should test them very carefully to ensure that you've set up the correct set of permissions.

Protecting Files With Flags

Sometimes you might need to ensure that no user, even the owner, inadvertently moves, changes, or deletes a certain file.

Mac OS X and other BSD-UNIX (Berkeley System Distribution) file systems support *flags,* in addition to permission modes. Flags help define what can be done to a file, such as deleting it or changing a symbolic link. The most important flag in Mac OS X is the uchg flag, which locks files. An ordinary user cannot change, move, or delete a file that has this flag set. The root user can override this flag, and the file owner can clear it.

If you set or clear the uchg flag from the command line, the Finder will update the icon the next time you click it.

The Finder uses the uchg flag to lock a file when you click Locked on the File Info window, as shown below. When you lock a file in the Finder, the file's icon changes to include a small lock image.

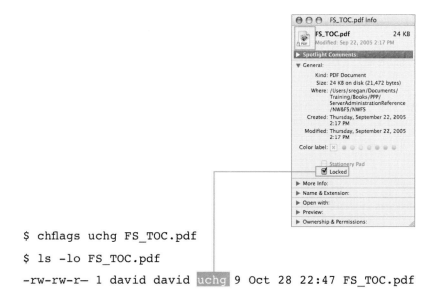

```
$ chflags uchg FS_TOC.pdf
$ ls -lo FS_TOC.pdf
-rw-rw-r— 1 david david uchg 9 Oct 28 22:47 FS_TOC.pdf
```

You can also set and clear the uchg flag from the command line. To set the flag from the command line, use

```
chflags uchg filename
```

If you have installed the developer tools, you can also use the SetFile command to set the uchg flag. Type */Developer/Tools/SetFile -a L filename.*

To list flags, type *ls -lo.* To clear the flag, type *chflags nouchg filename.*

This example shows the effect of the uchg flag:

```
$ rm Ffile
override rw-rw-r--  david/david uchg for Ffile? y
rm: Ffile : Operation not permitted
```

As the example shows, an ordinary user cannot delete a file with the uchg flag set. When the root user attempts to remove a file with the uchg flag set, the rm command automatically clears the uchg flag.

A file lock has no effect on the containing folder. That is, you can move a folder containing a file with the uchg flag set. As a result, locked files in folders moved to the Trash can cause problems later when you try to empty the Trash.

The chflags command and ls -o are unique to BSD variants of UNIX. Do not assume that all experienced UNIX system administrators know about them. Linux uses chattr and lsattr to set and view flags. Solaris has no equivalent.

> **WARNING ▶** A similar flag exists called schg that should generally never be used. If a file has the schg flag set, nobody can remove or modify the file, which will likely cause problems. Even system administrators and the root user can't modify the file. Unfortunately, this also means nobody can modify the flags of the file to remove the schg flag. If you do come upon a file with the schg flag set, you'll need to boot into single-user mode to remove it.

Monitoring and Troubleshooting Permissions and Flags

This section examines how to obtain information about permissions and flags and how to correct some common problems. You will learn how to use options to the find command to find files with specific permissions or flags set. You will also learn what Disk Utility's permission check does and does not do.

Finding Files by Permission Mode

You can use the -perm option to the find command to identify files with specific permissions. Specify +1000 to list folders with the sticky bit set. Specify +4000 to list setUID programs, +2000 to list setGID programs, and +6000 to list both.

For example, the following find command lines find setUID and setGID programs, respectively, and then perform a long listing on each one.

```
$ find . -perm +4000 -exec ls -l {} \;
-rwsr-xr-x  1 root  wheel  36516 23 Sep 23:39 ./ps
$ find . -perm +2000 -exec ls -l {} \;
-r-xr-sr-x  1 root  operator  23336 23 Sep 23:47 ./df
```

Finding Locked Files

Locked files in the Trash might cause the Finder's Empty Trash process to fail.

You can use the -flags option to the find command to identify files with specific flags set. Specify +uchg to list files locked with the uchg flag. For example:

```
$ cd /Applications/Adobe\ Acrobat\ 5.0/
$ find . -flags +uchg
./Distiller/Settings/eBook.joboptions
./Distiller/Settings/Press.joboptions
./Distiller/Settings/Print.joboptions
./Distiller/Settings/Screen.joboptions
```

Repairing Disk Permissions in Disk Utility

Occasionally a program or install package will modify permissions resulting in applications that are not running correctly. You can run Disk Utility to repair permissions on your system drive as a regular maintenance task.

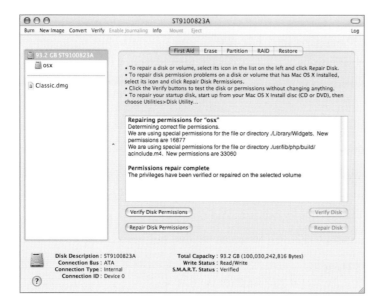

Disk Utility uses the receipts from the installation of Mac OS X or Mac OS X Server as a reference for file permissions. If files are not installed as part of an installer package, then Disk Utility will not be able to verify or repair the permissions on those files.

The permissions for installed files are stored in the bill of materials (BOM) files under /Library/Receipts. The Mac OS X installer uses a BOM to determine which files to install, remove, or upgrade. You can use the lsbom command to view the permissions in a BOM. For example:

```
$ lsbom -p ?Mf /library/Receipts/BSD.pkg/Contents/Archive.bom
root/admin   drwxrwxr-t    .
root/admin   drwxrwxr-x    ./Library
root/admin   drwxrwxr-x    ./Library/Documentation
root/admin   drwxrwxr-x    ./Library/Documentation/Commands
root/admin   drwxrwxr-x    ./Library/Documentation/Commands/bash
```

MORE INFO ▶ For more information on BOMs, see the man page for lsbom.

Because home folders are not part of any package, Disk Utility does not repair them. For example if the user changes permissions on files and folders they own, permissions on those will not be repaired.

What You've Learned

- ▶ Use the chmod command to set file and folder permissions from the command line.
- ▶ Some extra permissions not available from the Finder can be set from the command line.
- ▶ The umask controls default file permissions.
- ▶ You can lock or unlock files from the Finder or use the chflags command from the Terminal.
- ▶ Use the find command to find locked files and files with specific permissions.
- ▶ Disk Utility's permission check will return some, but not all, of the file permissions to their correct state.
- ▶ File-sytem ACLs are a powerful way to go beyond basic UNIX file permissions.

References

Administration Guides
"Mac OS X File Services Administration": http://images.apple.com/server/pdfs/File_Services_v10.4.pdf

Apple Knowledge Base Documents
The following Knowledge Base documents (located at www.apple.com/support) provide further information about file permissions and flags.

Document 106712, "Troubleshooting permissions issues in Mac OS X"

Document 302469, "Mac OS X: Resolving permissions (umask) issues in a server-based group folder environment"

URLs

File System Overview: http://developer.apple.com/documentation/MacOSX/Conceptual/
BPFileSystem/Articles/BSDInfluences.html#//apple_ref/doc/uid/20002286

Security Overview: Permissions: http://developer.apple.com/documentation/Security/
Conceptual/Security_Overview/Concepts/chapter_3_section_9.html

Grokking Darwin ACLs: www.afp548.com/article.php?story=20050506085817850&query=acls

UNIX Permissions Lesson and Quiz: www.lsa.umich.edu/lsait/admin/mac/PermQuiz.pdf

Lesson Review

1. Describe three useful folder permissions that you can set only from the command line.
2. Describe the difference between setUID and setGID.
3. You have rwx permission to a folder that has the sticky bit set. You are not the owner of the folder or the system administrator. You have rw- permission to another user's file in that folder. Can you delete the file? Can you edit the file?
4. You have written a script that uses the chflags command to lock and unlock files. You would like to use the script on other versions of UNIX. Will it work?

Answers

1. You can prevent users from seeing a long listing of a folder's contents by denying execute permission. If you set execute but not read permission on a folder, users who know the name of a file can get it, but other users cannot find it. If you set the sticky bit on a folder, a user may remove or rename files in that folder only if the user has write permission for the folder and the user is the owner of the file, the owner of the folder, or the system administrator.
2. When a program has the setUID bit set, that program always executes with the user ID of the owner of the file, regardless of who actually executes the program. A program with the setGID bit set executes with the group ID of the file's group.
3. You cannot delete the file, but you can edit it.
4. It should work on BSD-based versions of UNIX, but probably won't on other versions.

28

Time   This lesson takes approximately 1 hour to complete.

Goals   Identify the file-sharing services available in Mac OS X

Manipulate the configuration choices for personal file sharing

Locate specific contents of the smb.conf file and test them using
the testparm command

Differentiate between browsing for SMB services on Mac OS X
and Windows

Access an SMB service running on Mac OS X from a Windows computer

Connect to a shared FTP volume on a Mac OS X computer from Windows
and from UNIX and transfer files

Access FTP services from the command-line or using a Web browser

Network File Services

The last two lessons of this book focus on file sharing on Mac OS X. In this lesson, you'll learn about the three file-sharing services that Mac OS X provides, how to turn them on and off, and how to configure these services on your computer.

You will find out how to let users on other computers connect to yours using Apple Filing Protocol (AFP), Server Message Block (SMB), and File Transfer Protocol (FTP), and how to modify the behavior of the file-sharing service. Finally, you'll learn some monitoring and troubleshooting techniques.

Understanding Personal File Sharing

Personal File Sharing uses AFP. The process that provides AFP service is AppleFileServer. The executable file resides in /System/Library/CoreServices/AppleFileServer.app/Contents/ MacOS/, but you normally invoke it from a symbolic link, /usr/sbin/AppleFileServer. You start and stop AFP service from the Sharing pane of System Preferences. You can also start or stop service from the command line by starting the process directory.

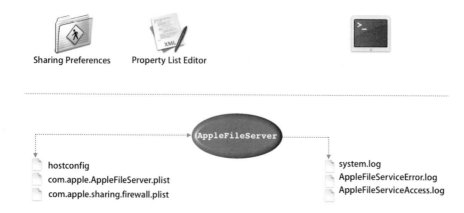

Sharing Preferences   Property List Editor

AppleFileServer

hostconfig
com.apple.AppleFileServer.plist
com.apple.sharing.firewall.plist

system.log
AppleFileServiceError.log
AppleFileServiceAccess.log

There are system plist files in /System/Library/CoreServices/AppleFileServer.app/ Contents that also control AFP, but you shouldn't touch those.

Two configuration files control AppleFileServer: /etc/hostconfig and /Library/ Preferences/com.apple.AppleFileServer.plist. In addition, a property in com.apple. sharing.firewall.plist controls whether the AFP port in the firewall is open. You can use Property List Editor to edit the two plist files. You can also edit these files with a text editor, but first you must convert them from binary to text XML format:

```
sudo plutil –convert xml1 /Library/Preferences/com.apple.AppleFileServer.plist
```

The system log, /var/log/system.log, contains entries for AFP startup and for abnormal shutdown. An error log and an access log also reside in /Library/Logs/AppleFileService.

Starting the Apple File Service

Starting Apple File Service consists of a series of steps:

1. You start Personal File Sharing in the Sharing pane of System Preferences.

2. The enable property for Personal File Sharing in /Library/Preferences/com.apple. sharing.firewall.plist changes from 0 to 1. This change opens a port in your computer's firewall for AFP connections.

    When AppleFileServer terminates, it writes the integer value serverStoppedTime to /Library/Preferences/com.apple.ServerAdmin.plist.

3. A line in the /etc/hostconfig file changes from AFPSERVER= –NO– to AFPSERVER=–YES–. When you restart your computer, the startup script /System/Library/StartupItems/ AppleShare/AppleShare starts AppleFileServer if the value in /etc/hostconfig is –YES–.

4. The AppleFileServer process handles communication with other computers over AFP.

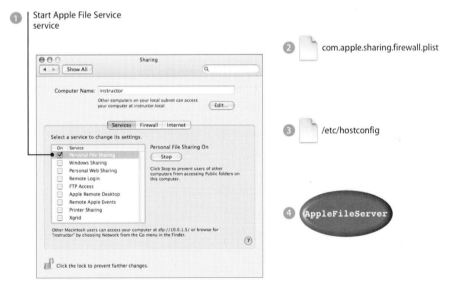

When you stop Personal File Sharing in the Sharing pane of System Preferences, the steps are reversed. That is, the configuration files are changed back and the AppleFileServer process quits.

As an alternative to using Sharing preferences, you can enable AFP service by performing these tasks, as root:

1   Edit com.apple.sharing.firewall.plist, using Property List Editor or a text editor (if using a text editor, you must use plutil first), and change the enable property under Personal File Sharing from 0 to 1.

2   Execute the program /usr/sbin/AppleFileServer.

3   Edit /etc/hostconfig to AFPSERVER=–YES– from AFPSERVER=–NO–.

To stop AFP service, you would reverse these steps, changing the file settings and killing the process.

Editing com.apple.AppleFileServer.plist

No graphical user interface exists that is specifically designed for modifying the behavior of AppleFileServer, but you can use Property List Editor or a text editor to edit the file com.apple.AppleFileServer.plist in /Library/Preferences.

Alternatively, you can use the defaults command. For example, to change the Boolean property admin31GetsSp from true to false, you would type the following:

sudo defaults write /Library/Preferences/com.apple.AppleFileServer admin31GetsSp -bool false

> **NOTE** ▶ Stop AppleFileServer before you make changes to its properties.

The following figure illustrates how changing items within the com.apple. AppleFileServer.plist affects users gaining access remotely.

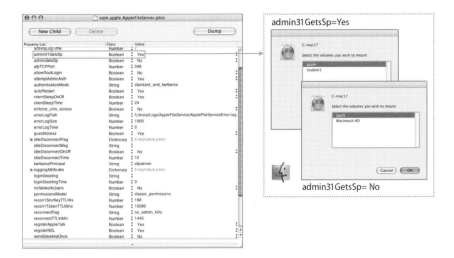

Two properties that you might need to edit are:

▶ admin31GetsSp: This property controls whether a user logging in as an administrator sees user share points or volumes. This field is set to true (yes) by default, so an administrator only sees share points. If you want administrators to see volumes, change the admin31GetsSp property to false (no).

▶ guestAccess: This property controls whether users can log in as guest if they do not have an account on your machine. It is set to true by default. If you do not want to allow guest access, change the guestAccess property to false.

Understanding Windows Sharing

A Common Internet File System (CIFS) comprises an entire suite of protocols that provide the browsing and sharing interface on Windows.

File sharing on Windows computers is based on the SMB protocol. Like other UNIX-based operating systems, Mac OS X uses the Samba server software to provide SMB file services.

As shown in the figure below, the two programs responsible for Windows Sharing are smbd and nmbd, which reside in /usr/sbin. The nmbd program provides NetBIOS name service, so that other computers running Windows or the Samba suite can resolve your computer's name. The smbd program is the actual SMB server daemon. Both of these processes are run as children of launchd, the systemwide daemon manager. Configuration files in /System/Library/LaunchDaemons/ control the startup of the two daemons. The file /etc/smb.conf controls the behavior of smbd and nmbd. The enable property in com. apple.sharing.firewall.plist controls whether the Samba port in the firewall is open.

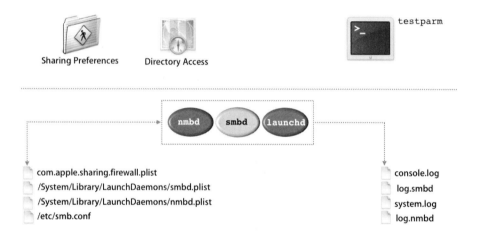

You use the Sharing pane of System Preferences to stop and start SMB file services. You use Directory Access to modify workgroup and wins server, which are two of the parameters in smb.conf. You must use a text editor to modify other parameters. The command testparm scans the smb.conf file and provides output that is useful for debugging.

Each of the two daemons has its own log file in /var/log/samba. You may also look in the other log files for mention of netbios_ssn and netbios_ns. As you know from Lesson 26, "Maintaining Local Volumes and Files," forked files may be problematic when using file-sharing protocols other than AFP.

Getting SMB Started

Starting Windows Sharing consists of several steps, as shown in the following figure:

1. You start Windows Sharing in the Sharing pane of System Preferences.

2. The enable property for Samba Sharing in /Library/Preferences/com.apple.sharing. firewall.plist changes from 0 to 1. This change opens a port in your computer's firewall for SMB connections.

3. The Disabled key is removed from both of the config files, /System/Library/ LaunchDaemons/smbd.plist and nmbd.plist.

4. launchd is notified of the changes to /System/Library/LaunchDaemons/smbd.plist and nmbd.plist. Because these files have been changed so that SMB and NMB are no longer disabled, the launchd process listens for NMB and SMB connections.

5. After a request, launchd starts the nmbd process.

6. When a user connects to your computer using SMB, launchd starts smbd to manage the connection.

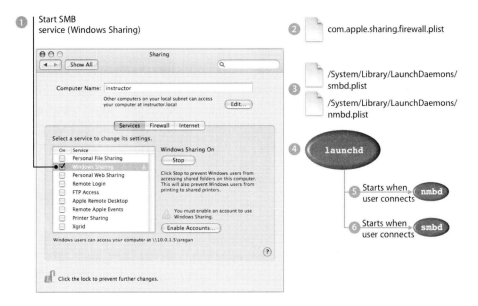

NOTE ▶ You'll also notice an Enable Accounts button for Windows Sharing. By default, each user's account on your computer will not have the necessary password hash stored to allow that user to connect via Windows Sharing. You can use that button to enable an account for Windows sharing, which will require you to reenter the password so it can be hashed in the appropriate format.

When you stop Windows File Sharing in the Sharing preferences pane, the files change back to their original state and launchd rereads its configuration file. The smbd process stops when the last connected user disconnects. The nmbd process stops shortly after that. You can also start or stop Windows File Sharing from the command line.

1 Change the enable property for Samba Sharing in com.apple.sharing.firewall.plist to 1 when starting or 0 when stopping.

2 Issue the following two commands to start Windows File Sharing:

    sudo launchctl load –w /System/Library/LaunchDaemons/nmbd.plist
    sudo launchctl load –w /System/Library/LaunchDaemons/smbd.plist

3 To stop Windows File Sharing, issue the same launchctl commands, but use unload instead of load, and change the firewall setting back to 0.

Configuring SMB Parameters With Directory Access

You may be familiar with Directory Access, the application you use to configure directory services and service discovery protocols on your Mac OS X computer. If you disable SMB in directory services, you will not be able to browse for SMB services using the Finder.

The file /var/run/smbbrowsing.conf is similar to smb.conf. It is generated from smb.conf at system startup.

Directory Access also provides a configuration interface for /etc/smb.conf. If you select SMB and click Configure, you see a dialog for configuring two SMB parameters, Workgroup and WINS server, as shown in the following figure. When you use Directory Access to change those parameters, a subprocess changes the corresponding settings in /etc/smb.conf and /var/run/smbbrowsing.conf. The following figure shows the entries in the SMB plug-in within Directory Access and the corresponding entries in the smb.conf file.

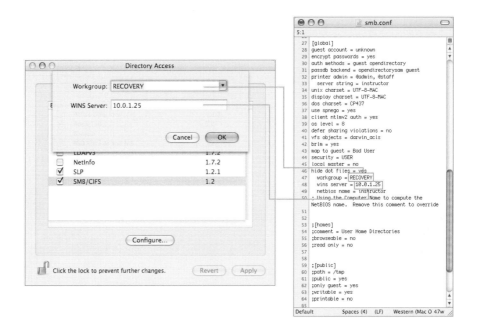

The Workgroup parameter controls which Windows workgroup your computer belongs to. Windows workgroups are simply collections of computers configured to advertise themselves as belonging to a workgroup. By default, Mac OS X computers and most Windows client computers belong to a workgroup called WORKGROUP. The workgroup name is case-sensitive. If you do not use workgroups on your network, leave this field blank.

Workgroups affect the browsing interface. When users on other Mac OS X computers open /Network in the Finder, they will see your computer in a folder that has the same name as that of your computer's Workgroup. Windows users can see computers listed by workgroup by clicking My Network Places on the desktop.

The WINS server field contains the NetBIOS name server. On Windows networks, the WINS server coordinates and manages the mapping of NetBIOS names to Internet Protocol (IP) addresses. A WINS server is necessary if a Windows network includes more than one IP subnet. It is not necessary if the whole Windows network is on one subnet, because the computers can use User Datagram Protocol (UDP) broadcasts to find out which computer is using which name. On the other hand, using a WINS server will reduce traffic. If you use one, all Windows (and Samba) computers should point to it.

Configuring SMB Parameters by Editing smb.conf

Following are some smb.conf parameters that you may want to change:

▶ server string: The description before the computer name when you browse from a Windows XP computer. The default server string is Mac OS X, as shown in the following figure.

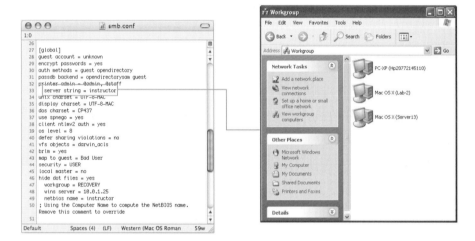

▶ max smbd processes: The number of users using SMB who can connect to your computer at the same time.

▶ create_mask: The creation mask that determines the default permissions on files.

▶ guest account: The account used for guest users. By default, it is set to unknown.

▶ hide dot files: When set to yes, files beginning with a period (dot) either are not displayed on a Windows client or appear dimmed, depending on the settings on the client.

▶ veto files: Specifies a list of files that the client will not see when listing a folder's contents.

The parameters in smb.conf and smbbrowsing.conf that correspond with Workgroup and WINS Server are workgroup and wins server. When Directory Access changes these parameters, it leaves the rest of smb.conf and smbbrowsing.conf untouched, so you can safely change other parameters with a text editor. You would normally use Directory Access to configure workgroup and wins server. If you must configure these parameters from the command line, restart the computer or the DirectoryService process so that Directory Access picks up the change.

NOTE ▶ Always keep smbbrowsing.conf consistent with smb.conf. You can make the same changes to both files, or you can edit smb.conf and restart the computer.

MORE INFO ▶ See the man page for smb.conf for more information. Also see the Samba manual on your Mac OS X computer at file:///usr/share/swat/using_samba/toc.html.

Browsing on Mac OS X and Windows XP

The computer names you see in Connect to Server on Mac OS X might not be the same as the ones you see when you browse on Windows, as the example in the following figure illustrates.

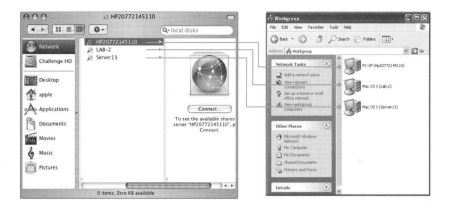

Browsing on Mac OS X has a few unique characteristics:

▶ When you view a Windows XP computer, the name you see is the computer name configured by the Windows administrator.

▶ When you view a Mac OS X or Mac OS X Server computer, you see one of the following: the DNS name, if there is DNS service on the network, or the Bonjour name (without .local) if there is no DNS service.

You'll also find some traits specific to browsing on Windows XP:

▶ When you view either a Windows XP computer or a Mac, the name you see consists of an initial string followed by a second string in parentheses.

▶ In a Windows XP computer name, the initial string is the computer description string, and the string in parentheses is the computer name configured by the Windows administrator.

▶ In a Mac OS X computer name, the initial string is the server string parameter in smb.conf. It is Mac OS X by default. The second string is one of the following: the DNS name, if there is DNS service, or the Bonjour name (without .local) if there is no DNS service.

Getting FTP Access

FTP is commonly used for transferring files. The process responsible for FTP service on Mac OS X is /usr/libexec/ftpd. Mac OS X Server uses a different FTP daemon (/usr/libexec/xftpd) with different configuration parameters. You use the Sharing pane of System Preferences to stop and start the FTP service.

The configuration file /System/Library/LaunchDaemons/ftp.plist controls the startup of the daemon when the computer is started. The files ftpchroot, ftpusers, and ftpd.conf in /etc control the behavior of the daemon. The files /etc/motd and /etc/ftpwelcome contain the welcome messages users see before and after logging in, respectively. A property in com.apple.sharing.firewall.plist controls whether the FTP Access port in the firewall is open.

Sharing Preferences

ftpd

/Systems/Library/LaunchDaemons/ftp.plist
/etc/ftpchroot
/etc/ftpusers
/etc/ftpwelcome
/etc/motd
/etc/ftpd.conf

ftp.log

The daemon writes messages to /var/log/ftp.log and the system log. In addition, launchd writes some FTP-related messages to the system log.

> **NOTE** ▶ FTP is not enabled by default because it is considered an insecure protocol. Before you enable FTP, consider the fact that it is not encrypted and passwords may be passed as clear text. As an alternative to FTP, there is another, more secure protocol called Secure FTP SFTP, which is included with Mac OS X as part of the Secure Shell Protocol (SSH).

Starting FTP

Starting FTP consists of the follwing steps:

1. You start FTP Access in the Sharing pane of System Preferences.

2. The value of the enable property for FTP Access in /Library/Preferences/com.apple. sharing.firewall.plist changes from 0 to 1. This change opens a port in your computer's firewall for FTP connections.

3. The Disabled key is removed from the configuration file /System/Library/ LaunchDaemons/ftp.plist.

4. launchd is notified of the changes to /System/Library/LaunchDaemons/ftp.plist. Because this file has been changed to indicate that FTP is no longer disabled, the launchd process listens for FTP connections.

5. When a user connects to your computer using FTP, launchd starts ftpd to manage the connection.

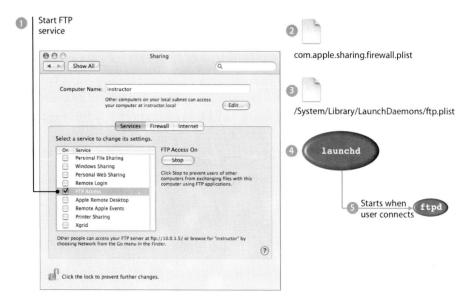

When you stop FTP Access in Sharing preferences, the files change back to their original state and launchd rereads its configuration file. The ftpd process stops when the last connected user disconnects.

You can start and stop FTP sharing from the command line by using one the following methods:

▶ Change the value of the enable property for FTP Access in com.apple.sharing.firewall.plist to 1 when starting and to 0 when stopping.

▶ Issue the following command to manage FTP sharing:
sudo launchctl load –w /System/Library/LaunchDaemons/ftp.plist

▶ To stop FTP access, issue the same launchctl command, but use unload instead of load, and change the firewall setting back to 0.

NOTE ▶ If you have an account with the name administrator, you will have to modify this file to grant that user access via FTP. For security reasons, do not grant FTP access to root.

Configuring FTP

There are several commands that enable you to customize some of FTP's features from the command-line interface.

ftpusers and ftpchroot

Sometimes you might need to prevent certain users from logging in to your computer using FTP. To do that, add the user's name to /etc/ftpusers. By default, the file contains the following list of users who are not allowed to log in using FTP:

    Administrator
    administrator
    root
    uucp
    daemon
    unknown
    www

Sometimes you need to restrict an FTP user's access to the file system. You can do that by changing the user's root folder for FTP sessions. For example, if you change student17's root folder to be his home folder, when the user logs in using FTP, commands like pwd, cd, and get will act as if "/Users/student17" is "/". This prevents student17 from seeing the rest of the file system.

To change a user's FTP root folder to be the user's home folder, create the file /etc/ftpchroot, if necessary, and add the user's name. If you want a user's FTP root to be a different folder, you must set the chroot (change root) directive in /etc/ftp.conf.

> **MORE INFO** ▶ For more information, see the man page for ftpusers and ftpchroot.

The following illustrates what happens when different users log in remotely via FTP. Depending on where the user's name is located, he or she will have different default directories and permissions to search other directories.

▶ The normal user would do the following to log in remotely via FTP:

ftp pwd

257 "/Users/david" is the current directory.

ftp cd /private

250 CWD command successful.

▶ The ftpchroot user would do the following to log in remotely via FTP:

ftp pwd

257 "/" is the current directory.

ftp cd /private

550 /private: No such file or directory.

ls /

-rw-r--r--	1	david	david	16	Jan 20 10:44	AUserFile
drwx------	3	david	david	102	Jan 20 10:44	Desktop
drwx------	3	david	david	102	Jan 20 10:44	Documents
drwx------	17	david	david	578	Jan 20 10:44	Library
drwx------	3	david	david	102	Jan 20 10:44	Movies
drwx------	3	david	david	102	Jan 20 10:44	Music
drwx------	3	david	david	102	Jan 20 10:44	Pictures
drwxr-xr-x	4	david	david	136	Jan 20 10:44	Public
drwxr-xr-x	5	david	david	170	Jan 20 10:44	Site

ftpd.conf

If you want a user's FTP root folder to be somewhere other than the user's home folder, you can use the chroot directive in ftpd.conf. For example, if you want all the users in ftpchroot to have /Users/special as their root, create /etc/ftpd.conf, if necessary, and add the following line:

chroot CHROOT /Users/special

Sometimes users might need to download large files from your computer. You could speed up the FTP downloads by converting all your files to a smaller format. Alternatively, you can keep your files in their original format and allow FTP to perform an automatic file conversion. To do that, you use the conversion directive in ftpd.conf. For example, if you want users to be able to gzip files before copying them, you could add the following line to ftpd.conf, as shown in the following figure:

conversion all .gz f xyz /usr/bin/gzip –c %s

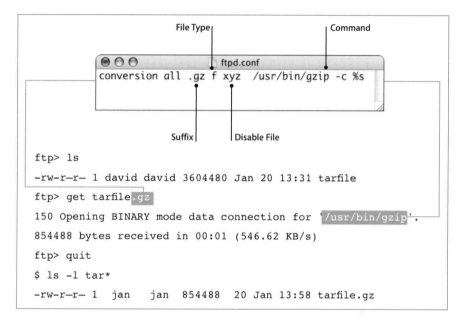

```
ftp> ls
-rw-r—r— 1 david david 3604480 Jan 20 13:31 tarfile
ftp> get tarfile.gz
150 Opening BINARY mode data connection for /usr/bin/gzip.
854488 bytes received in 00:01 (546.62 KB/s)
ftp> quit
$ ls -l tar*
-rw-r—r— 1  jan   jan  854488  20 Jan 13:58 tarfile.gz
```

The f means only files, not folders, can be converted. If the file xyz exists in the folder, it prevents conversion. These fields are mandatory.

Then, if the user types

get tarfile.gz

in a folder that contains a file called tarfile but not tarfile.gz, a shell on your computer will execute the command

/usr/bin/gzip –c tarfile

and copy the output of the command to the user's computer as tarfile.gz.

Monitoring and Troubleshooting

Once file-sharing services are enabled, you'll need to monitor them from time to time and ensure they are functioning properly. If not, you should know how to take corrective action.

Monitoring File-Sharing Processes

You can monitor file-sharing processes by using Activity Monitor and by examining the log files. For general troubleshooting of SMB or FTP service, use Activity Monitor to watch launchd start daemons. Choose All Processes Hierarchical from the pull-down menu in Activity Monitor. You might need to increase Activity Monitor's update frequency using the Monitor menu.

The log files for nmbd, smbd, and ftpd are /var/log/samba/log.nmbd, /var/log/samba/log.smbd, and /var/log/ftp.log, respectively. You can get more output from ftpd, nmbd, or smbd by invoking any of them with the –d option. You do that by editing the files under /System/Library/LaunchDaemons/. For example, if you change the ftp.plist ProgramArguments key from

```
keyProgramArguments/key
array
    stringftpd/string
    string–l/string
/array
```

to

```
keyProgramArguments/key
array
    stringftpd/string
    string–l/string
    string–d/string
/array
```

the next time ftpd executes, it will write more detailed output to /var/logs/ftp.log. The –d options to nmbd and smbd allow you to specify a debug level by putting an integer after the –d. A level of 3 should give you as much detail as you need. The following figure shows ftpd debug (–d) output to ftp.log.

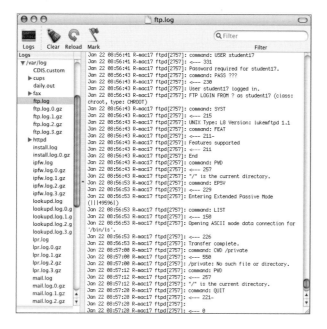

You can use the log files to debug AppleFileServer. Before it quits, AppleFileServer writes to the log /Library/Logs/AppleFileService/AppleFileService. In addition, configd writes messages to the system log when it starts AppleFileServer.

Troubleshooting Connection Failures

If users cannot connect to your system, you can take several steps to troubleshoot the problem.

First, determine whether the problem is specific to one protocol. If more than one protocol is affected, you should troubleshoot your network connection as described in Lesson 25, "Resolving Network System Issues."

If the problem is specific to AFP, determine how many other users are already connected. Mac OS X allows up to ten users to connect to your computer simultaneously using Personal File Sharing. If you need to let more users connect, you can upgrade to the unlimited-client version of Mac OS X Server.

If you click the Firewall button in the Sharing pane of System Preferences, you can add other ports and control their firewall settings.

For any of the file-sharing protocols, if users cannot connect, verify that the protocol's port is enabled in com.apple.sharing.firewall.plist. You can also get a real-time view of the current firewall settings by typing *sudo ipfw list*.

SMB-Specific Troubleshooting

If Windows File Sharing (SMB) clients cannot connect to your computer after you upgrade to a newer version of Mac OS X, change the password on each account on your computer. You should also verify that their account is enabled for Windows File Sharing in Sharing preferences.

It might take nmbd a few minutes to stop when you stop Windows File Sharing using the Sharing pane of System Preferences.

The testparm command checks the smb.conf file and reports errors. If you then press Return, it lists all configuration parameters, including defaults not specified in smb.conf, as shown in the following text.

```
testparm
Load smb config files from /private/etc/smb.conf
Processing section "[printers]"
Loaded services file OK.
Invalid combination of parameters for service printers.
Level II oplocks can only be set if oplocks are also set.
Server role: ROLE_STANDALONE
Press enter to see a dump of your service definitions


# Global parameters
[global]
        dos charset = CP437
        unix charset = UTF-8-MAC
        display charset = UTF-8-MAC
        workgroup = RECOVERY
        server string = instructor
        auth methods = guest, opendirectory
        map to guest = Bad User
        passdb backend = opendirectorysam, guest
```

```
        guest account = unknown
        client NTLMv2 auth = Yes
        client lanman auth = No
        client plaintext auth = No
        defer sharing violations = No
        os level = 8
        local master = No
        wins server = 10.0.1.25
        brlm = Yes
        printer admin = @admin, @staff
        vfs objects = darwin_acls

[printers]
        path = /tmp
        printable = Yes
        browseable = No
```

The workgroup name is case-sensitive. If, for example, some of your computers are assigned to Workgroup and others are assigned to WORKGROUP, you will see two workgroups in your browser window.

On some versions of Windows, a user who connects to a remote computer using SMB must have the same short name on the remote computer as on the local computer.

Mac OS X supports these Windows network authentication methods:

▶   Cleartext (off by default)

▶   NTLMv1 & 2

▶   SMB NT

What You've Learned

▶   You can start and stop each file-sharing service using the command line or the Sharing pane of System Preferences.

▶   Use the configuration file for each file service to customize their configuration beyond what their GUI setup screen provides.

► You can change a property that allows administrators to see entire volumes instead of share points when connecting over AFP.

► You can change the server string associated with your computer in the Windows XP browsing interface.

► There are several monitoring and debugging techniques for resolving problems users may have connecting to your computer.

References

Administration Guides

"Mac OS X Server Collaboration Services Administration": http://images.apple.com/server/pdfs/Collaboration_Services_v10.4.pdf

"Mac OS X Server File Services Administration": http://images.apple.com/server/pdfs/File_Services_v10.4.pdf

"Mac OS X Server Web Technologies Services Administration": http://images.apple.com/server/pdfs/Web_Technologies_Admin_v10.4.pdf

"Mac OS X Server Windows Services Administration": http://images.apple.com/server/pdfs/Windows_Services_v10.4.pdf

Books

Ts, Jay; Eckstein, Robert; Collier-Brown, David. *Using Samba, 2nd ed.* (O'Reilly, 2003).

URLs

Apple Filing Protocol Programming Guide: http://developer.apple.com/documentation/Networking/Conceptual/AFP/

Samba: www.samba.org/

Apache Web Server: www.apache.org/

WebDAV Resources: www.webdav.org/

Lesson Review

1. What file-sharing protocols are supported on Mac OS X?

2. What are the processes that implement these protocols?

3. At startup, which configuration file determines whether AFP will be started?

4. What happens at startup if SMB or FTP has been turned on in the Sharing pane of System Preferences?

5. What software suite is the Mac OS X implementation of SMB based upon?

Answers

1. AFP, SMB, and FTP

2. AppleFileServer for AFP, nmbd and smbd for SMB, and ftpd for FTP

3. The /etc/hostconfig file

4. The launchd daemon checks the configuration files in /System/Library/ LaunchDaemons/. If any of them has Disabled set to true, launchd will ignore it. Otherwise, launchd waits for a connection on that service's port, then hands the connection off to that service's daemon.

5. It is based on the Samba suite.

29

This lesson takes approximately 2 hours to complete.

Understand the concept of user share mounts

Differentiate between static mounts and dynamic mounts

Configure Mac OS X to automatically mount a volume on startup
or login

Use command-line tools such as mount, umount, and nfsstat to
troubleshoot mounts

Understand how disk arbitration manages the mounting and
unmounting of remote file systems

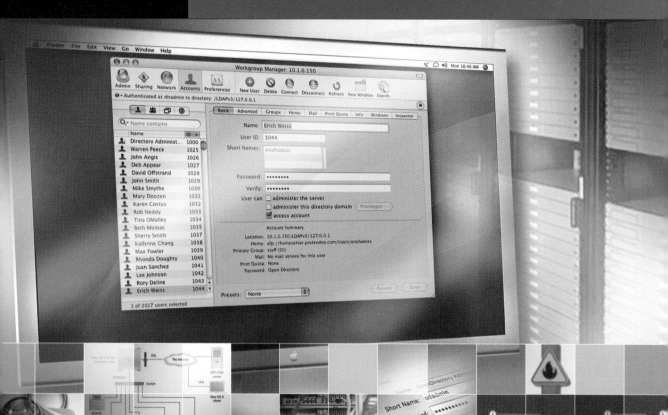

Mounting Remote File Systems

Mac OS X connects to various file-sharing services such as the Apple Filing Protocol (AFP), File Transfer Protocol (FTP), network file system (NFS), and Server Message Block (SMB) for Windows.

This lesson discusses the mechanics behind the connections, the various methods of mounting share points, and some variances that make the experience different, based on several criteria. While the easiest methods of connecting to a server are through the Network icon in the Sidebar or the Connect to Server option in the Go menu (both from the Finder), some additional methods, such as using the mount command from the command line, will also be examined in this lesson.

Understanding User Mounting

Service discovery protocols let you view a list of computers or volumes and click to initiate a mount. In Mac OS X, you view the list by clicking the Network icon in the Sidebar.

Apple supports four service discovery protocols: AppleTalk, Bonjour, Service Location Protocol (SLP), and SMB, as shown in the following figure. No single service discovery protocol discovers all file services on Mac OS X. None of the protocols discovers FTP, and only SMB discovers SMB. Browsing is not implemented for FTP, and NFS browsing is available only if the server is running Mac OS X Server. To manage those methods, you use Directory Access to enable and disable service discovery protocols.

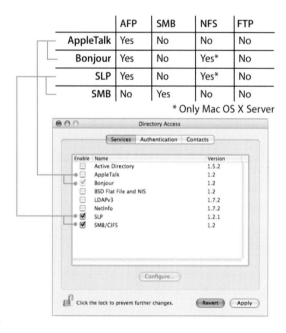

	AFP	SMB	NFS	FTP
AppleTalk	Yes	No	No	No
Bonjour	Yes	No	Yes*	No
SLP	Yes	No	Yes*	No
SMB	No	Yes	No	No

* Only Mac OS X Server

Discovering Services on a Windows Network

Windows users can browse SMB services by selecting My Network Places. Browsing is possible because Windows networks establish service discovery with a computer that maintains a list of available computers.

On each subnet of a Windows network, the workgroup members elect one computer as the Local Master Browser, as illustrated in the following figure. The Workgroup members may elect additional local browsers as backup browsers.

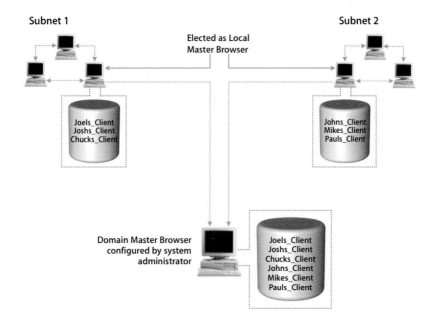

The system administrator can designate one server as the Domain Master Browser (DMB) to circulate browse lists outside of Internet Protocol (IP) subnets. The DMB registers with the WINS server. Local Master Browsers look for this name and send updates to the DMB, which then combines the lists and sends them back.

When a Windows user selects My Network Places, the client computer connects to a browser, obtains a copy of the browse list, and displays it.

Using the Network Browser

On Mac OS X, when you click the Network icon in the Sidebar, the Finder displays a list of browsable servers. You will see any local computers on your network, or you can select different network areas or workgroup names to see the servers they include.

To initiate a mount, as illustrated in the following figure, select a computer and click Connect, and enter the authentication information if necessary. Once you have mounted the server volumes, the contents of the server appear in the Finder window. The server (or share point) appears on the desktop and in the Sidebar, although this behavior can be modified by adjusting the Finder preferences.

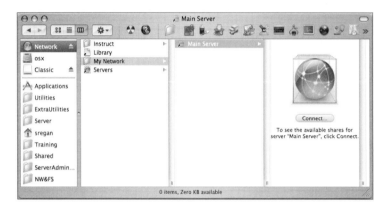

In Mac OS X, volumes mounted via the Network icon in the Sidebar actually mount in subdirectories under /Volumes. Later in this lesson, you will view these mounts from the command line.

Mounting Using Connect to Server

You invoke the Connect to Server command either from the Finder's Go menu or by pressing Command-K in a Finder window. As shown in the following figure, you specify the URL of a server, and the Finder attempts to connect.

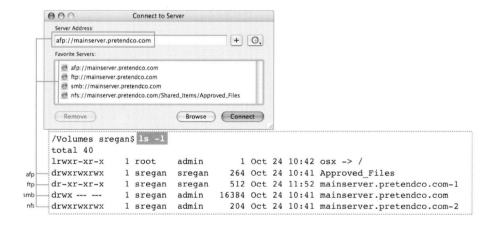

When you use Connect to Server to connect to an AFP server, AFP displays a list of volumes you can mount. Both administrators and regular users see a list of share points when mounting over AFP. It is also not necessary to type the letters *afp* before the IP address or name of the server, as Connect to Server will default to AFP.

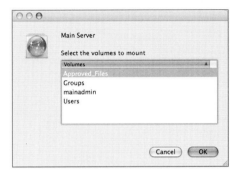

When you mount using Connect to Server, a volume icon appears on your desktop and in the Sidebar. You can change your Finder preferences so that you do not see volume icons on your desktop.

Connect to Server actually mounts each share point on a subdirectory of /Volumes that is named for the share point or server being mounted. You can see the actual mount points by choosing Go to Folder from the Go menu and typing */Volumes*, as shown in the following figure.

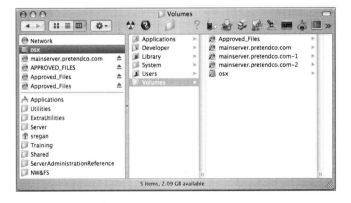

You can connect to all four service types (AFP, SMB, FTP, and NFS) using the Finder, but FTP mounts read-only, so you can download files but not upload them to the server.

Browsing is not implemented for FTP, and NFS browsing is available only if the server is running Mac OS X Server.

Mounting From the Command Line

To mount a volume using the mount command, you need a folder to mount on. Use mkdir or choose New Folder under the Finder's File menu to create the folder prior to mounting.

> **NOTE ▸** The commands disktool –e, disktool –u, diskutil eject, and diskutil unmount can unmount physically attached volumes and are preferable to umount for that purpose, although they may not work consistently when used on command-line mounts.

The following examples show how to use the mount command for AFP, SMB, FTP, and NFS:

▸ AFP Mount:

   mount –t afp afp://mainadmin:mypwd@mainserver.pretendco.com/Approved_Files /Users/sregan/
   Documents/MyAFPMount/

▸ SMB Mount:

   mount –t smbfs //mainadmin@MAINSERVER.PRETENDCO.COM/Approved_Files /Users/sregan/
   Documents/MySMBMount

▸ NFS Mount:

   mount –t nfs mainserver.pretendco.com:/Shared_Items/Approved_Files /Users/sregan/Desktop/
   MyNFSMount/

> **NOTE ▸** Though it's not possible to show it properly on the printed page, all of these URLs should be typed on one line with no paragraph returns.

The syntax for the three protocol types is similar in that each requires you to specify the type argument with the –t option to the mount command. Also, for all three protocols, you use %20 instead of a space because URLs cannot contain spaces. (In the previous examples, however, there were no spaces in the URL and so there was no need to use %20).

Other URL features, however, are different. For example, the syntax for AFP and SMB requires you to specify the share point on the server by the share name, but NFS syntax requires that you specify the full path to the shared folder. (That is, you must know where the folder resides on the NFS server in order to mount it from the command line.)

NFS requires no authentication, but AFP and SMB do. AFP and SMB will prompt for the user name and password if you don't supply them on the command line. For additional options you can pass to the mount command, see the mount man page.

When you mount from the command line, icons usually appear automatically. If an icon does not appear once the volume is mounted, type *disktool −r*.

> NOTE ▶ If you have mounted a volume from the command line, you should unmount it from the command line. If you try to unmount the volume by dragging the icon to the Trash, the Finder might stop responding. If that happens, relaunch the Finder.

Listing and Unmounting Mounted Volumes

The mount command, with no arguments, lists all mounted file systems:

```
instructor:~ sregan$ mount
/dev/disk0s3 on / (local, journaled)
devfs on /dev (local)
fdesc on /dev (union)
volfs on /.vol
automount −nsl [135] on /Network (automounted)
automount −fstab [150] on /automount/Servers (automounted)
automount −static [150] on /automount/static (automounted)
afp_005An80ZHyoM001Eic06SdO0−1.2c000006 on /Users/sregan/Desktop/MyAFPMount (nodev,
nosuid, mounted by sregan)
//MAINADMIN@*SMBSERVER/APPROVED_FILES on /Users/sregan/Desktop/MySMBMount (nodev,
nosuid, mounted by sregan)
mainserver.pretendco.com:Shared_Items/Approved_Files on /Users/sregan/Desktop/MyNFSMount
(nodev, nosuid, mounted by sregan)
```

The nodev option means you cannot use special files in /dev on the mounted volume. The nosuid option means the setuid/setgid bits on commands located on the server volume are not honored if you execute them from the client.

> NOTE ▶ All three protocols are used to mount the same directory, something that would not be practical in real-world use. It is shown here for comparison purposes.

The umount command unmounts a volume. (The command for unmounting is umount, not "unmount.") The following lines show unmounting the three volumes from the desktop.

```
instructor:~ sregan$ umount Desktop/MyAFPMount/
instructor:~ sregan$ umount Desktop/MySMBMount/
instructor:~ sregan$ umount Desktop/MyNFSMount/
```

Some details about using umount:

▶ Unmounting from the command line will not remove the directories created for the mounts when using NFS and SMB.

▶ If the directory created for the mount has items inside the directory, they will be hidden when the mount is made. When unmounted, the original data will be shown again. It may be necessary to relaunch the Finder to see the original files again.

▶ If the volume is in use, the umount command will fail unless you force an unmount by using the –f option.

Mounting a Volume at Login

To set up an automatic mount as a user, use Connect to Server or the Network browser in the Sidebar to mount the volume. Then select your account in the Accounts pane of System Preferences and click Login Items, as the following figure illustrates.

There are two methods for adding the volume to your startup items:

▶ Click the Add (+) button and locate the server in the Recent Servers folder in your home Library folder.

▶ Drag the volume's icon into the list of items.

Any user can add a mounted volume to her startup items so that it automatically mounts when she logs in.

Now each time you log in to your Mac OS X computer, the login dialog for the mount will appear. If you add your password to Keychain, or if a Kerberos infrastructure has been implemented, the mount will occur automatically. Note that this is specific to a single user, unlike automounting with the automount daemon.

If you start up the computer while the server is unavailable, you may experience a delay while automount attempts to mount the volume. To prevent this delay, hold the Shift key when logging in to disable login items.

Mounting With the automount Daemon

You can configure your computer to mount volumes automatically on startup by adding a mount record to the NetInfo database. When the automount daemon runs at startup, it reads the mount record and attempts to mount the volume. This type of automount is supported for AFP, SMB, and NFS. The following figure shows what tools are available to manage local automounts and what log file the automount daemon writes to.

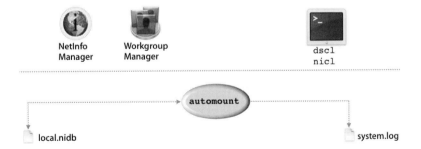

You can add the mount record from the command line using dscl or nicl, or from the NetInfo Manager utility. You can also download and install the Mac OS X Server tool Workgroup Manager and use it to configure mount records in the local domain.

This type of mount cannot be disabled during startup, so avoid using it on mobile computers or for mounting a server that is frequently unavailable.

> **NOTE ▶** To avoid having to include a password in the mount record, use this type of mount only for NFS servers or for AFP servers that allow guest access.

Using Mount Records

A mount record consists of the following properties:

▶ name: The server's name and the full path to the folder that is to be mounted; for example, mainserver.pretendco.com:/Users.

▶ vfstype: Set to nfs for NFS mounts and url for AFP or SMB mounts.

▶ dir: The local folder where clients will mount the share point. Dynamically mounted share points always have a value of /Network/Servers/.

▶ opts: Mount options. There may be both, one, or neither of the options net and url.

  • net indicates that the share point is to be dynamically mounted.

  • url is the URL path to an AFP share point; for example, url==afp://;NO%20USER%20AUTHENT@mainserver.pretendco.com:/Users.

The mount record shown in the following figure causes automount to mount the share called Users onto /Network/Servers/mainserver.pretendco.com. This occurs the first time a user attempts to list or access the volume. The name of the user who initiated the mount will appear in the output from the mount command. The automount daemon then unmounts the volume when the user logs out.

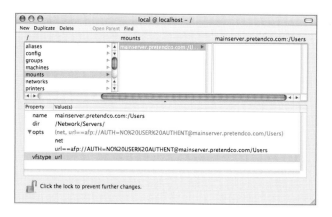

Troubleshooting

When attempting to mount volumes from another computer, you might encounter file-fork issues, the insecurity of NFS mounts, how Mac OS X reacts to the loss of a connection, more than one mounting of the same volume, and security issues related to Fast User Switching. You will also learn some tips for resolving browsing and mounting issues.

Using Forked Files Over AFP

The Hierarchical File System Plus, HFS Plus, supports forked files, but other file systems, such as UFS, do not. When copying files between local volumes, Mac-specific utilities handle forks correctly, as do command-line utilities such as cp and mv, but only on Mac OS X systems. (Apple engineered such command-line utilities to handle resource forks properly.) The Windows graphical user interface does not support resource forks as well. A similar issue exists with file-sharing services. Only AFP supports forked files; NFS, SMB, and FTP do not.

AFP was designed to handle forked files. When a forked file is written on a Mac OS X computer over AFP to a volume on a server, the File Manager on the Mac OS X computer treats the AFP mount point as if it were an HFS Plus file system. That is, it keeps the forked file intact. AFP also preserves the intact forked file as it is copied. Once the forked file is received on the server computer, the server's File Manager preserves the forked file if the volume is HFS Plus, or splits the file into two flat files if the volume is a flat-file system, such as UFS.

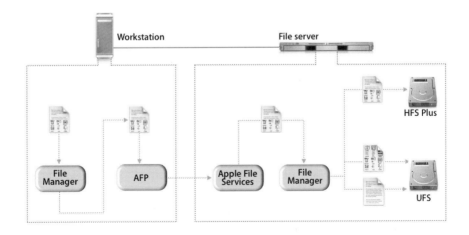

Using Forked Files Over NFS

NFS, SMB, and FTP were not designed to handle forked files. The example shown in the following figure illustrates what happens when you copy a forked file over NFS. (This example shows NFS but applies to other non-AFP file systems as well.)

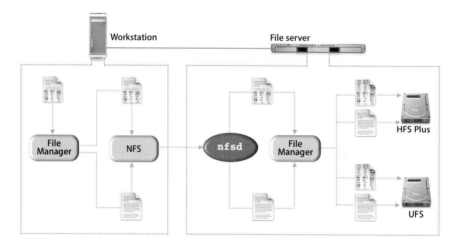

When you write a forked file on a Mac OS X computer over NFS to a volume on a server, the File Manager on the Mac OS X computer treats the NFS mount point as if it were a flat-file system. That is, it splits the file into two flat files. Because NFS on the server writes two separate files, the File Manager on the server computer stores the data as two flat files, regardless of the volume's file-system type.

When a forked file is stored as two flat files on an HFS Plus file system over NFS, the file looks like a normal file when viewed from Mac OS X, but not when viewed from the server. Mac OS X graphical user interface applications executing on the Mac OS X computer expect forked files on an NFS volume to be stored as two flat files, because the File Manager on the Mac OS X computer treats the NFS mount point as if it were a flat-file system. Applications executing on the server, however, expect files on an HFS Plus file system to be intact.

For the same reasons, when a forked file is created locally on an HFS Plus file system on the server and the volume is mounted on Mac OS X over NFS, the file looks normal when viewed from the server but not when viewed from Mac OS X.

Understanding NFS Security

NFS is inherently less secure than the other protocols because it does not authenticate users. The NFS server compares the IP address of your computer only with the list of computers that are authorized to mount the volume. The only time it does this comparison is when you mount the volume. Anyone with a packet sniffer can pretend to be an authorized client.

NFS was developed when only trusted people could create an account; in a few places, this assumption is still true, such as in small, standalone research networks.

In addition, NFS assumes that the user database on the client computer is exactly the same as the one on the server. If your user ID is 503 on your client computer, the NFS server believes that you are user 503 on the server. Potentially, this allows a client administrator to steal another user's identity on the server. All he would have to do is create a new user on his computer, and then change the user ID in his local NetInfo database. This is a tremendous security issue when root is enabled.

NFS has some options that help administrators work around this problem. An NFS server administrator can:

▶ Limit clients

▶ Share the volume as read-only

▶ Share the volume with root or all users mapped to nobody (uid –2)

▶ Restrict access to the mount point based on IP address or subnet

▶ Implement a policy of users creating and enabling encrypted disk images

> **NOTE** ▶ Know the security policy on NFS servers that you mount. If you believe that a server is insecure, caution users against storing sensitive documents there. If users need only to download from the server, you can mount it as read-only.

Disconnecting When Volumes Are Mounted

Sometimes your computer may lose its connection to a server due to circumstances beyond your control. If you lose your network connection while you have volumes mounted, or if a server from which you have mounted becomes unavailable, Mac OS X will display an error message asking whether to disconnect from servers whose volumes you have mounted.

The following figure shows the dialogs that appear when an AFP, SMB, or NFS share has been disconnected abruptly, whether from a network disconnection or a service shutdown. The dialogs with the thin bar across the top are called Inspector windows and appear over any windows. The larger dialogs with a thicker bar across the top may not appear over all windows, so anyone using the computer at that time may not be alerted to the shutting down of a server. The three dialogs with the red octagon appear when the service has stopped abruptly but the network connection to the server is still valid.

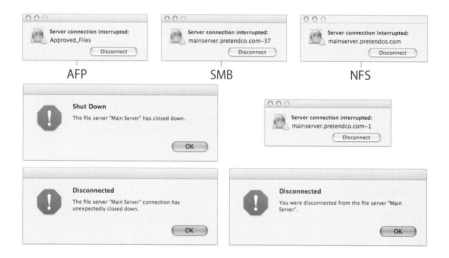

Mac OS X version 10.4 will reconnect automatically if a connection is lost. This information (the automount daemon and the kernel write messages about lost connections) is output to the system.log file.

Here is an example of a mount that was successful, followed by the physical network connection being lost, and then a reconnect minutes later. The volume reconnects automatically and attempts to reconnect every 10 seconds:

```
Oct 24 16:48:08 instructor kernel[0]: AFP_VFS afpfs_mount: /Volumes/Approved_Files, pid 402
Oct 24 16:48:22 instructor kernel[0]: UniNEnet::monitorLinkStatus – Link is down.
Oct 24 16:48:25 instructor launchd: Server 0 in bootstrap 1103 uid 0: "/usr/sbin/lookupd"[380]: exited
abnormally: Hangup
```

Oct 24 16:48:25 instructor configd[32]: posting notification com.apple.system.config.network_change

Oct 24 16:48:29 instructor lookupd[406]: lookupd (version 365) starting – Mon Oct 24 16:48:29 2005

Oct 24 16:49:59 instructor kernel[0]: AFP_VFS afpfs_Reconnect: doing reconnect on /Volumes/ Approved_Files

Oct 24 16:49:59 instructor kernel[0]: AFP_VFS afpfs_Reconnect: connect to the server /Volumes/ Approved_Files

Oct 24 16:49:59 instructor kernel[0]: AFP_VFS afpfs_Reconnect: connect on /Volumes/Approved_ Files failed 65.

Oct 24 16:50:04 instructor kernel[0]: AFP_VFS afpfs_Reconnect: posting to KEA retry for /Volumes/ Approved_Files delayCnt 6

Oct 24 16:50:04 instructor KernelEventAgent[43]: tid 00000000 received VQ_NOTRESP event (1)

Oct 24 16:50:04 instructor KernelEventAgent[43]: tid 00000000 type 'afpfs', mounted on '/Volumes/ Approved_Files', from 'afp_005An80ZHyoM001Eic06SdO0–1.2c000009', not responding

Oct 24 16:50:04 instructor KernelEventAgent[43]: tid 00000000 found 1 filesystem(s) with problem(s)

Oct 24 16:50:09 instructor kernel[0]: AFP_VFS afpfs_Reconnect: connect to the server /Volumes/ Approved_Files

Oct 24 16:50:09 instructor kernel[0]: AFP_VFS afpfs_Reconnect: connect on /Volumes/Approved_ Files failed 65.

The log is snipped here due to its length. A reconnect is attempted every 10 seconds between these entries.

Oct 24 16:50:29 instructor kernel[0]: AFP_VFS afpfs_Reconnect: connect to the server /Volumes/ Approved_Files

Oct 24 16:50:29 instructor kernel[0]: AFP_VFS afpfs_Reconnect: connect on /Volumes/Approved_ Files failed 65.

Oct 24 16:51:39 instructor kernel[0]: UniNEnet::monitorLinkStatus – Link is up at 100 Mbps – Full Duplex

Oct 24 16:51:40 instructor configd[32]: posting notification com.apple.system.config.network_change

Oct 24 16:51:40 instructor lookupd[427]: lookupd (version 365) starting – Mon Oct 24 16:51:40 2005

Oct 24 16:51:48 instructor kernel[0]: AFP_VFS afpfs_Reconnect: connect to the server /Volumes/ Approved_Files

Oct 24 16:51:48 instructor kernel[0]: AFP_VFS afpfs_Reconnect: Opening session /Volumes/ Approved_Files

Oct 24 16:51:48 instructor kernel[0]: AFP_VFS afpfs_Reconnect: Logging in with uam 10 /Volumes/ Approved_Files

Oct 24 16:51:48 instructor KernelEventAgent[43]: tid 00000000 received VQ_NOTRESP event (1)

Oct 24 16:51:48 instructor kernel[0]: AFP_VFS afpfs_Reconnect: Restoring session /Volumes/ Approved_Files

Eventually, automount unmounts the volumes, and they no longer appear in the Network browser, in the Sidebar or desktop, or in the output of the mount command.

NOTE ▶ If you reestablish your link to the network or the server becomes available again, the spinning ball icon might appear when you attempt to use the Finder. Relaunch the Finder to get rid of the icon.

Working With Multiple Mounts and Multiple Users

Normally, all mounted volumes unmount when a user logs out. However, if Fast User Switching is enabled and more than one user is logged in, mounted volumes are not unmounted automatically when a user logs out. The volumes remain mounted and are accessible to all users logged in to the computer.

The following output shows several volumes mounted by several users who have logged in using Fast User Switching. (The table before the output should help you decipher the text.)

Mount Points

Users	Approved_Files	Groups	Users
hadmin	✓		
amie	✓	✓	
dakota	✓		✓

Amie–iBook:~ hadmin$ mount
/dev/disk0s3 on / (local, journaled)
devfs on /dev (local)
fdesc on /dev (union)
volfs on /.vol
automount –nsl [117] on /Network (automounted)
automount –fstab [136] on /automount/Servers (automounted)

```
automount –static [136] on /automount/static (automounted)
afp_005An80ZHyoM001Eic06SdO0–1.2c000006 on /Volumes/Approved_Files (nodev, nosuid,
mounted by hadmin)
afp_005An80ZHyoM001Eic06SdO0–1.2c000007 on /Volumes/Approved_Files–1 (nodev, nosuid,
mounted by amie)
afp_005An80ZHyoM001Eic06SdO0–2.2c000008 on /Volumes/Groups (nodev, nosuid, mounted by amie)
afp_005An80ZHyoM001Eic06SdO0–1.2c000009 on /Volumes/Approved_Files–2 (nodev, nosuid,
mounted by dakota)
afp_005An80ZHyoM001Eic06SdO0–2.2c00000a on /Volumes/Users (nodev, nosuid, mounted by dakota)
```

If a disconnect happens, a collective inspector dialog appears after a few minutes, as shown in the following figure, informing the logged-in user that several mounts have become available and offering to disconnect the orphaned mount points. However, a successful rejoining of the server or the Mac OS X computer to the network will result in a reconnect.

Troubleshooting Browsing

If a computer does not appear in the Network browse list on your computers, try the following:

▶ Try other services from the same server. If more than one protocol is affected, you should troubleshoot your network connection.

▶ Check Directory Access. The service discovery protocol you need may have been disabled.

▶ If you're browsing for AFP service from a pre–Mac OS X computer, you might need AppleTalk. Be sure AppleTalk is enabled on only one network interface. The pre–Mac OS X computer must be able to make the connection via something other than AppleTalk, as AppleTalk can discover share points but cannot connect to them.

▶ Try browsing from a different computer. If the service appears there, find out what is different on that computer. Look at Network preferences and Directory Access settings, for example.

Troubleshooting Mount Issues

When attempts to mount a volume fail, several other dialogs commonly appear.

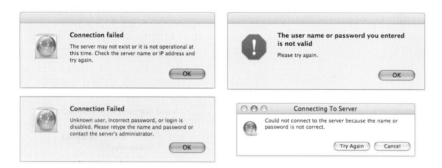

If you can browse a computer but cannot connect, try the following:

▶ Look for network problems. Check physical connections and try to ping the server. Try other services from the same server. If more than one protocol is affected, you should troubleshoot your network connection.

▶ Check whether a firewall is configured to block the port you are trying to access between the two systems.

▶ Restart automount with the –d flag to enable debug mode. Repeat the attempts to mount.

▶ Verify the permissions of the folder you're mounting on.

▶ Verify that the URL you are using is correct.

▶ Try connecting from a different computer. If the service appears on that computer, find out what is different. Look at Network preferences and Directory Access settings, for example.

► If you get a login dialog but cannot mount the volume, the connection is good and authentication is the problem. Verify the user name and password.

► If you have a problem mounting from the Finder, try mounting from the command line. You may get more information from error messages.

Recognizing Connection Errors

Sometimes when the Finder cannot connect to a server, it provides an error message. If the Finder detects an error before it attempts to mount, the message will not contain an error code. Two causes of this are nonexistent computers and bad authentication information, as shown in the following figure.

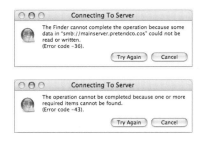 

If you try to mount a volume that is not being shared, you will get an error message with error code −36.

You might see some of the following error messages when mounting from the command line:

−36   Error in a URL

−43   Error in a URL, probably the volume name

−47   Already connected to the server as this user

−1069   Server does not exist

−5000   Access denied

−5019   Volume does not exist

−5023   Bad password

You can look up error codes on Mac OS X or Mac OS X Server by viewing the file /System/Library/Frameworks/CoreServices.framework/Versions/A/Frameworks/ CarbonCore.framework/Headers/MacErrors.h.

Sometimes processes write error messages to the system log. Look for the following process names in Console. The error might be related to file sharing.

Protocol	Process
AFP	/System/Library/Filesystems/AppleShare/asp_tcp.kext
AFP	/System/Library/Filesystems/AppleShare/asp_atp.kext
AFP	/System/Library/Filesystems/AppleShare/afpfs.kext
SMB	/sbin/mount_smbfs
SMB	/usr/sbin/smbd
SMB	/usr/sbin/nmbd
NFS	/sbin/mount_nfs
FTP	/System/Library/Filesystems/ftp.fs/mount_ftp

Checking Server Availability

If users cannot connect to a server, you should check access to the server itself.

You can use Port Scan in Network Utility to scan for open network ports on the server. There are several command-line utilities you can use to verify that SMB or NFS service is available on a server.

SMB

To see what an SMB server is sharing, type

```
smbclient –L hostname –N
```

The results should look something like this:

```
Domain=[RECOVERY] OS=[Unix] Server=[Samba 3.0.10]
        Sharename      Type       Comment
        _____      ____       _____
        Groups         Disk       macosx
        Public         Disk       macosx
        Users          Disk       macosx
        IPC$           IPC        IPC Service (Mac OS X)
        ADMIN$         IPC        IPC Service (Mac OS X)
Anonymous login successful
Domain=[RECOVERY] OS=[Unix] Server=[Samba 3.0.10]

        Server                 Comment
        _____              _____

        MY–MAIN–SERVER         Mac OS X

        Workgroup              Master
        _____              _____

        RECOVERY
```

Testing whether you can authenticate with a specific user name and password uses the format

smbclient //*hostname*/share –U user%*password*

where *password* is your password on the SMB server.

This should give you an smb: \> prompt. (Type *exit* to exit the prompt.) If you don't get the prompt, there's a problem with either the user name or password.

To check that the NetBIOS name maps to a particular IP address, type

nmblookup –U IPaddr hostname

where *IPaddr* is the IP address and *hostname* is the hostname of the SMB server. It should respond with the same IP address and hostname.

NFS

To query the state of an NFS server, you can use rpcinfo and showmount.

To see whether the NFS processes on the server have registered with portmap, type

rpcinfo –p servername

where *servername* is the name of the NFS server. The output should show nfs and mountd.

For example:

```
rpcinfo –p mainserver
```

program	vers	proto	port	
100000	2	tcp	111	portmapper
100000	2	udp	111	portmapper
100024	1	udp	1020	status
100024	1	tcp	1017	status
100021	0	udp	1008	nlockmgr
100021	1	udp	1008	nlockmgr
100021	3	udp	1008	nlockmgr
100021	4	udp	1008	nlockmgr
100021	0	tcp	1016	nlockmgr
100021	1	tcp	1016	nlockmgr
100021	3	tcp	1016	nlockmgr
100021	4	tcp	1016	nlockmgr
100005	1	udp	989	mountd
100005	3	udp	989	mountd
100005	1	tcp	1014	mountd
100005	3	tcp	1014	mountd
100003	2	udp	2049	nfs
100003	3	udp	2049	nfs
100003	2	tcp	2049	nfs
100003	3	tcp	2049	nfs

To see what volumes are being exported (shared) by the server and who is allowed to mount those volumes, use showmount –e *servername*.

For example:

> showmount –e mainserver

and

> showmount –e mainserver.pretendco.com

To see which other computers have mounted NFS volumes from the server, use showmount *servername*.

For example:

> showmount mainserver

and

> showmount mainserver.pretendco.com

What You've Learned

▶ Mac OS X supports four file-sharing protocols for maximum compatibility with other operating systems:

- AFP, primarily used by other Macintosh computers

- SMB, primarily used by Windows computers

- FTP, used by most computers

- NFS, primarily used by other UNIX-based systems

▶ You can use the Finder's Network browser to locate servers that offer share points over various protocols, such as AFP and SMB.

▶ To manage mounts from the command line, use mount to mount, umount to unmount, and nfsstat to troubleshoot NFS mounts.

▶ One way to have mounts at login is to first mount the volume, then drag it inside the Login Items tab of the Accounts preferences pane within System Preferences, which makes an alias for mounting at login.

▶ Knowing the specifics behind what happens when you use Connect to Server, such as where the mount occurs in the local file system, can help you better troubleshoot problems as they arise.

References

Apple Knowledge Base Documents

The following Knowledge Base document (located at www.apple.com/support) provides further information on file services.

Document 106439, "'Well Known' TCP and UDP Ports Used By Apple Software Products"

Books

Ts, Jay; Eckstein, Robert; and Collier-Brown, David. *Using Samba, 2nd ed.* (O'Reilly, 2003).

You can also find a copy of the book on your Mac OS X computer at /usr/share/swat/using_samba/toc.html.

URLs

Apple developer documentation: http://developer.apple.com/documentation

Samba: www.samba.org

NFS protocol specification: www.ietf.org/rfc/rfc3530.txt

Lesson Review

1. What are some important differences between AFP and NFS?
2. How do you configure your workstation to automount remote volumes on startup?
3. What process actually mounts volumes when you use the Network browser?
4. Where do volumes mount when you use the Network browser?
5. Where do volumes mount when you use Connect to Server?

Answers

1. Apple Filing Protocol was designed to handle forked files, and NFS was not. AFP performs user authentication, while NFS relies on IP address and user ID.
2. Add a startup item in your account preferences, or add a mount record to the NetInfo database using Workgroup Manager, NetInfo Manager, dscl, or nicl.

3. The automount daemon performs the actual mount.

4. In subdirectories of /private/var/automount/Network

5. In subdirectories of /Volumes

Part 4   Appendixes

vi Reference

This is a quick reference to the command-line editor, vi. It is not required that you use vi; you can use any way possible to edit flat text file, such as one of the two other command-line editors that come with Mac OS X, emacs, or pico. The goal when editing command-line files is to not have a file extension on the end. GUI applications such as BBEdit and SubEthaEdit will also permit you to save files without an extension.

vi Editor

The vi editor has two modes:

- ▶ Command mode, which is used for entering commands
- ▶ Edit mode, which is used to type text

The a, A, i, I, o, O, c, C, and R commands put vi into edit mode. To return to command mode from edit mode, press Escape. When you are in edit mode, you will see the word INSERT at the bottom left of the Terminal window.

The following table shows file-handling commands and their descriptions:

Command	Description
vi *file*	Edits the file named *file*. If the file does not exist, it will be created during a save.
vi -R *file*	Open file *file* in read-only mode.
:w	Write buffer to current file.
:w *file*	Write buffer to new file named *file*. Similar to a Save As.
:e *file*	Open file *file* for editing from within vi.
:q	Quit editing session. Will not quit unless changes have been saved.
:q!	Quit editing session. Will quit whether changes have been saved or not.

Keying a number before many of the navigation commands augments their behavior, as described in this table:

Command	Description
:*num*	Move to line number *num*.
G	Move to the last line of the buffer.
0	Move to the beginning of the current line.
$	Move to the end of the current line.
Arrow keys	Move the cursor in the direction of the key.

Command	Description
h j k l	Move the cursor. h and l are left and right; j and k are down and up.
w	Move to the beginning of the next word.
num	Move to column *num* in current line.
Control-F	Scroll forward one screen length.
Control-D	Scroll forward 1/2 screen.
Control-B	Scroll backward one screen length.
Control-U	Scroll backward 1/2 screen.

The following table shows miscellaneous commands and their descriptions:

Command	Description
Escape	Return to command mode.
Control-G	Display current line number.
.	Repeat last command.
J	Join current line with next line.
:shell	Bring up a shell from within vi. Type *exit* to exit the shell and return to vi.
:!*shell_command*	Execute *shell_command*. Returns to vi when *shell_command* has completed executing.

The following table shows how to set various preferences.

Command	Description
:set all	Display the current preferences settings.
:set showmode	Show or do not show editing mode.
:set noshowmode	

Command	Description
:set list	Display or do not display control characters in file.
:set nolist	
:set number	Display or do not display line numbers.
:set nonumber	
:set ignorecase	Ignore or do not ignore case when searching.
:set noignorecase	

Keying a number before many of the editing commands augments their behavior:

Command	Description
x	Delete the current character. Deleting using this command places the deleted character in the yank buffer.
i	Start inserting text at the cursor position.
I	Start inserting text at the beginning of the first nonblank character in the current line.
a	Start appending text after the cursor position.
A	Start appending text after the last character in the current line.
o	Open a line following the current line and enter insert mode.
O	Open a line above the current line and enter insert mode.
r*char*	Replace the current character with *char*.
R	Enter replace mode, overwriting all characters.
cw	Change the current word to whatever text follows. Changing using this command places changed characters in the yank buffer.
C	Change all characters from cursor to end-of-line. Changing using this command places changed characters in the yank buffer.

Command	Description
>>	Right indent.
<<	Left indent.
:r *file*	Insert file *file* at cursor position.
:r !*shell_command*	Insert the output of the shell command *shell_command* at the cursor position.
dw	Delete to the end of the current word. Deleting using this command places deleted characters in the yank buffer.
dd	Delete the current line. Deleting using this command places deleted lines in the yank buffer.
D or d$	Delete to end of line. Deleting using this command places deleted characters in the yank buffer.
u	Undo the last command that changed the buffer.
U	Restore the current line to its original state. Original state is defined as the state of the line when the cursor first moved to the line. When the cursor moves off of a line, the change is not undoable with this command; try the u command instead.
yw	Put the current word into the yank buffer.
"*letter*yw	By preceding yw with a quote and a letter, you can yank to the letter buffer. *letter* must be lowercase a–z.
yy	Put the current line into the yank buffer.
"*letter*yy	By preceding yy with a quote and a letter, you can yank to the letter buffer. *letter* must be lowercase a–z.
p	Paste text from the yank buffer at the cursor position.
"*letter*p	By preceding p with a quote and a letter, you can paste from the letter buffer. *letter* must be lowercase a–z.

Should there be an intro sentence here, too?

Search/Replace

Command	Description
/pattern	Search forward of the cursor for *pattern*.
?pattern	Search backward from the cursor for *pattern*.
n	Repeat last find in the same direction.
N	Repeat last find in the opposite direction.
:x,ys/old_string /new_string/flags	Substitution range is lines x through y. In place of x,y, % may be used to signify entire buffer as substitution range. With no x,y, substitution range is the current line. If flag c is used, confirmation is requested for each substitution. If flag g is used, all occurrences of old_string over substitution range are replaced; otherwise, only the first occurrence of each line is replaced.

Basic Command-Line Reference

The command-line interface has been around for a very long time. Its roots go back to the earliest computers. While there are literally hundreds of commands—and thousands of options within these commands—this appendix focuses on the commands that are an extension to the basic ones every administrator must know: cd, ls, and pwd. (Of course, the commands discussed here are by no means the only ones you should know.) You will get an overview of the following:

▶ Running commands to find files, manage processes, monitor usage, and manage disks and volumes

▶ Exchanging data between the Finder and the command line

Armed with this additional information, you should be able to better manage your Mac OS X server.

Finding Files Using locate and find

You can use both the find and locate commands to search the file system for files matching certain criteria. The locate command uses a database describing the known files on your system. The locate database is built and updated automatically as long as your system is running at the appropriate time. By default on Mac OS X and Mac OS X Server systems, the locate database is updated at 4:30 a.m. each Saturday. You can execute the script that updates the locate database using the command sudo /etc/weekly.

The locate command understands the wildcard characters that the shell uses (wildcards are discussed later in this appendix). To pass the wildcard character on to the locate command, you must escape the character so that the shell doesn't process it. For example, the command locate "*.rtf" or locate *.rtf will print a list of all files with names ending in .rtf, while locate *.rtf results in an error.

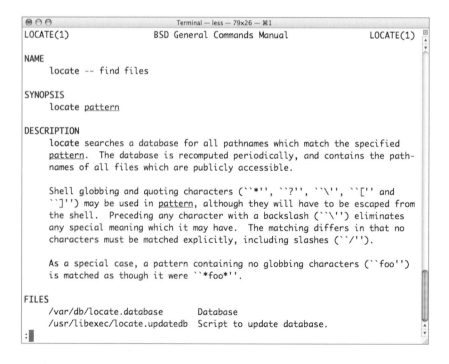

```
                            Terminal — less — 79x26 — ⌘1
LOCATE(1)                   BSD General Commands Manual                LOCATE(1)

NAME
     locate -- find files

SYNOPSIS
     locate pattern

DESCRIPTION
     locate searches a database for all pathnames which match the specified
     pattern.  The database is recomputed periodically, and contains the path-
     names of all files which are publicly accessible.

     Shell globbing and quoting characters (``*'', ``?'', ``\'', ``['' and
     ``]'') may be used in pattern, although they will have to be escaped from
     the shell.  Preceding any character with a backslash (``\'') eliminates
     any special meaning which it may have.  The matching differs in that no
     characters must be matched explicitly, including slashes (``/'').

     As a special case, a pattern containing no globbing characters (``foo'')
     is matched as though it were ``*foo*''.

FILES
     /var/db/locate.database        Database
     /usr/libexec/locate.updatedb   Script to update database.
:
```

The command find ~ -name *.rtf –print starts a search of the files in the user's home directory and prints on the screen all of the files with names ending in lowercase .rtf, while the command find ~ -iname *.rtf –print starts a search of the files in your home folder and lists all of the files with names ending in .rtf, regardless of whether the rtf is in lowercase or uppercase.

File Locations

Mac OS X introduces a number of predefined folders intended to contain files of particular types. Since many applications depend on the name and location of these folders, they should not be renamed or moved.

Most applications in the Mac OS X graphical user interface (GUI) reside in /Applications, and operating system files reside in /System. By convention, UNIX programs store their configuration information in /etc while most command-line tools are installed in /bin, /sbin, /usr/bin, or /usr/sbin. Shells search these four folders to find the programs whose names you enter on the command line. Programs in other locations may be executed by specifying an absolute or relative path to the executable.

> Most applications in the Mac OS X graphical user interface reside in /Applications.
> Operating system files that generally should not be touched are in /System.
> Many UNIX configuration files are in /etc.
> Most command-line tools are in one of the following directories:
> - /bin
> - /sbin
> - /usr/bin
> - /usr/sbin
> Command-line tools that ship with the Developer Tools are installed in /Developer/Tools.

For example, /Developer/Tools/GetFileInfo /Users executes the GetFileInfo command installed by the developer tools. The current folder is not part of the default search path on Mac OS X. This is important for Windows users, but it is a security risk to have a shell include the current folder in the search path, because it could allow unauthorized applications to execute.

Managing Processes From the Command Line

You can determine the currently running processes from the command line using the ps or top command. Use top to see a regularly updated view of system utilization, including memory usage, page faults, and the set of currently executing processes.

```
● ○ ○                    Terminal — top — 79x26 — ⌘1
Processes:  74 total, 2 running, 72 sleeping... 261 threads        14:10:48
Load Avg:  0.16, 0.20, 0.23     CPU usage:  12.3% user, 14.9% sys, 72.8% idle
SharedLibs: num = 205, resident = 35.6M code, 4.41M data, 8.27M LinkEdit
MemRegions: num = 14742, resident = 553M + 9.50M private,  140M shared
PhysMem:   107M wired,  570M active,  285M inactive,  963M used, 60.2M free
VM: 10.0G + 130M   183496(0) pageins, 134812(0) pageouts

  PID COMMAND      %CPU   TIME    #TH #PRTS #MREGS RPRVT  RSHRD  RSIZE  VSIZE
 4744 top         10.8% 0:00.85   1    18     22   540K   336K   2.29M  26.9M
 4743 mdimport     0.0% 0:00.28   4    63     52   988K   3.36M  3.08M  41.2M
 4726 less         0.0% 0:00.01   1    13     19   132K   364K   944K   26.7M
 4723 sh           0.0% 0:00.00   1     8     17    48K   744K   368K   27.1M
 4722 sh           0.0% 0:00.00   1    13     17    48K   744K   564K   27.1M
 4721 man          0.0% 0:00.01   1    13     17   128K   336K   836K   26.6M
 4515 bash         0.0% 0:00.08   1    14     17   208K   692K   872K   27.1M
 4514 login        0.0% 0:00.02   1    16     36   132K   340K   556K   26.9M
 4512 Terminal     2.4% 0:07.70   7   195    243   3.77M  13.9M+ 12.7M- 229M
 4389 Mail         0.0% 0:14.75   8   146    334   10.7M  18.8M  21.8M  247M
 4258 Safari       0.0% 0:55.20   7   135    505   35.4M  18.6M  46.0M  263M
 4194 lookupd      0.0% 0:01.70   2    34     38   536K   724K   1.29M  28.5M
 3812 Microsoft    0.0% 0:04.70   3    70    154   1.62M  7.28M  3.29M  205M
 3811 Microsoft    1.2% 8:09.51   8   128    699   26.7M  26.1M+ 42.4M  325M
 3806 Keynote      0.6% 2:22.05   4   108    499   29.4M  19.3M+ 36.3M  303M
 3761 Image Capt   0.0% 0:00.80   3    75    144   996K   4.36M  2.40M  202M
 3759 GraphicCon   0.0% 0:23.62   5   114    331   5.43M  22.3M  9.36M  302M
 3758 Adobe Phot   0.5% 3:29.05   6   117   1734   264K   29.0M  275M   664M
```

In the leftmost column of the top tabular output, you will find the process identifier (PID) associated with that process. You can also use the ps command to determine the PID of a process. The PID is used to send a message to a particular process. For example, the command ps -auxww | grep TextEdit prints the PID# and other information for just the TextEdit process.

When you have the PID# for a process, you can send it the command kill -9 *PID#*, where *PID#* is the number associated with the TextEdit process. This command asks the process with the given PID to terminate immediately. You can send a variety of commands to running processes, such as rereading a configuration file or logging additional information.

The killall command enables you to signal processes by name rather than by PID. The command killall -KILL TextEdit force-quits all processes that belong to you with the name TextEdit.

Monitoring System Usage

Many shell commands exist to help you monitor the system. The last command shows you which users have logged in most recently or when a specified user last logged in to your system.

```
000                    Terminal — bash — 74x26 — ⌘1
instructor:~ sregan$ last
sregan    ttyp2                     Sat Jul 16 12:47    still logged in
sregan    ttyp2                     Sat Jul 16 12:47 - 12:47  (00:00)
sregan    ttyp1                     Sat Jul 16 12:44    still logged in
sregan    ttyp1                     Sat Jul 16 12:44 - 12:44  (00:00)
sregan    console   instructor.local Fri Jul 15 09:35    still logged in
reboot    ~                         Fri Jul 15 09:35
shutdown  ~                         Fri Jul 15 09:19
sregan    console   instructor.local Fri Jul 15 01:50 - 09:19  (07:28)
reboot    ~                         Fri Jul 15 01:50
shutdown  ~                         Thu Jul 14 15:32
sregan    console   instructor.local Thu Jul 14 12:22 - 15:31  (03:08)
reboot    ~                         Thu Jul 14 12:22
shutdown  ~                         Thu Jul 14 12:21
sregan    ttyp1                     Thu Jul 14 12:09 - shutdown  (00:12)
sregan    ttyp1                     Thu Jul 14 12:09 - 12:09  (00:00)
test      console   instructor.local Thu Jul 14 10:14 - 12:21  (02:07)
sregan    ttyp1                     Thu Jul 14 09:36 - 12:09  (02:33)
sregan    ttyp1                     Thu Jul 14 09:36 - 09:36  (00:00)
sregan    console   instructor.local Thu Jul 14 08:40 - 10:14  (01:33)
reboot    ~                         Thu Jul 14 08:40
shutdown  ~                         Thu Jul 14 08:39
sregan    console   instructor.local Wed Jul 13 10:26 - 08:39  (22:13)
reboot    ~                         Wed Jul 13 10:25
shutdown  ~                         Wed Jul 13 09:57
sregan    console   instructor.local Wed Jul 13 09:35 - 09:57  (00:21)
```

The id command enables you to determine which groups a particular user has access to, or to determine the short name for a user given their user ID (UID).

Mac OS X systems maintain many log files. Viewing log files on your system or on another system using ssh can help you troubleshoot any number of problems. The command tail -n 10 /Library/Logs/Software\ Update.log displays the ten most recently installed software updates. The command tail -f /var/log/system.log displays the current contents of the system log, then continues to print new lines as they are added to the file.

Managing Disks and Volumes

You can get all of the functionality presently available in Disk Utility through two commands accessible from the command line:

▶   hdiutil, which handles disk-image management

▶   diskutil, which includes the rest of the features

You can read the man pages to learn how to use the different features, or you can type the command at the command line, and the different options you can use will appear.

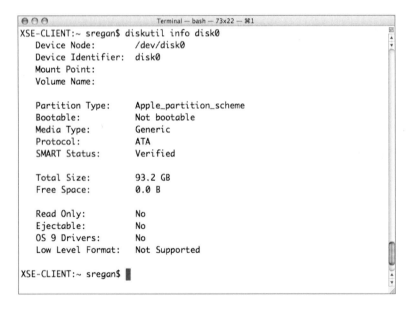

You can also use the df and du commands to determine free space and space utilization on a volume.

Working With the Command Line and the GUI

In Mac OS X, the command line and the GUI work hand in hand. Transferring data from one environment to the other and moving between the two environments is done very easily. You can select a group of files in the Finder and drag them to a Terminal window to add their paths to a command.

The open command enables you to open files and URLs as if you had double-clicked them in the Finder. For example, the command open ~/Documents/ReadMe.rtf launches TextEdit (or your preferred application for opening RTF files) and opens the specified ReadMe.rtf file. Similarly, the command open http://www.apple.com launches Safari (or your preferred Web browser) and opens the Apple home page.

Searching Text Files Using pipe and grep

Use the grep command to search the contents of the listed text file or files. For example, in grep domain /etc/resolv.conf, the file resolv.conf is searched for the word *domain* and the lines containing that word are displayed.

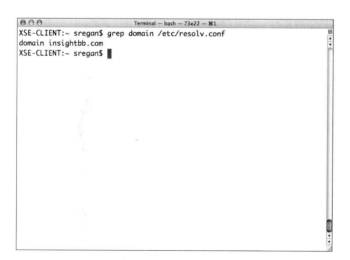

Often, the output of one command is used as input for another command. The UNIX pipe character (|) is used for this purpose. The command ps -auxww | grep Finder executes the ps command and "pipes" its output (the process list) to the grep command. The grep command reads the process list as input, looking for the word *Finder,* and displays any lines containing *Finder* in the process list.

Additional Shell Filename Wildcards

Other wildcard characters enable you to specify more complex patterns than you can with the * character. The shell wildcards supported by UNIX shells are *, ?, and [].

```
●●●                    Terminal — bash — 81x30 — ⌘1
ls: M*dd: No such file or directory
XSE-CLIENT:~/Music sregan$ ls -la M*d
Marshall Tucker Band:
total 0
drwxrwxrwx      3 sregan   sregan     102 May  2  2003 .
drwx------    674 sregan   sregan   22916 May 27 09:09 ..
drwxrwxrwx      3 sregan   sregan     102 Feb 14  2004 The Capricorn Years

Michael McDonald:
total 0
drwxrwxrwx      3 sregan   sregan     102 May 14  2003 .
drwx------    674 sregan   sregan   22916 May 27 09:09 ..
drwxrwxrwx      3 sregan   sregan     102 May 14  2003 Sweet Freedom

Michael Stanley Band:
total 16
drwxrwxrwx     14 sregan   sregan     476 Oct 25  2004 .
drwx------    674 sregan   sregan   22916 May 27 09:09 ..
-rw-rw-rw-      1 sregan   sregan    6148 May 26 00:05 .DS_Store
drwxrwxrwx      6 sregan   sregan     204 May  1  2003 Cabin Fever
drwxrwxrwx      6 sregan   sregan     204 Apr 30  2003 Greatest Hints
drwxrwxrwx      7 sregan   sregan     238 Apr 30  2003 Heartland
drwxrwxrwx      5 sregan   sregan     170 Feb 14  2004 Inside Moves
drwxrwxrwx      3 sregan   sregan     102 Apr 30  2003 Ladies' Choice
drwxr-xr-x      7 sregan   sregan     238 Feb 14  2004 MS-Live 2K
drwxrwxrwx      5 sregan   sregan     170 Apr 30  2003 MSB
drwxrwxrwx      4 sregan   sregan     136 Apr 30  2003 North Coast
drwxrwxrwx     15 sregan   sregan     510 Feb 14  2004 Stage Pass
drwxr-xr-x      3 sregan   sregan     102 Mar  8  2004 You Break It...You Bought It
drwxrwxrwx      3 sregan   sregan     102 Apr 30  2003 You Can't Fight Fashion
```

The ? wildcard matches any single character. The [] wildcard matches a single character in a list of characters appearing within square brackets. In the figure above, the list command is asked to show only those files whose names start with a capital *M* and end with a lowercase *d*, but can have any number of characters in between.

A few examples can help to build your understanding of wildcards. Consider a collection of five files with the names ReadMe.rtf, ReadMe.txt, read.rtf, read.txt, and It's All About Me.rtf:

▶ *.rtf matches ReadMe.rtf, read.rtf, and It's All About Me.rtf.

▶ ????.* matches read.rtf and read.txt.

▶ [Rr]*.rtf matches ReadMe.rtf and read.rtf.

▶ [A-Z]* matches ReadMe.rtf, ReadMe.txt, and It's All About Me.rtf.

Additional Mac OS X–Specific Commands

Additional Mac OS X–specific commands include:

▶ softwareupdate: Use to view the list of available updates and install updates that you specify.

▶ installer: Use to install certain packages and/or metapackages.

▶ pbcopy and pbpaste: Enable you to create data in one environment and use it in the other.

▶ atlookup: Use to view AppleTalk devices on your local network.

▶ plutil: Permits the conversion of binary files to XML style for editing.

▶ GetFileInfo and SetFile: Enable you to manipulate HFS files with resource forks, and get and set file attributes (such as type and creator) associated with HFS files. Both are located in the Tools folder inside the Developer folder.

What You've Learned

▶ You can use locate and find to find files.

▶ The last command helps you keep track of user logins.

▶ The id command helps you keep track of user and group IDs.

▶ The tail command helps you view recent activity in a log file.

▶ The command-line interface gives you another way to force-quit applications and processes.

References

Administration Guides

"Mac OS X Server Command-Line Administration": http://images.apple.com/server/pdfs/Command_Line_vl0.4.pdf

Apple Knowledge Base Documents

You can check for new and updated Knowledge Base documents at www.apple.com/support.

URLs

UNIX home page: www.unix.org

Lesson Review

1. The locate command is built into what script (and the location of the script) that runs automatically if the Mac OS X computer is on during that time period?

2. What does top show?

3. What command would you use to see a live continuous update of the system log file?

4. What does grep do?

Answers

1. /etc/weekly

2. The top command displays a regularly updated view of system utilization, including memory usage, page faults, and the set of currently executing processes.

3. tail –f /var/log/system.log

4. grep searches the contents of the listed text files or items.

Index